SQL Server 7: The Complete Reference

SQL Server 7: The Complete Reference

Gayle Coffman

Osborne/**McGraw-Hill**

Berkeley New York St. Louis San Francisco
Auckland Bogotá Hamburg London Madrid
Mexico City Milan Montreal New Delhi Panama City
Paris São Paulo Singapore Sydney
Tokyo Toronto

Osborne/**McGraw-Hill**
2600 Tenth Street
Berkeley, California 94710
U.S.A.

For information on translations or book distributors outside the U.S.A., or to arrange bulk purchase discounts for sales promotions, premiums, or fund-raisers, please contact Osborne/**McGraw-Hill** at the above address.

SQL Server 7: The Complete Reference

234567890 AGM AGM 90198765432109

ISBN 0-07-882494-X

Publisher
Brandon A. Nordin

Editor-in-Chief
Scott Rogers

Acquisitions Editor
Wendy Rinaldi

Project Editor
Ron Hull

Editorial Assistant
Debbie Escobedo

Technical Editors
Gil Milbauer
Brian Engler

Copy Editor
Sally Engelfried

Proofreader
John Gildersleeve

Indexer
Jack Lewis

Computer Designer
Michelle Galicia
Anne Sellers
Jani Beckwith

Illustrator
Lance Ravella
Brian Wells
Beth Young

Series Design
Peter Hancik

This book is dedicated to my husband Chris,
daughter Kelly Collins,
and son Christopher.

About the Author...

Gayle Coffman has been ensuring the integrity and recoverability of internal IT databases of major corporations for nearly two decades. In addition to experience that spans IDMS, Oracle, Sybase, and many other systems, she has extensive, in-depth knowledge of the SQL Server product line. The broad range of new database tools and advanced functionality in the latest Microsoft database, SQL Server 7, prompted her to make this the subject of her first book.

Contents at a Glance

Part II Installation

Part III Administration

Part IV Development—The Programming Language

Part V Reference Materials

Contents

Acknowledgments

I would like to especially thank my husband, Chris Coffman, who kept the ship afloat for the past year and shared his expert advice. Special thanks also go to Gil Milbauer and Brian Engler, technical editors, and Ron Hull, project editor, for correcting, formatting, and polishing. Finally, I have to express my gratitude to Danny Raphael at Microsoft, who gave me the encouragement to start, and to Wendy Rinaldi at Osborne/McGraw-Hill, who gave me the courage to finish.

Introduction

Microsoft SQL Server has been almost totally rewritten in version 7. Many brand new features are in place, many things have been simplified and streamlined to provide better performance. Built-in Internet integration allows you to conduct business on the Internet and build intranet sites. Performance has increased on many fronts with this version, and terabyte databases are supported. SQL Server 7 leads in price-performance by reducing administrative overhead and lowering total cost of ownership with a design that is geared toward dynamic configuration. Many of the day-to-day manual tasks of the database administrator have been automated. Dynamic locking, dynamic memory allocation, auto-grow tempdb, auto-grow log files, auto-grow database files, automatic creation of the database upon a restore, automatic index creation across an entire database, and many other new features help eliminate administrative tasks. Minimizing complexity for users, administrators, and developers allows applications to be deployed at a lower cost and in less time.

This book describes the new functionality and provides an overview of SQL Server 7—making it readily apparent that there is much to learn about the latest version of Microsoft SQL Server. The content of the book is based on years of experience administering the product and is intended for all administrators of SQL Server databases. *SQL Server 7: The Complete Reference* is a comprehensive resource that covers all facets of this robust product. It teaches new administrators how to use the product, and it shows experienced SQL Server users how to make the most of the newest features of SQL Server. This book is meant to be a reference that can be used frequently throughout the day. The Internet is emphasized, as is replication over the Internet. Transact-SQL syntax and system stored procedures are included, making this a reference worth having to answer your version-related questions. If you are brand new to SQL Server, you will get an introduction to some of the best database tools on the market. If you are a seasoned user, you will appreciate the detailed information and easy-to-read format designed to keep those hard-to-remember details at your fingertips.

How This Book Is Organized

There are many different ways to use SQL Server depending on whether you are a user, a developer, an administrator, or a manager. In order to best serve these different interests, this book is organized into five parts:

- Part I, "Welcome to Microsoft SQL Server 7," is a comprehensive overview of SQL Server—what it is, how it came to be, and where it is going. Architectural improvements, the new storage structure, Internet/intranet, Microsoft Transaction Server, the enterprise, Microsoft Management Console (MMC), SQL Server Agent, integration with Windows NT security, Transact-SQL enhancements, new and enhanced tools, replication enhancements, and simplifying the role of the database administrator are all covered in Part I.
- Part II, "Installation," contains instructions for installing SQL Server, installing SQL Mail, and upgrading SQL Server to version 7. These procedures are explained in detail with supporting illustrations.
- Part III, "Administration," discusses the tasks associated with database management and preventive maintenance, backups, remote and linked servers, and database monitoring with emphasis on maintaining the integrity, recoverability and the reliability of the database.
- Part IV, "Development—The Programming Language," contains development topics, such as database, referential, and transaction integrity; how to design and create a database; normalization; indexing; very large databases (VLDBs); approaches to database design; generalization; coding strategies; partitioning; concurrency; writing Transact-SQL, stored procedures and triggers; and data warehouses.
- Part V, "Reference Materials," includes Transact-SQL syntax, system tables, and system stored procedures. The entries in these chapters are arranged alphabetically so you can quickly find the information you need.

Conventions Used in This Book

The conventions used in this book are as follows:

- UPPERCASE for Transact-SQL keywords
- Italics for arguments supplied by a user
- A vertical bar (|) used for separating a choice of items
- Brackets for optional syntax
- Braces for required syntax
- Labels for a set of syntax used together

Part I

Welcome to SQL Server 7

The Complete Reference

Chapter 1

What Is Microsoft SQL Server?

Microsoft SQL Server is a relational database that runs on the NT operating system. SQL, or Structured Query Language, is a widely accepted industry standard for defining, changing, and managing data and controlling how changes to the database are made by using tables, indexes, keys, rows, and columns to store data. SQL was developed from the ideas of Dr. Edgar (Ted) F. Codd of International Business Machines (IBM) who helped develop the relational model while working at IBM's research labs in the 1970s.

History of Microsoft SQL Server

In a June 1992 interview with *ComputerWorld* magazine senior editor Jean Bozman, Dr. Codd remembered attending a lecture in the late 1960s about a database product of an IBM competitor. When he asked the lecturer about "predicate logic and existential and universal quantifiers" and the database expert did not recognize the description of relational technology, Codd became convinced that relational theory was a wide open field and that once people knew about relational theory, they would put it in a category with mathematics and accounting.

In 1969, Dr. Codd was continuing to define and advocate the pursuit of the relational database model. Meanwhile, IBM announced that its primary and probably only database system was to be IMS, which is a *non*relational database. Luckily, IBM's then head of research, Ralph Gamory, also advocated pursuing a prototype of a relational database that came to be called System R. There was widespread opposition to this fractious new relational concept that was in competition with IMS, their "one and only database management system." Dr. Codd said he was "accused once or twice of trying to undermine IBM," and his relational database was viewed as a competitor to IMS.

Even with the release of IMS, customers demanded easier ways to retrieve data than what the database could offer. They wanted better tools and the elimination of the obstacles that made it difficult for the average person to store and retrieve data. They wanted to be able to query a database in "human-like" language and the ability to redefine data relationships immediately rather than once every two weeks or whenever one could assemble a team of programmers. They wanted to simplify the process required to make data definition changes to the structure holding the data and, even more than that, to access the data without being forced to use the views defined when the database was originally built or updated.

The obstacles to accessing data in the nonrelational environment are many. In a network hierarchical database a person could not add a field to a file, change the length or datatype of the field, or delete the field because the physical structure that was originally designed to store the data had to remain unchanged. Changes to the structure were brought to database change meetings and the changes were made in batches. This created a development bottleneck that rested at the door of the database administrators, who usually made the accumulated database changes all at once in the off-business hours. Programs, usually written in COBOL, had to be written to unload the data from the database, and still more programs had to be written to reload the data back into the database after the physical structure was rebuilt. This was a time consuming process that took much effort.

Another obstacle in nonrelational databases is the inability of a network or hierarchical database to query data in a freestyle manner outside of the views of the logical structure that was originally defined. The manner in which data needs to be queried changes over time, and real business cases require that raw data be able to turn into the up-to-the-minute information necessary to run a business competitively. In the nonrelational databases, one could not view or query the data any differently than what was defined when the database was created unless custom programs and special processing occurred. The time and rigors of unloading data, rebuilding schemas, and reloading data made it impossible to have anything but a rigid, inflexible database that did not satisfy the information needs of the hour.

It's no wonder that programmers and customers involved in this time consuming and expensive process began to think about the budding technology concepts of the relational databases as defined by Dr. Codd. In 1984, I was designing a database that allowed the customer to look at their income statement and balance sheet in a myriad of different ways when my manager told me, "Too bad you don't have a relational database." That was when I first heard about this sort of database and what they could do.

The relational database overcomes many obstacles to accessing the data and offers the programmer a painless alternative. A one-line command as easy as **alter table** can change the structure. There is no unload, no reload, and the data is not disturbed at all (unloading being the act of separating the actual data from the database structure). Adjustments are easily made, and all the data elements in the database can be queried flexibly. Views of the data do not have to be predefined, and relationships can be built on a moment's notice.

By the mid-1970s it was recognized that relational databases were better suited to deliver the functionality the customers wanted. In order to deal with customer demand, IBM resurrected its System R project, and relational databases began to appear in the marketplace in the early 1980s. Dr. Codd stated in the 1992 *ComputerWorld* article, "Relational databases have a solid future, but they must be enhanced to perform faster and to be more openly accessible to end users. They also need to embrace new technologies."

From these early relational beginnings came Microsoft SQL Server. Microsoft originally licensed the basic building blocks of SQL Server from Sybase and made the product available on PC platforms running OS/2 and, more recently, Windows NT. A joint effort between Sybase, Ashton-Tate, and Microsoft in 1988 produced one of the first databases on the personal computer, making the relational database more openly accessible to end users, just as Dr. Codd had envisioned. Microsoft spearheaded the SQL Server project; Ashton-Tate withdrew when SQL Server was ported to the NT operating system from OS/2. Both Microsoft and Sybase sold the database on the PC hardware platform until version 4.21, but the Microsoft/Sybase partnership dissolved in 1993, Sybase since concentrating on the minicomputer platform and Microsoft on the personal computer platform.

Perhaps Bill Gates read the June 1992 *ComputerWorld* article since both he and Dr. Codd were interviewed in the same article and described as "25 People Who Changed the World" and SQL Server was in full development at Microsoft at the time of the article.

Microsoft, the personal computer, and the Internet are making Dr. Codd's vision of end user accessibility to data a reality in a way that others have failed to do.

Future of Microsoft SQL Server

Today the relational database is accepted as the preferred method of storing data and many companies, each with a different relational database, are competing to lead the SQL pack. The truth is that the future of databases, and thus SQL, is driven by both the demands of the customer and the marketplace, and these demands are the same as they were 30 years ago: bigger, faster, easier to use, and more accessible databases. This puts continuous long-term pressure on the developers of relational databases.

The ease of use demand places mainframe and minicomputer operating systems in a different category from the personal computer. Mainframe and minicomputer operating systems are costly, difficult to use, and not designed with a simple user interface. In addition, mainframe database systems require major funding and expensive expertise and many minicomputer databases are locked into the complex UNIX operating system.

Personal computers are the easiest computer on the market to use. Microsoft's extensive expansion of the graphical user interface in SQL Server 7 for the PC clearly shows that Microsoft is listening to the customer and is focused on meeting demands for ease of use and administration. Over the years, I have often wondered why the programmers that write databases do the convoluted things that they do. Microsoft has fixed and eliminated many of the mistakes and unnecessary complexities of their legacy design of the early 1980s, which was long overdue for an overhaul. Overall, the low-level rework is readily apparent, and database administrators will be enchanted with the enhancements in this area and will be particularly fond of job stream management. Microsoft calls this going after the low-end market so that a database administrator is not needed. I just call that common sense.

Today, personal computers are as powerful as the mainframes of times past and range from the individual platform (such as what I use) to the high-end SMP servers with 8 to 16 processors. Discussing the age-old problem of input/output being much slower than actual computing with *ComputerWorld*, Dr. Codd correctly predicted the solution would someday be "one small electronic computer for every disk unit. You can put one whole CPU on a single chip so it can manage the search and updates for that disk." He was clearly talking about distributed computing and personal computers.

Microsoft is placing data, and thus information, into the hands of the small business, the medium business, and the large business by way of the personal computer. After all, how many businesses can afford a mainframe with a sophisticated database? Only the very large ones with millions of dollars in operating capital can afford a mainframe system, and only a medium or large business can afford minicomputers. On the other hand, Microsoft SQL Server is affordable to the small business and can still scale up to meet the needs of the large corporation.

Microsoft clearly demonstrates how a large company can run its business on Microsoft SQL Server by using it for its own business needs. Every piece of software it sells is recorded on Microsoft SQL Server databases, creating tens of millions of data rows. Microsoft calls this "eating our own dog food," and it certainly appears as though their health has not suffered from it! All new releases of NT and Microsoft SQL Server are subject to the rigorous tests of Microsoft's internal applications, and the product makes the same functionality affordable for the small business owner.

Microsoft has already demonstrated scalability, and this is working well despite rumors to the contrary. Most people have not experienced the use of this product on a day to day basis inside a large corporation like Microsoft, but I can tell them from personal experience that it scales very well and will continue to improve as the technology advances.

The testimony of support analysts running databases in need of a design overhaul or suffering from the omission of code to harness a transaction can indicate a poor performance database. The Microsoft Transaction Server helps to free the developer of this overhead. There is a right way and a wrong way to design SQL Server databases and to code SQL, and a database in need of design improvement combined with less than optimal coding techniques can result in a slow database. If you have a good design, good coding techniques, and the appropriate hardware, Microsoft SQL Server can do the job.

Microsoft SQL Server's future is in cheaper, faster, easier access to data for small, medium, and large businesses. Their ongoing efforts to address the customer demands of the broader market make the future of SQL Server secure. As Microsoft continues to give the small business access to technology that was once only available to the privileged corporate few, the true strength and viability of Microsoft SQL Server becomes even more obvious.

Architectural Improvements

In this release, Microsoft has taken the core technology of the SQL Server database and redesigned it with more data warehouse functionality, a better optimizer, and a rewrite of the database storage engine. Also important is its improved scalability, an ongoing

Microsoft focus. Microsoft SQL Server can now store a terabyte, one thousand gigabytes, in each database. The Microsoft Enterprise concept is intent on meeting the needs of the high-end database market in the distributed computing environment and supplies all the tools to manage the many servers required in this type of computing environment, including the ability to access up to eight CPUs. The Microsoft Management Console (MMC) is where this all comes together. The *snap in* functionality of the MMC allows the insertion of third party tools to manage the environment and comes with all of the functionality of the Enterprise Manager which it houses. We'll discuss more about the MMC and what it can do in Chapter 3.

The architectural improvements are a major advance for the database, and Microsoft does not intend to stop here. The company will continue to take advantage of PC hardware advances and will come up with better ways of parallel processing on multiple CPUs. The database structure will continue to be improved to ensure performance and ease of use. Microsoft is totally focused on lowering the TCO (Total Cost of Ownership). This includes reducing, simplifying, and eventually eliminating the tasks of the database administrator.

New Storage Structure

The method of storing data is completely different in Microsoft SQL Server version 7 than it was in version 6.5. Instead of the *device* paradigm for storage that allows multiple databases per physical file, we now see databases stored as files with one database per file or group of files. In the past, the device moniker hid what was actually happening, which was the creation of an operating system file. Now a single database can reside in multiple files via the file group feature, though multiple databases will no longer exist together in a single file. This creates a dramatic improvement in performance and capacity. It also eases the initial burden of comprehension for a new user by simplifying the concepts and taking out the confusing references to devices and the extra steps involved in creating them. The **create database** command now specifies the name and size of the data and log files associated with the database; the **disk init** statement that was used in previous versions to create the actual physical database file and the requirement to reference size in terms of the number of 2K datapages is no longer necessary. (SQL Server 7 now uses 8K datapages.) Now the database size reference is in terms that most users are familiar with: kilobytes, megabytes, and gigabytes.

In addition to these changes in the storage structure, there are new disk formats for rows, extents, data files, and log files. These new formats will allow the desired scalability from low-end to high-end systems while improving performance. In an effort to improve space utilization, text and image data can now be shared by multiple rows. In previous versions, if a column contained a few bytes of text or image data it would take up an entire 2K page. Now free space on the new 8K page will be used by data belonging to other rows. There is also the provision of automatic database creation and alteration when a database is restored. Just the act of issuing a command to restore a database file will automatically create and/or alter the database. This way the database administrator won't have to figure out the size of the receiving database and then create it before restoration. This is merely one example of how SQL Server 7 is much easier to administrate.

SQL Server and the Internet

The combination of Microsoft SQL Server and Microsoft Internet Information Server (IIS) provides the framework to connect the relational database to the Internet while using Web browsers to display data. This is the beginning of the era of database end-user accessibility and was not possible before Internet visual browser technology matured. There are untold advantages to integrating the NT operating system with all of the NT Inter/Intranet capabilities and the SQL Server database: by using the ODBC connectivity built into the NT operating system, Microsoft SQL Server and the NT Internet Information Server database developers have the functionality to deliver interactive, online database content to the masses via an Internet Web Site. There is also improved support for distributed transactions and enhanced distributed management tools that allows for seamless replication and multiple platform implementations. Microsoft's total embrace of the Internet technology has made this possible in ways that were unimaginable just a few short years ago. Databases can now be replicated via the Internet and make data accessible to users in remote locations throughout the world. The improved image data type will help add rich content for the Internet user. Images are stored and managed as a tree structure of data fragments that appear as if they were stored in a table row. There are plans to support new data types, such as video and audio, to meet the emerging Internet technology. This is exactly what Dr. Codd was talking about when he said that the relational database should be able to support new technologies.

Intranets: SQL Server Behind the Firewall

The Microsoft Exchange Server can be used with the SQL Mail part of Microsoft SQL Server and the Microsoft BackOffice product line to build Intranet solutions. The Intranet is similar to the Internet, but the number of users is usually limited to employees within a corporation. The Intranet is also protected by a firewall. With an Intranet, a company can keep its data confidential yet still have the benefits of the Web environment.

Companies can use an Intranet to distribute information or collect information from their employees. Many companies are moving their internal applications to the Intranet and leveraging them once they are there. Think of entering the hours you work on the Intranet or entering your expense reimbursement data into an Intranet Web page which makes its way to a SQL Server database. Find out what the next department is doing by visiting their Web page on the Intranet. The possibilities are endless, especially as they incorporate the data stored in the corporate database onto the Web page. An Intranet can also be used as a proving ground for applications before moving them to the Internet.

Reliability, quick response time, and security are good reasons to embrace Intranet technology. Intranets are relatively immature now, but they are moving forward as the internal communication needs of companies grow. Businesses will not be competitive into the next century if they do not embrace the Internet and Intranet technologies. SQL Server 7 supports this philosophy by committing to a set of tools designed explicitly for this purpose. If data can be stored on a SQL Server 7 database, it can quickly be presented via browser technology.

Advent of the Microsoft Transaction Server

Scalability, the ability to add more hardware when the size of the data and the demand in number of users increases, has been a customer demand for many years. A distributed computing platform requires that this work well but, unfortunately, personal computer hardware has not stepped up to the task of distributed computing until recently. Now however, the PC hardware comes with differing processing capabilities and multiple CPUs, and it is up to the software to harness this newly acquired power. Microsoft SQL Server is accomplishing this with the parallel execution of a single query across multiple CPUs. The interesting part of this is that Microsoft SQL Server 7 is the only database designed to run in a distributed computing environment and can take advantage of many of the opportunities inherent in the PC platform in a way that other relational databases cannot.

The client/server model as we know it is two-tiered, which means two computers are involved, a client and a server. This does not fit well into the scalability equation when the servers are dealing with thousands of users, so the idea of a three-tiered or multitiered application has come into being to meet the physical challenges of the hardware. Multitiered means the insertion of another computer into the mix which, for example, can implement the business rules of the Enterprise and transform data.

Microsoft Transaction Server is an associated technology that keeps the developers from having to deal with connectivity and related issues. It is a complete two-tiered server environment for ActiveX and has automatic thread and process management and a database connection pool. The developer does not have to worry about beginning and ending transactions: if a component is flagged as transactional, the Microsoft Transaction Server creates a transaction around the processing, and those components referenced will also be included in the transaction. The product protects the developer from system-level tasks like thread management and is best used with DCOM. DCOM, sometimes referred to as COM+, is an extension to COM (Component Object Model), which will be used to build the next-generation applications for the distributed environment. A client gets access to one of the DCOM objects and calls routines through that pointer as if the object were running on the client. DCOM has a data binding feature that binds object and database fields. A COM server can create object instances of many object classes, and a COM object can have multiple interfaces, each representing a different way the object acts. The use of DCOM objects has been accelerated by the use of COM objects and other related technologies, and this architecture is the basis for the technology of the future on the Web for databases.

This product makes distributed server applications easier to deploy and scaleable in ways not matched by other vendors.

Enterprise Visionary

NT Server Enterprise Edition will have Microsoft Transaction Server (MTS) and Message Queue Server built in. SQL Server Enterprise Edition uses Cluster Server, scaleable to 16 nodes. SQL Server 7 has 64-bit addressing to support applications that need more than the 2GB of memory allowed by 32-bit software. Windows NT and SQL Server will scale to eight processors out of the box and can use up to 3GB of application memory. In a future unspecified release of SQL Server, the database will implement massive parallelism on large clusters. This is clearly a direction Dr. Codd could have appreciated.

Just as one can not help but hear about Dr. Codd when learning about relational databases, one can not help but mention Bill Gates when discussing the Enterprise. His vision of the Enterprise shows in the implementation of NT Server, Microsoft SQL Server, and the components that facilitate the distributed computing environment. Also included in this mix is BackOffice Server 4.0 Enterprise Edition. It will include the enterprise versions of NT, SQL Server, Exchange, and Site Server Enterprise Edition, which includes Commerce Server. In addition, Wolfpack APIs allow third parties to integrate their clustering products with the Microsoft technology. This is a strategy that allows third party products to build on the Microsoft technology. Win32 and OLE, part of the Component Object Model, are also part of the strategy and are being offered for licensing to third parties on other operating systems. The ultimate intent of the strategy is to move from the desktop to the Enterprise.

The server model is the predominant feature in the release of Microsoft software products. BackOffice has SQL Server, System Management Server, SNA Server, MS Mail Server, and Windows NT. Windows, Component Object Model, and OLE round out the Enterprise picture. What OLE adds is a programming model which is based on object-oriented interfaces and is defined using Microsoft Interface Definition Language (MIDL). OLE provides a consistent programming model across all components and objects and implements Microsoft's COM. Microsoft will begin to provide OLE interfaces for developers to use rather than APIs. The objects can be incorporated in applications using their OLE interfaces, the idea being to reuse the COM objects.

Microsoft's programming interface is the Win32 API, and this interface is the central part of the strategy. The goal is to make Win32 available on other operating systems in the form of link libraries that will allow programmers to link applications. The Win32 API has a preemptive scheduler for multitasking, multithreading, 32-bit linear memory-addressing, protected memory, symmetric multiprocessing capability, and other features.

An introduction to SQL Server 7 is not complete without mentioning clustering capabilities. Clustering through the use of Microsoft's Cluster Server API will constitute a major part of the Enterprise equation by linking servers together to provide application load balancing. When one database server fails, clustering moves them to another server, making the database a virtual database on a shared dish. Cluster Server gets services back online in case of failure and helps system administrators keep systems available during maintenance procedures. The system administrator can wait for a slow time and initiate the fail-over to do maintenance on the servers. A *fail-over* is when the secondary server monitoring the primary gets no response after two tries and the secondary server maintains a lock on the shared drive array with no complaint from the other server. When that happens, Cluster Server can move services back to the restored primary server. Cluster Server watches critical services and applications, and any protected program that becomes unavailable is restarted on the same machine or a different server. To deal with hardware failure, Cluster Server uses one server to monitor the other. The NT Server Enterprise will have built-in transaction processing and clustering. Microsoft SQL Server and the Microsoft Transaction Server MTS will create an Enterprise software solution. Cluster Server servers are currently linked via the SCSI bus, and both servers share an array of drives and monitor each other. Cluster Server uses polling to determine the availability of a server or subsystem.

After a complete fail-over, the secondary server begins to take the configuration of the primary server. IP addresses are remapped, the primary's NetBIOS server name is co-opted, and NetBIOS shares are put back online. Microsoft's SQL Server is designed to work with Cluster Server for load distribution or if one server fails, the other will support SQL Server on the shared disk.

Bill Gates, Microsoft CEO, summarizes the vision of the future of enterprise computing: "Any business of any size can now run its enterprise applications on Microsoft software and industry-standard hardware. Combining enterprise-class scalability with PC-industry volume economics will radically reshape the enterprise markets. The ongoing R&D investments by Microsoft and the industry will provide our customers still greater levels of scalability, interoperability, availability, and manageability in the future."

Chapter 2

Improvements in Capacity

Breaking the Memory Barriers

Memory is a major factor in the performance of Microsoft SQL Server, and not supplying enough memory to SQL Server will degrade performance. The minimum is stated at 16MB memory. Of course, as is the case for all NT-based applications, the more memory available, the better the application will perform. With memory prices at an all time low, a safe rule of thumb is to install as much memory as the machine will hold, at least in the case of single or dual CPU "non-specialized platforms."

Dynamic Allocation

The way that memory is sized is one of SQL Server 7's new features. When the software is installed, SQL Server dynamically allocates the amount of memory according to its needs and available memory by default.

If you decide to allocate memory yourself instead of letting SQL Server dynamically allocate memory, be sure to factor in a minimum of 12MB (although 24MB seems to be the effective minimum for bare bones use) for the NT operating system. Normally though, NT will need more memory, depending on what applications are running on the server in addition to SQL Server. It is never a good idea to run other resource intensive applications on a heavily used SQL Server. Take these extra services into account when allocating memory to SQL Server and periodically check to see what other services are running. Remove any outdated or unneeded services unnecessarily consuming memory.

In an effort to achieve better performance, memory can be locked as a working set. The server configuration *set working set size* can determine if memory is locked. This server configuration is set with *sp_configure* or by using the Microsoft Management Console (MMC). There is a new screen in the Enterprise Manager devoted to memory settings:

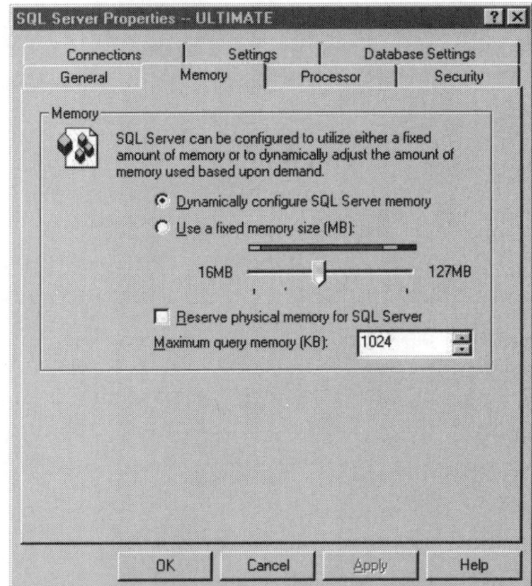

The check box called Reserve Physical Memory for SQL Server is the check box that corresponds to working set size. If this setting is 0 (off), NT will swap SQL Server pages. If the check box is checked or the value is 1 (on), Windows NT will not swap SQL Server pages even when SQL Server is not using them. Keep in mind that this will prevent other applications from using the memory resources also.

NT will allow you to allocate more virtual memory than there is physical memory; however, doing this will result in decreased performance. System overhead resource requirements change depending on what the configurations are. The more complex the SQL Server configuration, the more system overhead. It is better to let SQL Server dynamically control how much memory to allocate to avoid application problems caused by inadequate memory settings and memory contention with other applications.

Setting and Adding Memory

If you feel you must set your own memory, consider the following guidelines while remembering that NT needs at least 12MB of memory and you must leave enough for the NT operating system to function adequately:

Total Physical Memory (in MB)	**SQL Server Memory (in MB)**
16	4
24	8
32	16
48	28
64	40
128	100
256	216
512	464

These figures reflect the specified minimums. Even though Microsoft is working hard to reduce resource utilization, running NT, SQL Server, MTS, and IIS all on one platform will not be achieved effectively without significant amounts of memory.

If you are going to add memory to SQL Server, do it in large increments. Adding 4 or 8MB won't help that much, but moving from 32MB to 64MB will show significant improvement. Before you add memory, use the Performance Monitor to determine the memory behavior on your server. If the *cache hit ratio* is high (more than 85 percent), more memory will not help. The server is finding the stored procedures and indexes in memory most of the time, which indicates you have enough memory to store the commonly referenced objects. The cache hit ratio provides information about whether data is in memory or on disk. This rule does not apply to Very Large Databases (VLDB), as some of the data cannot fit into memory because the tables and indexes are so large.

The Page Faults/sec counter of the Memory object can tell you if SQL Server is generating page faults. If this is happening, SQL Server has too much memory allocated and not all of it is in the computer's physical memory. This depends on your system and how much physical memory is installed.

Use Windows NT Performance Monitor and use Add Data and select SQLSERVER in the instance box. You will see the counters in the drop-down list box.

Version 7 Memory Updates

Placing the *tempdb system database* in memory is no longer an option in SQL Server 7 as it was in earlier versions. Few applications used the tempdb in RAM option, and performance did not seem to improve when it was used. In addition, the sort pages and hash buckets server configuration options are no longer used and will cause an error if you try to use them, as will other abandoned options. Server configuration options no longer supported by SQL Server 7 include:

- backup buffer size
- backup threads
- free buffers
- hash buckets
- max lazywrite IO
- tempdb in RAM
- sort pages

A new option is **min memory per query** used to specify the minimum amount of memory (in kilobytes) that will be allocated for the execution of a query

Other configuration options that affect memory are min server memory and max server memory. To allocate a fixed amount of memory to SQL Server set min server memory and max server memory to the same amount. You can also set set min server memory and max server memory to span a range. This will keep SQL Server memory usage within a range and keep memory free for other applications. Min server memory is used to make sure SQL Server always has a minimum amount of memory. Max server memory is used to keep SQL Server from using more than the value in max server memory but can never be less than 4MB. SQL Server is capable of giving memory back to NT if some other application starts and NT has less than 5 megabytes of memory free. Since there is a delay between the time another application is executing and when SQL Server can release memory, you can use max server memory so that your users will not experience the wait. Do this only if your users are experiencing a noticeable problem.Use *DBCC MEMUSAGE* to determine the amount of memory of the largest objects in the buffer cache and the Perfomance Monitor counter Page Faults/sec of the Memory Object to show the number of times a virtual page is not in memory, meaning that the page is read from disk instead of from memory. High values for this figure either mean more physical memory should be added or the memory configuration for SQL Server should be inspected to see if more memory can be released back to NT.

Storage Capacity to a Terabyte

In this section we will see how various changes to the architecture will help the database scale to a terabyte, such as when a simplification in the interface between the SQL Server and the file system has occurred.

Space Management

Database pages have been increased from 2K to 8K to support row-level locking. This improves performance when accessing large amounts of data by retrieving more data for each I/O, which will help when scaling databases to the terabyte range. This will cause every SQL Server DBA in the world to pause for a moment when calculating space requirements with pages as a factor. A database page is defined four times bigger.

Databases are self-describing and autogrow attributes and database options follow a database moved to another SQL Server.

Database and Transaction Logs as Files

A SQL Server 7 database will always consist of two or more files. There is always at least one data file (.mdf or .ndf) and one log file (.ldf), and there are no longer multiple databases in one file. (The file extensions are a changeable default.) This helps to increase the scalability of SQL Server to one terabyte per database and was necessary to implement row-level locking. When a database is dropped, its associated files can be deleted. The new structure is one database per file and one database can have multiple files.

In addition, SQL Server 7 will allow a database file to grow and shrink as the data grows and shrinks without the interference of a database administrator. SQL Server 7 also has file groups. A file group is an allocated assembly of database files grouped for ease of administration. For example, you could have a file group for one database and group all the files for the database into a named or the default file group. The transaction log is now an operating system file instead of in the syslogs table in the database. There is no filegroup for the log file. By default you get one log file.

Transaction Log Enhancements

Enhancements to the transaction log also contribute to the viability of a terabyte database on SQL Server. Since files are now used to store data and logs, the *syslogs* system table no longer stores the transaction logs on datapages and in database tables, but rather in files. And, since the database and logs can no longer reside on a single file, there must now be at least two files for the database: one data file and one log file. The idea behind this is to read more at one time from the log file and to keep the logs from competing with data for space in memory which makes sense when you have a terabyte database.

The transaction log is now an operating system file instead of in the syslogs table in the database. There is no filegroup for the log file. By default you get one log file. The log file can be thought of as a circular entity, deleting from the beginning and writing to the end. You can accurately monitor transaction log space with DBCC SQLPERF (LOGSPACE).

Accessing Data with Indexes

The query processor will now use additional nonclustered indexes more effectively because the row locator is no longer the physical record identifier, and— the clustering key of the clustered index, if there is one, is the row locator instead. This has the effect of exposing the clustering key to the relational engine.

When a page splits on the clustered index, this new row locator, the clustering key, eliminates the update of all of the physical record identifiers (rids) of the *non*clustered indexes. Keep the clustered index small because you have to write the clustering key in each secondary index. When a page splits on the clustered index the row has to be physically relocated with a different physical record identifier (rid). If you have no clustered index on your table, you will have no clustering key but if there is *no* clustered index on the table, page splits on the clustered index do not happen, so it doesn't matter if the clustering key is not available. In this case, nonclustered indexes will still use the physical record identifiers (rids) to point to the location of the row.

If you create a clustered index in SQL Server 7, try to keep the clustering key as small as possible. A clustered index that is wide (multicolumn or character data) will not perform as well as a narrow index on an integer because the clustering key will have to be written on the nonclustered index entries, making the nonclustered indexes larger. These index access changes also help the performance in terabyte-size databases.

Tembdb Space Management

Tempdb is also an area that has constrained the reporting activities on very large databases. Tempdb used to be fixed in size, but it now grows as it is needed.

Dynamic Row-level Locking

The SQL Server 7 locking subsystem has been changed to incorporate full row-level locking for both data rows and index entries. This can keep SQL Server from locking entire pages, which interferes with the availability of unrelated rows that just happen to be on the same page as the desired row or rows. It can also help prevent the deadlocking and blocking that are commonly seen in SQL Server applications.

Row-level locking constitutes a long-awaited and major enhancement to SQL Server. The quest for row-level locking was so important to this release that it was what drove the page storage changes that have occurred. Concurrency, that is, the ability for multiple users in online transaction processing to use the data and still maintain the integrity of data access and changes, will be improved with the new locking behavior. There are latches which wait but don't deadlock and wait type codes in the *sysprocesses* system table have been enhanced to include latch. Access method changes have occurred and the system no longer locks two pages of data to insert a row as in previous versions.

There is also dynamic locking that occurs when row level locking is not the right choice and page or table locking is better. The optimizer determines the granularity for locking by measuring the concurrency cost resulting in an automatic multi-granularity solution.

In addition, the new lock solution completes lock requests with greater speed by dynamically managing its locks and varying its settings as the database gets larger. The locks configuration option no longer has to be tuned manually; SQL Server can now automatically decide to do a page-level lock or a row-level lock. Follow this general rule:

Page-level locking is best for:	**Row-level locking is best for:**
table scans	Insert
	Update
	Delete

There is a system table called syslockinfo that contains locking information as well as a system stored procedure called sp_lock that can give you information related to locking. The SQL Server Profiler can also give you information about locking.

The table hint in the SELECT statement, READPAST, reads past locked rows and skips them and the SET LOCK TIMEOUT statement determines the number of milliseconds a statement will wait for a lock to be released.

It must be noted that locking in the *tempdb* system database is significantly reduced in SQL Server 7. System deadlocks no longer occur in this version of SQL Server when tempdb is used. Latches wait but do not deadlock and since extents are no longer linked together there are no related deadlocks. System internal deadlocks have disappeared.

You can customize the Isolation Level (which is the level a transaction can accept inconsistent data) by using the SET TRANSACTION ISOLATION LEVEL statement for the session. The Isolation Level determines the locking behavior of SQL Server. You can also use DBCC USEROPTIONS to check which Isolation Level is in use for your session. A lower isolation level increases concurrency but also increases the chance of phantom rows and lost updates. Conversely, a higher isolation level alleviates lost updates, but can decrease concurrency. You can use the system stored procedures *sp_who* and the *sysprocesses* system table to assist you in viewing system concurrency (who is on the system now) showing users and the processes they are running.

Isolation levels impacting concurrency and locking that SQL Server 7 supports are the SQL-92 isolation levels:

- Read uncommitted (the lowest level)
- Read committed (SQL Server default level)
- Repeatable read
- Serializable (the highest level)

The isolation level of repeatable read or serializable prevents lost updates.

SQL Server 7 contains attempts to alleviate the manual overhead of administering SQL Server to make the entire process less complicated and less obscure. Everywhere possible, SQL Server has been automated to take over many of the little tweak-type tuning jobs that most database administrators neglect until there is a performance problem. If it made sense to remove an option because no one uses it or even knows what it means, the developers have taken it out or let SQL Server tune according to the demand or resource of the server. This is a good solid approach and has the effect of modernizing SQL Server.

Backup

SQL Server 7 backup features enhanced speed and performance, including:

- fuzzy backup
- differential backup
- automatic database creation upon a restore

In addition:

- Backups can be checked for consistency without restoring the database.
- SQL Server can restore and roll forward part of the database.
- Backups are supported in the Microsoft Tape Format.

SQL Server will automatically create the database for the restored file if it is not on the server and alter it if it is not the correct size for the backup file. The new *fuzzy backup* concept allows the backup to occur with less impact on SQL Server. Now, backing up a database does not cause SQL Server to slow down, nor do users notice that a backup is running on the system. This allows data to be backed up in an inconsistent manner, so a part of the logs are routinely backed up to provide the missing transaction integrity. The pages do not have to be locked when the backup occurs. This helps to make the running backup process transparent to the users who are logged on to SQL Server.

There is also a new concept of the *differential backup*. This is much like an differential backup of the file directory structure where a full backup is performed and then only the changed files are backed up in a given number of subsequent days until the next full backup is scheduled. This is yet another valuable change to the backup strategy in an effort to save time and reduce system overhead and can be used effectively for very large databases.

Another new backup feature allows database administrators to check the backup file for consistency without restoring it to a database. This reduces the amount of time and resource overhead if you want to determine if your backup file is good. SQL Server 7 can also restore or roll forward a portion of the database, shortening the amount of time it takes to recover one file of the database in the event of a system failure, such as disk problems or other hardware failure. Complying with the Microsoft Tape Format will allow database backup files to share the same tape as, say, an NT Backup file. This will make the whole backup exercise of the system administrator and the database administrator easier and faster.

Utilities for the Terabyte Database

To support a terabyte database, SQL Server utilities have been vastly improved, particularly in how fast they execute and fast roll forward is 2 to 10 times faster in the amount of time SQL Server takes to rollback a transaction.

Faster Database Consistency Checker

It used to be that if you had a huge database, running a Database Consistency Checker (DBCC) command on database would take more time that any SQL Server DBA would care to admit. It was very important when dealing with the possibility of terabyte databases that this be improved, and it has been. However, if your database is larger than 5GB, it is still advisable to run DBCC on a database you have loaded to your backup server. Also, DBCC still has to look at every page in the database in some circumstances. The larger your database, the longer it will take to read every database page.

DBCC CHECKDB is now the one-stop shop. It runs CHECKALLOC and CHECKCATALOG as well as the CHECKDB consistency checks and now you don't HAVE to run this utility. There is now a fail fast response by SQL Server when it recognizes that corruption may be occurring. The process is terminated or SQL Server shuts down. This is infinitely preferable to having to manually fix the resulting problem or restore from a backup.

DBCC has the capability to repair damaged databases. DBCC CHECKALLOC, DBCC CHECKDB, and DBCC CHECKTABLE have the ability to repair at a database (even a suspect database) and contain the following options:

- REPAIR_ALLOW_DATA_LOSS (allow SQL Server to do the best it can but the result could be some data loss as an entire page is removed if it is bad)
- REPAIR_FAST (fast safe repairs that can be done quickly, fix linkage, etc.)
- REPAIR_REBUILD (slow safe repairs like rebuilding indexes)

Each layer of repair includes the prior one. If you run this with no informational messages, only the errors are shown.

Reporting of spurious errors no longer occurs when the database is not in single user mode, and DBCC SQLPERF (LOGSPACE) returns accurate results.

Faster Bulk Copy

Bulk copy operations (the process of importing data into a database or exporting data out of a database) now validate constraints and fire triggers as the data is placed into the database. Additional improvements have been made to speed up the bulk copy processes to protect the referential integrity of the database, and bulk copy has been targeted for continuous improvement to make it faster. For more on bulk copy operations, see Chapter 8.

Rebuilt Query Processor

Any conversation about bigger and faster has to include a discussion about the query processor, the intelligence that is applied when data is requested from the database. The query processor has to retrieve the data in the fastest manner possible. With the idea of large databases and warehouses of data in mind, there are now hash and merge join and aggregation techniques to help the process of joining data on larger databases. These new techniques are being used on large databases instead of only using the nested-loop join. Within the query processor, new strategies have been applied to help complex queries perform better. SQL Server 7 now has the capability to filter the data through intersection and union algorithms, using the indexes before actually pulling the rows off the database.

The query optimizer is now cost-based and no longer has trouble picking the correct index to use. It also requires less tuning. Previously, the SQL developer had to use an optimizer hint to force the use of the desired index when the optimizer would not pick the optimal index.

The query processor communications with the data-storage components of SQL Server uses OLE DB. OLE DB is used to support distributed queries between many SQL Server 7 servers or ODBC data sources.

The SQL Server Query Analyzer *SHOWPLAN* output is now easier to read and has eliminated some of the outdated terminology and introduced new terminology. This was a smart move, because it used to be easy to forget to use *SHOWPLAN* to look at the execution plan when writing a query. Several other limitations have been removed, including the 16–work table limitation—now you can use up to 32 tables in a single query. All of this is helpful when scaling to the terabyte database.

More CPUs

SQL Server 7 can also access more CPUs, allowing parallel query execution across multiple processors. This means that portions of an execution plan can run in parallel on different CPUs and that the SQL Server application can figure out which queries can be completed faster if they are executed with a parallel execution plan. The work is then divided among the processors on the machine. Use the NT Performance Monitor to determine if your application is CPU-bound. You may need hardware CPU upgrades to build a better processor or to build up multiple processors for complex or large applications.

The Processor: percent Processor Time counter indicates the amount of time the CPU spends processing a thread. An average count of 80–90 percent should prompt you to look into adding or upgrading CPUs. You can also use the SQL Profiler Percentage CPU Usage data component to detect whether an application is CPU-bound.

Maximum Length for Char/Binary and Varchar/VarBinary

Storage of text and image data has been changed in SQL Server 7. Parallel retrieval of text and image data, which consists of character data and binary data, will allow data of the large datatypes to be returned to the user faster, which is what that user wants to see. Also, space is used more efficiently: if the row is too small to fit on a datapage, other rows can be placed on the page to use the available space instead of wasting the remaining space on the datapage, as in previous versions.

The maximum number of bytes in a row is now 8060 bytes (8K), and the length of character and binary data types has been increased to 8000 bytes from the 255 bytes of earlier versions. HTML documents can be stored as text datatypes, which also stores ASCII text files. The text datatype stores end-of-line characters, while the image datatype does not. The image (binary) data type stores binary data in excess of 8K and can store Microsoft Word files, Microsoft Excel files, bitmaps, and GIF and JPEG files, to name just a few.

The Complete Reference

Chapter 3

Microsoft Management Console

The Enterprise Manager is still very similar to previous versions with the exception of the new framework around the Enterprise Manager called the Microsoft Management Console (MMC), a new way of presenting the administration of BackOffice servers. The intention is to be able to "snap in" other tools to administer BackOffice servers in this same framework that will allow for a customizable and centrally located command center. The presentation is very similar to Microsoft Windows NT Explorer and appears as a list tree.

Adding Microsoft Management Console Snap-Ins

When you open the Microsoft Management Console, you will see an item called the Console Root. The window is divided into two parts, with the Scope Pane on the left and the Results Pane on the right. If this is your first look at the MMC, it may seem strange to you, but after drilling down through the Explorer-like items by expanding them, things will begin to look more familiar. You will see four downward-pointing pyramids in the command bar—Action, View, Tools, and Help—which represent menus. The Action menu contains the items you will see when you right-click an object and will bring up a short-cut menu for the object. The choices will vary depending on which object you select in the Scope or Results Pane. The SQL Server 7 MMC snap-in console is called SQL Server Enterprise Manager, shown in Figure 3-1.

Adding a New Server Group

To add a new server group within the hierarchy tree of the Enterprise Manager, go to the Command menu of the Enterprise Manager, click Action, and you will see an option for adding a New Server Group. Do not confuse the menu item New SQL Server Group in the Action Menu with the groups and roles of NT that I mentioned earlier in this book. The New SQL Server Group item in the Action Menu is a way to group servers together. This SQL Server Group allows you to build your Windows NT Explorer-like tree in a hierarchy of SQL Servers within the Enterprise Manager so that you can begin to build and expand the tree and see the hierarchy. You can place servers of the same type together, which is convenient when you have hundreds of servers. You can place the servers in easily recognized groups of servers, locate them in the list hierarchy, and get to them quickly when an administration crisis arises and more than one server needs immediate attention.

The dialog box shown below enables you to build a New Server Group. Notice there are two levels in this dialog box: the Top Level Group and the Sub-Group. Type

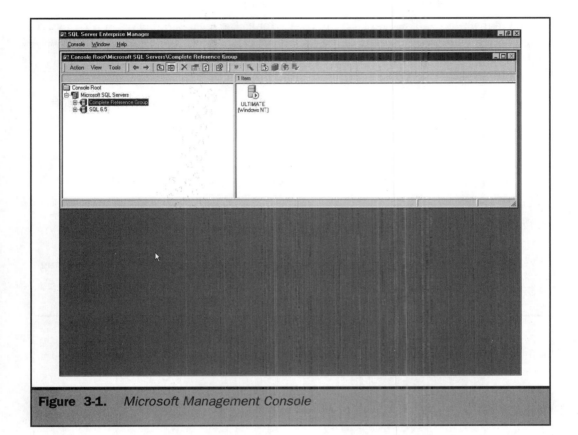

Figure 3-1. *Microsoft Management Console*

in the name of the SQL Server Group. The figures show a server group called the Complete Reference Group of SQL Servers that was created in the Manage Server Groups window.

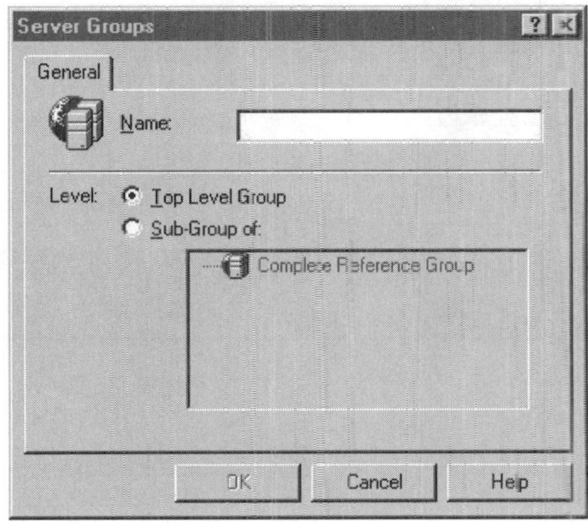

I have installed SQL Server 7 on my computer as the local SQL Server and named it Ultimate, which is also the name of the NT server. SQL Server will automatically use the NT machine name for the SQL Server name. To place Ultimate in the group of Complete Reference servers:

1. Click on the item called SQL Servers under the Console Root of the Microsoft Management Console (MMC).
2. Click on the server group created called Complete Reference Group.
3. From the Action Menu, select Register Server.
4. Click Next when the Register SQL Server Wizard screen shown in Figure 3-2 appears.
5. Select a server under the list of available servers.
6. Press the Add button.
7. Press the Next button. The Select Connection Option screen will appear, giving you the choice to connect to the server using NT Authentication or SQL Server

Figure 3-2. *First screen of the Register SQL Server Wizard*

Authentication. If you choose NT Authentication, you will connect using the NT account information you log into your computer with. You will not have to enter a password because the SQL Server trusts NT with a trusted connection. If you chose SQL Server Authentication you will have to type the login ID and password for the non-trusted connection.

8. Choose the connection option of your choice.
9. Press the Next button.
10. When the Select SQL Server Group screen appears, press the Add button to add the \\Ultimate server to the Complete Reference Group.
11. Press the Next button to move through the next screen.
12. Press the Finish button.

You have now registered a server and placed it in a server group that you have created. You can continue until you have registered all SQL Servers. Once you have accomplished this, you have a rich and powerful GUI tool set available to you for administering your SQL Servers. Tasks that take many minutes at the command line or by using Transact-SQL commands take seconds with the Enterprise Manager, a snap-in on the Microsoft Management Console.

If you select a SQL Server and right-click, you can choose Edit SQL Server Registration from the pop-up menu. You can check three other server-wide options if you would like them to apply to your server:

- Display SQL Server state in console
- Show System Databases and System Objects
- Automatically start SQL Server when connecting

If the Show System Databases and System Objects check box is not checked, the system databases, *master*, *msdb*, and *model* will not appear in the Enterprise Manager hierarchy tree.

Integrating SQL Server with External Tools

You can run any NT application from within the Microsoft Management Console and the Enterprise Manager. Expand your newly registered SQL Server by clicking on the plus sign beside the server name in the Enterprise Manager tree. Select SQL Servers in the Microsoft Management Console and you can access the Tools menu for the Enterprise Manager and select External Tools from there.

Selecting External Tools from the Tools menu will allow you to add an external tool that can be invoked from within the Enterprise Manager. The following dialog boxes are used to add an external tool to the Enterprise Manager.

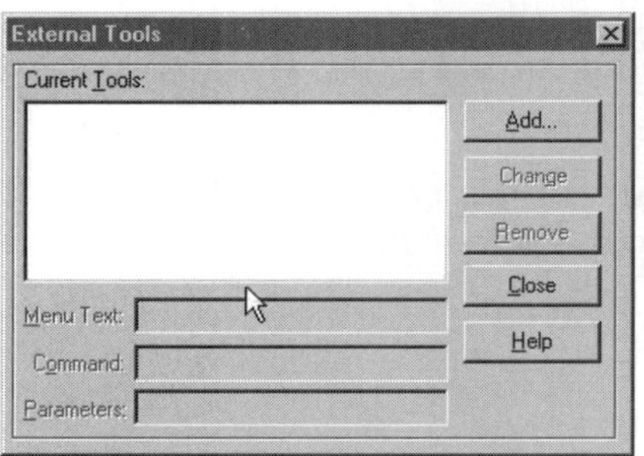

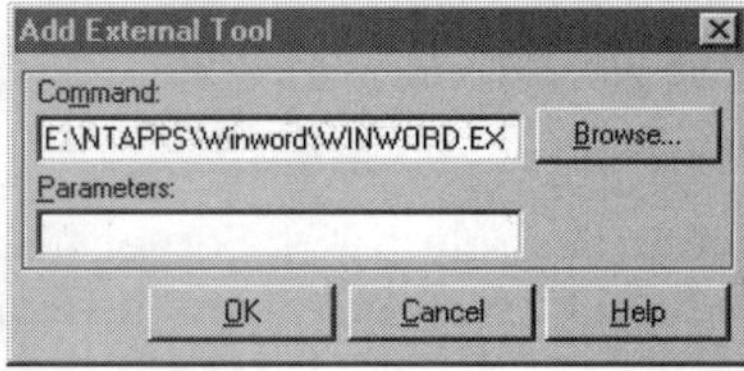

You will be able to invoke the NT application tool of your choice within the Enterprise Manager. In this case, I have added Microsoft Word NT application by simply pointing and clicking at some menu choices and browsing my disk for an application I wanted to include in the Microsoft Management Console. I will now be able to select and execute Microsoft Word from the Microsoft Management Console. I liked this so much that I added the rest of my favorite tools to this centrally located place and now have access to them at the bottom of the Tools menu

The other menu on the command bar within the Microsoft Management Console is called View. The items in this menu allow you to view the Results Pane in different ways. If you select Large, the Results Pane will show large icons like the view shown in Figure 3-3. The other view selections are Small (for small icons), List (for a list of icons), Detail (for a list with column headings providing more detailed information) and Taskpad.

Taskpad is an interesting view of the Enterprise Manager because it offers a plethora of tools and wizards to help with the processes involved in administrating your database environment. (When you select Tools, Wizards from the Enterprise Manager, you see 22 database, data transformation services, management, and replication wizards.) If Setting Up Your Database Solution is selected from the Taskpad Results pane in the Enterprise Manager shown in Figure 3-4, the next Taskpad formatted Results pane appears. Taskpad selections of Creating databases, Creating views, Creating indexes, Setting up security, and Creating stored procedures are wizards to guide you though these database tasks.

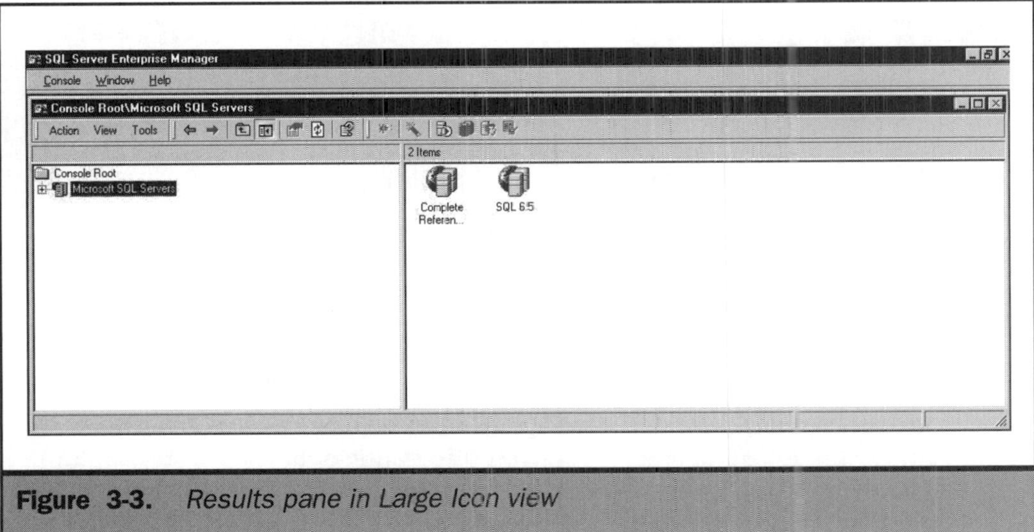

Figure 3-3. *Results pane in Large Icon view*

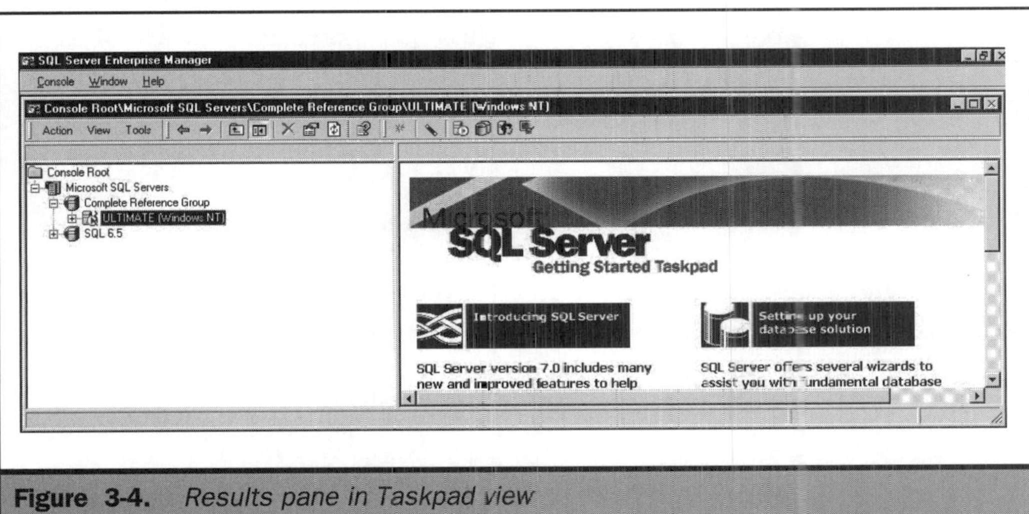

Figure 3-4. *Results pane in Taskpad view*

Enterprise Manager Functionality for Servers

The Enterprise Manager allows you to manage your SQL Servers and to perform the following server-wide functions:

Enterprise Manager Server Function	Descriptive Note
Register servers (allows them to be seen in the Enterprise Manager hierarchy tree)	Refer to the immediately preceding text and illustrations.
Assign a system administrator password if you are using SQL Server Authentication	This should be done immediately after installing SQL Server.
Configure local servers	This has become easier with fewer configuration options to worry about; many are now done automatically by the server.
Configure remote servers	This functionality works well and allows SQL servers to share data and communicate with each other.
Configure a multiserver environment	This is just like configuring a local server, which is what makes the Enterprise Manager deserve its name.
Set up login security	This has been more fully integrated into NT and made easier.
Create alerts	The server can perform actions such as paging and e-mailing on an error or event.
Administer and configure SQL Mail	SQL Server has the capability to send mail from inside the database, which makes it possible (and easy) to e-mail reports after a batch job has been completed—or upon a SQL Server alert.
Establish operators	You can easily e-mail or page a system administrator according to their scheduled work times.
Create and schedule jobs for a stand-alone environment	This has been greatly enhanced.
Create and schedule jobs for a multiserver environment	This has been greatly enhanced to include multiserver job scheduling.

Enterprise Manager Server Function	Descriptive Note
Create and manage replication scenarios	Replication has had a number of major enhancements.
Set the polling interval for SQL Server Enterprise Manager	This allows the DBA to set the interval that the Enterprise Manager is checking to see if the remote server is responding, which turns the indicator icon green or red on your computer screen and tells you if the server is started or stopped.

The procedure to perform each of the functions is explained in detail in the following paragraphs. It's extremely easy to administer SQL Servers using the Enterprise Manager. Without this tool, the DBA must write Transact-SQL code and possibly some other third-generation programming language to accomplish tasks that the Enterprise Manager can do with a point-and-click interface.

This GUI database tool vastly surpasses any of the UNIX database tools or any of the PC database tools on the market. The Enterprise Manager is *the* tool for the DBA. This represents as big an improvement in customer satisfaction and ease of use as moving from a network/hierarchical database to a relational database. There are major gains for the customer in terms of cost and reduction in database complexity. The Enterprise Manager represents a monumental step forward in the evolution of database tools.

Register Server

I described the server registration process in detail earlier in this chapter. (See under the heading "Adding Microsoft Management Console Snap-Ins.") This is the first step to bringing the SQL Server into the administrative jurisdiction of the Enterprise Manager. The Enterprise Manager will check your authentication before it will allow you to use the Enterprise Manager tool set to perform actions on SQL Server.

SQL Server 7 has a colorful Register Wizard within the Microsoft Management Console Enterprise Manager to help you through the SQL Server registration process.

Assign a System Administrator Password

The Enterprise Manager allows you to assign the System Administrator (SA) password with a point and a click. This should always be done right after you install SQL Server. If you do not do this then, the system administrator password is null and anyone can log into your SQL Server with system administrator privileges by simply typing **sa** as the login ID and leaving the password null.

Avoid this security risk by assigning the password immediately after you install SQL Server. This should be a part of your written procedures. Then store the password somewhere where no one can find it except you so that you don't forget what you set it to when you need to login as SA later. Or, if you are lucky enough to be in a well-tooled shop, you will have a tool for the SA that will give you the SA password for the server if you query the tool. You can also make something like this yourself by creating a table on a secured operations server and querying the table when you cannot remember the SA password for the server. This is much more secure than leaving the password lying on a piece of paper in one of your desk drawers. Something like this is necessary if you have a large number of servers to administer. The following steps demonstrate how easy it is to change the SA password.

This area of interest is located in the Microsoft Management Console | Enterprise Manager hierarchy tree under SQL Servers.

1. Expand the SQL Server in the Enterprise Manager hierarchy tree by clicking on the plus sign beside the server name.
2. Double-click on the Logins item under Security.
3. Right-click on the sa login ID, which is shown here:

4. Select Properties.
5. Type in the password for SQL Server Authentication for the sa (system administrator) login ID, as shown in Figure 3-5.
6. You will be asked to type it in again for verification.

Configure Local Servers

Configuring a server and a database has never been easier. All you have to do is visit a few screens in the Enterprise Manager and modify a few columns. The only difficult part is knowing your SQL Server well enough to know what the consequences of changing the numbers will be. The actual act of changing the configuration is very simple.

This area of interest is located in the Microsoft Management Console | Enterprise Manager hierarchy tree under SQL Servers.

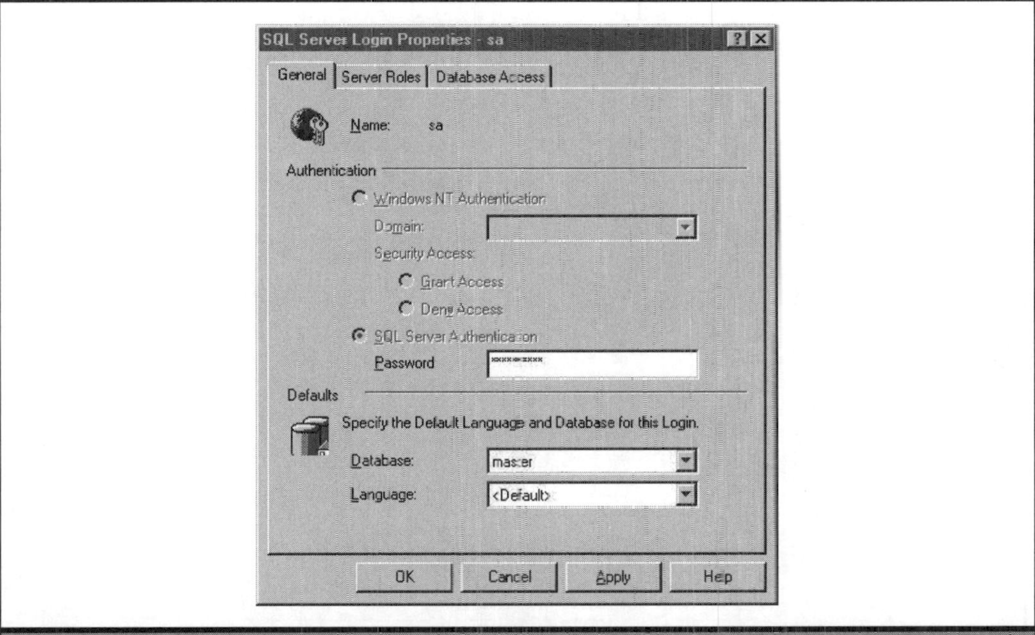

Figure 3-5. *Enter a password in the sa Properties dialog box*

1. Click on the server in the Enterprise Manager; (Local) is the representation of the local SQL Server called \\Ultimate.
2. Right-click on the server name (Local) to display a shortcut menu.
3. Select Properties from the shortcut menu.
4. The tabs for options to configure servers are displayed, as in Figure 3-6.

Configure Remote Servers

The real power of the Enterprise manager for the DBA is shown here. The process to configure a remote server is exactly the same as in the "Configure Local Servers" section. The remote server must be recognized on your network for the Enterprise Manager to locate the server and allow you to register it. After you register the remote server, it will appear on the Enterprise Manager hierarchy tree just as it does on the local server.

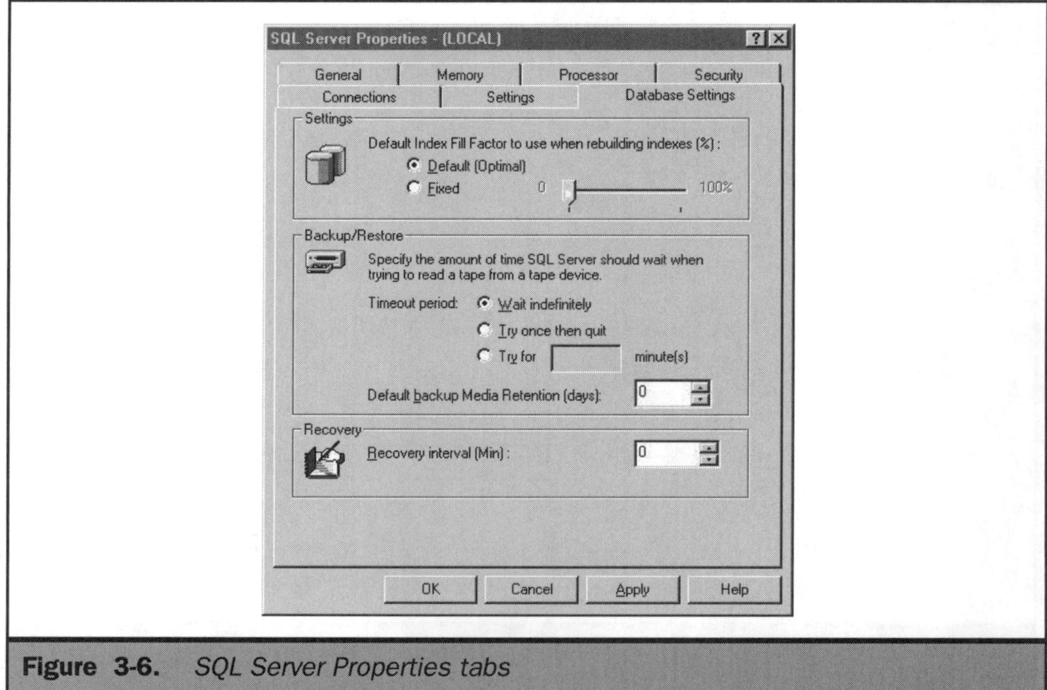

Figure 3-6. *SQL Server Properties tabs*

Configure a Multiserver Environment

Multisite management allows you to use a central SQL Server to manage a group of SQL Servers. The application of this technology is only as limited as your imagination. It allows you to create jobs and job steps, schedule jobs, logically influence the flow of the job steps with report success on success, failure on failure, failure on success and success on failure, and 'go to step' on success or failure. The failure or success logs are stored at the central SQL Server. This functionality considerably eases the burden of administration when doing job scheduling on each local server.

The Make Master Server Wizard steps you through the process of creating a multiserver environment. Define your central master server as an administrative server only without other NT applications running on it and forward events to this server. The act of creating target servers in called enlisting, and the act of unenlisting is called to defect from the enlistment. The master server is also referred to as the MSX master server.

The msdb database on the master server contains a table called the sysdownloadlist table. This table contains instructions like deleting a job, inserting a job, starting a job, and changing the polling interval on the target server. Entries are posted to the table by using the sp_post_msx_operation or by using other job-related stored procedures.

To view a master SQL Server Agent error log, right-click SQL Server Agent, select Multi Server Administration, and then Manage Target Servers on the Target Server Status tab, select a server, and View Errorlog.

To check the status of a target server, right-click SQL Server Agent, select Multi Server Administration, and then Manage Target Servers on the Target Server Status tab, select a server, and Check State.

Using SQL Server Enterprise Manager, a system administrator can define a multiserver configuration by right-clicking on SQL Server Agent in the Enterprise Manager hierarchy tree and selecting Multi Server Administration, then Make this a Master or Make this a Target. You can designate one server as the master server that distributes jobs, alerts, and event messages to target servers in the target server group.

The concept of a multiserver environment has been created to place servers in target groups, which then allows the application of a specific job to a targeted list of servers. The following new stored procedures are associated with this functionality. Keep in mind that we are talking about groups of target servers, not groups of users or groups of servers in the Enterprise Manager hierarchy.

Note *This area of interest is located in the Microsoft Management Console | Enterprise Manager | Tools Menu | Query Analyzer where you can run these stored procedures.*

Showing the system stored procedures and new system tables involved will help to explain this new concept and what is intended by it. The new system tables involved are systargetservers, systargetservergroups, and systargetservergroupmembers, which are located in the SQL Server system database called msdb. Only the system administrator can do this function. You must be in the msdb database in the Query Analyzer logged in as system administrator to execute the following stored procedures:

Multiserver Stored Procedure Name	Description of Functionality	Example
sp_add_ targetservergroup	Add the target server group	EXEC sp_add_targetservergroup 'Servers with Tax database'
sp_delete_ targetservergroup	Delete the target server group	EXEC sp_delete_targetservergrou p 'Servers with Tax database'

Multiserver Stored Procedure Name	Description of Functionality	Example
sp_help_ targetservergroup	Lists the servers in the specified target server group	EXEC sp_help_targetserver 'Servers with Tax database'
sp_add_ targetsvrgrp_member	Adds the specified group name or, optionally, if you give the server name, will add the specified server to the specified group	EXEC sp_add_targetsvrgrp_memb er 'Servers with Tax database', 'UncleSam''
sp_delete_ targetsvrgrp_member	Removes the specified target server group member	EXEC sp_add_targetsvrgrp_memb er 'Servers with Tax database', 'UncleSam;AuntSam''
sp_apply_job_to_targets	Adds the job to those servers where the job is not currently applied	EXEC sp_apply_job_to_targets 'Tax table update job','Servers with Tax database', 'UncleSam', 'APPLY'
sp_remove_ job_from_targets	Removes the specified job from those servers where the job has already been applied	EXEC sp_remove_job_from_target s 'Tax table update job','Server with Tax database,'UncleSam,AuntSa m'
sp_update_ targetservergroup	Changes the name of the target server group	EXEC sp_update_targetservergrou p 'Server with Tax database', 'Tax Servers'

The following select statement run in the Query Analyzer in the msdb database shows how the new row for the new target server group is added as a row in the system table that stores target server groups.

```
use msdb
go
select * from systargetservergroups
go

servergroup_id name
-------------- -------------------------
1              Servers with Tax database

(1 row(s) affected)
```

The following illustration shows the output from the Query Analyzer when the systargetservergroups system table is queried after adding the target server group:

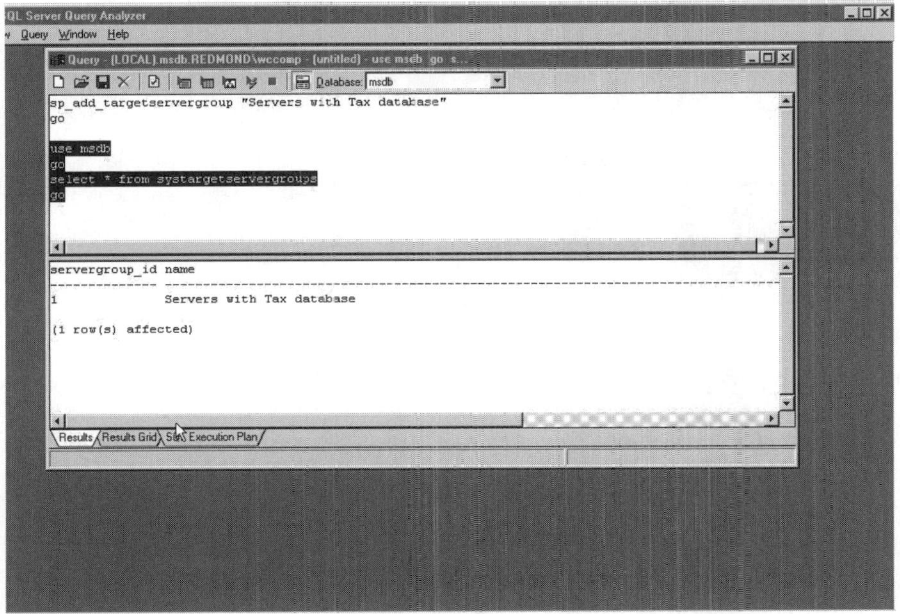

Set Up Login Security

The Enterprise Manager allows you to easily administer the security aspects of your servers, databases, and tables. You can control access by defining the database access of a login ID. See Figure 3-7. The two types of authentication are NT Authentication and SQL Server Authentication. This is described in more detail in Chapter 5 of this book.

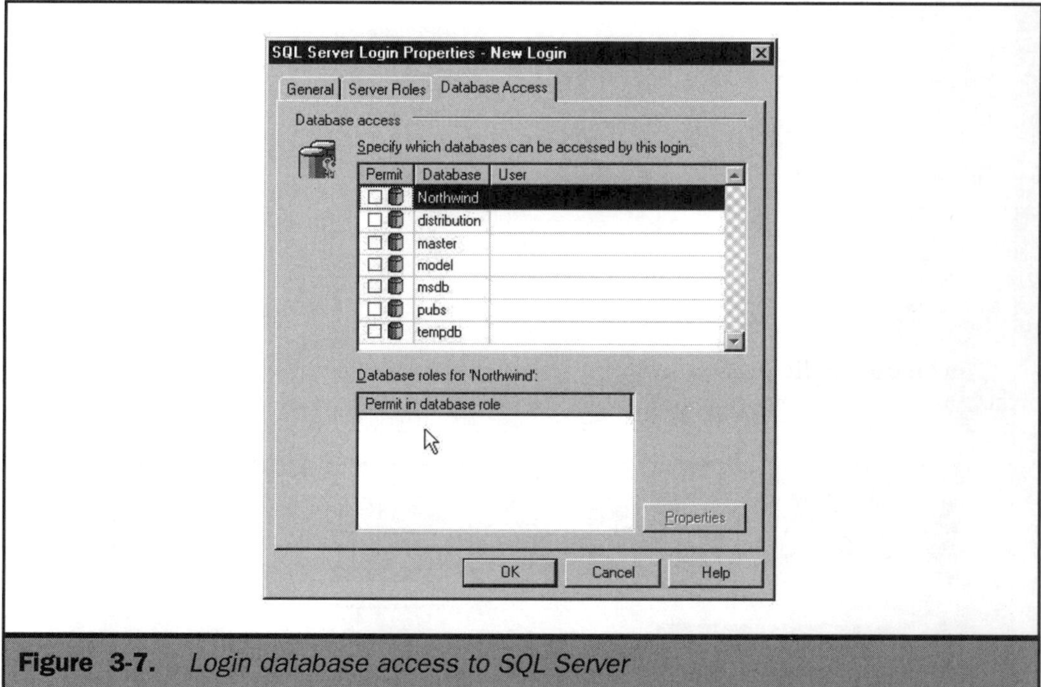

Figure 3-7. *Login database access to SQL Server*

The following steps show how to add a new login ID using the Enterprise Manager.

Note *This area of interest is located in the Microsoft Management Console | Enterprise Manager hierarchy tree under SQL Servers.*

1. Expand the server by clicking on the plus sign (+) in the Enterprise Manager hierarchy tree by the name of the desired server.
2. Select Logins and right-click. This will display the shortcut menu.
3. Select New from the shortcut menu. The SQL Server Login Properties screen will appear with three tabs.
4. Choose the General tab, which is shown in Figure 3-8.
5. Choose the desired authentication, either NT Authentication or SQL Server Authentication.

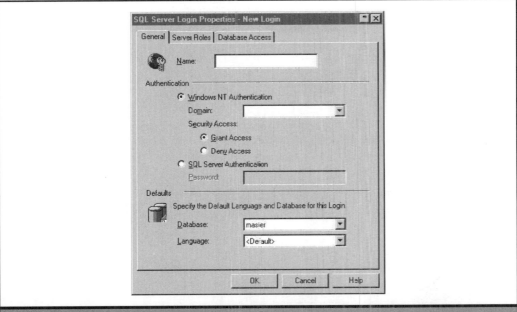

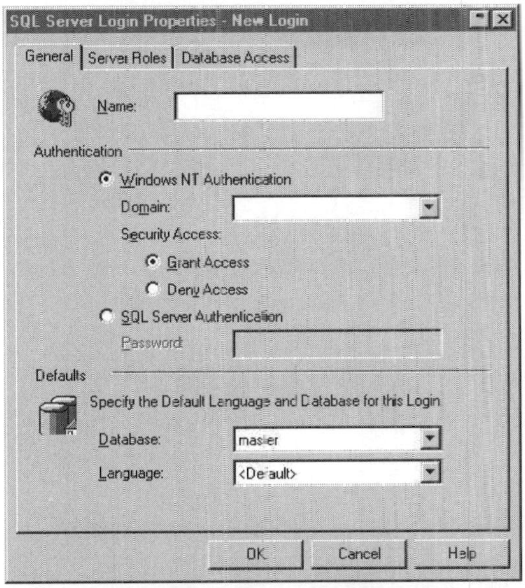

Figure 3-8. *General tab of the SQL Server Login Properties dialog box*

6. If SQL Server Authentication is chosen, enter the login ID and password.
7. If NT Authentication is chosen, enter the NT account and domain the SQL Server will use for the trusted connection.

The following steps show how to add the newly created login to a Server Role. Roles are discussed in detail in Chapter 5.

1. Expand the server by clicking on the plus sign in the Enterprise Manager hierarchy tree by the name of the desired server.
2. Select Logins and double-click. This will display existing logins.
3. Right-click on the desired login.
4. Select Properties from the shortcut menu. The SQL Server Login Properties screen will appear with three tabs.
5. Choose the Server Roles tab, which is shown in Figure 3-9.

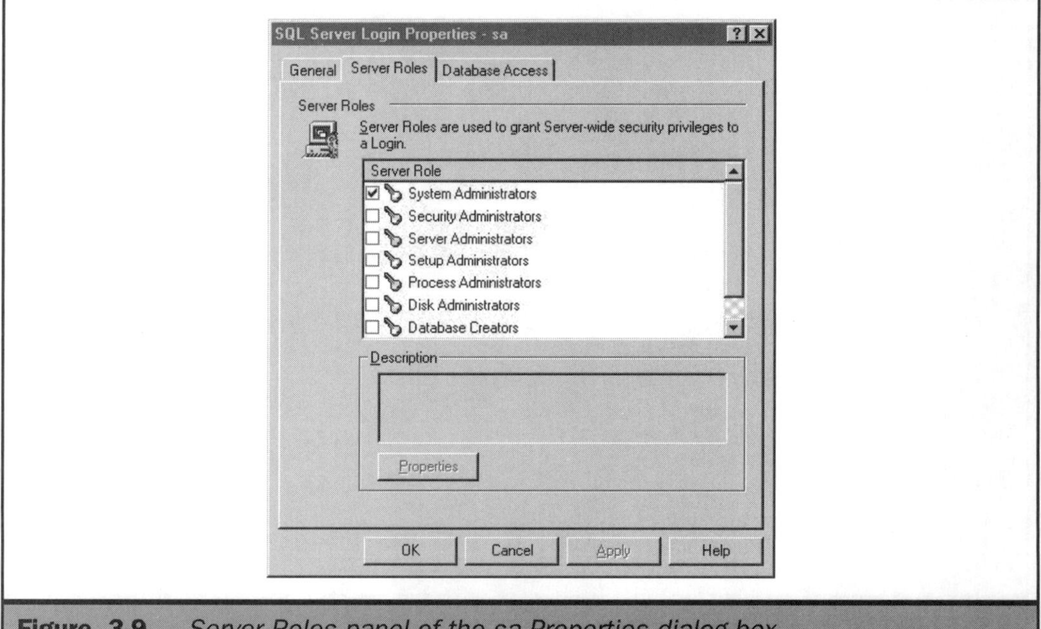

Figure 3-9. *Server Roles panel of the sa Properties dialog box*

6. Click on the check box for the desired Fixed Server Role or a user-defined Server Role for this login.

The following steps show how to give database access to the login ID. Database access can easily be assigned using the screen shown in Figure 3-10. Here you can assign access to a database and assign the login to Database Roles.

1. Expand the server by clicking on the plus sign in the Enterprise Manager hierarchy tree by the name of the desired server.
2. Select Logins and double-click. This will display existing logins.
3. Right-click on the desired login.
4. Select Properties from the shortcut menu. The SQL Server Login Properties screen will appear with three tabs.
5. Choose the Database Access tab.
6. Click on the check box for the desired database.
7. Click on the check box for the Database Role or a user-defined database role for this login.

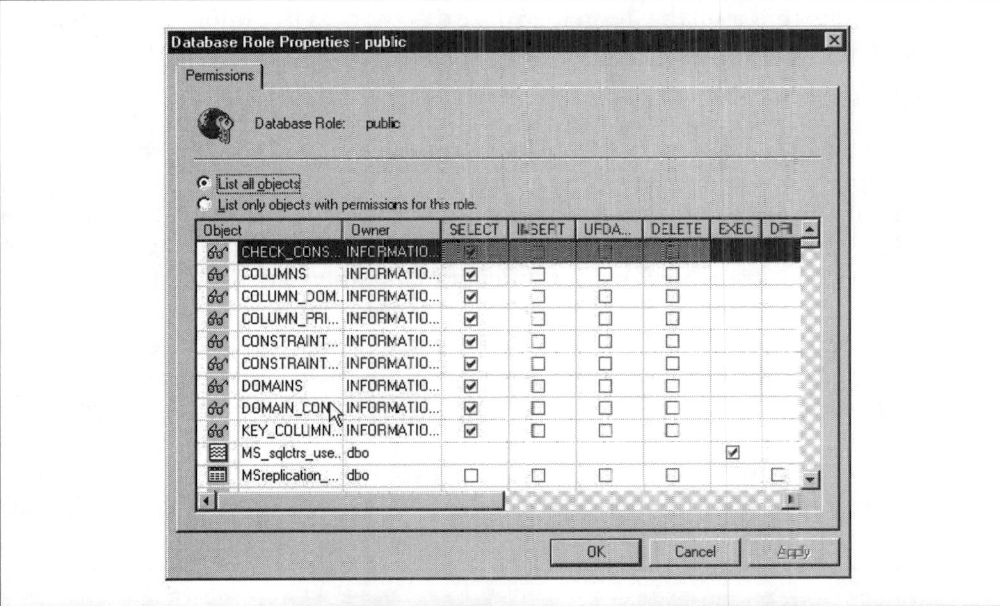

Figure 3-10. *To access the Permissions panel, click the Database Access tab, the Properties button, and then the Permissions button*

Create Alerts

The process of creating alerts to alert the operator to SQL Server errors has become very easy in SQL Server 7. To create a new alert using the Enterprise manager, follow these steps.

1. Expand the server by clicking on the plus sign (+) in the Enterprise Manager hierarchy tree by the name of the desired server.
2. Select the SQL Server Agent item under the expanded server name.
3. Expand the SQL Server Agent item by clicking the plus sign by the SQL Server Agent.
4. Click on Alert.
5. Right-click on Alert.
6. Select New Alert from the shortcut menu. The New Alert Properties Screen appears.
7. Enter the name for the new alert.
8. Select Find and enter the selection criteria and click on the button labeled … . This will give a list of existing alerts for SQL Server (see Figure 3-11).

9. Place your cursor on the desired error and press the OK button. This will place the error number in the New Properties Alert screen.
10. Select the Response tab.

Figure 3-11 shows the Manage SQL Server Messages screen. Use this screen to search for error messages and select errors to alert.

There are many error messages indicating the state of SQL Server that are stored in the *sysmessages* table. The Find list allows you to pick the message error number that defines the alert. This usually is an error number in the *sysmessages* table. Only *sysmessages* errors written to the NT event log can cause an alert to be sent.

Alerting an error means that when and if the error occurs you can receive a page or an e-mail telling you the error for which you have set the alert has occurred and then, optionally, execute a job. The Response screen in Figure 3-12 shows how easily this can be accomplished.

In the New Alert Properties Response panel, there is a very nice feature. When the response is defined as the execution of a job when the error occurs, a pop-up tells you

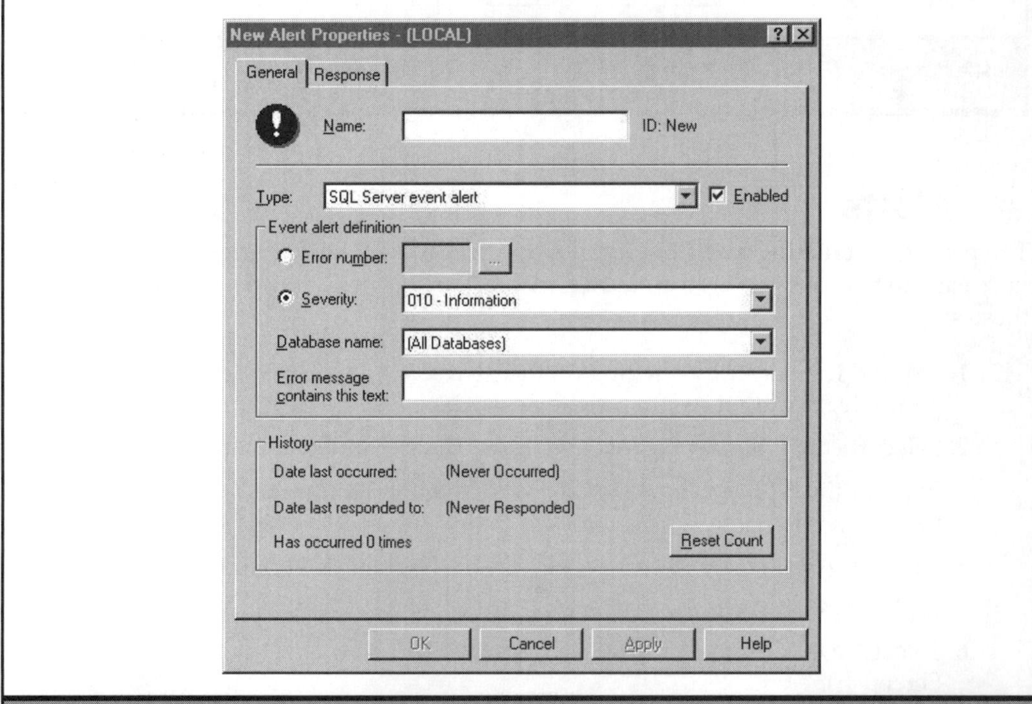

Figure 3-11. *In Enterprise Manager, right-click on SQL Server Agent, New, and then Alert*

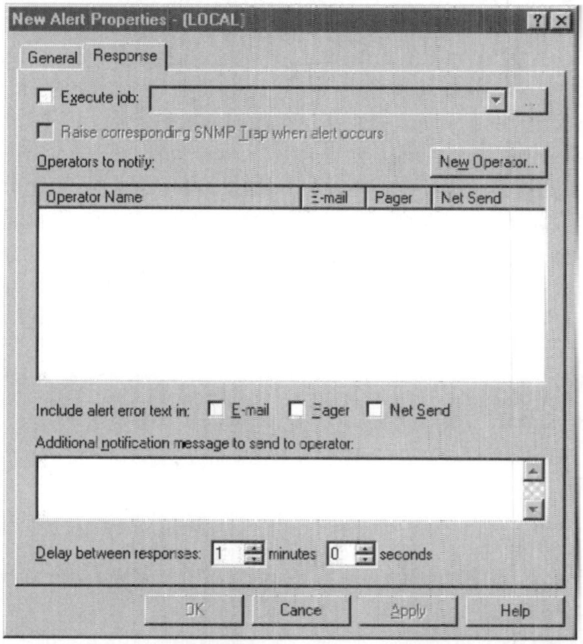

Figure 3-12. Response panel of the New Alert Properties dialog box

that you have no jobs and asks you if you would like to add a job. If you say yes, the screen to add the job appears.

Note *If the alert is not working correctly, check to see if the SQL Server Agent NT service is running, that the alert is enabled, and that the event is recorded in the NT event log.*

Instead of using the Enterprise Manager to create an alert, you can execute the following stored procedure within the msdb system database.

```
USE msdb
GO
EXEC sp_add_alert @name = 'Unexpected Shut Down', @message_id =
17061, @severity = 0, @notification_message = 'Error 17061 has
occurred. The server,Ultimate, has experienced an unexpected shut
down...', @job_name = 'Initialize After Unexpected Shut Down'
GO
```

Administer and Configure SQL Mail

The Enterprise Manager allows the administration and configuration of SQL Mail. SQL Mail is a MAPI-enabled application that is part of SQL Server and allows an application to send electronic mail. SQL Mail uses Microsoft NT Mail, Microsoft Exchange, or another MAPI provider as a vehicle for sending and receiving mail. Microsoft NT Mail is installed on the server with the server functioning as a Mail client. Installation of SQL Mail will be discussed in Chapter 12, "SQL Mail." There are many uses for SQL Mail, including sending e-mail when an alert or an event occurs on the server. You can also use it to send a report after a scheduled job. Messages can contain text strings, results of a query, or an attachment in the form of a file.

This area of interest is located in the Microsoft Management Console | Enterprise Manager | SQL Servers.

Administration

To administer SQL Mail from the Enterprise Manager, perform the following steps:

1. Expand the desired server in the Enterprise Manager hierarchy tree.
2. Right-click on SQL Mail.
3. Choose start or stop SQL Mail.

Configuration

To configure SQL Mail from the Enterprise Manager, perform the following steps:

1. Expand the desired server in the Enterprise Manager hierarchy tree.
2. Right-click on SQL Mail under Support Services.
3. Select Properties. The SQL Mail Configuration screen appears, as shown here:

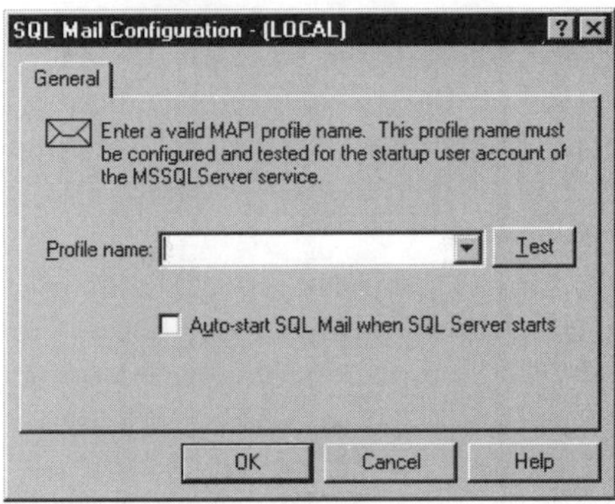

4. Enter a valid mail login Profile name.

Establish Operators

The Enterprise Manager allows you to perform the server function that establishes or defines an operator who becomes available for automatic notification in the event of a predefined error occurring on the server. This SQL Server 7 functionality facilitates the definition of operators which includes the name, e-mail name, pager e-mail name, net send address, and a pager on-duty schedule for a workday begin and workday end time representing when this operator is available.

The steps to define an operator are as follows:

1. Expand the desired server in the Enterprise Manager hierarchy tree.
2. Expand SQL Server Agent under Management.
3. Right-click Operator.
4. Click New Operator. The New Operator Properties dialog box, shown in Figure 3-13, appears.
5. Complete the General Tab information by giving the e-mail, pager e-mail, and net send address that has already been defined for the person designated as the new operator.
6. Click on the Notifications tab, shown in Figure 3-14, and complete the notification times for the new operator.

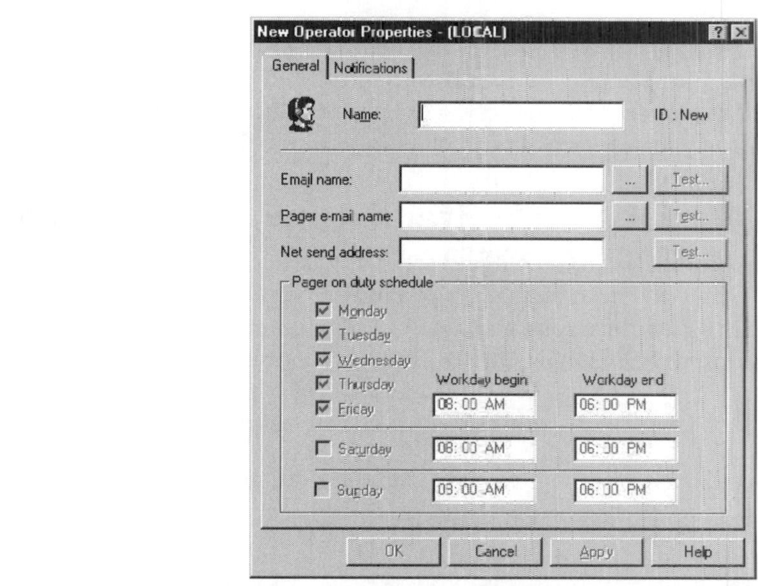

Figure 3-13. *General panel of the New Operator Properties dialog box*

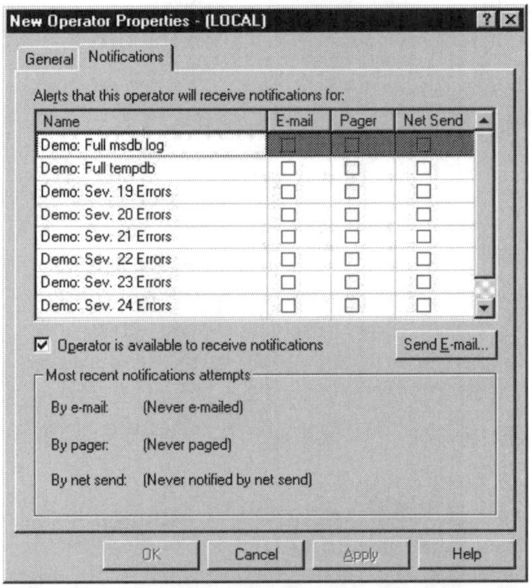

Figure 3-14. *Notifications panel of the New Operator Properties dialog box*

The screens include buttons to allow you to test the methods of notification you have selected for this operator. There is a check box to indicate if the operator is available to receive notifications, which makes it very easy to disable the notification in the event the operator is on vacation, sick, or otherwise temporarily unavailable.

Create and Schedule Jobs for a Stand-Alone Environment

The Enterprise Manager allows you to create and schedule jobs in a stand-alone environment to run at a time of your choice. This is handy if you have users on the database and you want to schedule resource-intensive jobs to occur in the off hours when contention for resources between on-line users and resource-intensive jobs is reduced.

The steps to create a job in a stand-alone environment are as follows:

1. Expand the desired server in the Enterprise Manager hierarchy tree.
2. Expand SQL Server Agent under Management.
3. Right-click on Jobs.
4. Click New Job.

5. Type a name for the job of up to 100 characters.
6. Select the owner responsible for the job from the drop-down list box of login IDs; the default is system administrator. Only the SA can assign a job owner.
7. Type in the job description in up to 512 characters.
8. Click the Steps tab.
9. Click New.

Each job must have one step, so you must fill out the information on the New Job step screen, including typing in the commands for the job. Transact-SQL commands can be entered. The Advanced tab in the New Job step screen allows you to enter an output file name and actions to perform in the event of job success or job failure and under which user permissions the job runs.

Now that a new job has been created, you can schedule a time for the job to run by performing the following steps:

1. Expand the desired server in the Enterprise Manager hierarchy tree.
2. Expand SQL Server Agent.
3. Click on Jobs. The available jobs appear in the Result Pane.
4. Right-click on the job you wish to schedule.
5. Select Properties from the short-cut menu.
6. Select the Schedules tab, shown in Figure 3-15.
7. Click New Schedule.
8. Enter the job name in the Name field.
9. Indicate when you want the job to run from the available options: Start automatically when SQL Agent starts, Start whenever the CPU(s) become idle, One time, or Recurring.

Notice the Enabled check box, allowing you to turn off the schedule without removing it. This new job step functionality is very important and powerful; it mimics the functionality that has been missing from the PC environment and was contained in the mainframe environment years ago. Instead of writing Job Control Language (JCL), the Enterprise Manager provides an easy-to-use point-and-click interface that can give the same functionality of setting up a job and job steps in a fraction of the time with a fraction of the effort.

Create and Schedule Jobs for a Multiserver Environment

Creating jobs for a multiserver environment uses the same steps as creating jobs in a stand-alone SQL Server environment. The major difference is that in a multiserver

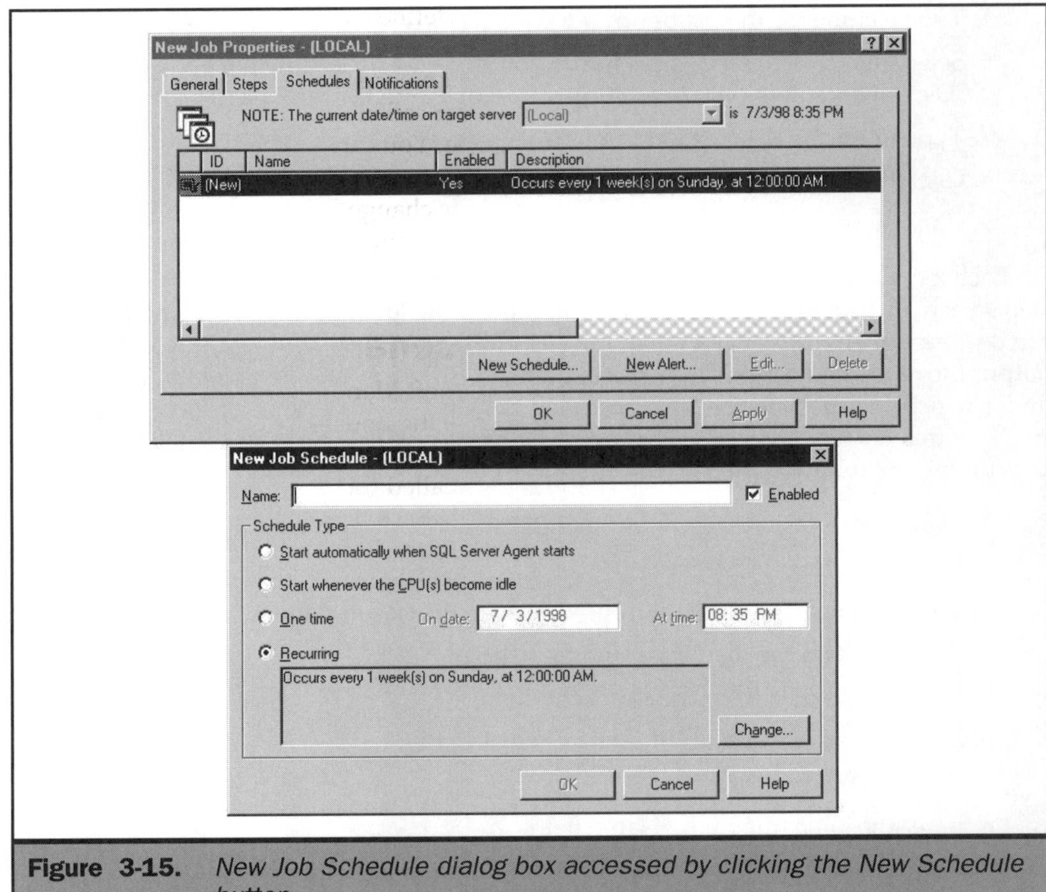

Figure 3-15. *New Job Schedule dialog box accessed by clicking the New Schedule button*

environment, you must use the target server group created earlier to determine which servers are in the multiserver environment (see "Configure a MultiServer Environment"). The screen that determines this is the New Job Properties screen and the radio button choice to Target local server or to Target multiple servers. If you select Target multiple servers, a list of target server groups appears from which you can select a target server group.

There are also a few differences and complexities involved with changes to jobs, such as changes in the steps, schedules, or job-to-server relationships, which require the changes be posted to a SQL Server Agent download list. This list, batch-like in its approach, provides the data to notify target servers of the changes and execute the job with the changes. The SQL Server Agent is the topic for discussion in the next chapter.

In a multiserver environment, you are able to define a master SQL Server and synchronize target servers to the SQL Server Agent download list where you post the changes to your job. The master SQL Server Agent records the jobs and the job step results in the system table on the local target server called *sysjobhistory* and in a system table on the master server called *sysjobservers* table. You can make sure that the job changes are in the job instructions to the enlisted servers by synchronizing the target servers when a job in a multiserver environment is changed.

The complete functionality for SQL Server Agent and job creation is covered in detail in Chapter 4.

Create and Manage Replication Scenarios

The Enterprise Manager running under the Microsoft Management Console also allows you to create and manage replication. You can use the Enterprise Manager from any workstation to set up replication across as many servers as your application needs. There is a built-in tool in the Enterprise Manager called the Replication Monitor that controls the replication processes. Additionally, the task list, task queue, and task history can be displayed and managed from within the Replication Monitor, which can set alerts on replication tasks to notify an operator when a certain event occurs and is used to troubleshoot problems at the distributor. The Replication Monitor has a distributor focus, meaning that it can only be seen in the Enterprise Manager hierarchy tree when the server is defined as a replication distributor. Making the server a replication distributor is accomplished by clicking on the desired server and choosing Replication from the Tools Menu in the command bar.

This wizard is invoked from the Tools menu of the Microsoft Management Console | Enterprise Manager | SQL Servers | Tools. The wizard will ask you to select the local machine as the distributor or configure another registered server as the distributor.

Replication is covered in detail in Chapter 9, "Replication Enhancements for Microsoft SQL Server 7."

Set the Polling Interval for SQL Server Enterprise Manager

The SQL Server Enterprise Manager allows you to set the interval of checking the status of the SQL Server, SQL Server Agent, SQL Agent, Replication Monitor, and the Distributed Transaction Coordinator to see if they are still running. The icon in the Scope Pane indicates if the server is running or not running. To do this, follow these steps:

1. Expand the desired server in the Enterprise Manager hierarchy tree.
2. From the Tools menu in the command bar, select Options.

3. Select the General tab, as shown in Figure 3-16.
4. The services SQL Server, SQL Server Agent, SQL Agent, Replication Monitor, and the Distributed Transaction Coordinator appear in the drop-down list box.
5. Set the Polling Interval seconds for each option on this screen.

There is a slightly different flavor of this called the server-down polling interval. This is how long the polling interval is to check for server-down and let the SQL Agent automatically restart the SQL Server. This is set on a different screen. To set the server-down polling interval, do the following steps:

1. Expand the desired server in the Enterprise Manager hierarchy tree.
2. Under Management, select the SQL Server Agent for the server.
3. Right-click on the SQL Server Agent.
4. Select Properties from the shortcut menu.
5. Click the Advanced tab, as shown in Figure 3-17.
6. Set the polling interval seconds for how often you want the server to be checked for server-down so that the SQL Agent can restart the server.

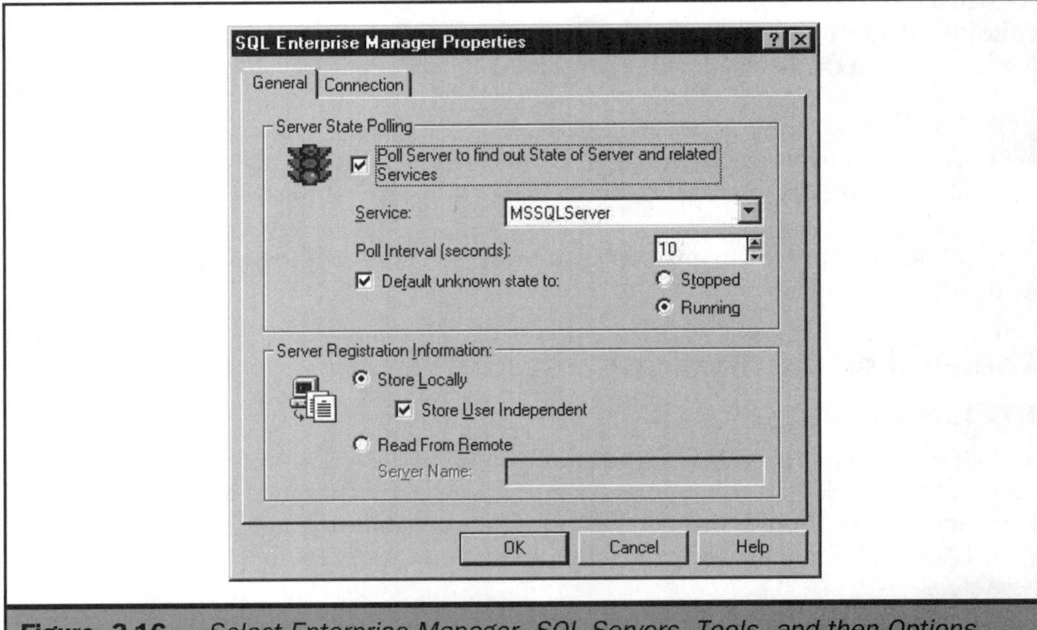

Figure 3-16. *Select Enterprise Manager, SQL Servers, Tools, and then Options*

In addition to server-wide functionality, the Enterprise Manager also offers a plethora of functionality to configure and manage databases.

The Enterprise Manager is a very advanced tool for the the database administrator and the SQL Server developer. In the evolution of database management tools, there has never been a tool that provides the standardized user interface and ease of use that is offered in the sophisticated functionality of the Microsoft Management Console Enterprise Manager.

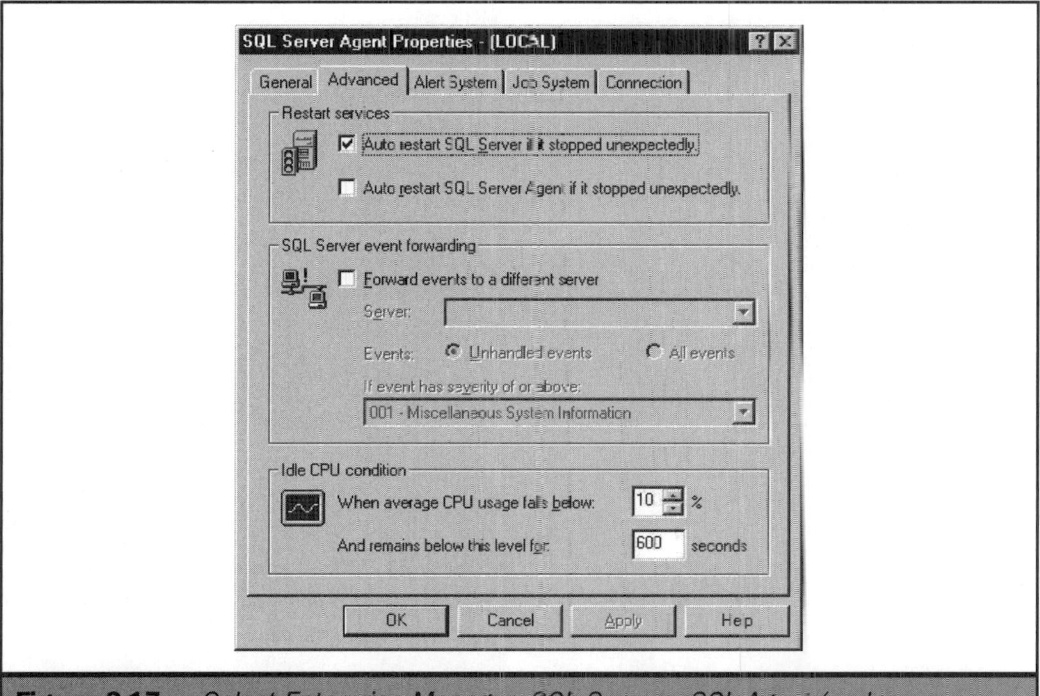

Figure 3-17. *Select Enterprise Manager, SQL Servers, SQL Agent (under Management), Properties, and then Advanced*

Chapter 4

SQL Server Agent

The SQL Executive has been renamed *SQL Server Agent* and provides the following functionality:

- Job scheduling
- Job execution
- Alert creation
- Notification of operators

This area of interest is located in the Microsoft Management Console | Enterprise Manager hierarchy tree under Microsoft SQL Servers | SQL Agent.

SQL Server Agent is an NT service that runs alongside SQL Server and communicates the job scheduling and alerting to SQL Server. All scheduling information is contained in the *msdb* system database that is automatically created when SQL Server is installed. There have been many enhancements to this extension of SQL Server, including the management of multiserver jobs. Figure 4-1 shows the entry of the SQL Server Agent in the Server Manager services list and Figure 4-2 shows the Create Job Wizard in the Enterprise Manager hierarchy list.

Note

This area of interest is located in the NT Service Control Manager | Computer menu | Services.

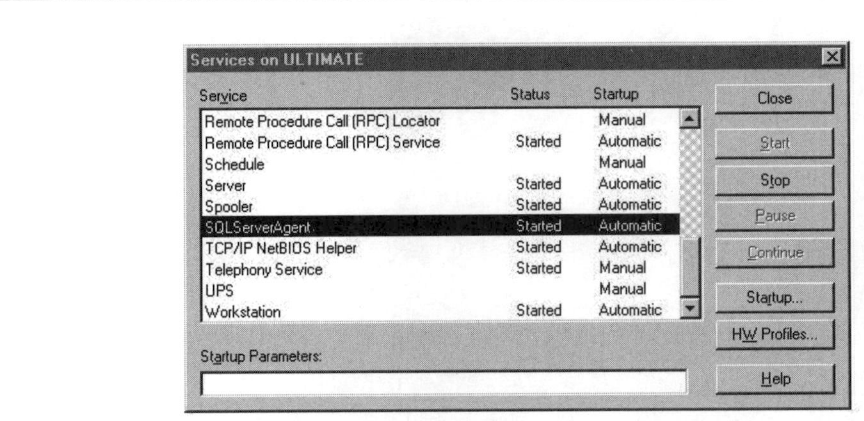

Figure 4-1. *To view the hierarchy list in NT Services Manager, go to the Computer menu and select Services | SQL Server Agent*

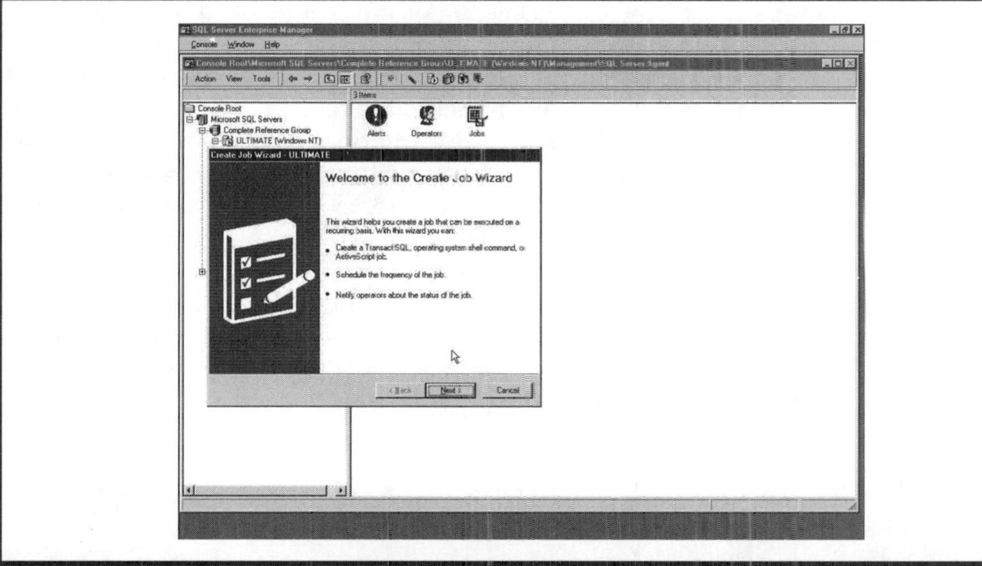

Figure 4-2. *In MMC, choose Enterprise Manager, Tools, Wizards, and then Create Job Wizard*

There are two ways to access the SQL Server Agent: the Enterprise Manager, which allows you to create jobs, operators, and alerts, and the NT Service Control Manager, which provides for starting and stopping the services manually and the startup configuration for SQL Server Agent.

After exploring the three Enterprise Manager categories, you will be shown the NT Service Control Manager. The three categories under the SQL Server Agent are:

- Operators
- Jobs
- Alerts

Defining Operators

The SQL Server Agent has been created as an adjunct to assist in large scale database operations. The functionality in the SQL Server Agent is made to order whether you are managing four or four thousand databases. The definition of database operators and the built-in alerting mechanisms are very useful.

Database Operators, the group responsible for keeping servers and databases accessible to the end users, are the key to database operations. These are the people that are notified when there is an interruption in the users' access to the data contained in the SQL Server database, and it is usually important to reach an operator as soon as the service interruption occurs. The SQL Server Agent provides this service by tying an operator to the occurrence of an interruption in service through the creation of custom alerts that attempt to notify the operator through e-mail, telephony services for paging, or network messaging in the event of error or failure. It is preferable to have the computer alert the operator instead of database users, who usually find the problem just when they have work to complete in a hurry. Rather than the database user having to figure out who to call and wait for the operator to arrive and to diagnose and fix the problem, a better scenario would be to have the computer page the operator based on an alert that generates a page. As long as an operator can get access to a network connection, the problem, in many cases, can be identified and corrected even before the user recognizes that there was an interruption in access to the data.

One of the first steps in setting up the SQL Server Agent environment is to define your operators. This is done by performing the following steps:

1. Click on the item called Microsoft SQL Servers under the Console Root of the Microsoft Management Console (also referred to as the MMC).
2. Expand the server group created called Complete Reference Group.
3. Expand the server you wish to use.
4. Expand SQL Server Agent under Management.
5. Right-click on Operators.
6. Select New Operator from the shortcut menu.
7. The New Operator screen will appear, as shown in Figure 4-3.

The New Operator screen allows you to enter the name, e-mail name, and pager e-mail name and to designate the scheduling of when the operator is to receive notification.

Choosing the Notifications tab on the New Operator dialog box allows you to determine at which severity of error the operator should be notified as well as the method of notification. It even has a selection that allows you to disable the notification of the operator in the event of vacation or illness as shown in Figure 4-4.

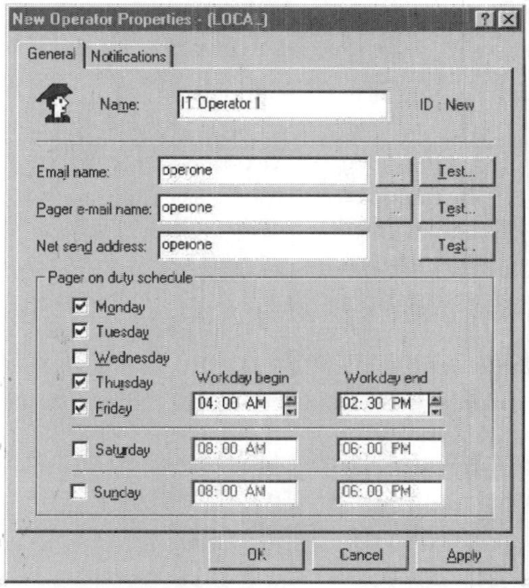

Figure 4-3. *In MMC, choose Enterprise Manager | Microsoft SQL Servers | SQL Agent | Operator | New Operator | General tab*

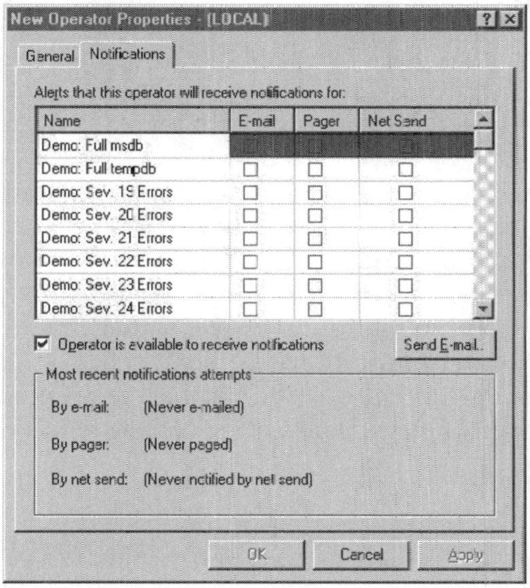

Figure 4-4. *You can disable notifications when you're away from the office*

Creating Jobs

After defining operators, you can move on to creating jobs and job categories. The following steps allow you to create a job:

1. Click on the item called Microsoft SQL Servers under the Console Root of the Microsoft Management Console (MMC).
2. Expand the server group created called Complete Reference Group.
3. Expand the server you wish to use.
4. Expand SQL Server Agent under Management.
5. Right-click on Jobs.
6. Select New Job from the shortcut menu. The New Job screen will appear.

The New Job screen has four different tabs that each equate to a full screen of functionality for a new job. Each of the four tabs will be discussed in detail. The four tabs are

- General
- Steps
- Schedules
- Notifications

The panel under the General tab has Name, Category, Owner, and Description as entry fields for a new job. This allows you to describe the job, name the job, designate an owner of the job, and place the job in a job category. This screen contains the selection that determines if this job is for a local server or if it targets multiple servers for the execution of the same job running on each server in the multiserver environment.

The panel under the Steps tab, shown on the next page, has the powerful capability of creating job steps. This mimics the jobstream environment familiar to mainframe users and provides a welcome functionality. The system administrator no longer has to write and compile code, as was required while using this job step functionality in the IBM mainframe world. With the Enterprise Manager, you can fill out fields on a screen, select items from a drop-down list box or click on selections, and press the OK button—the standard Windows controls that we are used to using. This is a much gentler interface for users than the mainframe Job Control Language (JCL) of times past.

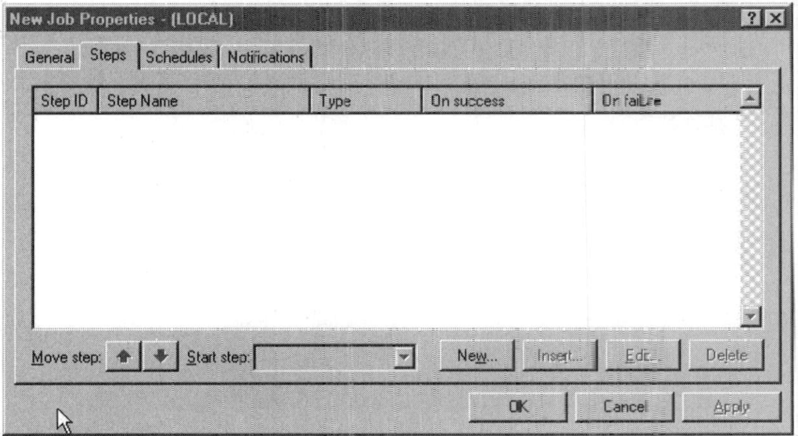

The Steps panel has a New button to add steps to the job. Pressing the New button reveals the New Job Step screen, and this is where it gets interesting. The General panel of the New Job Step screen has a Step Name and a Type drop-down list box which has the following selections:

- Active Scripting
- CmdExec
- Distribution
- Logreader
- Merge
- Snapshot
- TSQL

The interesting thing about the Type drop-down list box is that the General panel changes to be specific with every selection, as does the panel under the Advanced tab. Figure 4-5 shows the TSQL type (top) and the Active Scripting type (bottom) General tabs. Each screen is specially tailored to the type selected. Figure 4-6 shows the Advanced screen for both the TSQL type (top) and the Active Scripting type (bottom). As you can see, each screen differs depending on the type. This is true for all of the above listed types.

Notice the Open and Parse buttons are associated with the TSQL type. The Open button allows you to select a file; the well-placed Parse button checks the TSQL code for errors.

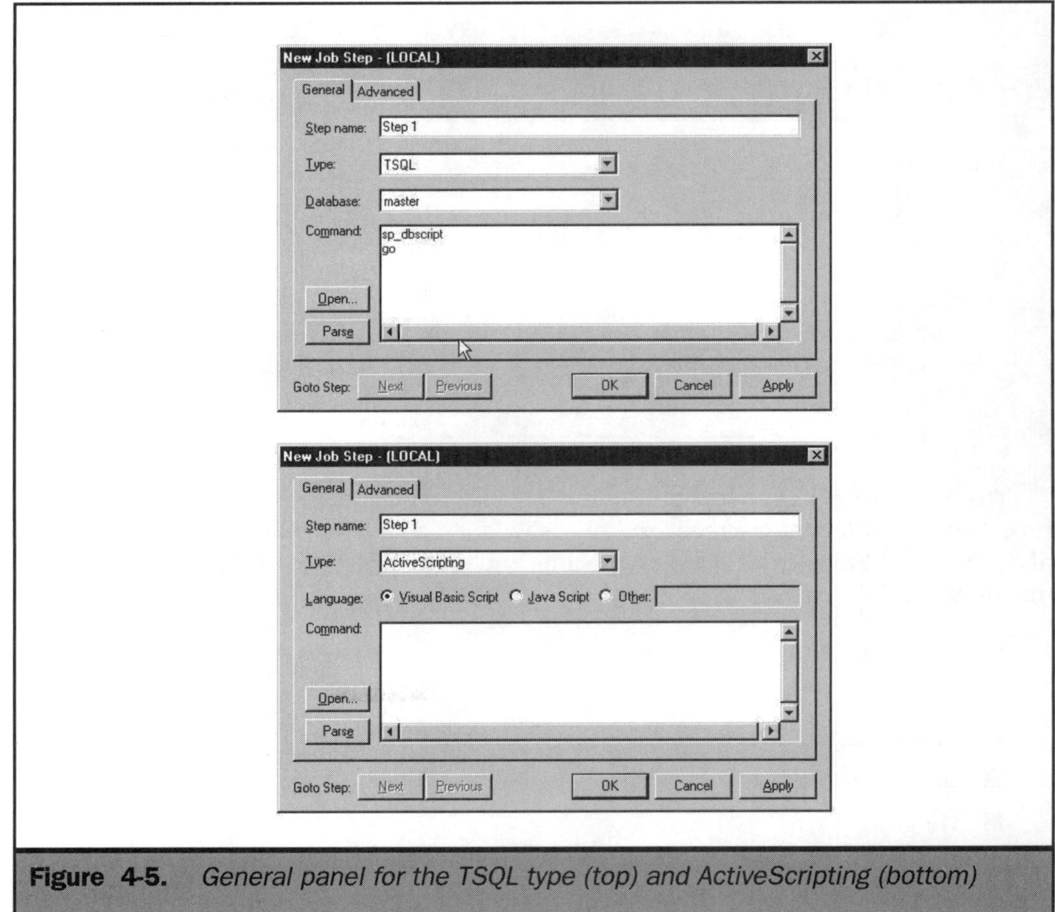

Figure 4-5. *General panel for the TSQL type (top) and ActiveScripting (bottom)*

The ActiveScripting General panel has radio buttons to indicate which language will be placed in the Command window. The choices are Visual Basic script, Java script, or Other, with a place to fill in the other language name.

The TSQL type Advanced panel has a field to enter the output file and a selection to indicate if you want to append to the designated file. It has a Run as User entry field and On Success/Failure Flow logic in the form of On Success or Failure action drop-down list boxes with several choices, including quit the job recording success, quit the job recording failure, and go to next step. There is a bona fide set of logic behind On Success, record failure or On Failure, record success.

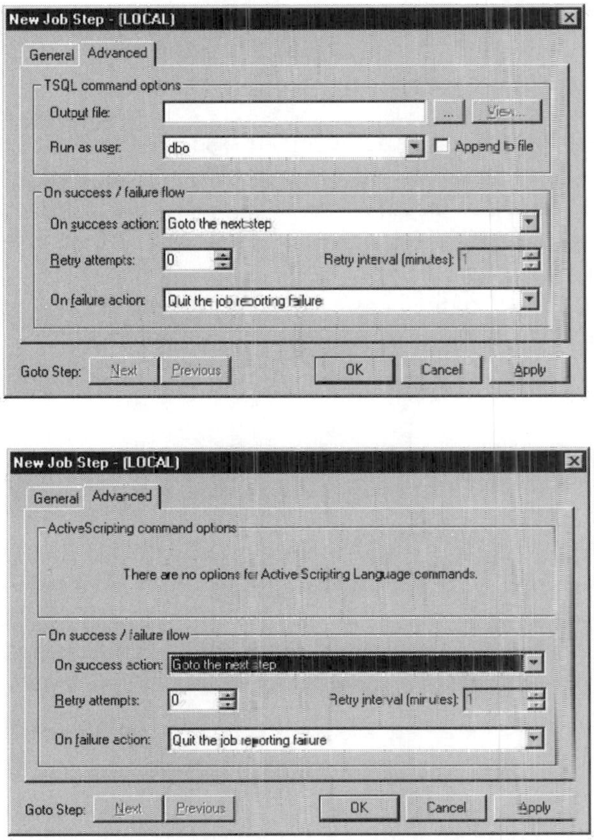

Figure 4-6. *Advanced panel for the TSQL type (top) and ActiveScripting (bottom)*

The ActiveScripting Advanced panel has the same On Success/Failure flow logic built into the screen as does the preceding TSQL type Advanced panel. It has the same Retry Attempts and Retry Interval settings that the TSQL type Advanced panel has.

The Schedules tab of the New Job screen allows you to schedule when your job will run. There are several scheduling options:

- Start automatically when SQL Server Agent starts
- Start whenever the CPU(s) become idle

- One time
- Recurring

A job to delete rows would be a good example of a job that could run whenever the CPU(s) became idle.

The recurring job option has another screen associated with it called the Edit Recurring Job Schedule screen. This screen, which is accessed by the Changes button under the New Job Schedules tab, allows you to determine if the recurring job will run daily, weekly, or monthly. If the job runs daily, you can further determine how many times per day the job will run.

The Notifications panel of the New Job dialog screen, shown here:

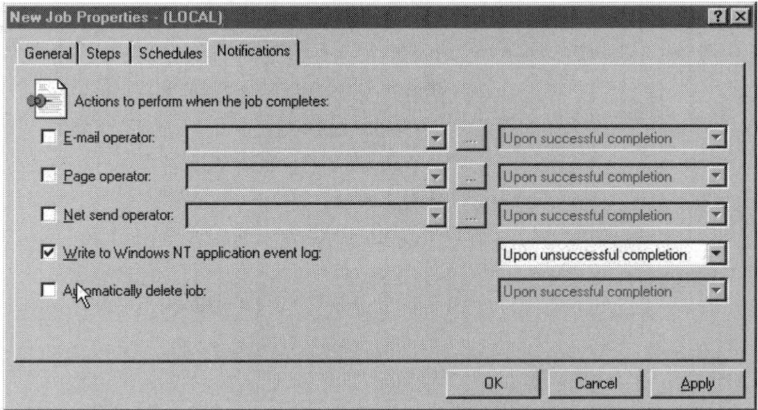

indicates actions to perform when the job completes, including who and by which method to notify of the operators you defined earlier. There is also a selection to indicate whether to write to the NT Event log. All of the actions have an associated drop-down list box that describes upon which event the actions should be performed. The choices in the drop-down list box are:

- Upon successful completion
- Upon unsuccessful completion
- Whenever the job completes

Creating Alerts

After creating jobs, you can move on to creating alerts. The following steps allow you to create an alert:

1. Click on the item called Microsoft SQL Servers under the Console Root of the Microsoft Management Console (MMC).
2. Expand the server group created called Complete Reference Group.
3. Expand the server you wish to use.
4. Expand SQL Server Agent under Management.
5. Right-click on Alerts.
6. Select New Alert from the shortcut menu.
7. The New Alert screen will appear.

The New Alert screen has two tabs, General and Response, that each equate to a full screen of functionality for a new alert. I discuss the General panel in detail here; I explain the Response panel later in this chapter.

The General panel of the New Alert dialog box has name, type, and event alert definition and history:

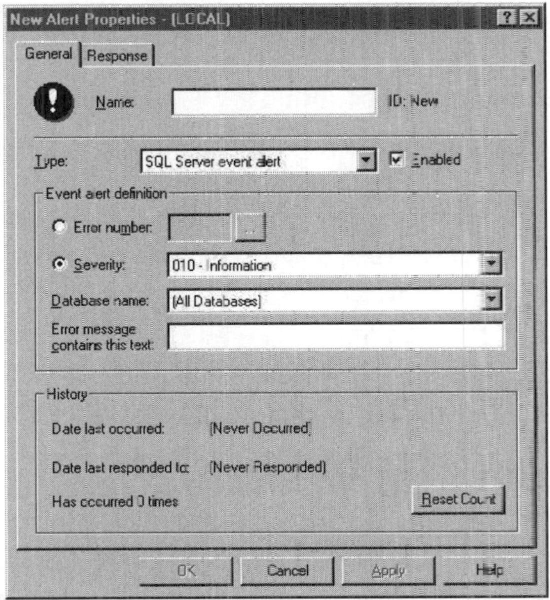

You can simply enter the name into the field and select the type from a drop-down list box, but the event alert definition is a little more involved.

There are two radio buttons, Error number and Severity. Since SQL Server generated errors are given a severity level, you can generate alerts on a particular error or on a group of errors of a certain severity. If you choose the Error number radio button, you can search for a valid SQL Server error by pressing the ... button. This button notation means go look for more or, in this case, go search for a valid error number. The ability to access this depth of error information formerly accessible programmatically provides an extremely useful feature that will be put to good use by SQL Server operators everywhere.

Since all the information is kept in the sysmessages table, it is very easy to query this as an aid in the design of enterprise operation alerting strategies. I have included a sample query which produced the results in Table 4-1 to demonstrate some of the error information contained within SQL Server itself. Execute this query in the Query Analyzer in the master database to see all of the error messages used by SQL Server:

```
SELECT severity, error, description FROM sysmessages
GO
```

Table 4-1 displays a sample of the errors available for alerting. A severity level of 21 is shown in the result set shown in Table 4-1.

Severity	Error	Description
21	601	Descriptor for system table '%ld' in database '%d' not found in the descriptor hash table.
21	602	Could not find row in Sysindexes for dbid '%d', object '%ld',index '%d'. Run DBCC CHECKTABLE on Sysindexes.
21	604	Could not find row in Sysobjects for object '%ld' in database '%.*ls'. Run DBCC checktable on Sysobjects.
21	605	Attempt to fetch logical page %S_PGID in database '%.*ls' belongs to object '%.*ls', not to object '%.*ls'.
21	607	Insufficient room was allocated in the session descriptor for object '%.*ls' for search arguments. Only %d search arguments were anticipated.
21	608	Buffer holding logical page %S_PGID of object '%.*ls' in database '%.*ls' was not kept in the first or second slot of the session descriptor for that object during a scan.

Table 4-1. *Sysmessages System Table Output for Severity 21*

Severity	Error	Description
21	611	Attempt made to end a transaction that is idle or in the middle of an update.
21	613	Request made to retrieve more rows from an already completed scan of object '%.*ls' in database '%.*ls'.
21	615	Unable to find database table id = %d, name = '%.*ls'.
21	618	A varno of %d was passed to opentable - the largest valid value is %d.
21	623	Attempt to retrieve row from page via RID failed because logical page %S_PGID is not a data page. %S_RID. %S_PAGE.
21	624	Attempt to retrieve row from page via RID failed because the requested RID has a higher number than the last RID on the page. %S_RID.%S_PAGE.
21	625	Could not retrieve row from logical page %S_PGID via RID because the entry in the offset table (= %d) for that RID (= %d) is less than or equal to 0.
21	629	Fatal attempt to delete clustered index entry for page %S_PGID—index row contains page %S_PGID
21	639	Attempt to fetch logical page %S_PGID dbid %d failed— page is not currently allocated.
21	644	The index entry for RID '%.*hs' was not found in index page %S_PGID indexid %d database '%.*ls'
21	649	Could not find the clustered index entry for Page %S_PGID Objid %ld status 0x%x. Index page %S_PGID was searched for this entry in database '%.*ls'
21	805	Unable to find descriptor for object '%.*ls' in database '%.*ls' in hash table when marking buffer dirty or flushing Syslogs.
21	806	Could not find virtual page for logical page %S_PGID in database '%.*ls'.
21	811	Attempt to grab buffer which is on descriptor chain.

Table 4-1. *Sysmessages System Table Output for Severity 21* (continued)

Severity	Error	Description
21	812	Attempt to grab a pinned buffer.
21	815	Unable to find buffer holding Sysindexes page in the cache—pageno = %S_PGID dbid = %d.
21	820	Attempt to dirty non-log buffer %S_BUF which is in I/O.
21	822	Could not start I/O for request %S_BLKIOPTR.
21	824	Attempt made to write page in buffer in database that has no entry in Sysdatabases. %S_BUF.
21	825	Attempt made to write page in buffer in database with no DBTABLE structure - Sysdatabases row marked as in use by process %d. %S_BUF.
21	834	bufclean called on dirty buffer (page %S_PGID, stat %#x/%#x, objid %#x, sstat%#x).
21	901	Unable to find descriptor for database '%d' object '%ld' in hash table after hashing it.
21	909	More than %d entries required to build the logical-virtual translation table for database '%.*ls'. The database is too fragmented.
21	912	DBTABLE descriptor cannot be found for database '%.*ls' which is supposed to be already open.
21	915	Descriptor for system catalog '%.*ls' not found in DBTABLE chain for database '%.*ls'—all system catalogs should reside permanently in this chain.
21	919	Database '%.*ls' has been marked 'suspect' by recovery. Please run DBCC to drop this database.
21	931	Database '%.*ls' cannot be opened because of a failure to initialize the global timestamp. This indicates that a problem exists in the log for the current database. Please contact Technical Support for assistance.
21	1103	Allocation page %S_PGID in database '%.*ls' has different segment id than that of the object to which we are allocating. Run DBCC CHECKALLOC.

Table 4-1. *Sysmessages System Table Output for Severity 21* (continued)

Severity	Error	Description
21	1108	Cannot deallocate extent %S_PGID, database %d. Object id %ld, index id %d, status %d in extent does not match object id %ld, index id %d, status %d in object being deallocated. Run DBCC CHECKALLOC.
21	1109	Attempt to read allocation page %S_PGID failed either because object ID is not correct (%ld) or the page ID is not correct %S_PGID.
21	1117	Extent chain for object %ld is not correctly linked.
21	1514	Page allocated to sort found to be busy. Page number %S_PGID. %S_BUF.
21	1525	Sort Failure. Rollforward of sort encountered sort descriptor timestamps out of sequence. Old timestamp in log: %04x %08lx. New timestamp in log: %04x %08lx. Timestamp in sort descriptor: %04x %08lx.
21	1528	Character data comparison failure. An unrecognized Sort-Map-Element type (%d) was found in the server-wide default sort table at SMEL entry [%d].
21	1529	Character data comparison failure. A list of Sort-Map-Elements from the server-wide default sort table does not end properly. This list begins at SMEL entry [%d].
21	1601	No resources available to start '%ls' process. Use sp_configure to increase the number of user connections.
21	1602	Unable to initialize network %d.
21	1603	Process priority %d invalid or no process slots available.
21	1604	Process not runnable or kpid %d not within range.
21	1605	Failed to open virtual socket for new connections.
21	1606	Failed to initialize network receive buffer.
21	1607	Failed to initialize network send buffer.

Table 4-1. *Sysmessages System Table Output for Severity 21* (continued)

Severity	Error	Description
21	1608	A network error was encountered while sending results to the front end. Check the SQL Server error log for more information.
21	1609	Kpid %d out of range.
21	1610	Could not kill process %d.
21	1611	Could not install quit function.
21	1612	Could not install attention function.
21	1613	Could not close network %d connection for server process %d.
21	1614	Could not yield process.
21	1615	Process unable to sleep.
21	1616	Failed to flush receive stream buffer.
21	1617	Could not infect process %d
21	1619	Could not open TEMPDB, unable to continue.
21	1620	Failure to open master db for the first time.
21	1808	Default devices are not supported.
21	1905	Could not find 'zero' row for index '%.*ls' the table in Sysindexes.
21	2202	Could not translate virtual read address to device and seek vaddr=0x%x.
21	2205	Could not translate virtual write address to device and seek vaddr=0x%x.
21	2208	Tried to read unopened device vaddr=0x%x.
21	2209	Tried to write unopened device vaddr=0x%x.
21	2603	No space left on logical page %S_PGID of index %d for object '%.*ls' when inserting row on index page—this situation should have been taken care of while traversing the index.

Table 4-1. *Sysmessages System Table Output for Severity 21* (continued)

Severity	Error	Description
21	2620	The offset of the row number at offset %d does not match the entry in the offset table of the following page: %S_PAGE.
21	2622	Insufficient room on this page to insert a row of length %d. %S_PAGE.
21	2623	The PG_DEALLOC bit is on in this page at runtime—should have been turned off by de-allocating page in recovery. %S_PAGE.
21	2624	Insert into table %S_DES fails because rowlength %d is less than minlen %d.
21	2626	Illegal attempt to insert duplicate key row in the clustered index for object '%.*ls' in database '%.*ls'.
21	2728	Could not find Sysobjects row for table '%.*ls'.
21	3001	Internal error. Could not find index for system catalog '%.*ls', unable to dump database.
21	3113	Database '%.*ls' does not have an entry in SYSUSERS for the DBO.
21	3114	Database '%.*ls' does not have an entry in Sysdatabases.
21	3301	Invalid log record found in Syslogs (logop %d).
21	3303	Failed to find SAVEPT in log for xact %S_RID, current number is %d, looking for %d.
21	3305	Page %S_PGID in database '%.*ls' read in during runtime or load xact was uninitialized.
21	3306	Process %d was expected to hold logical lock on page %S_PGID instead of process %d.
21	3307	Process %d was expected to hold logical lock on page %S_PGID.
21	3308	Page %S_PGID was expected to have %ls lock on it.

Table 4-1. *Sysmessages System Table Output for Severity 21* (continued)

Severity	Error	Description
21	3309	While in backout, process %d was chosen as deadlock victim while waiting for process %d to release lock on page %S_PGID.
21	3310	Cannot find log record with RID: (%ld, %d).
21	3313	Error while redoing logged operation in database %.*ls. Error at log record ID %S_LSN.
21	3314	Error while undoing logged operation in database %.*ls. Error at log record ID %S_LSN.
21	3401	Rec_init: getnext SCAN_RID of last checkpoint failed on Rid from Sysdatabases. %S_RID.
21	3404	Rec_complete: Could not open controlling database (id %d) of controlling database in multi-db transaction.
21	3412	Database %d, table %ld. Attempt to mark table as suspect. Getnext SCAN_CLUST on Sysobjects.objid failed.
21	3413	Database %d. Attempt to mark database as suspect failed. Getnext NC scan on Sysdatabases.dbid failed.
21	3417	Cannot recover the master database, exiting.
21	3418	Not enough descriptors to open model.
21	3421	Unable to recover database '%.*ls' because of a failure to initialize the global timestamp. This indicates that a problem exists in the log for the current database. Please contact Technical Support for assistance.
21	3423	Error recovering database '%.*ls' - could not find expected BEGIN TRANSACTION record at location: %S_RID.
21	3424	No more room in transaction table for transaction (%ld, %d).
21	3425	Transaction (%ld, %d) not found in transaction table.

Table 4-1. *Sysmessages System Table Output for Severity 21* (continued)

Severity	Error	Description
21	3429	Error recovering database '%.*ls'—could not connect to commit service to check completion status of xact: %S_RID.
21	3437	Error recovering database '%.*ls'—could not connect to the DTC to check completion status of xact: %S_RID.
21	3440	Database '%.*ls' (dbid %d): RECOVERDB command can only be run after a RESTORE command that used the WITH NORECOVERY option.
21	3441	Database '%.*ls' (dbid %d): RECOVERDB command failed accessing file '%ls'. Error was '%.ls'.
21	3442	Database '%.*ls' (dbid %d): Undo-file size is insufficient.
21	3443	Database '%.*ls' (dbid %d): was marked for standby/readonly use but has been modified. RESTORE LOG cannot be performed.
21	3444	Database '%.*ls' (dbid %d): could not find start of previous recovery operation. RESTORE LOG cannot be performed.
21	3445	Database '%.*ls' (dbid %d): File '%ls' is not a valid undo-file.
21	3501	Could not get Sysdatabases row for database '%d' at checkpoint time %S_RID.
21	3502	No checkpoint records found in Syslogs for database '%.*ls'.
21	3504	Sysindexes page # %S_PGID in database '%.*ls' is not in buffer cache at checkpoint after getindex call.
21	3904	Can't unsplit logical page %S_PGID in object '%.*ls' in database '%.*ls'—both pages together contain more data than will fit on one page.

Table 4-1. *Sysmessages System Table Output for Severity 21* (continued)

Severity	Error	Description
21	3905	Can't unsplit logical page %S_PGID in object '%.*ls' in database '%.*ls'—row number %d is used on both pages.
21	3907	Failed to receive results from PROBE. The distributed transaction named %.*ls has not been committed and data may be inconsistent across databases.
21	4003	ODS Error. Server is terminating this connection.
21	4202	Could not find BEGINXACT record in log while finding truncation page during dump transaction in database '%.*ls'.
21	4203	Could not find checkpoint record after truncate page in dump transaction in database '%.*ls'.
21	4802	Bulk_main: getindex of primary index row failed on BULK INSERT table.
21	4803	Received invalid row length %d from bcp client. Max rowsize is %d.
21	4804	Premature end-of-message while reading current row from host. Host program may have died.
21	4807	Received invalid row length %d from bcp client. Min rowsize is %d.
21	4815	Received invalid column length from bcp client.
21	4816	Invalid bcp object.
21	4905	ALTER TABLE failed because page %S_PGID of the system catalog Sysindexes in database '%.*ls' is not in the cache.
21	6501	Logical page %S_PGID in database '%.*ls' missing from buffer cache after fetching the index row.
21	6901	Overflow on High component of timestamp occurred in database %d. Database table possibly corrupt.

Table 4-1. *Sysmessages System Table Output for Severity 21* (continued)

Severity	Error	Description
21	6902	Page timestamp value falls between the old and new timestamps from log. Page #=%S_PGID, object id = %ld, page timestamp=%04x %08lx. Log: old timestamp=%04x %08lx, new timestamp=%04x %08lx.
21	6903	High order of timestamp indicates that timestamp structure may be incorrect.
21	6904	Mismatch between database table passed and the one found in the system structure when requesting new database timestamp. Database id passed in : %d. System database id: %d.
21	8646	The index entry for RID '%.*hs' was not found in indexid %d of table %d in database '%.*ls'.
21	9004	The log for database "%.*ls" is corrupt.

Table 4-1. *Sysmessages System Table Output for Severity 21* (continued)

Some examples of severity levels in the Severity drop-down list box that are available for alerting are shown in the following list:

Severity Level	Description
010	Information
011	Specified Database Object not found
012	Unused
013	User Transaction Syntax Error
014	Insufficient Permission Error
015	Syntax Error in SQL Statements
016	Miscellaneous User Error
017	Insufficient Resources
018	Nonfatal Internal Error
019	Fatal Error in Resource

Severity Level	Description
020	Fatal Error in Current Process
021	Fatal Error in Database Processes
022	Fatal Error: Table Integrity Suspect
023	Fatal Error: Database Integrity Suspect
024	Fatal Error: Hardware Error
025	Fatal Error
110	Non-sysmessages, Server Information
120	Non-sysmessages, Server Warning
130	Non-sysmessages, Server Error
140	Non-sysmessages, Abnormal Server Termination

As severity level descriptions show, error severity levels of 17 and above would interest a system administrator and be worthy of an automated alert to a SQL Server operator. If the SQL Server houses a mission critical application, a page would be in order; otherwise, an e-mail message could suffice.

The Response tab on the New Alert dialog enables you to define what action will be taken when the alert is raised. Here's what the panel under the Response tab looks like:

You can notify an operator or execute a job. There are options to include the error message in the page or e-mail notification message. You can send an additional notification message to the operator, press the New Operator button and create a new operator, designate the amount of time to delay between responses for a recurring alert (preventing having to send out continuous pages or messages if the alert is occurring every second), or even raise a corresponding SNMP trap when the alert occurs.

Now that you know how to access SQL Server Agent from the Enterprise Manager, here are the steps to access SQL Server Agent from the NT Service Control:

1. At a command prompt, type **srvmgr \\servername**. The Server Manager screen appears.
2. Select Computer from the Menu bar.
3. Select Services.
4. Scroll down and click on the SQLServerAgent service, shown in Figure 4-6.

You are now ready to stop and start the SQLServerAgent service or change the startup parameters. The startup parameters screen can be accessed by clicking the Startup button.

The startup parameters screen contains sections for Startup Type and Logon As. Startup types consist of the following:

Startup Types	**Description**
Automatic	SQLServerAgent service starts automatically when NT is rebooted.
Manual	SQLServerAgent service has to be manually started when NT is rebooted.
Disabled	SQLServerAgent service is disabled and cannot be started.

The Log On As options consist of the following:

Log On As	**Description**
System Account	Do not assign the MSSQLServer and SQLServerAgent services to the run in the Local System account due to the fact that there must be network access permissions. Without this, server-to-server remote procedure calls (RPC), replication jobs, and backups will fail.
This Account	Specify an account that has been specially set up to run SQL Server Agent. This account should have network access and the appropriate permissions if you are to run SQL Mail and SQL Server Agent.

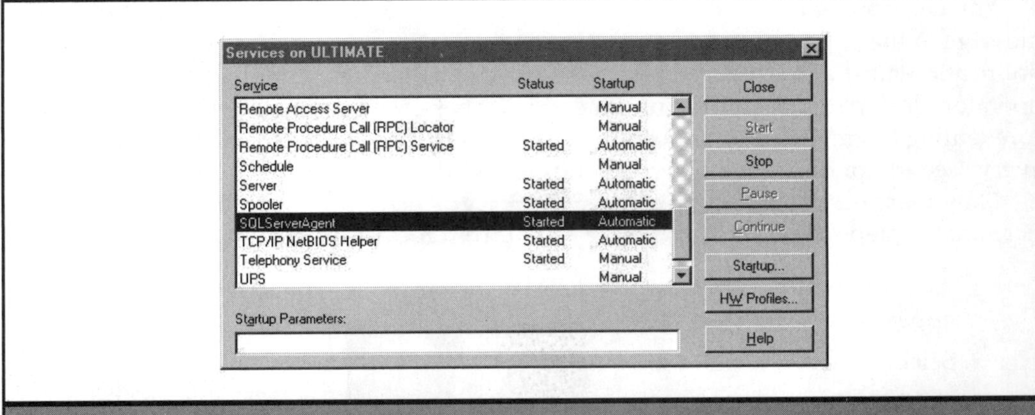

Figure 4-7. *NT Service Control Manager | Computer | Services*

Starting and stopping SQL Server Agent is easy from the NT Service Control Manager. Simply click on the SQLServerAgent service and press the Start or Stop button. The appropriate one will be selectable depending on the current stopped or started state of the SQLServerAgent service.

Multitask and Multischedule Jobs

SQL Server Agent allows you to create multi-task jobs through the creation of job steps that allow you to create a job with many steps and to run one task per step. The logic is built into the screens that define the steps to determine what action to take in the event of job step success and failure (see "Creating Jobs" earlier in this chapter).

SQL Server Agent also allows you to create multiple schedules for the same job. You may decide to run the job on a daily, weekly, and monthly schedule. Each of these schedules can be set up for the same job. The job will run at each scheduled time.

Microsoft SQL Server Agent is a powerful tool in the Microsoft quest for "lights out" management and databases that can automatically run tasks at night without the intervention of database administrators. For more information on multiserver jobs, see the section titled "Configure a Multiserver Environment" in Chapter 3.

The Complete Reference

Chapter 5

Integration with Windows NT Security

Database security exists to protect data from users that should not be viewing or adding, changing, or deleting the data. With access to databases being placed on the Internet and corporations growing much larger, controlling access to sensitive data has become more of a focus recently than in times past. Even the average person has an interest in this area—none of us wants such information as our credit reports or Social Security information accessed or changed by unauthorized or random users.

As database administrators, we are particularly interested in protecting the data under our care from users who are not supposed to see the data or change it. We are interested in systems that make this access easy to administer and maintain, because in the absence of proper procedures and standards, this access can become unmanageable, especially when we are responsible for the access of thousands of users.

The concept of separating the duties of users into groups and roles increases security because work can be divided so that two users have to do every task. Roles or groups can be assigned only the access they need to perform their work. For example, one worker could approve a check and another could actually print and mail the check.

The way that SQL Server and NT are integrated in checking the access and permissions of the user has been strengthened and simplified, and a whole layer of administration has been eliminated. There is now a hierarchical security system where roles and groups and users can be members of other roles, and permissions can now be assigned in many layers.

The Disappearance of the Security Manager

The Security Manager is no longer used and has been removed from the Microsoft SQL Server tool set. Administering secure user-access to a database and giving users specific and controlled permissions is now easier. The building blocks for accessing Microsoft SQL Server are logins, users, roles, and groups. First we will talk about the logins involved, which is the method for authenticating a user in Microsoft SQL Server. Then we will move on to users, roles, and groups.

There are now two parts to security when working with Microsoft SQL Server: authentication and permission validation. *Authentication* is the part of security that can identify the user and confirm that they have been allowed to connect to SQL Server. *Permission validation* is used to control access to the database and to the objects within the database. It also controls the activities the user can perform once access to the database is completed.

Authentication

There are now only two ways to identify a user and confirm that the user has permission to access a SQL Server: Windows NT authentication and SQL Server authentication. The SQL Server can be configured to use NT Authentication server mode or Mixed server mode of authentication. Mixed means both Windows NT authentication login ID and SQL Server authentication login ID can be used to gain access to the SQL Server. If the mode is NT Authentication mode, then only the Windows NT Authentication login IDs are allowed.

The first table that follows shows the authentication modes now available in Microsoft SQL Server, Mixed and NT Authentication. Mixed Authentication mode has both types of authentication, NT Authentication and SQL Server Authentication, while NT Authentication mode has NT Authentication type only. The second table shows the two types of authentication within the authentication mode, which are called NT Authentication and SQL Server Authentication. This table also shows the characteristics of the authentication types.

Authentication Mode = Mixed	Authentication Mode = NT Authentication
Windows NT Authentication login IDs and/or SQL Server Authentication login IDs	Windows NT Authentication login IDs only

Windows NT Authentication	SQL Server Authentication
Don't have to type login ID	Have to type login ID
Don't have to type in password	Have to type in password
An NT Administrator must have created the NT Account or NT Group	No NT account or group associated
Login ID is NT Account or NT Group	Login ID is SQL Server login ID not integrated with NT security—this is SQL Server security functionality only, Windows NT is not involved
Trusts NT (trusted)	Does not trust NT (nontrusted)

Windows NT Authentication Mode

A network connection to SQL Server with NT Authentication mode assumes a *trusted connection* between SQL Server and the client. The trusted connections are supported through network protocols (Named Pipes, Multi-protocol, and so forth) that support trusted connections between the server and the client. SQL Server does not validate the password or the account when NT establishes a trusted connection and passes the login ID and the password to SQL Server. It assumes the login ID and password is good because NT has already validated the user when the user came onto the network. SQL Server uses this same NT network user name and password to validate the user in SQL Server as NT uses to validate the user on the network or to access the operating system; in other words, there is no need for a separate login ID and password to gain access to the databases on SQL Server using Windows NT Authentication mode. This type of authentication is beneficial because it allows SQL Server to take advantage of the NT security features that are comprised of a much richer set of validation functions than those SQL Server supplies on its own. The user must enter the network and pass all of the NT validation functions before accessing SQL Server under his own network identity. For example, NT validation can be set so passwords expire after a given time.

Use the Microsoft Management Console, register your SQL Server into a server group, and refer to Figure 5-1.

To take advantage of Windows NT security, set up Windows NT Authentication Mode for your SQL Server:

1. Expand a server group.
2. Select a server, right-click on the server, and select Properties.
3. Click the Security tab.

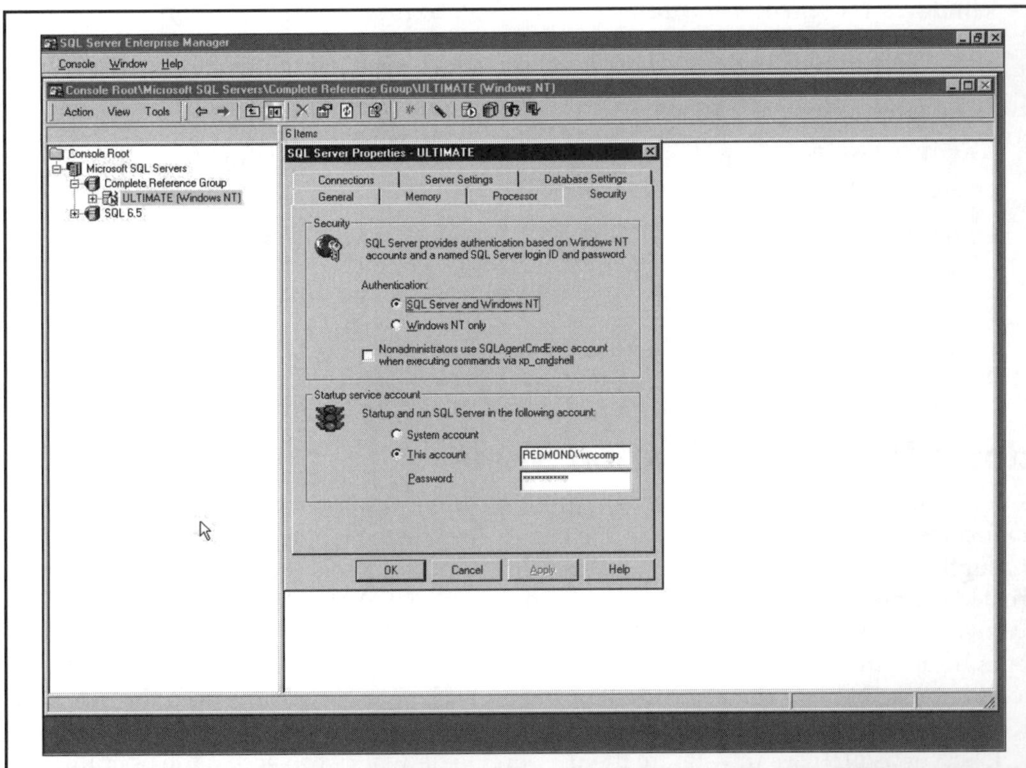

Figure 5-1. *Setting up Windows NT Authentication Mode*

4. Select Windows NT only or SQL Server and Windows NT.
5. Select the OK button.

To define the relationship between the Windows NT account or group and SQL Server login ID and to set up a trusted connection between Windows NT and SQL Server:

```
sp_grantlogin 'DomainName\NTusername'
```

An alternative syntax is:

```
sp_grantlogin [DomainName\NTusername]
```

Use the SQL Query Analyzer Tool found in the Tools menu on the Microsoft Management Console if cursor is placed on the server in the server group. Position yourself in the window and in the master database.

Windows NT users or groups need user or group permission to connect to Microsoft SQL Server. If all members of a Windows NT group will be connecting to SQL Server, you can add a SQL Server login account for the group as a whole. If a group shouldn't be collectively granted permission, you can add a SQL Server login specifically for a single Windows NT user.

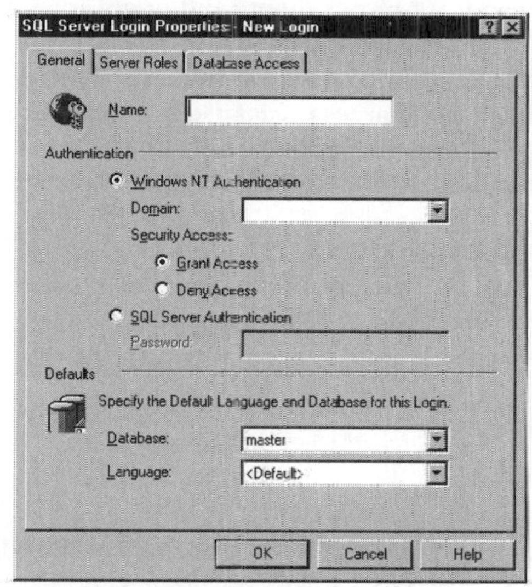

Figure 5-2. *Creating a Windows NT authenticated login ID*

Alternatively, you can use the Microsoft Management Console to add a SQL Server login for both Windows NT authentication and SQL Server authentication. Figure 5-2 shows Windows NT authentication.

Use the Microsoft Management Console, register your SQL Server into a server group, and refer to Figure 5-2.

1. Expand the server name.
2. Right-click on Logins and then select New Login.
3. Select Windows NT Authentication.
4. Type in the Windows NT account.
5. Set the default database for user.

SQL Server Authentication Mode

A network connection to SQL Server with SQL Server Authentication mode assumes a *nontrusted connection* between SQL Server and the client. A user types in a login name and password that has been set up as a SQL Server standard login. SQL Server will verify the login ID and the password itself and compare it to a login ID that has been predefined by the system administrator as a SQL Server login ID. If the system administrator has not set up the specified login ID, the connection will fail.

There are several good uses for SQL Server authentication, and many applications are written to use it. Many people prefer this method because they understand a login and a password and NT authentication can seem complicated and obscure. SQL Server authentication is also used for Internet clients and operating systems that are not Windows NT-based.

Sometimes an entire application as well as all of its users will use one SQL Server login and password. This type of access is easy to manage but creates a security risk by not tracking the identity of each user and should not be used for databases containing confidential information such as sales or personnel information.

Use the SQL Query Analyzer Tool found in the Tools menu on the Microsoft Management Console after positioning the cursor on the server in the server group.

To create a SQL Server login (SQL Server authentication):

```
sp_addlogin 'login', 'password', 'database', 'language',
'login_pid', 'sid'
```

All the arguments are optional except login, which is stored as the sysname in the syslogins table in the master database. The arguments are discussed in detail in Chapter 23, "System Stored Procedures."

Alternatively, you can use the Microsoft Management Console to add a SQL Server login for both Windows NT authentication and SQL Server authentication (Figure 5-3 shows SQL Server authentication). The steps are as follows:

1. Expand the server name.
2. Right-click on Logins and then select New Login.
3. Select SQL Server Authentication.
4. Type in a login name and password
5. Set the default database for user.

The main, immediately visible difference between the two types of login ID is that when the screen to connect to the SQL Server appears, the user with the Windows NT authenticated login ID does not have to type in a login ID and password, while the user with the SQL Server authentication login ID does. Windows NT authentication works because NT passes the login ID and password to SQL Server, which then checks to see if the NT account or group is a member of the syslogins table. Another difference is that if you enter the domain name after selecting Windows NT Authentication, the domain name automatically appears as the first part of the Name field. (The NT user must have been previously created.)

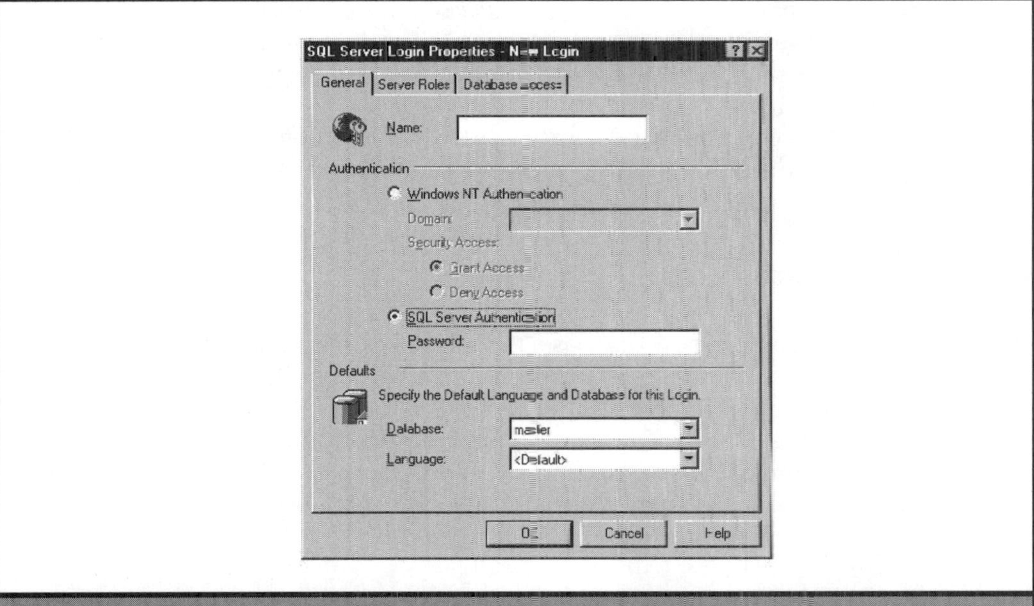

Figure 5-3. *Creating a SQL Server authenticated login ID*

To summarize, there are two types of logins, an NT authenticated login and a SQL Server authenticated login. A login ID is used for authentication, which identifies the user and confirms database access. The login ID has a default database that is used when the connection is established and is defined for the login ID when it is created.

Permission Validation

Now that we have seen how a user gains access to Microsoft SQL Server by using one of the two types of SQL Server login ID, we can talk about how this login ID is related to a SQL Server database user.

Database Users

One of the differences between a SQL Server login ID and a database user ID is that a SQL Server login ID is for the entire SQL Server. One login ID can be associated with multiple database users, and all databases can establish a relationship between the SQL Server login ID and the database user ID using the stored procedure *sp_grantdbaccess*. The database user ID, on the other hand, is good only in a specific database on SQL Server.

A relationship must be defined by a user in the role of db_accessadmin or db_owner between the SQL Server login ID and the database user ID. This is accomplished by creating a user inside the database and passing an established SQL Server login ID as a parameter to the *sp_grantdbaccess* stored procedure. A database user ID cannot be created unless it's associated with a valid SQL Server login ID in this manner. (Pre-SQL Server 7, the *sp_adduser* command was used; it is still supported for backward compatibility.)

The sp_grantdbaccess command connects an SQL Server login ID to a database user ID, and this is what allows the SQL Server login ID permissions on the specified database.

```
sp_grantdbaccess 'login', 'databaseusername'
```

This command creates a new database user in the *sysusers* system table in the database and relates the database user to the SQL Server login ID that was created using sp_grantlogin for a Windows NT authenticated user or using sp_addlogin for a SQL Server authenticated user. The *login* is a mandatory argument while the *databaseusername* argument is optional and, if left off, defaults to the *login* and makes both parameters the same. Conversely, to remove a database user, use the *sp_revokedbaccess* stored procedure.

The following are rules for using sp_grantdbaccess:

- Cannot be used within a user defined transaction

- SA login cannot be added to a database
- Windows NT accounts or groups need to be qualified by a domain name
- Can be executed only by users with certain database roles; *db_accessadmin* or *db_owner*

Here are rules for using sp_revokedbaccess:

- Cannot be used within a user defined transaction.
- Cannot remove public role, DBO user, or the fixed roles in database
- Cannot remove the Guest User account in the master and tempdb databases.
- Cannot remove a Windows NT user from an NT group.
- Can be executed only by users with certain database roles: *db_accessadmin* or *db_owner.*
- A user cannot be dropped if it owns objects within the database; you must change the owner of the objects with the stored procedure sp_changeobjectowner before using *sp_revokedbaccess.*

Note *Use the Microsoft Management Console and register your SQL Server into a server group.*

As an alternative to sp_grantdbaccess, you can use the Microsoft Management Console to create a new database user for both Windows NT authentication and SQL Server authentication (see Figure 5-4):

1. Expand the server and select the database.
2. Right-click on the database.
3. Select New, then New Database User.
4. Select the login name.
5. Type in the user name.
6. Select any roles in which to place the user.
7. Click OK.

This *sp_grantdbaccess* stored procedure is how the login (authentication) is mapped to a SQL Server database user used to control access to objects and actions performed in the database (permission validation). This actually connects the two parts of security, authentication and permission validation, to provide secured access and specified permissions. It is easier to administer if the login ID and the database user ID are the same name. You should consider setting this as a standard in your system.

To refine this access even further and to grant specific permissions to a collective bunch of users, groups and roles are used.

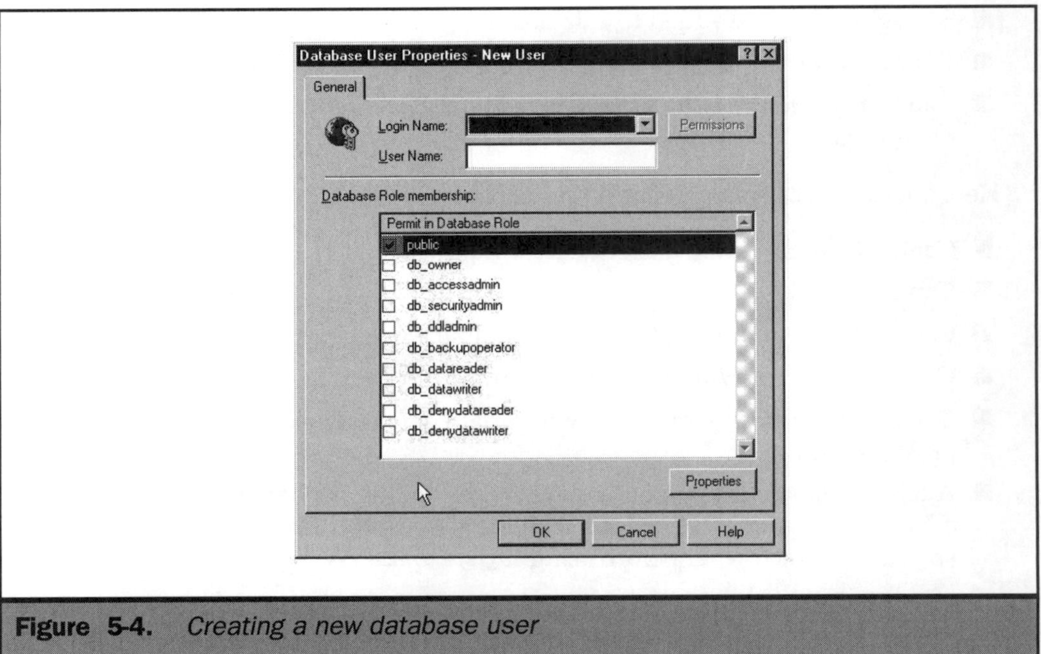

Figure 5-4. *Creating a new database user*

NT Groups and SQL Server Roles

Placing users into groups and roles makes it easier to administer permission to multiple users at once. A *group* is a way to administer users or other groups within Windows NT. A *role* is a way to administer users within SQL Server that contain SQL Server logins, Windows NT logins, groups, or other roles. The database groups in previous versions of SQL Server have been replaced by roles, which are much more powerful. Sp_addgroup, sp_changegroup, sp_dropgroup have been included for backward compatibility; but they are now just inferior methods of manipulating roles.

NT Groups

You can grant access to the logins of the entire NT group on SQL Server by creating a SQL Server login for the group. Then the **GRANT** statement is used to allow a user, role, or group permissions to access data or perform specific actions in the database. Permissions can only be granted for users in the current database. Conversely, the **REVOKE** command is used to take away granted permissions, and the **DENY** statement is used to prevent a user from ever gaining permission by someone else giving the **GRANT**. The great thing about setting up an SQL Server login for an NT group is that once it is set up, all you have to do is add a new user to the NT group. The SQL Server login and database permissions are already in place.

There are two types of permissions: *object* and *statement* permissions. Object permissions give the user access permission to use objects such as tables, views, procedures, and extended procedures that exist in the database. Statement permissions allow access to specific Transact-SQL statements such as **CREATE TABLE** or **EXECUTE PROCEDURE**.

When a group is a member of a higher-level group, all members of the group inherit the security settings of the higher-level group, in addition to the security settings defined for the group itself or user accounts.

SQL Server Roles

If there are no NT groups, you can still assemble users into a collective unit and administer the users together by using *roles*. You can create functional collections of users (both NT and SQL Server–authenticated), as well as other roles. This is a very powerful tool for simplifying administration of database permissions.

Note *Use the Microsoft Management Console (MMC), register your SQL Server into a server group, and refer to Figure 5-5.*

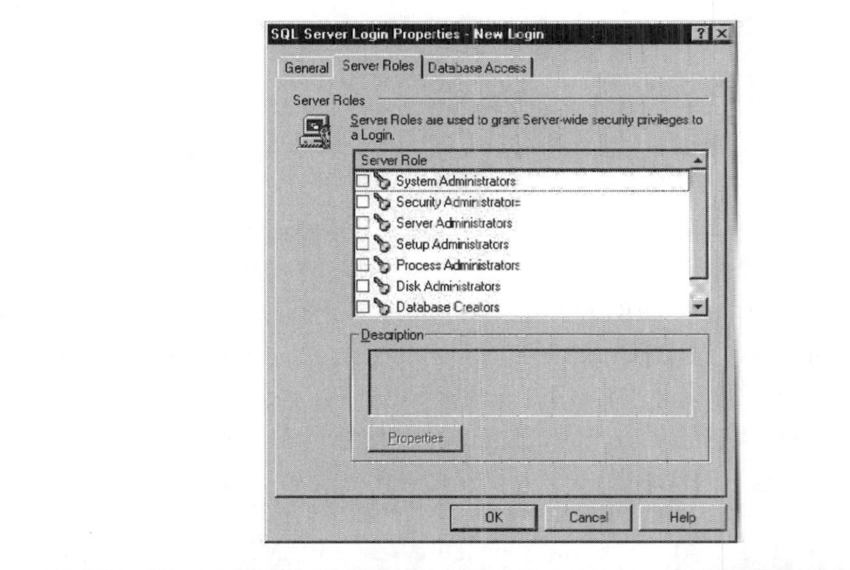

Figure 5-5. *Assigning fixed server roles*

You can use the Microsoft Management Console to assign a user to a fixed role for a SQL Server authentication login ID:

1. Expand the server name in the MMC.
2. Right-click on Logins and then select New Login.
3. Select SQL Server Authentication.
4. Type in a login name and password for SQL Server Authentication or NT account or user for Windows NT Authentication.
5. Set the default database for user.
6. Click on the Server Roles tab.
7. Click on the Roles you choose to give to the user.

FIXED SERVER ROLES Fixed server roles exist at the server level and outside of a specific database. A user must have NT login account or a SQL server login account to be added to a fixed server role. Any member of a fixed server role can add other logins to the role.

The following table shows the name of the Fixed Server Role and the permissions for the Fixed Server Role.

Fixed Server Role Name	What This Role Can Do
System Administrators, sysadmin	Permission to perform any activity in SQL Server
Server Administrators, serveradmin	Permission to configure server-wide settings
Setup Administrators, setupadmin	Permitted to install replication and manage extended procedures
Security Administrators, securityadmin	Permitted to manage server logins
Process Administrators, processadmin	Permitted to manage processes running in SQL Server
Database Creators, dbcreator	Permitted to create and alter databases
Disk Administrators, diskadmin	Permitted to manage disk files

To add a member to a fixed server role, see Figure 5-5 for the Microsoft Management Console, Enterprise Manager method, or use the following stored procedure:

```
sp_addsrvrolemember 'security_account', 'role'
```

The user will inherit all of the permissions of the role they are assuming. Fixed server roles mean exactly what they imply; they cannot be removed or changed. The only ones who have permission to execute *sp_addsrvrolemember* are other members of fixed server roles. The *syslogins* system table is updated to indicate which login ID is assigned to which fixed server role.

To delete a member from a fixed server role, see Figure 5-5 for the Enterprise Manager method or use the following stored procedure:

```
sp_dropsrvrolemember 'security_account', 'role'
```

It is not possible to drop the SA (system administrator) user from a fixed server role.

FIXED DATABASE ROLES Fixed database roles exist at the database level and inside of a specific database. A user must have an NT login account or a SQL server login account to be added to a fixed database role. Roles can also be added to a fixed database role. Any member of a fixed database role can add others to the role.

The following table shows the name of the Fixed Database Role and the permissions for the Fixed Database Role.

Fixed Database Role Name	What This Role Can Do
db_owner	As DBO, permitted to do all activities of all other database roles in addition to other Database Owner tasks
db_accessadmin	Permitted to allow access and disallow access to Windows NT groups/users and SQL Server users in the database
db_datareader	Permitted to see all data from all user tables in the database
db_datawriter	Permitted to modify data in all user tables in the database (Insert, Update, Delete)
db_ddladmin	Permitted to create, alter, and/or drop objects in the database
db_securityadmin	Permitted to administer roles and statement and object permissions in the database
db_dumpoperator	Permitted to do backups of the database
db_denydatareader	Not permitted see any data in the database
db_denydatawriter	Not permitted to modify any data in the database

To add a member to a fixed database role, see Figure 5-6, or use the following stored procedure:

```
sp_addrolemember 'role', 'security_account'
```

The user will inherit all of the permissions of the role they are assuming. If the security account is for a Windows NT user or group and they are not a user in the database, they will be automatically added as a user. Use the domain name in front of the security account for a Windows NT user or group, for example, **DomainName\SecurityAccount**, for the security account argument. If the security account is for a SQL Server user or role, these must exist in the database from which you execute the command. You *can* use a security account without the domain name prefix for the security account parameter when the security account represents a SQL Server user. If you have a user-defined role, do not try to add a fixed role to it at either the database level or the server level, as this will not work. Fixed database roles are exactly what they imply; they cannot be removed or changed. The sysusers system table is updated to indicate which database user is assuming which fixed database role.

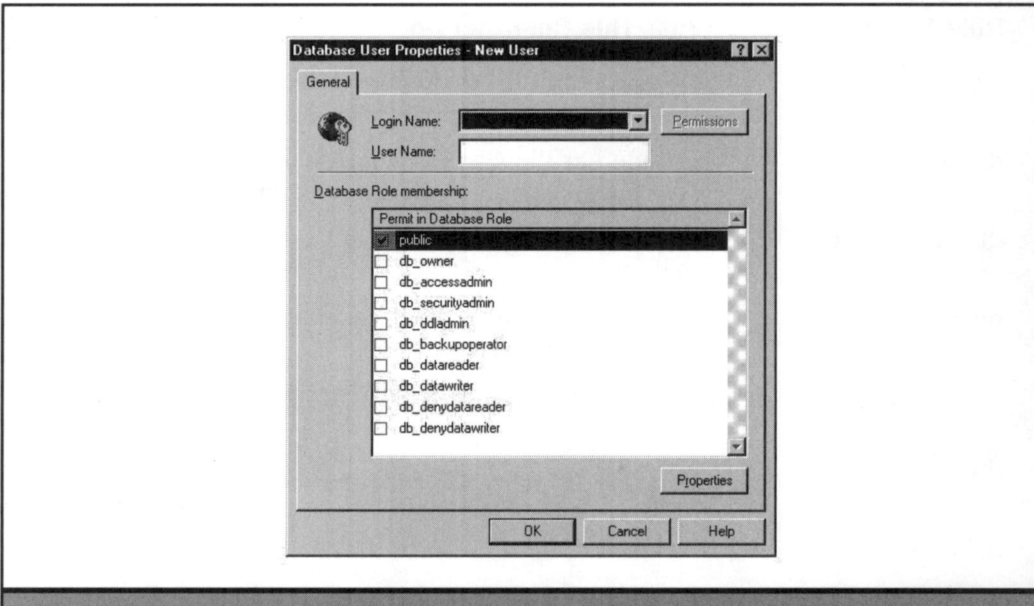

Figure 5-6. *Assigning fixed database roles*

In addition to the fixed database roles seen in Figure 5-6, there are two special user/role permissions for Microsoft SQL Server:

- **Guest user** If the user attempts to access a database and has not been established as a database user, the user will be established as a Guest user. This means they can access any objects that the Guest user has permission to use within that database.
- **Public role** If you want to give everyone in the database permission to some object or to perform some action, you can give permission to the Public role. Everyone is entitled to the permissions given to the Public role.

Use the following system-supplied stored procedure to show the permissions for each fixed database role:

```
sp_dbfixedrolepermission 'role'
```

The Query Analyzer is located in the Tools Menu in the Microsoft Management Console. You can execute stored procedures from the Query Analyzer window.

The output from the Query Analyzer has the following information:

DbFixedRole	Permission
db_owner	Everything in the database
db_accessadmin	Add member to db_accessadmin
db_accessadmin	sp_adduser
db_accessadmin	sp_dropuser
db_accessadmin	sp_grantdbaccess
db_accessadmin	sp_revokedbaccess
db_securityadmin	Add member to db_securityadmin
db_securityadmin	DENY
db_securityadmin	GRANT
db_securityadmin	REVOKE
db_securityadmin	sp_addrole
db_securityadmin	sp_addrolemember
db_securityadmin	sp_droprole

DbFixedRole	Permission
db_securityadmin	sp_droprolemember
db_ddladmin	Add member to db_ddladmin
db_ddladmin	All DDL but GRANT, REVOKE, DENY
db_ddladmin	sp_adduserobject
db_dumpoperator	Add member to db_dumpoperator
db_dumpoperator	CHECKPOINT
db_dumpoperator	DUMP DATABASE
db_dumpoperator	DUMP TRANSACTION
db_datareader	Add member to db_datareader
db_datareader	SELECT permission on any object
db_datawriter	Add member to db_datawriter
db_datawriter	DELETE permission on any object
db_datawriter	INSERT permission on any object
db_datawriter	UPDATE permission on any object
db_denydatareader	Add member to db_denydatareader
db_denydatareader	No SELECT permission on any object
db_denydatawriter	Add member to db_denydatawriter
db_denydatawriter	No DELETE permission on any object
db_denydatawriter	No INSERT permission on any object
db_denydatawriter	No UPDATE permission on any object

Everyone with access to the database can execute the stored procedures *sp_dbfixedrolepermission* and *sp_helpdbfixedrole.*

Use the following system-supplied stored procedure to show the names and descriptions for each fixed database role:

```
sp_helpdbfixedrole 'role'
```

The Query Analyzer is located in the Tools Menu in the Microsoft Management Console. You can execute stored procedures from this window.

The output from the Query Analyzer has the following information:

DbFixedRole	Description
db_owner	DB Owners
db_accessadmin	DB Access Administrators
db_securityadmin	DB Security Administrators
db_ddladmin	DB DDL Administrators
db_dumpoperator	DB Dump Operator
db_datareader	DB Data Reader
db_datawriter	DB Data Writer
db_denydatareader	DB Deny Data Reader
db_denydatawriter	DB Deny Data Writer

Note *Use the Microsoft Management Console, select a Server in Server Group; then select a Database and right-click on Database Role.*

To create a new-user defined role in the database, see Figure 5-7, or use the following stored procedure:

```
sp_addrole 'role' , 'owner'
```

The *owner* parameter defaults to DBO owner; however, if you specify an owner, the owner must be a database user or a database role in the *sysusers* system table in the database in which you are executing the command. Only *db_securityadmin* or *db_owner* roles are permitted to use the sp_addrole stored procedure. You can use GRANT or DENY statements to assign permission to the new database role.

To drop a database role from the database, execute the following stored procedure inside the database:

```
sp_droprole 'role'          --This removes standard database roles
sp_dropapprole 'role'       --This removes application database roles
```

The row that was inserted into the *sysusers* table is removed from the *sysusers* system table. You will be unable to drop fixed roles and the *public* role; you must first remove all the users from the role. Use the stored procedure *sp_droprolemember* to remove the database users from the role. Do not execute this stored procedure from within a user defined transaction. Only a member of the *db_owner* or *db_securityadmin* roles is permitted to use *sp_droprole*.

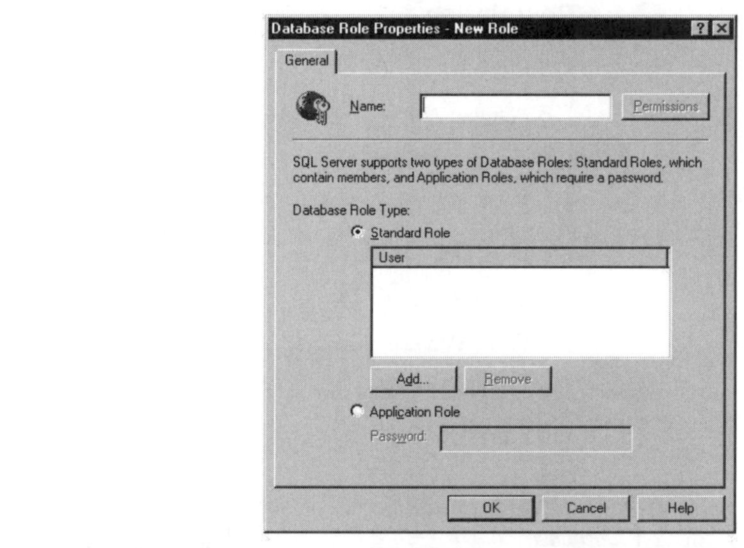

Figure 5-7. *Adding a user-defined database rule*

Granting Permissions

The permissions granted to a group or role are inherited by members of that group or role. Permission can be granted at different levels. Granting permission to a user can come into conflict with permissions granted to another role in which the user is a member. The restrictive deny and revoke permissions that prevent a user from accessing an object apply when there are conflicting permissions between roles if a user is in multiple groups or roles or has conflicting individual user permissions.

There are three states to a permission:

- Grant
- Revoke
- Deny

The GRANT Statement

Grant means one database user gives permission for another database user to see data, change data, and perform database actions. You can only grant from the current database to users in the current database. Now there is also a WITH GRANT option to the GRANT statement which allows you to grant permission to a database user to grant permission to others. John gives Jane permission WITH GRANT, which allows

Jane the permission to grant the same permission to Jay. If Jane gave Jay permission WITH GRANT, then Jay could grant the same permissions to Jerry. You can also grant collections of users this ability by granting WITH GRANT to groups and roles. However, the WITH GRANT permission is one you want to use with caution or you can lose control over who is granting permissions to whom.

The two kinds of permissions are:

- Statement permissions
- Object permissions

Statement Permissions

Statement permissions are given by the Transact-SQL GRANT statement and give a security account access to other Transact-SQL statements including the GRANT statement. The user can be given permission to use the following Transact-SQL statements when giving statement permissions:

ALTER DATABASE	EXECUTE
ALTER TABLE	GRANT
BEGIN TRANSACTION	GRANT on object
CHECKPOINT	INSERT
COMMIT TRANSACTION	KILL
CREATE DATABASE	RESTORE DATABASE
CREATE DEFAULT	LOAD TRANSACTION
CREATE INDEX	RAISERROR
CREATE PROCEDURE	READTEXT
CREATE RULE	RECONFIGURE
CREATE TABLE	REFERENCES
CREATE TRIGGER	REVOKE
CREATE VIEW	REVOKE on object
DBCC	ROLLBACK TRANSACTION
DELETE	SAVE TRANSACTION
DISK INIT	SELECT
DISK MIRROR	SET
DISK REFIT	SETUSER
DISK REINIT	SHUTDOWN

DISK REMIRROR	TRUNCATE TABLE
DISK UNMIRROR	UPDATE
DROP any object	UPDATE STATISTICS
BACKUP DATABASE	UPDATETEXT
DUMP TRANSACTION	WRITETEXT

Here is the syntax for statement permissions:

```
GRANT {ALL | statement[,…]}
TO security_account [,…]
```

The following table shows the Grant statement arguments for statement permissions and the description of the argument.

GRANT Argument for Statement Permission	Description
ALL	**Statement:** Gives the ability to use all statements when used as a statement permission. In the case of giving all statement permissions, only the System Administrator (SA) and the Database Owner (DBO) can give all permissions because they are the only ones that have all permissions themselves. SA, of course, has more than DBO because SA is server-wide and the DBO is database-wide.
Statement	CREATE DATABASE can be used if the user granting the permission is SA. If the user is not SA, CREATE DEFAULT, CREATE PROCEDURE, CREATE RULE, CREATE TABLE, CREATE VIEW, DUMP DATABASE, and DUMP TRANSACTION can be granted to another user. This action enables the grantee to use the statement. Also, insert, update, delete, select, references, and execute can be granted by object owners.
Security Account	The permissions are given to this user. The user can be a Microsoft SQL Server User, a SQL Server Role, a Windows NT User, or a Windows NT Group.

Here's an example of the GRANT statement for statement permissions:

```
GRANT CREATE DATABASE, CREATE TABLE
TO security_account
GO
```

Or, for a Windows NT authenticated user, use the DomainName\SecurityAccount:

```
GRANT CREATE DATABASE, CREATE TABLE
TO DomainName\SecurityAccount
GO

GRANT CREATE TABLE
TO rolename
GO
```

Object Permissions

Object permissions allow the user to have applicable permissions to objects such as tables, views, procedures, and extended stored procedures as they exist in the database. If you are a member of the *sysadmin* and *db_securityadmin* roles, you can grant all permission in all databases. If you are an object owner, you can grant permissions for any objects for which you are the owner. The db_owner role can grant any permission on any object in the database they own.

The syntax for object permissions is as follows:

```
GRANT
{{ALL | permission[,…]} [(column[,…])] ON {table | view}
| ON {stored_procedure | extended_procedure}}
TO security_account [,…]
[WITH GRANT OPTION]
[AS {group | role}]
```

The following are the GRANT arguments for object permissions:

GRANT Argument for Object Permissions	Description
ALL	**Object:** Transfers all permissions for the object when ALL is used to give a user permissions on an object.

GRANT Argument for Object Permissions	Description
Statement	CREATE DATABASE can be used if the user granting the permission is SA. If the user is not SA, CREATE DEFAULT, CREATE PROCEDURE, CREATE RULE, CREATE TABLE, CREATE VIEW, DUMP DATABASE, and DUMP TRANSACTION can be granted to another user. This action enables the grantee to use the statement. Also, insert, update, delete, select, references, and execute can be granted by object owners.
TO Security Account	The permissions are given to this user. The user can be a Microsoft SQL Server User, a SQL Server Role, a Windows NT User, or a Windows NT Group.
WITH GRANT OPTION	Gives the user the ability to grant the specified permissions to other users.
AS {*group* | *role*}	This indicates under which group or role the user granting the permission is acting. If the grantor is in multiple roles, there may be conflicting permissions and the grantor may indicate which role or group has permission to grant these permissions.
Permission	The object permission being granted by the grantor to the grantee. See the next table to see which objects have which permissions.
ON Table	The name of the table the user will be permitted to access with the assigned permissions.
ON Column	The name of the column the user will be permitted to access with the assigned permissions.
ON View	The name of the view the user will be permitted to access with the assigned permissions.
ON Stored_procedure	The name of the stored procedure the user will be permitted to access with the execute permission.
ON Extended_stored procedure	The name of the extended stored procedure the user will be permitted to access with the execute permission.

The following table specifies the permissions for the specific objects when a user is giving object permissions as opposed to statement permissions.

Object Name	Permissions for Object Name
Table or view permissions	SELECT, INSERT, DELETE, UPDATE, REFERENCES
Extended stored procedure permissions	EXECUTE
Column permissions	SELECT, UPDATE
Stored procedure permissions	EXECUTE

The following examples use GRANT statement for object permissions:

```
GRANT EXECUTE
ON storedprocedurename
TO security_account
WITH GRANT OPTION
GO

GRANT SELECT,UPDATE
ON tablename
TO public
GO

GRANT SELECT ON tablename
TO user AS rolename
GO
```

Special Rules When Granting Permissions

There are a number of special rules to note when granting permissions:

- You must use the *REFERENCES column* permission for the table if the user will be inserting or modifying a row in a table with a *FOREIGN KEY* constraint and does not have *SELECT* permission on the table or the column.
- Not all statements require permissions to use them. The ones that do require permission add objects to the database or administer the database.

- A user does not have the ability to grant some Transact-SQL statements. These have to be permitted by membership in a special system role such as sysadmin, the only one that can issue the SHUTDOWN statement to shut down the database.
- Statement permissions are broken up by roles. Certain roles have permission to execute certain statements. For example, the CREATE DATABASE permission is a defaulted permission of the *sysadmin* role.
- The option WITH GRANT only works for object permissions.
- If you have the sysadmin or db_owner role, you can test permissions by using the SETUSER to impersonate another user to see if you have given the permissions properly.
- A row is inserted into the *sysprotects* system table when a grant occurs.
- Use the sp_helprotect stored procedure to see the permissions for an object or a user.

The REVOKE Statement

The REVOKE statement can be used to remove a granted permission or to rescind the denial from a denied permission.

The REVOKE syntax for statement permissions is as follows:

```
REVOKE {ALL | statement[,…]}
FROM security_account [,…]
```

The REVOKE syntax for object permissions is:

```
REVOKE [GRANT OPTION FOR]
{ALL [PRIVILEGES] | permission[,…]}
{{[(column[,…n])] ON {table | view}
| {procedure | extended_procedure}}
FROM security_account [,…] [CASCADE]
[AS {group | role}]
```

The following table shows the arguments for the REVOKE statement and the description of the argument.

REVOKE Argument	Description
ALL	**Object:** Removes all permissions for the object when ALL is used to revoke permissions on an object. **Statement:** Removes all granted or denied permissions on statements when used as a statement permission. In the case of revoking all statement permissions, only the System Administrator (SA) and the Database Owner (DBO) can revoke all permissions because they are the only ones that have all permissions themselves with SA, of course, having more than DBO because SA is server-wide and DBO is database-wide.
Statement	CREATE DATABASE can be used if the user revoking the permission is SA. If the user is not SA, CREATE DEFAULT, CREATE PROCEDURE, CREATE RULE, CREATE TABLE, CREATE VIEW. DUMP DATABASE, and DUMP TRANSACTION can be revoked from another user. This action revokes the granted or denied permission.
Security_account	The permissions are revoked from this user. The security accounts can be a Microsoft SQL Server User, a SQL Server Role, a Windows NT User, or a Windows NT Group.
GRANT OPTION FOR	Removes the effects of WITH GRANT OPTION. The user can no longer grant the WITH GRANT OPTION to others but will retain their permissions.
PRIVILEGES	This is not required and can be included for ANSI compliance.
AS {*group* | *role*}	This indicates under which group or role the user revoking the permission is acting. If the person revoking is in multiple roles, there may be conflicting permissions, and this user may indicate which role or group has permission to revoke these permissions.
Permission	The object permission is revoked.
Table	The name of the table from which permissions are being revoked.

REVOKE Argument	Description
Column	The name of the column from which permissions are being revoked.
View	The name of the view from which permissions are being revoked.
Stored procedure	The name of the stored procedure from which permissions are being revoked.
Extended stored procedure	The name of the extended stored procedure from which permissions are being revoked.
FROM	Indicates a list of security accounts.
CASCADE	Removes permissions from the security accounts and also from all security accounts to which the security account granted privileges.

There are a number of special rules to note when revoking permissions:

- Do not attempt to revoke permissions from the system roles.
- If CASCADE is not used as an argument when revoking permissions from a user who was granted WITH GRANT OPTION permission, an error message is returned.
- The *sysprotects* system table has a row removed when the revoke statement is issued.

Here are some examples of the REVOKE statement:

```
REVOKE CREATE TABLE FROM security_account
GO

REVOKE CREATE TABLE
FROM DomainName\SecurityAccount
GO
```

To REVOKE a denied permission:

```
REVOKE INSERT ON tablename
FROM security_account
GO
```

The DENY Statement

Issuing a deny command keeps a user from assuming the permissions of group or role memberships and adds a row to the *sysprotects* system table indicating that the user cannot obtain the permission in the future until the DENY is revoked.

Here is the DENY syntax for statement permissions:

```
DENY{ALL | statement[,…]}
TO security_account[,…]
```

and the DENY syntax for object permissions:

```
DENY {ALL [PRIVILEGES] | permission[,…n]}
{[(column[,…])] ON { table|view}
|ON { table | view}[( column[,…])]
| {procedure | extended_procedure}}
TO security_account
[CASCADE]
```

The following table shows the arguments for the DENY statement and the description of the argument.

DENY Argument	Description
ALL	**Object:** Denies all permissions for the object when ALL is used to deny a user permissions on an object. **Statement:** Takes away the ability to use all statements when used as a statement permission. In the case of denying all statement permissions, only the System Administrator (SA) and the Database Owner (DBO) can deny all permissions because they are the only ones that have all permissions themselves with SA, of course, having more than DBO because SA is server-wide and DBO is database wide.
Statement	CREATE DATABASE can be used if the user denying the permission is SA. If the user is not SA, CREATE DEFAULT, CREATE PROCEDURE, CREATE RULE, CREATE TABLE, CREATE VIEW, DUMP DATABASE, and DUMP TRANSACTION can be denied to another user. This action denies the user permissions to use the statement.

DENY Argument	Description
Security_account	The permissions are denied to this user. The user can be a Microsoft SQL Server User, a SQL Server Role, a Windows NT User, or a Windows NT Group
PRIVILEGES	This is not required and can be included for ANSI compliance.
AS {*group* | *role*}	This indicates under which group or role the user denying the permission is acting. If the person denying is in multiple roles, there may be conflicting permissions, and this user may indicate which role or group has permission to deny these permissions.
Permission	The object or statement permission denied.
Table	The name of the table from which permissions are being denied.
Column	The name of the column from which permissions are being denied.
View	The name of the view from which permissions are being denied.
Stored_procedure	The name of the stored procedure from which permissions are being denied.
Extended_procedure	The name of the extended stored procedure from which permissions are being denied.
TO	Indicates a list of users.
CASCADE	Denies permissions to the user and also to all users to which the user granted permissions and to all users to which they granted permissions, and so on…

There are a number of special rules to note when denying permissions:

- If you deny an individual user and they are later added to group with the permission, they will not have permission.
- Use REVOKE to remove a denied permission for a user.
- The *sysprotects* system table has a row inserted when the deny statement is issued.

The following examples demonstrate use of the DENY statement:

```
DENY SELECT, INSERT, UPDATE, DELETE
ON tablename
TO security_account
GO

DENY CREATE TABLE TO rolename
GO
```

To change permissions in the Microsoft Management Console on an object, follow these steps:

1. Expand the server name.
2. Expand Databases and then the specific database name.
3. Select the object type in the scope pane.
4. Right-click the object in the results pane.
5. Select Task, then Manage Permissions.
6. Select List All Users/DB Roles.
7. Select the permission you want to change.

Recommendations to Implement Security

There are a number of actions a database administrator can take to implement security:

- Ascertain that there is a unique login ID for every user. Creating one login ID and allowing many users to gain access to the database with it is not a good implementation of a security system. There is no way to track who is doing what in the database.
- Set up groups and roles and collectively manage users. This cuts down on the amount of overhead to manage security and is more likely to ensure accuracy and standardization of access.
- Have DBO be the owner of all your database objects.
- It is best to have users perform all insert, update, and delete activity through the use of stored procedures. You simply have a greater level of control through Transact-SQL, and you know exactly what your users are doing to the data.
- Triggers can be used to prevent unwanted access to data to rollback undesired writes.
- For SA access, place the individual user in the sysadmin role.
- Use the organizational chart of the company to divide the access permissions into functional roles.

Ownership Chains

Objects can be dependent on other objects; this dependency is called an *ownership chain*. If a user owns all the objects and the dependent objects, everything is fine. However, it is when the user does not own all the objects referenced or needed by a view or stored procedure that things start to get complicated. This is called a broken ownership chain. SQL Server examines permissions on each object in the chain whose next link is owned by a different user.

If a user grants permissions to someone else to use a view or a stored procedure which has tables owned by that same user, they do not have to grant permissions to the individual tables referenced in the view or stored procedure.

xp_cmdshell

xp_cmdshell executes a given command string as an operating system command shell and allows the user to execute NT commands inside of SQL Server.

```
xp_cmdshell {'command_string'} [, no_output]
```

The following table shows the xp_cmdshell arguments and a description of the argument:

xp_cmdshell Arguments	Description
'*command_string*'	The operating system command where up to 255 characters are allowed
no_output	Optional parameter that returns no output to the user

The use of xp_cmdshell should be evaluated in an environment where the desire is to control access to operating system files either on the server or in the NT domain. The following bulleted points indicate where security risks can occur:

- If the account that is running Microsoft SQL Server has many permissions granted to it, such as a domain administrator, any user that is granted execute permission for xp_cmdshell will be able to execute any operating system command with the privileges of the account that is running Microsoft SQL Server. The default is a user account with local administration privilege, but if the account has domain administrator privileges the entire domain can be exposed.

- To restrict xp_cmdshell access, set the *xp_cmdshell - Impersonates Client* option in the Microsoft SQL Server setup program. When this check box is checked, only users who have connected to SQL Server through a trusted connection and who are members of the local Administrators group on that computer are allowed to use xp_cmdshell. When a non-SA executes xp_cmdshell with the Impersonates Client option set, the requested command runs in the SQLServerAgentCmdExec user account, which is the same account used by SQL Server Agent for scheduled tasks entered by all non-SA users.
- If you select the option *xp_cmdshell - Use SQLServerAgentCmdExec Account for NonSAs* and a user logs on to SQL Server as SA, the command is executed under SQL Server's security context instead of the SQLServerAgentCmdExec security context.

You can use the Query Analyzer—which is invoked from the Enterprise Manager Tools menu—to execute the xp_cmdshell extended stored procedure (see Figure 5-8).

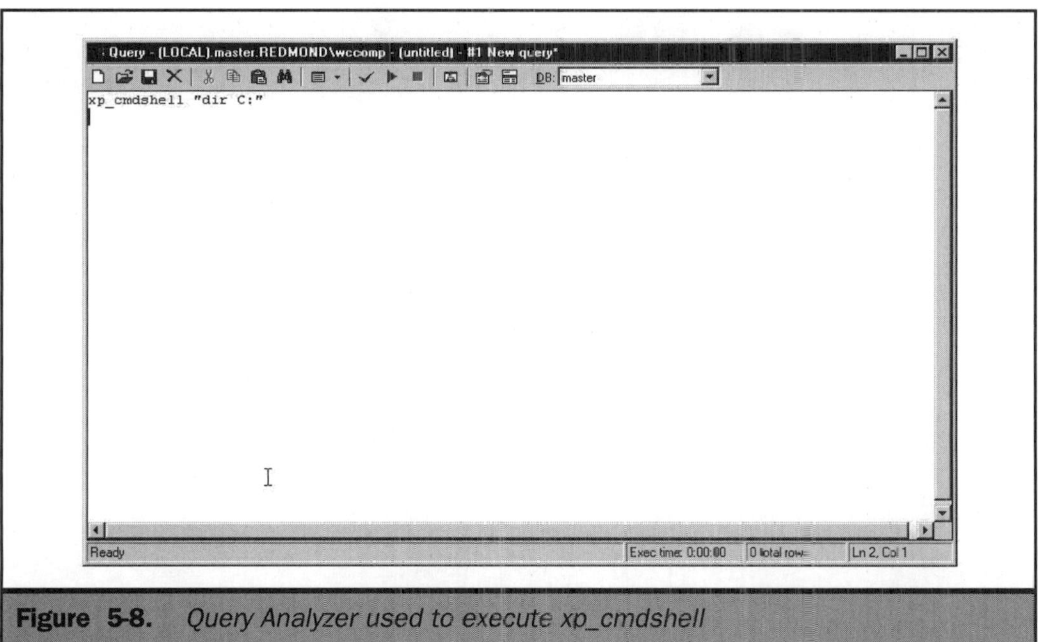

Figure 5-8. *Query Analyzer used to execute xp_cmdshell*

Chapter 6

Transact-SQL Enhancements

In this chapter, we will discover the extent of the Transact SQL enhancements that are part of the Microsoft SQL Server 7 release.

Stored Procedure Enhancements

A stored procedure is a compilation of Transact-SQL statements into an object that can be run using the statement, **EXECUTE *storedprocedurename***. The stored procedure can return a result set or sets, an integer return code, or an OUTPUT argument or parameter. Stored procedures are advantageous for many reasons: speed, reusability, business logic encapsulation, protection from queries that have not been optimized, reduced network traffic, and security (because permissions need only be granted to the stored procedure, not to the objects it accesses). Stored procedures are the basis of the Transact-SQL developers' interaction with the database and contribute to database performance and reliability.

Microsoft SQL Server provides the capability of permanent or temporary stored procedures. The temporary stored procedures are stored in the *tempdb* system database.

Delayed Name Resolution Behavior in Stored Procedures

Delayed name resolution saves time and effort for the Transact-SQL programmer by permitting the SQL Server developer to create a stored procedure, a batch file, or a trigger and reference objects in the Transact-SQL code that do not yet exist. In previous versions, a Transact-SQL programmer would have to create objects in a certain order. For example, in version 6.x, as you are creating the stored procedure, the object the stored procedure is referencing in the Transact-SQL code in the creation script has to exist on the database when the stored procedure is parsed (syntactically validated) and the stored procedure object is created. If the object the stored procedure is referencing is not found on the database, the stored procedure object will not be created. In previous versions, SQL Server returned an error stating that the referenced object did not exist, and you had to create the object in order to create the stored procedure (or it could also be a trigger) that referenced the object. This was a very time-consuming and illogical loop.

In Microsoft SQL Server 7, when the stored procedure is *parsed* (syntactically validated) as it is created and a referenced object does not exist, the SQL Server allows the stored procedure to be created and placed on the database even though the object referenced in the stored procedure or trigger was not found on the database. The name is resolved in the later runtime stage called *resolution*. The resolution stage is another validation stage which occurs at runtime instead of at object creation time. If the object is referenced by the stored procedure at runtime—which may be days later—and the referenced object still has not been created, the SQL Server will send a runtime error because the stored procedure did not pass the resolution stage.

This makes Transact-SQL development easier because there are many objects which may not exist when the stored procedure is created but will at runtime when it is executed. At runtime in the resolution stage the *query plan* is formulated.

Microsoft SQL Server uses information such as the amount of data in the table and the indexes that are present on the table to build the query plan. This data about the existing referenced object has to be present in the resolution stage but, because we are not actually executing the stored procedure object at that stage of the game, a referenced object name does not have to be present in the object creation syntax validation stage.

The SQL Server Optimizer must have information about *existing* objects in order to formulate the query plan and place the plan in memory (see Figure 6-1) in a place called the *procedure cache*. The query plan is then used by Microsoft SQL Server to execute the stored procedure object.

Alter Procedure Statement

Another welcome change in Microsoft SQL Server 7 is the ability to alter a stored procedure object instead of having to remove it from the database and the syscomments system table in order to change it. The ability to change stored procedures is important because they, along with triggers, carry other references and permissions that are destroyed when the object is dropped. Just changing the object

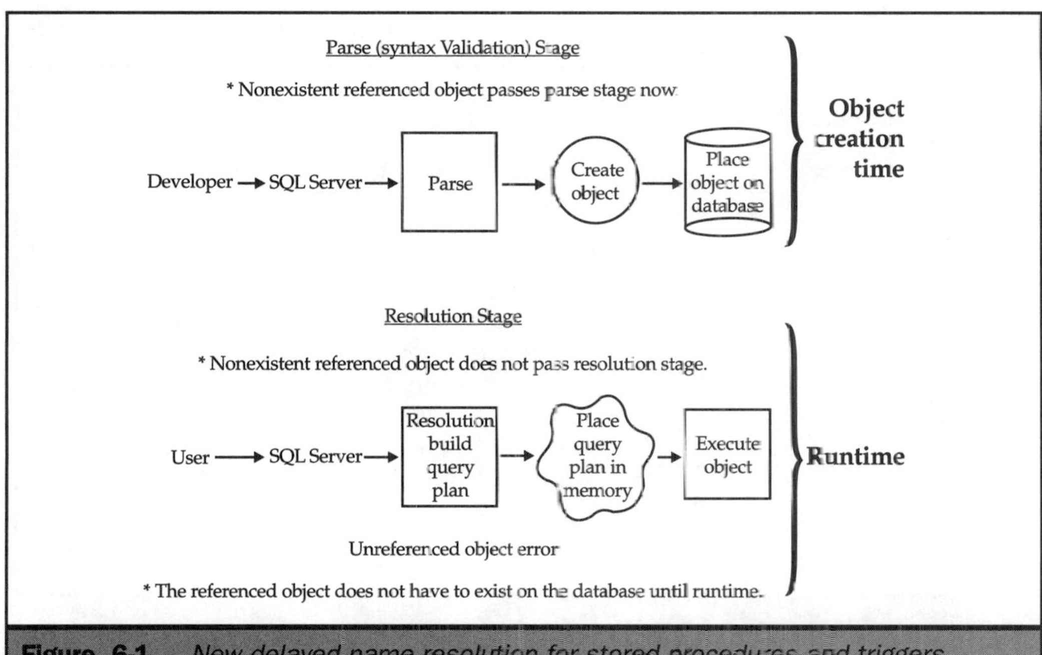

Figure 6-1. *New delayed name resolution for stored procedures and triggers*

instead of removing it retains the references and permissions that are associated with the object. The following table shows who is able to use the Alter Procedure statement:

Alter Procedure Usage

Stored Procedure Owner

Data Definition Language Administrators

DBO

The syntax for the **ALTER PROCEDURE** statement is:

```
ALTER PROC[EDURE] procedure name [;number]
[({@argument_name } data_type [= default] [OUTPUT])]
[,...]
WITH {RECOMPILE | ENCRYPTION | RECOMPILE , ENCRYPTION}]
[FOR REPLICATION]
AS
Transact-SQL statements [...]
```

Table 6-1 names the ALTER PROCEDURE parameters and gives a description of each parameter.

Alter Procedure Parameter	Description
Procedure Name	This parameter is the name of the procedure you desire to change or alter.
Number	This is used to group stored procedures of the same name. It is an optional parameter.
Argument Name	This parameter is the argument used to pass values to the stored procedure. Use an @ sign before the name. This indicates the user must pass the value to the stored procedure when it is executed. You may define your stored procedure to have none or up to 1,024 arguments.

Table 6-1. *Alter Procedure Parameters*

Alter Procedure Parameter	Description
Data Type	This indicates the datatype of the parameter. The only datatype you can not pass is the *image* datatype.
Default	You can give a default value for the argument.
OUTPUT	This indicates the argument is available for return after the stored procedure is executed.
RECOMPILE	The query plan is not saved in memory to be used next time the stored procedure is executed; a new query plan is generated every time the user requests the execution of the stored procedure. The RECOMPILE parameter is explicitly needed and will not default to what recompile was when the stored procedure was created if you do not give the recompile parameter.
ENCRYPTION	Stored procedures are stored in the *syscomments* system table on the database in encrypted format. You must use this with alter if you want them. The ENCRYPTION parameter is explicitly needed and will not default to what encryption was when the stored procedure was created if you do not give the encryption parameter.
FOR REPLICATION	Use FOR REPLICATION when creating or altering a stored procedure that acts as a filter and will be exclusively used by replication. This can not be used with the WITH RECOMPILE option.
AS	The word AS indicates that one or multiple Transact-SQL statements that comprise the stored procedure follow.
SQL Statements	These statements are the actual Transact-SQL code of the stored procedure.

Table 6-1. *Alter Procedure Parameters* (continued)

New System Stored Procedures

Many new system stored procedures have been created for Microsoft SQL Server 7. They fall into the following categories:

- Distributed Query Related
- Cursor Related
- Security Related
- Web Related
- Job Related
- Other

Details on the system stored procedures can be found in Chapter 23.

New Distributed Query Related System Stored Procedures

The new distributed query related stored procedures are for use with distributed queries and accommodate the new OLE DB connectivity facilities. Many of the tools have been converted to use the functionality of OLE DB. Table 6-2 describes the new distributed query related system stored procedures.

New Distributed Query Related System Stored Procedures	Description of New Functionality
sp_addlinkedserver	Creates a linked server
sp_droplinkedserver	Removes a linked server for use with distributed queries
sp_addlinkedsrvlogin	Creates or updates a SQL Server login mapping to a linked server
sp_droplinkedsrvlogin	Creates or updates a SQL Server login mapping to a linked server
sp_linkedservers	Shows a listing of linked servers for the local server
sp_catalogs	Shows the list of catalogs for the named linked server
sp_columns_ex	Shows the column information for the desired remote table

Table 6-2. *New Distributed Query Related Stored Procedures*

New Distributed Query Related System Stored Procedures	Description of New Functionality
sp_foreignkeys	Shows the foreign keys for the desired remote table
sp_primarykeys	Shows the primary key columns for the desired remote table
sp_indexes	Shows index information for the desired remote table
sp_tables_ex	Shows table information on the matching remote tables
sp_serveroption	Shows options for distributed queries

Table 6-2. *New Distributed Query Related Stored Procedures* (continued)

New Cursor Related System Stored Procedures

Table 6-3 describes the functionality of the new cursor related stored procedures. When you need to process the result set one row at a time, use cursors.

New Cursor Related Stored Procedure	Description of New Functionality
sp_cursor_list	The sp_cursor_list stored procedure shows information about currently open server cursors for the connection such as what type of cursor it is.
sp_describe_cursor	The sp_describe_cursor stored procedure shows the attributes of a server cursor.

Table 6-3. *New Cursor Related Stored Procedures*

New Cursor Related Stored Procedure	Description of New Functionality
sp_describe_cursor_columns	The sp_describe_cursor_columns stored procedure shows the attributes of the columns in the result set of a server cursor, examples being the name and data type of each cursor column.
sp_describe_cursor_tables	The sp_describe_cursor_tables stored procedure shows the attributes of the tables in the result set of a server cursor.

Table 6-3. *New Cursor Related Stored Procedures* (continued)

New Security Related System Stored Procedures

Table 6-4 describes the functionality of the new stored procedures. These procedures are for use with new security features available in Microsoft SQL Server 7 such as roles.

Enhanced Web Related System Stored Procedures

Table 6-5 describes the new and enhanced Web related stored procedures in Microsoft SQL Server.

New Security Related Stored Procedure	Description of New Functionality
sp_dbfixedrolepermission	The sp_ dbfixedrolepermission stored procedure shows the permissions for each fixed database role.
sp_helpdbfixedrole	The sp_ helpdbfixedrole stored procedure removes a linked server for use with distributed queries.

Table 6-4. *New Security Related Stored Procedures*

New Web Related Stored Procedure	Description of New Functionality
sp_savehtmltable	The sp_savehtmltable stored procedure imports an HTML table into the specified Microsoft SQL Server table.
sp_makewebtask	The sp_makewebtask stored procedure produces an HTML document containing data returned by executed queries by creating a task.

Table 6-5. *New Web Related Stored Procedures*

New Job Related System Stored Procedures

The SQL Server Agent uses the new job related stored procedures with the greatly expanded job processing scheduling tool. Use the SQL Server Agent to shield you from the complexity of streaming together these stored procedures, which are illustrated in Chapter 4 of this book via the SQL Server Agent. Table 6-6 describes the functionality of the new job related system stored procedures.

New Job Related Stored Procedure	Description of New Functionality
sp_add_alert	Adds an alert
sp_add_category	Adds a category for a job, alert, or operator
sp_add_job	Adds a job
sp_add_jobschedule	Adds a job schedule
sp_add_jobserver	Adds to list of servers available for jobs
sp_add_jobstep	Adds a job step
sp_add_notification	Adds an operator notification
sp_add_operator	Adds an operator
sp_add_targetservergroup	Adds a target server group for multiserver jobs

Table 6-6. *New Job Related Stored Procedures*

sp_add_targetsvrgrp_member	Adds a targetserver group member
sp_apply_job_to_targets	Applies the job to the target server
sp_delete_category	Deletes a category
sp_delete_job	Deletes a job
sp_delete_jobschedule	Deletes a job schedule
sp_delete_jobserver	Deletes a server available for jobs
sp_delete_jobstep	Deletes a job step
sp_delete_notification	Deletes a notification
sp_delete_operator	Deletes an operator
sp_delete_targetserver	Deletes a target server
sp_delete_targetservergroup	Deletes a target server group
sp_delete_targetsvrgrp_member	Deletes a target server group member
sp_downloaded_row_limiter	Limits the rows in the *sysdownloadlist* system table that exist with a downloaded status of 1 for the specified server
sp_help_category	Shows category information
sp_help_downloadlist	Lists all rows in the *sysdownloadlist* system table for the named job. Lists all rows if no job is given as a parameter
sp_update_notification	Updates a notification
sp_update_targetservergroup	Changes the name of a targetservergroup
sp_help_job	Shows information about a job
sp_help_jobhistory	Shows information about the history of a job
sp_help_jobschedule	Shows job schedule information
sp_help_jobserver	Shows job server information
sp_help_jobstep	Shows job step information
sp_help_operator	Shows operator information

Table 6-6. *New Job Related Stored Procedures* (continued)

sp_help_targetserver	Shows target server information
sp_help_targetservergroup	Shows target server group information
sp_manage_jobs_by_login	Manages jobs for the specified login
sp_msx_defect	Removes a server from multiserver operations
sp_msx_enlist	Adds a server to multiserver operations
sp_post_msx_operation	Inserts rows into the *sysdownloadlist* system table telling target servers to download posted job operations
sp_purge_jobhistory	Removes the history rows for jobs
sp_remove_job_from_targets	Removes the named job from target servers or target server groups
sp_resync_targetserver	Synchronizes the named server in the multiserver environment
sp_start_job	Runs a job
sp_stop_job	Stops a job
sp_update_category	Updates the category name
sp_update_job	Updates the attributes of a job
sp_update_jobschedule	Updates the settings of a job
sp_update_jobstep	Updates the settings of a job step
sp_update_targetservergroup	Updates the target server group name
sp_help_notification	Shows information about notifications
sp_update_operator	Updates operator information

Table 6-6. *New Job Related Stored Procedures* (continued)

Other New System Stored Procedures

Table 6-7 describes several other new stored procedures in Microsoft SQL Server.

New Stored Procedure	Description of New Functionality
sp_validname	The sp_validname stored procedure determines if the SQL-Server identifier name is valid.
sp_dbcmptlevel	The sp_dbcmptlevel stored procedure is a bridge to the new version 7 behavior and buys time until the application can be modified to take advantage of the new functionality of version 7 features.

Table 6-7. *Other New Stored Procedures*

New System Extended Stored Procedures

The new system extended stored procedures are rarely used in the context of everyday usage of Microsoft SQL Server unless it's by one of the Microsoft SQL Server GUI tools. The extended stored procedures in the following list are used by the SQL Profiler GUI tool formerly known as SQL Trace:

xp_trace_addnewqueue
xp_trace_deletequeuedefinition
xp_trace_destroyqueue
xp_trace_enumqueuedefname
xp_trace_enumqueuehandles
xp_trace_eventclassrequired
xp_trace_getappfilter
xp_trace_getconnectionidfilter
xp_trace_getcpufilter
xp_trace_getdbidfilter
xp_trace_getdurationfilter
xp_trace_geteventfilter
xp_trace_geteventnames
xp_trace_getevents
xp_trace_gethostfilter
xp_trace_pausequeue
xp_trace_restartqueue
xp_trace_savequeuedefinition
xp_trace_setappfilter
p_trace_setconnectionidfilter
xp_trace_setcpufilter
xp_trace_setdbidfilter
xp_trace_setdurationfilter
xp_trace_seteventclassrequired
xp_trace_seteventfilter
xp_trace_sethostfilter
xp_trace_sethpidfilter
xp_trace_setindidfilter
xp_trace_setntdmfilter
xp_trace_setntnmfilter

xp_trace_gethpidfilter
xp_trace_getindidfilter
xp_trace_getntdmfilter
xp_trace_getntnmfilter
xp_trace_getobjidfilter
xp_trace_getowneridfilter
xp_trace_getpercentfilter
xp_trace_getqueueautostart
xp_trace_getreadfilter
xp_trace_getserverfilter
xp_trace_getseverityfilter
xp_trace_getspidfilter
xp_trace_getuserfilter
xp_trace_getwritefilter
xp_trace_loadqueuedefinition
xp_trace_setobjidfilter
xp_trace_setowneridfilter
xp_trace_setpercentfilter
xp_trace_setqueueautostart
xp_trace_setreadfilter
xp_trace_setserverfilter
xp_trace_setseverityfilter
xp_trace_setspidfilter
xp_trace_setuserfilter
xp_trace_setwritefilter
xp_trace_getqueuedestination
xp_trace_setqueuedestination
xp_trace_startconsumer

These extended stored procedures are used by the SQL Server Profiler discussed in the next chapter on new database tools.

Triggers

There have been improvements in the functionality and behavior of triggers in Microsoft SQL Server. The following features have been added to triggers:

- Alter Trigger
- Triggers Can Call Themselves Recursively
- More Than One Trigger for a Trigger Action

Alter Trigger Statement

You now have the ability to alter a trigger object instead of having to remove it from the database and the syscomments system table. This is important because triggers carry other references and permissions that are destroyed when the object is dropped. Changing the object instead of removing it retains the references and permissions that are associated with the object. If you use the WITH APPEND option, more than one trigger can exist for each Update, Insert, and Delete, which means more than one trigger can fire for each Update, Insert, and Delete. The WITH APPEND capability is present in the compatibility level of 7 set by *sp_dbcmptlevel*. The following table describes who can use the Alter Trigger statement:

Alter Trigger Usage
Table Owner
Data Definition Language Administrators
DBO

The syntax is:

```
ALTER TRIGGER trigger_name
ON table
[WITH ENCRYPTION]
{FOR {[,] [INSERT] [,] [UPDATE] [,] [DELETE]}
[NOT FOR REPLICATION]
AS
sql_statement [...n]
}
|
{FOR {[,] [INSERT] [,] [UPDATE]}
[NOT FOR REPLICATION]
AS
IF UPDATE (column)
[{AND | OR} UPDATE (column) [,...n]]
sql_statement [...n]
}
```

Table 6-8 describes the arguments for Alter Trigger.

Here's an example of how the Alter Trigger statement can be used to alter an insert trigger:

Alter TriggerParameter	Description
TriggerName	The name of the trigger you are changing.
TableName	The table name on which the trigger will execute.
WITH ENCRYPTION	Encrypts the code in syscomments system table.

Table 6-8. *Arguments for the Alter Trigger Statement*

Alter TriggerParameter	Description
{[,] [INSERT] [,] [UPDATE] [,] [DELETE]} | {[,] [INSERT] [,] [UPDATE]}	Keywords indicating which statements will fire the trigger.
NOT FOR REPLICATION	If the sqlrepl login ID associated with replication modifies the table then do not fire the trigger.
AS	The Transact-SQL statements are next.
Transact-SQL statement(s)	The Transact-SQL statements that are the trigger.
IF UPDATE (ColumnName)	Provides IF logic based on whether it is an INSERT or UPDATE to a named column.
ColumnName	The name of the column to check for INSERT or UPDATE action.

Table 6-8. *Arguments for the Alter Trigger Statement* (continued)

```
ALTER TRIGGER mytrigger
ON tablename
FOR INSERT
AS RAISERROR ('mytrigger error', 1, 2)
```

Statements Not Allowed Within a Trigger

The Transact-SQL statements you can use in a trigger are limited. You cannot use the following Transact-SQL statements in a trigger:

ALTER DATABASE
ALTER TABLE
ALTER TRIGGER
LOAD LOG
RESTORE LOG
REVOKE

CREATE DATABASE
CREATE DEFAULT
CREATE PROCEDURE
CREATE RULE
CREATE TABLE
CREATE TRIGGER
DENY
DISK INIT
DROP DATABASE
DROP DEFAULT
DROP PROCEDURE
DROP RULE
DROP TRIGGER
DROP VIEW
LOAD DATABASE
SELECT INTO (because it creates a table)
TRUNCATE TABLE
ALTER PROCEDURE
ALTER VIEW
CREATE INDEX
CREATE TABLE
CREATE VIEW
DISK RESIZE
DROP INDEX
DROP TABLE
GRANT
RESTORE DATABASE
RECONFIGURE
UPDATE STATISTICS

Enabling Triggers to Call Themselves Recursively

A trigger can call itself recursively if the *sp_dboption* recursive trigger option is set and if an update is done to the table within the trigger.

Here's an example:

```
sp_dboption mydb, 'recursive triggers', true
```

This example sets the *recursive triggers* database option to true and allows triggers to call themselves recursively if an update is done to the table within the trigger.

More Than One Trigger for a Trigger Action

There can be more than one trigger for the database modification actions of Update, Insert, and Delete if the WITH APPEND option is indicated or if the compatibility level for *sp_dbcmptlevel* is set to 70.

New Data Types

There is new functionality for data types in Microsoft SQL Server to support the new enhancements. Table 6-9 describes the new functionality for data types.

New Data Type Functionality	Description
CAST conversion function	The ANSI/ISO synonym for the CONVERT conversion function
character data and binary strings	Expanded to 8000 bytes
uniqueidentifier	Data type for global unique identification numbers, GUIDs
nchar , nvarchar, and ntext	Unicode data types
+ (Add and String Concatenation) and - (Subtract)	Date and time addition and subtraction
Cursor behavior	Cursor variable

Table 6-9. *New Data Type Functionality*

Data Storage Enhancements

There have been some changes in data storage on the database, with the best being the ability to use ALTER TABLE to drop a column and the NOT FOR REPLICATION clause for IDENTITY property. Table 6-10 shows the storage statements affected and describes their enhancements.

Area of Interest	Enhancement Description
ALTER TABLE	DROP COLUMN clause
	Has a non-NULL default for a column
The ALTER VIEW	Global variables
CREATE TABLE	Nullable bit columns NOT FOR REPLICATION clause for IDENTITY property INSERT You do not have to execute SET IDENTITY_INSERT ON INSERT statement by a replication connection keeps the IDENTITY values
User-defined indexes	Maximum of 1024 bytes

Table 6-10. *Enhancements to Data Storage Statements*

New Property Functions

There are several new property functions that have been introduced by Microsoft SQL Server 7. Table 6-11 describes the new property functions.

Property Function	Description
COLUMNPROPERTY	Shows information about a column or procedure parameter
OBJECTPROPERTY	Shows information about objects in the database
TYPEPROPERTY	Shows information about a data type
DATABASEPROPERTY	Shows information about a database
INDEXPROPERTY	Shows information about a particular index

Table 6-11. *New Property Functions*

New Security Functions

There are new security functions to go with the security enhancements in Microsoft SQL Server 7 related to roles and the new Security Identification (SID) number. Table 6-12 describes the new security functions.

Security Function	Description
IS_MEMBER	Shows whether the current user is a member of the specified Windows NT group or SQL Server role
IS_SRVROLEMEMBER	Shows whether the current login ID or, optionally, another login ID is a member of the named server role
SUSER_SID	Shows the security identification number (SID) from the login name

Table 6-12. *New Security Functions*

Security Function	Description
SUSER_SNAME	Shows the login user name from the security identification number (SID or of the current user if no SID is given)

Table 6-12. *New Security Functions* (continued)

Other New Functions

Other new functions of the Microsoft SQL Server 7 release that are related to new functionality are described in Table 6-13.

Function	Description
LEN	Returns the number of characters in the string
NEWID	Makes a unique identification number (GUID)
REPLACE	Replaces the characters of the second string in the first string with a third string
SUBSTRING	Provides SUBSTRING functionality on text data
SYSTEM_USER niladic function	Shows the Windows NT domain and user names for the logged in user (Windows NT Authentication only)
FILE_ID	Shows you the file identification number for a named file
FILE_NAME	Shows you a file name for a named file identification number
FILEGROUP_ID	Shows you a filegroup identification number for a named filegroup
FILEGROUP_NAME	Shows you a filegroup name for a named filegroup identification number
NCHAR	Gives the Unicode character for a given character code value

Table 6-13. *Other New Functions*

Function	Description
UNICODE	Gives a Unicode integer value for a named Unicode character
PARSENAME	Gives a named piece of an object name
SET *@local_variable*	Delegates a value to the named local variable and can be used with cursor variables
DECLARE *@local_variable*	Creates a cursor variable
OPENROWSET	Gives OLE DB functionality to create a distributed query
QUOTENAME	Shows that a named character string is a valid quoted identifier
VAR	Shows the statistical variance
VARP	Shows the statistical variance for the population
STDEV	Shows the standard deviation
STDEVP	Shows the standard deviation for the population
CURSOR_STATUS	Shows whether the procedure returned a cursor and if a result was set for a given argument and whether it has any rows in it
GETCHECKSUM	Shows the checksum value

Table 6-13. *Other New Functions* (continued)

Enhancements to Queries

Microsoft SQL Server 7 has also brought some new changes to query processing including new optimizer hints, parallel processing of queries, and showplan enhancements in the **SET** statement.

Table 6-14 describes the query enhancements.

Query Enhancement	Description
ANSI views	Shows a system table-independent view of the SQL Server metadata; applications still work when system tables have been changed.
SET ANSI_NULLS	Only used in batches; not for use inside a stored procedure
SET SHOWPLAN_ALL	Shows how the Transact-SQL statements will be executed and estimates the resource requirements for the statements
SET SHOWPLAN_TEXT	A subset of SET SHOWPLAN_ALL
parallel execution of individual queries	Queries run in parallel on multiple processors
optimizer hints	The LOOP, HASH, MERGE, ROBUST PLAN, and FASTFIRSTROW are new hints. A READPAST optimizer hint is available for the **SELECT** statement. The optimizer hints are for giving information to the optimizer to help it perform better.
computed columns	Can be stored and retrieved from the database
SELECT	TOP, PERCENT, and WITH TIES options

Table 6-14. *Query Enhancements*

New Optimizer Hints

The new optimizer hints deserve some attention. They are used with **SELECT**, **INSERT**, **UPDATE**, and **DELETE** statements and communicate with the Query Analyzer to indicate how you want the query to execute. Table 6-15 describes the new optimizer hints.

Optimizer Hint	Description
READPAST	Reads past locked rows and skips them. This is the same as setting @@LOCK_TIMEOUT to 0. This is for **SELECT**.
{HASH | ORDER} GROUP	Aggregations in the GROUP BY or COMPUTE clause of the query use hashing or ordering.
{MERGE | HASH | CONCAT} UNION	Means that UNION should be performed by merging, hashing, or concatenating the sets. If more than one UNION hint is named, the optimizer will select the best strategy.
FAST	The query is optimized for fast retrieval of the first so many rows. After the first so many rows are sent, the query produces the entire result set.
FORCE ORDER	Says that the join order of the query should be maintained during query optimization.
ROBUST PLAN	Uses the upper limits for data resources during query optimization.

Table 6-15. *New Optimizer Hints*

Enhancements to Transactions

There has been some work in the transaction area of Microsoft SQL Server. COMMIT and ROLLBACK now take a user-defined transaction name, and optimizer hints have been added. See the details in the preceding section. Table 6-16 describes each transaction enhancement.

Transaction Enhancement	Description
COMMIT [WORK]	Indicates the end of a transaction and now accepts a user defined transaction name.
DELETE	Optimizer hints added: The LOOP, HASH, MERGE, ROBUST PLAN, and FASTFIRSTROW are new hints. The optimizer hints are for **SELECT**, **INSERT**, **UPDATE**, and **DELETE** statements.
INSERT INTO…SELECT	Optimizer hints added: The LOOP, HASH, MERGE, ROBUST PLAN, and FASTFIRSTROW are new hints. The optimizer hints are for **SELECT**, **INSERT**, **UPDATE**, and **DELETE** statements.
ROLLBACK [WORK]	Rolls back a user-specified transaction.
UPDATE	Optimizer hints added: The LOOP, HASH, MERGE, ROBUST PLAN, and FASTFIRSTROW are new hints. The optimizer hints are for **SELECT**, **INSERT**, **UPDATE**, and **DELETE** statements.

Table 6-16. *Transaction Enhancements*

Enhancements to System Tables

There are new system tables to support the new functionality seen throughout Microsoft SQL Server 7, many of which are related to the new job functionality in this version. Table 6-17 describes the new system tables.

System Table	Contents
sysfiles	Has rows for each database file
sysfilegroups	Has rows for each database filegroup
syscategories	Has rows for categories
sysdownloadlist	Has rows for the job downloadlist
sysjobhistory	Has rows for job history
sysjobs	Has rows for jobs
sysjobschedules	Has rows for job schedules
sysjobservers	Has rows for job servers
sysjobsteps	Has rows for job steps
systargetservergroupmembers	Has rows for target server group members
systargetservergroups	Has rows for target server groups
systargetservers	Has rows for target servers
systaskids	Has rows for tasks
sysvolumelabel	Has rows for the incremental volume labels used for backups
sysoledbusers	Has one row for each user and password mapping for the named linked server

Table 6-17. *New System Tables*

As you have seen in this chapter, Transact-SQL has gone through many changes in version 7. In the next chapter, we will review the new and enhanced tools for Microsoft SQL Server 7, also transformed from previous versions.

Chapter 7

New and Enhanced Tools

This chapter covers SQL Server 7's new and enhanced tools, which include:

- SQL Server Query Analyzer
- Data Transformation Services
- SQL Server Profiler
- Index Tuning Wizard
- Replay SQL Server
- Database Maintenance Plan Wizard
- Web Assistant Wizard
- Visual Database Tools
- Replication Monitor

SQL Server Query Analyzer

The most obvious change to ISQL/w is that it is now called SQL Server Query Analyzer. This is one of the best environments to author Transact-SQL statements. Now the color of each word changes as you enter a query in the window, much in the way that the C++ or Visual Basic programming editors color-code different structures of the language. The Query Analyzer's interface with SQL Server uses ODBC. Query results are displayed in the following three formats depending on which you have selected from the Query Menu:

- Execute
- Execute with Grid
- Display Execution Plan

Execute is the output window of previous versions, that is, it displays the columns. The problem with this view is that wide columns are sometimes difficult to read and you must scroll horizontally to see the results of all the columns.

The *Execute with Grid* option places the data in an easier to read columnar format that looks vaguely similar to a Microsoft Excel spreadsheet and allows more data to appear on the screen at once. To use the Execute with Grid option in the Microsoft Management Console, go to the Tools menu of the Enterprise Manager and select SQL Server Query Analyzer | Query | Execute with Grid. Figure 7-1 shows what the output looks like when you use this option.

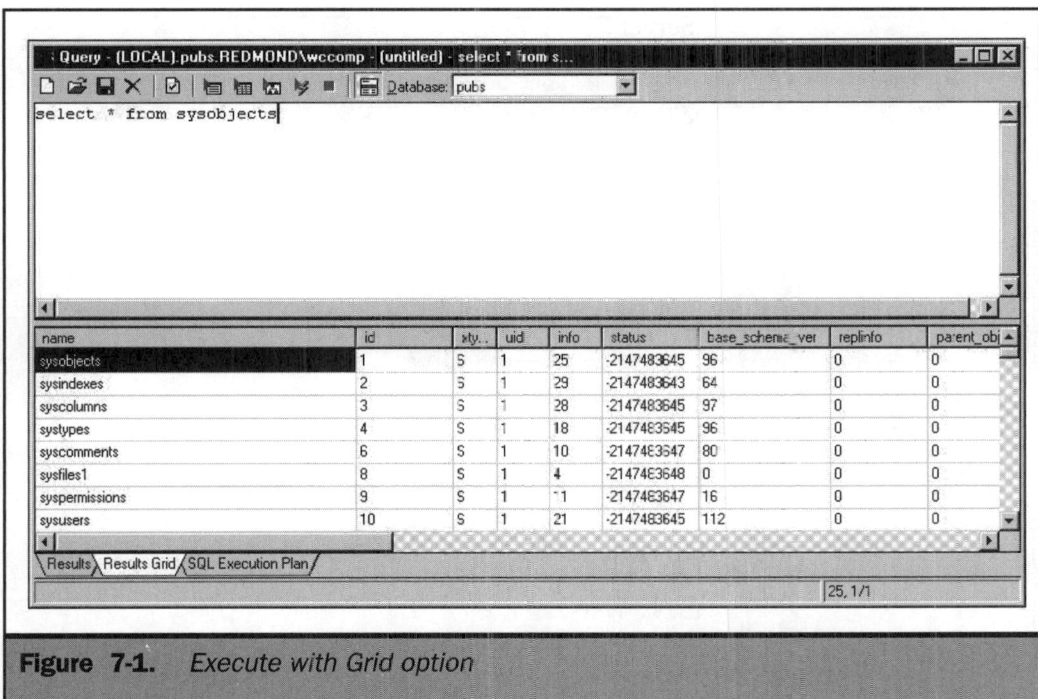

Figure 7-1. *Execute with Grid option*

The *Display Execution Plan* query view displays a graphical representation of the query. It has the interesting feature of displaying information as the cursor moves over an object in the query plan graph. This information includes:

- Type of Scan
- Physical Location
- Logical Location
- Estimated Rows
- Estimated IO
- Estimated CPU
- Average Row Size
- Total Subtree Cost
- Argument

The execution plan devised for a simple query is shown in Figure 7-2 .

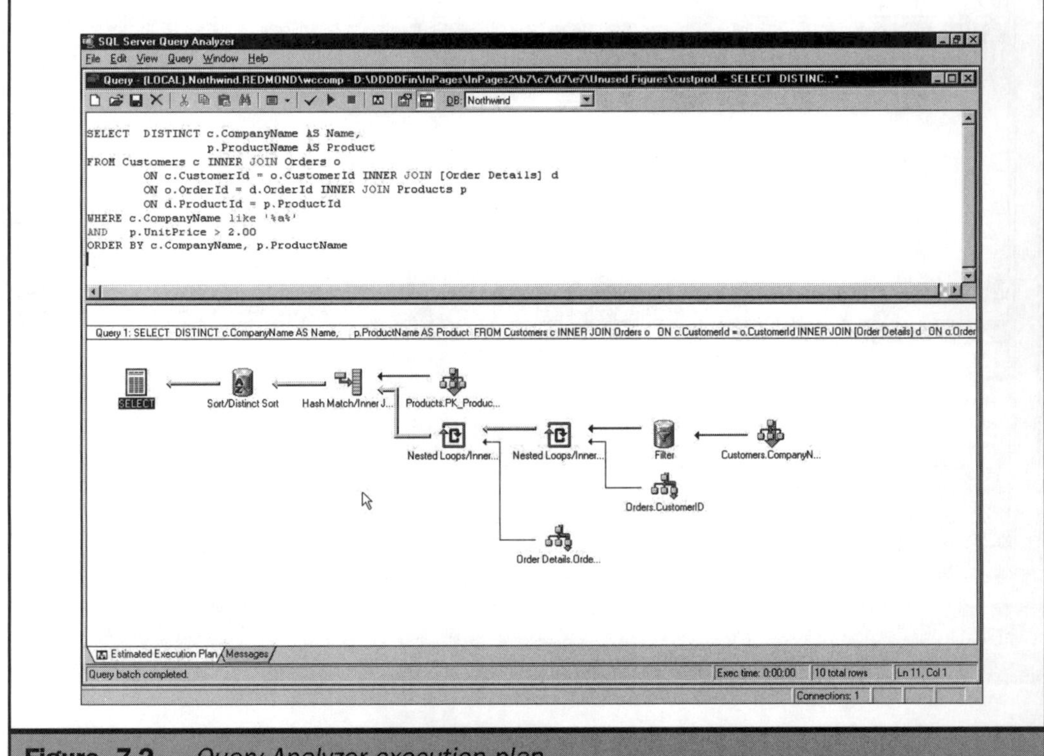

Figure 7-2. *Query Analyzer execution plan*

Data Transformation Services

Being able to move data from one environment to another is crucial in an organization, and among the most significant new features of SQL Server 7 is the capability to do this as easily as you can in Microsoft Access and Microsoft Excel. The Data Transformation Service (DTS) performs this function with the DTS Import Wizard and the DTS Export Wizard and provides even greater power than any of the Microsoft data import and export programs.

The DTS Import/Export Wizard can be invoked by expanding the server in the Enterprise Manager, right-clicking the Data Transformation Services entry under the expanded server, and selecting New Package. (A DTS wizard can be invoked by selecting Tools then Wizards from the command bar in the Enterprise Manager. All of the wizards are listed and the DTS Wizards can be invoked by selecting from the list.)

The DTS Import Wizard allows you to choose a data source, as shown in Figure 7-3. The Source drop-down list contains the following choices:

- dBase 5, III, and IV
- Microsoft Access
- Microsoft Data Link
- Microsoft Excel 3.0, 4.0, 5.0, and 8.0
- Microsoft Jet OLE DB Provider
- Microsoft OLE DB Provider for Oracle
- Microsoft OLE DB Provider for Plato
- Microsoft OLE DB Simple Provider
- Microsoft Remote
- Microsoft SQL Server (ODBC Driver)
- Microsoft SQL Server 7.0 only (OLE DB Driver)
- Microsoft Visual Fox Pro Driver
- Oracle (Microsoft Driver)
- Other (ODBC Data Source)
- Paradox 3.x, 4.x, and 5.x
- Text File

The screen fields change depending on which data source is chosen. If a database is involved, the fields that appear are server, database, login, password, and/or data set name. If files are involved, the file name is requested from the user.

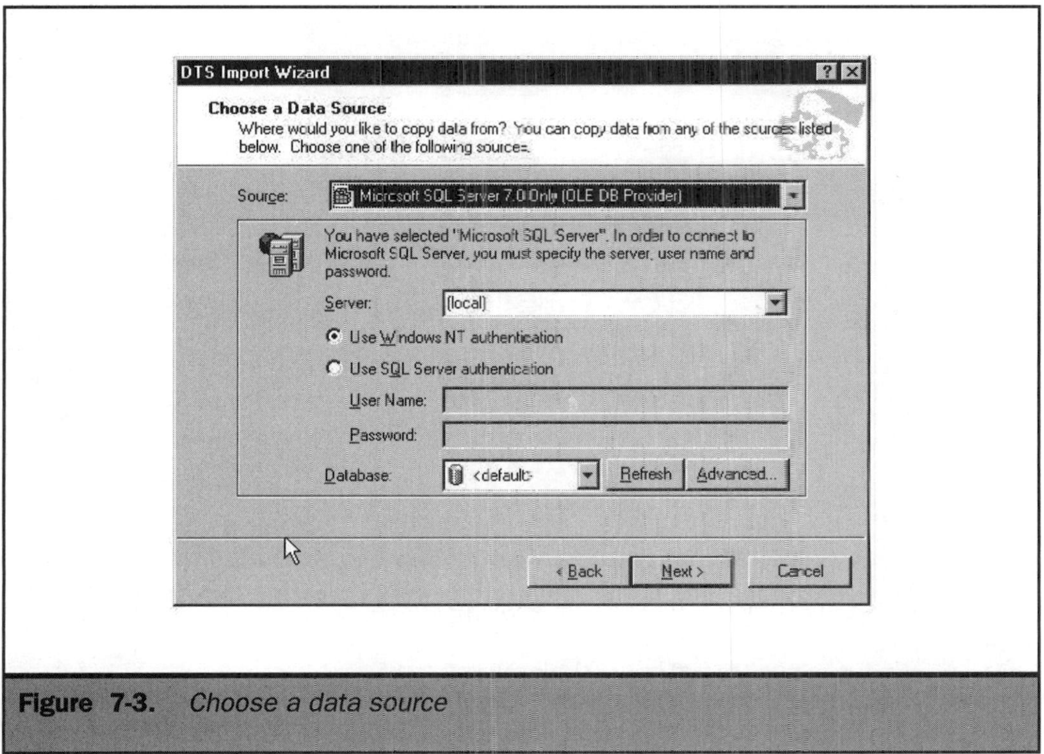

Figure 7-3. *Choose a data source*

The next screen in the Import Wizard, shown in Figure 7-4, requests that you choose a destination for your data. The same drop-down list box appears with the same choices as in the Data Source screen.

As you proceed to the next screen, you see a choice to Copy Table from the Source Database or Query the Source Database. If Query the Source Database is chosen, a screen appears that allows you to enter a query. The query window has a Query Builder button and a Parse button. You may enter a query to receive data from the source database for the data that you would like to import.

The Select Source Tables screen allows you to enter the destination table name, as shown in Figure 7-5.

As you again press the ... button on the Select Source Table screen and move deeper into the Data Transformation Service, you see the Column Mappings and Transformations screen. This screen has two tabs: Column Mappings and Transformations. The Column Mappings panel allows you to change the column name, datatype, nullability, and the size of the data as it is imported. The Transformations

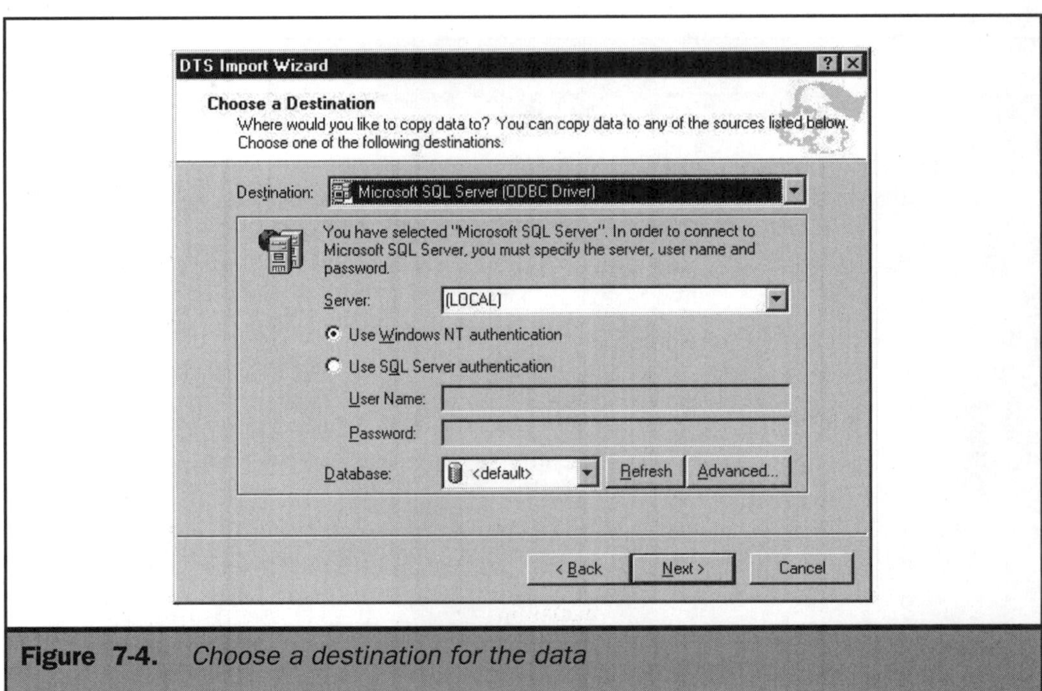

Figure 7-4. *Choose a destination for the data*

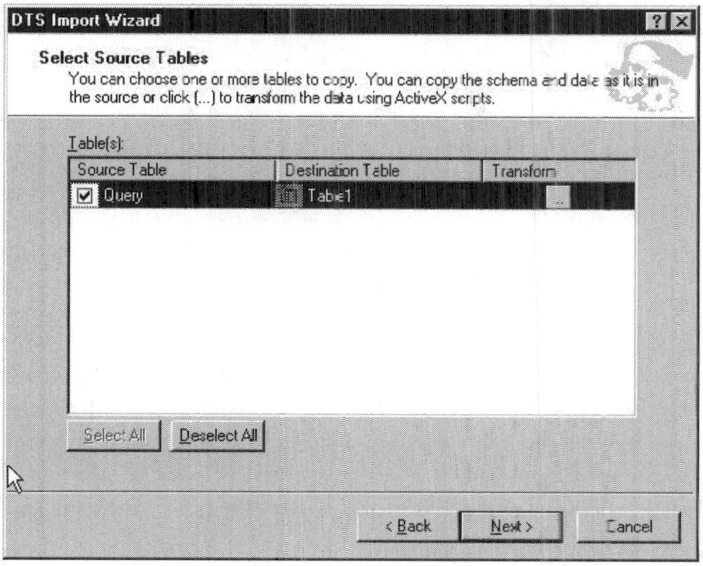

Figure 7-5. *Use this screen to name the destination table*

panel, shown here, contains the Active X script that will transform the data into the desired format as you import:

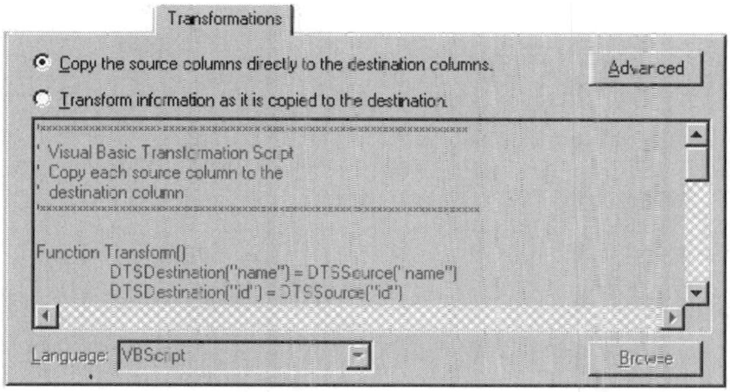

The Advanced button on the Transformations panel shows settings for Transformation Flags that define how the data is moved from the source to the destination and requests the selection of those Transformation Flags that may apply to your data import.

When you have completed the screens in the DTS Import Wizard, you will have created what is called the *DTS package*, which is a template of the steps you have defined. Use the Save and Schedule Package screen to save your work.

From this screen, the DTS package can be scheduled to run at a later time by selecting the Schedule DTS Package for later execution check box and then using the Edit Recurring Job Schedule screen.

Another way to create a DTS Package (using the DTS Designer) is to right-click on Data Transformation Services in the Enterprise Manager hierarchy tree. Using the DTS Designer, you can drag and drop icons and create a graphical representation of your DTS Package. As you drag and drop icons, screens appear that allow you to enter the required information. The graphical representation of a DTS Package and the DTS Designer are shown in Figure 7-6.

The DTS Designer has a workflow built into it reminiscent of the SQL Server Agent. The workflow contains the following elements:

Connection (Create an Open Connection)

Task (Set of Operations)

Precedence Constraint (Steps with On Success On Failure)

Package (Collection of Tasks)

Data Transformation (Movement of Data)

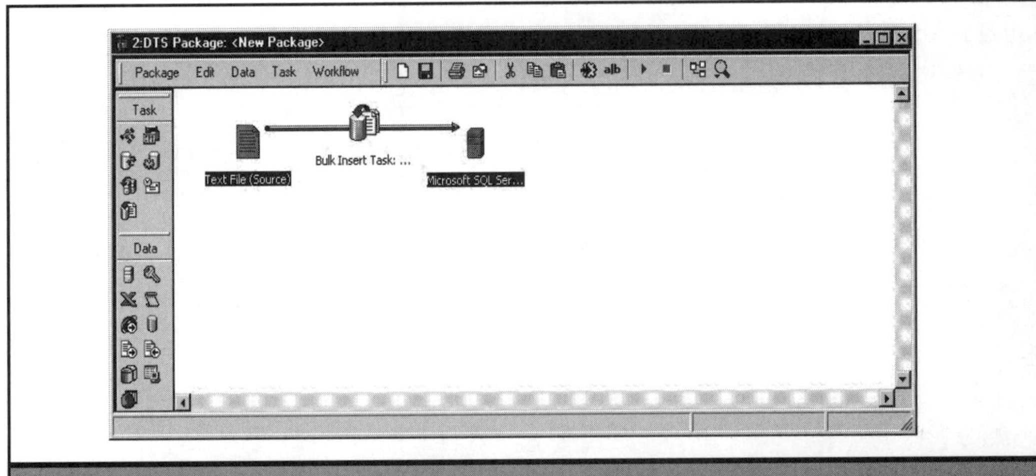

Figure 7-6. DTS Package: <New Package> in the DTS Designer

Using the elements to create a workflow while you are building a package is the purpose of the DTS Designer and is accomplished by using the following method:

1. Create connections in the DTS Designer
2. Enter information for the connections
3. Create tasks between source and destination connections
4. Add any custom tasks or Microsoft ActiveX scripts
5. Use precedence constraints

ODBC data sources accessible through the SQL Server Data Transformation Services using OLE DB ODBC provider are:

ODBC Data Source
Oracle
DB276
Microsoft Access
Microsoft Word

DTS does fast BCP and has the ability to create Excel pivot tables. DTS is able to use COM objects to provide additional transformations of data, if needed, for the creation of a data warehouse. Data Transformation Services (DTS) does not create objects such as stored procedures, views, or triggers between different relational databases or sources.

SQL Server Profiler

SQL Server Profiler is a database tool that monitors events on Microsoft SQL Server and replaces what used to be called SQL Trace. You can create traces to collect data about events such as Transact SQL statements and connections. This is a debugging tool designed to pinpoint problem queries, monitor the performance of the SQL Server, and debug applications. See Chapter 17 for more detailed information on SQL Server Profiler.

The SQL Server Profiler is invoked by choosing SQL Server Profiler from the Microsoft SQL Server menu that appears under the NT Start button or from the Tools Menu in the Enterprise Manager.

Trace Output File

To save trace output to a file, use the options under the General tab of the Trace Properties dialog box, shown here:

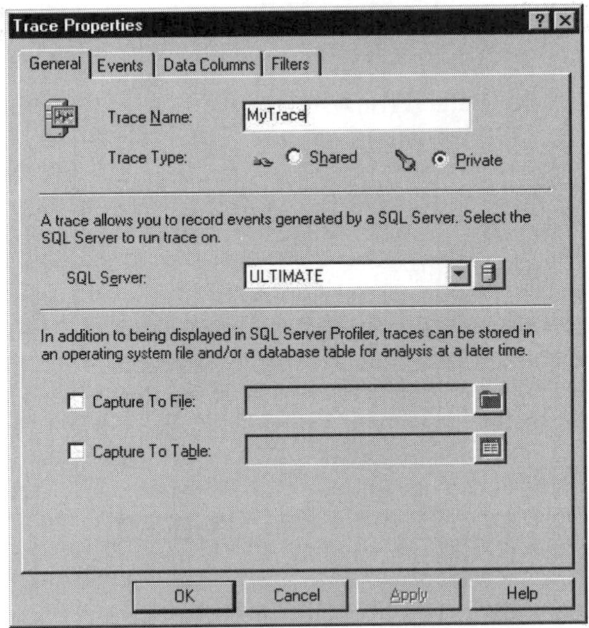

The file, called a *trace output file,* has several important uses:

- Captures events for resolution of SQL Server errors
- Debugs extended stored procedures
- Establishes metrics for server events over a period of time
- Assists in creating a workload file for the Index Tuning Wizard
- Creates input to replay SQL Server functionality in SQL Server Profiler

Index Tuning Wizard

The goal of the Index Tuning Wizard is to automatically index an entire database. The Index Tuning Wizard analyzes profile events to generate what if indexes and recommends the best index mix for the workload. You do not have to fully populate the index with a what if scenario. You may generate the index now or schedule the index creation for later and tune the database automatically on a weekly or monthly basis. If you like, you can have the Microsoft SQL Server e-mail the DBA in the morning with recommendations on how to improve performance of the workload by reworking the indexes.

The Index Tuning Wizard can be invoked within the Perform Index Analysis selection in the Query Analyzer selected from the Tools Menu in the Enterprise Manager or from the Tools Menu in the SQL Server Profile, and can optimize your databases by suggesting the creation of indexes. The Index Tuning Wizard accomplishes this by analyzing a workload (Transact-SQL script or a trace file from running the Microsoft SQL Server Profiler), using the SHOWPLAN cost formula to select the best indexes, and recommending a more efficient mix of indexes. The CREATE INDEX statements are automatically generated by the recommendation and can be run now or scheduled for later and will drop and create more efficient indexes for the workload.

Replay SQL Server

The Replay SQL Server functionality of SQL Server Profiler plays back the trace capture data file in real time or compressed mode. To replay trace capture data using the SQL Server Profiler, open a trace file and select the Replay menu then Settings to see the following Replay screen:

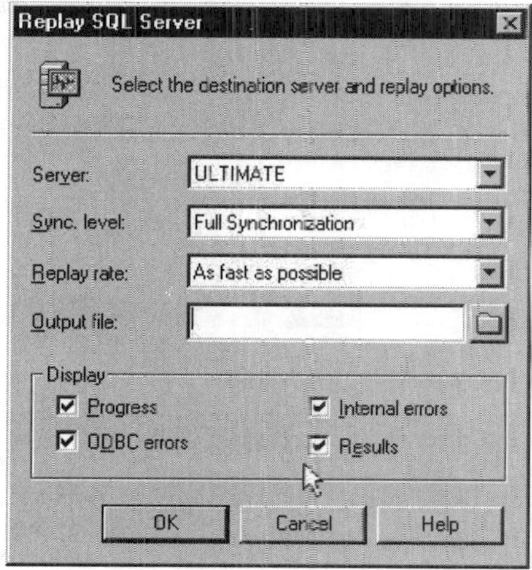

Replay SQL Server can read the following file types saved by the SQL Server Profiler:

SQL Server Profiler File Type	Description
filename.sba	SQL Server Profiler BCP ANSI
filename.scu	SQL Server Profiler Compact Unicode
filename.sbu	SQL Server Profiler BCP Unicode
filename.srw	SQL Server Profiler_70_raw

SQL Server Profiler_70_raw is raw event data which takes up the most disk resources and can be read the fastest.

Database Maintenance Plan Wizard

The object of the Database Maintenance Plan Wizard is to create a maintenance plan that you can schedule to run under the SQL Server Agent. The Database Maintenance Plan Wizard is invoked by expanding the server in the Enterprise Manager, right-clicking the Database Maintenance Plans entry under the expanded server, and selecting New Plan. You can use the maintenance plan to run database consistency checks, back up databases and transaction logs, update statistics, and rebuild indexes. It has become as simple as creating a maintenance plan and scheduling it to run in the off hours.

Check boxes in the Update Data Optimization Information screen in the Database Maintenance Plan Wizard allow you to reorganize data and indexes and update statistics. This screen also has the scheduling information that will be fed to SQL Server Agent for job scheduling of the maintenance plan.

From the Run Data Integrity Tests screen of the Database Maintenance Plan Wizard (Figure 7-7), you can choose to run Database Integrity Tests. These can also be

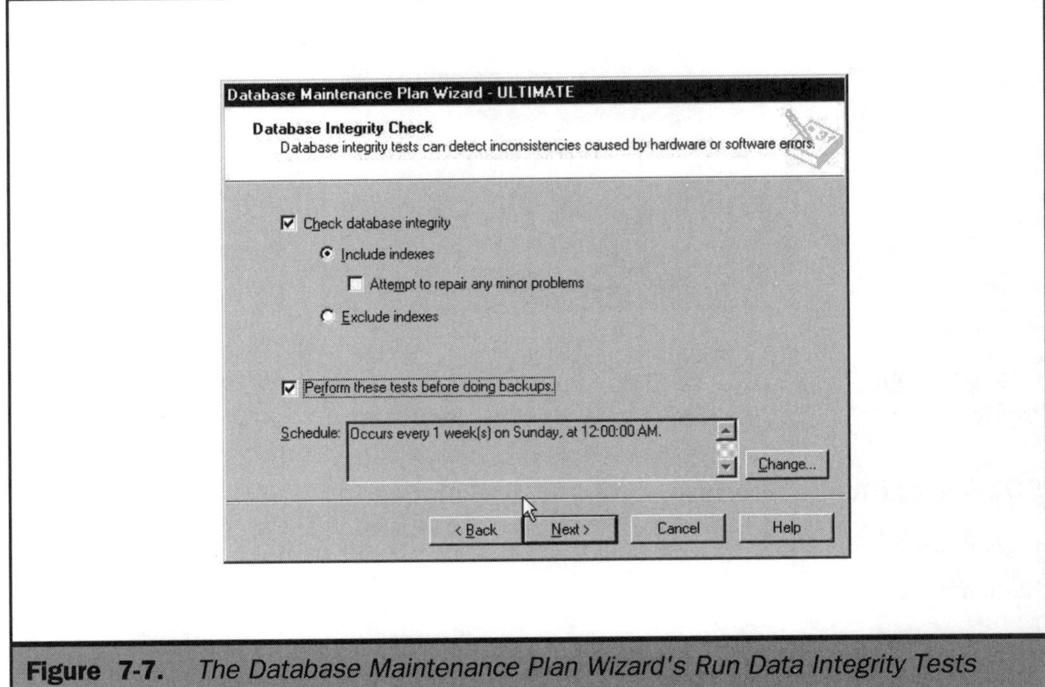

Figure 7-7. *The Database Maintenance Plan Wizard's Run Data Integrity Tests screen*

scheduled from this screen using the SQL Server Agent. These tests can be performed before backing up the database or the transaction log by checking the appropriate check box.

With the Specify the Database Backup Plan screen (Figure 7-8), you can set how and when to back up the database. You can verify the integrity of the backup on completion by checking the appropriate check box. The media can be either tape or disk and there is a note telling you that disk backup filenames are automatically created.

With the Specify the Transaction Log Backup Plan screen, you can set how and when to back up the transaction log. Again, you can verify the integrity of the backup on completion by checking the appropriate check box, the media can be either tape or disk, and there is a note telling you that disk backup filenames are automatically created.

With the Reports to Generate screen, you can send a report to a Web page, a file, or to a Database Administrator (one of the operators you set up earlier in the SQL Server Agent).

The final screen in the Database Maintenance Plan Wizard shows you in paragraph form what you have created as your maintenance plan. When everything is successfully created, you receive a message stating the plan has been completed.

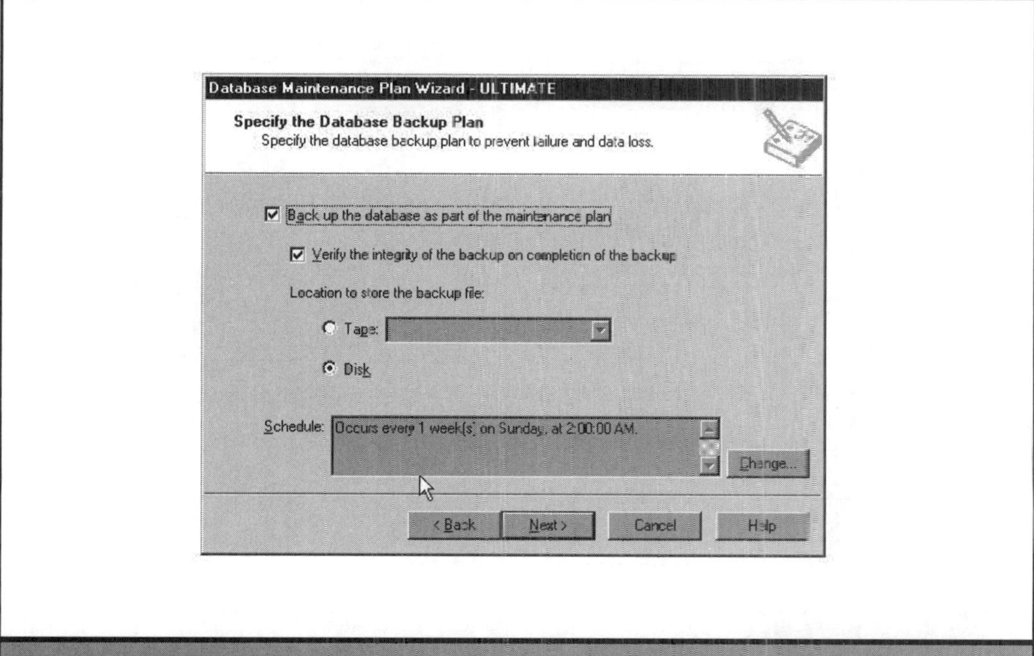

Figure 7-8. *Use the Database Maintenance Plan Wizard to specify a database backup plan*

Web Assistant Wizard

The Web Assistant Wizard is a handy database tool that provides an easy way to build a Web page to display the results of a query. It is invoked by expanding the server in the Enterprise Manager, right-clicking the Web Assistant Jobs entry, and selecting New Web Assistant Job. The first page of the Web Assistant Wizard lays out its capabilities.

The next screen in the Web Assistant Wizard asks you to select a database. Here you can open a window so that you may enter a Transact-SQL Query to select data from the desired table(s) for the Web page. The Schedule the Web Assistant screen schedules the job to update the HTML Web page when the wizard is completed, on demand, at a particular date and time, when the SQL Server data changes, or at regularly scheduled intervals.

The Publish Web Page screen holds the location of the path to publish the Web page. The locations can be a physical directory, a network directory, or an FTP path. The screen further notes that the location must be accessible to the MSSQLServer startup account.

The Format Web Page screen asks whether you want SQL Server to help format the Web page or if you want to select a template file, as shown in Figure 7-9. The template file defines the formatting of the HTML document, and the reference, <%insert_data_here%>, specifies where the query results will be located. In the template file, you can

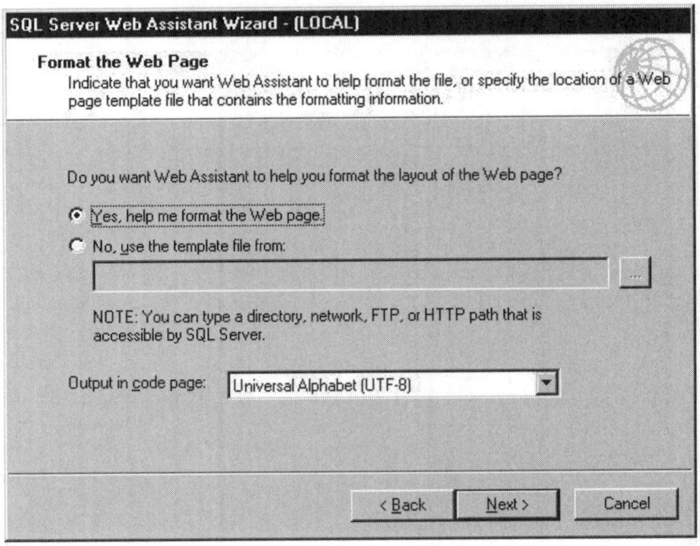

Figure 7-9. *Format the Web page*

alternatively specify how you would like to format the row yourself by using <%begindetail%> and <%enddetail%>, including <TR>, </TR>, <TD>, and </ TD> HTML tags. For each column in the result set, the <%insert_data_here%> tag must be inserted.

The next screen, Specify Titles, has input fields ready to accept the title of the Web page and the title of the HTML table with the data. You can also specify the size of the HTML table title font.

Formatting a table with the SQL Server Web Assistant requires that you answer whether you want the column names displayed in the HTML table and asks what font characteristics you would like to apply to the table data: fixed, proportional, bold, or italic. You can also check a box that will place a border around the table.

The Add Hyperlinks screen, shown in Figure 7-10, asks whether you would like to add one hyperlink, no hyperlinks, or a list of hyperlinks that you select from a SQL Server table where you have placed them earlier.

The Limit Rows screen of the Web Assistant limits the total number of rows returned by SQL Server and/or limits the number of rows displayed on the Web page. If you choose to limit the number of rows returned by SQL Server, it will return the first rows limited by the number you specify. By specifying how many rows appear on

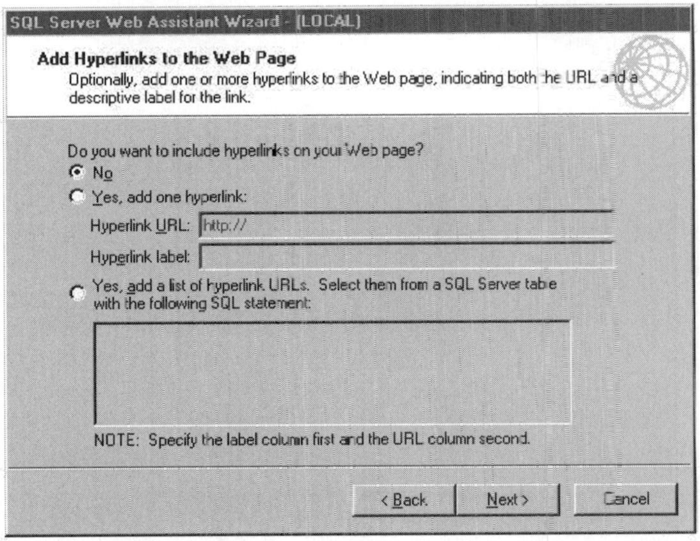

Figure 7-10. *Add Hyperlinks to the Web page*

each page, you may also adjust the placement of rows on the Web page, putting all the rows on one scrolling page or linking successive pages together.

The screen to Complete the Microsoft SQL Server Web Assistant Wizard shows in paragraph form what has been done to this point. Finally, the Web Assistant lets you know it has successfully completed your Web page. Now, use the NT Explorer and double-click on the .htm file to go to the directory where the newly created Web page was placed. Figure 7-11 displays the Internet Explorer with the Web page just as it was created by the Web Assistant.

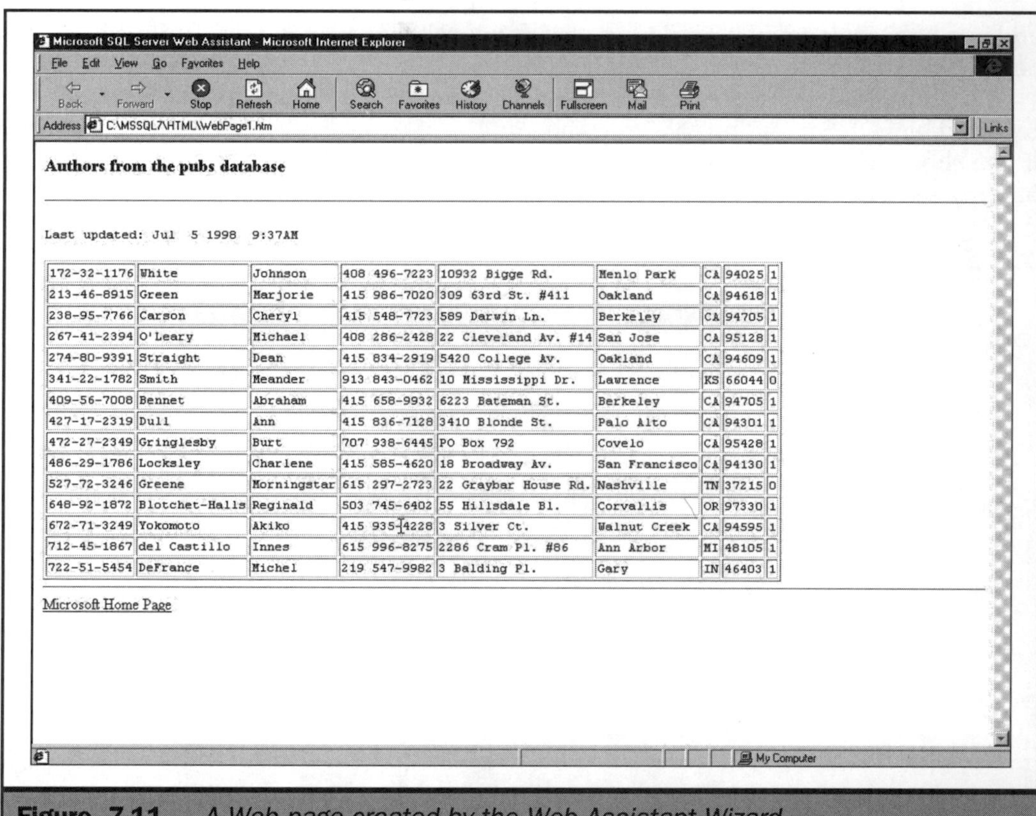

172-32-1176	White	Johnson	408 496-7223	10932 Bigge Rd.	Menlo Park	CA	94025	1
213-46-8915	Green	Marjorie	415 986-7020	309 63rd St. #411	Oakland	CA	94618	1
238-95-7766	Carson	Cheryl	415 548-7723	589 Darwin Ln.	Berkeley	CA	94705	1
267-41-2394	O'Leary	Michael	408 286-2428	22 Cleveland Av. #14	San Jose	CA	95128	1
274-80-9391	Straight	Dean	415 834-2919	5420 College Av.	Oakland	CA	94609	1
341-22-1782	Smith	Meander	913 843-0462	10 Mississippi Dr.	Lawrence	KS	66044	0
409-56-7008	Bennet	Abraham	415 658-9932	6223 Bateman St.	Berkeley	CA	94705	1
427-17-2319	Dull	Ann	415 836-7128	3410 Blonde St.	Palo Alto	CA	94301	1
472-27-2349	Gringlesby	Burt	707 938-6445	PO Box 792	Covelo	CA	95428	1
486-29-1786	Locksley	Charlene	415 585-4620	18 Broadway Av.	San Francisco	CA	94130	1
527-72-3246	Greene	Morningstar	615 297-2723	22 Graybar House Rd.	Nashville	TN	37215	0
648-92-1872	Blotchet-Halls	Reginald	503 745-6402	55 Hillsdale Bl.	Corvallis	OR	97330	1
672-71-3249	Yokomoto	Akiko	415 935-4228	3 Silver Ct.	Walnut Creek	CA	94595	1
712-45-1867	del Castillo	Innes	615 996-8275	2286 Cram Pl. #86	Ann Arbor	MI	48105	1
722-51-5454	DeFrance	Michel	219 547-9982	3 Balding Pl.	Gary	IN	46403	1

Figure 7-11. *A Web page created by the Web Assistant Wizard*

Visual Database Tools

Visual Database Tools are fully integrated into Microsoft Management Console's Enterprise Manager and can be invoked at various places in the Enterprise Manager. For example, if you use the Enterprise Manager to expand the server, expand the database, choose Tables, and select a table, you can then right-click on the table, select Open Table, and view and update the data in the table as shown in Figure 7-12. This

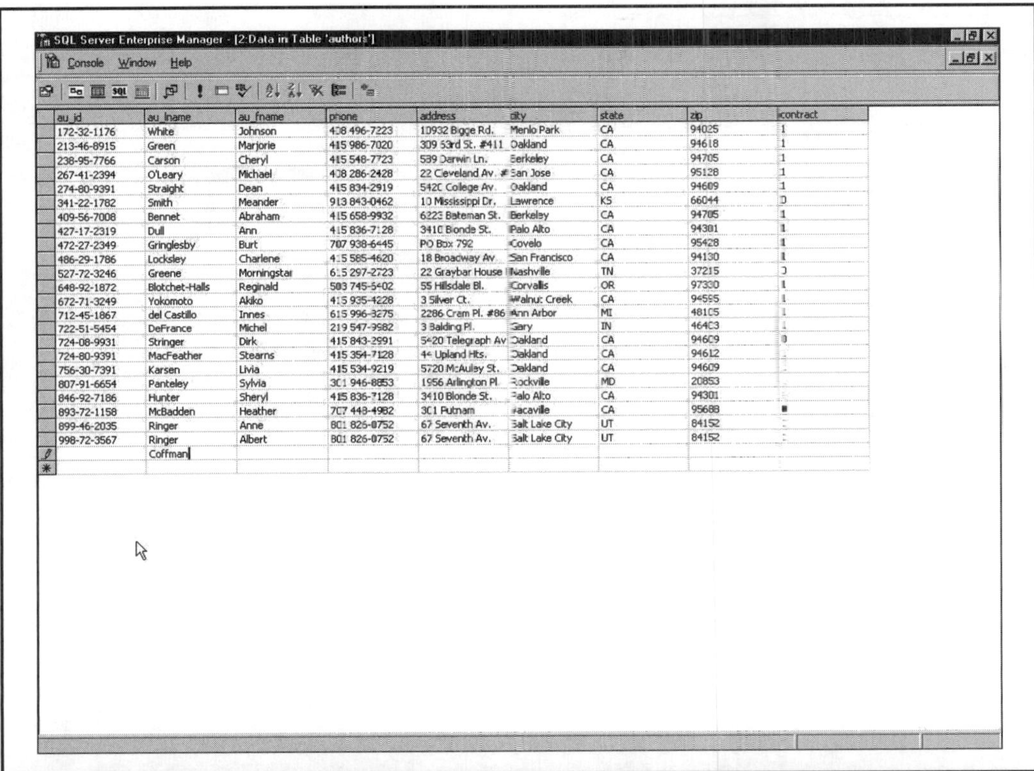

au_id	au_lname	au_fname	phone	address	city	state	zip	contract
172-32-1176	White	Johnson	408 496-7223	10932 Bigge Rd.	Menlo Park	CA	94025	1
213-46-8915	Green	Marjorie	415 986-7020	309 63rd St. #411	Oakland	CA	94618	1
238-95-7766	Carson	Cheryl	415 548-7723	589 Darwin Ln.	Berkeley	CA	94705	1
267-41-2394	O'Leary	Michael	408 286-2428	22 Cleveland Av. #	San Jose	CA	95128	1
274-80-9391	Straight	Dean	415 834-2919	5420 College Av.	Oakland	CA	94609	1
341-22-1782	Smith	Meander	913 843-0462	10 Mississippi Dr.	Lawrence	KS	66044	0
409-56-7008	Bennet	Abraham	415 658-9932	6223 Bateman St.	Berkeley	CA	94705	1
427-17-2319	Dull	Ann	415 836-7128	3410 Blonde St.	Palo Alto	CA	94301	1
472-27-2349	Gringlesby	Burt	707 938-6445	PO Box 792	Covelo	CA	95428	1
486-29-1786	Locksley	Charlene	415 585-4620	18 Broadway Av.	San Francisco	CA	94130	1
527-72-3246	Greene	Morningstar	615 297-2723	22 Graybar House	Nashville	TN	37215	0
648-92-1872	Blotchet-Halls	Reginald	503 745-6402	55 Hillsdale Bl.	Corvallis	OR	97330	1
672-71-3249	Yokomoto	Akiko	415 935-4228	3 Silver Ct.	Walnut Creek	CA	94595	1
712-45-1867	del Castillo	Innes	615 996-8275	2286 Cram Pl. #86	Ann Arbor	MI	48105	1
722-51-5454	DeFrance	Michel	219 547-9982	3 Balding Pl.	Gary	IN	46403	1
724-08-9931	Stringer	Dirk	415 843-2991	5420 Telegraph Av.	Oakland	CA	94609	0
724-80-9391	MacFeather	Stearns	415 354-7128	44 Upland Hts.	Oakland	CA	94612	[illegible]
756-30-7391	Karsen	Livia	415 534-9219	5720 McAuley St.	Oakland	CA	94609	[illegible]
807-91-6654	Panteley	Sylvia	301 946-8853	1956 Arlington Pl.	Rockville	MD	20853	[illegible]
846-92-7186	Hunter	Sheryl	415 836-7128	3410 Blonde St.	Palo Alto	CA	94301	[illegible]
893-72-1158	McBadden	Heather	707 448-4982	301 Putnam	Vacaville	CA	95688	[illegible]
899-46-2035	Ringer	Anne	801 826-0752	67 Seventh Av.	Salt Lake City	UT	84152	[illegible]
998-72-3567	Ringer	Albert	801 826-0752	67 Seventh Av.	Salt Lake City	UT	84152	[illegible]
	Coffman							

Figure 7-12. *Use the Enterprise Manger to update rows in a table*

has never been possible before within the Enterprise Manager. You can also select Design Table from the same menu and use the Visual Database Tool to design a table.

Another place to invoke the Visual Database Tools functionality from within the Enterprise Manager is when you expand the server, expand the database, and select Database Diagram. You will be able to see an existing database diagram and to create a new database diagram by defining the relationships between the tables in your database. I created this Database Diagram (Figure 7-13) of the pubs database by using the Create Database Diagram Wizard.

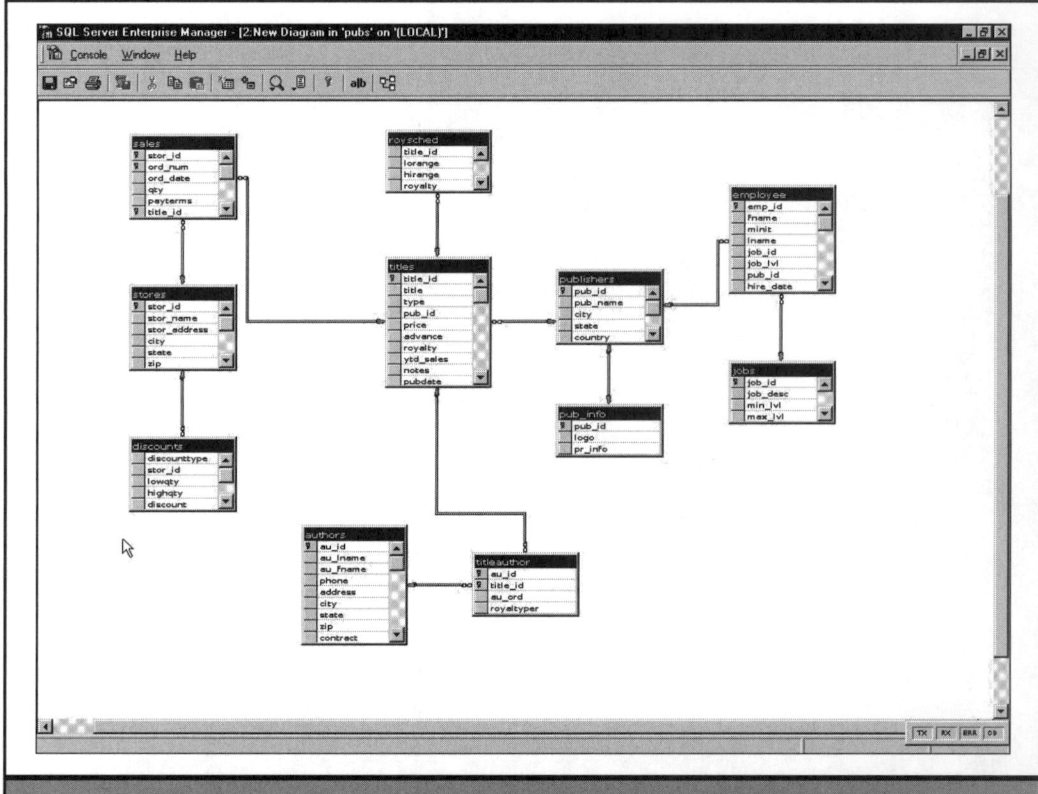

Figure 7-13. *Created by the Create Database Diagram Wizard in the Enterprise Manager*

The Visual Database Tools will also be available with Microsoft Access. The tools have the following functionality:

- Create database schema diagrams
- Create tables
- Build queries
- Connect to any ODBC-compliant database
- Author complex queries
- Add, update, and delete data in the database
- Create SQL objects such as databases (from diagrams), tables, stored procedures and trigger Microsoft SQL Server and Oracle databases

The four parts of Microsoft Visual Database Tools are called:

- Data View
- Database Designer
- Query Designer
- Source Code Editor

Data View

The Data View displays:

- **Live connections to the databases** SQL Server Login IDs that connect to SQL Server
- **Database diagrams** Illustrations that show the relationships between tables on a database
- **Tables** Rows and columns that comprise database objects used to store data
- **Triggers** Stored procedures that automatically run in the event of an UPDATE, INSERT, or DELETE to a row in a table
- **Views** Virtual tables that consist of queries stored and maintained on the database server
- **Stored procedures** Procedures written using Transact-SQL that can contain program flow, logic, and queries against the database

Database Designer

The Database Designer creates and modifies:

- The structure of Microsoft SQL Server databases
- Database objects such as tables, relationships, indexes, and constraints
- Data Definition Language commands
- Scripts of the Transact-SQL code for the database diagram changes

Query Designer

The Query Designer builds and executes queries against any ODBC-compliant database. It also enables you to:

- Use a visual query diagram
- Use a criteria grid to specify search criteria, sort order, output columns
- Generate the SQL
- Edit data in your tables

Source Code Editor

The Source Code Editor is a tool to:

- Edit stored procedures and triggers
- Execute stored procedures

Replication Monitor

The Replication Monitor feature of Enterprise Manager allows you to view the status of Replication Agents. In order to see the Replication Monitor in the Enterprise Manager, you must enable the server as a Distributor by performing the following steps:

1. Log in with SA privileges.
2. Use SQL Server Enterprise Manager.
3. Expand the server.
4. Choose Tools | Replication.
5. Use the Configure Publishing and Distribution Wizard.

Note *The Configure Publishing and Distribution Wizard is invoked by expanding the server in the Enterprise Manager, selecting the Tools menu, and selecting Replication.*

You can either configure the SQL Server as a *publisher and distributor* or as a *dedicated distributor*. In the Configure Publishing and Distribution Wizard, use the Configure with Defaults screen to configure with defaults or customize the distribution database name, the location of the distribution database file, and the distribution database transaction log file.

If you choose to customize the publishing and distribution configuration, choose the option to customize the settings and you will see the screens that enable publishers, enable databases for publication, and enable subscribers. After you have enabled the SQL Server as a distributor, you can use the Replication Monitor to see a list of Publishers, Publications, and Subscribers; see scheduled Replication Agents; monitor how each agent is performing; and see the history of the Replication Agent. You can even set up alerts for replication events. Replication is discussed in greater detail in the chapter on Replication later in this book.

In the next chapter, SQL Server 7 utility changes are described. Utilities are command line tools, as opposed to the GUI (Graphical User Interface) tools described in this chapter.

Chapter 8

Utility Changes

The main objective of the Microsoft SQL Server utilities is to improve functionality, performance, and reliability. With the move to support a terabyte database, the database utilities also have to be able to handle a larger amount of data, and the Microsoft SQL Server utilities have been improved to do just that, particularly in how fast they execute.

The following utilities are discussed in this chapter with an emphasis on the new functionality of each utility:

- Bulk Copy Program (BCP)
- Backup
- Restore
- Database Consistency Checker (DBCC)
- OSQL and ISQL
- SQLMaint

BCP

The *Bulk Copy Program (BCP)* utility is a command-line executable run from a DOS command prompt. This utility copies the data from the database to an operating system file. It is also capable of taking data from an operating system file and placing the data in a table on a Microsoft SQL Server database. The BCP utility has been completely reworked in version 7, and, from a design and architectural point of view, it is one of the most improved and interesting areas in the new release.

The architecture of the BCP utility has been changed so that it no longer uses the DB_Library bulk copy API; it now uses the ODBC bulk copy API. Formerly, the bulk copy laid data down in preformatted rows, which was an endless source of error. Now the bulk copy utility uses a Tabular Data Stream (TDS) result set. This means that the primary insertion path for SQL Server is used, and any optimization that occurs will occur across all aspects of the data insertion path. After the bulk load portion receives the TDS result set, OLE DB takes over and moves the row set to the Relational Engine. OLE DB then moves the data from the Relational Engine to the Storage Engine while formatting the data into pages and storing the data on the database.

The good news is that Microsoft SQL Server has been working hard on the art of transferring data, and there is more than one way to solve this problem. Ventures have been made to make it possible for the "other" vendors' databases to move data in and out of SQL Server via an Import/Export functionality of the Data Transformation Services tool in Microsoft SQL Server 7. This tool was covered in Chapter 7.

The entire format and insertion path of the BCP utility has changed, and new features have been added so that BCP is quite handy when you want to move data in a job as a command file. You can also choose whether or not to log the BCP event and whether to enforce constraints or fire triggers. If you do not wish to log the BCP transactions, set the database option SELECT INTO / BULKCOPY. To do this in Enterprise Manager, expand the server, select a database, right-click, select Properties from the shortcut menu, select the Options panel, and click the checkbox called Select Into/Bulk Copy (see Figure 8-1). If you wish to enforce constraints, use the CHECK_CONSTRAINTS arguments of BCP described in the following table.

The BCP utility can be used to:

- Get data out of a database, sometimes in a recovery situation
- Put data into a database, sometimes from another vendor's database or a nonrelational file format from a legacy application
- Move large amounts of data into and out of a database into a flat file format
- Copy data from a query to a datafile (new functionality). See the QUERYOUT argument of bcp in Table 8-1.
- Move data in and out of servers in batch jobs and job steps
- Move data from the database into a spreadsheet or another type of database such as Microsoft Excel or Microsoft Access.

In addition, some applications write BCP into the application by using the bulk copy API in DB Library, ODBC, or OLE DB programs.

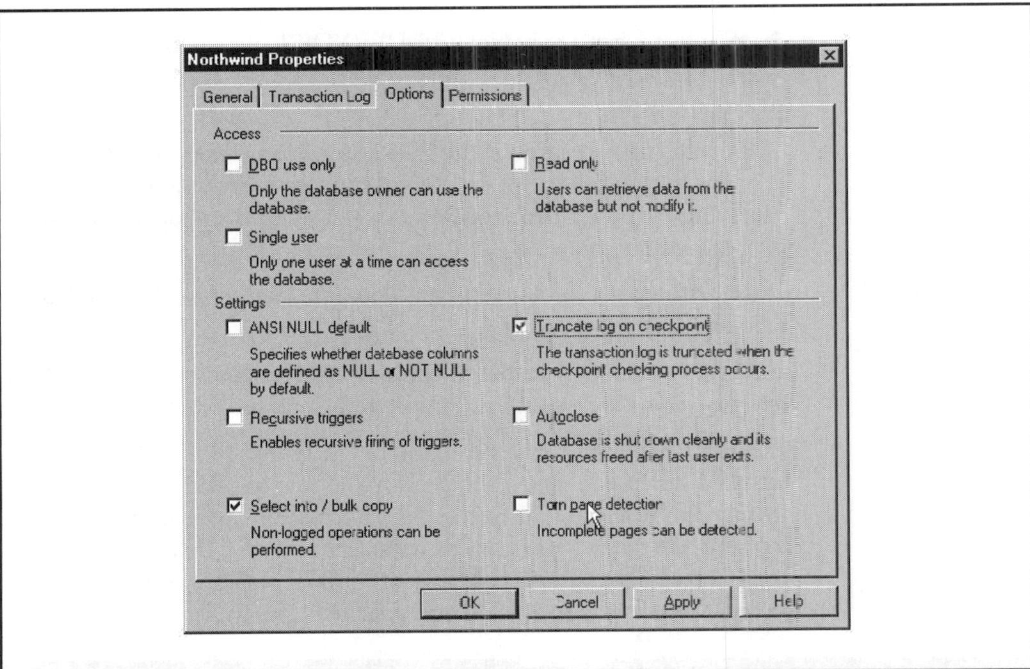

Figure 8-1. *Select Into/Bulk Copy database option*

The syntax for using the BCP utility is:

```
bcp [[databasename.]tableowner.]tablename {in | out | format} datafile
[-m] [-f] [-e] [-F] [-L] [-b] [-n] [-c] [-w] [-6] [-E][-t] [-r] [-i] [-o]
[-U] [-P] [-S] [-v] [-a][-T] [-q] [-k] [-h]
```

Table 8-1 describes the BCP utility arguments. An asterisk (*) appears next to arguments that are important. This is not to say the others are not required or important, but you should definitely decide whether you need to use the asterisked arguments if you are not already.

BCP Argument	Description
DatabaseName	Names the database involved.
TableOwner	Names the owner of the table.
TableName	Shows the database table or view.
IN OUT	Indicates whether you are copying data into or out of the database or creating a format file.
QUERYOUT	An example of QUERYOUT is: bcp "select * from Sysobjects" QUERYOUT objects.txt -c -S*servername* -U*sa* -P*password*
FORMAT	A format file is created if the FORMAT argument is used depending on the -n, -c, -w, or -6 arguments and the table delimiters. If the format option is used, then the -f option needs to be specified as well.
DataFile	Names the path to the data file. The data file path can be up to 255 characters.
-m *	Sets the *maximum* number of errors that can occur before execution stops. If you do not set this, it will default to ten errors.
-f	Names the entire path and name of the *format* file. A format file is created when you answer the command line questions and is used to communicate to SQL Server the information it needs about the columns in the file. This file is created once with a default name bcp.fmt and is used thereafter by other BCP sessions as the fixed format of the data moved. If you specify -n, -c, -w, or -6 arguments

Table 8-1. *BCP Utility Arguments*

BCP Argument	Description
	with no -f, you will not enter into the format command line questionnaire. If you want to avoid this dialog altogether, you can use the -c argument, which will use the char datatype for the column or field. If -c is used, BCP does not prompt for each column, the default storage type is char, tab is the default column separator, and new line is the default row terminator.
-e *	Names the entire path and name of the *error* file. This is where all "bad" rows go. The database will not accept these rows. If you do not use -e, no error file will be created.
-F	Determines the row to mark as the *first* row to start copying. If -F is not used, the first row will be marked as the first row to start copying.
-L	Determines the row to mark as the *last* row to finish copying. If –L is not used, the last row will be marked at the last row to finish copying.
-b *	Sets the number of rows per *batch* to copy. Each batch becomes one transaction. If -b is not used, all the rows will be placed in one transaction. This is not available for use with the -h (hint) "ROWS_PER_BATCH = bb" argument, which is where the data file is sent to the server as one transaction. It is up to the server to optimize the load by using ROWS_PER_BATCH bb.
-n *	Copies the data using the databases' datatypes as the default; this is called the *native* datatype and BCP will not prompt you for the datatypes of each column or field. This argument is associated with the format file command line interaction with SQL Server.
-c *	Copies the data using the *char* datatype as the default, and BCP will not prompt you for the datatypes of each column or field, the default storage type is char, tab is the default column separator, and new line is the default row terminator.
-w *	Copies the data using *Unicode* characters as the default, and BCP will not prompt you for the datatypes of each column or field; the default storage type is nchar, tab is the default column separator, and new line is the default row terminator.

Table 8-1. *BCP Utility Arguments* (continued)

BCP Argument	Description
-6 *	When used with the -c argument or the -n argument, uses *6.x datatypes* as the default and BCP will not prompt you for the datatypes of each column or field. This is useful when you have to use BCP files from a SQL Server 6.x database. This is associated with the format file command line interaction with SQL Server.
-E *	Used when identity columns are defined on the tables involved and the identity values already exist in the data file. Preserves the identity values that *exist* in the file. This is especially useful if the identity column is a primary key and other table(s) exist that have foreign keys linked to this column.
-t *	Allows you to specify the default field *terminator* after the argument. If it is to be tab, use \t.
-r *	Allows you to specify the default *row terminator*. If it is to be new line, use \n.
-i	Specifies the name of the redirected *input* data file to BCP.
-o	Names the redirected *output* data file for BCP.
-U	Indicates the *user login ID* under whose permissions the BCP will operate.
-P	Names the *password* for the login ID.
-S	Names the Microsoft *SQL Server* you are using and to which you are trying to connect.
-v	Tells you the current BCP *version*. This can become important when you are using multiple versions of Microsoft SQL Server on a network or have users using outdated, out-of-version or beta copies of the BCP executable.
-a	Allows you to *override* the server configuration option (sp_configure) for the number of bytes per network packet sent over the network. 4096 is the Microsoft SQL Server default and 4096–8192 is usually the range for the speediest BCP. You can see what packet size is used in the BCP output to the screen or to the output file.
-T *	Requests a *trusted connection* to Microsoft SQL Server.

Table 8-1. *BCP Utility Arguments* (continued)

BCP Argument	Description
-q	Specifies the *quoted identifier* BCP option that corresponds to the ANSI quoted identifier convention you can set for every SQL Server connection. This can be used if you have a name that contains characters that are not usually valid in an identifier name, such as a table name. Double quotes delimit this type of identifier.
-k *	When the field is NULL in the data file, the database column *keeps* a NULL value rather than allow any default operations to occur on the populated database column.
-C	The code page needs to be given if the data contains *char, varchar,* or *text* columns longer in length than 127 or shorter in length than 32 where ACP=ANSI/Microsoft Windows (ISO 1252), OE=-default code page, RAW=no conversion to a code page happens or you can supply a code page number.

-h	Passes a *hint* to be used when moving data into a table with BCP. This is used only with a version 7 database. You may use more that one of the following hints:
	`ORDER (column_list)where column_list = {column [ASC | DESC] [,…]}`
	The use of a sorted data file can improve BCP speed by placing the data in the table in the order of the existing clustered index. The BCP default is no ordering.
	`ROWS_PER_BATCH = bb`
	With this hint the data file is sent to the server as one transaction; it is up to the server to optimize the load by using the ROWS_PER_BATCH value.
	`KILOBYTES_PER_BATCH = nn`
	You can use the KILOBYTES_PER_BATCH hint to indicate the number of kilobytes per batch.
	`TABLOCK`
	This optimizer hint provides an exclusive table lock for the entire BCP operation. The default is no table lock, and this may mean contention for the table. This hint is required for parallel BCP data loads.
	`CHECK_CONSTRAINTS`
	This hint means that the table constraints of the receiving Microsoft SQL Server table are honored. If this is not used, constraints are not honored.

Table 8-1. *BCP Utility Arguments* (continued)

Backup

What used to be called "dumping" a database or transaction log in previous versions is now called BACKUP. This change corresponds to the new data structures contained in Microsoft SQL Server 7 that provide the following functionality:

- Backs up an entire database
- Backs up files and filegroups
- Backs up a transaction log

Part of the BACKUP procedure sometimes involves the creation of a *dump device,* which is the logical name for a physical file. The database, file, filegroup, or log then dumps to this logical device name which is associated with the physical file.

After you have created your dump devices, you may begin to back up and restore your database. There are many different variations of the BACKUP and RESTORE statements. Chapter 21, "Transact-SQL Programming Reference," contains examples of the different variations and provides the arguments.

Restore

What used to be called *loading* a database transaction log in previous versions is now called RESTORE, and the change corresponds to the new data structures contained in Microsoft SQL Server 7 that provide the following functionality:

- Restores an entire database
- Restores files and filegroups
- Restores a transaction log

There are two new options of the RESTORE utility in addition to the others that have existed previously: RESTART and REPLACE. If you use REPLACE, SQL Server will destroy the database and recreate it according the specification in the backup set. Under the following conditions, the database will not be restored if you do not use the REPLACE option:

- The database already exists on the server
- The database name is different from the database name in the backup set
- The set of files in the database is different from the set of database files contained in the backup set

File size differences are not recognized by Microsoft SQL Server in the restore process, and they are not checked when a restore occurs.

RESTART is the option that restarts the restore if it was interrupted. To do this, repeat the RESTORE command and specify RESTART option. However, there is a caveat to this option: It can only be used for restores that are from tape media and are written across multiple tape volumes.

Another great new feature is RESTORE VERIFYONLY. This feature checks to see if the backup set is all there and that the data can be read. It does not check the database tables for corruption.

There are a few more variations of the RESTORE statement that are useful:

- RESTORE FILELISTONLY   Returns a result set with a list of the database and log files contained in the backup set.
- RESTORE VERIFYONLY   Checks to see if the backup set is all there and that the data can be read. It does not check the database tables for corruption.
- RESTORE HEADERONLY   Displays all the header information for all backups for a backup file.

Database Consistency Checker

The Database Consistency Checker (DBCC) is used to scan different parts of the database to check for inconsistencies. It looks for errors and reports its findings in the form of a DBCC output report. As your exposure increases in this area, you will become familiar with DBCC errors by number and know what they are, how critical they are, and what to do about them as is specific to your environment. There are many different ways to implement your usage of DBCC, and each environment gets different DBCC errors depending on which parts of the database functionality you are exercising with your application. The factors that can influence how DBCC is used are the size of the database, how many users are on the database, and the importance of the data. In version 7, CHECKDB is a one-stop shop that runs CHECKCATALOG and CHECKALLOC. Due to the fail-safe, fail-fast philosophy of version 7, it does not have to be run as much. Spurious errors no longer occur if the database is not in single-user mode, and there are options for repairing the database in CHECKDB, CHECKALLOC, and CHECKTABLE.

DBCC Scenarios

The following three scenarios demonstrate how DBCC can be implemented to run in different environments depending on usage and size.

DBCC SCENARIO #1: Important Data, Small to Medium Size Database, Business Hours Usage

If you have a database, such as an Accounting database, containing very important data that is not in the multi-gigabyte range and is used mostly during the day, you may want to use DBCC after hours in the following manner:

- Run DBCC CHECKDB
- Check the DBCC output for errors
- If errors are discovered, ascertain the criticality of the error (some errors are due to space allocation and are not regarded as critical errors)
- Check the Knowledge Base to determine what to do about the error
- Follow the Knowledge Base procedures to correct the error
- Dump the database

The Knowledge Base mentioned above is a Microsoft tool that records various errors that have been historically noted. It will give you either a workaround or a corrective action for each error. In an environment with many servers and databases the Knowledge Base is a very important tool, and I have become dependent on it because it is a fast way to analyze everything about an error that has recently occurred. Access to the Knowledge Base is available via the Internet, or by contacting Microsoft Technical Support to determine how you can get access to it. If you do not have access to the Knowledge Base, call Microsoft Technical Support if you have a critical error.

Microsoft SQL Server has the ability to notify the DBA that corrective action is required, so the entire procedure of running DBCC in off business hours can be automated. To take advantage of this, databases should be ranked in order of priority, and you should specify whether to page a DBA immediately or e-mail the DBA in the morning when they arrive at work. A database that is heavily used by both Americans and Europeans is heavily used 24 hours a day and may require 24-hours-a-day/7-days-a-week pager support or some other sort of immediate notification in the event of a critical DBCC error. In this situation, DBCC would probably not be run on the server but on another server. This leads us to the next DBCC scenario.

DBCC SCENARIO #2: Important Data, Very Large Database (VLDB), Around-the-Clock Usage

If you have a database that has important data, is a very large multi-gigabyte database, and users are using it around the clock, you may consider the following:

- Acquire a backup server
- Run DBCC CHECKDB on your backup server in single user mode

This is a difficult scenario to administer because you have to take extra steps to ensure the integrity and recoverability of your data. The best bet here is to get another server (which you should have anyway with a database like this in case you have to move your application overnight to another server due to hardware anomalies or some other hardware related issue). Use this backup server to run DBCC checks on the database; it can also function as a reporting server (see the next section).

There are all kinds of good, solid reasons to have a backup server for a database of this importance. On multi-gigabyte databases, DBCC must look at the database at the page level. This can take so long on larger databases that it becomes impossible to maintain a good computing environment for the customer, but a DBA can take advantage of a backup server to run DBCCs against the database in single-user mode after the database is restored to the backup server.

DBCC SCENARIO #3: Reporting Server, Duplicate Database Restoring from Another Database, Read-only Database, Round-the-Clock Usage

If you have a reporting server whose databases are actually restored from another database, you may want to consider the following:

- There may be no need to run DBCC on the server of origin
- Make sure that DBCC CHECKDB is being run on either the database of origin or the reporting server

If DBCC is not being run on the database of origin and it makes more sense to run DBCC on this reporting server, you should consider the possibility of getting another reporting server. This will allow a maintenance window for upgrades and activities centered around preventative maintenance of the databases and will allow your users access to the database at all times. Monitor your environment to determine when your number of users and your usage times are being stretched. Try to be on top of your hardware needs and add servers as your number of users and usage times increase. It will save a lot to stay ahead of the curve.

Most DBCC errors show up in the error log prior to the run of DBCC. The error log is something that every Microsoft SQL Server writes to and, in environments with many servers, it is important to use SQL Server's ability to create automated alerts to e-mail or page a DBA when the error occurs in the error log. This will be the first alert to trouble. The alerts can be in order of the error's severity, and you can specify whether to notify on an error of a certain severity or to not notify at all on certain errors. It is now very easy to set up automated alerts on SQL Server errors; Chapter 4 on the SQL Server Agent can show you the mechanism for doing this.

Functionality of DBCC

There are different types of Database Consistency Checks to run against a database, and each one does different things. The following sections describe the most commonly used types.

DBCC CHECKCATALOG

DBCC CHECKCATALOG checks to see if the system tables are consistent. This should be run every time you have DBCC scheduled to run on your database. This checks the integrity of *syscolumns* with *systypes* and *sysobjects* with *syscolumns*. Every data type in syscolumns must have a row in systypes, and every table and view must have a minimum of one column in syscolumns.

DBCC CHECKDB

DBCC CHECKDB checks the integrity of every object on the database. Any errors found should be fixed. You do not have to run DBCC CHECKALLOC or DBCC CHECKTABLE if you run DBCC CHECKDB. Indexes and data pages for each table are checked for correct page linkage and consistent pointers. Indexes are further checked to make sure the entries are properly sorted and that offsets and data on each page are reasonable. Sizes of text, ntext, and image pages for each table are checked. Page allocation is checked for all pages.

OTHER DBCC STATEMENTS

There are many other DBCC statements that are a subset of the functionality of DBCC CHECKDB or that perform some other utility type function. The syntax, descriptions, and arguments can be found in Chapter 24, "Transact-SQL Programming Language Reference."

- DBCC CHECKALLOC checks the allocation of data pages in the database. NOINDEX means that nonclustered indexes on user tables will not be checked. NO_INFOMSGS tells SQL Server to not display informational messages, and only error messages are displayed.
- DBCC CHECKIDENT returns the current identity value for the named table or corrects the identity value.
- DBCC SHRINKDATABASE shrinks the size of the data files in a database.
- DBCC SHRINKFILE shrinks the size of a data file. Targetsize is an integer and is the size you want the file to be in megabytes; it is not used by SQL Server if you also specify TRUNCATEONLY. If you do not use targetsize, the file will be reduced as much as SQL Server can shrink it. NOTRUNCATE means the space will remain in the database file(s). TRUNCATEONLY means unused space will be added to the free space in the directory without relocating rows.
- DBCC CHECKFILEGROUP looks at the allocation and integrity of all tables in the file group. NOINDEX means that nonclustered indexes on user tables will not be checked. NO_INFOMSGS tells SQL Server to not display informational messages; only error messages are displayed.
- DBCC UPDATEUSAGE updates the sysindexes table to indicate up-to-date values for the size data (rows, used, reserved, and dpages) of the table(s).

NO_INFOMSGS tells SQL Server to not display informational messages; only error messages are displayed.

- DBCC UPDATEUSAGE WITH COUNT_ROWS updates the *sysindexes* system table with the current number of rows in the table for *sysindexes* rows with an indid of 0 or 1. COUNT_ROWS can take time on large tables.
- DBCC DBREINDEX rebuilds one or all indexes for a table. This is very useful to preserve uniqueness and primary key constraints that could be lost if a drop/recreate were done on the index(es). Fillfactor is a percentage of how much data is on each index page. If you give 0 (zero) as a fillfactor, the original fillfactor from when the index was created will be used. NO_INFOMSGS tells SQL Server to not display informational messages; only error messages are displayed.
- DBCC OPENTRAN shows the oldest active transaction and replicated (distributed and nondistributed) transactions. WITH TABLERESULTS gives the results in a format that can be loaded into a table. NO_INFOMSGS tells SQL Server to not display informational messages; only error messages are displayed.
- DBCC PINTABLE means that SQL Server will not flush the table from memory. The table will have its own place in memory.
- DBCC UNPINTABLE means that SQL Server can flush the table from memory.
- DBCC CHECKTABLE checks the integrity of a specific table (data, index[es], text, ntext, image pages) on the database. NOINDEX means that nonclustered indexes on user tables will not be checked. NO_INFOMSGS tells SQL Server to not display informational messages: only error messages are displayed.
- DBCC SHOWCONTIG tells you if there is fragmentation on a named table and named index.
- DBCC TEXTALLOC checks the allocation of text or image columns for a table. FULL tells SQL Server to produce an allocation report.
- DBCC MEMUSAGE shows the memory usage of the SQL Server and the procedure cache for the SQL Server expressed in 8K pages
- DBCC PERFMON shows performance information about three statistics, IOSTATS, LRUSTATS, and NETSTATS.
- DBCC DBREPAIR drops a database that can not be recovered. This command is only included for backward compatibility. Use Drop Database instead.
- DBCC TEXTALL selects tables in the database that have text, ntext, or image columns and runs TEXTALLOC against the tables. FULL tells SQL Server to produce an allocation report.
- DBCC USEROPTIONS shows the SET options for the current session.

- DBCC dllname (FREE) takes the named extended stored procedure out of memory.
- DBCC SQLPERF (LOGSPACE) shows the transaction log space in the databases on the Microsoft SQL Server.
- DBCC TRACEON turns on the named trace flag.
- DBCC TRACEOFF turns off the named trace flag.
- DBCC TRACESTATUS tells you which trace flags are in use on the server.
- DBCC PROCCACHE shows information about the procedure cache.

DBCC is a powerful tool that performs a wide variety of functions. The more familiar you are with the functionality of DBCC, the better you will be able to manage your server and keep the databases in good condition.

OSQL and ISQL

The OSQL utility is functionally similar to ISQL except it uses ODBC instead of DB-Library to connect to and communicate with Microsoft SQL Server 7. You can run Transact-SQL statements, system procedures, and script files from both OSQL and ISQL. Both utilities are started directly from the operating system and have case-sensitive arguments. You can use both to run interactively with the results sent to STDOUT or you may run ISQL in a command file in batch mode by passing arguments with the results sent to a named file.

Not only Transact-SQL statements can be run within ISQL and OSQL. There are also commands specific to both utilities:

- **GO** runs the statements.
- **RESET** resets your session by clearing any statements entered.
- **ED** invokes the editor.
- **!!** executes an operating-system command.
- **QUIT or EXIT( )** exits from ISQL and OSQL.
- **CTRL+C** terminates a query but does not exit.

You can also issue operating system commands by beginning a line with two exclamation points (!!) followed by the command in both utilities. In addition, you can read a file from the operating system file structure into the ISQL or OSQL buffer by interactively entering either of the utilities by typing the following syntax at the prompt within the utility:

```
:r filename
```

To include comments in a Transact-SQL statement submitted to SQL Server from ISQL or OSQL, use two hyphens per each line beginning (--) or use the common C programming syntax (/*...*/). The syntax, descriptions, and arguments can be found in Chapter 21, "Transact-SQL Programming Reference."

SQLMAINT

The sqlmaint utility can be used to create a job to backup databases and can be run from a command prompt. In version 7 this can be used in lieu of a Database Maintenance Plan if you are not satisfied with the way the Database Maintenance Plan backs up a database to a new backup file name every time it is run, which can lead to space problems on the server. SQL-DMO must be registered on the SQL Server to run sqlmaint.

The sqlmaint Utility performs maintenance operations on a database(s) and is handy because it is run at the command prompt or from the SQL Server Agent. It can be used to back up a database, check database consistency, run UPDATE STATISTICS, verify the backup, back up the database only if the database consistency checks are clean, and is capable of placing the results in an HTML file or e-mailing the results to an operator.

The syntax is:

```
[-?] |
[
[-S server]
[-U "login_ID" [-P "password"]]
{
[ -D database_name | -PlanName name | -PlanID guid ]
[-Rpt text_file [-DelTxtRpt <time_period>] ]
[-To operator_name]
[-HtmlRpt html_file [-DelHtmlRpt <time_period>] ]
[-RmUnusedSpace threshold_percent free_percent]
[-CkDB | -CkDBNoIdx]
[-CkAl | -CkAlNoIdx]
[-CkTxtAl]
[-CkCat]
[-UpdSts]
[-UpdOptiStats sample_percent]
[-RebldIdx free_space]
[-WriteHistory]
[
{-BkUpDB [backup_path] | -BkUpLog [backup_path] }
```

```
{-BkUpMedia
{DISK [ [-DelBkUps <time_period>]
[-CrBkSubDir ] [ -UseDefDir ]
]
| TAPE
}
}
[-BkUpOnlyIfClean]
[-VrfyBackup]
]
}
]

<time_period> ::=
number[minutes | hours | days | weeks | months]
```

The arguments are described in Table 8-2.

sqlmaint Argument	Description
-?	Displays the syntax for sqlmaint.
-S server	Server is the target server.
-U "login_ID"	Login ID is the permission to se when connecting to SQL Server
-P "password"	Password is the password for the login ID.
-D database_name	Database is the name of the database to perform the maintenance.
-PlanName name	Name is the name of a database maintenance plan.
-PlanID guid	Guid is the globally unique identifier (GUID) of a database maintenance plan.
-Rpt text_file	Text_file is the fully qualified path and name of the file.
-DelTxtRpt <time_period>	Time_period is used to delete the any files whose names match the text_file* that are older than the time period.

Table 8-2. *sqlmaint Utility Arguments*

sqlmaint Argument	Description
-To operator_name	Operator_name is the operator to send the report to through SQLMail.
-HtmlRpt html_file	Html_file is the fully qualified path and name of the file to place an HTML report.
-DelHtmlRpt <time_period>	Time_period is used to delete the any files whose names match the html_file* that are older than the time_period.
-RmUnusedSpace threshold_percent free_percent	RmUnusedSpace instructs SQL Server to remove unused space from the database for databases that automaticaly expand. Threshold_percent is the megabytes the database must be before unused space is removed. Free_percent is how much unused space can stay in the database. This is a percentage of the database size.
-CkDB | -CkDBNoIdx	-CkDB | -CkDBNoIdx instructs SQL Server to run DBCC CHECKDB with or without the NOINDEX option.
-CkAl | -CkAlNoIdx	-CkAl | -CkAlNoIdx instructs SQL Server to run DBCC NEWALLOC with or without the NOINDEX option.
-CkTxtAl	-CkTxtAl instructs SQL Server to run DBCC TEXTALL.
-CkCat	-CkCat instructs SQL Server to run DBCC CHECKCATALOG.
-UpdSts	-UpdSts instructs SQL Server to run update statistics on all database tables.
-UpdOptiStats sample_percent	-UpdOptiStats sample_percent instructs SQL Server to run update statistics on all user created database tables using the WITH SAMPLE option of UPDATE STATISTICS.
-RebldIdx free_space	-RebldIdx free_space instructs SQL Server to rebuild indexes on tables in the database by using the free_space percent value as the inverse of the fill factor. For example, if free_space percentage is 10, then the fill factor used is 90. If a free_space equals 100, the original fill factor is used.

Table 8-2. *sqlmaint Utility Arguments* (continued)

sqlmaint Argument	Description
-WriteHistory	-WriteHistory writes a row to the sysdbmaintplan_history table in the msdb system database.
-BkUpDB [backup_path] | -BkUpLog [backup_path]	-BkUpDB [backup_path] | -BkUpLog [backup_path] defines which backup operation to perform. -BkUpDb back up the whole database. -BkUpLog backs up the transaction log. [backup_path] is the name of the backup directory. [backup_path] is not necessary if the argument -UseDefDir is supplied and will not be used if both are supplied. The file name for a database backup is created by the system as: dbname_db_yyyyMMddhhmm.BAK. or dbname_log_yyyymmddhhmm. You must also supply the -BkUpMedia parameter.
-BkUpMedia DISK | TAPE	-BkUpMedia DISK | TAPE is the backup media type.
-DelBkUps <time_period>	-DelBkUps <time_period> instructs the system to delete any backup file in the directory if it is older than the time_period. number[minutes | hours | days | weeks | months] is an integer and represents the time, for example, 12weeks, 3months, or 15days. If only an integer is supplied, weeks is the default.
-CrBkSubDir	-CrBkSubDir will create a system named subdirectory in the [backup_path] directory, a way to place the backups for each database into its own subdirectory without changing the [backup_path] argument.
-UseDefDir	-UseDefDir instructs SQL Server to place the backup file in the default backup directory overriding whatever the [backup_path] argument is. For a vanilla SQL Server install this is the C:\Mssql7\Backup directory.

Table 8-2. *sqlmaint Utility Arguments* (continued)

sqlmaint Argument	Description
-BkUpOnlyIfClean	-BkUpOnlyIfClean keeps the backup from happening if -Ck checks find DBCC errors in the data. However, maintenance operations are positional and run in the order they appear as arguments. Put any –Ck checks before the -BkUpDB/-BkUpLog arguments if you are using this argument or you will not get what you expect.
-VrfyBackup	-VrfyBackup instructs SQL Server to run RESTORE VERIFYONLY on the backup after it is finished.

Table 8-2. *sqlmaint Utility Arguments* (continued)

All of SQL Server's utilities have been improved in version 7, and great care has been taken to address the performance problems that have been experienced in the past. Microsoft knows that these utilities must be able to run on a database as large as a terabyte, and the utilities have been changed dramatically to meet this goal. In the next chapter, we will review the replication enhancements to SQL Server 7.

Chapter 9

Replication Enhancements for SQL Server 7

Replication is used to distribute data from one SQL Server to other SQL Servers in other locations. This is accomplished by establishing an original copy of the data and then setting up SQL Server to synchronize the data thereafter by moving the data from one server to another using a Publisher and a Subscriber. There is only one Publisher, but a Publisher can have many Subscribers. In SQL Server 7, the Subscribers can update data at the Publisher, as opposed to the traditional model in which data can only be changed at the Publisher. Subscribers can also be Publishers.

The addition of two new Agents to SQL Server 7 has enhanced its replication abilities. Now, along with the Log Reader and the Distribution Agents, we have the Snapshot and the Merge Agents, and there are three major choices when you want to replicate data:

- Merge Replication
- Snapshot Replication
- Transaction Replication

The replication enhancements covered in this chapter are:

- Multi-site Update Replication
- Merge Replication
- Snapshot and Data Transformation Services
- Partitioned Transactional Replication
- Updating Subscriber
- Push and Pull Subscriptions
- Anonymous Pull Subscriptions
- Internet Replication Enhancements
- Data Encryption
- Heterogeneous Data-Replication Services
- Creating Replication Scripts

Multi-site Update Replication

Along with replication comes the problem of how and when the data is updated across all the servers involved in the replication scenario. How can multiple sites update the same data at the same time without having one site as the owner of the replication scenario? What if the updates occur at the same time? Who will update first and who will have to wait until the locks are released? There are problems involved with replication such as lost updates and availability uncertainties with the two-phase commit. One machine may become unavailable while it waits to update all the remote servers. Applications have different needs in these areas, depending on how your users are viewing and using the data.

To solve the complex problems of allowing multiple sites to update replicated data, Microsoft SQL Server has come up with a number of ways to implement multi-site update replication depending on the needs of the application:

Application Need	**Multi-site Update Replication Choice**
Autonomy most important	Merge Replication
Latency; consistency	Snapshot and Data Transformation Services
Partition application to avoid conflicts; latency is only a matter of seconds	Partitioned Transactional Replication
Subscribers must be consistent	Updating Subscribers

A replication tool has to abide by the laws of physics and networks while attempting to answer the needs of the customer for a replicated copy.

Merge Replication

Merge replication is a multi-site update replication choice in Microsoft SQL Server 7 that is used when the autonomy of the SQL Server is the most important consideration. In this process, data moves only during pair-wise reconciliation when a scheduled merge occurs. The merge process connects to both servers, and the Reconciler merges the data while resolving any conflicts that arise. Arriving values are merged with existing values, and conflicts are resolved according to reconciliation rules that can be extended and customized with COM/OLE. Alternatively, conflicts can be resolved based on priorities previously assigned. Data moves from the changed SQL Server to the one that needs to be synchronized.

In the case of merge replication, the log reader and transactions are not used for the reconciliation; rather, the actual data is used. You may change the column many times, but only the last row image is used in reconciliation. You can configure Merge Replication by using the Configure Publishing and Distribution Wizard. To access the wizard in Enterprise Manager, expand a server and select Tools | Wizards | Replication | Configure Publishing and Distribution Wizard. This wizard will enable your Publishing databases for Merge Replication.

First you must choose a distributor. This process will create a *distribution* database. You may create the distribution database on the Publishing server or use a different server to house your distribution database after you have configured the server to be a distributor. Figure 9-1 shows the Enable Publisher screen. You may register other servers as Publishers for this screen if you choose.

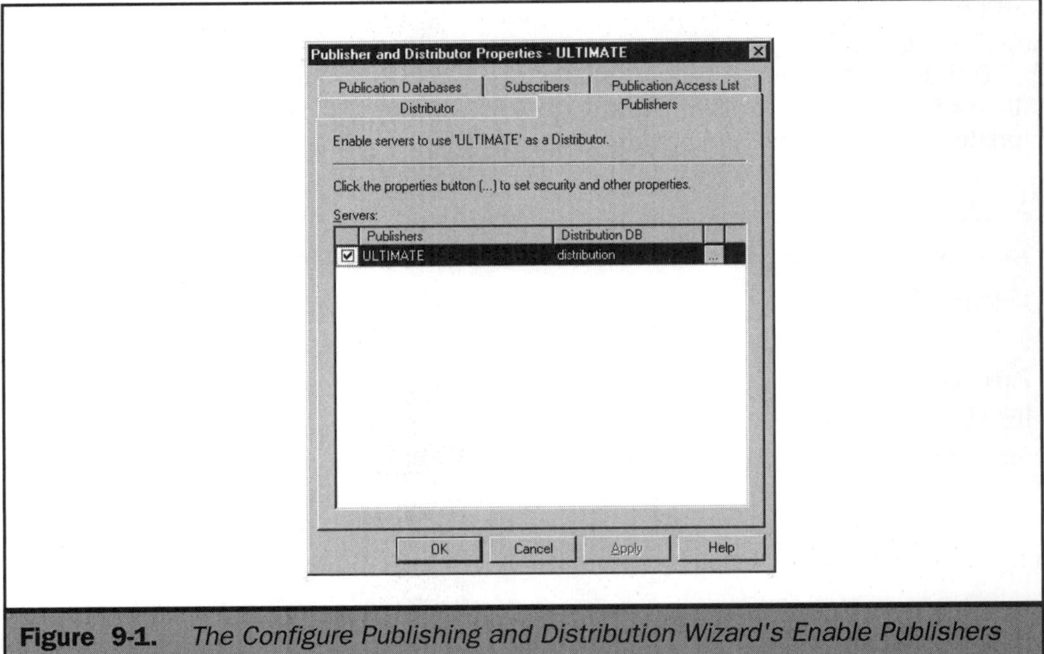

Figure 9-1. *The Configure Publishing and Distribution Wizard's Enable Publishers screen*

You may also click the ... button in the list box to see the options for the Publisher, which include the working folder information and how the Replication Agents will log on to the Publishing server. The next screen shows the check boxes that enable the Publishing databases for Merge Replication.

The next screen shows the process for enabling the Subscriber. In this case, the Publisher, the Distributor, and the Subscriber are all on the same SQL Server. The next screen shows Options for the Subscriber, including a description of how Replication Agents log on to the Subscriber. The next screen shows the successful completion of the Publishing and Distribution Wizard configuring the distribution database.

If you decide to back out of the creation of the distribution database and the configuration, you can use the Disable Publishing and Distribution Wizard to remove the distribution database and the Publisher and Subscribers just created. To access that wizard in Enterprise Manager, expand the server, go to the Tools menu, and select Replication | Configure Publishing and Distribution Wizard | Disable the Publishing and Distribution Wizard.

Just as you can configure a Publisher for Merge Replication and disable and remove a Distributor and Publisher, you can also configure the *Publication* for Merge Replication. To do so, you first need to access the Publish and Push Subscriptions window (Figure 9-2) in Enterprise Manager by expanding the server and selecting Tools | Wizards.

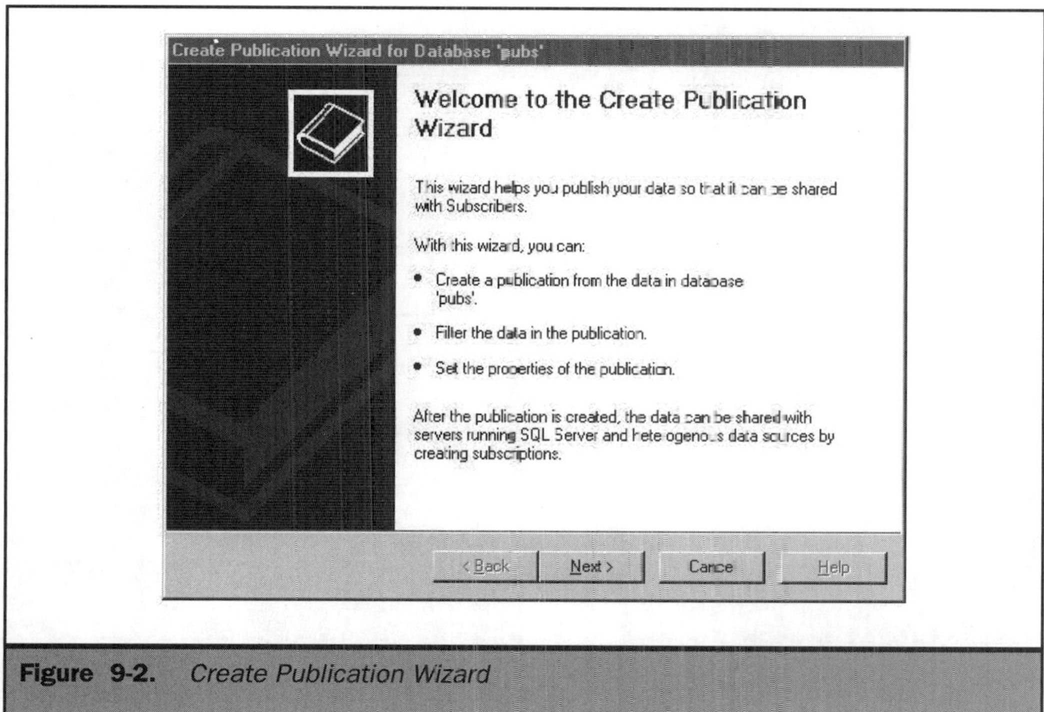

Figure 9-2. *Create Publication Wizard*

Next, select Wizards, double-click on Replication, and select the Create Publication Wizard. This wizard will let you choose the Publication type: Snapshot, Transactional, or Merge. The Create Publication Wizard asks you to specify the Publication name and description. The next screen shows the successful completion of the Create Publication Wizard. After the screens of the Create Publication Wizard close down, the new publication appears in the Enterprise Manager hierarchy tree under the Replication Monitor, as shown in Figure 9-3.

The Subscription must now be created as a Merge subscription. For purposes of this example, we will pull the subscription from the Subscriber using the Pull Subscription Wizard, as opposed to pushing the publication from the Publisher. Select the Pull New Subscription button, and the Pull Subscription Wizard screen appears.

A publication must be chosen for the subscriber. From the Choose Publication screen, choose the Publication. The next screen gives you the choice of initializing the subscription now or waiting to do the Merge until the agents are scheduled to run, and the following screen lets you create the Merge Agent schedule.

Click the Change button on the Set Merge Agent Schedule screen and the scheduling screen, now called the Edit Recurring Job screen, appears. This is the same scheduling screen presented in previous versions of Microsoft SQL Server and is very similar to the old Task Schedule screen.

The next screen that appears (Figure 9-4) allows you to set your subscription priority.

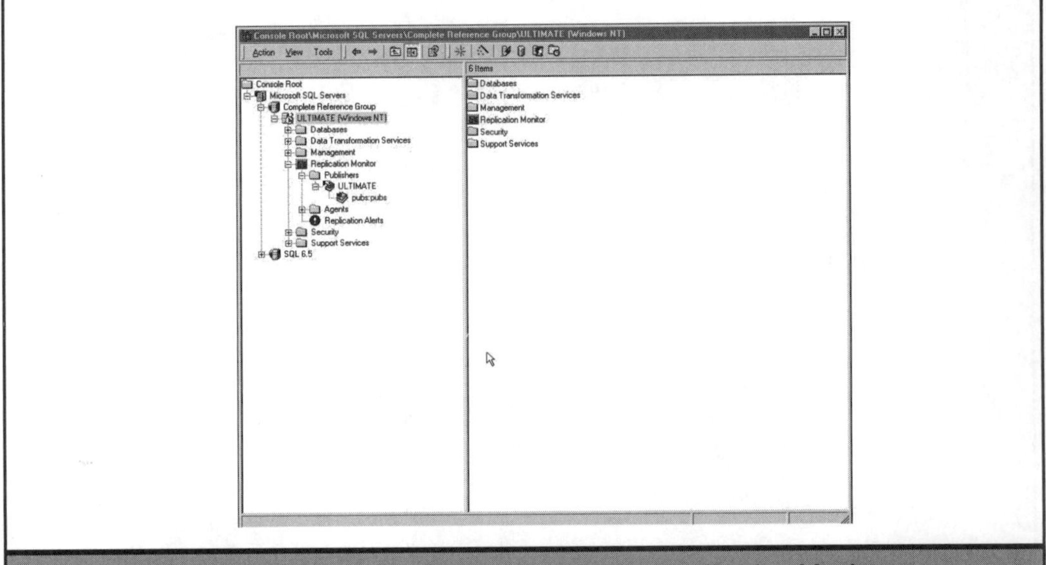

Figure 9-3. *The new publication appears under the Replication Monitor*

This is how multi-site updates resolve update conflicts. If two Subscribers are updating the same column in a row of data, the column will show the update of the server who has the highest priority.

The final screen completes the process of creating a Merge Replication Pull Subscription.

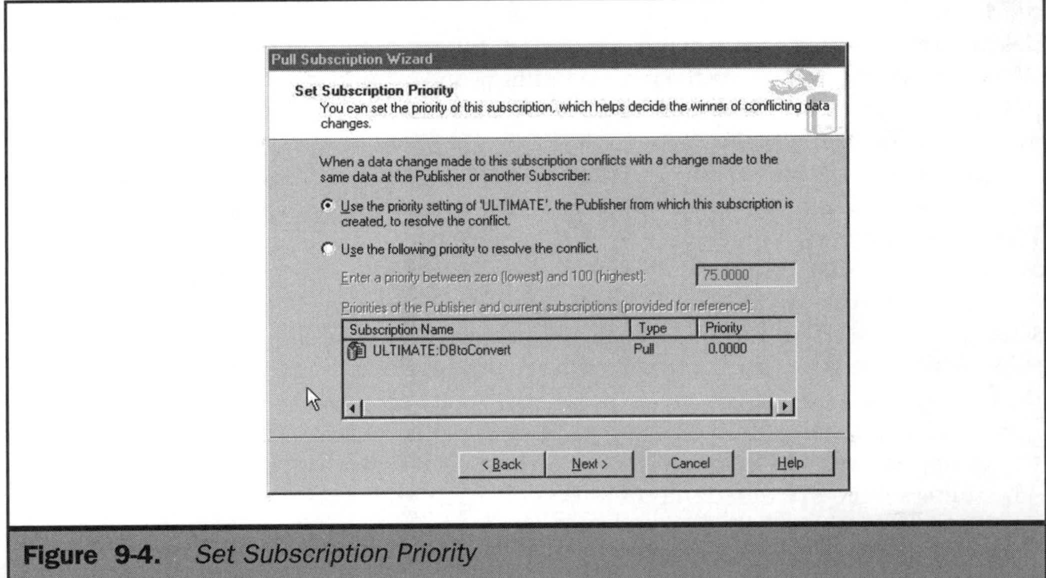

Figure 9-4. *Set Subscription Priority*

Snapshot and Data Transformation Services

The snapshot multi-site update replication choice takes a picture of the database schema and data at a specific point in time. This is the basis for the first synchronization. The BCP utility is used to move the schema and data. After this, updates are applied to destination servers in scheduled table-refreshes of the data. As scheduled in replication configuration, a new snapshot is taken and applied to the server on a periodic basis.

This choice has the benefit of reducing the administrative overhead in dealing with the logreader and the transaction logs. There is latency involved in it, but the data remains in a consistent state. This is the easiest replication scenario to administer and configure.

Note *The Create Publication Wizard is invoked by expanding the server in the Enterprise Manager, selecting the Tools menu | Wizards.*

The Choose Publication Type screen in the Create Publication Wizard has three choices which represent the three main types of replication:

- Snapshot Publication
- Transaction Publication
- Merge Publication

The Choose Publication Type screen briefly describes each of these types of replication, as shown in Figure 9-5.

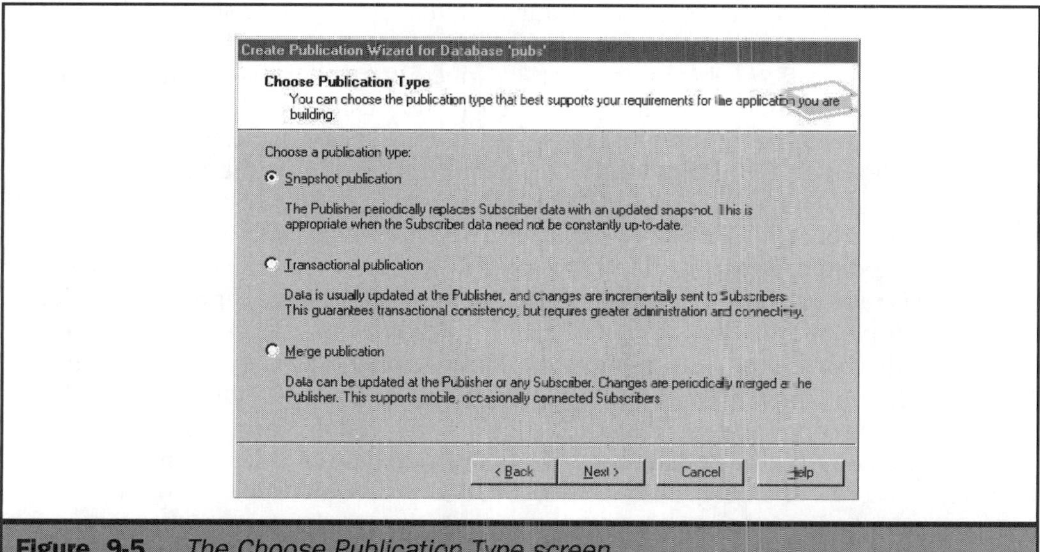

Figure 9-5. *The Choose Publication Type screen*

Partitioned Transactional Replication

Partitioned Transactional Replication is best used when your application needs consistency between Publishers and Subscribers within seconds of a transaction. Partitioning is a great tool in designing a replication scenario. It is much better to partition the application to avoid update conflicts rather than try to resolve them when they occur. Conflict resolution has a winner and a loser, and any time there is a loser there is a transaction that may not get applied. Avoid this situation by partitioning your data and using transaction replication.

Transactional replication has a Publisher and one or more Subscribers. A Publisher sends data to the Subscriber in the form of Articles. The transaction log is used to log the changes to the data and then place the changes on a distribution database where they are then sent to the Subscriber in the same order they are made to the Publisher. This process requires a network connection between the Publisher and the Subscriber and replicates with just seconds of latency.

The Snapshot Agent, Log Reader Agent, and the Distribution Agent participate in transactional replication. You can configure transactional replication with updatable Subscribers and pull subscriptions or anonymous pull subscriptions.

Updating Subscriber

An *updating Subscriber* is a replication Subscriber that can perform simultaneous updates to the Publisher as data is updated on the Subscriber. This is done via a two-phase commit and the Distributed Transaction Coordinator (DTC). This feature, called *synchronous transactions,* is a new replication feature—available for the first time in SQL Server 7. It is available for either transactional replication or snapshot replication, both of which can be set up by checking a check box in the Create Publication Wizard. To enable updatable Subscribers, expand the server in Enterprise Manager and select Tools | Replication | Publish and Push Subscriptions | Create Publication | Create Publication Wizard | Choose Publication Type, Snapshot (or Transaction) Publication | Allow Updatable Subscriptions. Select the Yes radio button in the Allow Updatable Subscriptions window, shown in Figure 9-6.

Different parts of SQL Server work together to create what is known as the Immediate Updating Subscriber. The Microsoft Distributed Transaction Coordinator (MS DTC) is responsible for the two-phase commit, while triggers capture the updates at the Subscriber and send them to the Publisher. Updates are differentiated between those actually changed at the Subscriber and those applied by the Publisher to the Subscriber in the normal process of replication by using the NOT FOR REPLICATION clause when the triggers were created. This means the Update, Insert, or Delete trigger will only fire when a user updates the Subscribing database and not when a replication transaction occurs. The trigger uses a remote stored procedure call to a stored procedure on the Publisher; if it returns success, the transaction is committed.

Before the transaction is committed, it must go through a series of checks to see what has happened to that piece of data on the Publisher. If the data was updated on

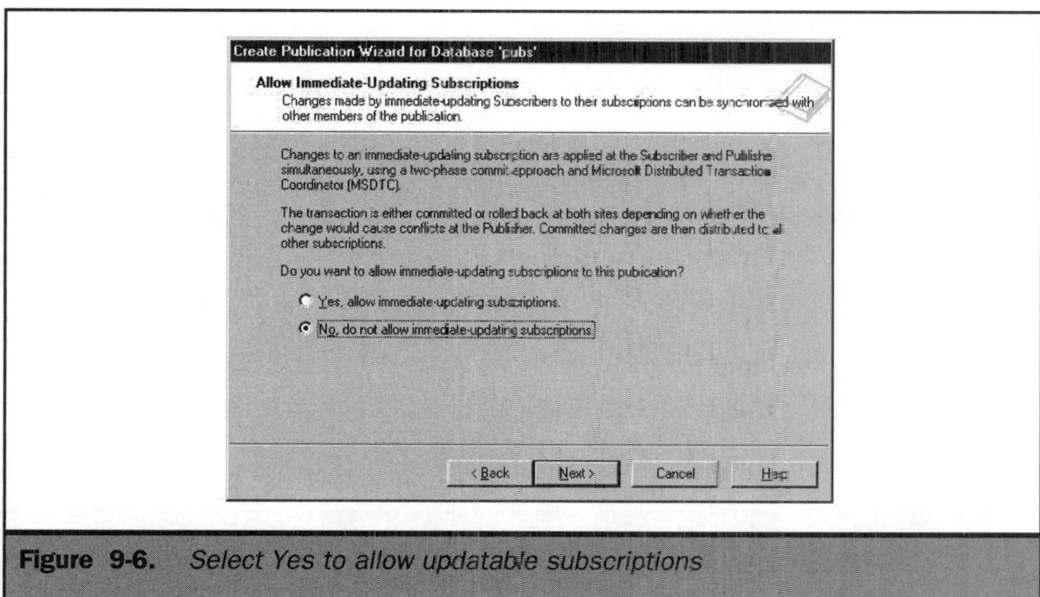

Figure 9-6. *Select Yes to allow updatable subscriptions*

the Publisher before the transaction from the Subscriber could be applied, the transaction is rolled back. SQL Server checks to see if there is a timestamp on the article. If there is, it compares timestamps and will not apply a transaction if the same data has been changed on the Publisher. If there is no timestamp, a row compare occurs. If the rows are the same on the Publisher and the Subscriber using the view of the data before it was changed on the Subscriber, then the transaction is applied. If the rows are different, meaning the Publisher was updated before the Subscriber tried to update the data, the Subscriber's update will not be applied. In this case, the Publisher wins. A process called *loopback detection* keeps the Subscriber updates from replicating back to the Subscriber during replication by the Publisher only if the article has a timestamp.

Push and Pull Subscriptions

There are two options for moving data to a Subscriber: the Publisher can *push* the data to the Subscriber or the Subscriber can *pull* the data from the Publisher. A single Publication can move data using both methods.

When a Publisher is pushing data to the Subscriber, the Subscriber is not involved in asking for the data or determining when the data comes. The Subscriber gets the data when the Publisher is ready, which can occur as soon as the data is changed or when the Publisher schedules the data to be pushed to the Subscriber. To enable this type of replication, select the Push Subscription Wizard from the Tools menu | Wizards in Enterprise Manager. The Push Subscription Wizard is shown in Figure 9-7. A push subscription is best used when the changes must be seen on the Subscriber as

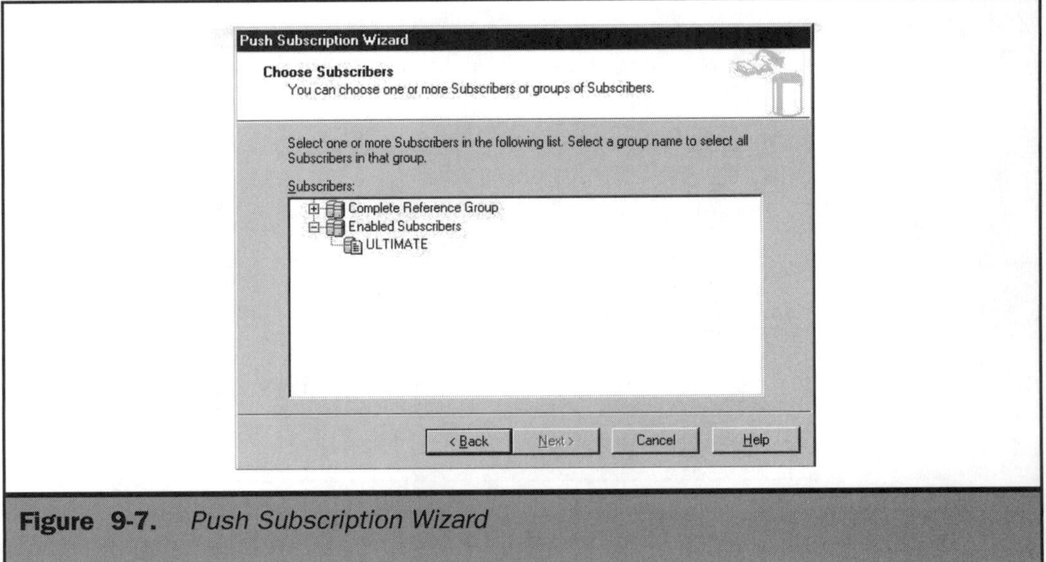

Figure 9-7. *Push Subscription Wizard*

soon as they occur on the Publisher and when an application needs security. Changes can also be pushed to Subscribers on a scheduled basis.

It is best for the Subscriber to pull data from the Publisher when there are multiple Subscribers on the Internet. To use this method, in the Enterprise Manager, select Pull Subscription from the Tools menu | Wizards. The Pull Subscription Wizard is shown in Figure 9-8. The Subscriber can receive changes from the Publisher on a schedule set by the Subscriber or whenever it is convenient. This method is less secure than the push method.

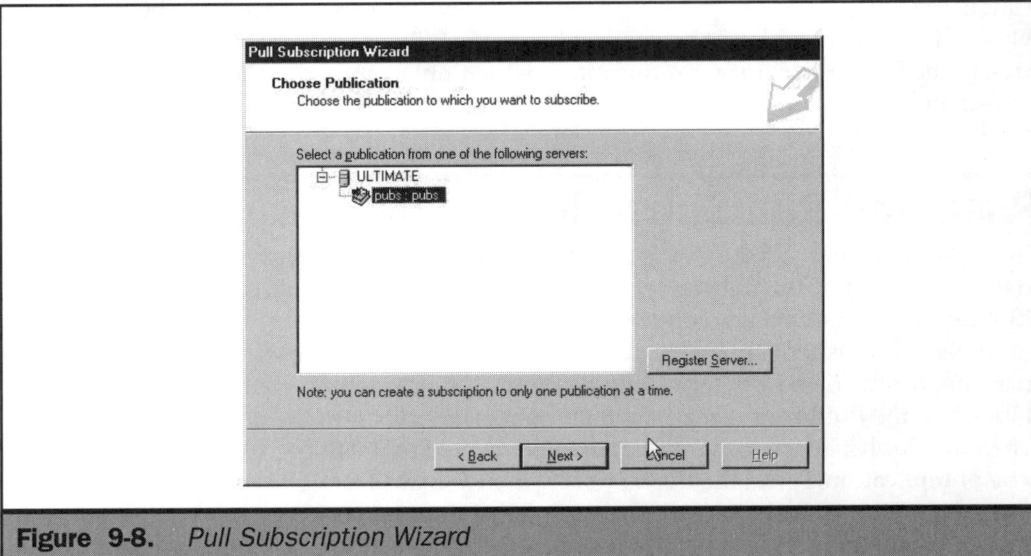

Figure 9-8. *Pull Subscription Wizard*

Internet Replication Enhancements

Microsoft SQL Server has made it easy to use the Internet to get data from the Publisher to a Subscriber. There are a few rules that apply. If you have a firewall, the Publisher and the Distributor must be on the same side of the firewall. If you do not have a firewall, the Publisher and the Distributor must have a direct network connection.

Connecting to Microsoft SQL Server from the Internet is easy. It can be done from the SQL Server Query Analyzer utility or a client application using ODBC or DB-Library. To accomplish this, the client and the server computer have to be connected to the Internet and require the use of the TCP/IP or Multi-Protocol Network Libraries. Using the Multi-Protocol Network Library requires that TCP/IP support be enabled. An administrator can use the Multi-Protocol network library to establish an encrypted connection with SQL Server for one user or for all users. TCP/IP Windows Sockets, NWLink IPX/SPX, and Named Pipes are supported under the Multi-Protocol Net-Library, which communicates over one or many Interprocess Communication (IPC) mechanisms supported by Windows NT. The Multi-Protocol Net-Library takes advantage of the Remote Procedure Call (RPC) facility of Windows NT, which provides integrated security. For the Multi-Protocol network library, clients determine the server's address by simply using the server's name.

Anonymous Pull Subscriptions

An anonymous pull subscription is a subscription that does not have information about each Subscriber stored at the Publisher and the Distributor. If the server is not a Subscriber to the Publisher and the Publisher is configured for anonymous subscriptions, the Pull Subscription wizard will create an anonymous subscription for the Subscriber. Pull subscriptions require that the Subscriber initiate the subscription and the data pulls from the Publisher. This can be used by Internet Subscribers.

Replication for Internet publication has been enhanced with the Replication Distribution Agent Utility, which facilitates the distribution of copies of data from the source server (Publisher) to a destination server (Subscriber). This is initially set up on one or more servers and then runs either real-time, on a schedule, or on demand to distribute the data to the remote server. The beauty of this feature is that the Subscriber can be physically located in a remote area and any data changes can reach the Subscriber over the Internet as they are made on the source server.

To allow many Internet data subscribers, the idea of an anonymous subscription has been formulated. This is a new functionality which is a special kind of pull subscription. In the past, the data was pushed from the source server; now it can be pulled from the subscriber server. Information about the anonymous subscriber is not stored at the publisher, and the Subscriber becomes the responsible party to keep the anonymous subscription in sync. However, for a large number of subscribers the overhead of storing the information is not desirable.

The same steps are used to create an anonymous subscription as are used to create a pull subscription. In addition, the publication must be enabled for anonymous subscriptions and the server cannot be registered as a Subscriber at the Publisher. Use the Replication Distribution Agent Utility to add an anonymous subscription.

The Replication Distribution Agent Utility is a wizard, meaning it is a user interface that helps the user perform tasks previously requiring programming. The wizard sets up and starts the replication task that moves the transactions and snapshot jobs held in the distribution database tables to the subscription server.

Data Encryption

The Multi-Protocol network library has the capability to encrypt data sent to and from SQL Server, which is obviously useful in the Internet environment. Encryption can be set up for one user or for all users. This is a process that requires the use of the Microsoft SQL Server Client Network utility, located in the Microsoft SQL Server program group, to turn on encryption for the Multi-Protocol Network Library.

Use the Client Network Utility and the Server Network Utilities (which are located in the SQL Server 7 program group).

On the computer running the client (run the Client Network Utility) and the SQL Server (run the Server Network Utility), follow these steps once on each client and once on the SQL Server:

1. In the Microsoft SQL Server program group, start the SQL Client Network Utility (or the Server Network Utility if you are on the SQL Server).
2. Click the General tab.
3. Press the Add button in the General tab, select Multi-Protocol, and type in the server alias as shown in Figure 9-9.
4. Select OK button.
5. On the SQL Server there is an additional step in the Server Network Utility. Edit the Multi-Protocol selection and select the Enable Multi-Protocol encryption check box.

Privacy on the Internet: Microsoft Proxy Server

To ensure privacy on the Internet, Microsoft SQL Server can be connected through Microsoft Proxy Server, which is closely integrated with Windows NT Server user authentication. Proxy Server is a program providing secure access to the data stored on Microsoft SQL Server databases. The Proxy Server is a stand-alone program that

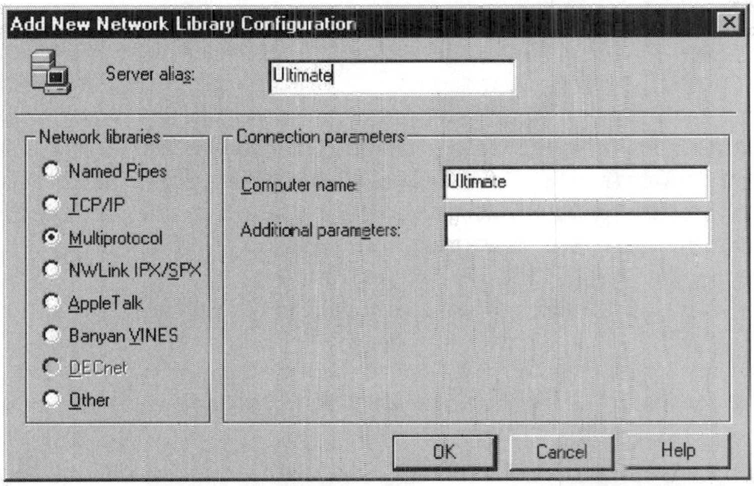

Figure 9-9. *Client Network Utility / Add New Network Protocol*

provides secure access by controlling the listening port and not allowing unwanted users access to the port by blocking access to ranges of IP address, domains, or users.

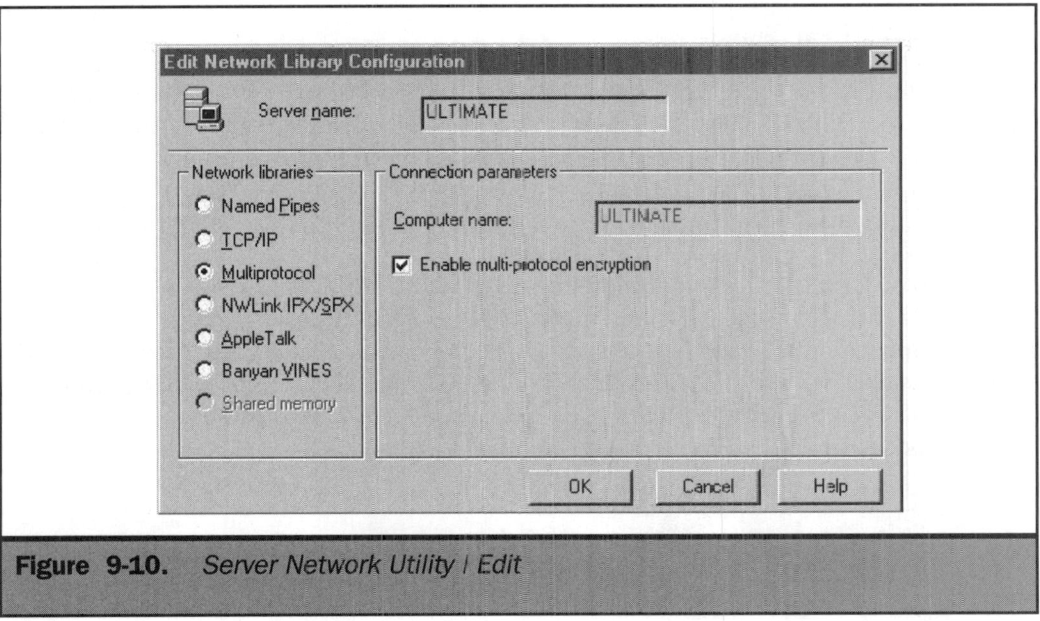

Figure 9-10. *Server Network Utility / Edit*

TCP/IP Sockets can also be used in combination with Microsoft Proxy Server. This allows SQL Server to communicate using standard Windows Sockets as the IPC method across the TCP/IP protocol. By default, Windows 95 uses TCP/IP sockets.

If you set up SQL Server to listen on TCP/IP, you must enter the TCP/IP port number in the Port number box. By default, SQL Server uses 1433, the official Internet Assigned Number Authority (IANA) socket number for Microsoft SQL Server, when accepting connections from TCP/IP sockets clients. When SQL Server is configured in setup to listen on a proxy server using Microsoft Proxy Server over TCP/IP Sockets, you must enter the proxy server address in the Remote WinSock proxy address box when you set up the TCP/IP Sockets network library.

The following steps describe how to connect to SQL Server using Microsoft Proxy Server and TCP/IP:

Note *Use the Microsoft SQL Server Setup in the SQL Server program group.*

1. In the Microsoft SQL Server Setup, select Work with an existing SQL Server, and then select Next.
2. Select the Change Network Support option and select the Next button.
3. Click the TCP/IP Sockets box.
4. In the Port Number box, type the port number (SQL Server default is 1433).
5. In the Remote Winsock proxy address box, type the node name or the IP address of the proxy server.
6. Select Finish, and then select Install Now.
7. Stop and start SQL Server.

The people I know who have used this remote Winsock proxy client part of Proxy Server and the TCP/IP Network Library were satisfied with the result, stating that the performance was similar to a slow WAN—and they were on the Internet from New Zealand to Washington state. To listen remotely by way of Remote Winsock (RWS), define the local address table (LAT) for the proxy server so that the listening node address is outside the range of LAT entries.

A person can also integrate IBM mainframe and AS/400 computers and data with PC systems and Microsoft SQL Server using Microsoft SNA Server. Microsoft SNA Server supports Intranet and Internet access. Each PC uses a local area network (LAN) protocol such as TCP/IP, IPX/SPX, NetBEUI, Banyan VINES, or AppleTalk to connect to Microsoft SNA Server computers, which then connect to mainframes using IBM SNA protocols.

SQL Server Data Transformation Services provides the functionality to import, export, and transform data from multiple heterogeneous sources using an OLE DB-based architecture. OLE DB is an important part of the Internet picture and provides support for transforming and publishing HTML data to the Internet.

Heterogeneous Data-Replication Services

Non-Microsoft SQL Server third-party databases and data sources can become Publishers. SQL-DMO, Visual Basic, C, and C++ programming can be used to make Microsoft SQL Server replication services available to third-party products. SQL-DMO is used to create publications, articles, and subscriptions. The other programming languages are used to store the transactions in the SQL Distributor. After this is accomplished, the SQL Distribution Agent and the Enterprise Manager can be used to forward the transactions and monitor replication. You can find samples of Visual Basic SQL-DMO on your Microsoft SQL Server installation CD in the \samples\sqlrepl\samppub\sqldmo directory with a sample C program in the samples\sqlrepl\samppub\repdist directory. The Replication Distributor Interface is the interface that allows the SQL-DMO and programming languages to interface with the Microsoft SQL Server replication framework. The Replication Distributor Interface stores the replicated transactions in the distribution database. The Replication Distributor Interface uses OLE DB connections and objects. Use Visual C++ and the OLE library to access these objects.

Creating Replication Scripts

You can now create a Transact-SQL script to use if you have to rebuild your replication scenario from scratch (see Figure 9-11) once you have completed your replication scenario by selecting Tools | Replication | Generate Replication Scripts in the Enterprise Manager. From the Enterprise Manager, simply run the scripts you have created after building your replication scenario.

With Microsoft SQL Server 7 it has never been easier to use the Internet to replicate data. From the encryption techniques offered to the replication scripts, every step is simplified.

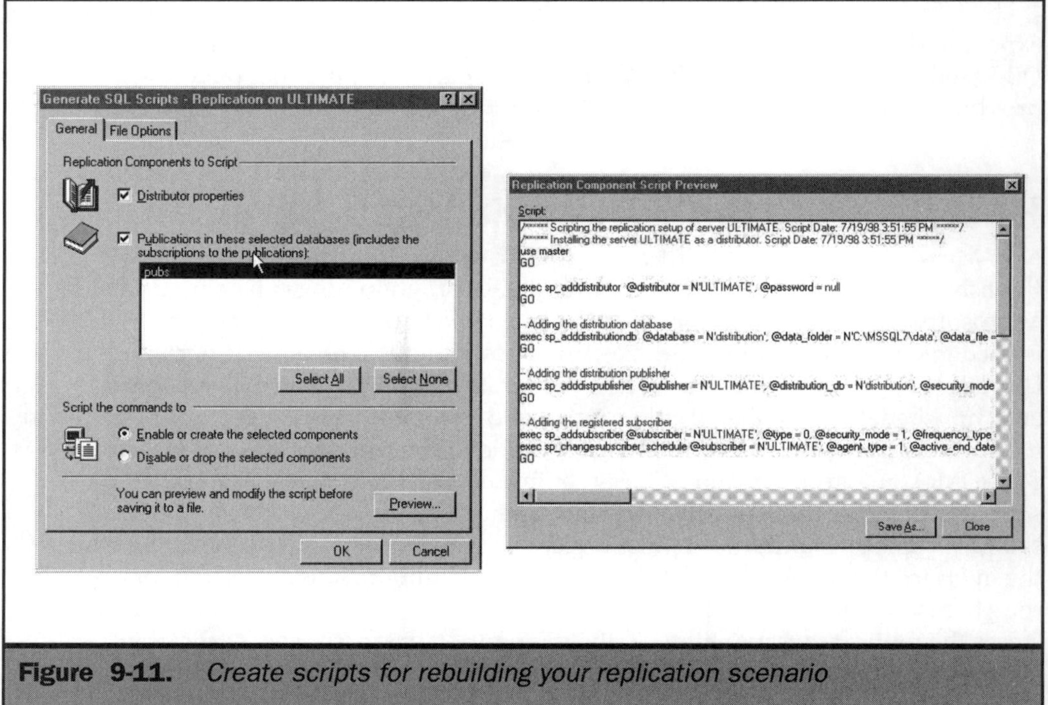

Figure 9-11. *Create scripts for rebuilding your replication scenario*

Chapter 10

Simplifying the Role of the Database Administrator

One of Microsoft's goals is to lower the total cost of ownership of the Microsoft product line that includes Microsoft SQL Server. One of the ways they've achieved this goal is by simplifying the tasks related to database maintenance with the Enterprise Manager, which makes database administration straightforward and easy. This won't put any DBAs out of work, but it will enable them to perform database maintenance tasks with speed and efficiency.

Some of the enhancements that simplify the role of the Microsoft SQL Server database administrator are covered in this chapter.

- Automatic and Dynamic Configuration
- Memory
- Locks
- Database Files Expand Automatically
- Autogrow TempDB and Startup Reset
- Automatic Database Creation and Alteration When Restoring
- Transact SQL Version Compatibility Levels
- Simplification of Configuration Options
- Dynamic Schema Management
- Drop a Column
- Alter a View, Trigger, or Procedure
- UNIQUE IDENTIFIER Datatype and the Globally Unique Identifier (GUID)

Automatic and Dynamic Configuration

In SQL Server 7 there are server configuration options set automatically and dynamically, a behavior that is sometimes called self-tuning. Formerly, these options had to be set manually, and they kept the same value until the database administrator manually changed the configuration value again. With this self-tuning behavior in SQL Server 7, many of the configuration values are changed frequently and dynamically by the SQL Server as resources are available.

Memory

Microsoft SQL Server can now use memory dynamically. Memory is configured automatically and grows and shrinks depending on what is available on the NT server. If the memory server configuration option is set to zero (0), memory is automatically and dynamically allocated to SQL Server. If the memory option is set to a nonzero setting, memory available to SQL Server does not go above that amount. To configure memory usage, expand the server group in Enterprise Manager, select a server, right-click on it, choose Properties, and select the Memory tab (see Figure 10-1).

The lazy writer scans the system to determine how much physical memory is free. The goal is to keep NT from paging but to give memory to SQL Server. The lazy writer process keeps within 200K of 5MB free at all times. If there are not 5MB free, it will decrease the amount of memory available to SQL Server and give it to NT. When more memory becomes available, the lazy writer will increase the SQL Server buffer cache again and make memory available to SQL Server with 5MB (plus or minus 200K) of free physical memory.

Locks

The maximum number of available locks configuration setting is set to zero (0) by default. At this setting, SQL Server automatically and dynamically allocates the locks memory to 96 bytes per lock. No more than 40 percent of memory in the SQL Server

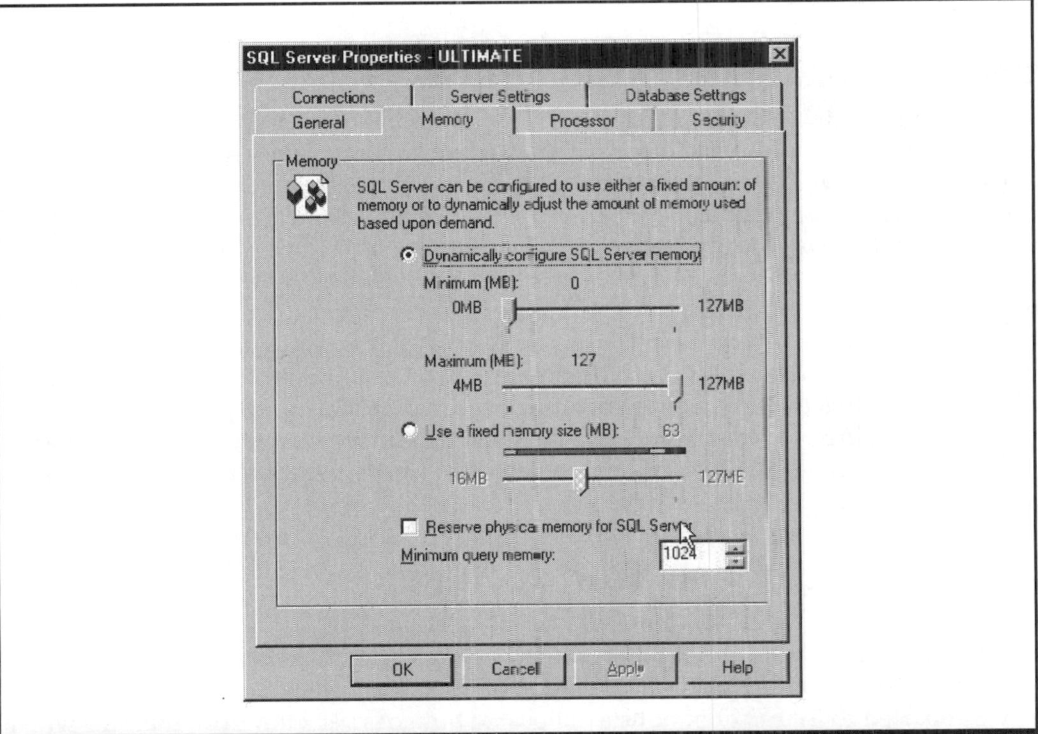

Figure 10-1. *Memory panel of the SQL Server Properties dialog box*

cache buffer will be used for locks, with an initial allocation of 2 percent of SQL Server's total memory allocation.

If you wish to set the locks option yourself, you must first use the *sp_configure* system stored procedure to set another server configuration option, *Show Advanced Options* to 1 (true). You can do this in a Query Analyzer window or using the OSQL utility at the command line.

```
EXEC sp_configure 'show advanced options', 1
GO
RECONFIGURE WITH OVERRIDE
GO
EXEC sp_configure 'locks', yourintegervalue
GO
```

The Query Analyzer can be invoked by selecting a server in the hierarchy tree and then the Tools Menu in the Enterprise Manager.

Database Files Expand Automatically

Traditionally, an important task for the database administrator has been to manage the space that the database uses. This was a manual process requiring the intervention of a knowledgeable database administrator when the database grew to a point where it used all of its allocated space. SQL Server 7 removes this obstacle and automatically expands the database file while there is still space left on the drive. Now the only problem becomes making sure there is space on the drive and that you do not insert millions of rows after accidentally creating a Cartesian product with the insert query. Manual intervention is required when the disk is full. However, you can control the maximum growth of the database with the CREATE DATABASE statement argument, MAXSIZE. Set this to the desired maximum size for the database to prevent your drives from filling past capacity. This is an important improvement; in the past when the database reached its allocated limit, it ceased to function until a DBA could fix the problem by expanding the database.

Autogrow TempDB and Startup Reset

Tempdb is the system database that is the working storage area of the database. This database now grows as needed when you make a query with an ORDER BY clause or other complex queries requiring the creation of temporary workspace tables. However, space allocated to *tempdb* does not stay allocated but goes back to its original size when the SQL Server is stopped and started.

Automatic Database Creation and Alteration When Restoring

There is a new argument when issuing a RESTORE command: REPLACE. This argument means that SQL Server will destroy the database and recreate it according to the specification in the backup set. If you do not use the REPLACE option, the database will not be restored under the following conditions:

- The database already exists on the server
- The database name is different from the database name in the backup set
- The set of files in the database is different from the set of database files contained in the backup set

File size differences are not recognized by Microsoft SQL Server in the restore process, and they are not checked when a restore occurs.

Transact SQL Version Compatibility Levels

The *sp_dbcmptlevel* system stored procedure is the key to setting compatibility levels. After you have upgraded your databases to SQL Server 7 (see Chapter 13, "Upgrading SQL Server"), the compatibility level for your user databases can be set to what it was before you upgraded, and your application will behave as it did before you upgraded.

System databases will have a SQL Server 7 compatibility level. The compatibility level for the *model* system database is set to 70 initially. You can now change it to 60 or 65, and thereafter all your new databases will be created with the compatibility level you set in the model system database.

```
sp_dbcmptlevel [databasename, compatibilitylevel]
```

Each database can be assigned its own compatibility level.

Keywords change depending on the compatibility level. For 70, BACKUP, PERCENT, RESTORE, TOP are reserved words but are not at lower compatibility levels. For 65, AUTHORIZATION, CASCADE, CROSS, DISTRIBUTED, ESCAPE, FULL, INNER, JOIN, LEFT, OUTER, PRIVILEGES, RESTRICT, RIGHT, SCHEMA, WORK are reserved words but are not at compatibility level 60.

Simplification of Configuration Options

Many of the server configuration options from the Sybase legacy were obscure, and documentation on what to do with the options was scarce. The following configuration options have been *removed* from SQL Server 7:

- backup buffer size
- backup threads
- free buffers
- hash buckets
- LE threshold maximum
- LE threshold minimum
- LE threshold percent
- logwrite sleep
- max lazywrite IO
- open databases
- procedure cache
- RA cache hit limit
- RA cache miss limit
- RA delay
- RA pre-fetches
- RA slots per thread
- RA worker threads
- recovery flags
- remote conn timeout
- SMP concurrency

The following list shows what server configuration options are available in SQL Server 7:

- affinity mask
- allow updates
- cost threshold for parallelism
- cursor threshold
- default language
- default sortorder id
- fill factor (%)
- index create memory (KB)
- language in cache
- language neutral full-text
- lightweight pooling
- locks
- max async IO
- max degree of parallelism
- max server memory
- max text repl size
- max worker threads
- media retention
- min memory per query
- min server memory
- nested triggers
- network packet size
- open objects
- priority boost
- query governor cost limit
- query wait
- recovery interval
- remote access
- remote login timeout option
- remote proc trans
- remote query timeout
- resource timeout
- scan for startup procs
- set working set size
- show advanced options
- spin counter
- time slice (ms)
- Unicode comparison style
- Unicode locale id
- user connections
- user options

The updated server configuration options present a much clearer list of tuning opportunities on SQL Server. The sp_configure system stored procedure can be executed in the *master* system database to change the value of the configuration option.

```
sp_configure [configurationoption, value]
```

Some of the server configuration options are presented in the Enterprise Manager in a set of screens that you can access by selecting the SQL Server from the Enterprise Manager hierarchy tree, right-clicking, and selecting Properties. The General tab shows server information.

The Memory tab determines whether SQL Server will dynamically and automatically allocate memory or allow the user to set the memory. This corresponds to the memory server configuration options. The Processor tab allows you to set *max worker threads, priority boost, number of processors and minimum query plan threshold for considering queries for parallel execution.* The Security tab determines the authentication mode and SQL Server startup account as well as non-administrators use of SQLAgentCmdExec account when executing commands via xp_cmdshell.

The Connections tab sets the server configuration options of *maximum concurrent user connections, default connection options, remote server connections, remote query timeout, and enforcement of distributed transactions (MTS).* The Settings tab contains the options for *nested triggers, allow updates,* and *default language.* SQL Mail settings are also on this screen. Some options are considered Advanced Options. These are not present on the above screens and have to be set after you use the sp_configure system stored procedure to set the server configuration option to Show Advanced Options:

```
sp_configure 'Show Advanced Options', 1
GO
RECONFIGURE WITH OVERRIDE
GO
```

You can immediately change the configuration of server options that are considered dynamic, without stopping and starting the SQL Server, by using RECONFIGURE WITH OVERRIDE. Otherwise, the SQL Server must be stopped and restarted to change the runtime value.

Dynamic Schema Management

The ability to easily change a database schema is an important part of making the work of the database administrator more straightforward and more efficient. The ability to drop a column has been available in other relational products for years but has been missing from SQL Server. Now it is included in SQL Server 7, along with the ability to alter a view, trigger, or procedure.

Drop a Column

The ALTER TABLE Transact-SQL command now has the capability to drop a column. The DROP COLUMN argument to ALTER TABLE makes this possible.

```
ALTER TABLE tablename DROP COLUMN columnname
```

Alter a View, Trigger, or Procedure

ALTER VIEW, ALTER TRIGGER, and ALTER PROCEDURE are new Transact-SQL commands for SQL Server. This is helpful for the database administrator because permissions, dependent stored procedures, and triggers are not affected when these commands are executed. In previous versions, the views, triggers, and stored procedures had to be dropped and recreated. Permissions then had to be reapplied, and dependent stored procedures and triggers had to be recompiled.

UNIQUE IDENTIFIER Datatype and the Globally Unique Identifier

The uniqueidentifier datatype solves the problem of dealing with more than one table with an identity column that needs uniqueness among all the rows in all the tables. Now the union of the two tables still produces rows with globally unique identifiers. In previous versions, Transact-SQL programming was required to produce this globally unique ID.

The only operations that are allowed against a uniqueidentifier datatype are equality comparison operators (=, <, and >) and the IS NOT NULL and IS NULL operators. There is a new function called NEWID() that can be used to initialize a uniqueidentifier column or variable. To initialize a variable with a globally unique identifier (GUID):

```
DECLARE @var_1 uniqueidentifier
SET @var_1 = NEWID()
```

To initialize a column to a globally unique identifier:

```
UPDATE tablename
SET columnname = NEWID()
WHERE columnname = columnvalue
```

In summary, all of these new features contribute to making the role of the database administrator easier, more efficient, and more enjoyable.

Part II

Installation

Chapter 11

Installing SQL Server

This chapter will cover how to install SQL Server 7. If you have an existing SQL Server database from an earlier version, see Chapter 13, "Upgrading SQL Server." Figure 11-1 shows the first screen in the installation process, which is accessible by inserting the SQL Server CD-ROM and accessing the CD-ROM drive. The setup.exe program will automatically run, and a Windows graphical user interface screen appears and begins the install of SQL Server 7. If the setup.exe program does not run automatically or you are accessing it on a network drive, run the setup.exe program from the appropriate directory.

SQL Server offers three installation types:

- Typical
- Minimum
- Custom

Following are the indicators for which installation type to use. Read the indicators to figure out which installation type is best for your circumstances.

Perform a *typical installation* if the following conditions apply:

- No existing data to convert
- Network Protocols are Named Pipes, TCP/IP Sockets, and Multi-Protocol
- Default character set, 1252—ISO Character Set
- Default sort order, dictionary order, case-insensitive
- Default Unicode collation, general, case insensitive
- You wish to install all Client Management Tools
- You wish to install Online Books
- You wish to keep the default program file location of \MSSQL7
- You wish to keep the default data file location of \MSSQL7
- 148MB disk space is available

Perform a *minimum installation* if the following is true:

- You have a minimal disk space usage of 112MB
- You do not need Online Books

Use a *custom installation* if you need to convert SQL Server 6.x databases to SQL Server 7 (see Chapter 13, "Upgrading SQL Server") or if you need to change any of the following installation options:

- Network protocols
- Character set

- Sort order
- Unicode collation
- Server components to install
- Installation of online documentation
- Program file location
- Data file location
- Logon account for SQL Server
- Logon account for SQL Server Agent
- Autostart of SQL Server

Note *Use the Installation CD for SQL Server 7*

After you figure out which installation type to use, you will need to think about pre-installation preparation.

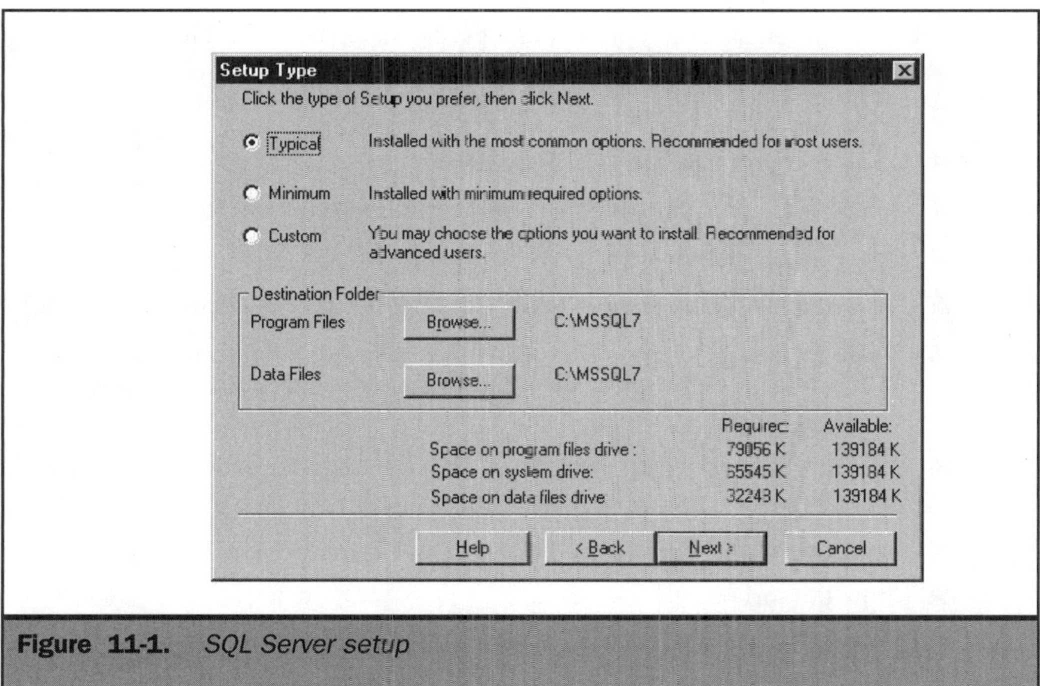

Figure 11-1. *SQL Server setup*

Pre-installation Preparation

It is always a good idea to prepare as much as possible before you install any type of application like SQL Server. First, verify that the write-caching disk controller is disabled on the computer running SQL Server 7. Failure to do this could result in database corruption later when you least expect it. There are some drives whose write-cache is safe for SQL Server. Discuss this with the hardware vendor and explain that SQL Server is a database system that depends on the write-ahead mechanism for recovery and there can be no loss of dirty pages. More and more write-caches come with battery backups and other mechanisms to help ensure this. Following are the physical tasks you need to perform before starting the installation process:

- Verify that you have enough disk space to install SQL Server 7
- Back up any existing SQL Server 6.x databases
- Close any other applications or applets running on the server before running the SQL Server setup program

You will also need to gather information and make some decisions before you start the setup program. Review the installation options and use the pre-installation preparation list provided below to write down your choices so that you will know what to select when you run the setup program.

The following pre-installation preparation list can help you assemble the information you need to install SQL Server 7:

- Verify that you have the required hardware
- Verify that you have the required software
- Decide which installation type (typical, minimal, custom) to use.
- Know the domain name
- Know the SQL Server name (taken from the Windows NT computer name)
- Create or use an existing Windows NT user account that starts the SQL Server services (SQL Server, SQL Server Agent and MSDTC can use the same or different accounts)
- Have a Windows NT user account with Administrator privileges to run SQL Server setup
- Know the character set
- Know the sort order
- Choose the default Unicode Collation or know which one to use
- Choose a SQL Server authentication mode (NT authentication or mixed)
- Know the primary SQL Server user name

- Know the company name
- Know you serial number
- Know which network protocols you are going to use
- Decide whether to install Online Books
- Know the location to place SQL Server data files
- Know the location to place program files
- Decide whether to use autostart for SQL Server

If you have questions about installation options items in the pre-installation preparation list, the following section, "Setup Options and Requirements," contains information that can help you make a decision.

Setup Options and Requirements

The following sections provide details about the components and requirements to consider in pre-installation preparation.

Equipment Needed

You will need both hardware and software in working order before you install SQL Server 7. The following tables cover the hardware and software requirements.

Hardware Component	Requirements
Computer	DEC Alpha AXP and compatible systems
	Intel and compatible systems 486/33 MHz or higher
	Pentium or Pentium PRO processor
Memory	Minimum 32MB of RAM. Don't skimp here. Install as much memory as you can afford or that your machine will hold. Sizing memory correctly will greatly enhance performance and give it enough room to support your application's use of SQL Server. When you have big tables with indexes, the system will perform better if it can retrieve from memory rather than paging the index to disk. If you do not have large amounts of data, you can install less memory.

Table 11-1. *Hardware Requirements*

Hardware Component	Requirements
Disc drive	Standard CD-ROM drive
Hard disk space—minimum installation	80MB
Hard disk space—typical installation	185MB
Hard disk space—custom installation	185MB *plus more* if you are upgrading from SQL Server 6.x
	If you are upgrading, you will need to plan for 1.5 times the space required by SQL Server 6.x non-system databases *in addition* to the 185MB. This is covered in the Chapter 13, "Upgrading SQL Server."
NT supported network adapter	Required only if you intend to use SQL Server on a network. For a stand-alone installation of SQL Server you will not need a network adapter.

Table 11-1. *Hardware Requirements* (continued)

Software Component	Requirements
Operating system	Windows NT Server 4.0 or workstation, Service Pack 4 and any subsequent version
Clients	Windows 95/98, Windows NT Workstation, UNIX, Apple Macintosh, and OS/2
	Small Business Server
Internet	Internet Explorer 4.01

Table 11-2. *Software Requirements*

Software Component	Requirements
Network software	If you are using Banyan VINES or AppleTalk ADSP, you will need additional network software.

Table 11-2. *Software Requirements* (continued)

Default Domain

If you intend to use a network, SQL Server is interested in the name of the default Windows domain for network users of trusted connections. When SQL Server is adding a security account, it prefaces the account name with the name of the default domain. You can see the domain name by using the Microsoft Windows Control Panel to access the Network icon.

Try not to install SQL Server on a Primary Domain Controller (PDC) or a Backup Domain Controller (BDC). These NT machines are busy taking care of the accounts database, authentication, and NT replication. Instead, install SQL Server on a Member server of a Domain. You can specify a Member server when you install Windows NT.

SQL Server Name

The first character of a SQL Server name can be alpha or underscore with no embedded spaces. Keep in mind that the name is actually the computer name chosen when the Microsoft Windows operating system was installed on the computer. You can easily change the name: go to the Windows Control Panel, click on the Network icon, the Identification tab, and the Change button. You will have to reboot the computer after the name is changed for the change to take effect.

SQL Server and SQL Server Agent and MSDTC Logon Accounts

If a domain user account (for interaction with other computers for distributed processing and replication) instead of a local system account is selected during installation, a Windows user account must be created prior to running the SQL Server setup program. Use the Windows NT User Manager to create the account.

Note *The User Manager can be invoked by pressing the Start Menu button, selecting Programs, Administrator Tools (Common), User Manager for Domains, New User.*

Select the Password Never Expires and User Can Not Change Password check boxes to avoid the problem of the password being changed at the user NT level rather than the SQL Server startup account level. This causes SQL Server to fail to start if a user tries to change the password. Clear the others. See Figure 11-2 to see this screen.

The new account must be a member of the Administrators group. Use the Group button on the New User screen to place the account in the Administrators or Domain Admins group.

When the user account has been given administrator privileges, it must be given Log on as a service right. After you select the user, select Policy. From the User Manager main menu in the command bar, select User Rights. At this screen, click in the Advanced Rights check box. If this check box is not checked, the Log on as service right will not appear in the drop down list box. Select Log on as Service right for the user account.

The screen shown in Figure 11-3 can be accessed by using the Microsoft Windows NT Start Menu | Programs | Administrator Tools (Common) | User Manager for Domains, then selecting User | Policy | User Rights, checking the Advanced Rights check box and, finally, selecting "Log on as a service" from the drop-down list.

You may set up separate accounts for SQL Server, SQL Server Agent and MSDTC, or you may use the same account. Choose the Use a Domain User Account in the setup program for SQL Server, SQL Server Agent and MSDTC.

Windows NT User Account with Administrator Privileges to Run SQL Server Setup

When you are installing SQL Server, log on to the system under a user account that is a member of the NT Administrators group or the Domain Admins group. Use the NT

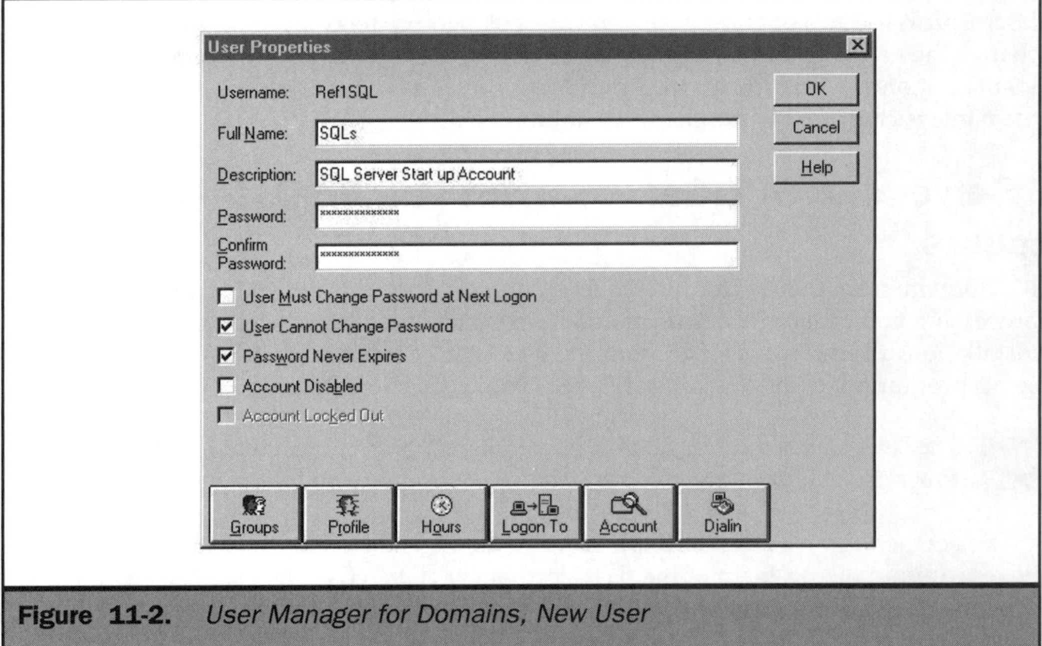

Figure 11-2. *User Manager for Domains, New User*

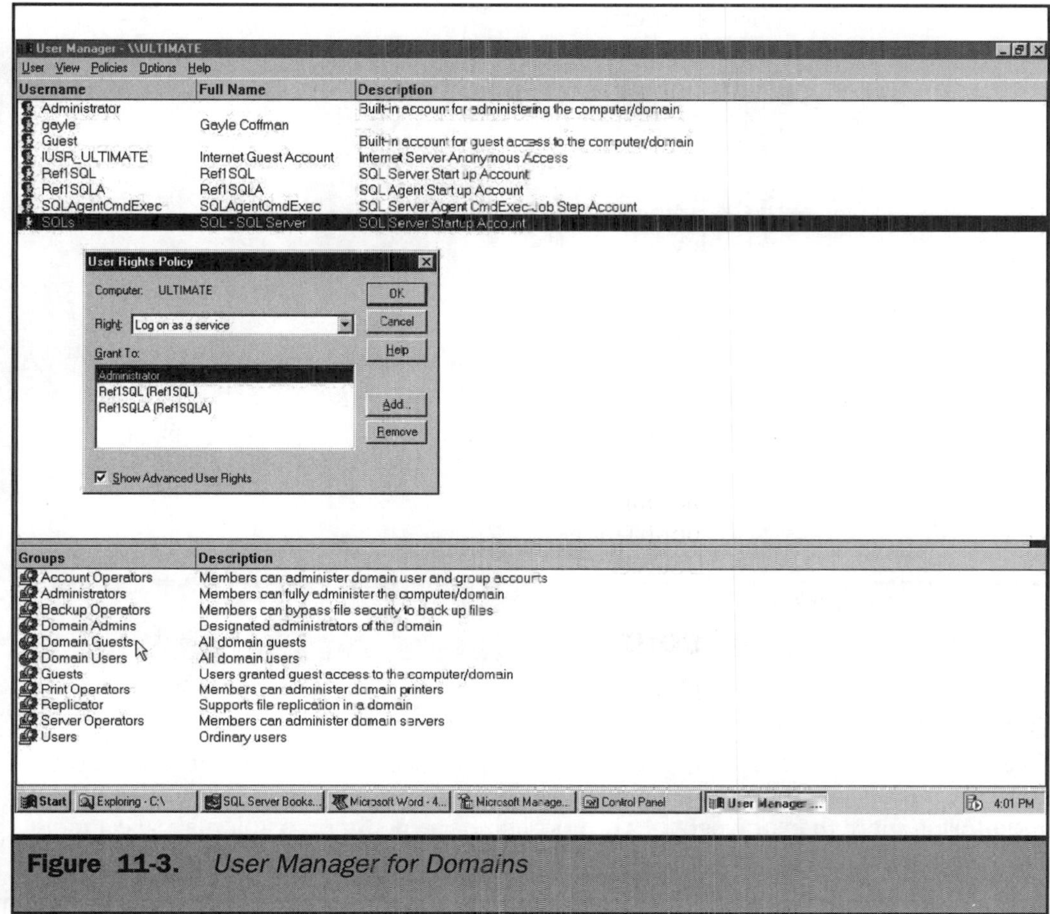

Figure 11-3. *User Manager for Domains*

User manager to verify that the account you are using to run setup is an account with system administration privileges.

User Name, Company, and Serial Number

You must enter the name of the primary responsible user of the SQL Server in the installation process. The company and serial number should be entered for purposes of support. You can find the serial number on the box in which your SQL Server installation CD was packaged

Convert Existing SQL Server Data to SQL Server 7

The process to convert existing SQL Server 6.x data is an option that exists when doing a custom installation. This process will be covered in detail in Chapter 13, "Upgrading SQL Server." For purposes of this discussion, however, we are not converting, and the radio button entitled "Yes, run the SQL Server Upgrade Wizard" is not checked, as shown in Figure 11-4.

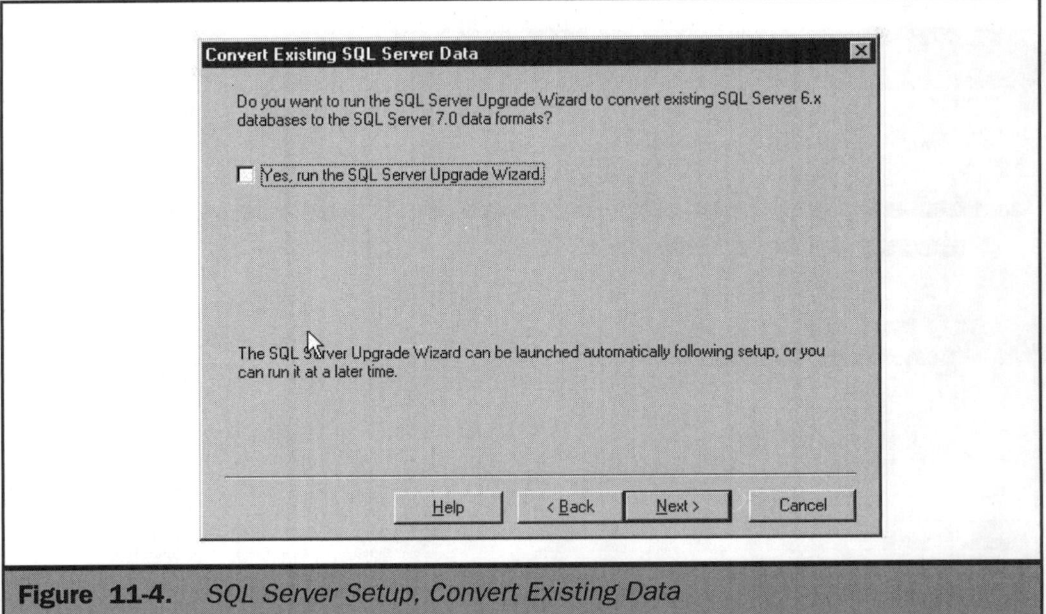

Figure 11-4. *SQL Server Setup, Convert Existing Data*

Network Protocols

The Network Protocols setup option allows you to choose which network libraries to use to communicate between the clients and the server. SQL Server is capable of monitoring more than one network protocol at the same time, so you may select more than one of the network protocols listed in Table 11-3.

Network Protocol	Description
Named Pipes	Named Pipes is the default for SQL Server running on Windows NT. SQL Server listens on the standard pipe, \\.\pipe\sql\query, for named pipe connections.
TCP/IP Sockets	TCP/IP Sockets is the default for Windows 95. Windows Sockets are used and you are required to type the port number. The default is 1433, the official Internet Assigned Number Authority (IANA) socket number for SQL Server. If you set up SQL Server to listen on a proxy server using Microsoft Proxy Server over TCP/IP Sockets, see the section, "Data Encryption" in Chapter 9.

Table 11-3. *Available Network Protocols*

Network Protocol	Description
Multiprotocol Net-Library	The Multiprotocol Net-Library uses the Windows NT remote procedure call (RPC) facility. Windows NT Authentication moves over the TCP/IP Windows Sockets, NWLink IPX/SPX, and Named Pipes protocols. Multiprotocol supports encryption; see Chapter 9.
NWLink IPX/SPX	This net library is used for Novell IPX clients. You will be asked for the Novell Bindery service name (the default is the computer name of the SQL Server) to register SQL Server on the Novell network.
AppleTalk ADSP	Apple Macintosh-based clients use this to connect to SQL Server. When installing this net library, you will be asked for the AppleTalk service object name. You may enter the SQL Server computer name if you choose.
Banyan VINES	Banyan VINES support for Windows NT-based clients and servers is available only for SQL Server on the Intel platform. You will be asked for a StreetTalk service name that can be created using the Vines software program called MSERVICE. Servicename@group@org is the format to enter the StreetTalk service name.

Table 11-3. *Available Network Protocols* (continued)

The network protocols available to SQL Server are shown in Figure 11-5.

Character Set

It is important that the correct character set for your application is chosen *during* the installation process. The default character set is code page 1252 (ISO Character Set).

A character set is a set of 256 uppercase and lowercase letters, digits, and symbols. The last 128 characters differ from one character set to another. These are the characters that SQL Server can store in the database. Different languages use a different set of the last 128 characters. In order for SQL Server to store the special characters of these different languages, the character set has to be the right one for the language. Table 11-4 describes some of the character sets.

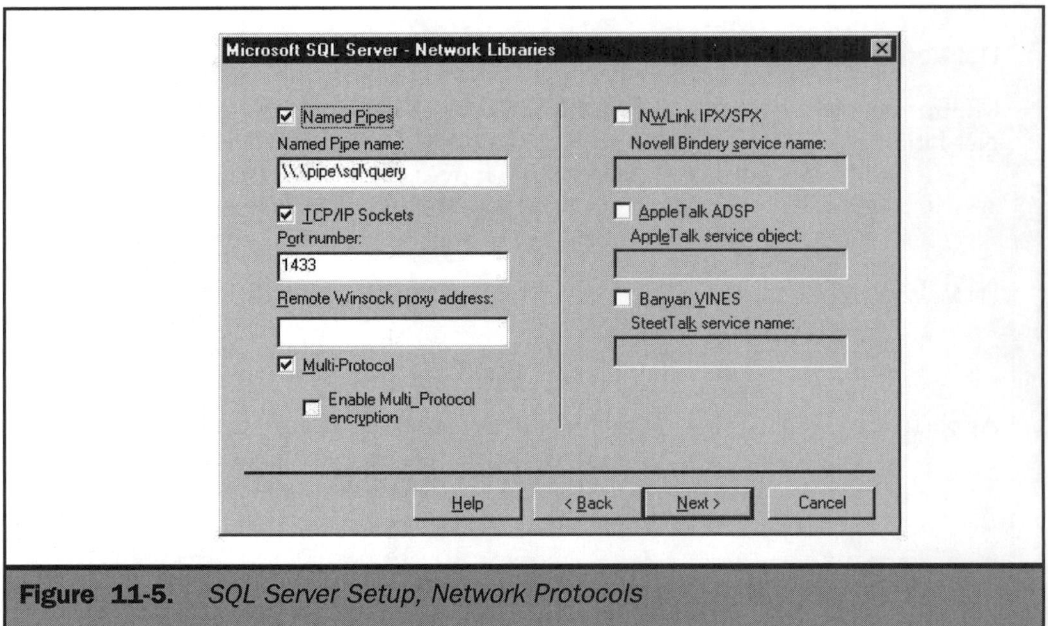

Figure 11-5. *SQL Server Setup, Network Protocols*

SQL Server Character Set	Description
Code page 1252	ISO Character Set—the SQL Server default character set. This character set is also called the ANSI character set.
Code page 850	Multilingual—the character set for European, North American, and South American languages. This is good for MS DOS applications using extended characters.
Code page 437	U.S. English—includes graphics not normally used in databases. Use code page 1252 (the default) instead to get more compatibility with other languages besides U.S. English.
Code page 932	Japanese
Code page 936	Chinese, simplified

Table 11-4. *SQL Server 7 Character Sets*

SQL Server Character Set	Description
Code page 949	Korean
Code page 950	Chinese, traditional
Code page 1250	Central European
Code page 1251	Cyrillic
Code page 1253	Greek
Code page 1254	Turkish
Code page 1255	Hebrew
Code page 1256	Arabic
Code page 1257	Baltic

Table 11-4. *SQL Server 7 Character Sets* (continued)

There is a new feature called the Unicode datatype that allows columns to store data from more than one character set. This is handy if you get into a situation where you need to import data from other languages into a SQL Server database.

Sort Order

It is important that the correct sort order for your application is specified *during* the installation process. The default sort order is Dictionary sort order, case insensitive. Sort order specifies how the data is sorted when Transact-SQL statements are issued that have GROUP BY, ORDER BY, and DISTINCT clauses. There is a different set of sort orders to choose from for every character set. For example, the sort orders you can choose from for the default character set of Code Page 1252, ISO Character Set are:

- Dictionary order, case-insensitive
- Binary order
- Dictionary order, case-sensitive
- Dictionary order, case-insensitive, uppercase preference
- Dictionary order, case-insensitive, accent-insensitive
- Danish/Norwegian dictionary order, case-insensitive, uppercase preference
- Icelandic dictionary order, case-insensitive, uppercase preference

- Swedish/Finnish (standard) dictionary order, case-insensitive, uppercase preference
- Swedish/Finnish (phonetic) dictionary order, case-insensitive, uppercase preference

Each character set has a different list of available sort orders.

Unicode Collation

If you have Unicode datatypes in your database, a Unicode collation is specified which determines how to sort the Unicode columns. This is different from the regular sort order. The installation program will offer you default Unicode collation depending on the character set and sort order you have chosen. Know what you are doing if you choose a Unicode collation other than the default. Your SQL Server 6.x objects may fail the conversion to SQL Server 7 unless you choose the default Unicode collation, as shown in Figure 11-6.

Management Tools

There are several utilities that are always installed by the setup program:

- BCP
- ISQL
- OSQL

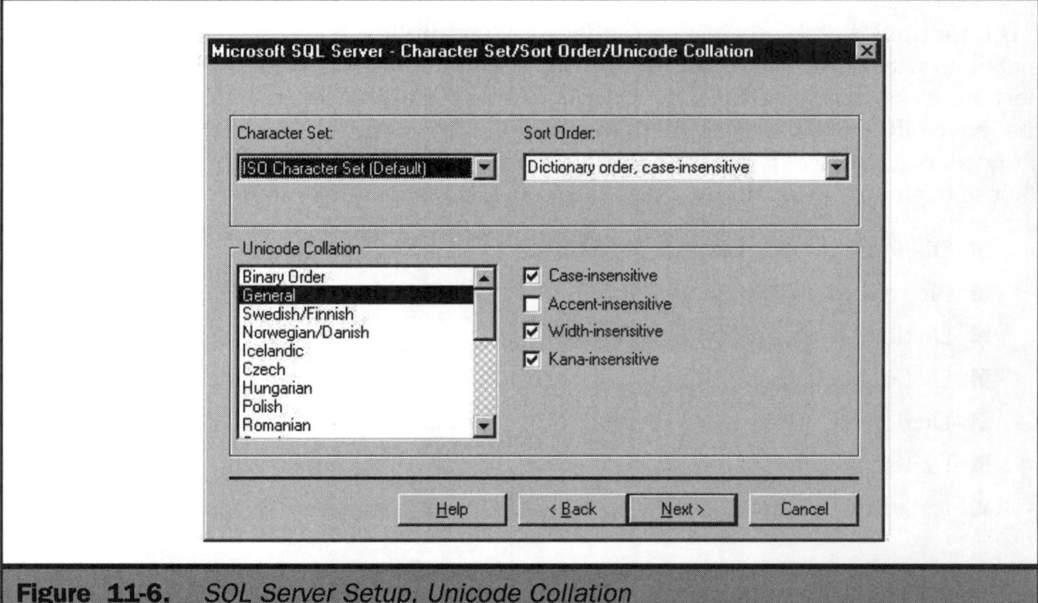

Figure 11-6. *SQL Server Setup, Unicode Collation*

There are other optional utilities you can also install during the setup installation process.

The Select Components screen gives you choices to install Server Components (Server, Upgrade Tools, Replication Support or Full Text Search), Management Tools (Enterprise Manager, Profiler, Query Analyzer, DTC Client Support, Replication Conflict Resolution), Client Connectivity, Books Online, and Development Tools (Headers and Libraries, Virtual Device Interface).

Authentication Mode

The SQL Server 7 authentication modes are:

Authentication Mode	Type of Login Allowed
Windows NT Authentication	Windows NT logins
Mixed Authentication	SQL Server and Windows NT logins

If you are unsure which to use refer to Chapter 5, "Integration with Windows NT Security" for an explanation of your choices. You can choose this after you have installed and registered SQL Server 7. Use the Enterprise Manager to register and select the server, right-click and then select Properties, and then select the Security tab (see Figure 11-7).

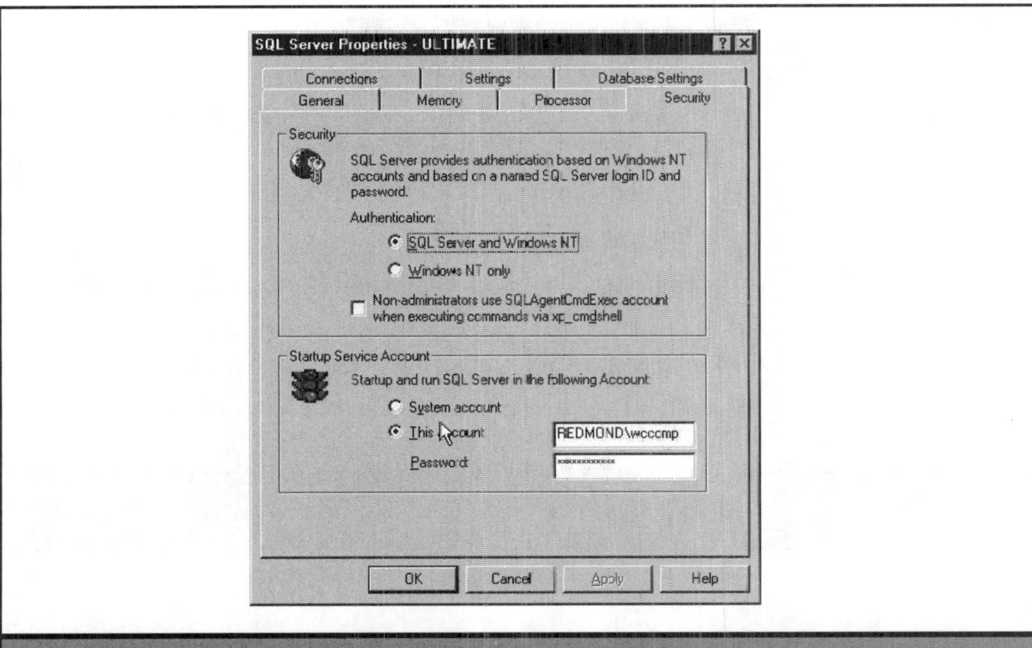

Figure 11-7. *Enterprise Manager, Security*

Location of Program Files

The default location is C:\ MSSQL7 for Windows NT and Windows 95 installations; however, you may change the location of the installation to another drive and directory name. You must conform to the "eight-dot-three" naming convention for the directory name you use to replace MSSQL7. The subset of directories listed in Table 11-5 is created upon installation under the drive and directory you specify in the installation setup and contains the program files.

Location of Management Tools Files

The default location is C:\ MSSQL7 for Windows NT and Windows 95 installations. The subdirectories listed in Table 11-6 are created upon installation under the drive and directory you specify in the installation setup and contain the utility files.

Subdirectory	Program Files
\Bin	Client executable files, Windows DLL files
\Binn	Client and server executable files, DLLs, and online Help files
\Books	SQL Server Books Online files
\Charsets	Character set and sort order files
\Include	OLEDB include (*.h) files
\Install	Installation scripts and associated output files created during the install of SQL Server
\Lib	OLEDB library (*.lib) files
\Samples	Programming example files
\Snmp	Simple Network Management Protocol (SNMP) files
\Symbols	Libraries that can be used to generate stack backups and traces for Windows NT 4.0 and subsequent versions
\Upgrade	Files used and created during the upgrade from SQL Server 6.x to SQL Server 7

Table 11-5. *Subdirectories Containing Program Files*

Subdirectory	Utility Files
\Binn	Client executable files
\Books	SQL Server Books Online files
\HTML	Help files
\Include	OLEDB include (*.h) files
\Lib	OLEDB library (*.lib) files
\Samples	Programming example files
\Upgrade	Files used for upgrading
\System32 directory for Windows	DB-Library and Net-Library DLLs

Table 11-6. *Subdirectories Containing Tools Files*

Location of Data Files

The default location is C:\ MSSQL7 for Windows NT and Windows 95 installations; however, you may change the location of the installation to another drive and directory name. You must conform to the "eight-dot-three" naming convention for the directory name you use to replace MSSQL7. The subdirectories listed in Table 11-7 are created upon installation under the drive and directory you specify in the installation setup and contain the data files.

Subdirectory	Data Files
\Backup	Backup files
\Data	Data files and database log files
\Log	Error log files
\Repldata	Replication working directory for replication files

Table 11-7. *Subdirectories Containing Data Files*

Autostart SQL Server and SQL Server Agent

The setup program initially determines whether you want the SQL Server service and the SQL Server Agent service to start automatically when NT is started. The default is for the service not to start automatically. If you have a production system, you will probably want the service to start automatically. This will prevent SQL Server from becoming inaccessible in the event that NT is restarted. After the installation process is complete, you can change the autostart properties of the service at a later time if you decide you would like to do it differently. You can change this later by using the Enterprise Manager, selecting your server, and then right-clicking and selecting Properties from the shortcut menu.

Server Standards

It is a good idea to establish a set of installation standards for installing SQL Server on an NT server. If you have a large corporation with different server sizes, standardize the size of your servers and establish standards for each size.

Establish which type of hardware recovery you will have on each partition. Figure out where your Program Files and Data Files are to go, and stay with the standard when you install SQL Server on different machines.

Removing SQL Server

If you need to remove SQL Server from your computer, use the Remove SQL Server option of the setup program. There are check boxes in this process that can be checked that will remove program files and data files. You may remove only the program files and/or the databases. You may also issue a command at the command prompt to remove SQL Server.

```
C:\Mssql7\Binn\Setup /t RemoveAll = WARN
```

Maintaining Installation Standards Using Unattended Installation

An unattended installation is made possible by creating an initialization file with settings for each installation option. You can start setup.exe from the command prompt and Use SQL Server Agent running on another machine to perform the installation at a scheduled time. To create the file, install SQL Server as you would like to see the options set and look for the SQLInstS.ini in the C:MSSQL7\INSTALL directory. You can use this file as a starting point and edit it as requirements and standards change. You edit it and enter the password for the accounts that run the SQL Server and SQL

Server Agent services. Use only the Local Installation Option, as the Remote Installation option is not available for unattended installations.

To create a Setup initialization file, you may use any text editor to create a file to enter the setup information in the same format as the SQLInstS.ini in the C:MSSQL7\INSTALL directory. Save the file with the *.ini* extension, making sure it has correct values, as there is no built-in error checking. You can also create a custom script and run it during installation. The path\filename must be referenced in the Setup initialization file.

The command line syntax to run an unattended installation is:

```
Setup /t IniFilePath = setupinitializationfilename
```

The Setup initialization file must be edited both before and after you use it because it contains the password for the SQLServerAgent service startup account, and you do not want this information in an operating system file. If you run the following command line syntax you will see the documentation for the setup parameters.

```
Setup /?
```

Remote Installation

As you install SQL Server, you may install SQL Server locally or remotely. If you would like to install SQL Server on a machine other than the computer on which you are running the setup program, choose the Remote option. You must be able to reach the remote machine on your network and enter the name of the remote machine and the disk drive to install SQL Server.

The Complete Reference

Chapter 12

Installing SQL Mail

SQL Mail is the mail service that uses the mail application programming interface (MAPI), an application programming interface (API) that enables SQL Server to send and receive e-mail messages. SQL Mail uses extended stored procedures that come with the installation of Microsoft SQL Server.

Windows NT Messaging Service

The NT server has built-in Messaging services that work with SQL Server and enable it to send e-mail. SQL Mail is often used with Microsoft Outlook, Microsoft Exchange, Microsoft Windows NT Mail, or some other MAPI to send and receive electronic mail.

NT messaging may not have been installed when Windows NT was installed. When you need to install SQL Mail, you may have to install the NT Messaging Service first if it is not already installed.

The steps are:

1. Log on to NT as the account that is running the SQL Server service on the local machine.
2. Double-click on the Inbox icon. A message appears asking if you would like to install Windows NT Messaging. This indicates wheter or not it is installed.
3. You will need access to the NT installation CD ROM drive and the I386 directory. If the system prompts you to overwrite new files, respond in the negative.

The MAPI interface requires that a client mail program be installed on the Windows NT server in order for SQL Mail to work. Microsoft Outlook or Microsoft Exchange works well with SQL Mail and can be installed on the Windows NT server to create a mail client.

Setup of SQL Mail

In order for SQL Mail to run successfully on Microsoft SQL Server, you must have installed a client mail application on the server. In addition, a Mail post office, which is located on another server, must be available. Finally, you must start the Mail client under the SQL Server startup account. This means that SQL Server must be configured to use a mail account that is either the same as the MSSQLServer startup account or is an Exchange mailbox owned by the MSSQLServer startup account.

SQL Mail Prerequisites

Before you start the configuration and setup of SQL Mail, it is helpful to know the SQL Mail prerequisites:

- A mail client program installed on the Microsoft SQL Server computer
- An Exchange mailbox owned by the SQL Server service startup account
- An NT account that functions as the SQL Server service startup account and that owns the Exchange mailbox
- The name of the Exchange mail server

The NT Account

You will need an NT account which owns the Exchange mailbox and can be used as the SQL Server startup account.

You can run the Service Manager to view the SQL Server startup account by typing the following at a command prompt:

```
srvmgr \\servername
```

When the Service Manager starts, choose Computer | Services and select the MSSQLServer service from the list of services as shown in Figure 12-1.

Press the Startup button to see the account used to start the MSSQLServer service as shown in Figure 12-2.

Make this Windows NT account the owner of the mailbox.

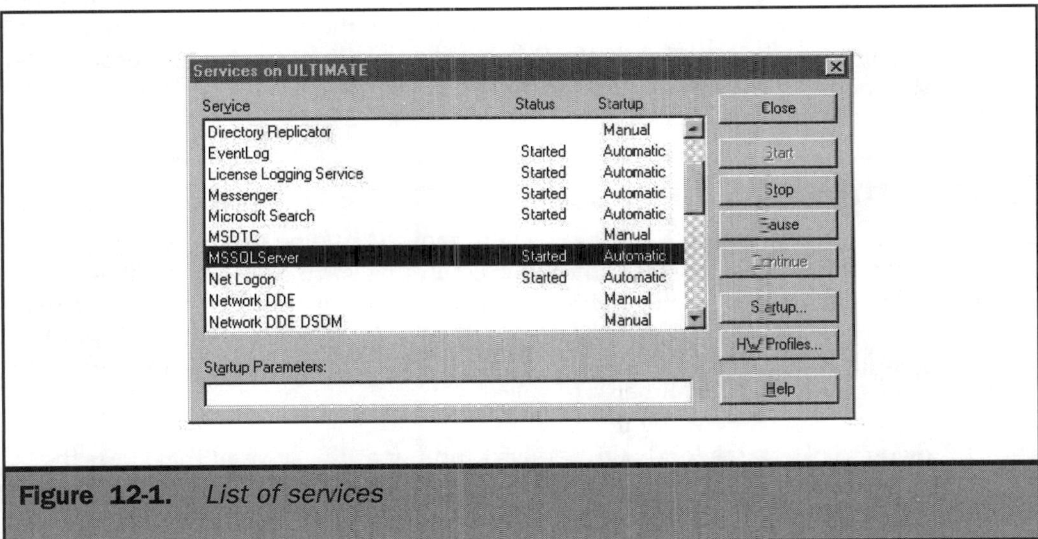

Figure 12-1. *List of services*

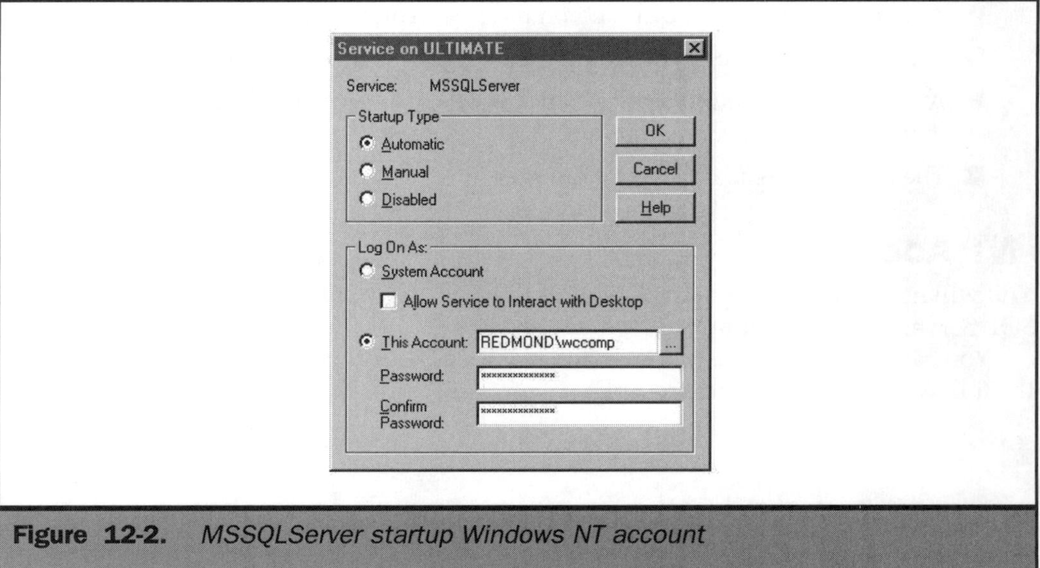

Figure 12-2. *MSSQLServer startup Windows NT account*

The Exchange Mailbox

Let us use the Microsoft Exchange mail program on the SQL Server computer and start by having the mail administrator make the owner of the mailbox the same NT account that starts SQL Server. It is possible to have co-owners of the mailbox. Users of the mailbox can also be configured to be the Database Administrators that are responsible for SQL Mail on SQL Server.

Installing the Microsoft Exchange Mail Client

If you choose to use Microsoft Exchange as your mail client, you will probably want the owner of the mailbox to be the same NT account that starts SQL Server (it is possible to have co-owners of the mailbox, and users of the mailbox can be configured to be the Database Administrators that are responsible for SQL Mail on SQL Server). Follow these steps to install Exchange as a client on the SQL Server computer:

1. Log on to NT on the local SQL Server computer as the account that starts the SQL Server service.
2. Install the Exchange Mail Client on the SQL Server by running the mail program's setup.exe.
3. Select a Typical installation and press the button.

4. When asked for a name, enter the name of the Exchange mailbox owned by the SQL Server service startup Windows NT Account.
5. Finish the Exchange client installation.
6. Start Exchange on the client by double-clicking on the icon created on the desktop by the installation of the mail client or by selecting it from the NT menu.
7. Remove any services that are not Microsoft Exchange Server.
8. Continue through the screens on remote usage (select no) and Personal Address Book.
9. When prompted for allowing Exchange to start automatically when NT is started, select Do Not Add.
10. Complete the installation.
11. Start Exchange. Choose Tools | Options and the Send tab. Uncheck the Save a Copy of the Item in the Sent Items Folder check box. This prevents you having to clear the sent items when the folder becomes full.
12. Go back to the Inbox and send mail to verify the install.
13. Choose File | Exit and log off the Exchange client program.
14. Use the Enterprise Manager to configure the properties.
15. Check the Auto Start Mail Client check box and enter the mailbox name in the Profile name field as shown in Figure 12-3.
16. Stop and then restart SQL Server.
17. Check the SQL Server error log to see if SQL Mail started.

If SQL Mail fails to start or you see errors in the SQL Server error log, see the following section on problem solving.

Problem-solving Techniques If SQL Mail Fails To Start

If SQL Server fails to start, check for the following:

- MAPI errors in the SQL Server error log:
  - Is SQL Server running under the NT account that owns the mailbox?
  - Is the SQL Server Mail login in the setup program correct for SQL Server and SQL Server Agent?
  - Exchange running on the SQL Server, started under the SQL Server service startup account?

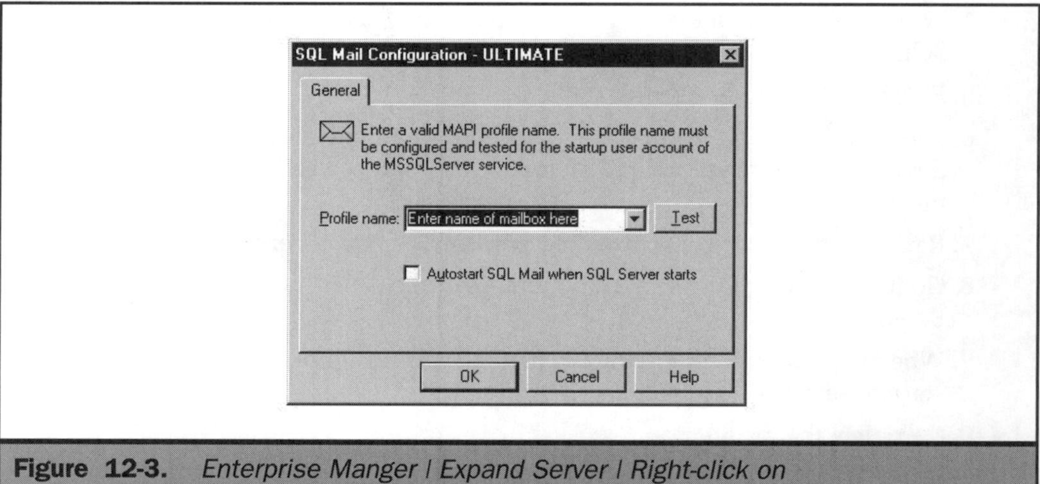

Figure 12-3. *Enterprise Manger | Expand Server | Right-click on SQL Mail | Properties*

- If SQL Mail stops responding, cycle SQL Server.
- Make sure the Mail Messaging service is installed on Windows NT by double-clicking on the inbox icon on the desktop. If you are asked if you want to install the service, it means that Windows NT Messaging is not installed, so proceed through the installation.

SQL Mail Extended Stored Procedures

Extended stored procedures that are used with SQL Mail include xp_startmail, xp_stopmail, xp_sendmail, xp_readmail, xp_processmail, xp_findnextmsg, and xp_deletemail. Only the system administrator (SA) can execute the SQL Mail extended stored procedures; however, the SA can grant execution of the extended stored procedures to other users. See Chapter 23, "System Stored Procedures," for more information on the use of the SQL Mail extended stored procedures listed above.

Starting and Stopping SQL Mail

There are a couple of different ways to stop and start SQL Mail. You can use the Enterprise Manager or execute the extended stored procedures provided with SQL Server for this purpose. You can also choose the Query Analyzer from the Tools Menu in the Enterprise Manager and use the xp_startmail or xp_stopmail extended stored procedures within the Query Analyzer window.

The following command can be executed in the Query Analyzer window to start SQL Mail.

```
xp_startmail
GO
```

The following command can be executed in the Query Analyzer window to stop SQL Mail.

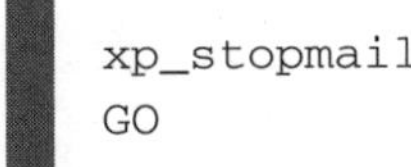

```
xp_stopmail
GO
```

To use the Enterprise Manager, expand the server and right-click on SQL Mail. The shortcut menu will give you the choice whether to Stop or Start SQL Mail.

Sending Mail from SQL Server

You can e-mail a simple message, a query result set, or an attachment from SQL Mail. Use the Query Analyzer located in the Tools menu of the Enterprise Manager to issue the xp_sendmail stored procedure.

A simple way to check if SQL Server is capable of sending mail is to issue the following command from the Query Analyzer window:

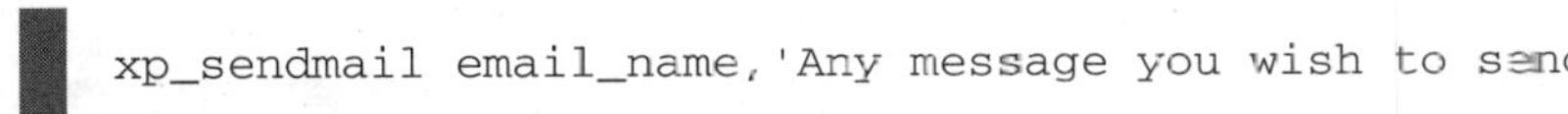

```
xp_sendmail email_name,'Any message you wish to send'
```

The message Mail Sent will appear, and the e-mail will appear in the email_name inbox.

See Chapter 23, "System Stored Procedures," for more information on the use of the SQL Mail extended stored procedure listed above. SQL Mail also has the capability to e-mail you with the results of a query.

SQL Mail and SQL Server Agent

If you want to use SQL Mail to work with the SQL Server Agent in order to notify a database administrator via e-mail when an alert occurs or when a scheduled task has succeeded or failed, you must set up the SQL Mail profile for SQL Server Agent. In order to accomplish this task, expand the server in the Enterprise Manager and select SQL Server Agent. Right-click on SQL Server Agent and then on Properties (see Figure 12-4). Select the SQL Mail button in the General tab and enter the NT account name that is the same as the MSSQLService startup account.

If you are using SQL Mail with the SQL Server Agent, you can set SQL Mail to automatically start whenever the SQL Server Agent service is started—even when SQL Server Agent stops and then restarts. Messages can be sent wherever the extended stored procedures can be invoked, such as at a call from a trigger or stored procedure

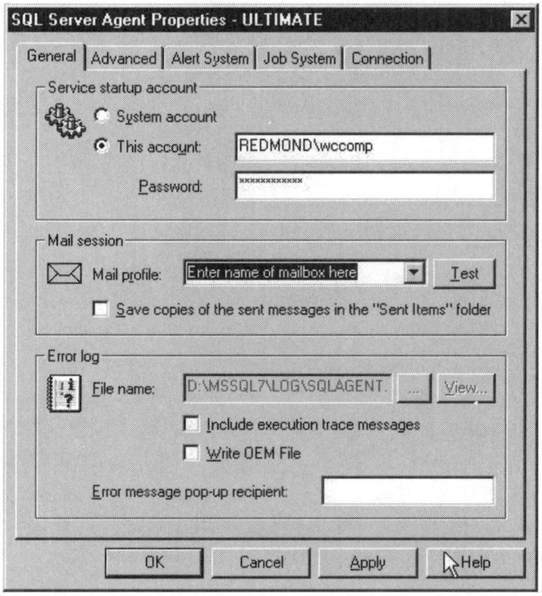

Figure 12-4. *SQL Server Agent Properties in Enterprise Manager*

or from within a script file. SQL Mail can also be used with the SQL Server Profiler to send mail when a performance threshold is reached.

The SQL Server Agent (formerly known as SQL Executive) has been enhanced to take full advantage of SQL Mail installed on SQL Server. See Chapter 4, "SQL Server Agent," for details on how to use the SQL Server Agent and SQL Mail together to notify you in the event of an alert or job failure.

The Complete Reference

Chapter 13

Upgrading SQL Server

You might think that upgrading to Microsoft SQL Server 7 is a complex process fraught with difficulty. Actually, it is a simple process to get your application up and running on version 7 and looking and running just as it did on your previous version because the compatibility level is set by default to the current user's previous version. However, you do need double the disk space so you can retain the 6.x version. This allows you to start developing and taking advantage of the new version 7 functionality at your own pace.

The compatibility level can also be changed to 60 (version 6.0), 65 (version 6.5), or 70 (version 7.0) behavior after the upgrade. You are still getting version 7 functionality, for example, the lowest cost locking strategy (row, page, or table based on input from the Query Optimizer at runtime). But keep in mind that after the upgrade, the compatibility level of the *model* system database is at 70. This means that all new databases will be created with version 7 behavior unless you execute the *sp_dbcmptlevel* stored procedure and set the compatibility level in the *model* system database to 65.

One of the great features of SQL Server's upgrade process is that the two versions can exist side by side on one computer. Every step of the upgrade process has been designed to protect the 6.x databases. However, installing Microsoft SQL Server version 7 replaces several common library files on your system, and uninstalling version 7 does not automatically return your SQL Server 6.x or Windows NT Server installation to its original state.

The installations that may encounter problems are those applications that are referencing the system tables directly and those that have management-type tools using SQL DMO. Since SQL DMO, tasks in SQL Executive, replication, and many configuration settings have changed. If your application is changing configuration settings dynamically or using these features, you may need to change your code. User objects created in the master system database will assume version 7 behavior because the *master* system database must remain at a compatibility level of 70 for SQL Server to function correctly. You cannot change the compatibility level in the master system database.

Microsoft thought long and hard about the conversion process and decided that the architecture must be changed to set the stage for the next 20 years in terms of quality, performance, scalability, and flexibility, so the conversion of your databases from version 6.x to version 7 requires an on-disk change. Your objects will be compiled and the data will move from version 6.x disk format to version 7 disk format because the size of the datapage has changed from 2K in version 6.x to 8K in version 7.0.

When to Upgrade

It is best to upgrade to new service packs and new versions as soon as they become available. Sometimes this can become a problem if you have an application that is developed by an outside vendor and the vendor is slow to move to the new service pack or version. Encourage the vendor to upgrade in a timely manner. If you do not think you can upgrade your production system, then upgrade your test systems or even a desktop computer so you can stay on top of the learning curve. The Microsoft SQL Server database technology is moving very fast. These improvements are what make Microsoft SQL Server such an exciting product to use year after year, but if you are facing a full-version upgrade there will be many new things to learn at once.

Upgrade Planning

The most important point in the planning process is to avoid surprises. Plan a training period and a dress rehearsal to familiarize yourself with the upgrade process and to determine if your application has problems such as stored procedures referencing a non-existent table, code-referencing system tables that have changed in version 7, and any other problems that are specific to your application. Give yourself enough time to identify and address anything that may occur. Microsoft support can be contacted to answer any questions, although most applications will not experience any problem at all. Microsoft has converted over 1,000 database in their 1K Challenge conversion program and they have anticipated and coded for many of the problems that can arise. SQL DMO, tasks in SQL Executive, replication, and many configuration settings have changed, so it is a good idea to set up a test system and run through the upgrade on a non-production machine if possible. This may not be possible for large systems because of hardware constraints. In that case, you can back out of this process at any time with your 6.x environment intact. In fact, you can even stop in the middle of the process and restart the process where you left off.

There are some things that you will want to do before you begin the upgrade:

- Back up your SQL Server 6.x environment.
- Make sure that your tempdb system database is at least 25 MB in your 6.x version.
- Make sure that your SQL Server 6.x version has an adequate amount of memory to run DBCC efficiently, as this will speed up the process (version 7 sizes memory dynamically).
- Make sure all the database users in your user databases have SQL Server logins in the *master* system database and correct any that are orphaned (*sysusers* system table, *syslogins* system table joined by *suid*). Check your *sysalternates* system table entries as well.
- Make sure the MSSQLServer service startup account is a Domain user account and not a LocalSystem account for both SQL Server versions.
- Make sure the SQLExecutive and SQLServerAgent service startup accounts are Domain user accounts and not LocalSystem accounts.
- Make sure you have at least 200MB free disk space to perform the Microsoft SQL Server 7 installation and upgrade, plus enough free space to copy the

objects and data in the databases you have chosen for upgrade. See the "Side-by-Side (Single Machine)" and "Computer-to-Computer (Two Machines)" sections later in this chapter for more details.

- If you have replication, install the latest 6.5 Service Pack, stop replication, and let the logreader empty.
- Make sure that you are running, at a minimum, Windows NT Server 4.0, Service Pack 4.
- If your databases are referencing objects in each other, upgrade all dependent databases at the same time.
- Make sure the default database for each login ID is upgraded with the databases you are upgrading or that the default database already exists in version 7.
- Close all your applications and stop your SQL Server services before beginning the upgrade process.

Before You Upgrade

Before you upgrade, read the section below that applies to the version you are currently running.

Upgrading from Version 4.2.1

If you need to upgrade from Microsoft SQL Server version 4.2.1, you must first upgrade to version 6.5 and the latest service pack before you can perform the upgrade to version 7. You will also need to upgrade NT Server 4.0 to the latest service pack available.

Upgrading from Version 6.0

It is best to upgrade your Microsoft SQL Server 6.0 installation to Microsoft SQL Server 6.5 and the latest service pack. However, it is possible to upgrade from Microsoft SQL Server 6.0 to 7.0. There can be some anomalies with the way GRANT/REVOKES worked in 6.0. As you know, there is a sp_dbcmptlevel 60 option designed to maintain compatibility with 6.0.

Upgrading from Version 6.5

When you are upgrading from Microsoft SQL Server 6.5 to version 7.0, you must apply the latest SQL Server service pack before starting the upgrade.

Version Upgrade Utility

You may either perform a side-by-side upgrade or a computer-to-computer upgrade with the Version Upgrade Utility. The Utility is optionally installed with SQL Server 7 and is available as a choice in the Microsoft SQL Server Program group on the NT Menu. This type of utility is not usually presented, but since about 80 percent of SQL Server was rewritten for version 7 and many of the key components were changed, this utility is necessary to perform the complicated process of converting a 6.5 database to a 7.0 database. The Version Upgrade Utility is very useful, especially considering the entire database and all of the associated data has to be rewritten into the Microsoft SQL Server 7 disk format.

The amount of disk space required affects which of the upgrade scenarios you will use. Additionally, if you have replication, you must use a side-by-side upgrade scenario. Whatever the scenario, you will need at least double the space taken by your current database to convert from 6.x to version 7.0. Many corporate budgets will be impacted by this disk space requirement unless the database technicians were schooled early in what to expect regarding space needs for upgrades and communicated the need to budgeters in the corporation.

You can choose your upgrade options as shown in Figure 13-1. Export and Import options as well as the data transfer method can be selected.

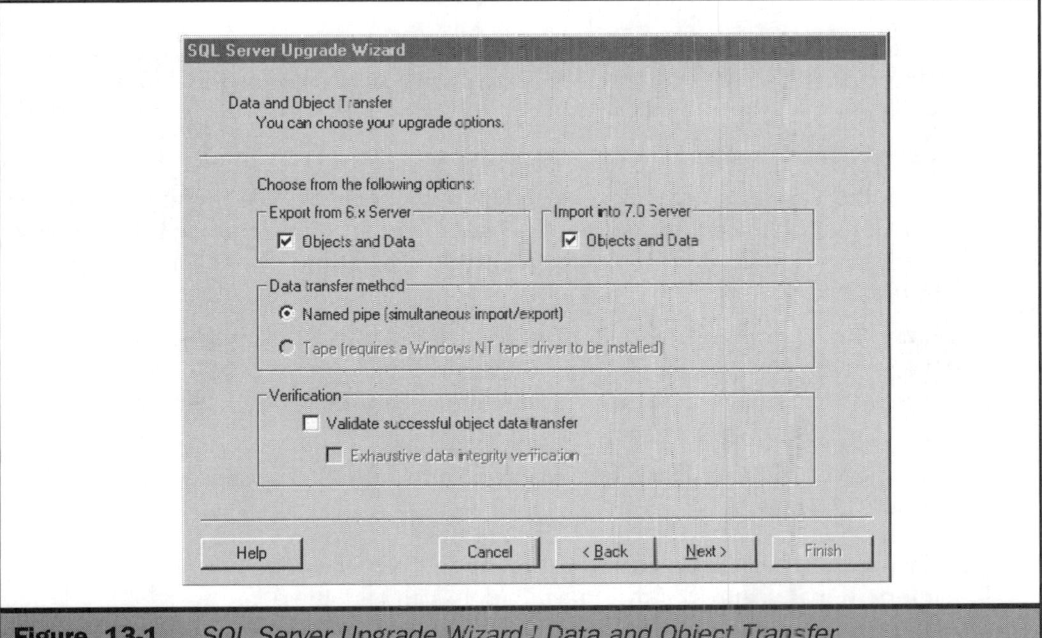

Figure 13-1. *SQL Server Upgrade Wizard ! Data and Object Transfer*

Side-by-Side Upgrade (Single Machine)

A side-by-side upgrade scenario means that you are installing Microsoft SQL Server version 7 on a computer that already has Microsoft SQL Server version 6.x. The data moves through one of the following methods:

- A disk-to-disk named pipe connection
- A tape drive backup
- A network share

A disk-to-disk named pipe connection is the fastest method and is used when you have enough disk space on your computer and can move data directly through a named pipe connection. You need 1.5 times the size of the databases and the associated log files if you are to use the disk-to-disk named pipe connection.

If you do not have enough disk space, you can use the Version Upgrade Wizard to export the version 6.x catalog, data, objects, and databases to a tape drive or network share. The Version Upgrade Wizard removes the SQL Server 6.x devices and reuses the disk space. Run the Version Upgrade Wizard again to import and upgrade the exported data, objects, and databases from the tape drive backup or network share.

Here are the steps you should follow to perform a side-by-side version upgrade:

1. Choose the Version Upgrade Wizard from the SQL Server 7 program group.
2. At the wizard screen, click the Next button.
3. Select Objects and Data check boxes from Export From 6.x and Import To 7.0 blocks on the screen (these selections are already marked as the default selections).
4. Click Named Pipe or Disk or Tape as the data transfer method.
5. Click the Validate successful object data transfer check box. If you feel you need to run the Database Consistency Checker to verify your database is free of any corruption, click Exhaustive data integrity verification. Then click the Next button.
6. Enter the Login information for the Export and the Import servers, including the SA password. In the Startup Command-Line Options box, if applicable, type any trace flags or startup parameters to be used for SQL Server 6.x and click the Next button as shown in Figure 13-2.
7. SQL Server switches between version 6.5 and 7.0 as the upgrade continues (see Figure 13-3).
8. The Code Page Selection screen allows you to enter a code page (for some international users), but most installations can take the default.

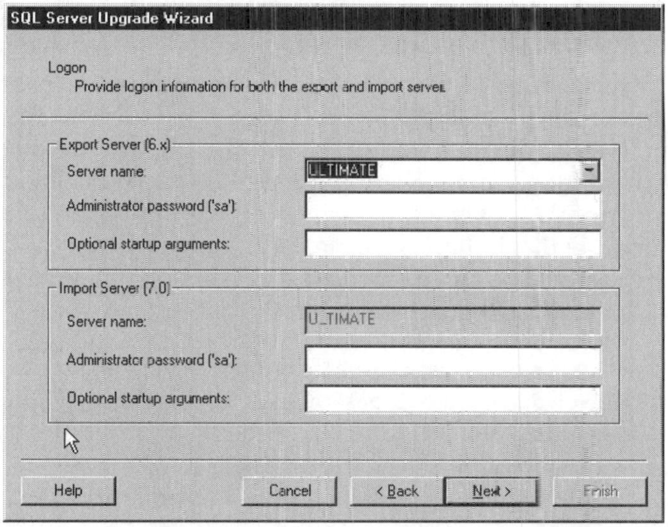

Figure 13-2. *Provide login information for import and export server*

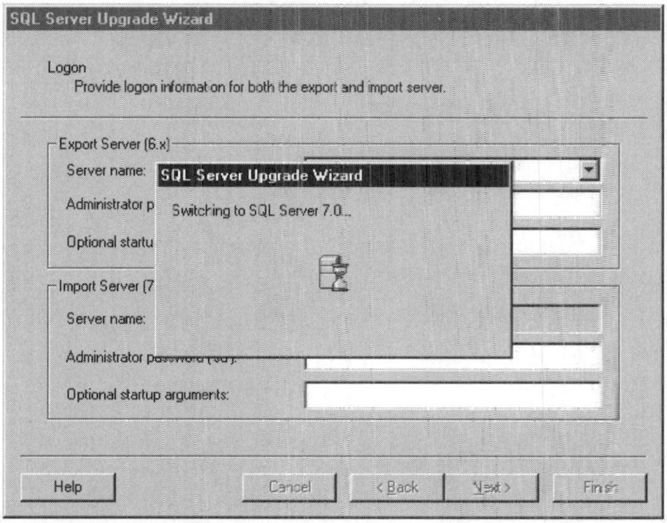

Figure 13-3. *SQL Server switching between versions during upgrade*

9. Exclude the databases you do not want to upgrade to version 7.0. (Note: It is best to upgrade them all at once, if possible. If you don't, the login's default database in the *syslogins* system table can be affected.) Click the Next button.
10. The Database Creation screen lets you see the proposed version 7.0 database layout and to view what SQL Server is allocating in terms of space. Press the Edit button to see the graphical representation of the new version 7.0 database and log files. Press the Advanced button to see the layout and a summary of available drive space. Under the Drive Summary in Figure 13-4, there is an icon next to drive C: that indicates it is not large enough to hold all the database files and that they must be moved to another drive. You can also see that SQL Server will shrink the database to conserve space during the upgrade process.
11. If you need to move the database files to another drive because you are out of space, double-click on the database file. This will allow you to edit the location of the database file and change other database file properties simply by editing the screen fields. Keep changing the drives until you have enough space and the Drive Summary no longer displays the icon next to drive C:.
12. Press the Accept button when you have figured out the best place for your database files.

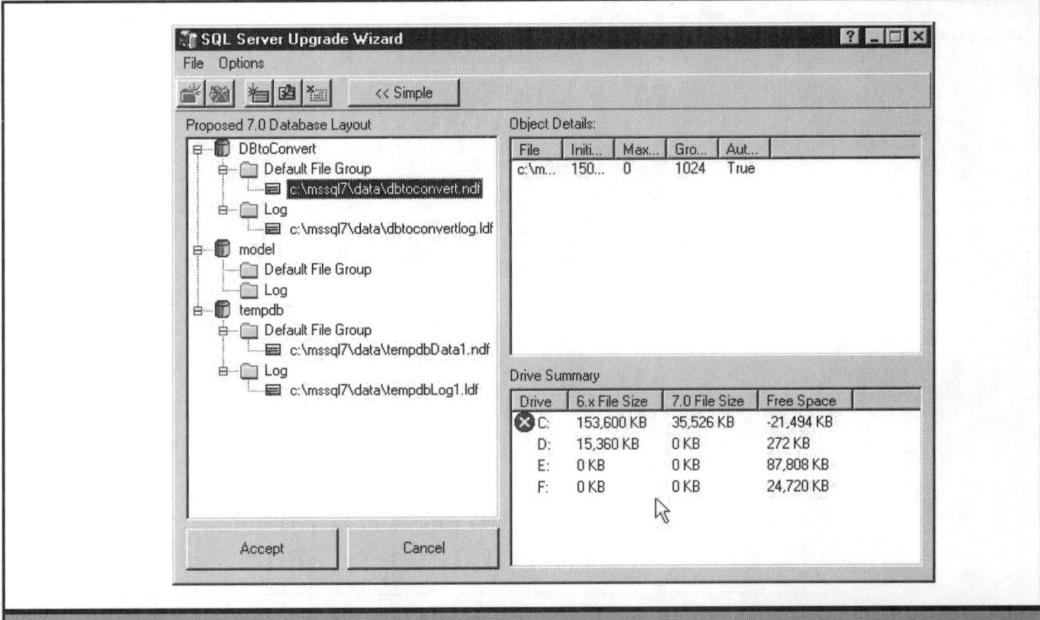

Figure 13-4. *Version Upgrade Utility | Database Creation | Edit | Advanced | Drive Summary*

13. Select the System Objects types you want to transfer.
14. For Quoted Identifiers, select Mixed if you are not sure if your objects were created with QUOTED_IDENTIFIERS OFF or ON. Select OFF or ON if you know. Note that if any of your objects fail to get created because Quoted_Identifiers was set wrong during the upgrade, you can re-execute the appropriate file after the upgrade (from the .prc, .viw, and other files in the upgrade directory) with the option set correctly. Examine the files in the C:\MSSQL7\Upgrade directory (or the directory where you installed SQL Server 7) to see the Transact-SQL executed by SQL Server during the upgrade process.
15. For ANSI Nulls, choose the default of OFF if ANSI nulls should not be used when stored procedures are created, or choose ON if ANSI nulls should be used. Then click the Next button. The final screen before the upgrade appears in Figure 13-5.
16. Click the Finish button.
17. The upgrade begins, providing a progress report as it upgrades to Microsoft SQL Server 7 (see Figure 13-6).

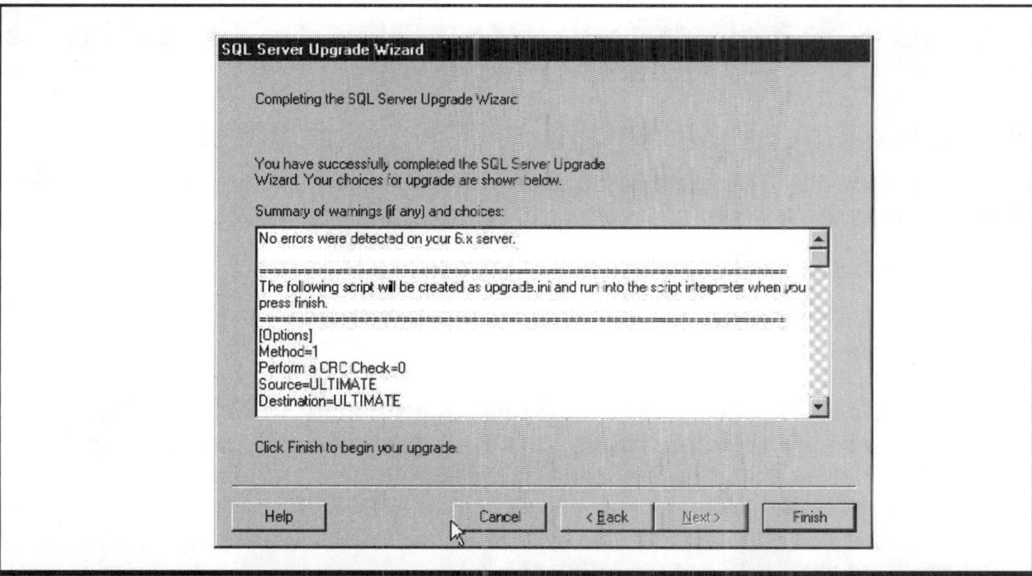

Figure 13-5. *The final screen of the SQL Server Upgrade Wizard before upgrade begins*

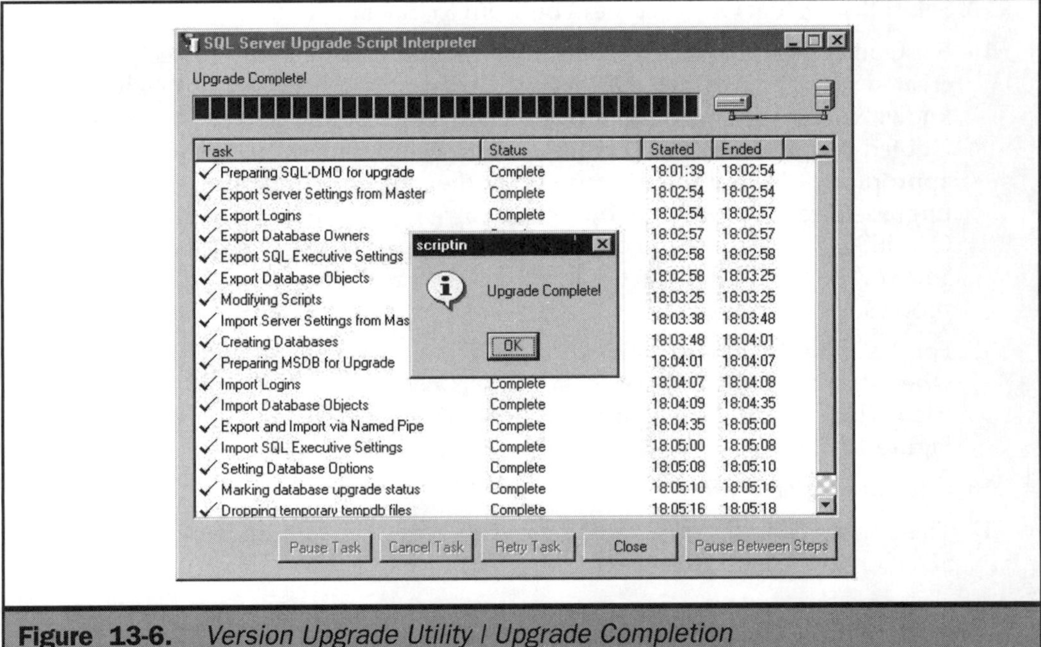

Figure 13-6. *Version Upgrade Utility / Upgrade Completion*

Computer-to-Computer Upgrade (Two Machines)

You can perform a two-machine upgrade if the computers are connected by a network. The data moves through one of the following methods:

- A direct pipeline
- A tape drive backup
- A network share

Follow the same steps outlined in the side-by-side upgrade in the preceding section but, when you name the Export and Import servers (as shown in Figure 13-2), indicate the SQL Server name that is on the remote computer.

Replication and Upgrading

You will be able to upgrade your replication servers and run replication even if your servers are at different version levels. However, a few rules apply if your replication topology will include version 6.x and version 7.0 SQL Servers as to which replication servers can be on which version.

- If you are publishing from a 7.0 server to a 6.x Subscriber, you must run a script (C:\MSSQL7\Install\Replp70.sql) and then execute the stored procedure the script installs (sp_addpublisher70) at a 6.x Subscriber.
- You must upgrade the distribution database before you upgrade the Publisher. You can use a 7.0 distributor and a 6.5 Publisher if they are on different machines.
- You can push subscriptions to SQL Server 6.x servers from a 7.0 Publisher but you cannot pull them.
- 7.0 installations can replicate between servers with different code pages, but this is not possible in version 6.x.

With these installation rules in mind, you can choose how to set up your replication topology if you still need to include 6.x SQL Servers.

Transactional replication should convert right over if you perform the upgrade as a side-by-side upgrade. Examine the new replication functionality in Chapter 9, "Replication Enhancements for SQL Server 7." There are two new Replication Agents, the Snapshot Agent and the Merge Agent, in addition to the version 6.x Log Reader Agent and the Distribution Agent.

Post-upgrade Tasks

When you have finished the upgrade to Microsoft SQL Server 7, you can register your server and/or add a new server group in the Enterprise Manager hierarchy. You may want to check your configuration settings and change any that you deem necessary. To perform any post-upgrade changes, use the Enterprise Manager or the SQL Server setup program. Keep your 6.x SQL Server installation until you are sure the upgrade was a success.

Service Pack

A *service pack* is a collection of bug fixes that have accumulated over a period of time as the bugs are identified. It is important to keep your system current by applying service packs as they become available. The service pack will typically replace system database objects such as system stored procedures or operating system files such as SQL Server executable program files. The service pack is very easy to apply and the steps usually consist of backing up the databases and stopping the SQL Server services before running a program that applies the service pack. A readme.txt file comes with the service pack that will guide you through the steps and let you know what the service pack is fixing.

Hotfix

A *hotfix* is similar to a service pack but usually targets a specific bug that a particular installation has found. It is a temporary fix that is sent to the customer until a service pack is released containing the bug fix. A hotfix is easy to apply and amounts to a quick replacement of a database object or operating system file. It comes with a readme.txt file with instructions. It is important to be informed about the latest available hotfixes in order to determine whether you need to apply it to your SQL Server. If, for example, the hotfix is for replication and you do not use replication, you may choose to wait until the next service pack.

Upgrading is not a difficult task and typically gives you new features and a smoother behavior pattern on the database. Upgrades are one of the best ways to keep your systems in good working order and running with the best available technology and should be installed whenever they become available.

Part III

Administration

Chapter 14

Database Management

Administrative Tool Set

The administrative tool set has been expanded in Microsoft SQL Server 7.0 and is covered in detail in Chapter 7. The following is a listing of available 7.0 tools for the database administrator:

- SQL Server Query Analyzer
- Data Transformation Package
- SQL Server Profiler
- Index Tuning Wizard
- Replay SQL Server
- Database Maintenance Plans
- Web Assistant
- SQL Mail
- Visual Database Tools built into the Enterprise Manager
- Replication Monitor

Refer to Chapter 8 for command line type utilities such as bulk copy (BCP) and OSQL, a new ISQL-type command line utility that uses ODBC to communicate with the server.

System Stored Procedures

SQL Server system stored procedures have been written to provide the functionality to perform all of the database administration tasks while preventing users from accessing the system tables directly. You can see a listing of system stored procedures by using the Enterprise Manager, expanding the server and the master database, and double-clicking on stored procedures.

Select a specific system stored procedure and double-click to see the Transact-SQL code for the selected system stored procedure. Other system stored procedures are located in the MSDB system database and can be accessed by using the same method but expanding the MSDB database instead of master. Other replication system stored procedures can be found in the replication distribution database or the user database if the procedure has been marked for replication.

System stored procedures can be grouped by functional area in the following categories:

- **Catalog** Data dictionary functionality
- **Cursors** Cursor functionality
- **Distributed Queries** Distributed query functionality
- **SQL Server Agent** Task management functionality

- **Replication** Replication functionality
- **Security** Security management functionality
- **System** SQL Server maintenance functionality
- **Web Assistant** Web functionality
- **Extended Procedures** SQL Server interface to external programs
- **OLE Automation** OLE automation within Transact-SQL

The system stored procedures are listed and described in Chapter 23, "System Stored Procedures."

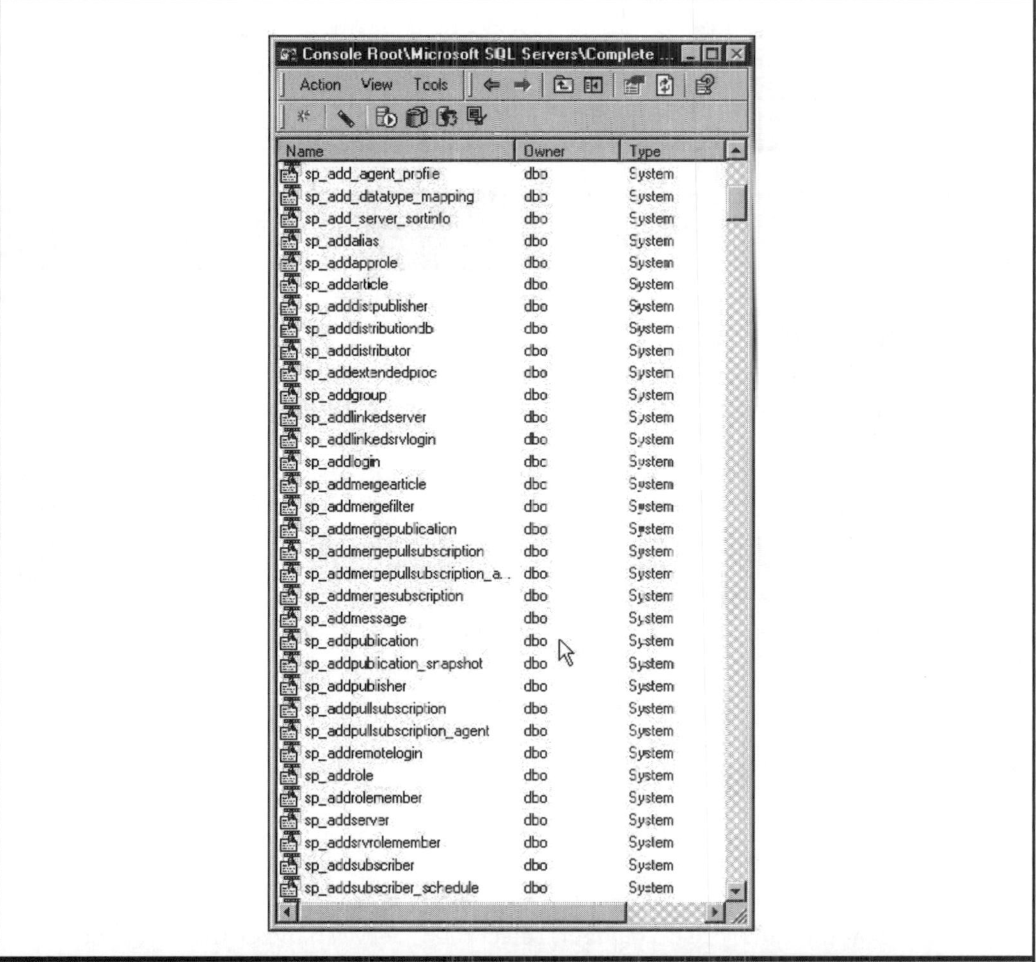

Figure 14-1. *System stored procedures in the master system database*

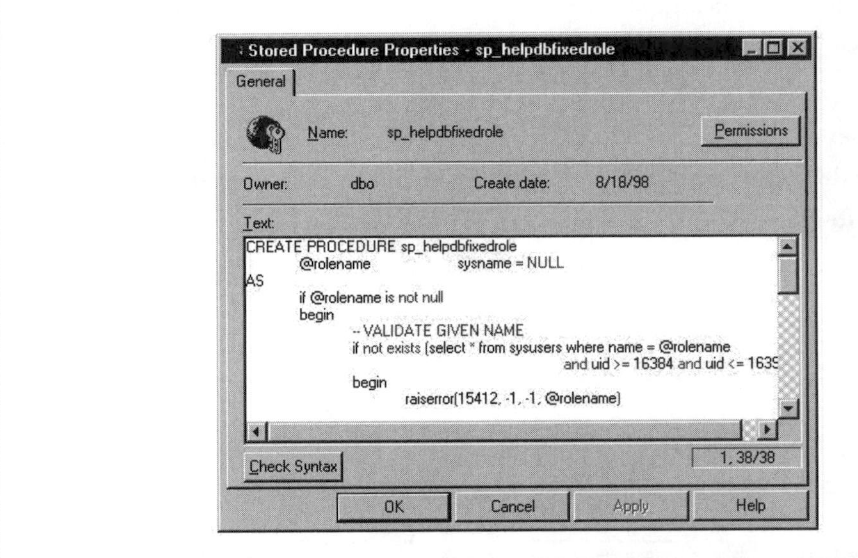

Figure 14-2. *Transact-SQL code for a system stored procedure*

The System Tables

The system tables function as a catalog or data dictionary for Microsoft SQL Server. Information relating to SQL Server, each database, and the database objects is stored in the system tables.

The configuration option that determines whether ad hoc updates without the use of system stored procedures can be made to the system tables is called **allow updates**. This option by default is set to off (0), which prevents ad hoc updates to the system tables. Keep in mind that any stored procedures created while the **allow updates** option is set to on (1) will continue to have the ability to update system tables even after the **allow updates** option is set back to off (0). It is a good idea to start SQL Server in single user mode before you set **allow updates** to on, or true (1).

The syntax to allow ad hoc updates to system tables is:

```
sp_configure 'Allow Updates', 1
GO
RECONFIGURE WITH OVERRIDE
GO
```

You can run the Enterprise Manager, select the Query Analyzer from the Tools Menu and run the sp_configure system stored procedure to set the **allow updates** option to true (1) as shown in Figure 14-3.

Every database in Microsoft SQL Server contains system tables of some sort. The *master* system database contains most of the system tables (see Figure 14-4) but each database contains a set of its own system tables depending on the functionality of the database. The MSDB system database contains system tables for the SQL Server Agent with job scheduling functionality. The *distribution* system database and user databases marked for replication contain system tables relating to replication. All of the system databases and user databases contain a subset of the system tables in the master database, and this subset of system tables contains information related to the objects contained in each database. The system tables are listed and described in Chapter 22, "System Tables."

SQL Errors and Error Logs

SQL errors can occur. If they do and the severity is high enough, they will be written to the SQL Server error log. The error log is an important method of determining the health and well being of SQL Server, and it is important to address any errors reported there by learning more about the nature of the error. Microsoft SQL Server *and* SQL

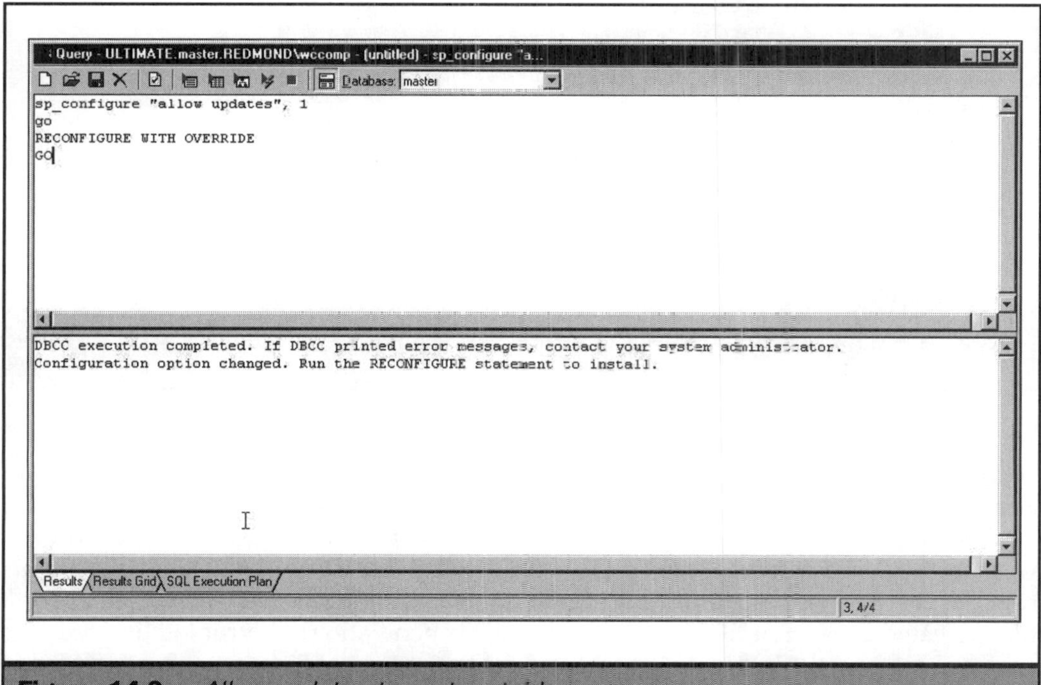

Figure 14-3. *Allow updates to system tables*

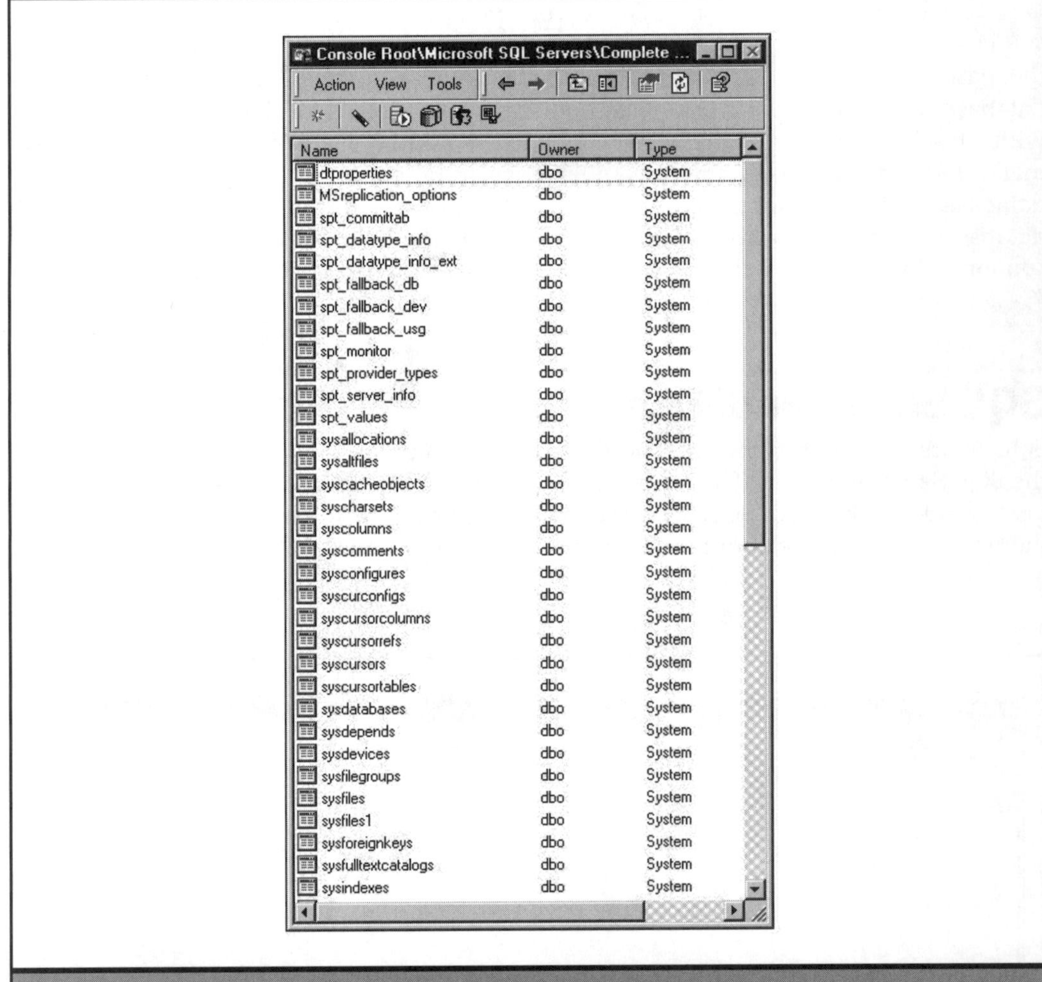

Figure 14-4. *System tables in the* master *system database*

Server Agent have error log files. The SQL Server Agent error log contains information about errors related to jobs and tasks from the SQLServerAgent service.

The SQL Server error logs can be found in the location chosen when SQL Server was installed. The default location is C:\Mssql7\Log\Errorlog. The default location of the SQL Server Agent error log file is C:\Mssql7\Log\Sqlagent.out. A new error log file is created every time SQL Server is started. Six generations of error log files are accumulated and the integer extension of errorlog.1, errorlog.2, errorlog.3, and so forth through errorlog.6 are stored in the location chosen upon install or in the default location, if it was not changed. There are at least two main ways to view the error log:

- SQL Server Enterprise Manager
- Opening the file with a text editor

To view the error log for SQL Server in the Enterprise Manager, expand the Error Logs entry in the Enterprise Manager hierarchy tree after you have selected your server, as shown in Figure 14-5.

Using the Enterprise Manager, the SQL Server Agent error log can be viewed by right-clicking on the SQL Server Agent entry in the Enterprise Manager hierarchy tree

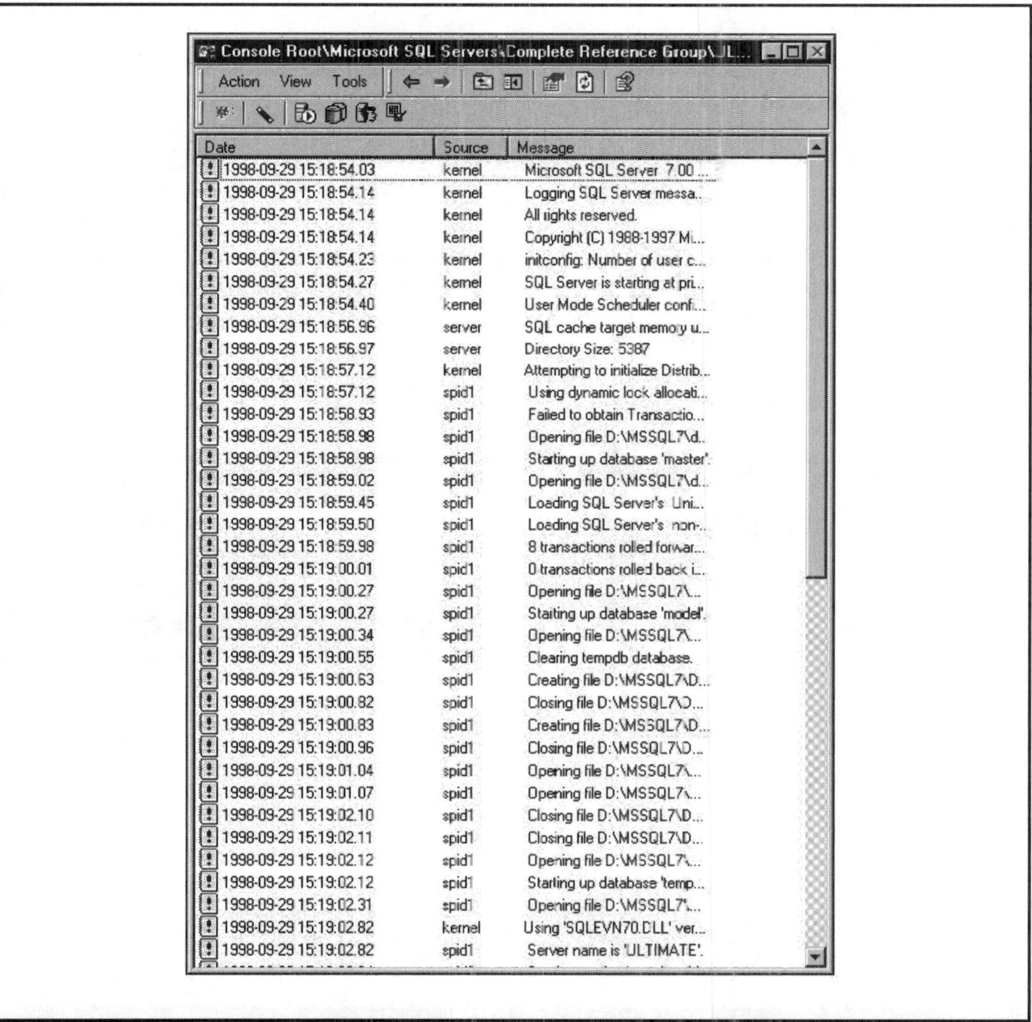

Figure 14-5. *SQL Server error log*

after you have selected your server and then selecting Display Error Log from the shortcut menu. An example of a typical error log is shown in Figure 14-6.

You can access the screen to set options for the SQL Server Agent error log by right-clicking on the SQL Server Agent entry in the Enterprise Manager hierarchy tree and selecting Properties from the shortcut menu. Options that can be set are:

- The name and location of the SQL Server Agent error log
- Whether to include trace execution messages in the error log
- A field for the NT login of the person you would like to receive a pop-up message via net send on their computer every time a SQL Server Agent error occurs

On the screen shown in Figure 14-7, you can see the field where you can change the name and location of the SQL Server Agent error log. There is also a check box that allows you to include execution trace messages in the SQL Server Agent error log. Keep in mind that performance will be affected if the server must write many entries to the error log. The error log has the capability of growing at an alarming rate under some circumstances and requires the use of caution when selecting this option. This is not one to check and forget about. If you check the include execution trace messages option, monitor the SQL Server Agent error log file to make sure you have enough

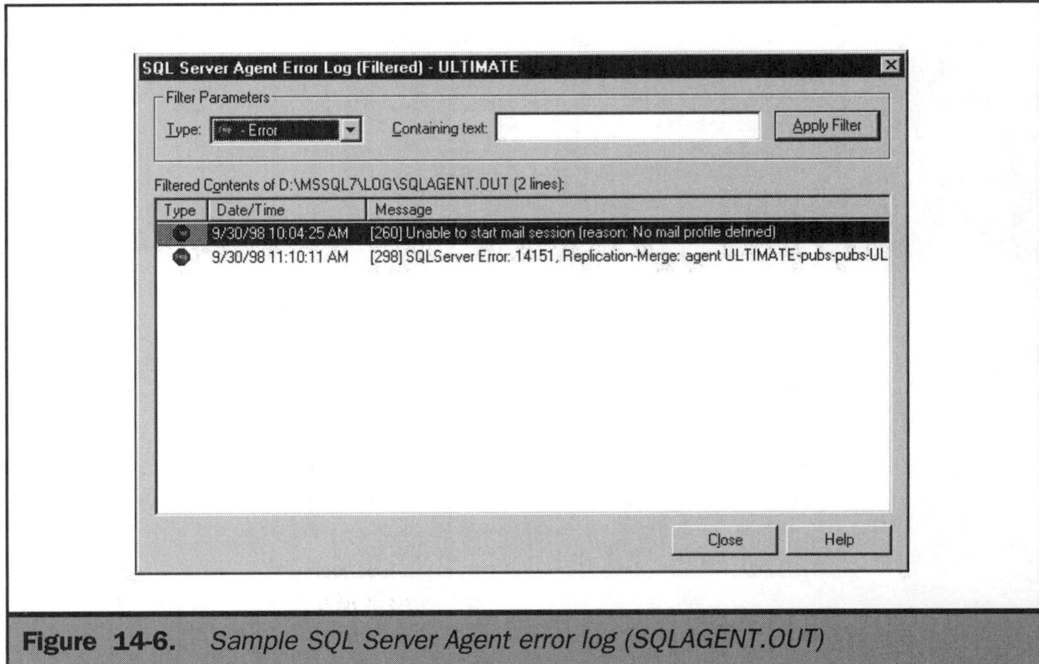

Figure 14-6. *Sample SQL Server Agent error log (SQLAGENT.OUT)*

space on your hard disk to support the growth of this file. If you decide to send a pop-up message via net send, the recipient would typically be a computer operator or a database administrator charged with the responsibility of resolving errors in the job stream associated with the SQLServerAgent service.

Monitoring the Error Logs

It is a good idea to monitor Microsoft SQL Server error logs to determine which events are occurring on SQL Server. Events related to SQL Server and SQL Server Agent are written to their respective error logs and also to the Windows NT application log that can be viewed using the NT Event Viewer. If you experience a problem, check not only the SQL Server error log or the SQL Server Agent error log but also the NT application error log. The combination of all of the information generated by the SQL Server and the NT operating system will give a more complete indication of the problem than will just looking at one or the other log. Both logs automatically time-stamp all recorded events.

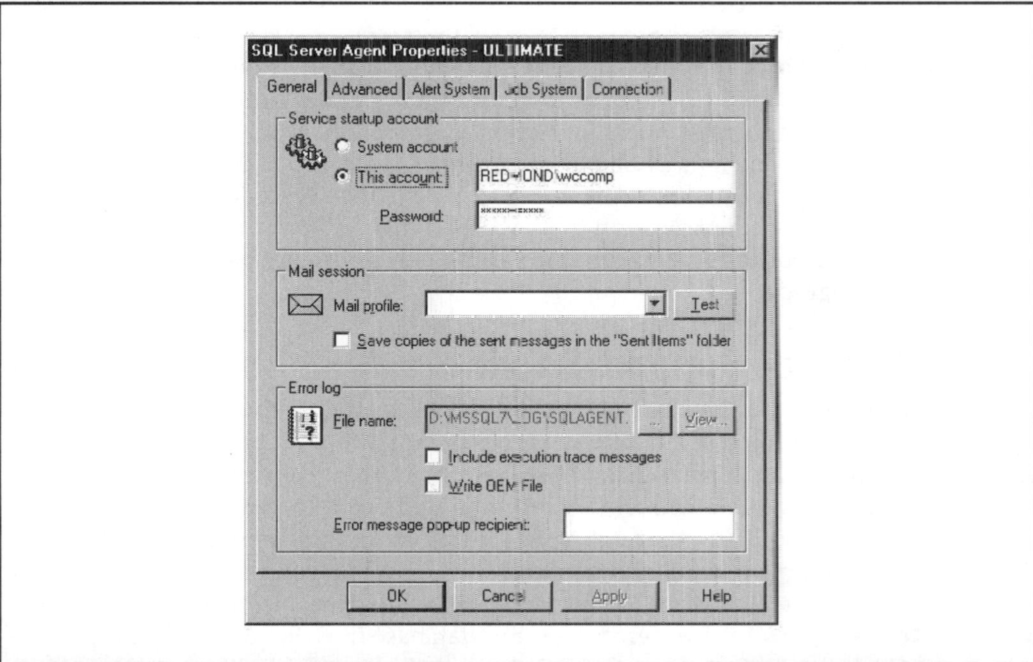

Figure 14-7. *Set error log options in the SQL Server Agent Properties dialog box*

TechNet and Knowledge Base Articles

Microsoft TechNet Monthly Issues is an indispensable resource if you really want to be able to manage your SQL Server errors effectively. TechNet (Technical Information Network) is a little loose-leaf notebook packed full of CD ROMs containing information about Microsoft products, including Microsoft SQL Server. Technical notes, case studies, resource kits, product facts, and Microsoft Knowledge Base give up-to-date information to allow you to support Microsoft SQL Server in the most effective way possible. You do not have to depend on your employer to give you access to this information. TechNet is available to the ordinary person for a few hundred dollars a year and is worth every penny to keep you up-to-date on Microsoft products and to give you detailed, specific, historical information about errors occurring on your SQL Server.

The Knowledge Base articles contained in the TechNet CD-ROM contain information about the error, and in many cases a work-around is offered for the problem related to the error. Many of the errors you will experience have occurred on other SQL Servers around the world and have been reported to Microsoft. The error and the solution are then documented in Knowledge Base articles and made available to other users who experience similar problems. It is important to search for the error in the Knowledge Base and to follow any recommendation you may find in the article.

Many of the errors are corrected in subsequent service packs, which is why it is important to keep SQL Server upgraded to the latest service pack available. Service packs undergo meticulous testing by Microsoft's internal business applications and are released internally to undergo more testing months before being offered to the public. Rest assured that you are receiving a service pack that has been subjected to the most rigorous business applications available in the world in terms of size and pushing-the-envelope technology. There is very little that can escape the pounding the service pack receives inside Microsoft by the Sales, Finance, Web, and SAP applications. My experience has taught me that the healthiest SQL Server is the one with the latest upgrade.

Microsoft Product Support Service

Once you have reviewed the Knowledge Base articles related to the error and have decided you need additional help or that you have run into a situation that no one has yet reported, you need to contact Microsoft Product Support Service (PSS). A PSS Engineer will assist you and will require information related to your environment. Be cooperative and prompt about providing this information, and try to provide the PSS Engineer with a complete detailed description of the problem and the symptoms. Make sure that you have a way to send Microsoft the large files they may need to debug the problem. They may ask for your error logs and database files. Be prepared and provide Microsoft with what is needed to troubleshoot the problem. This will go a long way toward a timely resolution of your problem.

SQL Server Strategy if an Error Occurs

The version 7.0 strategy is to have SQL Server kill the process ID that is having the problem and record the error in the error log. This is to keep from causing corruption by a process that may have run into a SQL Server bug or is breaking the rules of transaction processing. It is important to follow up with TechNet and the Knowledge Base articles to find information about the problem. You may have to report it to Microsoft if you believe you have run into a new, unreported bug.

Researching Errors

When you see an error in the error log, search for the error number in the Knowledge Base on TechNet. When you receive a list of Knowledge Base articles from your query, read all the Knowledge Base articles and decide which one is closest to your situation. Pay attention to the version in which the error was reported and compare it to your current version. Follow the work-around suggested in the article.

If you cannot find the error or if you need additional help, call Microsoft Product Support Services to report the error and receive assistance. Some errors are in Knowledge Base articles internal to Microsoft and the information will not yet have appeared on TechNet.

Recognizing Severe Errors

You can figure out how severe the problem is by reading the Knowledge Base article and looking for the severity level. Try to do this as soon as the error appears in the error log. That is why it is a good idea to set up your SQL Server to use SQL Server Agent to page or e-mail an operator or a database administrator as soon as an error is written to the error log.

Cycling SQL Server

Some errors that can cause damage can be avoided if SQL Server is cycled (stopped and started), and you'll want to know immediately if this is the case so that you have the option of preventing further corruption by stopping and starting SQL Server. The Knowledge Base will let you know if you have an error that requires you to cycle SQL Server.

Many times the problem is happening within the tempdb system database, a working database that is initialized when SQL Server is stopped and started. If the tempdb system database is reporting corruption, it is a good time to cycle SQL Server.

Drive Management

If you have a large SQL Server with a significant business application, you need to know the details on managing your disk drives. The best performing configuration is when RAID is implemented at the hardware level. A less costly configuration is to implement RAID at the operating system level.

Redundant Array of Inexpensive Disks

Redundant Array of Inexpensive Disks (RAID) is best implemented at the hardware level if possible and is a method of disk striping that offers fault tolerance in RAID levels 1 through 5 by providing parity information for redundancy. Data is spread out over multiple disks so that disk I/O can occur simultaneously. RAID-0 provides no fault tolerance; RAID-5 provides the most. It is best to use a combination of RAID levels 0, 1, and 5 with Microsoft SQL Server.

Database Files: RAID-0 or RAID-5

Using RAID technology with SQL Server improves performance, and the way that RAID is implemented can directly affect the performance of SQL Server. You can achieve the best performance by placing the database files on RAID-0 (also known as a hardware-based stripe set because of the way that the data is divided and placed across all the disks in an array). However, if one disk fails, the entire RAID-0 stripe set becomes inaccessible, not just the data on the failed disk.

If you have a system that cannot be down for any reason at any time but you are still concerned about performance, use RAID-5 for the database files (files with .mdf or .ndf for the extension). Parity calculations occur on RAID-5 providing redundancy because the data and parity are always stored on different disks. RAID-5 is similar to RAID-0 but includes fault tolerance and redundancy, as parity is written across all the disks. Using RAID-5 implemented at the hardware level for the database files spares the processor the work of calculating parity, thereby improving the performance of the processor.

Transaction Log Files: RAID-1 (Disk Mirroring)

It is best to use RAID-1 (disk mirroring) implemented at the hardware level for the drive containing your database transaction log files (files with .ldf extension) because RAID-1 has the best redundancy. RAID-1 uses a mirrored set to provide a redundant copy of a disk and is a good performer reading data; however, it slows down the disk writes. If you have a critical application, it is a good idea to protect your transaction logs with mirrored drives. In general, you have to weigh the risks of losing data with your desire for performance when deciding how to manage your disk drives.

Stripe Sets

Remember that RAID striped sets with parity can be implemented at the NT operating system level (software level) as well as the hardware level. The processor is then required to perform the parity checking consuming processor cycles. If you are concerned with cost more than with the use of processor cycles, it is cheaper to implement RAID at the NT operating system level, and you will still see an increase in performance. NT Windows RAID striped sets is a good solution for those of you who are interested in improving performance and containing cost.

Moving Databases

When you are faced with the task of moving a database to another server, there are a number of things to consider:

- Is the sort order and character set the same on both servers?
- Are the SQL Server Authentication Modes the same on both servers?
- Are any Trace Flags set?
- Are there user stored procedures in the master system database?
- Is the ANSI to OEM option on or off in NT Registry?
- Are the memory and versions on both servers compatible?
- Are SQL Server logins and remote logins the same on the servers?
- Are the sysservers system tables the same?
- Are there any special alerts on the server?
- Are any jobs or tasks scheduled to run on the server?
- Are the NT groups on the servers the same?
- Are the database options the same?
- Are transaction logs being backed up at a scheduled time?

All of the above questions must be answered and verified if you are moving a database from one server to another. The database has to move to an environment that is compatible and similar to the server from whence it came in order to behave in the same manner and have the same characteristics it exhibited before the move.

Re-creating SQL Server

You should be doing the following tasks every day to make sure you have a re-creation scenario in case you have to re-create your entire server, hardware and all, which can happen if you need to move to a bigger server or if you experience catastrophic hardware failure. Setting up a re-creation scenario requires using SQL Server Agent to set up the following tasks to run once each day. This way you will have the basic files to re-create SQL Server.

- Run the system stored procedures sp_configure, sp_helpdevice, sp_helpntgroup on SQL Server every day and save the results to a disk drive different from the one on which your master database is located.
- Back up all of your databases.
- Use the BCP utility to copy the master database system tables to flat files.
- Have standards for the locations of files on the drives in a written document.
- Have standards for installing NT and SQL Server in a written document.

Once you have the basic files, you can follow these steps to re-create the server:

1. Procure your hardware.
2. Install NT according to your standards (these standards should be written down).
3. Install SQL Server according to your standards (these standards should be written down).
4. You will not be restoring the master database, so anything in master must be re-created. Know what is in your master database and, as a general rule, do not create user stored procedures in the master system database.
5. Re-create the NT groups on the new server.
6. Re-create your master system tables by reviewing what is in the flat files that were BCP'd out and re-creating the values on SQL Server. In version 6.5, I used to BCP the system tables in. Be more careful now when doing this since there are drastic changes in the system tables from version 6.5 to version 7 and the foreign key relationships may be different.
7. Restore your databases.
8. Test the configuration with your application and your users to see if they can still log in and run the application.
9. Be prepared to troubleshoot any problem area.

These are the general steps to re-create your server when this becomes necessary for whatever reason. Run the systems in parallel for a while to test the applications attached to each database.

Administering Mission-Critical Applications

If you have a database containing information that is critical to your business, you may want to implement some of the following methods and move towards gaining fault tolerance, redundancy, and fail-over strategies on your server:

- Use transaction log backups and run full database backups at least once each week.
- Run Database Consistency Check utility (DBCC) on a regularly scheduled basis (every day for system databases, at least once each week for user databases).
- Send severe (severity level 21–25) SQL Server errors to a pager by using the SQL Server Agent so that you can respond immediately to a fatal error.
- Use hardware level RAID-5 on the drives holding the database files.
- Use hardware level RAID-1 (mirroring) on the drives holding the transaction log files.
- Consider using Microsoft Transaction Server (MTS) for fail-over strategies.
- Consider using NT Clustering for fail-over strategies.
- Possess a backup server in a different location and replicate to it.

It is particularly important to back up your databases religiously and to alert severe errors using the SQL Server Agent. An immediate response can minimize damage, and implementing this process long term makes you familiar with resolving errors. This is a remarkably easy process to implement when you use the SQL Server Agent as described in Chapter 4. Over time, you will become familiar with the errors that concern you that are different from application to application and version to version.

Administering Very Large Databases

Very large databases (in the realm of the multi-gigabyte) present a challenge for the database administrator because ordinary maintenance tasks such as backups and database consistency checks take a long time. Microsoft SQL Server 7.0 addresses these problems directly by improving the utilities that have historically taken so much time on the larger databases. DBCC has been dramatically improved to run much faster, and backups can be taken without interfering with other activities on the server or degrading performance. A backup now takes under 5 percent of CPU capability and can run virtually undetected by the other database users.

If you have a Very Large Database (VLDB), be sure to have another server as a backup on which to run database consistency checks and perform testing. This also provides a starting point if, in the event of catastrophic hardware failure, it ever becomes necessary to move from your current server.

Starting and Stopping the SQL Server

You can start Microsoft SQL Server automatically or manually, and all methods cause SQL Server to run as an NT service, except when running sqlservr.exe with the –c argument from a command prompt. If you choose to start SQL Server automatically, you can specify automatic startup when you install SQL Server or you can use the Enterprise Manager after SQL Server is already installed. This is invoked by right-clicking on the selected server in the Enterprise Manager hierarchy tree and selecting Properties. If you check the check box for Auto start SQL Server when NT starts, SQL Server will automatically start the next time your Windows NT Server is started.

Starting and stopping SQL Server is easiest to do using the Enterprise Manager. Simply right-click on the selected server in the Enterprise Manager and select Start or Stop. You can also Pause SQL Server from here. This means new logins are not allowed but logins already in are allowed to continue. You will not be able to use this method if SQL Server has been started from the command prompt with the –c option.

Another way to manually start and stop SQL Server and related services like SQL Server Agent and Distributed Transaction Coordinator is to use the SQL Server Service Manager. This is invoked by selecting it from the SQL Server program group in the Windows NT Start menu. Double-click on the green light to start SQL Server, the yellow light to pause SQL Server, or the red light to stop SQL Server. The services can be selected from the drop-down list box on the screen.

A third way to start and stop SQL Server is to select Services from the Control Panel to view a listing of services running on the computer. Select MSSQLServer and choose the Start or the Stop button. You can also start and stop the SQLServerAgent service and the Microsoft Data Transaction Coordinator (MSDTC) service with the Control Panel method.

Still another way to start and stop SQL Server is from a command prompt. SQL Server behaves differently when it is started this way and allows you to pass arguments to prevent SQL Server from running as a service and to start SQL Server in single user mode or minimal configuration. The next section outlines the parameters and tells how to start SQL Server from the command prompt.

Starting SQL Server from a Command Prompt

Microsoft SQL Server can be started from a command prompt by selecting Run from the NT start menu and typing any of the following three commands:

The syntax is:

```
net start mssqlserver
```

or

```
sqlservr
```

or

```
net start SQLServerAgent
```

The default arguments are:

- **-dmaster_file_ path** This argument represents the path for the master database file with the default upon installation being C:\Mssql7\Data\Master.mdf. Values in the NT Registry are used if you do not specify this argument.
- **-eerror_log_path** This argument represents the path for the error log file with the default upon installation being C:\Mssql7\Log\Errorlog. Values in the NT Registry are used if you do not specify this argument.
- **-lmaster_log_path** This argument represents the path for the master database log file with the default upon installation being C:\Mssql7\Data\Mastlog.ldf.

Other startup arguments are:

- **-c** This argument starts SQL Server where SQL Server does not run as a Windows NT service. All system messages will be displayed in the window where SQL Server was started, and you cannot pause or stop SQL Server using SQL Server Enterprise Manager, SQL Server Service Manager, the Services application in Control Panel, or any net commands. In addition, before logging off your session you have to stop SQL Server.
- **-f** This argument starts SQL Server with a minimal configuration with no CHECKPOINT execution. Use this if the server does not start for reasons such as the configuration options being set too high. This argument turns on the **allow updates** option to the system tables option and starts SQL Server in single user mode, so you must remember to stop SQL Server Agent or it will take your only connection. Temporary changes to memory usage, user connections, open databases, locks, open objects, language information in cache, asynchronous I/O, total procedure, and buffer cache are set to the minimum values. In addition, procedure cache is set to 50 percent, remote access and read-ahead are disabled, and startup stored procedures are ignored. Change what you need to change and restart SQL Server in the normal manner.
- **-m** This argument starts SQL Server in single-user mode. Stop SQL Server Agent or it will take your only connection. Only a single user can connect. The **allow updates** option is turned on, meaning this startup method can be used if you need to update system tables and you don't want anyone else to login to SQL Server while **allow updates** to the system tables is true.
- **-n** Starting SQL Server with this argument specifies that the Windows NT Event log will not be used to log SQL Server events. Use this with the –e argument or SQL Server events will not be logged to the SQL Server error log either.
- **-pprecision_level** This argument determines the maximum level of precision for decimal and numeric data types. The SQL Server default is 28, and if no precision level is supplied with the –p argument, the system will use the maximum precision level of 38.

- **-sregistry_key** The use of this argument starts SQL Server by using an alternate set of startup parameters from the NT Registry stored under registry_key (the Server subkey), which can exist as multiple previously defined startup configurations.
- **/Ttrace_number** This uppercase argument starts SQL Server with a specified trace flag.
- **-x** This argument does not keep CPU time and cache-hit ratio statistics which can improve performance.

Another way to stop SQL Server is by using the SHUTDOWN command within a Transact-SQL session.

SHUTDOWN and SHUTDOWN WITH NOWAIT

You can also stop SQL Server by running the SHUTDOWN Transact-SQL statement from OSQL or the Query Analyzer, or for that matter any other query tool where you can issue a Transact-SQL statement. This statement disables all logins, lets any Transact-SQL statements that are executing finish, and checkpoints every database. Because all these things are allowed to finish, recovery time is less when SQL Server is started again. Using the SHUTDOWN WITH NOWAIT does not finish anything, and SQL Server is immediately stopped; however, recovery time is increased.

If you have the time, the best way to stop SQL Server is using the SHUTDOWN statement, because all logins are disabled, any Transact-SQL statements that are executing are allowed to finish, and the CHECKPOINT statement is executed for every database.

Archiving

Another important topic in database management is managing your disk space by archiving old data off of the database. Periodic purging and archiving of historical data in the database is as necessary as starting and stopping them in managing your databases and will actually improve performance.

It is important to build your application with archiving functionality built into the design from the beginning. It is too late to start thinking about archiving when the database is full of unused data that you have to get off by the end of next week. Archiving takes planning and design, especially if the data is financial and tax laws govern the amount of time the data must be kept. This is not an easy problem to address, and addressing this gargantuan task with no planning or foresight can lead to big problems down the road for the database administrator and the entire company. The database structure and the relationships contained therein change over time, and it is not enough to lay the data down in flat files. You must also consider the relationships involved and have good strategies in place should you ever need to restore the data and make sense of it. Unfortunately, due to time constraints when applications are built, archiving is often considered the least important thing in the rush to produce an application. In reality, it is one of the most important elements in application design and implementation.

The Complete Reference

Chapter 15

Preventive Maintenance of Databases

Microsoft SQL Server 7 makes it easy to perform preventive database maintenance by offering a Maintenance Plan Wizard that walks you through the steps of creating a maintenance plan. The wizard uses the job scheduling functionality of the SQL Server Agent and allows you to reorganize data and index pages and to update statistics on a regularly scheduled basis. The Maintenance Plan Wizard also lets you run integrity tests on the database and specify the database backup plan and the free space percentage of a data page. Results reports can be generated to a file or a Web page. All this functionality is built into the few screens that comprise the Database Maintenance Plan Wizard. This is an incredible advance in technology for the database administrator because it is simple to perform and it eliminates coding this functionality in Transact-SQL. A database maintenance plan may not answer all of your requirements and you many choose to use the sqlmaint utility in a SQL Server Agent job to supplement or change the functionality offered here. The sqlmaint utility is discussed in Chapter 8, "Utility "Changes."

Update Statistics

UPDATE STATISTICS is a Transact-SQL statement that was added to the Database Maintenance Plan. This statement can be run to update the statistics on the distribution of values in the system tables if the number of rows in the table changes in a dramatic way.

The cost-based query optimizer uses these statistics to estimate the cost of using an index and tries to use the index with the least cost. The statistics must be updated as rows are added or removed from the table or as the distribution of values in the column changes, or the query optimizer will not have the latest statistical information when formulating the query plan. This could cause the optimizer to make a less than optimal decision about which index to use. It could even do a table scan on a million-rows table if the statistics information is indicating 0 rows. Figure 15-1 shows the Database Maintenance Plan Wizard. By using the Database Maintenance Plan Wizard you can indicate what number of rows or what percentage of the table should be sampled for extra large tables. If you enter a value that's too low, SQL Server will correct your entry based on the number of rows in the table and use the minimum number of values to make the sample representative and useful. If you do *not* use the FULLSCAN argument when issuing the UPDATE STATISTICS statement, SQL Server will perform a sampling on the table to collect the statistical information stored in the system tables that the query optimizer needs to formulate the query plan. This will save time on large tables because only the sample rows are scanned to collect the statistical information, not the entire table.

Running update statistics is one of the most commonly neglected database maintenance tasks and, if the required statistics are not up to date when formulating the query plan, can affect SQL Server query performance. The syntax and arguments for the UPDATE STATISTICS statement can be found in Chapter 21.

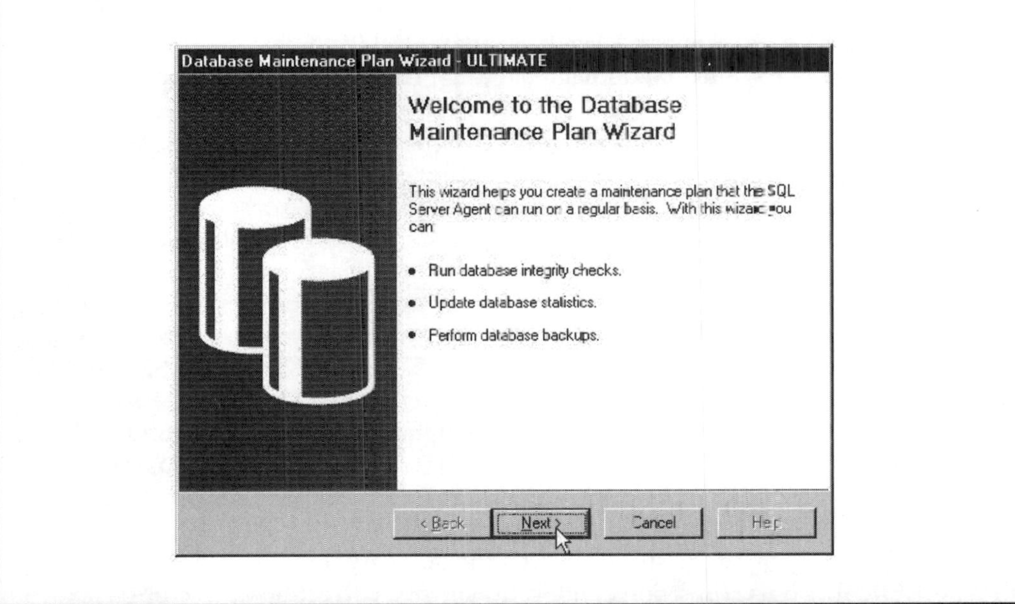

Figure 15-1. *The Database Maintenance Plan Wizard*

Database Consistency Checker

Just as it is necessary to run checks on your hard disk by using the CHKDSK utility for periodic maintenance, it is also necessary to check your database and verify that it is logically and physically consistent by running the Database Consistency Checker (DBCC) as part of your regular maintenance plan. It is best to run DBCC CHECKCATALOG and DBCC CHECKDB right before the database is backed up. In doing this you can ensure that you are not overwriting your last good backup with a backup that may contain errors. Check the DBCC output files, resolve any errors that may have occurred, and back up your database. Plan to run DBCC at a time when users are not on the system. If you have a database with large tables or one that is more than 5GB, you may want to run DBCC on a back up server after you have restored the database or use the NO_INDEX option which omits a scan of the nonclustered indexes. You should still check your nonclustered indexes, but perhaps on a less frequent basis than your data pages and clustered indexes. For more specific information on DBCC scenarios, see Chapter 8.

DBCC CHECKDB checks the integrity of every object on the database. Any errors found should be fixed. You do not have to run DBCC CHECKALLOC or DBCC CHECKTABLE if you run DBCC CHECKDB. Indexes and data pages for each table are checked for correct page linkage and consistent pointers. Indexes are further checked to make sure the entries are properly sorted and that offsets and data on each page are reasonable. Sizes of text, ntext, and image pages for each table, as well as page allocation, are checked for all pages.

DBCC CHECKCATALOG checks to see if the system tables are consistent. This should be run every time you have DBCC scheduled to run on your database. This checks the integrity of *syscolumns* with *systypes* and *sysobjects* with *syscolumns*. Every data type in syscolumns must have a row in systypes, and every table and view must have at least one column in syscolumns.

There are some notable changes in DBCC behavior in Microsoft SQL Server 7. You will no longer have to run DBCC DBREPAIR to drop a database marked as suspect; DROP DATABASE will do the job. In addition, DBCC SHRINKDATABASE should be used instead of DBCC SHRINKDB because DBCC SHRINKDB is no longer supported.

DBCC also has the capability of repairing the database if errors are found. DBCC CHECKTABLE, DBCC CHECKDB, and DBCC CHECKALLOC have a repair option that can have the values REPAIR_FAST (quick, small, low risk repairs are done such as extra space in nonclustered indexes), REPAIR_REBUILD (includes FAST repairs plus repairs that take longer yet are still low risk), and ALLOW_DATA_LOSS (includes REPAIR_REBUILD plus correction of allocation errors, correction of row or page errors and even includes the removal of corrupted text objects).

Another change in DBCC behavior is that both DBCC NEWALLOC and DBCC ROWLOCK are supported only for backward compatibility. DBCC NEWALLOC has been replaced by DBCC CHECKALLOC in Microsoft SQL Server 7, and you may remove any DBCC ROWLOCK statements because row level locking is a standard feature in Microsoft SQL Server 7.

The new index structure in Microsoft SQL Server 7 requires SQL Server to rebuild all nonclustered indexes on a table when the clustered index is dropped. Use DBCC REINDEX rather than DROP INDEX to drop a clustered index. Lastly, expect to see changes to any DBCC output you have created in previous versions. See Figure 15-2 for DBCC CHECKDB output for Microsoft SQL Server 7.

Techniques to Fix DBCC Errors

Consult the Knowledge Base first to research the error. Chapter 14, which describes TechNet and Knowledge Base Articles, contains more information on this subject. Also, see Figure 15-3, which shows a list of Knowledge Base articles within the Microsoft TechNet.

If the research on the error indicates that an index is corrupt, a fix is as simple as dropping and recreating the index. If the research on the error indicates that a table is corrupt, the data can often be salvaged by using SELECT INTO to move the data into another table. The old table can be dropped and the new table renamed back to the old table name. Indexes can be recreated as well as any dependent objects such as stored procedures and permissions which you should script out before dropping the indexes.

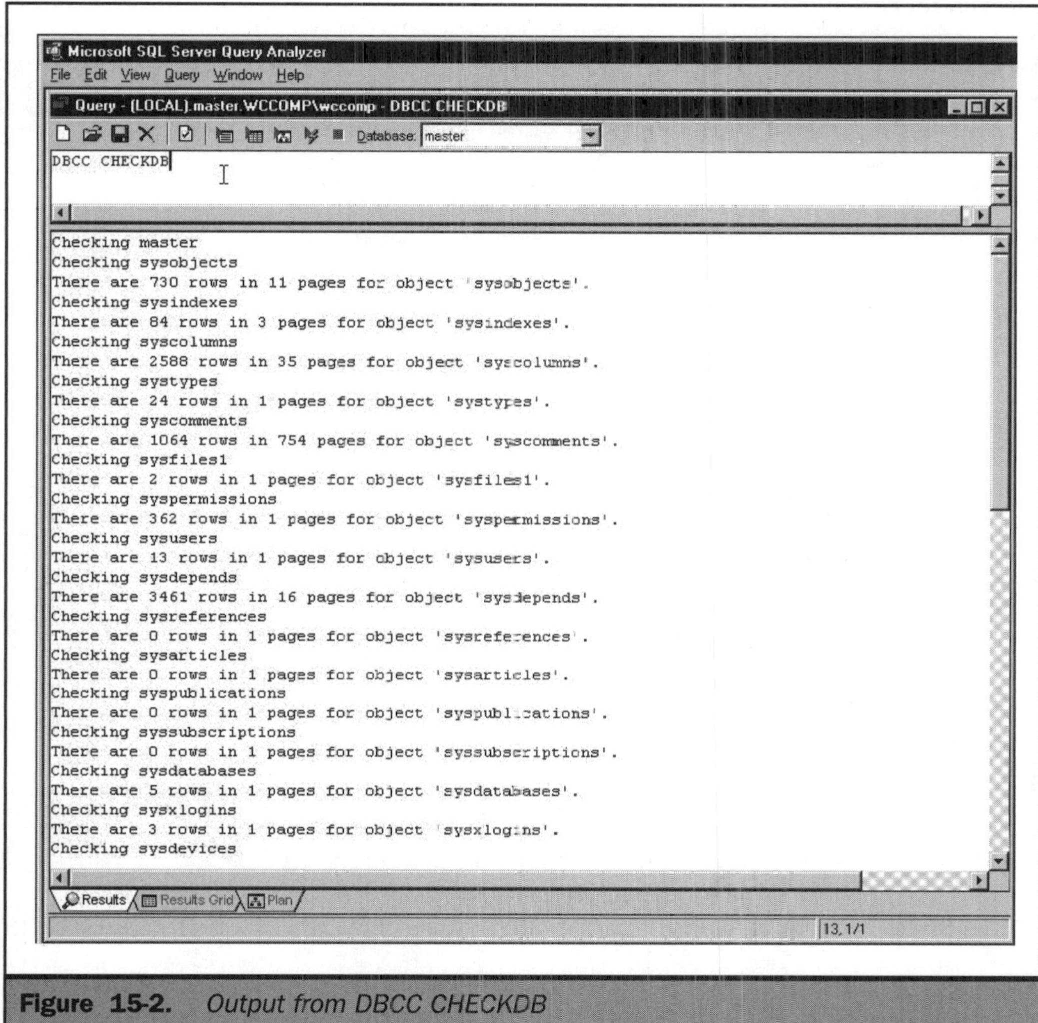

Figure 15-2. *Output from DBCC CHECKDB*

It can also be useful to try to use the BCP utility to export the data to an operating system file. If DBCC identifies a specific row or column of corrupt data, it may be better to delete the row or update the column rather than lose the entire table. If you have consulted the Knowledge Base and realize you need additional help, call Microsoft Technical Support and they will help you with the error. Figure 15-4 shows an example of a search for error 2546 and the resulting list of Knowledge Base articles

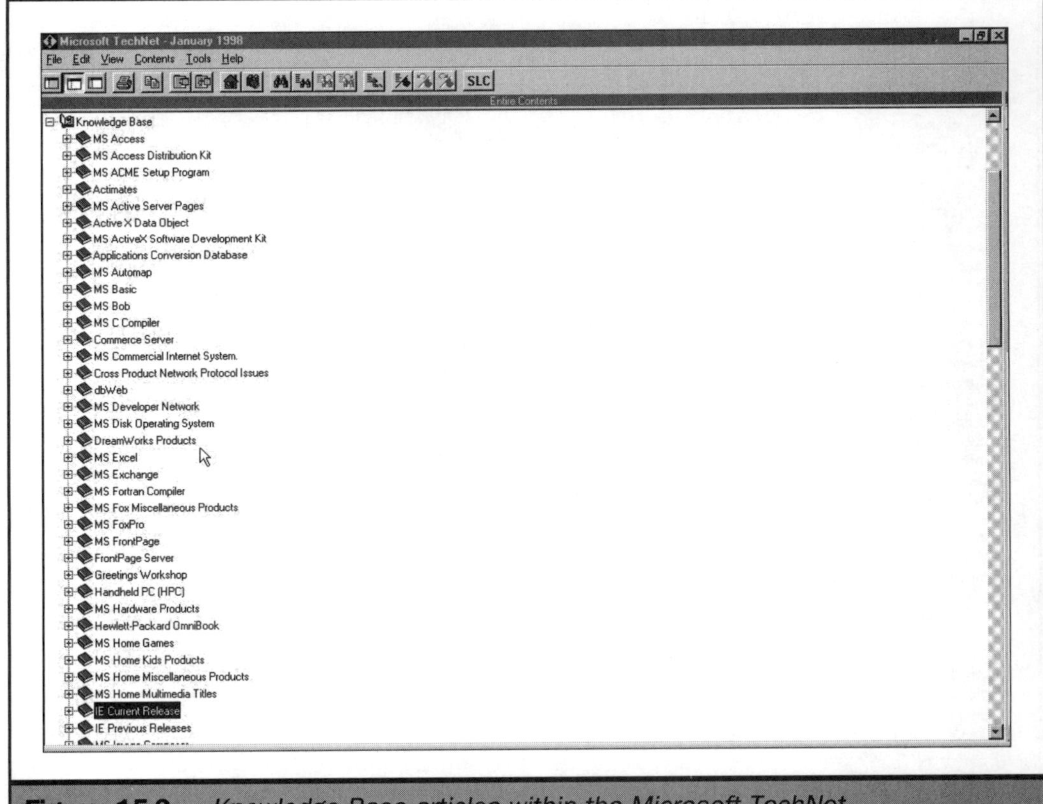

Figure 15-3. *Knowledge Base articles within the Microsoft TechNet*

related to the error. This information is invaluable in helping you to troubleshoot the errors you may see in the DBCC output file.

DBCC UPDATEUSAGE

DBCC UPDATEUSAGE is a Transact-SQL statement that can be run anywhere you can run a Transact-SQL statement. It works on a database, table, or index to evaluate and correct any inaccuracies in the *sysindexes* table for tables and clustered indexes. The most common indication that you should run DBCC UPDATEUSAGE is when the system stored procedure *sp_spaceused* is returning what you think is inaccurate information. This can happen after indexes have been dropped. You can also use the argument **updateusage** with *sp_spaceused* that will run DBCC UPDATEUSAGE before

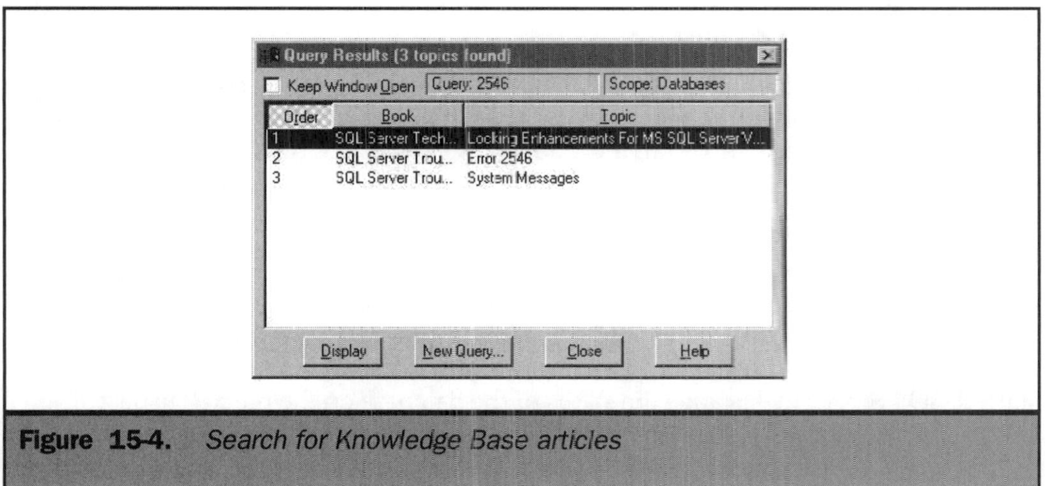

Figure 15-4. *Search for Knowledge Base articles*

it returns the space used information to you; however, be aware that this operation can take a while on a large database.

DBCC OPENTRAN

DBCC OPENTRAN is used to detect a long-running transaction that is preventing your transaction log from being truncated. It indicates the oldest distributed and non-distributed transactions marked for replication. An open transaction can prevent the transaction log from being cleared and the log can become full, and you may even be unable to truncate the log by issuing DUMP TRANSACTION statements. When this situation occurs, you have to be able to diagnose and fix the problem by knowing which transaction is problematic so you can dispense with it and bring the SQL Server back into its properly functioning state. The causes of a long-running query and an open transaction can be anything from less than perfect programming techniques to a SQL Server bug. SQL Server will not truncate an open transaction such as a transaction that has been issued the BEGIN TRANSACTION statement with a pending COMMIT TRANSACTION statement until that COMMIT TRANSACTION is issued. If an open transaction exists in the log, DBCC OPENTRAN displays the system process identification number (SPID) so that you may "kill" the process.

If you use the WITH TABLERESULTS argument, you will be able to accumulate the output of the DBCC OPENTRAN statement into a table. Analysis of this table will provide information about problem transactions and you may be able to fix a coding problem or find a work-around if there is a SQL Server bug or otherwise troubleshoot the situation as needed.

Suspect Databases

SQL Server changes the status of the database to "suspect" if it detects an event that compromises the integrity of the database. The database will become unavailable for use and the data contained within the database will be inaccessible.

Recovering a Suspect Database

There are certain times when it is wise to reset the suspect status in the *sysdatabases* system table and unmark the database as being suspect. Under certain circumstances the database is recoverable and the integrity of the database is intact. For example, if a backup of operating system files locks the database file right before SQL Server is started, SQL Server will change the status of the database on the file to "suspect" because it can not open the database file. Once the database file is unlocked, starting SQL Server will open the file, but the database will still be marked suspect and will be inaccessible until this status is removed.

Another example of this situation is SQL Server being unable to complete recovery on a database because the database or log is full. Use the following code listing to unmark a suspect database:

```
EXEC SP_CONFIGURE ALLOW UPDATES',1
RECONFIGURE WITH OVERRIDE
BEGIN TRAN
UPDATE sysdatabases
SET status = status - 256
WHERE name = databasename
AND status & 256=256
ROLLBACK TRAN

EXEC SP_CONFIGURE 'ALLOW UPDATES',0
RECONFIGURE WITH OVERRIDE
```

Use the ROLLBACK statement to check if there is more than one row updated. If only one row is updated, run the UPDATE statement again and use a COMMIT TRAN statement in place of the ROLLBACK TRAN statement. This will commit the change to the database. If more than one row is affected, you should make sure the ROLLBACK TRAN statement is performed and fix your where clause, because there should be only one database with a particular name.

Recovering a Suspect Database with the RESTORE Statement

You can attempt to recover the suspect database by using the RESTORE statement. The FROM clause of the RESTORE statement usually specifies the backup devices you are using to restore the backup. There is an implied subtle usage here. If the FROM clause is *not* used when the RESTORE statement is issued, a recovery occurs instead of a restore. You can use this when you need to recover the database after unmarking it suspect and/or repairing it, or you may want to use this technique to recover a database that has been restored with the NORECOVERY option. You can also use this technique when moving over to a standby server.

Adherence to Standards

One of the more important aspects of preventive maintenance is to enforce a set of standards across your servers. A set of standards may include the following:

- Directory structure (the location of database, log, operating system, program, Internet content, SQL backup, and application related files)
- RAID levels for fail over and redundancy on disk drives
- Frequency of DBCC and BACKUP maintenance procedures
- Procedures when an error is discovered in the DBCC output file
- The group having system administrator (SA)
- The group having database owner (DBO) access
- Naming conventions of user created objects
- Character set and sort order
- Guest access
- A central area of control over NT groups and domain accounts
- Installed communication protocols
- Security mode
- Versions of SQL Server and NT in use in production
- Password change intervals
- Memory

- IIS standards (FTP installation standards, home directories, directory permissions, privileges on virtual roots, services installed, member server versus primary, or backup domain server)

Standardization simplifies the database maintenance processes and contributes to a more efficient and organized operation. The standards should be documented and placed on a network share. This will be time well spent and will result in keeping database maintenance time to a minimum.

Backup Solutions

Backups offer an additional level of data protection after conditions occur where transaction recovery safeguards cannot meet data protection challenges. Providing the second level of data protection by maintaining current backup files is an important part of database maintenance responsibilities.

Database Backup

There are two fundamental types of database backups with variations of each, database backup and transaction log backup.

If you chose to only perform a database backup, you will be able to recover to the time of your last database backup. If you perform both database backups and transaction log backups, you will be able to recover your data up to the time that a failure occurred. The latter gives you the greater protection. The recovery solution is to restore your last database backup and then each transaction log backup until near the point in time that the corruption or loss of data occurred. You schedule your database backup to occur with the Database Maintenance Plan Wizard (see Figure 15-5). You schedule transaction log backups with the SQL Server Agent, as explained a little later in this chapter under the heading "Transaction Log Backups."

If you are backing up your databases with something other than a Database Maintenance Plan (such as the sqlmaint utility), you may want to add your database backup devices using either the *sp_addumpdevice* system stored procedure or the Enterprise Manager, expanding the server, and right-clicking on Backup Devices in the Enterprise Manager hierarchy tree. If you have not used a device to back up your database or log files and have used disk or tape files, you will have to use FROM DISK = or FROM TAPE = syntax to indicate from where the data will be restored. See Chapter 21 for the complete and detailed syntax of the BACKUP and RESTORE statements.

Differential Database Backup

A differential backup is an argument of the BACKUP DATABASE statement that, if used, backs up only the part of the database that has changed since the last full

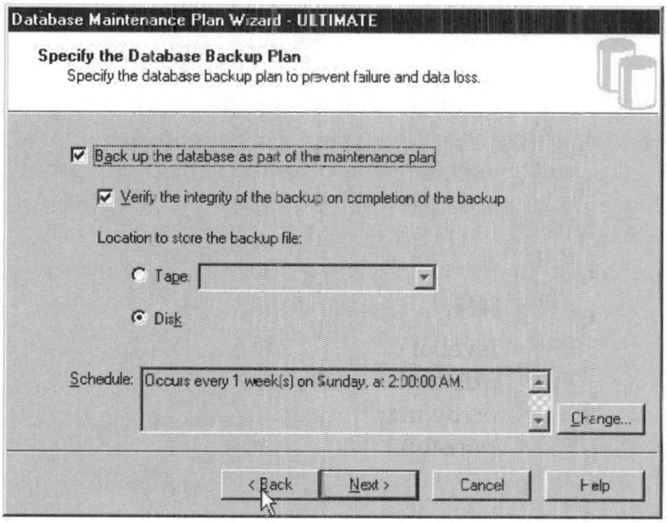

Figure 15-5. *Schedule database backups with Database Maintenance Plan Wizard*

database backup. This will usually result in a smaller backup file and can save time and space when you have a large database. A typical way to use a differential backup is to make a weekly full database backup and a daily incremental backup. These intervals can be changed according to your needs, of course.

You may also combine database, differential, and log backups to decrease the amount of time it takes to restore. If you choose to do this, you will restore the latest full database backup, restore the differential backups, and restore all log backups created after the differential backup in the exact sequence that the files were created.

Issue the following syntax to back up the database using a full database backup in conjunction with a differential backup:

```
BACKUP DATABASE database_name
TO database_device1
WITH INIT
GO
```

At a later point in time, issue the following syntax for your differential database backup:

```
BACKUP DATABASE database_name
TO database_device1
WITH DIFFERENTIAL
```

If you run into trouble later and need to restore, issue the syntax below to restore the database by first restoring the full backup and then the differential backup. Use the NORECOVERY argument if logs exist and need to be restored, or use the RECOVERY argument if no logs need to be restored after the differential backup is restored.

Full database RESTORE syntax:

```
RESTORE DATABASE database_name
FROM database_device1
WITH FILE = 1, NORECOVERY
```

Differential database RESTORE syntax:

```
RESTORE DATABASE database_name
FROM database_device1
WITH FILE = 2, NORECOVERY
```

Use NORECOVERY if you have additional transaction logs to RESTORE or RECOVERY if you have no transaction log backups to restore. Use the syntax outlined in the following section on transaction log backups to restore any existing transaction logs.

If you have not used a device to back up your database or log files and have used disk or tape files, you will have to use FROM DISK = or FROM TAPE = syntax to indicate from where the data will be restored. See Chapter 21 for the complete and detailed syntax of the BACKUP and RESTORE statements.

Transaction Log Backups

Transaction log backups can be run from a Database Maintenance Plan or by using the SQL Server Agent. Use the Database Maintenance Plan Wizard, or you can enter the Transact-SQL syntax for the transaction log backup by right-clicking on the SQL Server Agent in the Enterprise Manager and selecting New and then Job from the shortcut menu. Make sure that the *trunc.log on chkpt.* database option is false if you want to save transaction logs for recovery. You can schedule your transaction log backup to occur by using the Microsoft SQL Server Agent's automatic job scheduling functionality and choosing the Schedules Panel contained within the New Job screens. Try backing up the transaction log every 10 to 30 minutes and adjust the interval according to the number of new transactions and the amount of recoverability desired. You may also set an alert on the job step to page or e-mail a database administrator if the transaction log backup job step fails. Figure 15-6 shows the New Job Step screens. Notice the tabs in the New Job Properties window labeled Schedules and Notifications. Click these tabs to enter your schedule for running the job and to set up notification in the event of job failure or success.

If you have been backing up your logs every half hour and your failure occurs during that time interval, Microsoft SQL Server 7 allows you to use the RESTORE LOG STOPAT = 'Mar 7, 1998 12:00 AM' argument with any given time to restore only that part of the transaction log prior to the failure. You must use the WITH NORECOVERY argument of the RESTORE statement if you are restoring more than one log file except on the last log file, where you must use the WITH RECOVERY argument. Finally, you must remove all database users to restore a database and be connected as sysadmin (SA).

You will need to add your database backup devices using the *sp_addumpdevice* system stored procedure or use the Enterprise Manager, expanding the server and right-clicking on Backup Devices in the Enterprise Manager hierarchy tree. If you have not used a device to back up your database or log files and have used disk or tape files, you will have to use 'FROM DISK = ' or 'FROM TAPE =' syntax to indicate from where

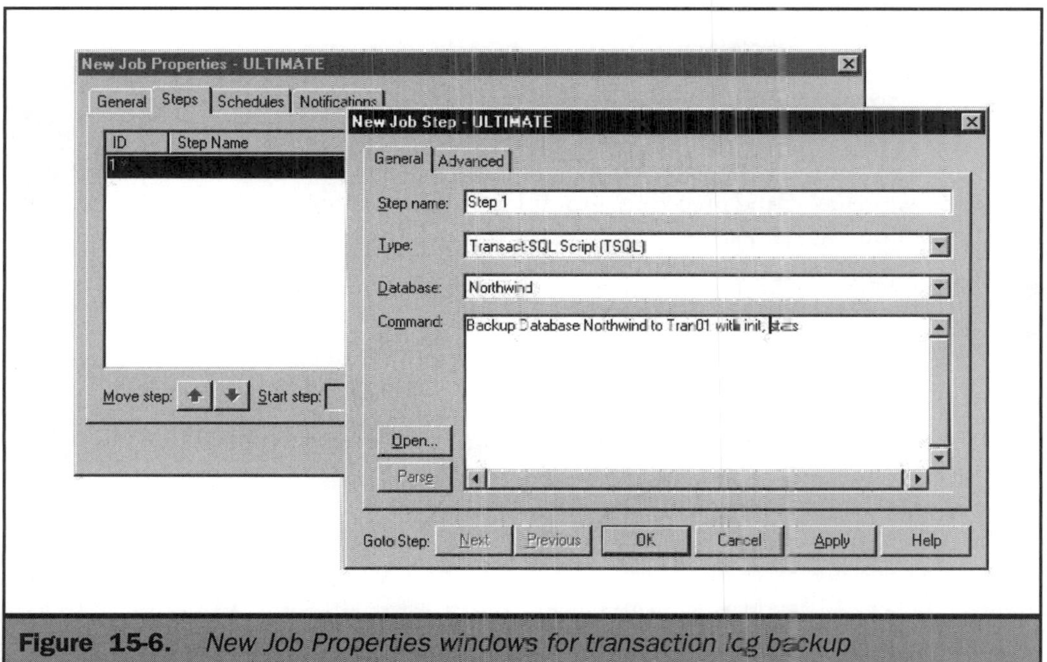

Figure 15-6. *New Job Properties windows for transaction log backup*

the data will be restored. See Chapter 21 for the complete and detailed syntax of the BACKUP and RESTORE statements.

To back up a transaction log, use the following syntax:

```
BACKUP LOG database_name
TO LOG_device1
WITH INIT
```

To restore when using a full database backup and transaction logs, the syntax depends on whether you are restoring only one transaction log or multiple transaction logs.

If you are restoring only one transaction log, first use the full database RESTORE syntax:

```
RESTORE DATABASE database_name
FROM database_device1
```

Then use the transaction log RESTORE syntax for only one transaction log:

```
RESTORE LOG database_name
FROM log_device1
WITH RECOVERY
```

If you have more than one transaction log to restore, you must first perform a full database restore (as in the preceding example) and then restore the first transaction log using the following syntax:

```
RESTORE LOG database_name
FROM log_device1
WITH NORECOVERY
```

Then restore the second transaction log using the following syntax:

```
RESTORE LOG database_name
FROM log_device2
WITH RECOVERY
```

You can see how WITH NORECOVERY is used on the first log file restored in a case of multiple transaction logs but WITH RECOVERY is used to restore the last transaction log file.

There are tradeoffs to using transaction log backups. You will be able to recover to the point of failure, but the BACKUP and RESTORE procedures are more involved. Remember that as part of your maintenance job steps you will have to clean up and remove the transaction log files from the operating system every time a full database backup occurs because SQL Server—at this point in time—does not automatically do this for you. See Chapter 25 for the complete and detailed syntax of the BACKUP and RESTORE statements.

Backups Using Multiple Backup Devices

If you have a very large database, if you copy backup files across the network on a scheduled basis, or if you want the BACKUP and RESTORE operations to occur more quickly, you may want to consider using a database striped backup to multiple backup devices. This will take advantage of SQL Server's capability to perform parallel IO to multiple devices and will decrease the amount of time it takes to back up or restore a database.

If you are using tape media and are using multiple backup devices, you will already have multiple tape drives installed. You will need to add your database backup devices using the *sp_addumpdevice* system stored procedure or using the Enterprise Manager, expanding the server and right-clicking on Backup Devices in the Enterprise Manager hierarchy tree.

The syntax to back up a database to multiple devices is:

```
BACKUP DATABASE database_name
TO database_device1, database_device2, database_device3, . . .
```

The syntax to RESTORE a database from multiple devices is:

```
RESTORE DATABASE database_name
FROM database_device1, database_device2, database_device3, . . .
```

See Chapter 25 for the complete and detailed syntax of the BACKUP and RESTORE statements.

Backup of Individual Database Files or Filegroups

If you perform a full database backup, you will be able to restore individual files or filegroups without ever having to back up just the individual file or filegroup. This means that if a known part of the database is lost and you know the file or filegroup on which it resides, you can restore only the individual file or filegroups rather than the entire database. This is useful for the very large databases (VLDBs) in the event a disk fails on a multiple file database. To maintain consistency with the remainder of the database after you have restored the file, you must restore the transaction logs beginning at the time the last full backup occurred. If you use this technique and the data has been modified, you must back up your transaction logs and restore them so that the database will be in a consistent state. This technique cannot be used with differential backups.

These types of restoration techniques are employed when the database is very large and the backup window is very small. You may use individual file and filegroup backups to back up half the files one night and the rest another night. If you choose to back up using this method, you must also maintain transaction log backups in order to bring the restored file or filegroups to the same point in time as the rest of the database.

If a table spans multiple files or filegroups, SQL Server will let you know you cannot restore a filegroup containing only a part of the table. In addition, if an index spans multiple files or filegroups, you must restore at the same time all the files and filegroups containing the index. If you implement files and filegroups across your databases, design the physical file structure of your databases with the rules for backup and restoration of files and filegroups in mind.

To back up an individual file or filegroup, use the following syntax:

```
BACKUP DATABASE database_name
file_or_filegroup , . . .
TO backup_file , . . .
WITH INIT
```

To restore an individual file or filegroup, use the following syntax:

```
RESTORE DATABASE database_name
file_or_filegroup , . . .
FROM backup_file , . . .
```

You must also restore the transaction logs files from the last database or file/filegroup backup to keep your database in a consistent state. You may also restore an individual file or filegroup from a full database backup without ever performing the individual file or filegroup backup. See Chapter 21 for the complete and detailed syntax of the BACKUP and RESTORE statements.

Backup/Restore Tape Restart Capability

The RESTART argument for the BACKUP and RESTORE statements provides the capability to restart the BACKUP or RESTORE operation if it was interrupted. This technique involves repeating the same BACKUP or RESTORE statement and adding the RESTART argument; however, there are some important caveats: This capability only applies to backups on tape media and for backups that span multiple tape volumes. This argument can save time if something happens in the middle of the tape backup or restore operation, and a restart becomes necessary.

Standby Servers

A *standby server* is another defense against loss of data. It is an entirely different set of hardware that is an exact configuration of the primary server and is kept current by initially restoring a full database backup and then restoring transaction logs on a scheduled periodic basis to maintain synchronization with the primary server (this is another task for the Microsoft SQL Server Agent). The server can be used to support ad hoc queries or to run DBCC checks when the transaction log restores are not running.

In the event of failure, the amount of time it takes to recover and provide the users access to the data will be substantially reduced, especially if the databases are very large. You will have to provide some mechanism to switch to a standby server in your application code because the server name and IP address will be different. The Microsoft Cluster Server used with SQL Server provides this fail-over support.

If you are using a standby server, use the WITH NO_TRUNCATE argument of the BACKUP LOG statement to save the complete log. This will allow recovery up to the time of failure. Restore this transaction log to the standby server, but be aware that any transactions not committed at the time of failure will be lost. When the primary server becomes available, the databases will have to be restored back to the primary server.

Keep in mind that the more frequently the transaction log is backed up the less time it will take to restore the transaction log to the standby server. Restore the database using the NORECOVERY argument of the RESTORE statement and restore each transaction log to the standby server using the STANDBY option of the RESTORE statement. Use the RECOVERY option to restore the final transaction log from the primary server. The NORECOVERY and STANDBY options of the RESTORE statement mean that checkpoints are not taken, so it is not necessary to set the *no chkpt. on recovery* database option on the database on the standby server.

In this chapter, we have covered the aspects of database preventive maintenance and data protection. The Microsoft SQL Server Agent and the Enterprise Manager can be used to perform your database maintenance tasks in an automated, scheduled manner. It is a time saver to take advantage of the new Maintenance Plan functionality and the new job step and scheduling functionality of the SQL Server Agent.

The Complete Reference

Chapter 16

Linked Servers and Remote Servers

Linked servers and remote servers both use the Microsoft Distributed Transaction Coordinator (MS DTC), albeit in different ways. Linked servers use OLE DB providers and data sources if the OLE DB distributed transaction interface is supported, whereas calls to stored procedures on remote servers use the ODBC CALL escape sequence or Transact-SQL EXECUTE syntax. Of the two mechanisms for remote servers, the ODBC CALL escape sequence is preferred because it is faster.

In this chapter, the Microsoft Distributed Transaction Coordinator is discussed, including how it performs updates to linked and remote servers through the use of the distributed transaction and the two-phase commit.

Microsoft Distributed Transaction Coordinator

The Microsoft Distributed Transaction Coordinator (MS DTC) is a service that Microsoft SQL Server adds to the Control Panel upon installation; it coordinates transactions among servers across a network of Microsoft Windows-based systems and can update data on more than one SQL Server or OLE DB data source.

An advantage to the MS DTC is that it guarantees the integrity of the transaction when the transaction includes many sources of data from different SQL Servers or OLE DB data sources (if the OLE DB distributed transaction interface is supported). In addition, stored procedures can be called on remote SQL Servers. The service guarantees that all of the data sources involved are updated or that none of them are updated if errors occur and the integrity of the entire transaction is not intact.

Updating different data sources connected over a network means that any number of things can go wrong. The network could be down, a computer could be down, or the database or application could experience errors. If any of these things happen, the application program must be able to keep the integrity of the transaction intact. An application programmer would not want to update a dollar amount on one data source and not have it updated on another because of a failure. Not only would the programmer then have to answer to accountants and production managers, it would prove difficult for the program itself to recover from the loss of data integrity.

If applications are written in Transact-SQL, C, or C++; use DB-Library or ODBC; and need to update data in one transaction on different data sources, MS DTC can simplify matters. Visual Basic applications can also use MS DTC by calling Transact-SQL stored procedures designed for the purpose of interfacing to MS DTC.

Transact-SQL applications can use the Transact-SQL BEGIN DISTRIBUTED TRANSACTION statement or they can let SQL Server automatically control MS DTC transactions. If a remote stored procedure on some other SQL Server is called, SQL Server and MS DTC work together to automatically coordinate the participation of all the remote servers referenced in any of the successively called stored procedures in the transaction.

If one remote stored procedure calls other remote stored procedures, all referenced SQL Servers automatically fall under the protective cover of the distributed transaction.

This will happen whether or not the Transact-SQL BEGIN DISTRIBUTED TRANSACTION statement is used with the remote stored procedure or not. If errors occur and the successively called SQL Servers cannot be reached, the entire transaction is rolled back on all the participating SQL Servers.

Even though SQL Server and MS DTC automatically coordinate distributed transactions for applications written in Transact-SQL, the Transact-SQL programming language cannot directly access MS DTC transaction objects.

For a higher level of control over DTC transaction objects, applications need to use C or C++ so that the transaction coordinator can be selected, transaction options objects can set a time out value for a transaction, and a description of the transaction can be given. Additionally, using C or C++ allows your application to avoid blocking the calling thread by using asynchronous Commit or Abort calls.

The MS DTC Administrative Console is provided within the Microsoft SQL Server program group on the NT Start Menu, or it can be invoked in the Enterprise Manager as a graphical user interface. The console allows you to view statistics about, as well as the status of, distributed transactions, and it provides the ability to stop and start the service. You can view all the transactions that are currently running, stop active transactions, or force transactions to commit or rollback. You can even remove a transaction from the transaction log of a coordinating MS DTC server. The panels in the MS DTC Administrative Console are shown in Figure 16-1.

The Trace panel in the MS DTC Administrative Console shows the event log and trace information. The capability to filter by severity level is present.

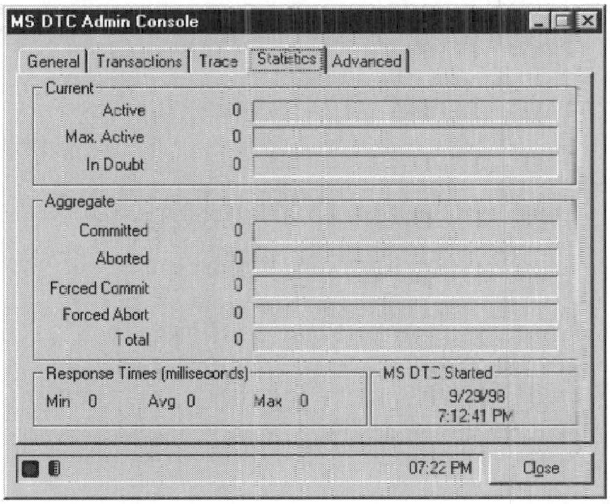

Figure 16-1. *MS DTC Administrative Console*

The MS DTC Statistics panel shows the current number of active transactions; the maximum number of concurrent transactions; and the number of committed, aborted, in-doubt, and administratively resolved transactions. In addition, the total number of processed transactions, transaction response times, and the date and time the MS DTC session started are displayed within the MS DTC Administrative Console panels.

The MS DTC Advanced configuration panel allows you to change MS DTC refresh frequencies and checkpoint and flush timers. It also lets you specify how old the displayed transactions are and the location of the MS DTC log file.

In the next section, we will see how the Microsoft Distributed Transaction Coordinator manages the two-phase commit.

Two-Phase Commit

The two-phase commit is a protocol to make transactions atomic and durable when more than one data source in involved in the transaction. It is coordinated by each MS DTC installation with one MS DTC installation assuming the responsibility for instructing the other MS DTC installations on the network to conduct the two-phase commit protocol with their local SQL Servers.

The main MS DTC installation is called the commit coordinator or the parent node. It is responsible for ensuring that the transaction either commits or aborts on all the servers involved and informs the application whether the transaction was committed or rolled back. The commit coordinator is always the MS DTC installation where the transaction originates.

The commit coordinator is chosen by the application after you install the MS DTC client utility on a client computer. If the transaction does not originate on the client, the application will not choose the commit coordinator, and the default commit coordinator will be the one referenced in the local system registry of the client computer. You can then configure MS DTC by choosing MS DTC from the NT Control Panel and choose the default commit coordinator for the client computer.

DB-Library Two-Phase Commit Functions

DB-Library two-phase commit functions can only be used in applications developed in SQL Server 6.5 and earlier. Your move to Microsoft SQL Server 7 should include plans to use the Microsoft Distributed Transaction Coordinator (MS DTC) instead of DB-Lib two-phase commit functions.

In the next section, we will see how the MS DTC manages the two-phase commit between a Subscribing and a Publishing SQL Server inside a remote stored procedure.

MS DTC, Replication, and the Updating Subscriber

Microsoft Distributed Transaction Coordinator (MS DTC) uses the Transact-SQL BEGIN DISTRIBUTED TRANSACTION statement to manage the two-phase commit between a Subscriber and Publisher inside a SQL Server remote stored procedure call. Using a SQL Server remote stored procedure will automatically enlist the capabilities of SQL Server and MS DTC to commit or roll back the transaction on all the referenced SQL Servers, whether the BEGIN DISTRIBUTED TRANSACTION statement is explicitly programmed in the remote stored procedure or not.

Conflict Detection for Publisher and Updating Subscriber

There are two methods used on the Publisher to detect conflict in transactions submitted from Subscribers:

- Timestamp conflict detection
- Row compare conflict detection

Timestamp conflict detection is used when a published table has a column with a timestamp data type. The Subscriber passes the timestamp to the Publisher, and the value is compared to the current timestamp on the Publisher for the row. If the values are the same, it means that the row on the Publisher has not changed after it was replicated to the Subscriber, so the transaction is committed.

Row compare conflict detection is used when a published table has no timestamp column. All of the Publisher column values in the row are compared to the updating Subscriber.

Loopback Detection for Timestamp Conflict Detection

Once a transaction is committed on the Publisher from the updating Subscriber, it is unnecessary to send the change back to the Subscriber using replication. SQL Server uses loopback detection only when there is a timestamp on the column. Add a timestamp column to your table if you wish to take advantage of this efficiency.

Distributed Transactions

To start a distributed transaction, use the BEGIN DISTRIBUTED TRANSACTION statement. A distributed query for linked servers or remote stored procedure calls for remote servers will be issued from the commit coordinator. This controlling server automatically calls MS DTC to enlist the linked and remote servers in the distributed transaction. When a COMMIT or ROLLBACK statement is issued, the commit coordinator, also known as the controlling SQL Server, calls MS DTC to manage the two-phase commit process by either committing or rolling back the transaction.

If a distributed query to a linked server is issued within a local transaction and the OLE DB distributed transaction interface is supported, the transaction automatically becomes a distributed transaction. If the data source does not support the OLE DB distributed transaction interface, only SELECT read-only statements are valid. Using the Transact-SQL COMMIT TRANSACTION, COMMIT WORK, ROLLBACK

TRANSACTION, or ROLLBACK WORK statements to complete a distributed transaction automatically calls MS DTC to manage the transaction.

Session-Level REMOTE_PROC_TRANSACTIONS Option

The REMOTE_PROC_TRANSACTIONS option can be turned on or off by using the Transact-SQL SET statement. When this session-level option is OFF, MS DTC transactions are not automatically promoted for remote stored procedure calls or linked server distributed queries with a local transaction. The Transact-SQL syntax to set this session-level option is:

```
set remote_proc_transactions {ON|OFF}
```

If REMOTE_PROC_TRANSACTIONS is set to OFF, remote stored procedure calls issued with a local transaction are not rolled back if the local transaction is rolled back. The changes to the remote server are committed when the remote stored procedure is finished executing on the remote server.

REMOTE PROC TRANS Server Configuration Parameter

REMOTE PROC TRANS is a server configuration controlled by using the sp_configure statement. This server configuration parameter sets the default setting of the REMOTE_PROC_TRANSACTIONS session-level option described in the preceding section.

REMOTE PROC TRANS is much the same as the session-level option in what it does, but it enables or disables implicit MS DTC transactions for an entire SQL Server system instead of just one session. The following syntax shows how to configure the SQL Server REMOTE PROC TRANS server configuration parameter:

```
sp_configure 'remote proc trans', 1
reconfigure with override
```

When using the REMOTE PROC TRANS server configuration parameter, 1 means ON and 0 means OFF. If REMOTE PROC TRANS is set to OFF, remote stored procedure calls issued with a local transaction are not rolled back if the local transaction is rolled back. The changes to the remote server are committed when the remote stored procedure is finished executing on the remote server.

MS DTC and COM

MS DTC is a part of the COM architecture, and transactions are a necessary part of distributed applications. The transaction idea was combined with COM in such a way that the installation, management, and use occurs automatically. The OLE transaction interfaces are implemented by using MS DTC. Expect the functionality and the extent of MS DTC to grow in the future by adding resource managers other than SQL Server.

Linked Servers

A linked server is a virtual server defined with the SQL Server stored procedure sp_addlinkedserver, which creates a linked server for the execution of distributed, heterogeneous queries against OLE DB data sources. After a linked server is added, the reference linked_server_name.catalog.schema.object_name can be used in Transact-SQL statements to reference data objects in the linked server.

Linked_server is the name of the linked server housing the data object. Catalog is the catalog name of the data object, schema is the schema name of the data object and object_name is the name of the data object. The combination of the names identifies a specific data object.

You can use the following system stored procedures to return metadata on linked servers:

- sp_linkedservers
- sp_catalogs
- sp_column_privileges
- sp_columns_ex
- sp_foreignkeys
- sp_primarykeys
- sp_indexes
- sp_table_privileges
- sp_tables_ex

See Chapter 23 for detailed information on system stored procedures.

Microsoft SQL Server uses mappings to connect to the OLE DB provider as the current SQL Server login. The current SQL Server login mapping to a remote SQL Server login is similar to the Remote Procedure Call (RPC) mappings, except that a different syntax is used. Also, with linked servers and distributed queries, the mapping is done at the source server instead of the receiving server as is the case with RPC mappings.

The system stored procedures *sp_droplinkedsrvlogin* and *sp_addlinkedsrvlogin* create the explicit mappings and the default mappings that permit all users to map to their corresponding user login on the linked server. They are created when a linked server is added using the system stored procedure *sp_addlinkedserver*. Chapter 23 contains detailed information about system stored procedures such as *sp_addlinkedserver*.

How to Define a Remote Server

To facilitate connections between SQL Servers in an organization, SQL Server adds remote servers. In this way a SQL Server can authenticate connections originating from other SQL Servers. Each individual SQL Server on a network can control access to it by listing the SQL Servers from which it accepts connections in its *sysservers* system table.

Use the following syntax to define a remote server. This syntax can also be used to define the name of the local server.

```
sp_addserver 'remote_server_name'
```

This stored procedure executes on a remote server and adds the remote server to the *sysservers* system table in the *master* system database.

Calling Remote Stored Procedures

Mechanisms to call remote stored procedures consist of the ODBC CALL escape sequence and the Transact-SQL EXECUTE statement. The ODBC CALL escape sequence is the best performing mechanism.

Using ODBC means that an application is used to retrieve the return codes of stored procedures. The SQL Server ODBC driver uses a protocol that has been optimized to send remote stored procedure calls between SQL Servers, and a lot of the processing and parsing is eliminated to increase performance.

Remote Configuration Options

You can view and set remote server configuration options in the Enterprise Manager by right-clicking on a server and selecting Properties and then the Connections panel (see Figure 16-2). The configuration to allow other SQL Servers to connect remotely via RPC can be changed here, as well as the number of seconds to wait before returning from a query. The default is zero, which means wait forever or until SQL Server is restarted. Hopefully, it will finish before then!

You can also change the setting to enforce distributed transactions used for the Microsoft Transaction Server (MTS) and set the maximum concurrent users. This is a value between 0 and 256 with a default of 10 and determines the maximum number of allowable remote servers that can connect concurrently. Remote server connections must be permitted on the SQL Server before a value for the maximum number of remote servers can be set. Changing these configuration options requires a stop and a start of the SQL Server.

You must change the configuration options on both servers for the settings to take effect.

Accessing Remote Servers Using Remote Logins

To access remote servers using remote logins, explicit mappings must be set up to a specific user ID and password for SQL Server logins. However, it is very easy to map

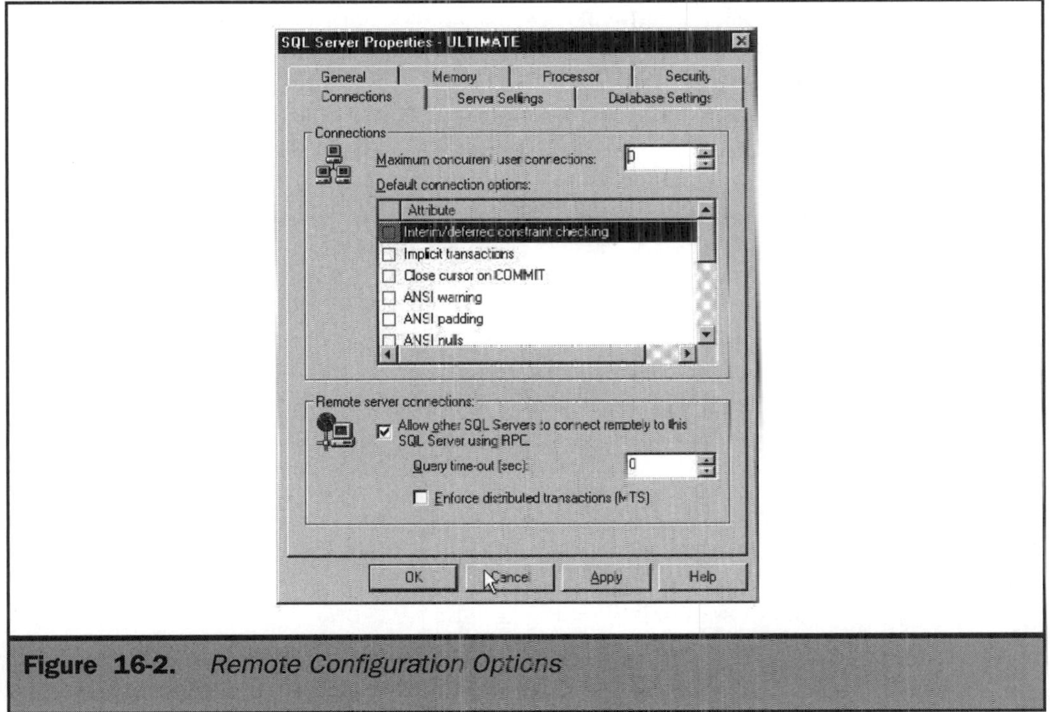

Figure 16-2. *Remote Configuration Options*

all users, and this can be done by using only the **remoteserver** argument of the system stored procedure, *sp_addremotelogin*.

The following syntax explicitly adds a remote login:

```
sp_addremotelogin {'remoteserver'} [, 'login' [, 'remote_name']]
```

How the parameters are used determines the extent of the login mappings. Using only the remoteserver argument means that all users on the remote server are mapped to existing logins of the same name on the local server. The local login matches the login on the remote server.

If the remoteserver and login arguments are given, all users on the remote server are mapped to the given local login. When users on the remote server connect to the local SQL Server, they connect as the login that is given.

If the remote name argument is given in addition to the other two arguments, then only the user named by the remote name argument is mapped to the given login on the local server. When the remote name on the remote server connects to the local SQL Server, they connect as the given login.

The default status of the remote login is not NT Authentication (trusted security). If you do not want the password check to occur, use the *sp_remoteoption* system stored procedure to change the status of the password. Details about the system stored procedure *sp_remoteoption* and how to use it can be found under the *sp_remoteoption* system stored procedure in Chapter 23.

In summary, the steps to add a system administrator (SA) connection to a remote server are:

Execute on the local server called server1:

```
sp_addlinked server     server2
GO
```

Execute on the remote server called server2:

```
sp_addlinked server     Server1
GO
sp_add remotelogin Server1, sa, sa
GO
sp_serveroption   Server1, 'data access', TRUE
GO
```

Note *Use sp_addserver and sp_configure 'remote access' when adding servers with a version earlier than version 7.*

Use the following syntax to keep from having to enter a password:

```
sp_serveroption   Server1, sa, sa, trusted, TRUE
```

In this chapter, we covered linked servers and remote servers and the way they use the Microsoft Distributed Transaction Coordinator (MS DTC) to perform the two-phase commit. In the next chapter, we will take a look at the SQL Server Profiler to explore ways of troubleshooting performance problems.

Chapter 17

Tools to Monitor Server Performance

It is important to monitor Microsoft SQL Server to make sure you are not experiencing performance bottlenecks. The three key areas that can become problematic are performance, throughput, and concurrency. Your queries can be slow, your transactions per second can be less than desirable, and your total number of concurrent users can cause locking and poor performance if your hardware is not scaled correctly or the application is not written correctly. Configuration options can be changed to tune the server if you experience problems in any of the three key areas, and applications problems can be identified and program changes can be made if the application is the culprit.

There are two graphical tools that provide the capability to keep an eye on the activities affecting your server's performance, the SQL Server Profiler and the SQL Server Performance Monitor. The more proficient you become at using these tools, the faster you can detect a problem and the sooner you can fix it.

The SQL Server Profiler has taken the place of SQL Trace and has the capability to provide real-time data on activities happening on the server. This data can be captured for analysis by saving it to a table or a file, and a baseline for SQL Server performance can be established.

Of the two tools, SQL Server Profiler provides more information about database performance. However, SQL Performance Monitor has the additional capability of scheduling jobs and generating alerts when performance thresholds are exceeded.

SQL Server Profiler

SQL Server Profiler is designed to be an application debugging tool for the system administrator. It provides visibility to Transact SQL statements and connections and identifies problem queries, inserts, updates, and other events occurring on SQL Server. This tool also monitors remote procedure calls.

The SQL Server Profiler is invoked by choosing SQL Server Profiler from the Microsoft SQL Server menu that appears under the NT Start button or from the Tools Menu in the Enterprise Manager.

SQL Server Profiler Queue

SQL Server Profiler uses a queue to hold the events to be captured. The size of the queue can be changed within the SQL Server Profiler by selecting Options from the View menu and changing the number of items to buffer for display to the console, as shown in Figure 17-1.

The queue functions just as any buffer does: the first thing in is the first thing out. Each trace is produced by different modules of computer code called producers, one producer for each event category that is busy sending events to the queue in chronological order. SQL Server controls the queue by pausing producers until space is available. If the timeout period passes before a producer can write to the queue, SQL

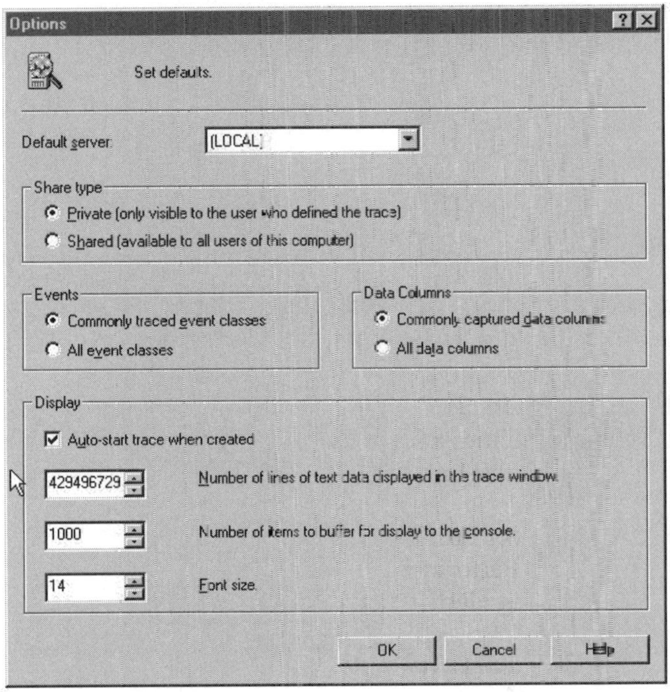

Figure 17-1. *SQL Server Profiler, Queue options*

Server pauses *all* the producers; this is called the autopause state. Producers continue to collect the event data but do not write to the queue during the autopause state.

If you would like to boost the thread priority to move more events from the buffer and get out of the autopause state, go to the File menu and click Properties. Select a Trace Name from the General Panel and click the button next to the SQL Server drop-down list box. You will see the server queue settings so you can change them to boost the thread priority on the screen shown in Figure 17-2.

Categories were established for related events traced by the SQL Server Profiler. In the next section we will look at trace event categories.

Trace Event Categories

Trace events are grouped in the following categories:

- Lock
- Misc

- Objects
- SQL Operators
- Scan
- Session
- Stored Procedures
- TSQL
- Transaction

Let's take a closer look at some of the categories to see what specific events we can trace that could give an idea of the performance of the server.

Lock Events

The SQL Server Profiler lock category contains the following trace events:

- Acquisition of a lock
- Canceled lock requests
- Deadlocks
- Lock releases
- Lock timeouts

Locking problems on Microsoft SQL Server usually occur when an application is not written correctly. Unfortunately, nearly every application in its infancy experiences locking problems. Getting as much information about the cause of the problem as

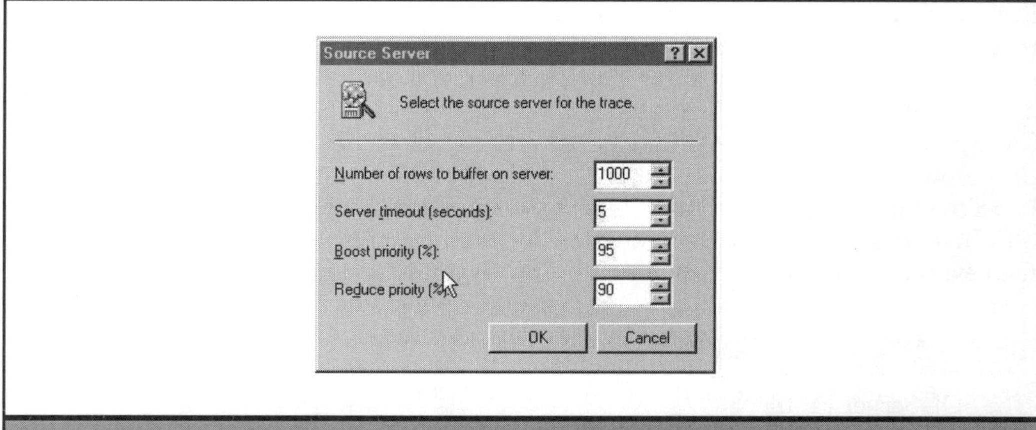

Figure 17-2. *SQL Server Profiler Trace Name properties*

possible makes it easier and faster to pinpoint the code involved in the locking problem using SQL Server Profiler.

Miscellaneous Events

The SQL Server Profiler miscellaneous category contains the following trace events:

- Attention
- Auto-UpdateStats
- CursorOpen
- ErrorLog
- EventLog
- HashBail
- LoginFailed
- Recompile(NoHints)
- ServiceControl

The miscellaneous event descriptions include interrupted or broken connections, events around the automatic running of update statistics, SQL Server cursor opening events, events writing to the SQL Server error log and the event log, hashing operations reverting to an alternate plan, unsuccessful login attempts, stored procedures and triggers recompiling without the given optimization hints, and pausing or restarting SQL Server.

Objects Events

The SQL Server Profiler objects category contains the following trace events:

- Object:Closed
- Object:Created
- Object:Deleted
- Object:Opened

The objects event descriptions include when an open object has been closed for SELECT, INSERT, or DELETE statements; when an object has been created, deleted or accessed; when a SQL INSERT, DELETE, or SELECT has taken place; the degree of parallelism; and when a table or index scan starts and stops.

Session Events

The SQL Server Profiler session category contains the following trace events:

- Connect

- Disconnect
- ExistingConnection

The session event descriptions include all connection events, all disconnect events, and activity by users logged on before the trace began.

Stored Procedure Events

The SQL Server Profiler stored procedure category contains the following trace events:

- SP:CacheHit
- SP:CacheInsert
- SP:CacheMiss
- SP:CacheRemove
- SP:Completed
- SP:ExecContext
- SP:Recompile
- SP:Starting
- SP:StmtStarting

Stored procedure trace events include finding a stored procedure in the procedure cache, removing or inserting a stored procedure into the procedure cache, completed stored procedures, the local state for the executing procedure, recompiling or starting stored procedures, and the beginning of a statement contained within a stored procedure.

TSQL Events

The SQL Server Profiler TSQL category contains the following trace events:

- RPC:Completed
- RPC:Starting
- SQL:BatchCompleted
- SQL:BatchStarting
- SQL:StmtStarting

TSQL trace events include completed remote procedure calls, remote procedure calls that have started, completed batch of Transact-SQL statements, when a batch of Transact-SQL statements is starting, and when each Transact-SQL statement is starting.

Transaction Events

The SQL Server Profiler Transaction category contains the following trace events:

- DTCTransaction
- SQLTransaction

Transaction trace events include MS DTC two-phase commit transactions between databases and begin, commit, save point, and rollback transactions.

As you can see, the SQL Server Profiler allows you to trace a number of important events. Don't forget to use this tool when you are experiencing difficulties on your server. The following section covers how to create a trace.

Creating a Trace

To create a SQL Server trace, select the SQL Server Profiler from the Microsoft SQL Server program group. When the Profiler is running, select New from the File menu, then Trace. Type in a name for the trace in the Trace Name dialog box on the General panel, select the SQL Server from the drop-down list box and decide if you want to capture the output to a file or to a table, and enter the location. Click the Events panel and select the events you would like to trace. Figure 17-3 shows the Events panel. After

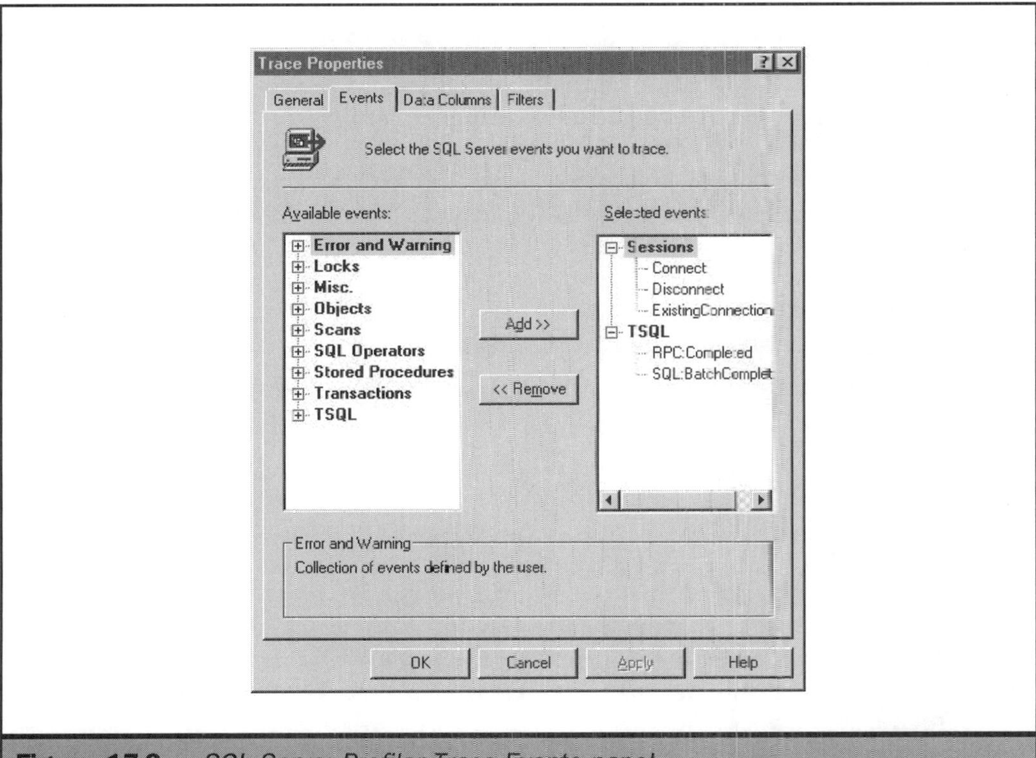

Figure 17-3. *SQL Server Profiler Trace Events panel*

selecting your trace events, select the Data Columns panel, select any additional columns you wish to include in the trace output and, finally, in the Filters panel, filter any events you do not wish to see.

Select the OK button and the trace starts immediately, sending the results to your selected destination. If you did not pick file or table, results are sent to the screen.

Working with an Existing Trace

To start a SQL Profiler trace that you have already created, select the SQL Server Profiler from the Microsoft SQL Server program group. When the Profiler is running, select Run Traces from the File menu and select the trace you would like to start from the list of existing traces.

You can also stop, pause, and delete traces from the File menu. Traces must be stopped before they can be deleted. All active traces must be stopped before you can close the SQL Server Profiler window.

You can select Properties from the File menu to modify an active trace after you have selected Run Traces, and the trace will appear on the screen or output to a table or file. Select the General, Events, Data Columns, or Filters panels for the characteristics you wish to modify.

If you have multiple active traces and wish to clear the trace window to see other traces, select Clear Trace Window from the File Menu.

Trace Output File

If you have chosen to save the data to a trace file in the General panel, as shown in Figure 17-4, the trace output will be saved to a file. This .scu file has several important uses:

- Capturing events for resolution of SQL Server errors
- Debugging extended stored procedures
- Establishing metrics for server events over a period of time
- Assisting in creating a workload file for the Index Tuning Wizard
- Inputting to Replay SQL Server functionality in SQL Server Profiler

Replay SQL Server

The Replay SQL Server functionality of SQL Server Profiler plays back the trace capture data file in real time or compressed mode. This will actually apply the Transact SQL in the file to the database. You can select the Replay SQL Server functionality from the SQL Server Profiler menu. See Chapter 7 for more information on Replay SQL Server.

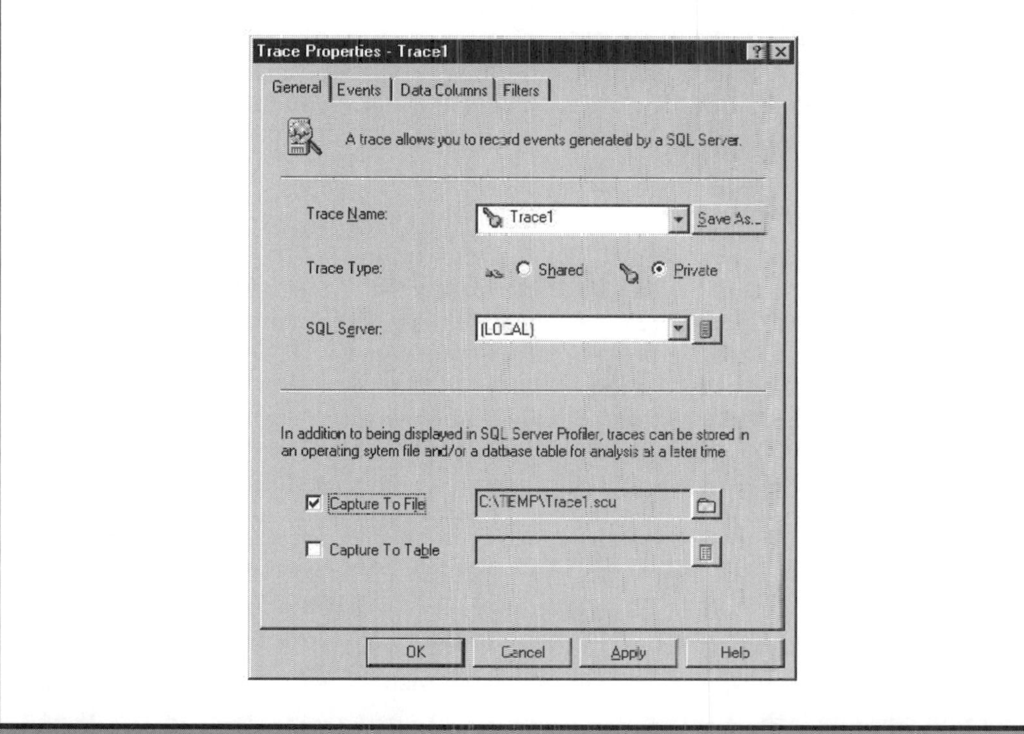

Figure 17-4. *SQL Server Profiler General panel*

SQL Server Performance Monitor

SQL Server Performance Monitor also provides the ability to monitor server performance and activity. The additional capability exists to set thresholds on selected counters and generate alerts when a threshold is reached.

The SQL Performance Monitor comes with the installation of SQL Server and is available as a selection from the Microsoft SQL Server program group.

Starting SQL Server Performance Monitor

From the NT Start menu, select the SQL Server program group and then select the SQL Server Performance Monitor. SQL Server Performance Monitor has charts that you can create, view, and save. You can also select objects and counters and add them to a chart. The charts display different colors to represent different counters. To keep a chart small and readable, create different charts to monitor different types of statistics.

Select New Chart from the SQL Server Performance Monitor File menu, then select the Edit menu and Add to Chart to bring up counters to select for monitoring. Select the counters you wish to monitor by adding them to the chart. When this task is complete, you will see the different colors in the chart monitoring different types of statistics.

Generating an Alert

This section explains how to generate an alert when a threshold is exceeded in the SQL Server Performance Monitor. Select the Performance Monitor from the Microsoft SQL Server program group. From the Performance Monitor View menu, select Alert. The Alert Log screen will display. From the Edit menu, select Add to Alert and then an object of interest and a counter. In the Alert If box, select the radio button for Over or Under and enter a threshold number. Finally, enter a sqlalrtr70 command in the Run Program on Alert box.

Here's the syntax of the sqlalrtr70 command to enter in the Run Program on Alert box:

```
sqlalrtr70 -E error_number [-S server_name] [-P password]
[-D database_name] [-V severity] [-T ]
```

In the preceding syntax, the error that will be raised on the server is whatever the error number is after the –E argument. The sqlalrtr70 parameters -E, -S, -P, -D, -V, and -T are case-sensitive, so be sure to enter them in uppercase. You may also choose to run the alert First Time or Every Time.

But wait, you are not finished yet! To generate an alert from a SQL Server Performance Monitor threshold, you are required to set up two different alerts; along with the SQL Server Performance Monitor alert described in the preceding text, you must set up a SQL Server alert.

The first part of creating a SQL Server alert is to create a user-defined event error message by using the Enterprise Manager to expand a server, then select SQL Server Agent and Alerts from the Enterprise Manger hierarchy tree. Select an alert in the Result pane by double-clicking it, or right-click an alert in the Result pane and select Properties. Click the browse button (…) to display the Manage Server Messages dialog box as shown in Figure 17-5.

Click the New button to create a user-defined message. You can use this error message to create a SQL Server alert when the error is raised by the Performance Monitor. Enter the same error number you plan to use in the sqlalrtr70 command in the Run Program on Alert box in the Performance Monitor. Error numbers for user-defined messages begin at 50001. SQL Server reserves the numbers less than 50001 for itself.

The last step is to create a new SQL Server alert that will go off when the error is raised. To create an alert using your user-defined error number, expand a server in the Enterprise Manager hierarchy tree, expand SQL Server Agent, right-click Alerts, and

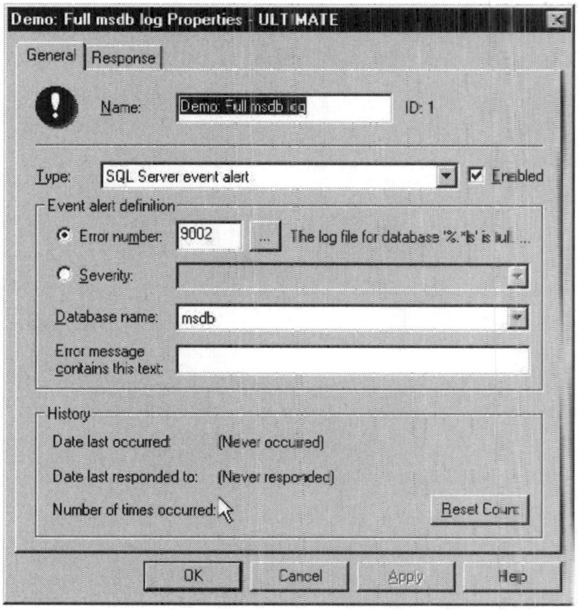

Figure 17-5. *Creating a user-defined error message*

select New Alert. Type in a name for the alert, select the Error Number radio button, press the browse button (…) and select the error number that you just created and that is referenced in your sqlalrtr70 command. The alert is enabled by default. Be sure to select the database from this screen if you want the alert to run in only one database. See Figure 17-6.

Select the Response panel to indicate what, whom, and how to notify when the alert goes off.

The SQL Server Performance Monitor and the SQL Server Agent service must be running for the alert to go off.

When the SQL Server Performance Monitor threshold is exceeded, the SQL Server Performance Monitor alert is generated, which in turn starts the sqlalrtr70 utility. This utility communicates with SQL Server Agent, the isql utility, and SQL Server Performance Monitor. The isql utility connects to the SQL Server and runs the RAISERROR WITH LOG Transact-SQL statement, which will write the event to the Windows NT application log. SQL Server Agent notices the event, and the SQL Server alert goes off and notifies whomever you selected in the Response panel when you created the new SQL Server alert.

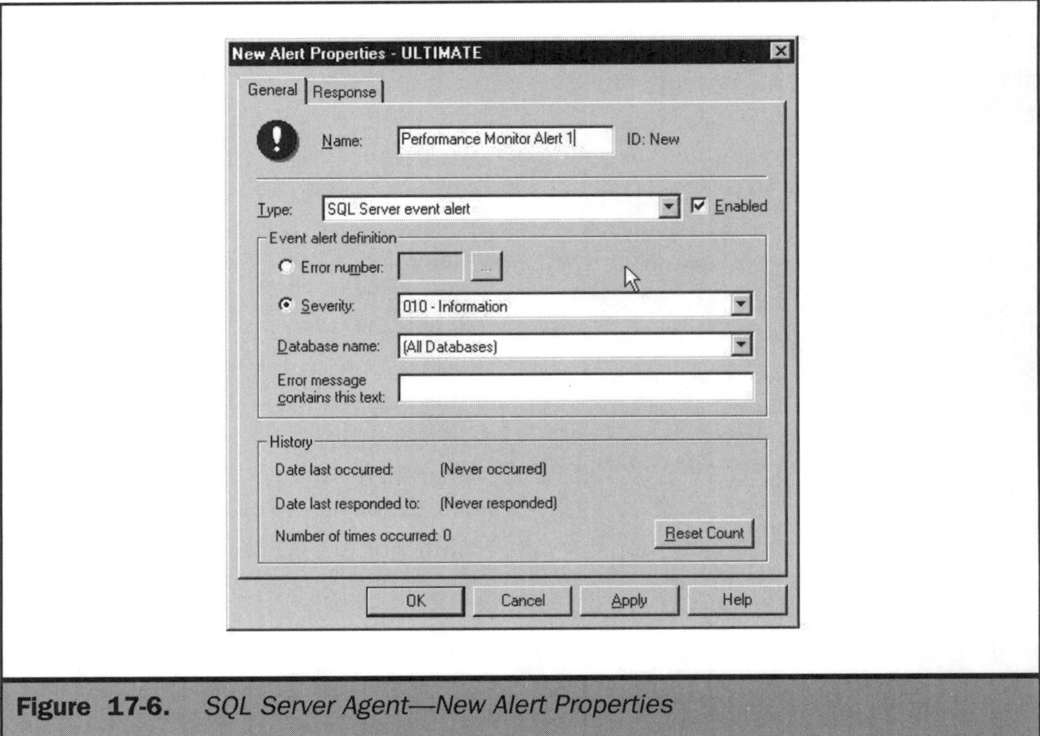

Figure 17-6. *SQL Server Agent—New Alert Properties*

Objects and Counters

SQL Server Performance Monitor collects information from performance counters grouped within a performance object. SQL Server counters you may find useful to monitor are:

- **Access Methods Object—Page Splits/sec** Caused by index pages that are too full.
- **Access Methods Object—Table Lock Escalations/sec** Number of times per second locks on a table are escalated.
- **Access Methods Object—Extents Allocated/sec** Extents allocated per second by database objects storing data.
- **Access Methods Object—Extents deallocated/sec** Extents deallocated per second by database objects storing data.
- **Access Methods Object—Worktables Created/sec** Number of worktables that were created in the previous second.

- **Buffer Manager Object—Buffer Cache Hit Ratio** Percentage of time that a request was found in the buffer cache in memory rather than read from disk. This ratio should approach 100 percent; the higher it is, the better the server performance.
- **Buffer Manager Object—Checkpoint Writes/sec** Dirty pages per second written to disk via a checkpoint.
- **Buffer Manager Object—Page Reads/sec** Number of physical page reads per second and the total number of physical page reads per second across all databases. If this value is high, your application should be examined in the areas of indexes, query efficiency, and design of the database.
- **Buffer Manager Object—Readahead Pages/sec** Number of physical I/O requests per second to read ahead and get the page before it is actually needed.
- **Cache Manager Object—Cache Hit Ratio** Percentage of time that a request was found in the data cache in memory rather than read from disk. This ratio should approach 100 percent; the higher it is, the better the server performance.
- **Databases Object—Transactions/sec** Number of Transact-SQL command batches executed per second. High transactions/sec is indicative of good throughput.
- **Databases Object—Active Transactions** Number of active transactions on the database.
- **Databases Object—Log Growths** Number of times the log has to be increased in size.
- **Latches Object—Average Latch Wait Time** Wait time in milliseconds when latches had to wait (latches are part of the new version 7 locking paradigm).
- **Locks Object—Number of Deadlocks/sec** Number of locks per second that became deadlocked.
- **Replication Logreader Object—Delivery Latency** The latency in seconds of the logreader.
- **Replication Logreader Object—Delivery Rate** Number of logreader commands inserted per second.
- **Replication Merge Object—Conflicts** Conflicts in the updating subscriber are counted. A value greater than zero means a loser and the conflict must be managed.
- **Replication Snapshot Object—Bulk Copy Rate** Number of rows bulk copied each second.
- **General Statistics Object—Logins/sec** Number of logins per second.

Performance Considerations

The SQL Server Performance Monitor can degrade performance on your server depending on how long it is run and what you are monitoring as well as the hardware platform, the number of counters, and the update interval you have chosen.

Permissions Needed to Connect to SQL Server

The SQL Server Performance Monitor uses Windows NT Authentication only. Be sure that the Windows NT account running SQL Server Performance Monitor has access to connect to SQL Server and is a member of the SQL Server public role. See Chapter 5, "Integration with Windows NT Security," for more information on Windows NT Authentication and the public role.

Running the Performance Monitor from a Remote Workstation

The Performance Monitor can be run from a remote workstation by installing the client utilities for SQL Server on a workstation (see Chapter 11, "Installing SQL Server") and selecting Performance Monitor from the SQL Server program group on the NT Start menu.

If SQL Server is not configured with the Named Pipes network protocol, SQL Server Performance Monitor will not be able to connect to the SQL Server selected. If you are having trouble connecting, check the network protocols for SQL Server by running the Server Network Utility from the SQL Server program group on the NT Start menu at the console of the computer installed with SQL Server. Verify that Named Pipes is an installed network protocol. Press the Add button to add it if it is not in the list.

Part IV

Development—The Programming Language

Chapter 18

Development Topics

In this chapter, we will explore different topics related to developing applications with SQL Server 7. Row-level locking and deadlock avoidance, lock escalation, and better query performance in this version will directly benefit developers, as well as SQL Server's integration with other Microsoft development tools with which you can debug your stored procedures, such as Visual C++ and Visual Basic. You can use the sample programs provided in the Samples directory where SQL Server 7 is installed.

One item that is particularly useful is the creation of the database diagram discussed in the next section. This is the map of your database and is important to those who inherit the system and need to provide database maintenance after the development process is complete. It also benefits developers coming into a project after it has started.

Database Diagram

The Visual Database Tools in Microsoft Visual Studio provide the capability to create a database diagram. The Database Designer has a special graphical user interface with which you can create and change the structure of not only Microsoft SQL Server databases but also Oracle databases. You can use "what if" designs without impacting your current design until you are ready to pass the scripts created by the Database Designer to your database administrator. Relationships, indexes, and constraints, as well as the modification of database objects and data definition language changes, can be done without writing a single line of Transact-SQL code.

The Visual Database Tools are being integrated into the Enterprise Manager, and we will see more and more of this integration as time goes on. Negotiating a complex database without a database diagram is difficult, so it is best to keep database diagrams of complicated database schemas up-to-date.

Data Integrity

There are many compelling reasons to enforce data integrity on your database, and Microsoft SQL Server provides many avenues and vehicles to guarantee the quality of your data. There are four aspects of data integrity:

- Entity integrity
- Domain integrity
- Referential integrity
- User-defined integrity

Each of these aspects is explained in the following sections as well as the methods of achieving them. Adopting the methods and implementing them on your database will not only achieve data quality but will prevent the costly data auditing and subsequent data cleansing tasks that evolve from lack of data integrity.

Entity Integrity

It is very important to make sure that every row is unique in a table and that the row can be pinpointed and accessed without involving any other row. Entity integrity in the form of uniqueness is accomplished through the creation of primary key constraints, unique indexes, unique constraints, or IDENTITY properties.

A primary key is a column or multiple columns containing values that are not the same in other rows in the table. There can be only one primary key per table, and the primary key columns should not allow nulls. When a primary key is created, SQL Server implements table uniqueness by creating a unique index for the primary key column(s). The implementation of a primary key on a table not only creates the desired result of making the row unique but also allows you to retrieve your data faster when accessing the table with the primary key index.

A more elaborate and sophisticated method of enforcing uniqueness on a table is the creation of an identity column. Defining the column with an IDENTITY property is often done for primary keys. The benefit to this is that the value in the column is automatically created by SQL Server at the time the row is inserted, and the application does not have to know or store the next value for the column. Since data access is faster where the index is an integer, performance is increased.

If the IDENTITY property is used and a row is inserted into the table and the insert fails, the value will not be used in the table and the next available number is still incremented. So, if you insert row 10 and the insert fails for whatever reason, the value 10 will never exist in that column; the next time the insert to the table succeeds, 11 will appear after row 9. However, you can manipulate the identity values in the table to use the unused values by using the statement SET IDENTITY_INSERT ON and giving the integer that you want inserted into the row if it does not already exist in the table. You will want to use the statement SET IDENTITY_INSERT OFF when you are finished. You may also find the DBCC CHECKIDENT statement useful to check and change the IDENTITY value.

There can only be one primary key per table, and you may have a situation where you need unique values in columns that are not the primary key. The UNIQUE constraint can also be used to create a unique index in a different column. When a duplicate row is inserted, SQL Server issues an error message telling the user a duplicate row already exists, preventing the insertion of the duplicate row. By default, primary key constraints use a CLUSTERED index, and UNIQUE constraints use NONCLUSTERED indexes. If your primary key is long, you may want to specify a NONCLUSTERED index, since NONCLUSTERED indexes now use the clustered key instead of a row-identifier.

Domain Integrity

Domain integrity means that only a range of values is valid for a column. The enforcement of only allowing certain values in a column is accomplished using data types, CHECK constraints and RULES, DEFAULT values, NOT NULL definitions, and FOREIGN KEY constraints.

Data types are used to define the types of data that can be placed in columns, local variables, and stored procedure parameters. You can use the data types that SQL Server provides or you can define your own data types. This will limit what can be inserted into a column; for example, you can not insert character data into a column created with a data type of integer. A CHECK constraint defines the values or formatting of values that can be placed in a column in a table, such as a phone number or a zip code. You can define more than one CHECK constraint for a single column, and you can add constraints to new or existing tables.

RULES are used in SQL Server 7 for backwards compatibility and do the same thing as CHECK constraints except that only one rule can exist for a column. Use CHECK constraints instead of RULES for SQL Server 7. RULES also requires the additional overhead of having to be bound to a column, while CHECK constraints are created when the table is created or altered.

Default values can be used to place a value in a column when you may not know the value, the data is coming in with a null value and the column does not allow nulls, or you do not want a null in the column. You can define a default value for the column by using the DEFAULT keyword when creating or altering a table. For example, if you want to average a column but you do not want the column to contain a null and be ignored entirely, placing a default zero in each row in the column makes your average valid and inclusive of all rows in the table.

Defining a column as NOT NULL at table creation time will prevent the placement of a NULL value into the column and is another method of ensuring data integrity, specifically, domain integrity. NULL in a column means the value is unknown and NULL behaves differently than empty or zero values because you can not compare NULL values and they are not equal. NULLS can create headaches later because, when using Transact-SQL statements, each statement can react differently to NULL values.

A FOREIGN KEY constraint is used with a primary key or a unique constraint to make sure that the only values inserted into the column are also contained in the primary key column in another table. This not only is used for domain integrity but also for referential integrity covered next.

Referential Integrity

Using referential integrity means that the relationships defined between tables are preserved and no orphan rows are allowed on your database. This means that SQL Server will prevent a user from adding a row to a child table where there is not a parent row in the parent table. It will also prevent the deletion or update of a parent row when there are children in another table.

SQL Server prevents this through the implementation of the FOREIGN KEY constraint and the CHECK constraint described in the preceding section.

If none of the standard SQL Server implementations to ensure integrity satisfies your requirements, you can define your own user-defined business rules in the form of CONSTRAINTS, TRIGGERS, and STORED PROCEDURES covered in the next section.

User-defined Integrity

User-defined integrity means that you can specify your own particular business rules for a table or a column. Triggers and stored procedures allow you to do this in a much more elaborate manner. You can use the full richness of the Transact-SQL language to control the elements inserted into your tables and columns in a much more complex manner using flow control language such as IF statements. Writing stored procedures and triggers is covered in Chapter 19.

Designing a Database

Designing a database is much easier than one would imagine, so try not to make this more complicated than it is. There are a few basic rules that apply, and sticking to these rules becomes intuitive after you have designed a few databases. I have never seen a perfectly designed database. All of them have their imperfections because they are designed by human beings, who are also imperfect. We cannot envision how others will access the data next year or how the business requirements will change, so just jump in there and give it your best shot. The great thing about relational databases is that they are easy to change, unlike the networking and hierarchical databases of days past.

The building blocks of a database design are:

- Entities
- Attributes
- Relationships

An *entity* is a person, place, thing, concept event, or anything else that can be named as a noun with information kept about it. There can be instances of the noun with each instance uniquely identified with a primary key. These nouns correspond to tables and should be named in the singular. Call the customer table customer, not customers. There is also the concept of associative entities, those entities grouped together in common relationships.

An entity may end up with more than one attribute that could be the primary key. If any part of the primary key can be empty or missing or NULL (unknown), that candidate for the primary key is disqualified and becomes what is called an alternate key.

Attributes are facts or properties about each entity, with some attributes grouped in a category of being a primary key attribute. Other types of keys include candidate keys, alternate keys, foreign keys, and surrogate keys. *Surrogate keys* are single-attribute keys for large composite (multi-column) keys. Surrogate keys make Transact-SQL programming easier because you do not have to reference multiple columns in your code when selecting with a query.

Relationships are the soul of the database design and contain the business rules. They are defined as the association between two and only two entities, yet they are represented in groupings of associative entities. A discussion of relationships carries with it the idea of cardinality, statements which define how many instances of the parent are connected to how many children, one-to-many, many-to-many, one-to-many identifying, one-to-many nonidentifying, one-to-many recursive, many-to-many recursive.

Many-to-many relationships are also known as nonspecific relationships and must be resolved. Relationships can also be considered entities, and the resolution of a many-to-many relationship can be resolved through the use of a junction table.

Identifying relationships result when the parent primary key is part of the primary key of the child. Nonidentifying relationships are when the parent primary key is not part of the primary key of the child.

A recursive relationship is a nonidentifying relationship in which the same instance of the entity is both the parent and the child.

Approaches to Database Design

A database design can be approached in one of three ways:

- Top down
- Middle out
- Bottom up

Using a top-down approach is the chronological sequencing of events such as requirements gathering, the development of a logical and physical design. This type of modeling is used in the requirements definition phase. However, in the fast-paced environments of today, you may not have the luxury of this expensive and time-consuming process. Sometimes you just have to jump in there and work with what you already have, which may be a limited budget or a legacy system with interfaces that will not allow you to change the physical structures much. In this case other approaches are needed.

A bottom-up is appropriate when you are installing an existing software package. A middle-out approach can be used effectively when you are doing revisions or extensions of existing systems.

In the next section, we will discuss a controversial topic: normalization. Keep in mind that the implementation of correct business rules and database performance are much more important than a perfectly normalized database.

Normalization

The logical design of the database, the tables, and the relationships between tables determine how the database will perform. Normalization techniques are rules to separate the data into tables. A certain amount of normalization will often improve performance, but only to a point. Remember that the higher the degree of normalization, the more complicated joins become, and too many complex relational joins involving many tables can affect the performance of the database in a negative way. Most systems only normalize to Third Normal Form, although there are five normal forms.

If you are using a bottom-up or a middle-out design approach, you may normalize a large table into several smaller tables. If you have the benefit of accessing your database through stored procedures, you could use views, and your application may not know you did it.

The Rules of Normalization to reach Third Normal Form are:

- A table should have a primary key to uniquely identify each row in the table. To achieve First Normal Form, create a unique primary key for each table created.
- To achieve Second Normal Form, you must have a First Normal Form database and then move redundant data attributes to a separate table.
- To reach Third Normal Form, eliminate columns not dependent upon the primary key of the table. One table should hold the data for only one type of entity.

Keep tables small instead of trying to cram the whole world into one large table. Large tables impede database performance. Keep nullable columns to a minimum; use null values in columns only when it makes sense to do so.

Try to strike an intelligent balance between normalizing too much, which can cause complicated joins with many of the tables involved, and not normalizing enough, which might mean having just a few wide tables with wide columns. Either extreme can slow down the performance of the database.

Generalization

Human beings automatically categorize, and this is especially true when we are designing databases. We always think that things come in types. This is called generalization. You can include the concept of generalization in your database design and create a common table with a primary key, a type column, and all the attributes that the types have in common. This would give you separate tables with the same primary key used as a foreign key in the parent table and all the attributes that the types do not have in common in the child table as illustrated in Figure 18-1.

The design in Figure 18-1 is correct if you have the situation "this type OR that type". However, if you have the situation "this type AND that type", you would have to

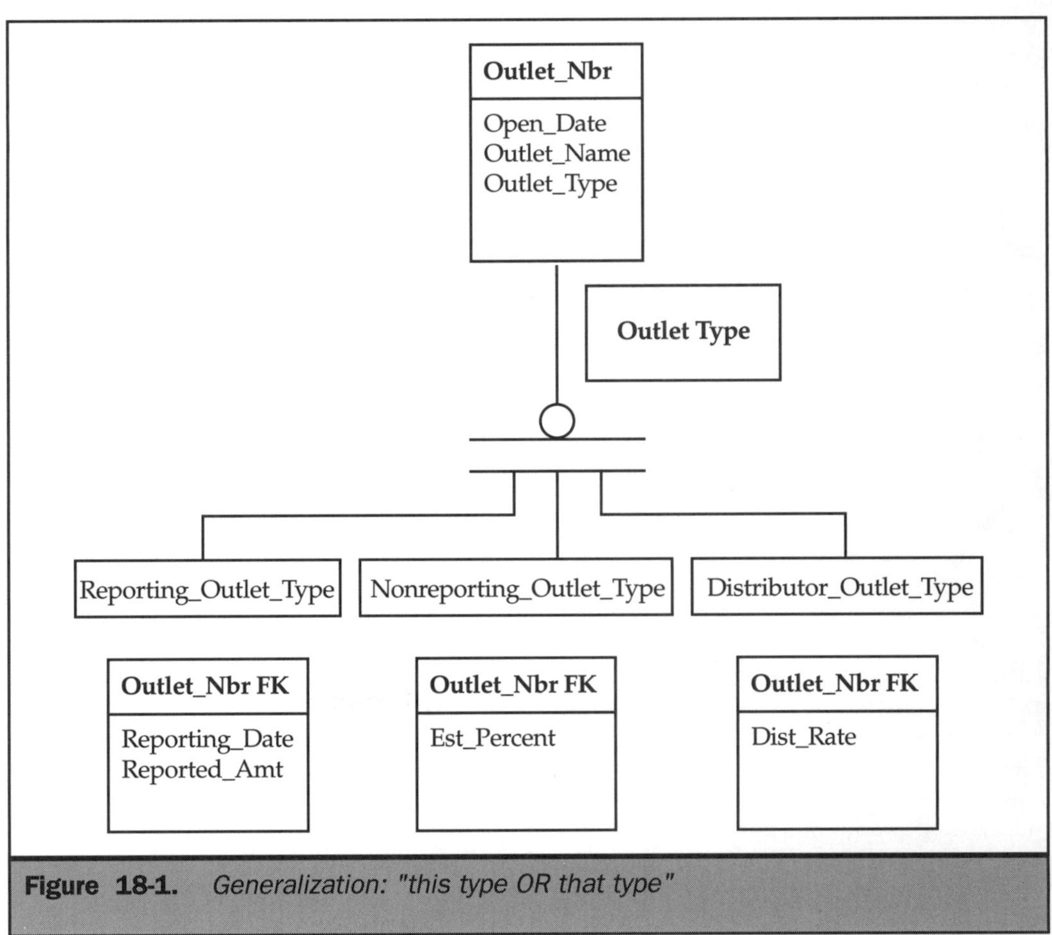

Figure 18-1. *Generalization: "this type OR that type"*

have a slightly different database design with a column for each type in the parent table instead of just one column for type, as shown in Figure 18-2.

There is yet a third scenario when generalizing, and that is "this type OR that type" *and* "this type AND that type". In a scenario of mixed ors and ands, an outlet can be a reporting outlet or a nonreporting outlet and also a distributor outlet. The mixed ors and ands–type scenario is represented in Figure 18-3.

Now that we have explored how to design a database, let's see how easy the Enterprise Manager makes it for us to create a database.

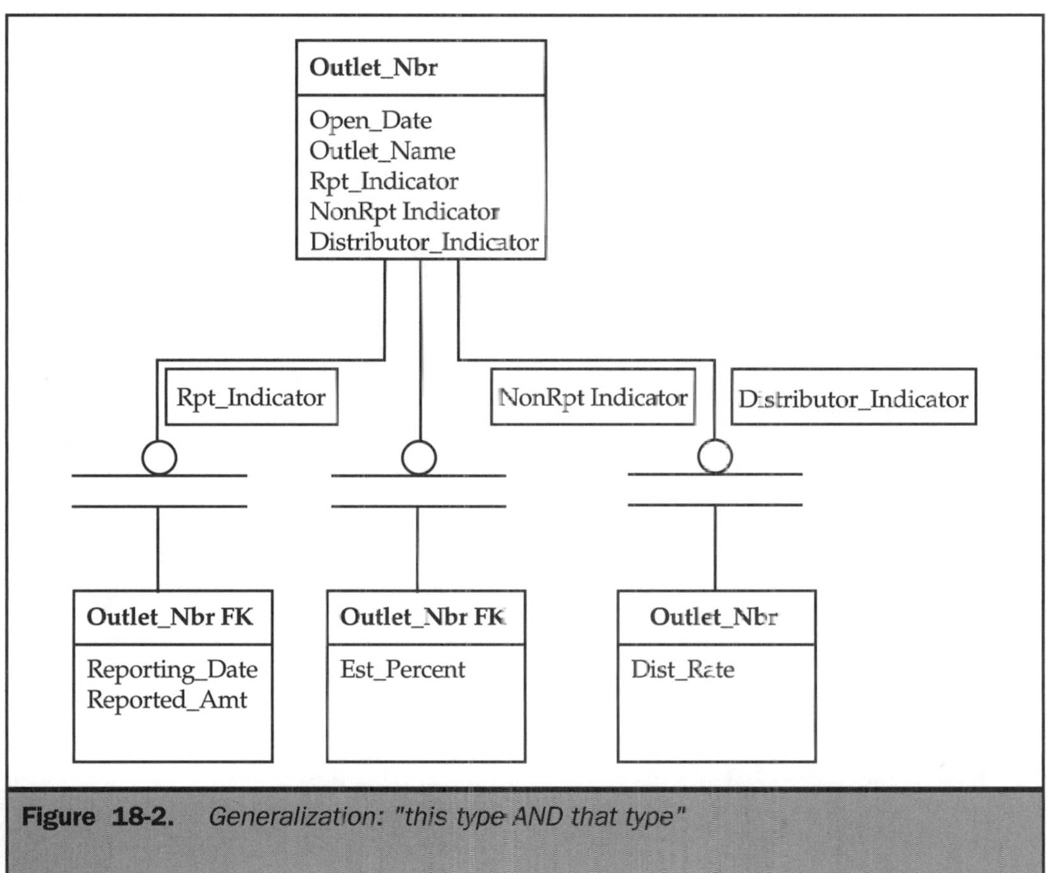

Figure 18-2. *Generalization: "this type AND that type"*

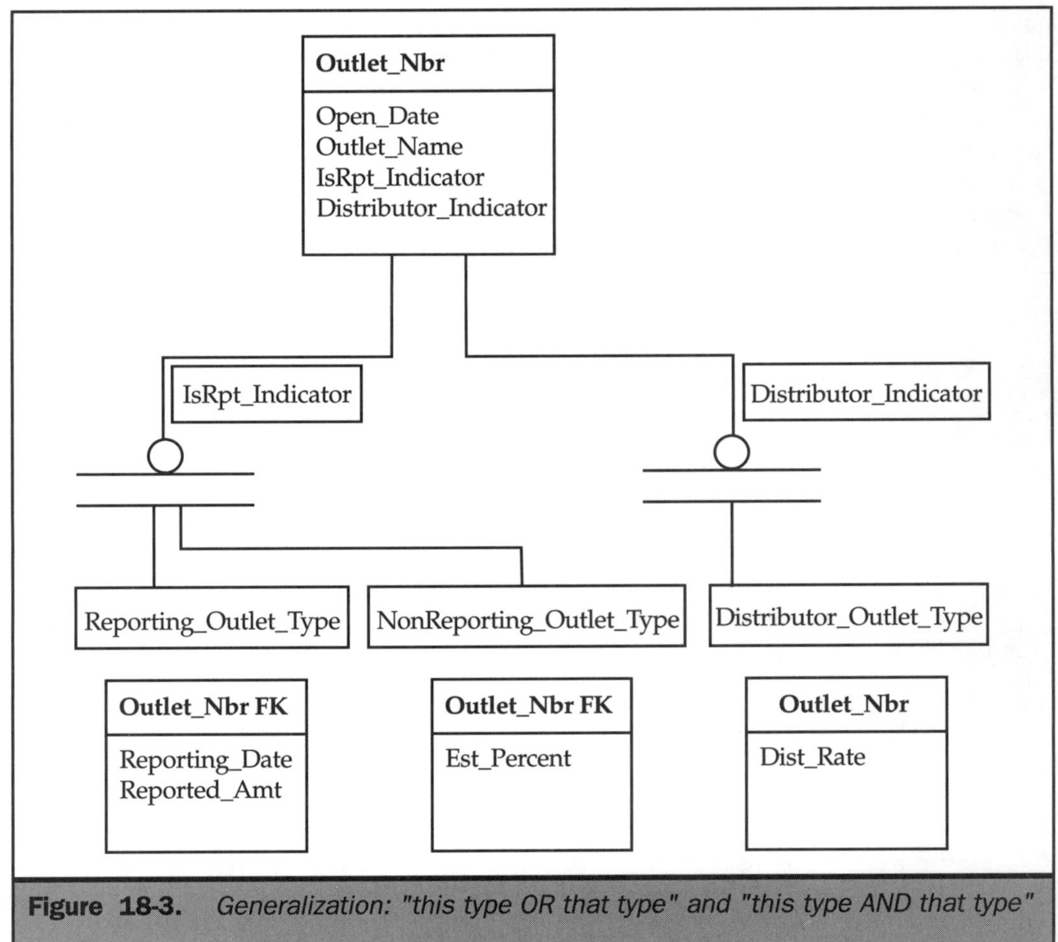

Figure 18-3. *Generalization: "this type OR that type" and "this type AND that type"*

How to Create a Database

The easiest way to create a database is to use the Enterprise Manager and run the Create Database Wizard, as follows:

1. Invoke the SQL Server Enterprise Manager by selecting it from the SQL Server program group in the Windows Start menu.
2. Expand your Server Group, then your SQL Server in the Enterprise Manager hierarchy tree.
3. Select Wizards from the Help Menu in the Microsoft Management Console. You'll see a list of wizards to choose from, as shown in Figure 18-4.

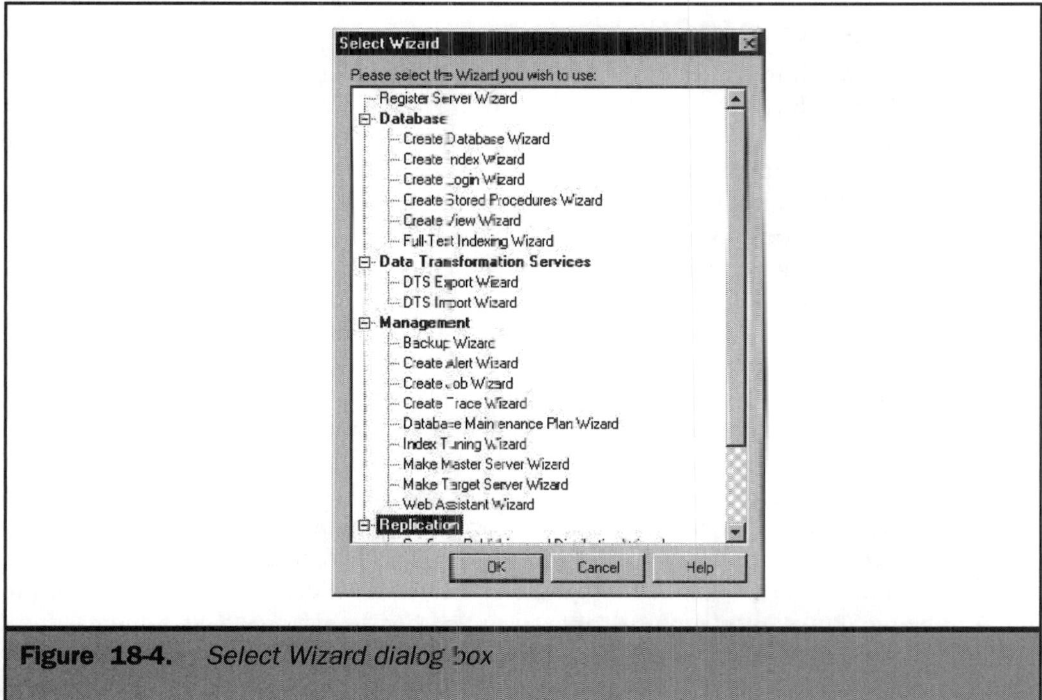

Figure 18-4. *Select Wizard dialog box*

4. Double-click on the Create Database Wizard selection and answer the question posed by the wizard. Follow the defaults or put in your own parameters.

You can also use the CREATE DATABASE Transact-SQL syntax found in Chapter 21, "Transact-SQL Programming Language Reference."

Very Large Databases (VLDBs)

Many aspects of SQL Server have been changed with the very large database in mind. The additional benefit of less contention with the workload during a backup, the differential backup, and the ability to restore a file or a filegroup instead of the entire database will help in the administration of the very large database. If you are backing up a very large database to tape, you now have the option of restarting the backup or a restore if something interrupts.

The Database Consistency Checker has gone through a significant performance improvement, and the large databases are experiencing major gains in this area. There is nothing but good news for the very large database with the SQL Server 7 release.

Coding Strategies

The major coding strategy to pursue when using SQL Server is to take advantage of using stored procedures instead of burying Transact-SQL in your application code.

The benefits of using stored procedures are many, including the fact that they provide the key to modular programming. This way, you can create the stored procedure and then call it because it is stored in the *syscomments* system table in the database. You can modify your stored procedures without having to recompile your application code or search through thousands of lines of code to find the Transact-SQL code that a database design change may require you to change in more than one place. So, use stored procedures, call them with your programs, and change the Transact-SQL your application uses in one place.

Your application will execute faster when you are using stored procedures because Transact-SQL code is already parsed and optimized. If someone has recently called the stored procedure, the query plan will be in memory. On the other hand, Transact-SQL coming from a client machine embedded in the application code will be compiled and optimized every time it is sent to SQL Server over the network for execution. Stored procedures reduce this network traffic. In addition, they can be used as a part of your security design because a user can be granted permission to execute a stored procedure without being allowed access to the tables using ad hoc Transact-SQL statements.

Indexing

An index increases the speed at which rows are retrieved from a database. The index can consist of one column or it can be a composite index composed of many columns.

The two types of SQL Server indexes are:

- Clustered
- Nonclustered indexes

A clustered index means that the data is sorted and placed in the table in sorted order sorted on what columns are contained in the index. Since the rows are in sorted order and an entity can exist in sorted order only once, there can be only one clustered index per table. The data rows are actually part of the index. A table should have at least one clustered index unless it is a very small table. It is best if a clustered index is a unique primary key.

In a nonclustered index, the data rows are not part of the index. A nonclustered index stores pointers to the data rows in the table and is not as efficient as a clustered index but is much preferable to doing a table scan and examining every row in the table until you find those that meet the query criteria.

Indexes can be defined in the following two ways:

- Unique
- Nonunique

A unique index means each row has its own value for the index key column(s). A nonunique index means that multiple rows can have the same value in the index key column.

The following statements can be used to create indexes:

- CREATE INDEX statement
- CREATE TABLE statement, PRIMARY KEY clause
- CREATE TABLE statement, UNIQUE clause
- CREATE TABLE statement, PRIMARY KEY clause
- CREATE TABLE statement, UNIQUE clause

Use the SORTED_DATA or SORTED_DATA_REORG option of CREATE CLUSTERED INDEX if you know your data is already sorted. This will speed up the creation of a clustered index. The fill factor controls how much space is placed between each index entry on the index page for nonclustered indexes or on the data page for clustered indexes. If you know that a table will have many inserts and deletes, create the index with a low fill factor; if you have a read-only table, use a high fill factor. Fill factors do not stay the same over time. The index will eventually gravitate to a certain density and stay there until the index is re-created.

There are some items to note about indexes:

- Smaller indexes are faster than larger ones with multiple columns. Integer or IDENTITY keys are the fastest.
- SQL Server will not use a composite index if the first column of the index is not referenced in the WHERE clause.
- It is best if there are a lot of different values in a column that is used for the index key. Otherwise, the result may be a table scan.
- Try to find out how users are going to retrieve the data and decide the best placement and use of the more efficient clustered index as opposed to the nonclustered index.

Index tuning is the major way to increase the performance of the database. Microsoft SQL Server offers the Index Tuning Wizard within the Query Analyzer, an isql/w similar window selected from the Tools menu of the Enterprise Manager. You can use the Index Tuning Wizard in combination with the SQL Server Profiler to analyze a workload that you provide by capturing the workload in the trace file with the SQL Server Profiler tool. It can then recommend the best index configuration for your database. Chapter 7 has more detailed information about how to use the Index Tuning Wizard.

Partitioning

Large tables present a performance problem. Partitioning a database into smaller tables costs a query less time because there is less data to scan. Rebuilding indexes is easier and faster.

If you cannot split your tables, you can partition tables by placing them on individual disk drives. Your goal is to have multiple drives reading at once, so place your tables accordingly. Use the new SQL Server functionality of filegroups to physically place the tables on different drives and use disk arrays to stripe across multiple disk drives.

Horizontal Partitioning

Horizontal partitioning means you are placing the table into multiple tables with the same structure. You can partition by month, alphabet, or however else your data naturally segments itself. You will want your queries to access as few of the partitioned tables as possible to avoid too many unions of the partitions to bring them back into one table.

Vertical Partitioning

Vertical partitioning is accomplished through normalization and row splitting. Row splitting splits the table into tables with fewer columns. Joining the two tables recreates the same row that was there before you split the table.

Again, queries are scanning less data. If you have a large table and your database users only use a few of the columns regularly, place the unused columns in another table. Partitioning a table can make many operations on a large table faster and easier.

Concurrency

Concurrency refers to performance issues related to multiple users accessing the data while maintaining transactional integrity via locking. If you are developing systems for a large number of concurrent users, it is best to keep your transactions a short duration. Exclusive locks keep other transactions from reading the rows, and these types of locks are held until the transaction is either committed or rolled back.

Transaction isolation level settings determine whether SELECT statements acquire locks that are held until the transaction is committed or rolled back. Unnecessary blocking can occur if a developer requires input or attempts to browse more data in the middle of a transaction or accesses more data in the middle of a transaction than is actually needed. Explore options in using the lower isolation levels of read-committed. Using isolation levels is a trade-off between risk of certain integrity problems or greater concurrent access to data rows. The higher levels offer more isolation and hold more restrictive locks. The transaction levels are, from low to high:

- READ UNCOMMITTED
- READ COMMITTED
- REPEATABLE READ
- SERIALIZABLE

See Chapter 21, "Transact-SQL Programming Language Reference," for the details and arguments to SET TRANSACTION ISOLATION LEVEL Transact-SQL statement. If your data has a low probability of being changed at the same time you are using it, figure out where it may make sense to use lower cursor transaction isolation levels when you are using cursors.

If your session is in implicit transaction mode, a new transaction will start after a COMMIT or a ROLLBACK and you will not even be aware of it. You may be requesting input from a user in the middle of a transaction and not even know you are doing it. Use the Transact-SQL SET statement in your code to set implicit transaction mode to OFF after a COMMIT or ROLLBACK, or the next Transact-SQL statement will start an implicit transaction. Any of the following Transact-SQL statements will do this: ALTER TABLE, FETCH, REVOKE, CREATE, GRANT, SELECT, DELETE, INSERT, TRUNCATE TABLE, DROP, OPEN, UPDATE. The transaction will remain open until you issue a COMMIT or a ROLLBACK.

In this chapter, we have covered development topics. In the next, we will cover writing Transact-SQL queries, stored procedures, and triggers.

The Complete Reference

Chapter 19

Using Transact-SQL

In this chapter, we will cover how to use Transact-SQL. Even a simply written query is extremely powerful, and it is very easy to start writing Transact-SQL queries: you use the SQL Server Query Analyzer to begin typing in simple queries and receiving result sets. The Query Analyzer is accessed from the Microsoft SQL Server program group or from the Tools menu inside the Enterprise Manager. See Chapter 11 if you wish to know more about how to install SQL Server 7.

As you gain experience with SQL Server, you can advance to writing more complex queries. In the next section we can explore the following topics related to using Transact-SQL:

- Writing queries
- Writing stored procedures
- Writing triggers
- Smart and big input/output
- Query processor
- Multi-index covered queries
- SHOWPLAN
- Joining tables
- Tempdb
- Cursors
- Recompiling stored procedures
- Heterogeneous distributed queries

You can also use the sample programs provided in the Samples directory where SQL Server 7 is installed. The first topic we can discuss is how to write queries.

Writing Queries

In its simplest, most effective form, a query can be a Transact-SQL SELECT statement with a simple WHERE clause. Here's an example of a simple SELECT statement:

```
SELECT    *
FROM MyAccountTable
WHERE Past_Due_Amt > 100000
```

In this example, the * means "show me all the columns and the values in the columns in the MyAccountTable, but I'm not naming them all because I may not know what they are called."

From this very simple query comes a lot of relevant and important information from which you can gather even more information. For example, if there was a CustomerID column in the result set, you might want to take the values from that column and run a query like the following to find the CustomerName and phone number:

```
SELECT    *
FROM CustomerTable
WHERE CustomerID = 3876098
```

In this example, you would most likely get the name and phone number of the customer returned, or at least another reference to phone that could lead you to another table with the phone number. You could continue to explore the database with little else but different queries in the form of very simple SELECT statements.

If you issue the following query, you can see all the user-defined table names in the database and can query them all to see what is in them.

```
SELECT name
FROM sysobjects
WHERE type = 'U'
ORDER BY name
```

In this example, the name of an object with a "U" in the type column in the sysobjects system table is a user-defined table. The tables are usually connected to each other because they each contain the same value in a similarly named column. This connection is called a relationship.

That is the fun part of Transact-SQL, and it is quite powerful in its most simple form. However, it can get quite complicated in its application, and this is what keeps it challenging and fun for beginners and experts alike. In the next section we will look at how to write stored procedures.

Writing Stored Procedures

Like queries, stored procedures are extremely easy to write in their simplest state but are also very powerful. Stored procedures are Transact-SQL statements compiled and stored on the database. They execute more quickly because the compilation and parsing process does not have to occur at the time the stored procedure is invoked.

Another advantage to them is that they are stored in one central area instead of scattered in the code throughout the application. As your business rules change, it is easier to locate the Transact-SQL code and change it in one place. The stored procedure is a database object.

Here's an example of a simple stored procedure:

```
CREATE PROCEDURE MajorPastDue
    AS
SELECT    *
FROM MyAccountTable
WHERE Past_Due_Amt > 100000
GO
```

In this example, we simply added the CREATE PROCEDURE AS syntax to the simple SELECT statement we were working with in the preceding section. CREATE PROCEDURE creates the set of Transact-SQL statements as a database object and stores the query on the database.

The following example shows how to execute the stored procedure after a successful compilation created in the example above:

```
EXECUTE MajorPastDue
```

In this example, the stored procedure that we just created is executed and returns the result set for the SELECT statement.

From this simple starting point it starts getting much more advanced and complicated. You can use local variables and parameters to pass information into the stored procedure, and you can call other stored procedures from within a stored procedure. The OUTPUT option allows you to pass variables from the stored procedure to the calling stored procedure. The next few examples will advance in levels of complexity.

Here's an example of a stored procedure using arguments, also called parameters:

```
CREATE PROCEDURE ProcWithParm
    @customer_id int
AS
SELECT Customer_Name
FROM Customer
WHERE Customer_ID = @customer_id
```

In this example, the name of the customer is returned and the customer ID is passed to the stored procedure.

Here's an example of how to execute a stored procedure with a parameter:

```
EXECUTE ProcWithParm 10034
```

In this example, the stored procedure created in the previous example called ProcWithParm is executed and the customer ID 10034 is passed to the stored procedure as an argument or parameter.

The complexity and length of your stored procedures can increase, as shown in the following example which incorporates a cursor and runs UPDATE STATISTICS on every table in the database.

```
/**************************************************************************
Description: UpdStatsAll is a stored procedure that uses a cursor to run
             Update Statistics on every table in the database.
             Execute this stored procedure in a user database.
**************************************************************************/
IF EXISTS (SELECT * FROM sysobjects
         WHERE id = object_id ('dbo.UpdStatsAll')
         AND   type = 'P')
BEGIN
    PRINT 'Dropping procedure UpdStatsAll'
    DROP PROCEDURE UpdStatsAll
END
GO
PRINT 'Create Procedure UpdStatsAll '
GO
CREATE PROCEDURE UpdStatsAll
AS
DECLARE @table_name varchar(128),
        @table_name_msg varchar(95),
        @errmsg varchar(85)
SELECT 'Starting Update Statistics ', getdate()
DECLARE cursor1 CURSOR
FOR SELECT name
    FROM sysobjects
    WHERE type = 'U'
    ORDER BY name
OPEN cursor1
FETCH NEXT FROM cursor1
INTO @table_name
WHILE (@@FETCH_status <> -1)
BEGIN
    IF (@@FETCH_status <> -2)
    BEGIN
        SELECT @table_name_msg = ' System is running Update Statistics on ' +
               RTRIM(@table_name)
        PRINT @table_name_msg
        EXEC ('UPDATE STATISTICS ' + @table_name)
    END
    ELSE
        BEGIN
```

```
            SELECT @errmsg = 'FETCH error has occurred.'
            GOTO err_rtn
        END
    FETCH NEXT FROM cursor1
    INTO @table_name
END
SELECT 'Finished with Update Statistics ', getdate()
DEALLOCATE cursor1
RETURN
err_rtn:
    DEALLOCATE cursor1
    RAISERROR 500000 @errmsg
    RETURN -100
GO
```

In this example, a stored procedure is used to run UPDATE STATISTICS on every table in the database.

Writing Triggers

A trigger is really just a special stored procedure and is used to perform some action when an INSERT, UPDATE, or DELETE occurs on a row in a table. The system automatically executes the trigger when the event occurs. The following example shows how to send an e-mail when an INSERT, UPDATE, or DELETE occurs in a table:

```
IF EXISTS (SELECT name FROM sysobjects
        WHERE name = 'CustChgTr' AND type = 'TR')
    DROP TRIGGER CustChgTr
GO
CREATE TRIGGER CustChgTr
ON Customer
FOR INSERT, UPDATE, DELETE
AS
    EXEC master..xp_sendmail 'CUSTSERV',
        'The data in the customer table has changed.'
GO
```

In this example, e-mail is sent to the Customer Service alias when the data in the Customer table has changed.

Another important aspect of triggers is the concept of a virtual table that is a copy of the table with the trigger that can be programmatically referenced as the table is inserted or deleted.

Here's an example of a trigger using the inserted table:

```
IF EXISTS (SELECT name FROM sysobjects
        WHERE name = 'reminder' AND type = 'TR')
    DROP TRIGGER reminder
GO
CREATE TRIGGER MyTrigger
ON MyTable
FOR INSERT, UPDATE
AS
DECLARE @MyFlag tinyint

SELECT @MyFlag = d.Disc_Type
    FROM Artist a INNER JOIN inserted i ON a.art_id = i.art_ID
    JOIN Discipline d ON d.disc_id = i.disc_id
IF (@MyFlag = 0)
BEGIN
    RAISERROR ('This artist does not have a discipline.',16,-1)
    ROLLBACK TRANSACTION
END
```

In this example, the trigger fires after checking the contents of the inserted table. Since UPDATES are mostly treated as an INSERT and a DELETE, the inserted table is used for both.

A trigger cannot call itself in response to a second update of the same table inside the trigger unless the Recursive Triggers database option is set. You can use *sp_dboption* to set this database option. Recursive trigger functionality is new to SQL Server 7.

Smart and Big Input/Output

Smart and Big input/output are designed into the 7.0 release of SQL Server and are a major step forward in the technology that will take SQL Server into the twenty-first century. The Microsoft vision emphasizes scalability and performance—and where else to accomplish this goal but at the input/output level? In this version, pages are bigger and parallel I/O is the norm.

Big I/O

Big I/O is telling us that, at 8KB, pages are four times larger than 2KB. Extents are also four times larger, at 64KB instead of 16KB, and result in an I/O that is four times larger.

Smart I/O

Smart I/O was conceptualized to achieve performance with the query processor functioning as a data pump. We have Big I/O and lots of read-ahead (number of pages placed into the cache for the query), physical row order scans, and parallel I/O reading from files. Read-ahead is for nonclustered as well as clustered indexes. The query processor drives the read-ahead, giving hints about the next pages needed.

Multi-Index Covered Queries

SQL Server 7 can use more than one index per table in a query accomplished through index intersection. There are actually shared row indicators written in the indexes so SQL Server can join the indexes to produce a result set in less time, which enhances the performance of a query.

Query Processor

The query processor behaves differently in SQL Server 7 than in previous versions and now supports very large databases and complex queries. The new execution strategies, plus hash join, merge join, and hash aggregation techniques, work better than the nested-loop join and can accommodate the larger databases.

Index intersection and union techniques on multiple indexes filter data before retrieval is attempted. All indexes on a table are updated concurrently and constraints are evaluated within the query plan.

The newly designed query processor gets information from the statistics and verifies statistics using fast sampling techniques. This allows the query processor to use more current statistics.

Improvements in the costing model and enhancements at compile time drastically improve the quality of a query plan. Use the SHOWPLAN functionality discussed in the next section to view the performance of the query processor.

SHOWPLAN

SQL Server 7 showcases the SHOWPLAN functionality by placing it in a prominent place in the Query Analyzer tool. You can now easily view how the query processor is planning to execute a query by typing a query into the Query Analyzer window, selecting Display Execution Plan from the Query menu, executing the query, and selecting the Execution Plan tab of SQL Server Query Analyzer for the SHOWPLAN output.

In SQL Server 7 a single query can now reference 32 tables, and the number of internal worktables that a query can use is no longer limited to 16. You can also use

Transact-SQL statements to execute SHOWPLAN if you would like to see the information returned in text format instead of graphical format. When SHOWPLAN_TEXT or SHOWPLAN_ALL is set, the query will not be executed. Instead, you will see the output for how the query execution plan is formulated by the query optimizer. Use the following examples of SHOWPLAN and run the query to see the text format:

```
SET SHOWPLAN_TEXT ON
```

In this example, after this Transact-SQL statement is executed, you see the output in a readable text format.

The next example is similar to the example above:

```
SET SHOWPLAN_ALL ON
```

In this example, the output is in a format that provides output for you to programmatically analyze the query plan.

SHOWPLAN Trees

SHOWPLAN_TEXT or SHOWPLAN_ALL are the Transact-SQL statements that show the query execution plan. When SHOWPLAN_TEXT or SHOWPLAN_ALL is set to ON, the query is not executed. What the query optimizer returns is a result set of the detailed query execution plan as if it is rows from a table.

If the input is a stored procedure or Transact-SQL statement, it establishes itself as the root of the tree. The statements called by the stored procedure are represented as a branch of the tree.

If the input is a Data Manipulation Language (DML) statement, such as SELECT, INSERT, DELETE, or UPDATE, the statement is the root of the tree with up to two branches: the execution plan and a trigger, if one is present.

SHOWPLAN represents conditional statements, such as IF..ELSE, by dividing into three branches. The IF..ELSE statement is the root of the tree with the *if* condition becoming a subtree branch. The *then* and *else* conditions are represented as statement blocks, and WHILE and DO-UNTIL statements are represented using a similar three-branch plan.

Operations performed by the query engine such as table scans, joins, and aggregations are represented as branches on the tree. Each branch contains information such as the relational algebra operator and the algorithm for that operator, for example, hash join, merge join, and nested loops. The cost estimates for the operator are shown because the optimizer is cost-based and chooses the most efficient plan with the least cost.

The OPEN CURSOR statement is shown as the root of the tree with its statement as a branch on the tree. Next, we will cover interesting information about joining tables.

Joining Tables

Tables are joined for the purpose of retrieving related data from two or more tables by comparing the data in columns and forming a new table from the rows that match. A logical operator, for example =, <, or > sandwiched between the columns from each table, specifies that only the rows meeting the join criteria are returned.

The WHERE clause is where the join of two tables is defined. The WHERE clause contains a join operator such as an equal sign, and it usually gives the name of the columns you are joining in the two tables. In the case of equality, the columns contain the same values in the rows to be selected back to the client. If you join two tables without a WHERE clause, you can get a Cartesian product, which is all possible combinations of all rows from each table participating in the join—a less than desirable result set that produces more rows than you may want to see. You can use relational operators in your WHERE clause to create a join. Another new feature allows you to use nested outer joins or inner joins nested within an outer join when using the ANSI-style syntax for joined tables.

The types of joins are:

INNER JOIN — An INNER JOIN is the usual join operation using a comparison operator (e.g., =). It displays only the rows with a match (true value of the join condition) for both join tables.

OUTER JOIN — An OUTER JOIN includes the left outer join, right outer join, and full outer join, which are described in the information below.

CROSS JOIN — A CROSS JOIN results in the cross product of two tables and returns the same rows as if no WHERE clause was specified in an old, non-ANSI-style.

The relational operators for an *outer join* are:

LEFT JOIN — LEFT JOIN returns the results all the rows from the first table in the JOIN clause with NULLS for the second table's columns if no matching row was found in the second table.

RIGHT JOIN — RIGHT JOIN returns the results all the rows from the second table in the JOIN clause with NULLS for the first table's columns if no matching row was found in the first table.

FULL [OUTER]	When a FULL [OUTER] JOIN occurs and a row from either the first table or the second table does not match the selection criteria, the row is selected and the columns of the other tables are set to NULL.

The relational operators for an *inner join* are:

=	Equal to
>	Greater than
> =	Greater than or equal to
<	Less than
< =	Less than or equal to
< >	Not equal to (ANSI standard)
! >	Not greater than
! <	Not less than
! =	Not equal to
LIKE	like
NOT	not
OR	or

You can use the substring function to join text and image columns by comparing the first characters, depending on the length of the column. This is the only way to join columns of these data types. The new joining techniques of the query processor are discussed next: the Merge Join and the Hash Join.

Merge Join

A new method called a Merge Join is employed by the query optimizer when it receives a request for a join with sorted inputs. It is most effectively used for equality joins, when both inputs are ordered on the join key, and when the request for ordering is on the clustering key.

The Merge Join algorithm is: get next row from outer table, get next row from inner table with the same key; if it is found, return the row and loop on the inner table; if it is not found, loop on the outer table. The Hash Join is another new join the query optimizer performs in version 7.

Hash Join

The Hash Join is another new way to process joins without ordered inputs when there are no indexes or requirements for ordered output and the join is an equality join. This is used for ad hoc queries and when a query is formulated and the indexes have not been planned.

The Hash Join algorithm is: read the smaller table, hash the key value, and put the key and the row ID in a hash bucket. Loop until there are no more rows in the smaller table, read the larger table, hash the key value and see if it is in the hash bucket; if it is, return the key and both row IDs, and loop until the outer table is finished. The final type of join used by the query optimizer is the familiar Nested Loop join.

Nested Loop Join

The Nested Loop Join is the old standby that was in previous versions of SQL Server. It is used when one input is small and the other input is large. This is the general purpose algorithm and works for nonequality joins and when more specialized Hash and Merge Joins are not applicable.

The Nested Loop algorithm is: get next row from outer table, get next row from inner table; if they match, return the result, loop through the inner table; when finished with the inner table, go back to first row of inner table and continue to loop through the outer table.

Tempdb

The *tempdb* system database expands automatically in version 7 if more space is needed. SQL Server sends the *tempdb* system database to its original size the next time SQL Server is started. *Tempdb* is the working area of the database. This new functionality is useful when running ad hoc queries or in month- or year-end processing where the *tempdb* requirements are greater but only for a short while.

Cursors

Cursors should really be called scrollers because that is what they do. They scroll through the data by "fetching" the next, previous, relative, or absolute row to become the current row. The overall syntactical framework of a cursor is always close to the same, albeit there are a few different types. In its simplest format, a cursor looks like the example below and is relatively easy to understand: just picture a cursor scrolling through a returned set of rows resulting from a SELECT statement:

```
DECLARE cursor1 CURSOR
FOR SELECT name
    FROM sysobjects
    WHERE type = 'u'
    ORDER BY name
OPEN cursor1
FETCH NEXT FROM cursor1
INTO @table_name
WHILE (@@FETCH_status <> -1)
BEGIN
    IF (@@FETCH_status <> -2)
    BEGIN
        SELECT @table_name_msg = " System is running Update Statistics on " +
               RTRIM(@table_name)
        PRINT @table_name_msg
        EXEC ("UPDATE STATISTICS " + @table_name)
    END
    ELSE
        BEGIN
            SELECT @errmsg = 'FETCH error has occurred.'
            GOTO err_rtn
        END
    FETCH NEXT FROM cursor1
    INTO @table_name
END
SELECT "Finished with Update Statistics ", getdate()
DEALLOCATE cursor1
RETURN
err_rtn:
    DEALLOCATE cursor1
    RAISERROR 500000 @errmsg
    RETURN -100
GO
```

In this example, the names of the user-defined tables are scrolled by fetching the next row in a loop through the SQL Server returned set of data from the SELECT FROM *sysobjects* system table. We get a return set, we scroll through it by getting the next row one by one and then doing something with the row—in this case, fetching the name of the user-defined table and running UPDATE STATISTICS on that table. SQL

Server 7 now has much better ways to run UPDATE STATISTICS on every table on a recurring basis by using the Database Maintenance Plan and scheduling a job to run every so often.

Some details about cursors have changed in version 7. A cursor can now be either Local or Global, with each Local cursor deallocated at the end of its scope. There is also a new cursor variable in Transact-SQL which allows a stored procedure to create a Local cursor and pass it around for processing. There are different types of cursors. For more detail on the different cursors you can employ, see "Cursors" in Chapter 21.

Recompiling Stored Procedures

There are events that happen on a database that a stored procedure query plan does not take into consideration. Consequently, if these events occur—for example when indexes are added or data is redistributed in indexed columns—the stored procedure should be recompiled to reflect the changed environment. But don't be alarmed if you haven't recompiled your stored procedures lately. This takes place automatically after SQL Server is restarted and the procedure is next executed and when a table used by the procedure is changed.

There are two ways to force a recompile of a stored procedure, and they differ substantially. If you use the *sp_recompile* system stored procedure, the recompile of the stored procedure occurs when the stored procedure is next run. You can also use the WITH RECOMPILE option of the CREATE PROCEDURE statement to force the recompile of a stored procedure every time it is run. This is a performance degradation and should only be done with that in mind. However, sometimes tradeoffs are required when the parameters vary substantially and affect the proper plans chosen within the stored procedure. A stored procedure query plan will not notice if an object is dropped and recreated as long as the object with the same name is there when the stored procedure executes.

Heterogeneous Distributed Queries

SQL Server 7 supports heterogeneous distributed queries by having Transact-SQL queries use data from any OLE DB data source without having to use Open Data Services to write server applications serving as gateways to other database systems.

In this chapter, we have covered some of the highlights of using Transact-SQL in SQL Server 7. For the syntax for the Transact-SQL language, refer to Chapter 21.

Chapter 20

Data Warehouses and the Data Marts

The concept of a data warehouse has emerged to solve the problems that occur when online analytical processing (OLAP) that involves decision support activities interferes with online transaction processing (OLTP).

A large number of concurrent users adding and changing rows of data while an OLAP query is running at the same time can cause contention, such as the OLTP users experiencing unacceptable performance and the OLAP users reporting that the OLAP query is taking too long to run. Providing a copy of the database on a regularly scheduled basis can help, but as the data grows, it is sometimes necessary to redesign the databases and to configure a data warehouse that is specifically designed for loading and querying large volumes of data. Another database or set of databases can be designed for OLTP or operational type of activities, and yet another database or set of databases can be a subset of the data warehouse used for reporting activities at the departmental level. The data warehouse gets particularly useful when large volumes of data requiring summarization is involved.

The difference between an OLTP system and an OLAP system is in the way the data is stored. In an OLTP system, the data is stored in a highly normalized manner at the detail level. The data in the data warehouse, an OLAP system, is stored in a very denormalized summarized manner to improve query performance of OLTP decision support processing.

A data warehouse provides summarized historical read-only data to facilitate decision support activities and usually consolidates data from different operational data sources. It also contributes to standardization across the organization as data is analyzed for consistency, and it is organized to contain only key performance indicators as it is brought into one location. Extraneous information needed at the lower levels to run the business that is unrelated to executive reporting is left behind.

Information is summarized and kept in the data warehouse for long periods of time to provide historical analysis and trend reporting. Data is usually not changed in a data warehouse unless it must be reprocessed because it is wrong. The only operations that occur are loading and reporting of data. Data warehouses use star schemas to improve response times.

Star Schemas

The star schema uses one "fact" table for the subject area and many dimension tables describing the fact table. Information stored in the fact table is summarized to improve performance. A dimensional key is a unique identifier that is used as a foreign key to join the fact and the dimension table. A data warehouse database can contain long, narrow fact tables and small, wide dimension tables when it is using the star schema. Queries retrieve dimension keys in the smaller dimension tables to key into the main fact table, reducing the amount of disk scanning. Since the data is already summarized as it is loaded, queries are faster.

Fact Tables

Fact tables are entities that are related to events and contain data aggregation per time period and per geographical or historical grouping. A sale, transaction, disaster, computer breakdown, request for service, publication of a book, construction of a house, and a hospital stay, all qualify as events and can vary immensely depending on your business. OLAP requires a historical and higher-level view in its aggregated form to detect trends and analyze the success of business practices and to support business decision-making by executives.

Fact tables can contain millions and billions of rows of historical read-only data. They should contain numeric data, not character data with integer foreign keys, into dimension tables to perform their role as the central part of the star schema. If a central fact table becomes too large, it can become a performance bottleneck and should be partitioned by splitting it into multiple logical tables around some natural division such as date.

Dimension Tables

Dimension tables are much smaller tables (hundreds or thousands compared to millions or billions) and reference the data stored in the fact table with descriptions, names, and other character data. Putting the character data in small dimension tables off to the side of the huge numeric fact tables allows the query to key into a small dimension table, pick up the index key to the large fact table, and scan a much smaller set of data. The result of processing the fact table first for distinct descriptions or names results in a much slower query scanning huge regions of data with huge worktable requirements in the *tempdb* system database. The design of the star schema with the decision tables revolving around the summarized fact table keeps the disk scanning and *tempdb* usage to a manageable level when huge amounts of data are involved.

While the data in the fact tables does not change unless it is wrong, the data in a dimension table is designed to account for changing values. A dimension table has an integer primary key, also called a dimensional key, and consists of predominantly character data. All the rules of normalization are broken when designing dimension tables. The goal is to denormalize the data into single tables. The trick is to know how the data is accessed and design the access method in the most convenient and fastest way possible to eliminate table joins required from indirect referencing of data. Multiple joins are the enemy in a database of this size and must be designed out by denormalizing the dimension tables. In other words, if a commonly used query requires a join of four tables, design a special dimension table for that query. If district is stored in another table (e.g., vendor table) remove it, place it in its own dimension table, and add a dimension key of district_id to the fact table. This can also be done with date or period data. Fiscal year, period, week, month, and year are all examples of date dimension tables. This method increases performance dramatically.

Approach the fact and dimension tables with careful deliberation by determining the core business events on which the data warehouse will focus to create the fact tables. Then determine the way the events will be analyzed to create the dimension tables.

Data Marts

A data mart is a smaller part of the data warehouse placed in its own database and used by a specific focused area of the business. A data mart can contain data at the detail level and/or at the summary level. Since the volume of data is smaller, the data mart is easier and faster to query.

There are many different ways to design a data warehouse and its corresponding data marts. The only limiting factors are your imagination and your business needs. You can create a data warehouse from the data marts or create the data marts from the data warehouse. You can use a top-down, middle-out, or bottom-up approach. The important activity is to correctly define the key, fundamental, and underlying business events and the analysis surrounding the events. You don't have to completely redo everything to start building a data warehouse. Start by identifying a key business event, such as sales, and build your data warehouse starting with one key event. Provide analysis and trend reporting that can provide key information needed by the decision-makers within the business. Rome was not built in a day and neither is a data warehouse, but the benefits from a data warehouse are significant enough to warrant steps in that direction.

Microsoft OLAP Server

Microsoft OLAP Server is a middle-tier server that allows analysis on large volumes of data. This product is to support online analytical processing (OLAP) applications and does reporting, data modeling, and decision support.

Microsoft Desktop Data Cube Service provides client access to OLAP data for custom applications. OLAP technology is designed to provide answers to questions that otherwise might require substantial time to answer. OLAP technology can provide answers to such questions in seconds because they query consistent and efficiently designed data warehouses. OLAP servers preprocess data into "cubes," summarizing into dimensions such as time and geography. Microsoft OLAP Server supports the three technologies—multidimensional (MOLAP), relational (ROLAP), and hybrid (HOLAP)—used to store OLAP data.

OLAP solutions are available for the reporting and analytical requirements of large businesses. They have traditionally been very expensive until now. Microsoft OLAP Server and Desktop Data Cube Service have graphical user interfaces and wizards to help create an OLAP database from an existing data warehouse quickly and inexpensively.

Data Explosion

Data explosion happens when all possible aggregations of data are precalculated and the resulting rows are more than those existing in the fact table. The Microsoft OLAP Server can automatically choose a subset of all possible aggregations and calculate the remainder of the aggregations from the subset as they are needed.

The Aggregation Design Wizard provides the functionality to manipulate the tradeoff between disk storage requirements and the amount of precalculated aggregation. Microsoft OLAP Server can partition cubes and store data across several servers. Microsoft OLAP Server has data model flexibility by supporting a full MOLAP implementation, a full ROLAP implementation, and a HOLAP solution, giving the OLAP database designer a choice of data models most closely matching the requirements of the organization.

Desktop Data Cube Service—Mobile Solution

You can run Microsoft Desktop Data Cube Service on your client workstations and use Microsoft Visual Basic or other languages to develop custom applications that can make use of OLAP data from Microsoft OLAP Server or data from relational databases that use Microsoft OLE DB. This allows the Microsoft OLAP Server to have multiple clients using the same cubes. The cubes can be stored on a client machine that is a notebook computer. This provides a mobile solution for presentation and analysis that allows you to analyze data without being connected to Microsoft OLAP Server.

Microsoft ActiveX controls and Microsoft Office implementations are being created to provide familiar graphical end-user interfaces. There are also open interfaces for other software vendors to develop third-party applications.

Multidimensional Database Cube

A cube is the main object in a multidimensional database. Each cube contains a set of dimensions according to how you analyze and categorize your data with hierarchical dimensioning being common. Measures are the quantitative data placed in cubes according to dimension. A cube can hold a number of aggregations.

Microsoft OLAP Manager

The Microsoft OLAP Manager is a snap-in in the Microsoft Management console. Within this tool you can create a new database and define a data source after setting up a System data source name DSN in the ODBC Data Source Administrator.

Create new dimensions by right-clicking on the Public Dimensions folder under your newly created databases and choosing New Dimension from the shortcut menu. The Dimension Wizard will lead you through the steps of creating a new dimension. The final step of the Dimension Wizard will take you to the Dimension Editor, where you can create levels to the dimension.

When you are finished with the dimensions, you can build the cube by right-clicking on the Cubes folder under the database and choosing New Cube from the shortcut menu. The Cube Wizard will lead you through the steps to creating a cube. The final step of the Cube Wizard will take you to the Cube editor, where you can add more public dimensions and private dimensions and select measures for the cube.

You are now ready to determine aggregations and process the cube by right-clicking the new cube in the hierarchy tree and selecting Process from the shortcut menu. The Aggregations Wizard will lead you through the steps to designing aggregations. The final step of the Aggregations Wizard will process your cube and show you the progression of the calculations.

Server Partitions

Partitions place one logical OLAP database into different physical stores. A single partition is created by default for each OLAP database. Segmenting the database into multiple partitions is how you allow different storage modes to take advantage of the MOLAP, ROLAP, or HOLAP characteristics that Microsoft's OLAP Server supports.

Single server partitions are multiple partitions created on a single server with a single DSN where you can tune your aggregations. You can store rarely used historical data in ROLAP with a small percentage of preaggregations to save disk space, and you can store current data in MOLAP with a high percentage of preaggregations to provide performance.

Multiple server partitions are created on multiple servers and use multiple DSNs processing in parallel. You can have the same database structure for different data, perhaps partitioned by year or geographical category.

In the hierarchy tree of the Microsoft Management Console, select the Partitions folder under your cube and choose New Partition from the shortcut menu. The Partition Wizard will lead you through the steps to create a partition.

You can use the ADO MD, an extension of ADO, as a programmatic object model for multidimensional data access. ADO MD is a language-independent data access interface for use with multidimensional databases. You can use Microsoft Visual Basic with ADO MD as the data access interface to data in multidimensional storage.

In this chapter, we have glimpsed the world of the data warehouse and Microsoft's new OLAP Server. In the next chapter, we will look at the syntax of the Transact-SQL programming language.

Part V

Reference Materials

Chapter 21

Transact-SQL Programming Language Reference

Transact-SQL is the the programming language for Microsoft SQL Server and is the enhanced version of structured query language (SQL) that was first developed by IBM. It is used to retrieve data from a database and to perform data definition (DDL), data manipulation (DML), and data control (DCL) operations of the SQL language. Transact-SQL is continuously moving towards—and in many cases improving upon—the American National Standards Institute (ANSI) standard.

Transact-SQL uses the following formats to categorize the syntax:

<table>
<tr><th>Syntax Format</th><th>Indicates</th></tr>
<tr><td>UPPERCASE</td><td>Keyword</td></tr>
<tr><td>italic</td><td>User-supplied</td></tr>
<tr><td>| (vertical bar)</td><td>Choose one, corresponds to the word 'or'</td></tr>
<tr><td>[ ] (brackets)</td><td>Optional syntax</td></tr>
<tr><td>{} (braces)</td><td>Required syntax</td></tr>
<tr><td>[,...n]</td><td>Repeat preceding and separate by commas or blanks</td></tr>
<tr><td><label> ::=</td><td>Labels a possible multiple-occurring lengthy unit of syntax</td></tr>
</table>

Add (+) and String Concatenation (+)

The plus sign (+) functions in two ways. It can indicate the addition arithmetic operator, adding two numbers together or adding days to a date. It can use column names, numeric constants, and expressions.

A second use of the plus sign is as an operator in a string expression concatenating two or more character or binary strings. Put a character string in quotes and be prepared to use the CONVERT or CAST function for noncharacter to character, and nonbinary to binary expressions.

Syntax

The syntax is:

```
expression + expression [ + [... n]]
```

The arguments are:

Expression	For the arithmetic operator, expression is an int, smallint, tinyint, numeric, decimal, float, real money, smallmoney, datetime or smalldatetime data type. When performing date calculations, provide one datetime or smalldatetime expression; the other expression must be a number of days to operate on the date expression. For concatenation, put a character string in quotes and be prepared to use the CONVERT or CAST function for noncharacter to character and nonbinary to binary expressions.
n	n means the preceding entry is repeatable.

Examples

Here's an example of the addition arithmetic operator adding two numbers together expressed as numbers and then as column names:

```
SELECT 9 + 7
```

and

```
SELECT salary + bonus
FROM mymoneytable
```

In the preceding examples, the numbers nine and seven are added together. Alternatively, you may represent the numbers as column names and use a FROM clause.

Subtract (-)

Subtract is an arithmetic operator that subtracts two numbers. You can also use the subtraction arithmetic operator to subtract days from a date, and it can use column names, numeric constants, and/or expressions.

Syntax

The syntax is:

```
expression - expression [ - [... n]]
```

The arguments are:

Expression	For the arithmetic operator, expression is an int, smallint, tinyint, numeric, decimal, float, real money, smallmoney, datetime or smalldatetime data type. When performing date calculations, provide one datetime or smalldatetime expression; the other expression must be a number of days to operate on the date expression.
n	n means the preceding entry is repeatable.

Example

Here's an example of the subtraction arithmetic operator:

```
SELECT 4 - 2
```

In this example, the SELECT statement calculates four minus two.

Multiply (*)

Multiply is an arithmetic operator used for multiplication and it can use column names, numeric constants, and/or expressions.

Syntax

The syntax is:

```
expression * expression [ * [... n]]
```

The arguments are:

expression	For the arithmetic operator, expression is an int, smallint, tinyint, numeric, decimal, float, real money, or smallmoney.
n	n means the preceding entry is repeatable.

Example

Here's an example of the multiplication arithmetic operator:

```
SELECT 7 * 8
```

In this example, the number seven and the number eight are multiplied.

Divide (/)

Divide is an arithmetic operator that performs division. It can be used with column names, numeric constants, and/or expressions.

Syntax

The syntax is:

```
expression / expression [ / [... n]]
```

The arguments are:

expression	For the arithmetic operator, expression is an int, smallint, tinyint, numeric, decimal, float, real money, or smallmoney.
n	n means the preceding entry is repeatable.

Example

Here's an example of the division arithmetic operator:

```
SELECT 56 / 8
```

In this example, the number 56 is divided by the number 8.

Modulo and Wildcard Character (%)

The % symbol is used for two different actions. It can provide the remainder of one number divided by another number. It can also be used as the wildcard character when looking for a string using column names, numeric constants, and/or expressions. You can use the LIKE keyword and wildcard characters to look for datetime, char, and varchar data types. You cannot search for seconds. It is a good idea to use LIKE when you search for datetime values due to heterogeneous data parts. If you want to search for the %, use square brackets.

Syntax

The percent sign (%) can be used as the modulo arithmetic operator (%) that returns the remainder when dividing:

```
SELECT dividend % divisor
```

Or as the wildcard character (%):

```
string_expression [NOT] LIKE string_expression
```

The arguments are:

Dividend	As a modulo arithmetic operator (returns the remainder when dividing) the numeric expression to divide, int, smallint, or tinyint.
Divisor	In a modulo artithmetic operation (returns the remainder when dividing), the numeric expression with which you want to divide the dividend, int, smallint, or tinyint.
string_expression	A string of characters and the wildcard character (%) enclosed in quotation marks.
NOT	NOT is the negative indicator of a boolean expression.
LIKE	LIKE does pattern matching.

Examples

Here's an example of the modulo arithmetic operator returning a remainder:

```
SELECT 87 % 9
```

In the preceding example, the number 87 is divided by the number 9 returning the remainder of 6.

Here's an example of the wildcard character (%):

```
SELECT *
FROM authors
WHERE name
like 'Heming%'
```

In this example, pattern matching is looking for a name that has Heming as the first 6 characters in the string.

Bitwise AND (&)

Int, smallint, or tinyint data type values are translated to binary representation and bitwise AND operations are performed on the binary representation.

Syntax

The syntax is:

```
expression & expression
```

The argument, expression, is an int, smallint, or tinyint translated to a binary number.

Example

Here's an example of the bitwise AND:

```
SELECT (integer & integer)
00010101   -- integer binary representation, A
01101011   -- integer binary representation, B
------------
00000001
```

In this example, the result is 0 when bit A is 0 and bit B is 1. The result is 1 when both bits of A and B are 1 and 0 when both bits of A and B are 0. It is also 0 when bit A is 1 and bit B is 0.

Bitwise OR (|)

Int, smallint, or tinyint data type values are translated to binary representation and bitwise OR operations are performed on the binary representation.

Syntax

The syntax is:

```
expression | expression
```

The argument, expression, is an int, smallint, or tinyint translated to a binary number.

Example

Here's an example of the bitwise operator OR:

```
(integer | integer)
10101010   -- integer binary representation, A
11001011   -- integer binary representation, B
------------
11101011
```

In this example, the result is 1 when both bits of A and B are 1. The result is 0 when bit A is 0 and bit B is 0. The result is 1 when bit A is 0 and bit B is 1, and it is 1 when bit A is 1 and bit B is 0.

Bitwise Exclusive OR

Int, smallint, or tinyint data type values are translated to binary representation and bitwise exclusive OR operations are performed on the binary representation.

Syntax

The syntax is:

```
expression ^ expression
```

The argument, expression, is an int, smallint, or tinyint translated to a binary number. The bitwise exclusive OR returns the data type of the expression.

Example

Here's an example of the bitwise exclusive OR:

```
SELECT (A ^ B)
10101010   -- integer binary representation, A
01001011   -- integer binary representation, B
------------
11100001
```

In this example, the result is 0 when both bits of A and B are 1. The result is 0 when bit A is 0 and bit B is 0. The result is 1 when bit A is 0 and bit B is 1, and it is 1 when bit A is 1 and bit B is 0.

Bitwise NOT (~)

Int, smallint, or tinyint data type values are translated to binary representation and the bitwise exclusive NOT operation is performed on the binary representation.

Syntax

The syntax is:

```
SELECT ~ expression
```

The argument, expression, is an int, smallint, or tinyint translated to a binary number. The bitwise NOT returns the data type of the expression. Be consistent with which data types you use when storing the decimal values, because tinyint, smallint, and int each store different numbers of bytes.

Example

Here's an example of the bitwise exclusive NOT:

```
~ 11001100
```

In this example the result is 00110011. All 1s become 0s and all 0s become 1s.

Equals (=)

The Equals sign is a comparison meaning that two expressions are equal to each other.

Syntax

The syntax is:

```
expression = expression
```

The argument, expression, is any valid expression and can be a variable or a column name. Compare only similar dataypes.

Example

Here's an example of the equals comparison operator:

```
SELECT *
FROM MyTable
WHERE column1 = column2
```

In this example, a column value in a table is compared to another column value and the rows with column values that are equal are selected.

Greater Than (>)

Greater Than is a comparison operator which compares expressions to see which is greater.

Syntax

The syntax is:

```
expression > expression
```

The argument, expression, is any valid expression and can be a variable or a column name. Compare only similar dataypes.

Example

Here's an example of the Greater Than comparison operator:

```
SELECT *
FROM MyTable
WHERE column1 > column2
```

In this example, the value contained in column1 in a table is compared to column2 to see if it is greater than column2. If it is, the row is selected.

Less Than (<)

Less Than is a comparison operator which compares expressions to see which value is less.

Syntax

The syntax is:

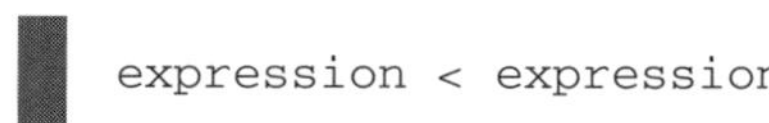

```
expression < expression
```

The argument, expression, is any valid expression and can be a variable or a column name. Compare only similar dataypes.

Example

Here's an example of the Less Than comparison operator:

```
SELECT *
FROM MyTable
WHERE column1 < column2
```

In this example, the value contained in column1 in a table is compared to column2 to see if it is less than column2. If it is, the row is selected.

Greater Than or Equal To (>=)

Greater Than or Equal To is a comparison operator which compares expressions to see which is greater than or equal to the other.

Syntax

The syntax is:

```
expression >= expression
```

The argument, expression, is any valid expression and can be a variable or a column name. Compare only similar dataypes.

Example

Here's an example of the Greater Than or Equal To comparison operator:

```
SELECT *
FROM MyTable
WHERE column1 >= column2
```

In this example, the value contained in column1 in a table is compared to column2 to see if it is greater than or equal to column2. If it is, the row is selected.

Less Than or Equal To (<=)

Less Than or Equal To is a comparison operator which compares expressions to see which is lesser than or equal to the other.

Syntax

The syntax is:

```
expression >= expression
```

The argument, expression, is any valid expression and can be a variable or a column name. Compare only similar dataypes.

Example

Here's an example of the Less Than or Equal To comparison operator:

```
SELECT *
FROM MyTable
WHERE column1 <= column2
```

In this example, the value contained in column1 in a table is compared to column2 to see if it is less than or equal to column2. If it is, the row is selected.

Not Equal (<>)

The Not Equal sign is a comparison meaning that two expressions are not equal to each other.

Syntax

The syntax is:

```
expression <> expression
```

The argument, expression, is any valid expression and can be a variable or a column name. Compare only similar dataypes.

Example

Here's an example of the not equal comparison operator:

```
SELECT *
FROM MyTable
WHERE column1 <> column2
```

In this example, a column value in a table is compared to another column value and the rows with column values that are not equal are selected.

Not Less Than (!<)

Not Less Than is a comparison operator which is used to compare expressions to see which value is not less than the other.

Syntax

The syntax is:

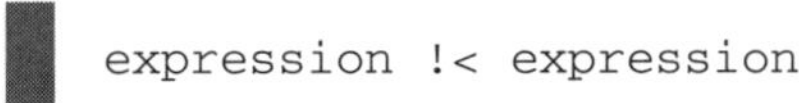

```
expression !< expression
```

The argument, expression, is any valid expression and can be a variable or a column name. Compare only similar dataypes.

Example

Here's an example of the Not Less Than comparison operator:

```
SELECT *
FROM MyTable
WHERE column1 !< column2
```

In this example, the value contained in column1 in a table is compared to column2 to see if it is not less than column2. If it is not less than, the row is selected.

Not Equal (!=)

This version of the Not Equal sign is a comparison meaning that two expressions are not equal to each other.

Syntax

The syntax is:

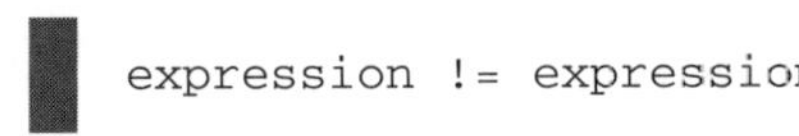

```
expression != expression
```

The argument, expression, is any valid expression and can be a variable or a column name. Compare only similar dataypes.

Example

Here's an example of the not equal comparison operator:

```
SELECT *
FROM MyTable
WHERE column1 != column2
```

In this example, a column value in a table is compared to another column value and the values that are not equal are selected.

Not Greater Than (!>)

Not Greater Than is a comparison operator which compares expressions to see which is greater.

Syntax

The syntax is:

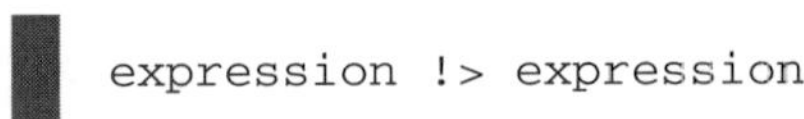

```
expression !> expression
```

The argument, expression, is any valid expression and can be a variable or a column name. Compare only similar dataypes.

Example

Here's an example of the Not Greater Than comparison operator:

```
SELECT *
FROM MyTable
WHERE column1 !> column2
```

In this example, the value contained in column1 in a table is compared to column2 to see if it is not greater than column2. If it is not greater than, the row is selected.

Comment (--)

Comments are ignored by the server, and you can place a comment with this syntax at the end of a line containing Transact-SQL syntax or by itself as a separate line. Do not include a GO statement in the comment.

Syntax

The syntax is:

```
-- Whatever your comment is
```

The argument, whatever your comment is, can be any character string.

Example

Here's an example of the comment:

```
SELECT * -- Any character string can be placed on a comment line
FROM MyTable
```

In this example, two dashes indicate the start of a comment. SQL Server will not syntactically validate the remainder of the line after the two dashes.

Comment (/*...*/)

Comments are ignored by SQL Server. You can place a comment with this syntax in the middle of a line containing Transact-SQL syntax or by itself as a separate line or lines. Do not include a GO statement in the comment.

Syntax

The syntax is:

```
/* Whatever your comment is */
```

The argument, whatever your comment is, can be any character string.

Example

Here's an example of the comment:

```
/* Any character string can be placed on a comment line
and can span multiple lines.*/
```

In this example, /* indicates the start of a comment and */ indicates the end of the comment. SQL Server will not syntactically validate the content of the line between /* and */.

Wildcard Characters to Match ([])

In a wildcard search, the square brackets indicate to SQL Server to search for any character inside the square brackets. The values inside the square brackets can also specify a range of values.

The escape clause provides a mechanism to tell SQL Server that certain characters that SQL Server normally uses as wildcard syntax are not to be used in the wildcard context but as a value in the string you are searching for. In other words, you would like to find the character in the string rather than use the character as wildcard syntax.

Syntax

The syntax is:

```
string_expression [NOT] LIKE string_expression[ESCAPE
'escape_character']
|[NOT] string_expression LIKE string_expression[ESCAPE
'escape_character']
```

The arguments are:

string_expression	String expression is a string of characters and wildcard characters. It can contain the square brackets for searching within a range of values.
NOT	NOT is the negative indicator of a boolean expression.
LIKE	LIKE does pattern matching.
ESCAPE 'escape_character'	This means that instead of the character functioning as wildcard syntax, you mean to instead search for the specific character in the string.

Example

Here's an example of the wildcard characters to match when searching for a range of alpha characters in the column:

```
SELECT *
FROM table2
WHERE column2 LIKE '[C-H]urry'
```

In the preceding example, any value in column2 that starts with the letters C through the range of the alphabet to the letter H and ending in the letters "urry" will be selected from the table.

Here's an example of searching for a bracket in the column:

```
CREATE TABLE table1
( column1 char(30))
INSERT Table1 VALUES ('[Searchforbracket')
INSERT table1 VALUES ('Donotsearchforbracket')
SELECT column1
FROM table1
WHERE column1 LIKE '[[Searchforbracket' ESCAPE '['
```

In the preceding example, the ESCAPE clause and the specific escape character [is used to find the exact character string of '[Searchforbracket' in the column. This means do not use the bracket as a wildcard character but search for it in the column.

Wildcard Characters Not to Match ([^])

In a wildcard search, the ^ indicates to SQL Server to search for any character not inside the square brackets. The values inside the square brackets can also specify a range of values not to include in the search.

The escape clause provides a mechanism to tell SQL Server that certain characters that SQL Server usually uses as wildcard syntax are not to be used in the wildcard context, but instead is not a value in the string you are searching for. In other words, you would like to not find the character in the string instead of using the character as wildcard syntax.

Syntax

The syntax is:

```
string_expression [NOT] LIKE string_expression[ESCAPE
'escape_character']
|[NOT] string_expression LIKE string_expression[ESCAPE
'escape_character']
```

The arguments are:

string_expression	String expression is a string of characters and wildcard characters and any string is placed in quotation marks. It can contain the square brackets for searching within a range of values.

NOT	NOT is the negative indicator of a boolean expression.
LIKE	LIKE does pattern matching.
ESCAPE 'escape_character'	This means that instead of the character functioning as wildcard syntax, you mean to instead search for the specific character in the string.

Example

Here's an example of the wildcard characters not to match when searching for a range of alpha characters in the column:

```
SELECT *
FROM table2
WHERE column2 NOT LIKE '[^I-Z]'
```

In the preceding example, any value in column2 that starts with the letter *I* through the letter *Z* in the alphabet will not be selected from the table.

Wildcard to Match One Character (_)

In a wildcard search, the underscore indicates to SQL Server to search for a single character that can by anything followed by the rest of the values in the string_expression. The escape clause provides a mechanism to tell SQL Server that certain characters that SQL Server normally uses as wildcard syntax are not to be used in the wildcard context but instead is a value in the string you are searching for. In other words, you would like to find the character in the string instead of using the character as wildcard syntax.

Syntax

The syntax is:

```
string_expression [NOT] LIKE string_expression[ESCAPE
'escape_character']
|[NOT] string_expression LIKE string_expression[ESCAPE
'escape_character']
```

The arguments are:

string_expression	String expression is a string of characters and wildcard characters and is any string is placed in quotation marks. It can contain the square brackets for searching within a range of values.

NOT	NOT is the negative indicator of a boolean expression.
LIKE	LIKE does pattern matching.
ESCAPE 'escape_character'	This means that instead of the character functioning as wildcard syntax, you mean to instead search for the specific character in the string.

Example

Here's an example of the wildcard characters to match when searching for a single character that can be any value followed by the rest of the characters in the string:

```
SELECT *
FROM table2
WHERE column2 LIKE '_urry'
```

In the preceding example, any single character followed by the letters "urry" will be selected from the table.

@@connections

This global variable holds the amount of logins and unsuccessful logins since Microsoft SQL Server was last started.

Syntax

The syntax is:

```
SELECT @@connections
```

@@cpu_busy

The global variable @@cpu_busy holds the amount of ticks (3.33 milliseconds) the CPU spent performing SQL Server commands since Microsoft SQL Server last started.

Syntax

The syntax is:

```
SELECT @@cpu_busy
```

@@cursor_rows

The global variable @@cursor_rows holds the number of rows in the cursor that was opened last.

If the cursor is populated asynchronously, the value returned (-m) is the number of rows currently in the keyset. If the cursor is fully populated, the value returned (n) is all the rows in the cursor. If no cursors are open, the value 0 (zero) is the value returned.

Syntax

The syntax is:

```
SELECT @@cursor_rows
```

Example

Here's an example of the ways to use @@cursor_rows:

```
SELECT @@cursor_rows
DECLARE cursor1 CURSOR FOR
SELECT customer_name FROM customer
OPEN cursor1
FETCH NEXT FROM cursor1
SELECT @@cursor_rows
CLOSE cursor1
DEALLOCATE cursor1
```

In this example, the first occurrence of @@cursor_rows will return 0 because no cursors are open. In the next occurrence of @@cursor_rows within the example, –1 will be returned because there is only one row in the asynchronous population of the cursor by the FETCH NEXT statement.

@@datefirst

The global variable @@datefirst contains the value of SET DATEFIRST, which is set to indicate what the SQL Server considers the last day of each week with the return values of 1 for Sunday, 2 for Monday, 3 for Tuesday, 4 for Wednesday, 5 for Thursday, 6 for Friday, and 7 for Saturday.

Syntax

The syntax is:

```
SELECT @@datefirst
```

@@dbts

The global variable @@dbts holds the value of the current timestamp for the current database.

Syntax

The syntax is:

```
SELECT @@dbts
```

@@error

The global variable @@error holds the error number of the last Transact-SQL statement executed in the session. @@error is set to zero (0) if no error occurred when the Transact-SQL statement executed. If there is a SQL Server error, @@error holds the number of the error in the *sysmessages* system table. It will only hold the value until the next Transact-SQL statement is executed. The only time you can check the @@error global variable is immediately after the Transact-SQL statement and before another Transact-SQL statement has executed. Therefore, check it immediately following the statement or save it to a local variable if you have logic that will need the value in @@error later in the Transact-SQL code.

Syntax

The syntax is:

```
SELECT @@error
```

Example

Here's an example of a way to save @@error to a local variable:

```
DECLARE @error_number int
SELECT *
FROM table1
SELECT @error_number = @@error
```

In this example, the value in @@error is saved to the local variable @error_number.

@@fetch_status

The global variable @@fetch_status holds the status of a cursor FETCH statement where zero (0) means the fetch is successful, -1 means the fetch failed, and –2 means that the row fetched is no longer available.

Syntax

The syntax is:

```
SELECT @@fetch_status
```

Example

Here's an example of using @@fetch_status:

```
DECLARE cursor1 CURSOR FOR
SELECT customer_name
FROM table1
FETCH NEXT FROM cursor1
WHILE @@fetch_status = 0
BEGIN
FETCH NEXT FROM cursor1
END
CLOSE cursor1
DEALLOCATE cursor1
```

In this example, @@fetch_status is used to control a cursor.

@@identity

The global variable @@identity holds the integer of the identity value that was used last. The @@identity global variable changes by issuing an INSERT or SELECT INTO statement or whenever a bulk copy insert to a table takes place. If the actions happen to a table with no identity column, the @@identity value is set to null for the session. If the actions are rolled back, the @@identity value does not get reset and keeps its incremented value.

Syntax

The syntax is:

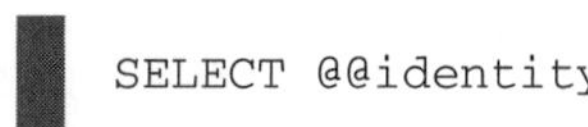

```
SELECT @@identity
```

Example

Here's an example of using @@identity:

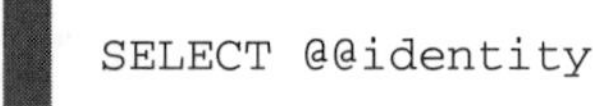

```
SELECT @@identity
```

In this example, the @@identity value displays. Use this after an insert into a table with an identity column to see the value you have just inserted into the identity column.

@@idle

The global variable @@idle holds the amount of 3.33 milliseconds SQL Server has been unused since it was started.

Example

Here's an example of using @@idle:

```
SELECT @@idle
```

In this example, the @@idle amount of time SQL Server was idle displays.

@@io_busy

The global variable @@io_busy contains the amount of 3.33 milliseconds SQL Server has been doing input and output operations since it was started.

Example

Here's an example of using @@io_busy:

```
SELECT @@io_busy
```

In this example, the @@io_busy is the amount of time SQL Server spent on input and output operations since it last started displays.

@@LANGID

The global variable @@LANGID returns the local language ID of the language currently in use.

Syntax

The syntax is:

```
@@LANGID
```

@@language

The global variable @@language holds the language name of the language currently used for Microsoft SQL Server.

Syntax

The syntax is:

```
SELECT @@language
```

Example

Here's an example of using @@language:

```
SELECT @@language
```

In this example, the @@language variable displays the language name you are using for SQL Server.

@@lock_timeout

The global variable @@lock_timeout holds the lock timeout setting, in milliseconds, for the running session.

Syntax

The syntax is:

```
SELECT @@lock_timeout
```

@@max_connections

The global variable @@max_connections holds the maximum number of simultaneous connections for Microsoft SQL Server that have been configured for SQL Server using the sp_configure run-time value.

Syntax

The syntax is:

```
SELECT @@max_connections
```

@@max_precision

The global variable @@max_precision holds the level of precision used by decimal and numeric data types with a default value of 28. You can change this by starting Microsoft SQL Server with the /p switch used with sqlservr invoked from the command prompt.

Syntax

The syntax is:

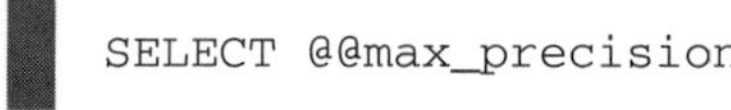

```
SELECT @@max_precision
```

@@nestlevel

The global variable @@nestlevel holds the nesting level of the current stored procedure at a point in time. When a stored procedure calls another stored procedure, nesting level is incremented from 0. The limit is 32.

Syntax

The syntax is:

```
SELECT @@nestlevel
```

@@options

The global variable @@options holds information about the SET options currently in effect for each user. Using the sp_configure configuration option "user options" changes the settings in their entirety and is what @@options represents. The SET command can be used to change language and query options. You can use the SET command to change an option and then immediately check for the value of the option in @@options.

Syntax

The syntax is:

```
SELECT @@options
```

@@pack_received

The global variable @@pack_received holds the number of input packets Microsoft SQL Server has received and read since it was started the last time.

Syntax

The syntax is:

```
SELECT @@pack_received
```

@@pack_sent

The global variable @@pack_sent holds the number of output packets Microsoft SQL Server has sent since it was started the last time.

Syntax

The syntax is:

```
SELECT @@pack_sent
```

@@packet_errors

The global variable @@packet_errors holds the number of packet errors since Microsoft SQL Server was started the last time.

Syntax

The syntax is:

```
SELECT @@packet_errors
```

@@procid

The global variable @@procid holds the ID of the currently executing stored procedure.

The syntax is:

```
SELECT @@procid
```

@@remserver

The global variable @@remserver is in the login record and holds the name of the remote server.

Syntax

The syntax is:

```
SELECT @@remserver
```

@@rowcount

The global variable @@rowcount holds the number of rows affected by the Transact-SQL statement that has just executed for those statements where rows are affected such as SELECT, INSERT, UPDATE, and DELETE statements.

Syntax

The syntax is:

```
SELECT @@rowcount
```

@@servername

The global variable @@servername holds the name of the local Microsoft SQL Server.

Syntax

The syntax is:

```
SELECT @@servername
```

@@servicename

The global variable @@servicename holds the name of the registry key for Microsoft SQL Server, MSSQLServer.

Syntax

The syntax is:

```
SELECT @@servicename
```

@@spid

The global variable @@spid holds the process ID of the process that is currently running.

Syntax

The syntax is:

```
SELECT @@spid
```

@@textsize

The global variable @@textsize holds the current value of the SET option TEXTSIZE, an option determining the longest length for text or image data that can be returned by a SELECT statement.

Syntax

The syntax is:

```
SELECT @@textsize
```

@@timeticks

The global variable @@timeticks holds how long a computer-dependent tick is, expressed in microseconds per tick. The operating system considers a tick to be 31.25 milliseconds, or 1/32 seconds.

Syntax

The syntax is:

```
SELECT @@timeticks
```

@@total_errors

The global variable @@total_errors holds the number of total read/write errors occurring on disk that Microsoft SQL Server has seen since it was started the last time.

Syntax

The syntax is:

```
SELECT @@total_errors
```

@@total_read

The global variable @@total_read holds the number of total disk reads that Microsoft SQL Server has seen since it was started the last time.

Syntax

The syntax is:

```
SELECT @@total_read
```

@@total_write

The global variable @@total_write holds the number of total disk writes that Microsoft SQL Server has seen since it was started the last time.

Syntax

The syntax is:

```
SELECT @@total_write
```

@@trancount

The global variable @@trancount holds the number of active transactions open for the user that is currently in session.

Syntax

The syntax is:

```
SELECT @@trancount
```

@@version

The global variable @@version holds the version date, version, and type of processor that is currently in use for the Microsoft SQL Server.

Syntax

The syntax is:

```
SELECT @@version
```

ABS

The ABS function returns the positive absolute value of a numeric expression.

Syntax

The syntax is:

```
ABS(numeric_expression)
```

The argument, numeric expression, can be an int, smallint, tynyint, decimal, float, money, numeric, real, or smallmoney data type.

ACOS

The ACOS function is a mathematical function that returns the radians for the angle, the arc cosine.

Syntax

The syntax is:

```
ACOS(float_expression)
```

The argument, float expression, is of the float data type and represents the arc cosine of the angle.

ALL

ALL returns either a true or a false. True is returned when everything returned by the subquery matches the expression, and false is returned when not all match or none match.

Syntax

The syntax is:

```
[NOT] expression { = | <> | != | > | >= | !> | < | <= | !< } ALL (subquery)
```

The arguments are:

NOT
: NOT is the negative indicator of a boolean expression.

Expression
: An expression can be a column name(s), a constant, a function, a variable, a subquery, constants, and functions.

{ = | <> | != | > | >= | !> | < | <= | !< }
: These symbols represent the arithmetic operators.

Subquery
: The ORDER BY clause, the COMPUTE clause, and the INTO keyword are not allowed in the subquery.

ALTER DATABASE

ALTER DATABASE changes database size and files.

Syntax

The syntax is:

```
ALTER DATABASE database
{ ADD FILE <filespec> [,…n] [TO FILEGROUP filegroup_name]
| ADD LOG FILE <filespec> [,…n]
| REMOVE FILE logical_file_name
| ADD FILEGROUP filegroup_name
```

```
| REMOVE FILEGROUP filegroup_name
| MODIFY FILE <filespec>
| MODIFY FILEGROUP filegroup_name filegroup_property
}
<filespec> ::=
(NAME = 'logical_file_name'
[, FILENAME = 'os_file_name' ]
[, SIZE = size]
[, MAXSIZE = { max_size | UNLIMITED } ]
[, FILEGROWTH = growth_increment] )
```

The arguments are:

DATABASE	The database you are altering.
ADD FILE	ADD FILE adds a file or a filegroup.
NAME	Name is the logical name of the file.
FILENAME	File name is a filename on the operating system.
SIZE	Size is the beginning size of the file expressed in MB for megabytes (default, minumum 1MB) and KB for kilobytes. If the size value is not given, the SIZE argument defaults to 3MB for data and 1MB for log.
MAXSIZE	MAXSIZE is the largest size the file can expand to expressed in MB (default) or KB. If this argument is not provided, the file will expand until the disk is full.
UNLIMITED	UNLIMITED means let the file expand until the disk is full.
FILEGROWTH	FILEGROWTH is by how much to grow the file at a time (default 256KB, mimimum 64KB) with zero (0) meaning none.
TO FILEGROUP	TO FILEGROUP adds the file to the filegroup.
FOR RESTORE	This is a backward compatibility argument (this used to be FOR LOAD in version 6.5) which creates the file without initializing it because the database will be restored.
ADD LOG FILE	ADD LOG FILE adds a log file to the database.
DROP LOG FILE	DROP LOG FILE drops a log file from the database.

CREATE FILEGROUP	CREATE FILEGROUP names the filegroup to create.
filegroup_name	Filegroup names the filegroup for adding or dropping.
REMOVE FILEGROUP	REMOVE FILEGROUP names the filegroup to drop.
MODIFY FILE	MODIFY FILE instructs SQL Server that FILENAME, SIZE, and MAXSIZE are modified for the file.
MODIFY FILEGROUP filegroup_name filegroup_property	MODIFY FILEGROUP gives a filegroup property to the filegroup. The filegroup properties are: READONLY=readonly filegroup READWRITE=Updates are allowed DEFAULT=filegroup is the default filegroup where new tables and indexes are created

Example

Here's an example of the ALTER DATABASE statement:

```
ALTER DATABASE mydatabase
ADD FILE ( NAME = 'mddat2',
FILENAME = 'c:\mssql7\data\mddat2.ndf',
SIZE = 10MB,
MAXSIZE = 100MB,
FILEGROWTH = 2MB)
```

In this example, a file is added to mydatabase, 10MB large with a maximum size of 100MB, and the file grows in 2MB increments.

ALTER PROCEDURE

The ALTER PROCEDURE changes an existing stored procedure while not affecting permissions and dependent objects. You must use WITH ENCRYPTION or WITH RECOMPILE with ALTER PROCEDURE if you wish to keep the option.

Syntax

The syntax is:

```
ALTER PROC[EDURE] procedure_name [;number]
[({@parameter_name | parameter} data_type [= default]
[OUTPUT])][,...n]
WITH {RECOMPILE | ENCRYPTION | RECOMPILE , ENCRYPTION}]
[FOR REPLICATION]
AS
sql_statement [,...n]
```

The arguments are:

procedure_name	Procedure is the name of the procedure you wish to modify.
;number	Number groups stored procedures together so that they can all be dropped at once.
{@parameter_name | parameter}	The argument or parameter(s) of the stored procedure.
data_type	Data type is the data type of the argument or parameter. The image data type is not supported.
Default	Default is the default value for the argument or parameter.
OUTPUT	OUTPUT means the argument or parameter is used to return a value.
n	n means more arguments or parameters can be listed, with a maximum of 1,024 arguments or parameters.
{RECOMPILE | ENCRYPTION | RECOMPILE, ENCRYPTION}	RECOMPILE means the procedure is recompiled every time it executes. ENCRYPTION means the syscomments system table rows holding the CREATE PROCEDURE statement will be encrypted.
FOR REPLICATION	FOR REPLICATION filters stored procedures executed only by replication and created with the FOR REPLICATION clause. They cannot execute on the subscriber and cannot be used with the WITH RECOMPILE argument.
AS	The commands of the stored procedure follow the AS keyword.
sql_statement	Transact-SQL statements create the stored procedure.
n	n means more than one Transact-SQL statements comprise the stored procedures, and they can be listed.

Example

Here's an example of the ALTER PROCEDURE statement:

```
ALTER PROCEDURE MyProcedure
WITH ENCRYPTION
AS
SELECT col1, col2
FROM MyTable
WHERE col1 = 5
GO
```

In this example, the stored procedure becomes encrypted.

ALTER TABLE

The ALTER TABLE statement changes the definition of the named table by dropping columns, adding columns, adding table or column level constraints, or disabling or re-enabling constraints or triggers.

Syntax

The syntax is:

```
ALTER TABLE MyTable
{
[WITH CHECK | WITH NOCHECK]
{  [ALTER COLUMN column_name
{
[ new_data_type [ (precision[, scale] ) ]
[ NULL | NOT NULL ] ]
| [ {ADD | DROP} ROWGUIDCOL ]
}
]
| ADD
{  [ <column_definition> ]
| column_name AS computed_column_expression
| [ <table_constraint> ]
}[,...n]
| DROP
{  [CONSTRAINT] constraint
| COLUMN column
}[,...n]
| {CHECK | NOCHECK} CONSTRAINT
{ALL | constraint[,...n]}
| {ENABLE | DISABLE} TRIGGER
{ALL | trigger[,...n]}
}
```

```
}
<column_definition> ::= { column_name data_type }
[ NULL | NOT NULL ]
[ IDENTITY [(seed[, increment] )
[NOT FOR REPLICATION] ] ]
[ ROWGUIDCOL ]
[ <column_constraint> ::=
[CONSTRAINT constraint_name]
{   { PRIMARY KEY | UNIQUE }
[CLUSTERED | NONCLUSTERED]
[WITH [FILLFACTOR = fillfactor]
[[,] {SORTED_DATA
| SORTED_DATA_REORG}]]
[ON filegroup]
| [FOREIGN KEY]
REFERENCES ref_table
[ ( ref_column ) ]
[NOT FOR REPLICATION]
| DEFAULT constant_expression
| CHECK [NOT FOR REPLICATION]
(logical_expression)
}
] [ ...n]
<table_constraint> ::= [CONSTRAINT constraint_name]
{  [  { PRIMARY KEY | UNIQUE }
[ CLUSTERED | NONCLUSTERED]
{ ( column[,...n] ) }
[ WITH [FILLFACTOR = fillfactor]
[[,] {SORTED_DATA
| SORTED_DATA_REORG} ]
]
[ON filegroup]
]
|  FOREIGN KEY
[(column[,...n])]
REFERENCES ref_table [(ref_column[,...n])]
[NOT FOR REPLICATION]
|  DEFAULT constant_expression
[FOR column]
|  CHECK [NOT FOR REPLICATION]
(search_conditions)
}
```

The arguments are:

Table	Table is the name of the table you are altering.
WITH CHECK | WITH NOCHECK	WITH CHECK | WITH NOCHECK determines if validation is performed for a new constraint (WITH CHECK is the default for new constraints) or reenabled (WITH NOCHECK is the default for reenabled constraints) FOREIGN KEY or CHECK constraint.
ALTER COLUMN	ALTER COLUMN refers to the column being modified.
column_name	Column name is the name of the column to be modified, added, or dropped and cannot be text; image; ntext; timestamp; the ROWGUIDCOL for the table; a computed column; a replicated column; an indexed column; used in a CHECK, FOREIGN KEY, UNIQUE, or PRIMARY KEY constraint (changing the length of a variable length column used in a constraint is okay); or used with a default.
new_data_type	New Data Type refers to the new data type for the modified column.
Precision	Precision is the precision for the data type.
Scale	Scale is the scale for the data type.
[{ADD | DROP} ROWGUIDCOL]	These arguments tell if the column is added to or dropped from the table and has the ROWGUIDCOL property (a global unique identifier column that can be assigned only to a uniqueidentifier column.)
ADD	ADD means you are adding column definitions, computed column definitions, or table constraints.

AS computed_column_expression	A computed column is a virtual column and is a new option. Computed columns can now be stored and retrieved, but you cannot INSERT or UPDATE a computed column and you cannot use a computed column as a key column or in a PRIMARY KEY, UNIQUE, FOREIGN KEY, or CHECK constraint.
DROP [CONSTRAINT] constraint | COLUMN column	DROP CONSTRAINT or COLUMN means remove it from the table.
N	The preceding item can be repeated.
CHECK | NOCHECK	The CHECK option enables the constraint, the NOCHECK option disables it. Disabling the constraint means that when an INSERT or UPDATE occurs, the constraint conditions are not used. This applies only to FOREIGN KEY and CHECK constraints.
ALL	ALL is in reference to enabling or disabling all the constraints with the CHECK or NOCHECK option.
{ENABLE | DISABLE} TRIGGER	ENABLE or DISABLE TRIGGER means the trigger still exists as an object on the database but if it is disabled, INSERT, UPDATE, and DELETE statements will not fire the trigger.
ALL	ALL is in reference to enabling or disabling all the triggers with the ENABLE or DISABLE TRIGGER option.
Trigger	Trigger is the name of the trigger you are going to ENABLE or DISABLE.
data_type	Data type is in reference to the SQL Server data type for the new column. If you are using the uniqueidentifier data type and you have existing rows in the table, you may want to use a DEFAULT constraint with the NEWID() function to generate the unique identifier values in the new column for the already existing rows.

NULL | NOT NULL	NULL or NOT NULL determines if a column can hold NULL values or if it cannot. If your table has existing rows and you are using NOT NULL, use the DEFAULT constraint WITH VALUES and the new column for your existing rows will automatically contain the default value.
IDENTITY	IDENTITY is a property used to place incrementing integers in a new column. If you have existing rows in the table and you add a column with the IDENTITY property, the new column added for the existing rows will automatically contain the incremental integer in each new column for the existing rows. This is also true when adding future rows.
Seed	Seed refers to the value of the integer you want in your first row if you are adding a column with the IDENTITY property and indicates from where you want the value in the new IDENTITY column to start. If you do not use this keyword, SQL Server will seed the column with the value 1.
Increment	If you are adding a column with the IDENTITY property, Increment is by how much you want the value in the new IDENTITY column to increment when a new row is added. If you do not use Increment, SQL Server will increment the value by 1 from the value in the last row added.
NOT FOR REPLICATION	If you are using replication and are adding a column with the IDENTITY property, use this to tell SQL Server not to enforce the IDENTITY conditions when a SQL Server system replication login (e.g., sqlrepl) inserts data into the table.

CONSTRAINT	The CONSTRAINT option is how a PRIMARY KEY, UNIQUE, FOREIGN KEY, CHECK, or DEFAULT constraint is created. CONSTRAINTS are used to manage data integrity and adding a CONSTRAINT can create indexes.
constraint_name	Constraint name is the name of the newly created CONSTRAINT. If you do not name the CONSTRAINT, SQL Server will.
PRIMARY KEY	PRIMARY KEY is a constraint (only one per table) that creates a unique index on the column(s) and designates the column(s) as the primary key of the table.
UNIQUE	Column values can be unique for the table but not necessarily designated as the primary key. The UNIQUE constraint creates a unique index on the column(s).
CLUSTERED | NONCLUSTERED	If you are creating a PRIMARY KEY (default CLUSTERED) or a UNIQUE (default NONCLUSTERED) constraint, CLUSTERED or NONCLUSTERED determines which kind of index you are adding. If you already have a clustered index, you cannot use CLUSTERED unless you remove the existing CLUSTERED index since there can only be one per table. If you already have a clustered index and you add a PRIMARY KEY constraint, it will default to NONCLUSTERED.
WITH FILLFACTOR = fillfactor	WITH FILLFACTOR describes how much data is on each index page. Available values are 1 to 100 with a default of 0, indicated in percentage. The lower the fillfactor, the more space is available between index entries on the page, which leaves more space to insert new rows on the page without forcing SQL Server to allocate more space for the new rows.

SORTED_DATA | SORTED_DATA_REORG	SORTED DATA tells SQL Server the data is already sorted and SQL Server does not have to sort the data when adding a clustered index. SQL Server will perform a check to be sure the data is in sorted order by checking the index value. If the check fails, an error is returned and the ALTER table will fail. On the other hand, SORTED_DATA_REORG tells SQL Server the data is already sorted but to reorganize the data on the disk. Use this when you are using the FILLFACTOR OPTION and you change the way the data is stored on the pages. Use DBCC SHOWCONTIG to determine if your table is fragmented and needs to be reorganized.
ON filegroup	ON filegroup determines where the index created for the constraint will reside on disk. If you do not use ON filegroup, the index will be placed on the same filegroup as the table. Use this when adding a PRIMARY KEY CLUSTERED index or UNIQUE CLUSTERED index and the result will be that the entire table will move to the named filegroup since the data of a clustered index is on the bottom leaf of the clustered index.
FOREIGN KEY…REFERENCES	FOREIGN KEY…REFERENCES creates a constraint to enforce referential integrity by ensuring that each entry in the column exists in the column of the referenced table.
ref_table	Ref table is the name of the table referenced by the FOREIGN KEY constraint.
ref_column	Ref column is the column referenced by the FOREIGN KEY constraint.
NOT FOR REPLICATION	If you are using replication and are adding a column with the IDENTITY property, use this to tell SQL Server not to enforce the IDENTITY conditions when a SQL Server system replication login (e.g., sqlrepl) inserts data into the table.

DEFAULT	DEFAULT is a constraint that determines which value is inserted into the column if no value is specified for the column on an INSERT. You cannot use this for a column with a timestamp data type, the IDENTITY property, or another DEFAULT constraint, since there can only be one value in a column. Drop the old default if you need to add another. DEFAULTS are powerful in that they can add values to new columns in existing rows.
VALUES	VALUES is used with DEFAULT and is the new values for existing rows; it is used for new columns added with ALTER TABLE.
constant_expression	Constant expression is used with DEFAULT and is the default value for the column; it can be a constant, a NULL, or a system function.
CHECK	CHECK is a constraint that limits the values that can be inserted into a column.
logical_expression	Logical expression can reference other columns in the same row and returns true or false.
column[,...n]	Column represents the list of columns for a constraint.
FOR column	FOR column is the column to be used with a DEFAULT constraint.

Example

Here's an example of the ALTER TABLE statement:

```
ALTER TABLE MyTable ADD col1 int null
CONSTRAINT myconstraint UNIQUE
GO
```

In this example, a unique constraint and a column are added to the table.

ALTER TRIGGER

Transact-SQL now has the ability to alter a trigger object instead of having to remove it from the database and the *syscomments* system table to change it. The ability to change a trigger is important because triggers carry other references and permissions that are destroyed when the object is dropped. Just changing the object instead of removing it retains the references and permissions that are associated with the object. If you use the WITH APPEND option of the CREATE TRIGGER statement, more than one trigger can exist for each Update,Insert,Delete. This means more than one trigger can fire for each Update,Insert,Delete. This WITH APPEND capability is present in compatibility level of 7.0 set by *sp_dbcmptlevel*. The WITH APPEND is only needed with compatibility level 65 or 60, because it is the default behavior when the compatibility level is 70.

Triggers are limited in what Transact-SQL statements you can use in a trigger. You cannot use the following Transact-SQL statements in a trigger:

- ALTER DATABASE
- ALTER TABLE
- ALTER TRIGGER
- CREATE DATABASE
- CREATE DEFAULT
- CREATE PROCEDURE
- CREATE RULE
- CREATE TABLE
- CREATE TRIGGER
- DENY
- DISK INIT
- DROP DATABASE
- DROP DEFAULT
- DROP PROCEDURE
- DROP RULE
- DROP TRIGGER
- DROP VIEW
- LOAD DATABASE
- LOAD LOG
- RESTORE LOG
- REVOKE
- SELECT INTO (because it creates a table)
- TRUNCATE TABLE
- ALTER PROCEDURE
- ALTER VIEW
- CREATE INDEX
- CREATE TABLE
- CREATE VIEW
- DISK RESIZE
- DROP INDEX
- DROP TABLE
- GRANT
- RESTORE DATABASE
- RECONFIGURE
- UPDATE STATISTICS

Syntax

The syntax is:

```
ALTER TRIGGER trigger_name
ON table
[WITH ENCRYPTION]
{FOR {[,] [INSERT] [,] [UPDATE] [,] [DELETE]}
[NOT FOR REPLICATION]
AS
sql_statement [...n]
}|{FOR {[,] [INSERT] [,] [UPDATE]}
[NOT FOR REPLICATION]
AS
IF UPDATE (column)
[{AND | OR} UPDATE (column) [,...n]]
sql_statement [...n]}
```

The arguments are:

TriggerName	The name of the trigger you are changing.
TableName	The table name on which the trigger will execute.
WITH ENCRYPTION	Encrypts the code in syscomments system table.
{[,] [INSERT] [,] [UPDATE] [,] [DELETE]} | {[,] [INSERT] [,] [UPDATE]}	Keywords indicating which statements will fire the trigger.
NOT FOR REPLICATION	If the sqlrepl login ID associated with replication modifies the table then do not fire the trigger.
AS	Means that the Transact-SQL statements are next.
Transact-SQL statement(s)	The Transact-SQL statements that are the trigger.
IF UPDATE (ColumnName)	Provides IF logic based on whether it is an INSERT or UPDATE to a named column.
ColumnName	The name of the column to check for INSERT or UPDATE action.

Example

Here's an example of the ALTER TRIGGER statement:

```
ALTER TRIGGER mytrigger
ON tablename
FOR INSERT
AS RAISERROR ('mytrigger error', 1, 2)
```

In this example, the trigger, mytrigger, is altered.

ALTER VIEW

ALTER VIEW has the ability to alter a view object instead of having to remove it from the database and the *syscomments* system table in order to change it. The ability to change a view is important because views carry other references and permissions that are destroyed when the object is dropped. Just changing the object instead of removing it retains the references and permissions that are associated with the object. In the SELECT statement do not reference a temporary table or include ORDER BY, COMPUTE, or COMPUTE BY clauses or the INTO keyword.

Syntax

The syntax is:

```
ALTER VIEW view_name
column [, ...n]))]
[WITH ENCRYPTION]
AS
select_statement [WITH CHECK OPTION]
```

The arguments are:

view_name	The name of the view you are changing.
Column [, ...n])	Column is the name of column name(s), comma delineated, that are part of the view.
WITH ENCRYPTION	Encrypts the code in *syscomments* system table.
AS	Means that the Transact-SQL statements are next.
`select_statement [WITH CHECK OPTION]`	The SELECT statement that is the basis for the view; the WITH CHECK OPTION means that SQL Server will check to ensure that any data modification statements to the view will match any boundaries set within the select_statement contained in the view.

Example

Here's an example of using the ALTER VIEW statement:

```
CREATE VIEW MyView
AS
SELECT column1, column2
FROM MyTable
```

In this example, the view is changed instead of dropped and re-created.

AND

The AND statement strings together two conditions and is true when both of the conditions are true. AND operators are evaluated first by SQL Server before other logical operators, but if you use parentheses, you affect the order that logical operators are evaluated.

Syntax

The syntax is:

```
[NOT] <predicate> AND [NOT] <predicate> [,...n]
```

The arguments are:

NOT	NOT is the negative indicator of a boolean expression.
Prepredicate [,...n]	Predicate is also called an expression, comma delineated, and returns TRUE or FALSE.

Example

Here's an example of the AND statement:

```
SELECT *
FROM MyTable
WHERE column1 = column2
AND column3 = column4
```

In this example, the column1 has to equal column2; in addition, column3 must equal column4 in the table for the rows to be selected.

ANY

Using the ANY keyword returns TRUE and FALSE even when used with a subquery. (The subquery rows are not returned, only TRUE or FALSE.)

TRUE is returned when the data retrieved in a subquery satisfies the comparison in the expression.

FALSE is returned when the comparison is false for all of the rows in a subquery or when the subquery finds no rows.

Syntax

The syntax is:

```
[NOT] expression { = | <> | != | > | >= | !> | < | <= | !< } {SOME | ANY}
(subquery)
```

The arguments are:

NOT	NOT is the negative indicator of a boolean expression.
Expression	An expression can be a column name(s), a constant, a function, a variable, a subquery, constants, or functions.
{ = | <> | != | > | >= | !> | < | <= | !< }	These symbols represent the arithmetic operators.
Subquery	The ORDER BY clause, the COMPUTE clause, and the INTO keyword are not allowed in the subquery.

Example

Here's an example of the ANY keyword:

```
IF @myvar>= ANY (SELECT au_lname FROM authors)
PRINT 'OK, this value is not less than all the names in the table'
ELSE
PRINT 'Sorry, you cannot use a value less than all the names in the table'
```

In this example, TRUE is returned.

APP_NAME

A char or varchar program name with a maximum length is returned for the running session if the program sets the function. You can determine which client applications are running Microsoft SQL Server with this function.

Syntax

The syntax is:

```
APP_NAME()
```

Example

Here's an example of the function APP_NAME():

```
SELECT APP_NAME()
```

In this example, selecting the content of APP_NAME returned "MS SQL Query Analyzer" because it was run in the Query Analyzer and the Query Analyzer sets the function.

ASCII

The ASCII function returns an integer representing the ASCII code value of the leftmost character of a character expression.

Syntax

The syntax is:

```
ASCII(character_expression)
```

The alphanumeric argument, character_expression, can be a constant, a variable, or a column.

Example

Here's an example of the ASCII function:

```
SELECT ASCII("AB")
```

In this example, 65, which is the ASCII code value of the character A, is returned, because no matter what other characters are placed after A, it returns the ASCII code value of the leftmost character in the character expression.

ASIN

The mathematical function ASIN returns the radians of the angle for the expression. This is also commonly referred as the arc sine. If you see the error message "Domain error occurred", Microsoft SQL Server is telling you that the angle value is outside of the valid range of the ASIN function.

Syntax

The syntax is:

```
ASIN(float_expression)
```

The argument, float expression, is a float data type.

Example

Here's an example of the ASIN function:

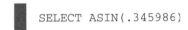

```
SELECT ASIN(.345986)
```

In this example, the value 0.35328948592348308, which is the angle expressed in radians, is returned for the float expression whose sine is 345986.

ATAN

The mathematical function ATAN returns the radians of the angle whose tangent is the float expression passed to the function as the argument. This is also commonly referred as the arc tangent.

Syntax

The syntax is:

```
ATAN(float_expression)
```

The argument, float expression, is a float data type.

Example

Here's an example of the ATAN function:

```
SELECT ATAN(.345986)
```

In this example, the value 0.33309440694206421, which is the angle expressed in radians, is returned for the float expression whose tangent is 345986.

ATN2

The mathematical function ATN2 returns the radians of the angle whose tangent is between the float expressions passed to the function as arguments. This is also commonly referred as the arc tangent.

Syntax

The syntax is:

```
ATN2(float_expression, float_expression)
```

The argument, float expression, is a float data type and must be given twice.

Example

Here's an example of the ATN2 function:

```
SELECT ATN2(.34 , .35)
```

In this example, the value 0.77090642433194834, which is the arc tangent of the angle expressed in radians that is between the two float expressions .34 and .35, is returned.

AVG

AVG is an aggregate function that averages the values for numeric columns ignoring null values in a given expression. If DISTINCT is used, the average is performed only on the unique values.

Syntax

The syntax is:

```
AVG([ALL | DISTINCT] expression)
```

The arguments are:

ALL	The aggregate function is used on all the values. ALL is the default.
DISTINCT	Only the unique instances of the values are averaged.
Expression	Expression is a constant, column name, function, subquery, and arithmetic, bitwise, and string operators.

Example

Here's an example of the AVG aggregate function:

```
SELECT AVG(age)
FROM table1
```

In this example, the column, 'age', in table1 is averaged and returned. If there is a NULL value in any of the rows, the row is ignored.

BACKUP

The BACKUP statement backs up an entire database, transaction log, file(s) or filegroup(s).

Syntax

To back up an entire database the syntax is:

```
BACKUP DATABASE {database_name | @database_name_var}
TO <backup_device> [,...n]
[WITH
[BLOCKSIZE = {blocksize | @blocksize_variable}]
[[,] DESCRIPTION = {text | @text_variable}]
[[,] DIFFERENTIAL]
[[,] EXPIREDATE = {date | @date_var}
| RETAINDAYS = {days | @days_var}]
[[,] FORMAT | NOFORMAT]
[[,] {INIT | NOINIT}]
[[,] MEDIADESCRIPTION = {text | @text_variable}]
[[,] MEDIANAME = {media_name | @media_name_variable}]
[[,] [NAME = {backup_set_name | @backup_set_name_var}]
[[,] {NOSKIP | SKIP}]
[[,] {NOUNLOAD | UNLOAD}]
[[,] [RESTART]
[[,] STATS [= percentage]]
]
```

Syntax

To back up named files or filegroups belonging to a database, the syntax is:

```
BACKUP DATABASE {database_name | @database_name_var}
<file_or_filegroup> [,...n]
```

```
TO <backup_device> [,…n]
[WITH
[BLOCKSIZE = {blocksize | @blocksize_variable}]
[[,] DESCRIPTION = {text | @text_variable}]
[[,] EXPIREDATE = {date | @date_var}
| RETAINDAYS = {days | @days_var}]
[[,] FORMAT | NOFORMAT]
[[,] {INIT | NOINIT}]
[[,] MEDIADESCRIPTION = {text | @text_variable}]
[[,] MEDIANAME = {media_name | @media_name_variable}]
[[,] [NAME = {backup_set_name | @backup_set_name_var}]
[[,] {NOSKIP | SKIP}]
[[,] {NOUNLOAD | UNLOAD}]
[[,] [RESTART]
[[,] STATS [= percentage]]
]
```

Syntax

To back up a transaction log the syntax is:

```
BACKUP LOG {database_name | @database_name_var}
{
[WITH
{ NO_LOG | TRUNCATE_ONLY }]
}
|
{
TO <backup_device> [,…n]
[WITH
[BLOCKSIZE = {blocksize | @blocksize_variable}]
[[,] DESCRIPTION = {text | @text_variable}]
[[,] EXPIREDATE = {date | @date_var}
| RETAINDAYS = {days | @days_var}]
[[,] FORMAT | NOFORMAT]
[[,] {INIT | NOINIT}]
[[,] MEDIADESCRIPTION = {text | @text_variable}]
[[,] MEDIANAME = {media_name | @media_name_variable}]
[[,] [NAME = {backup_set_name | @backup_set_name_var}]
[[,] NO_TRUNCATE]
[[,] {NOSKIP | SKIP}]
```

```
[[,] {NOUNLOAD | UNLOAD}]
[[,] [RESTART]
[[,] STATS [= percentage]]
]
}
<backup_device> :: =
{
{backup_device_name | @backup_device_name_var}
|
{DISK | TAPE | PIPE} =
{'temp_backup_device' | @temp_backup_device_var}
}
<file_or_filegroup> :: =
{
FILE = {logical_file_name | @logical_file_name_var}
|
FILEGROUP = {logical_filegroup_name | @logical_filegroup_name_var}
}
```

The arguments are:

DATABASE	If this is used, it instructs Microsoft SQL Server to do a complete backup of the database. You can also use this with a list of files or filegroups; this limits the database backup to the files and/or filegroups named. Microsoft SQL Server 7 version now backs up only enough of the log to create the database with transaction integrity when the backup file is restored.
databasename	This argument is the name of the database involved in the backup procedure. You can pass in the database name in the form of a variable or a constant string. databasename = @dbvariable or databasename = plaintextname
backupfilename	This argument is the logical name for the backup device created by *sp_addumpdevice*. This must follow the naming conventions for identifiers 1-128 characters. You can pass in the backup file name in the form of a variable or a constant string. backupfilename = @BFNvariable or backupfilename = plaintextname

{ DISK | TAPE | PIPE } = PATHFILENAME	This argument allows you the freedom of backing up directly to a file rather than a logical backup device. The files are newly created the first time the backup occurs and are then reused for subsequent backups. In regard to temporary backup files: DISK DISK backup files are created new each time. Use complete path and filename. TAPE Use WITH FORMAT for a valid Microsoft Tape format data set. Use complete path and filename, e.g., \\.\tape0. PIPE The client name of the named pipe used by the client application. You can pass in the temporary backup file name in the form of a variable or a constant string. tempbackupfilename = @TBFvariable or tempbackupfilename = plaintextname
NOUNLOAD	This argument determines that the tape will not automatically unload from the tape drive after a backup. This setting is set this way until the UNLOAD is given in a backup command to change the setting.
UNLOAD	This argument determines that the tape automatically rewinds and unloads when the backup is complete. This is the default setting for this tape drive behavior. This setting is set this way until the NOUNLOAD is given in a backup command to change the setting.
DESCRIPTION	This is a user-defined text used to provide information about the backup. You can enter up to 255 characters to describe the contents and perhaps the date or any other information pertinent to the identification of the backup later.

BLOCKSIZE	Specifies the physical block size, in bytes. DISK Not used TAPE Use only if the tape is being overwritten using FORMAT; otherwise the backup program can determine the best block size unless you override this by giving the tape blocksize yourself. PIPE Microsoft SQL Server uses 65,536 unless you tell it the blocksize.
FORMAT	This argument rewrites the backup file and the media header. You can use format to reinitialize a striped backup set. If you use this argument, you do not have to use the SKIP and INIT arguments because they are automatically invoked with FORMAT. As with all FORMAT commands, this wipes out data and header information, too; consequently, use with care. FORMAT also wipes out password information.
NOFORMAT	Is just the opposite of FORMAT. This does not rewrite the media header on all volumes, nor does it rewrite the backup file.
MEDIANAME	This argument can be up to 128 characters of user-defined text that is the media name for the backup media set. If you give the media name, it will attempt to match the media name on the backup volume. If you do not give the media name or the SKIP argument is used, there is no check for a match on media name. If this argument is used with the FORMAT argument, this is what will become the media name. Tapes shared with NT backup must have a media name.
MEDIADESCRIPTION	This argument can be up to 255 characters and is user-defined text that describes the media set.

INIT	This argument means that any data on the device will be overwritten and only this backup file will be on the media of DISK or TAPE. This differs from FORMAT because the media header is not overwritten. It also differs from FORMAT in that the password information prevents SQL Server from writing to the device. Use FORMAT to overwrite media with passwords. To overwrite media that is either password-protected or encrypted, specify the WITH FORMAT option. The backup media will not be overwritten if either all backup sets on the media have not yet expired (for more information, see the EXPIREDATE and RETAINDAYS options) or the backup set name given in the BACKUP statement, if provided, does not match the name on the backup media (for more information, see the NAME option). Note that SQL Server backups can coexist on tape media with Windows NT backups because the Microsoft SQL Server 7.0 backup format conforms to Microsoft Tape Format (MTF), which is the same format used by Windows NT tape backups. Use the SKIP option to override these checks
NOINIT	This argument determines that the backup set should be appended to the device rather than overwriting the last backup. In a backup command, NOINIT is the default if you do not specify INIT or NOINIT.
EXPIREDATE	Using this argument means that your backup set will not be overwritten until the expiredate. You must define this for all backup sets on the media for this to be in effect. Using the SKIP argument overrides this argument. You can pass in the expire date in the form of a variable or a constant string: expiredate = @Evariable or expiredate = "constantstring"

RETAINDAYS	Using this argument means that your backup set will not be overwritten until the the number of retain days has past. You must define this for all backup sets on the media for this to be in effect. Using the SKIP argument overrides this argument. You can pass in the retain days in the form of a variable or an integer: retaindays = @Rvariable or retaindays = integer Use this option with INIT for it to be in effect. EXPIREDATE or RETAINDAYS defaults to the Media Retention configuration setting of sp_configure. The overwrite prevention settings are only used by Microsoft SQL Server to keep Microsoft SQL Server from overwriting its backups.
DIFFERENTIAL	This is one of the new backup features. This argument means only back up the parts of the database that have changed since the last full backup. This option saves backup time and space. Microsoft SQL Server 7.0 now backs up only enough of the log to create the database with transaction integrity when the backup file is restored.
NAME	This argument follows the rules of identifiers of 1 to 128 characters and can be left blank. It is the name of the backup set.
RESTART	This is another of the new features available in Microsoft SQL Server 7.0 and allows Microsoft SQL Server to restart an interrupted backup operation. To implement this restart capability, repeat the BACKUP statement with the RESTART argument. This is only available for TAPE.
NOSKIP	This argument forces the checking of the media name and the expiration date and retain days. When the SKIP and NOSKIP arguments are given, they override any setting defined when the backup device was created.

SKIP	If you use this argument, the expiration date and media name checking is not used to prevent overwriting the backup set and mismatching the media name in the backup set. When the SKIP and NOSKIP arguments are given, they override any setting defined when the backup device was created.
STATS	This argument lets you see how far your backup has progressed and is displayed to the screen or output file in terms of percent complete.
FILE FILEGROUP	Use this argument when the size of the database is so large that a full database backup is not advisable in terms of performance. This can be one file or multiple files or one filegroup or multiple filegroups. Backing up files and/or filegroups is incompatible with the trunc. log on checkpoint option. If tables and their indexes reside on different files or filegroups, then all of these files must be backed up together.
LOG	This argument means you are backing up the transaction log and not the database. You will get all changes to the database that occurred since the last successful LOG backup.
TRUNCATE_ONLY NO_LOG	If you use these arguments and you are doing transaction log dumps, you should back up your entire database. The arguments delete the inactive portion of the log (without making a backup copy of the log) and truncate the log. After backing up the log using NO_LOG, database changes in the log cannot be applied to recover a database. That is why it is necessary to do a backup of the database.
NO_TRUNCATE	Backs up the log but does not truncate it.

Example

Here's an example of a backup for an entire database:

```
BACKUP DATABASE Customer TO customer_db1
```

In this example, the customer database is backed up to the dump device customer_db1.

Example

Here's an example of a backup for an entire database and the transaction log:

```
BACKUP DATABASE Customer TO customer_db1
GO
BACKUP LOG Customer TO customer_log1
GO
```

BEGIN...END

The BEGIN...END statements group Transact-SQL statements together so that when you use flow control statements like IF...ELSE, the entire group of statements is performed with the flow control logic instead of just the one statement immediately after the IF statement.

Syntax

The syntax is:

```
BEGIN
{sql_statement | statement_block}
END
```

The argument, {sql_statement | statement_block}, is any series of Transact-SQL statements.

Example

Here's an example of the BEGIN...END statements:

```
IF   @var1 = 5
BEGIN
SELECT @var2 = 6
PRINT 'I am also doing this print if var1 = 5'
END
```

In this example, the SELECT and the PRINT are both executed together if @var1 = 5.

BEGIN DISTRIBUTED TRANSACTION

The BEGIN DISTRIBUTED TRANSACTION statement indicates the beginning of a Transact-SQL distributed transaction controlled by the Microsoft Distributed Transaction Coordinator (MS DTC).

Syntax

The syntax is:

```
BEGIN DISTRIBUTED TRAN[SACTION] [transaction_name]
```

The argument, transaction_name, is named by the user and is used by the MS DTC to refer to this transaction.

Example

Here's an example of the BEGIN DISTRIBUTED TRANSACTION statement:

```
BEGIN DISTRIBUTED TRANSACTION
UPDATE mylocaltable
SET col1 = 'N/A'
EXECUTE remote.db1.dbo.reset_col1 'N/A'
COMMIT TRAN
```

In this example, the UPDATE statement updates the local database and the remote stored procedure updates the remote database using a two-phase commit.

BEGIN TRANSACTION

The BEGIN TRANSACTION statement indicates the beginning of a Transact-SQL local transaction.

Syntax

The syntax is:

```
BEGIN TRAN[SACTION] [transaction_name]
```

The argument, transaction_name, is a named by the user and refers to this transaction.

Example

Here's an example of the BEGIN TRANSACTION statement:

```
BEGIN TRANSACTION
UPDATE mylocaltable
SET col1 = 'N/A'
EXECUTE reset_col1 'N/A'
COMMIT TRAN
```

In this example, the UPDATE statement updates the local database, and the remote stored procedure updates the remote database using a two-phase commit.

BETWEEN

The BETWEEN includes the two values in a range.

Syntax

The syntax is:

```
[NOT] expression [NOT] BETWEEN expression AND expression
```

The arguments are:

NOT	NOT is the negative indicator of a boolean expression.
Expression	Expression is a constant, column name, function, and subquery and arithmetic, bitwise, and string operators.
AND	The AND statement strings together two conditions.

Example

Here's an example of the BETWEEN statement:

```
SELECT *
FROM tableX
WHERE col1 BETWEEN 1 AND 5
```

In this example, the rows are selected that have a value in a column between 1 and 5. Rows with 1 and rows with 5 will be selected in the query.

binary

You can use the fixed length binary data type to hold binary data when the values in the column are about the same length. Use the variable length varbinary data type when there is an inconsistency in length.

Syntax

The syntax is:

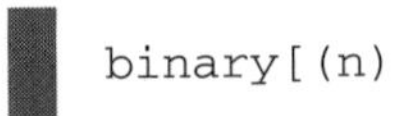

```
binary[(n)]
```

The argument (n) is the number of characters that is stored with a maximum of 8,000 bytes. Even if the column is shorter than (n), (n) is still the amount of space taken for the storage. If your columns do not exceed 15, use 15 for (n) and avoid making your columns too much bigger than the data you are to store. The query processor may not handle the situation well if the row exceeds 8,000 in a temporary table.

Defaults for length (if not provided) are 1 long in a data definition situation and 30 when using CONVERT. If the data is too long to fit in the column, it will be truncated.

bit

The bit data type hold 1 or 0 and is usually used to indicate 1 = yes and 0 = no. If you attempt to insert anything in a bit data type other than 0 or 1, 1 will be inserted.

Syntax

The syntax is:

```
Bit(n)
```

The argument (n) is an integer that determines the length of the bit column. Storage size is 1 byte where 1 byte holds 8 bits. Columns with the bit data type cannot be indexed.

BREAK

The BREAK statement is used in Transact-SQL flow control language to exit the WHILE loop.

Syntax

The syntax is:

```
BREAK
```

Example

Here's and example of BREAK in a WHILE loop:

```
WHILE … --something is true
BEGIN
IF … --something else is true
BREAK
ELSE
CONTINUE
END
```

In this example, if something else is true while inside the WHILE loop, the loop will be exited.

BULK INSERT

BULK INSERT places a data file into a database table in a given format.

Syntax

The syntax is:

```
BULK INSERT [['database_name'.]['owner'].]{'table_name FROM data_file}
[WITH
(
[ BATCHSIZE [ = batch_size]]
[[,] CHECK_CONSTRAINTS]
[[,] CODEPAGE [ = ACP | OEM | RAW | code_page]]
[[,] DATAFILETYPE [ =
{'char' | 'native'| 'widechar' | 'widenative }]]
[[,] FIELDTERMINATOR [ = 'field_terminator']]
[[,] FIRSTROW [ = first_row]]
[[,] FORMATFILE [ = 'format_file_path']]
[[,] KEEPIDENTITY]
[[,] KEEPNULLS]
[[,] LASTROW [ = last_row]]
[[,] MAXERRORS [ = max_errors]]
[[,] ORDER ({column [ASC | DESC]} [, …n])]
[[,] ROWTERMINATOR [ = 'row_terminator']]
[[,] TABLOCK])]
```

The arguments are:

'database_name'	Database_name is the name of the database housing the table.
'owner'	Owner is the name of the table owner.
'table_name'	Table_name is the table to bulk insert data.
data_file	Data_file is the path of the data file.
BATCHSIZE [= batch_size]	Batchsize is the number of rows in a batch.
CHECK_CONSTRAINTS	CHECK_CONSTRAINTS means constraints on a table are checked during the bulk insert. The default behavior is that constraints are not checked.

CODEPAGE [= ACP | OEM | RAW | code_page]	CODEPAGE is the code page of the data in the data file for char, varchar, or text columns with character values greater than 127 or less than 32. Raw is the fastest because no conversion occurs. The others are converted to the SQL Server codepage.
<value>	<value> is the code page number.
DATAFILETYPE [= {'char' | 'native' | 'widechar' | 'widenative'}]	DATAFILETYPE instructs the BULK INSERT to do the bulk insert using the default for the given type. Char is the default with \t (tab character) as the default field separator and \n (newline character) as the default row terminator. Native does the bulk copy operation using the native data types of the data as the default. There is no prompting for each field. Widechar uses Unicode characters as the default with no prompting and a default of nchar as the default storage type, \t (tab character) as the default field separator and \n (newline character) as the default row terminator. Widenative is the same as native except char, varchar, and text columns are saved as Unicode characters. This is faster than widechar and is for use transferring data from one SQL Server to another using a data file.
FIELDTERMINATOR [= 'field_terminator']	Field_terminator is the field terminator to be used for char and widechar and the default is \t.
FIRSTROW [= first_row]	First_row is the number of the first row to copy with default of 1.
FORMATFILE [= 'format_file_path']	Format_file_path is the full path of the format file with responses from a previous use.
KEEPIDENTITY	KEEPIDENTITY means identity columns are in the file; it takes the values for the identity columns from data file.

KEEPNULLS	KEEPNULLS means to keep nulls instead of applying the defaults.
LASTROW [= last_row]	Last_row is the number of the last row to copy with a default of 0; it means the last row physically present in the file.
MAXERRORS [= max_errors]	Max_errors is the maximum number of errors before the bulk copy operation stops with a default number of 10.
ORDER ({column [ASC | DESC]} [, ...n])	ORDER tells how the data in the data file is sorted. By default, the bulk copy operation assumes the data file is unordered. If the order is the same as the clustered index on the table, performance is faster.
n	N means the preceding entry is repeatable.
ROWTERMINATOR [= 'row_terminator']	Row_terminator is the row terminator to be used for both the char and widechar with a default of \n.
TABLOCK	TABLOCK means a table-level lock is acquired for the duration of the bulk copy operation. More than one client can insert into a table if there are no indexes on the table and TABLOCK is used. The default is the acquisition of row-level locks on the table.

Example

Here's an example of the BULK INSERT Transact-SQL statement:

```
BULK INSERT Mydb..MyTable
FROM 'a:\myfile.txt'
WITH ( FIELDTERMINATOR = ',',ROWTERMINATOR = '\n')
```

In this example, the data from myfile is inserted into the table, MyTable in the database, Mydb with a field terminator of comma and a row terminator of new line.

CASE

The CASE statement is the vehicle for using conditional values in Transact-SQL expressions.

Syntax

The syntax for a simple CASE statement is:

```
CASE expression
{WHEN expression THEN result}[, ...n]
[ELSE result]
END
```

The syntax for a searched CASE statement is:

```
CASE
WHEN Boolean_expression THEN result_expression [,...n]
[ELSE else_result_expression]
END
```

The arguments are:

expression	Expression is a constant, column name, function, and subquery and arithmetic, bitwise, and string operators.
Result	Result is returned when the expression matches the WHEN clause.
n	This indicates you can repeat the WHEN clause more than once.
Boolean_expression	The boolean expression indicates if the THEN clause will be executed.
ELSE result	ELSE result returns if the WHEN clause fails. NULL will be returned if you do not use ELSE and the WHEN clause fails.

Example

Here's an example of the CASE statement:

```
SELECT name = CASE Software
WHEN 'Word Processor' THEN 'Microsoft Word'
WHEN 'Spreadsheet' THEN 'Microsoft Excel'
END
FROM table1
WHERE company = 'Microsoft'
```

In this example, the values of "Microsoft Word" or "Microsoft Excel" are returned if "Word Processor" or "Spreadsheet" are the values found in the Software column in table1.

CAST

The CAST statement is the same thing as the CONVERT statement and is used for data type conversion in Transact-SQL.

Syntax

The syntax is:

```
CAST(expression AS data_type)
```

The arguments are:

expression	Expression is a constant, column name, function and subquery and arithmetic, bitwise, and string operators.
data_type	A data type is any system data type into which the column can be converted.

Example

Here's an example of the CAST statement:

```
CAST (MyDate AS varchar)
```

In this example, the MyDate value changes to a varchar data type instead of a datetime data type.

CEILING

The CEILING function is used in a mathematical context to return the smallest integer greater than or equal to the given numeric expression.

Syntax

The syntax is:

```
CEILING(numeric_expression)
```

The argument, numeric_expression, is a decimal, float, int, money, numeric, real, smallint, smallmoney, or tinyint data type.

Example

Here are some examples of the CEILING function:

```
SELECT CEILING(1.45)
```

In this example, the integer 2 is returned.

```
SELECT CEILING(-1.45)
```

In this example, the integer 1 is returned.

char data type

You can use the fixed length char data type to hold alphanumeric data when the values in the column are about the same length. Use the variable length varchar data type when there is an inconsistency in length.

Syntax

The syntax is:

```
char[(n)]
```

The argument, (n), is an integer representing the length of the column.

CHAR string function

CHAR is a string function used to change an ASCII code integer to a character.

Syntax

The syntax is:

```
CHAR(integer_expression)
```

The argument, (integer_expression), is a positive integer between 0 and 255.

Example

Here's an example of the CHAR string function:

```
SELECT 'BACKUP DATABASE  ' + name + ' to'  + name +
_dump with init,stats + CHAR(13) + 'GO'
FROM master..sysdatabases
WHERE name NOT LIKE 'tempdb'
```

In this example, the output appears as the syntax below and in a master, slave SQL SELECT statement method to create Transact-SQL code. This means the master SQL statement creates the slave SQL statement to run later. You will need to edit out any lines with the "(4 row(s) affected)" text before you run the slave Transact-SQL. Or, you can set NOCOUNT to on before the SELECT statement and the "(4 row(s) affected)" will not print. You can include the line of dashes because it will be interpreted as a comment.

The preceding SELECT statement will create the syntax to back up all the databases on SQL Server. CHAR(13) provides the new line character required for the GO statement to be the first character in a new line as is required for the GO statement. The ASCII code 13 is the new line character.

```
BACKUP DATABASE  master to master_dump with init, statsGO
BACKUP DATABASE  model to model_dump with init, statsGO
BACKUP DATABASE  msdb to msdb_dump with init, statsGO
BACKUP DATABASE  pubs to pubs_dump with init, statsGO
```

CHARINDEX string function

CHARINDEX string function returns the starting position of the pattern when searching for a pattern in a string.

Syntax

The syntax is:

```
CHARINDEX('pattern', expression [, start_location])
```

The arguments are:

pattern	Pattern is the alphanumeric values you are searching for.
expression	Expression is any valid SQL Server string expression.
start_location	Start location is the position within the column to start searching for the pattern. If this optional argument is not provided, SQL Server will start looking in the first position.

Example

Here's an example of the CHARINDEX string function:

```
SELECT CHARINDEX('find me in row 4', Column2, 10)
FROM MyTable
WHERE Column1 = '4'
GO
```

In this example, an integer is returned as the position of where in Column2 the pattern "find me in row 4" starts at or after the tenth character.

CHECKPOINT

CHECKPOINT in the current database issues the command to SQL Server to write to disk all pages updated since the last checkpoint. Issuing the CHECKPOINT statement checkpoints the database. Other checkpoints are automatically performed by SQL Server according to the setting of the *sp_configure* option called "recovery interval" set to determine what is the maximum acceptable recovery time in minutes.

Syntax

The syntax is:

```
CHECKPOINT
```

CLOSE

The CLOSE statement closes an open cursor. The data structures are left so that you can reopen a closed cursor.

Syntax

The syntax is:

```
CLOSE { { [GLOBAL] cursor_name } | cursor_variable_name }
```

GLOBAL	GLOBAL indicates a global cursor.
cursor_name	Cursor name is the name of the open cursor you are closing and is the GLOBAL cursor if GLOBAL is an argument and the local cursor if the GLOBAL keyword is not used.
Cursor_variable_name	Cursor variable name is the name of a variable containing the open cursor name that you wish to close.

COALESCE

COALESCE returns the first NOT NULL value it finds in a sequential check of each of its arguments. SQL Server will check the first argument, a column, or expression and, if it is NULL, SQL Server will check the next argument. If that one is NULL, the next argument is checked until an argument is checked that is NOT NULL; that will be the one returned.

Syntax

The syntax is:

```
COALESCE(expression [, ...n])
```

The arguments are:

Expression	Expression is a constant, column name, function, and subquery and arithmetic, bitwise, and string operators.
n	N means the preceding entry is repeatable.

Example

Here's an example of the COALESCE function:

```
SELECT COALESCE(Column1, Column2,     Column3)
FROM MyTable
WHERE Column4 < 9
GO
```

In this example, Column1 is analyzed for a NOT NULL. If Column1 is NOT NULL, the value in Column1 is returned, but if Column1 is NULL, Column2 is analyzed for a NOT NULL value. If Column2 has a value for Column2, the value is returned and so forth until a NOT NULL value is found in the arguments for the COALESCE function.

COL_LENGTH

COL_LENGTH returns the length of a column in bytes.

Syntax

The syntax is:

```
COL_LENGTH('table', 'column')
```

The arguments are:

Table	Table is the name of the table and can be in the form owner.tablename.
Column	Column is the name of the column.

Example

Here's an example of the COL_LENGTH function:

```
SELECT COL_LENGTH('MyTable', 'Column1')
```

In this example, the length (an integer) of Column1, a column in the table, MyTable is returned.

COL_NAME

COL_NAME returns the name of a database column after you give the function, the table identification number, and column identification number.

Syntax

The syntax is:

```
COL_NAME(table_id, column_id)
```

The arguments are:

Table_id	Table is the system ID of the table.
Column_id	Column is the system ID of the column.

COLUMNPROPERTY

COLUMNPROPERTY returns information on a column or procedure argument.

Syntax

The syntax is:

```
COLUMNPROPERTY(id, column, 'property')
```

The arguments are:

id	Id is the ID of the table or procedure argument.
column	Column is the name of the column or procedure argument.
property	Property is the type of information to be returned for the table or procedure argument. Possible values for property are, 'AllowsNull', 'IsIdentity', 'IsIdNotForRepl', 'IsOutParam', 'IsRowGuidCol', 'Precision', 'Scale', and 'UsesAnsiTrim'.

Example

Here's an example of the COLUMNPROPERTY function:

```
SELECT COLUMNPROPERTY(
OBJECT_ID('MyTable'),'Column1','PRECISION')
```

In this example, the precision of Column1 in MyTable is returned.

COMMIT TRANS[ACTION]

COMMIT TRANSACTION or COMMIT TRANS is the end of a transaction at which time all changes to the data since the start of the transaction become a permanent part of the database.

Syntax

The syntax is:

```
COMMIT [TRAN[SACTION] [transaction_name] ]
```

The argument, transaction_name, is used only by the programmer to tell which COMMIT belongs to which BEGIN.

Example

Here's an example of the COMMIT TRANS[ACTION] statement:

```
BEGIN TRANSACTION
UPDATE Mytable
SET Column1 = 3
WHERE Column2 = 8
GO
COMMIT TRANSACTION
GO
```

In this example, the transaction begins with a BEGIN TRANSACTION and ends with a COMMIT TRANSACTION.

COMMIT [WORK]

COMMIT WORK is the end of a transaction at which time all changes to the data since the start of the transaction become a permanent part of the database. This is exactly the same as COMMIT TRANSACTION and was added for ANSI SQL-92 compliance.

Syntax

The syntax is:

```
COMMIT [WORK] ]
```

The argument WORK is optional. The single word COMMIT does the same thing as COMMIT WORK.

Example

Here's an example of the COMMIT [WORK] statement:

```
BEGIN TRANSACTION
UPDATE Mytable
SET Column1 = 3
WHERE Column2 = 8
GO
COMMIT
GO
```

In this example, the transaction begins and ends with a COMMIT.

CONTAINS

CONTAINS searches character-based data types columns for precise or other matches, such as a word or phrase, the prefix of a word or phrase, a word that is near another word, a word that is inflectionally generated from another (such as make and made), and a word that has a higher designated weighting than another word. This function depends on the database/table/columns being enabled for full text searching. See the full text stored procedures in Chapter 22, "System Stored Procedures."

Syntax

The syntax is:

```
CONTAINS
( {column | *}, '<contains_search_condition>'
)
<contains_search_condition> ::=
{
<simple_term>
| <prefix_term>
| <proximity_term>
| <generation_term>
```

```
| <isabout_term>
| (<contains_search_condition>)
}
[ {
{AND | AND NOT | OR} <contains_search_condition>
}
] [...n]

<isabout_term> :: =
ISABOUT
( {
<generation_term>
| <prefix_term>
| <proximity_term>
| <simple_term>
}
[WEIGHT (weight_value)]
)

<generation_term> :: =
FORMSOF (INFLECTIONAL, <simple_term>)

<prefix term> ::=
word * | "phrase * "

<proximity_term> ::=
{<simple_term> | <prefix_term>} {NEAR() | ~}

<simple_term> ::=
word | " phrase "
```

The arguments are:

column	Column is the name of a character-type column. The columns must have been registered for full-text searching.
*	* means all columns in the table eligible to be searched (those registered for full-text searching). Qualify with the table name if there is more than one table in the FROM clause.
<contains_search_condition>	<contains_search_condition> is the text to search for in the column.

word	Word is a string of characters with no spaces and punctuation.
phrase	Phrase is one or more words with spaces.
<isabout_term>	<isabout_term> determines that the rows returned match the list of words and phrases that could each have a weighting value.
ISABOUT	ISABOUT is the <isabout_term> keyword.
WEIGHT (*weight_value*)	Weight_value defines a weight value, a number between 0.0 and 1.0. Each part in the <isabout_term> can have a *weight_value*.
AND | AND NOT | OR	AND | AND NOT | OR are logical operators.
<generation_term>	<generation_term> is the match of words when the <simple_terms> have differences from the original search word.
INFLECTIONAL	INFLECTIONAL means that plural and singular forms of nouns and tenses of verbs are matches.
<prefix_term>	Specifies a match of words or phrases beginning with the specified text (e.g., "MS*" searches from any string starting with MS).
<proximity_term>	<proximity_term> defines the match of words or phrases that are close to each other.
NEAR() | ~	NEAR() | ~ means that the string or word or phrase on one side of the NEAR() or ~ is close to the word or phrase on the other side of the NEAR() or ~.
<simple_term>	<simple_term> determines a match for an exact word or phrase (put double quotes around phrases).
n	N means the preceding entry is repeatable.

Example

Here's an example of the CONTAINS keyword:

```
SELECT MyFullTextEnabledColumn
FROM MyTable
WHERE CONTAINS(MyFullTextEnabledColumn, 'computer* OR hardware*')
```

In this example, values in MyFullTextEnabledColumn containing the strings supplied are displayed as a result set.

Example

Here's an example using CONTAINS with proximity syntax:

```
SELECT MyFullTextEnabledColumn
FROM MyTable
WHERE CONTAINS(MyFullTextEnabledColumn, 'Diana NEAR Princess')
```

In this example, values in MyFullTextEnabledColumn with the supplied words in proximity to each other are displayed.

Example

Here's an example using CONTAINS with inflectional syntax:

```
SELECT MyFullTextEnabledColumn
FROM MyTable
WHERE CONTAINS(MyFullTextEnabledColumn, ' FORMSOF (INFLECTIONAL, agree) ')
```

In this example, values in MyFullTextEnabledColumn with the supplied words in the form of the word are displayed (agreeable, agreed, agreeing, agrees, etc.).

Example

Here's an example using CONTAINS with weighted syntax:

```
SELECT MyFullTextEnabledColumn
FROM MyTable
WHERE CONTAINS(MyFullTextEnabledColumn, 'ISABOUT (dolphin weight (.8),
whale weight (.4), fish weight (.2) )' )
```

In this example, a search occurs for rows with MyFullTextEnabledColumn containing the words dolphin, whale, or fish with associated weightings.

CONTAINSTABLE

CONTAINSTABLE returns a table for those columns with exact or not so exact matches to words and phrases, words close to another word, or weighted matches. It can be used in a FROM clause of the a SELECT statement like any table name. A rank for each row is also returned. See CONTAINS for more information.

Syntax

The syntax is:

```
CONTAINSTABLE (table, {column | *}, '<contains_search_condition>')
<contains_search_condition> ::=
    {
        | <generation_term>
        | <prefix_term>
        | <proximity_term>
        <simple_term>
        | <weighted_term>
        | (<contains_search_condition>)
    }
    [    {
            {AND | AND NOT | OR} <contains_search_condition>
        }
    ] [...n]
<weighted_term> ::=
    ISABOUT
        (    {    {
                    <generation_term>
                    | <prefix_term>
                    | <proximity_term>
                    | <simple_term>
                }
                [WEIGHT (weight_value)]
            }  [, ...n]
        )
<generation_term> ::=
    FORMSOF (INFLECTIONAL, <simple_term> [, ...n] )
<prefix term> ::=
    { "word * " | "phrase * " }
<proximity_term> ::=
    {<simple_term> | <prefix_term>}
    {    {NEAR | ~} {<simple_term> | <prefix_term>} } [...n]
<simple_term> ::=
    word | " phrase "
```

The arguments are:

table	Table is the optionally qualified name of the table that has been enabled for full-text search.
column	Column is the name of the full-text enabled column you intend to search.
*	* means that all columns in the table enabled for full-text searching.
<contains_search_condition>	Contains_search_condition is the text (not a variable) to search for in the full-text enabled column.

CONTINUE

The CONTINUE statement is sometimes used with an IF statement and is used to restart a WHILE loop with anything after the CONTINUE not executed. See WHILE.

Syntax

The syntax is:

```
CONTINUE
```

CONVERT

CONVERT is used in the explicit conversion of an expression from one data type to another and can be used anywhere an expression can be used.

Syntax

The syntax is:

```
CONVERT (data_type[(length)], expression [, style])
```

The arguments are:

data_type	Data type is the nonuser-defined data type you wish the expression to be.
Length	Length is an optional length that you wish the expression to be.
Expression	Any valid expression.

Style	Style is the style of date format you want when you are converting datetime or smalldatetime data to character data and can be char, varchar, nchar, or nvarchar data types. When you are using the string format to convert float, real, money, or smallmoney data to character data, data types can be char, varchar, nchar, or nvarchar data types. **Styles for datetime or smalldatetime converted to character** (adding 100 gives the year in yyyy format instead of yy format): - 0 or 100 mon dd yyyy hh:miAM or PM 1 or 101 USA mm/dd/yy 2 or 102 ANSI yy.mm.dd 3 or 103 British/French dd/mm/yy 4 or 104 German dd.mm.yy 5 or 105 Italian dd-mm-yy 6 or 106 - dd mon yy 7 or 107 - mon dd, yy 8 or 108 - hh:mm:ss - 9 or 109 Default + milliseconds mon dd yyyy hh:mi:ss:mmmAM or PM 10 or 110 USA mm-dd-yy 11 or 111 JAPAN yy/mm/dd 12 or 112 ISO yymmdd - 13 or 113 Europe default + milliseconds dd mon yyyy hh:mm:ss:mmm(24h) 14 114 - hh:mi:ss:mmm(24h) - 20 or 120 ODBC canonical yyyy-mm-dd hh:mi:ss(24h) - 21 or 121 ODBC canonical (with milliseconds) yyyy-mm-dd hh:mi:ss.mmm(24h) **Styles for float or real datatypes converted to character**: 0 (the default) = 6 digits or less1 = 8 digits 2 = 16 digits **Style for money or smallmoney converted to character**: 0=No commas and 2 digits decimal (e.g., 1234.11). This is the default. 1=Commas and 2 digits decimal (e.g., 1,234.11) 2=No commas and 4 digits to the right of the decimal point (e.g., 1234.1111)

Example

Here's an example of the CONVERT function:

```
SELECT 'My Birthday is Today ' + CONVERT(varchar(12), getdate())
```

In this example, a string can be concatenated with a date by converting the date to a string and using the plus sign to concatenate the character data types.

COS

COS is a mathematical function returning the cosine of the angle in the expression.

Syntax

The syntax is:

```
COS(float_expression)
```

The argument, float_expression, is of the float data type.

COT

COT is a mathematical function returning the cotangent of the angle in the expression.

Syntax

The syntax is:

```
COT(float_expression)
```

The argument, float_expression, is of the float data type.

COUNT

COUNT is an aggregate function that returns an integer representing the number of values in the expression (usually a column). Using DISTINCT with COUNT returns the number of unique values.

Syntax

The syntax is:

```
COUNT({[ALL | DISTINCT] expression] | *})
```

The arguments are:

ALL	ALL is the default and counts all values while ignoring NULLs.
DISTINCT	Using DISTINCT with COUNT returns the number of unique values.

Expression	Expression is a constant, column name, function, and subquery and arithmetic, bitwise, and string operators.
*	* means all rows.

Example

Here's an example of the COUNT aggregate function:

```
SELECT COUNT(Column1)
FROM Mytable
```

In this example, the COUNT function will count the number of rows without null values in Column1 of Mytable. If a * was used instead of a column name, the number of all the rows in the table is returned.

CREATE DATABASE

CREATE DATABASE is the statement that creates a new database with its associated files.

Syntax

The syntax is:

```
CREATE DATABASE database_name
[ ON [PRIMARY]
[ <filespec> [,...n] ]
[, <filegroup> [,...n] ]
]
[ LOG ON { <filespec> } ]
[ FOR LOAD | FOR ATTACH ]

<filespec> ::=

( [ NAME = logical_file_name, ]
FILENAME = 'os_file_name'
[, SIZE = size]
[, MAXSIZE = { max_size | UNLIMITED } ]
[, FILEGROWTH = growth_increment] ) [,...n]

<filegroup> ::=

FILEGROUP filegroup_name <filespec> [,...n]
```

The arguments are:

database_name	The name of the new database you are creating using the rules for identifiers
[ON [PRIMARY] [<filespec> [,...n]] [, <filegroup> [,...n]]	If you use ON you are supplying the disk file names to store the data. The ON is followed by a list of files that are to become the data files for the primary filegroup and may optionally have a list of user created filegroups. If the PRIMARY keyword is not used, the first file listed is stored as the primary file.
PRIMARY	PRIMARY means that the filespec list contains the files in the primary filegroup containing system tables and objects not defined in filegroups. There can be only one PRIMARY file and it names the starting file of the database. If the PRIMARY keyword is not used, the first file listed is stored as the primary file.
n	This indicates you can repeat the files named more than once.
LOG ON	If you use LOG ON you are supplying the log file name(s) for the transaction logs. The LOG ON is followed by a list of files that are to become the log files of the database. If you omit this from the CREATE DATABASE statement, one log file with a name chosen by SQL Server will be created with a size 25 percent of the data files named.
FOR LOAD	Backward compatibility only. Not needed in version 7.0 because SQL Server can create a database when restoring.
FOR ATTACH	FOR ATTACH indicates that you have an existing set of operating system files. You must supply a filespec to define the first primary file. You also need filespec listings for files with a different path if different than when the database was first created or last attached. Use sp_attach_db instead of CREATE DATABASE FOR ATTACH unless you must list more than 16 filespec entries.
NAME	NAME means we are referring to the logical name of the file.

logical_file_name	The logical name used for the file.
FILENAME	FILENAME means we are referring to the physical or operating system file name for the file.
'os_file_name'	The operating system filename used and the path on the local server.
SIZE	SIZE means you are going to give a size of the file(s) you have named.
size	Size is the beginning size of the file. Use MB or KB with the number to indicate megabytes or kilobytes; the default is MB. The smallest allowed value for size is 1MB. If you do not use SIZE, the files will be created with 3MB for data files and 1MB for log files.
MAXSIZE	MAXSIZE means you will supply the maximum size the files can grow.
max_size	MAXSIZE is the maximum size the files can grow. If max_size is not specified, the file will grow until the disk is full. You should use the SQL Server Agent to generate an alert when your disk is approaching a certain capacity percentage.
UNLIMITED	UNLIMITED means the file(s) can grow until the disk is full.
FILEGROWTH	FILEGROWTH means you are going to suppy the amount the file should increment as it grows, not to exceed the MAXSIZE.
growth_increment	Growth_increment (default of 256KB, minimum 64KB) is given here with the growth increment supplied rounded to the nearest 64KB.

Example

Here's an example of the CREATE DATABASE statement:

```
USE master
GO
CREATE DATABASE mydb
ON
( NAME = mydb_dat1,
```

```
  FILENAME = 'c:\mssql7\data\mydbdat.mdf',
  SIZE = 100,
  MAXSIZE = 900,
  FILEGROWTH = 5 )
LOG ON
( NAME = 'mydb_log1',
  FILENAME = 'd:\mssql7\data\mydblog.ldf',
  SIZE = 25MB,
  MAXSIZE = 200MB,
  FILEGROWTH = 5MB )
GO
```

In this example, a new database is created on a data file and a log file.

CREATE DEFAULT

The CREATE DEFAULT statement creates an object that needs to be bound to a column or user-defined data type (which is why it is best to use the DEFAULT clause of the CREATE or ALTER TABLE statement). The default determines what value is inserted into the column or into all the columns with the user-defined data type when no value is supplied when the row is inserted. If the default is used over and over, use the CREATE DEFAULT statement because it is more efficient to code the CREATE TABLE statements.

Syntax

The syntax is:

```
CREATE DEFAULT default
AS constant_expression
```

The arguments are:

default	Default is the name of the default using the rules for identifiers.
constant_expression	A constant expression is constant values and not the names of database objects. You can use any constants, functions, mathematical expressions, and global variables. Place single quotes around characters and dates. Binary data is prefixed with 0x, and money is prefixed by a dollar sign ($).

Example

Here's an example of a CREATE DEFAULT statement:

```
CREATE DEFAULT Phone_Default AS 'No Phone Number'
GO
sp_bindefault Phone_Default, 'Mytable.Telephone_Nbr'
GO
```

In this example, the Phone_Default is created that inserts the characters 'No Phone Number' into the column when no value is given for the Telephone_Nbr column in Mytable using an INSERT statement.

CREATE INDEX

The CREATE INDEX statement creates an index on a table, but you must be the owner of the table. If the index you are creating is the PRIMARY KEY, use the PRIMARY KEY constraint in the CREATE TABLE or ALTER TABLE statements. You can create indexes in tables in another database by qualifying the table name using database.tableowner. tablename and qualifying the database and owner.

Syntax

The syntax is:

```
CREATE [UNIQUE] [CLUSTERED | NONCLUSTERED]
INDEX index_name ON table (column [, ...n])
[WITH
        [PAD_INDEX]
        [[,] FILLFACTOR = fillfactor]
        [[,] IGNORE_DUP_KEY]
        [[,] DROP_EXISTING]
        [[,] STATISTICS_NORECOMPUTE]
]
[ON filegroup]
```

The arguments are:

UNIQUE	UNIQUE means you are creating a unique index that keeps any two from having the same value(s) for the column(s) that comprise(s) this key. SQL Server ensures this by checking for duplicates. SQL Server will not let you place an index on existing rows with duplicate columns. You will have to update or remove the duplicate rows even if they are null before you can create the unique index.

CLUSTERED	A CLUSTERED INDEX means that the physical order of rows is the same as the indexed order of the rows with the leaf pages of the clustered index holding the data rows. If a clustered index is created, all the nonclustered indexes on the table are also rebuilt. This means you should create the clustered index first, especially if you have scripts that drop and re-create indexes. A clustered index is a sorted table, so creating a clustered index and using the ON *filegroup* clause moves the sorted table to a new filegroup designated in the CREATE INDEX statement. Make sure you have enough space in your files (1.2 times the space needed for the table).
NONCLUSTERED	A NONCLUSTERED index determines how a table is logically ordered. Unlike a CLUSTERED index, the logical order and physical ordering is different. The NONCLUSTERED index contains pointers to the actual physical rows, and the pointer may be the clustering key that is now stored in the NONCLUSTERED index instead of the Row ID (RID) as in versions past. If the table has no CLUSTERED index, the pointer is a pointer to the row consisting of the file ID, page number, and row ID. You can have as many as 249 NONCLUSTERED indexes per table but, as you know, the more indexes there are on a table the longer it takes to INSERT rows.
index_name	Index name is the name of the index and must be unique per table (but not per database) while following the rules for identifiers.
Table	Table is the name of the table that contains the column you are indexing. If you give the database and table owner and you have permission, you can create the index in another database.
column	Column is the name of the column(s) upon which you are creating an index. Listing more than one column name separated by commas in the parenthesis in the order you would like to prioritize the sort creates a composite index. Text, image, bit, and computed columns need not apply and cannot be used as columns for any index. The maximum is 16 columns for a composite index. The maximum size of a composite index is 900 bytes.

n	N means the preceding column is repeatable.
PAD_INDEX	PAD_INDEX means apply the FILLFACTOR to interior (non-leaf) index pages (nodes) as well as to leaf pages.
FILLFACTOR = *fillfactor*	FILLFACTOR determines how full each index page is and only applies when the index is first created, but the actual fullness of the pages changes over time. Valid values are from 1 through 100, and it defaults to 0 if the value is not supplied. Use sp_configure to change the FILLFACTOR default. When FILLFACTOR is 0, space is left in the index node for at least two entries where an entry is an index pointer in an index page. When FILLFACTOR is 100, all the data is packed together at 100 percent full; this is only recommended for a read only table. Of course, the FILLFACTOR determines the amount of space your index and data (in the case of a clustered index) takes up on disk. The lower the user-defined FILLFACTOR, the more space the index or data page needs to store data.
IGNORE_DUP_KEY	IGNORE_DUP_KEY determines the result when a duplicate key is inserted along with other row(s) into a unique clustered index. A warning is issued by SQL Server, but the other rows in the INSERT that are not duplicated keys are inserted. The duplicate key rows are ignored and not inserted. If IGNORE_DUP_KEY is not used, all the rows will fail to insert, not just the duplicate key rows.
SORTED_DATA_REORG	SORTED_DATA_REORG tells SQL Server the data is already sorted but to reorganize the data on the disk. Use this when you are using the FILLFACTOR OPTION and you change the way the data is stored on the pages. Use DBCC SHOWCONTIG to determine if your table is fragmented and needs to be reorganized.
DROP EXISTING	Using DROP EXISTING will drop and re-create the clustered index. At the same time, all existing nonclustered indexes are updated. This is more efficient than a DROP and CREATE because only one update is performed rather than updating once after the drop of the clustered index and again after the clustered index is re-created.

STATISTICS_NORECOMPUTE	STATISTICS_NORECOMPUTE is also used for efficiency and means that the index statistics are not automatically recomputed. Using this could hurt you by not providing the query optimizer distribution statistics to formulate query plans later.
ON *filegroup*	ON filegroup indicates in which filegroup the index will be placed. If you do not use ON filegroup, the index will be placed on the same filegroup as the table.

Example

Here's an example of the CREATE INDEX statement:

```
CREATE INDEX Column1_2_ind ON Mytable (Column1,Column2)
```

In this example, a composite index is created.

CREATE PROCEDURE

The CREATE PROCEDURE statement creates a stored procedure which is a compiled set of Transact-SQL statements optionally accepting arguments.

Syntax

The syntax is:

```
CREATE PROC[EDURE] procedure_name [;number]
[
({[@]parameter data_type} [VARYING] [= default] [OUTPUT])
]
[,…n]
[
WITH {RECOMPILE | ENCRYPTION | RECOMPILE, ENCRYPTION}
]
[FOR REPLICATION]
AS
sql_statement [...n]
```

procedure_name	Procedure_name is the name of the new stored procedure using the rules for identifiers, and stored procedure names are unique for database and owner. Temporary stored procedures can be created by prefixing the name with a single pound sign for local temporary procedures or a double pound sign for global temporary procedures to the stored procedure name. Stored procedures can also be created as startup stored procedures executed automatically when SQL Server starts by using the *sp_makestartup* system stored procedure. The total store procedure name cannot exceed 128 characters, including the pound (#) sign.
;number	Number is an integer used to group procedures of the same name so it is easy to drop them all with a single DROP PROCEDURE statement. Stored procedures named samename;1, samename;2, etc. can be dropped together with "DROP PROCEDURE samename", which drops the entire group. Once you have grouped like this, you have lost the ability to drop each individually.
[@]parameter	@parameter is a parameter or argument in the procedure. Zero, one, or more than one argument can be declared in a CREATE PROCEDURE statement. The value of each declared argument is supplied by the user when the procedure is executed if a default has not been coded. The maximum number of arguments is 1,024, and each is local to the stored procedure.
data_type	Data_type is referring to the data type of the argument or parameter. The cursor data type may only be used on OUTPUT arguments, and VARYING must also be used.

VARYING	VARYING defines the result set as an output parameter and is used for the cursor data type.
default	Default refers to the default value for the argument or parameter and must be a constant. With a default the stored procedure can be executed without supplying the value for the parameter or argument. Wildcard characters (%, _, [], and [^]) can be used if you are using the argument later with LIKE. The default can be NULL.
OUTPUT	OUTPUT means the parameter or argument is a return parameter. The value is returned to the calling procedure. Text parameters need not apply, as they cannot be used as OUTPUT parameters or arguments, but the OUTPUT keyword can hold a cursor placeholder.
n	N means the preceding entry is repeatable.
{RECOMPILE | ENCRYPTION | RECOMPILE, ENCRYPTION}	RECOMPILE means recompile this stored procedure every time it is executed. ENCRYPTION instructs SQL Server to encrypts the rows stored in the *syscomments* system table for the stored procedure.
FOR REPLICATION	FOR REPLICATION means that stored procedures created specifically for replication by this clause cannot be executed on the subscribing server; it is used to create a filter stored procedure executed only by replication. FOR REPLICATION cannot be used with the RECOMPILE option.
AS	AS precedes the statements the procedure is to execute.
sql_statement	SQL statement means there are multiple Transact-SQL statements to be executed in the stored procedure.
n	N means there can be multiple SQL Statements.

Example

Here's an example of CREATE PROCEDURE:

```
CREATE PROCEDURE MyProcedure
AS
SELECT Column1, Column2
FROM Mytable
WHERE Column3 = 8
GO
```

In this example, a stored procedure is created.

CREATE RULE

CREATE RULE creates a database object, a *rule*. A rule can be bound to a column or a user-defined data type and determines which values can be placed in a column. Look into using CHECK CONSTRAINTS instead because multiple constraints can be defined on a column or multiple columns where only one rule can be bound to a column.

Syntax

The syntax is:

```
CREATE RULE rule
AS condition_expression
```

The arguments are:

rule	Rule is the name of the rule using the rules for identifiers.
condition_expression	The condition_expression is any expression valid in a WHERE clause that defines the rule. A rule cannot reference any other columns or database objects. The new value of the column is represented within the rule in the form of an identifier prefixed by '@'.

Example

Here's an example of the CREATE RULE statement:

```
CREATE RULE Color_Rule
AS
```

```
@color IN ('Red', 'Blue', 'Yellow')
GO
sp_bindrule 'Color_Rule', 'Mytable.Column3'
GO
```

In this example, a rule is created as a database object and bound to a column. You can also bind the rule to a user-defined data type. Use sp_unbindrule to unbind the object.

CREATE SCHEMA

CREATE SCHEMA creates a schema, the database structure without data which can be used for development or test environments.

Syntax

The syntax is:

```
CREATE SCHEMA
[AUTHORIZATION owner]
[schema_element [schema_element2[...schema_elementn]]]
```

The arguments are:

AUTHORIZATION *owner*	AUTHORIZATION owner is the logon ID of a valid security account in the database.
schema_element = {*table_definition* | *view_definition* | *grant_statement*}	*table_definition* = CREATE TABLE statement which creates a table in this schema. *view_definition* = CREATE VIEW statement which creates a view in this schema. *grant_statement* = GRANT statement which grants permissions to a user or group of users in this schema.

Example

Here's an example of the CREATE SCHEMA statement:

```
CREATE SCHEMA AUTHORIZATION MyAccount
GRANT SELECT on View1 TO public
CREATE VIEW View1(Column1) AS SELECT Column1 from MyTable
CREATE TABLE MyTable(Column1 int)
```

In this example, the MyAccount schema is created for the database objects owned by my security account.

CREATE TABLE

CREATE TABLE creates a new table in a database.

Syntax

The syntax is:

```
CREATE TABLE table_name
(    {     <column_definition>
        | column_name AS computed_column_expression
        | <table_constraint>
    } [, ...n]
)
[ON {filegroup | DEFAULT}]
[TEXTIMAGE_ON filegroup]


<column_definition> ::= { column_name data_type }
[ NULL | NOT NULL ]
[ IDENTITY [(seed[, increment] )
            [NOT FOR REPLICATION] ] ]
[ ROWGUIDCOL ]
[ <column_constraint> ::=
    [CONSTRAINT constraint_name]
    {     { PRIMARY KEY | UNIQUE }
            [CLUSTERED | NONCLUSTERED]
            [WITH [FILLFACTOR = fillfactor]
            [ON filegroup]
        | [FOREIGN KEY]
            REFERENCES ref_table
            [ ( ref_column ) ]
            [NOT FOR REPLICATION]
        | DEFAULT constant_expression
        | CHECK [NOT FOR REPLICATION]
            (logical_expression)
```

```
    }
] [ ...n]
<table_constraint> ::= [CONSTRAINT constraint_name]
{     [ { PRIMARY KEY | UNIQUE }
        [ CLUSTERED | NONCLUSTERED]
        { ( column[,...n] ) }
        [ WITH [FILLFACTOR = fillfactor]
    ]
        [ON {filegroup | DEFAULT}]
    ]
    | FOREIGN KEY
            [(column[,...n])]
            REFERENCES ref_table [(ref_column[,...n])]
            [NOT FOR REPLICATION]
    | CHECK [NOT FOR REPLICATION]
        (search_conditions)
}
```

The arguments are:

Table	Table is the name of the table you are creating.
column_name	Column name is the name of the column to be created. You can leave it out for the timestamp data type and Timestamp will be the column name used by SQL Server.
AS computed_column_expression	A computed column is a virtual column and is a new option. Computed columns can now be stored and retrieved, but you cannot INSERT or UPDATE a computed column, and you cannot use a computed column as a key column in a PRIMARY KEY, UNIQUE, FOREIGN KEY, or CHECK constraint.
ON filegroup	ON filegroup determines where the table created for the constraint will reside on disk. If you do not use ON filegroup, the table will be placed on the default filegroup.

data_type	Data type is in reference to the SQL Server data type for the new column. If you are using the uniqueidentifier data type and you have existing rows in the table, you may want to use a DEFAULT constraint with the NEWID() function to generate the unique identifier values in the new column for the already existing rows.
NULL | NOT NULL	NULL or NOT NULL determines if a column can hold NULL values or if it cannot.
IDENTITY	IDENTITY is a property used to place incrementing integers in a new column. This is also true when adding future rows.
Seed	Seed is in reference to the value of the integer you want in your first row if you are adding a column with the IDENTITY property; it means from where you want the value in the new IDENTITY column to start. If you do not use this keyword, SQL Server will seed the column with the value 1.
Increment	If you are adding a column with the IDENTITY property, Increment is by how much you want the value in the new IDENTITY column to increment when a new row is added. If you do not use Increment, SQL Server will increment the value by 1 from the value in the last row added.
NOT FOR REPLICATION	If you are using replication and are adding a column with the IDENTITY property, use this to tell SQL Server not to enforce the IDENTITY conditions when a SQL Server system replication login (e.g., sqlrepl) inserts data into the table.
ROWGUIDCOL	The ROWGUIDCOL property is a global unique identifier column that can be assigned only to a uniqueidentifier column with one per table.

CONSTRAINT	The CONSTRAINT option is how a PRIMARY KEY, UNIQUE, FOREIGN KEY, CHECK, or DEFAULT constraint is created. CONSTRAINTS are used to manage data integrity, and adding a CONSTRAINT can create indexes.
constraint_name	Constraint name is the name of the newly created CONSTRAINT. If you do not name the CONSTRAINT, SQL Server will.
PRIMARY KEY	PRIMARY KEY is a constraint (only one per table) that creates a unique index on the column(s) and designates the column(s) as the primary key of the table. It is necessary to have a PRIMARY KEY if you plan to have FOREIGN KEYs in other tables that reference this table.
UNIQUE	Column values can be unique for the table but not designated as the primary key. The UNIQUE constraint creates a unique index on the column(s).
CLUSTERED | NONCLUSTERED	If you are creating a PRIMARY KEY (default CLUSTERED) or a UNIQUE (default NONCLUSTERED) constraint, CLUSTERED or NONCLUSTERED determines which kind of index you are adding.
WITH FILLFACTOR = fillfactor	WITH FILLFACTOR describes how much data is on each index page. Available values are 1 to 100 with a default of 0, indicated in percentage. The lower the fillfactor, the more space is available, which leaves more space to insert new rows on the page without forcing SQL Server to allocate more space for the new rows.

ON filegroup	ON filegroup determines where the index created for the constraint will reside on disk. If you do not use ON filegroup, the index will be placed on the same filegroup as the table.
FOREIGN KEY…REFERENCES	FOREIGN KEY…REFERENCES creates a constraint to enforce referential integrity by ensuring that each entry in the column exists in the column of the referenced table.
ref_table	Ref table is the name of the table referenced by the FOREIGN KEY constraint.
ref_column	Ref column is the column referenced by the FOREIGN KEY constraint.
NOT FOR REPLICATION	If you are using replication and are adding a column with the IDENTITY property, use this to tell SQL Server not to enforce the IDENTITY conditions when a SQL Server system replication login (e.g., sqlrepl) inserts data into the table.
DEFAULT	DEFAULT is a constraint that determines which value is inserted into the column if no value is specified for the column on an INSERT. You cannot use this for a column with a timestamp data type, the IDENTITY property, or another DEFAULT constraint since there can only be one value in a column.
constant_expression	Constant expression is used with DEFAULT and is the default value for the column and can be a constant, a NULL, or a system function.
CHECK	CHECK is a constraint that limits the values that can be inserted into a column.
logical_expression	Logical expression can reference other columns in the same row and returns true or false.
column[,...n]	Column represents the list of columns for a constraint.

Example

Here's an example of a CREATE TABLE statement:

```
CREATE TABLE Mytable
(
 MyTableID int identity,
 MyDate datetime,
 UsedByName AS USER_NAME()
)
```

In this example, a table is created and the USER_NAME system function is used as the computed column UsedByName.

CREATE TRIGGER

CREATE TRIGGER creates a trigger defined as a special kind of stored procedure that is executed when a user issues an INSERT, UPDATE, or DELETE statement affecting a table. If there are CONSTRAINTS on the table they are checked prior to the trigger firing. If the CONSTRAINT validation fails, the trigger will not fire. There can now be multiple triggers for any INSERT, UPDATE, or DELETE statement.

Syntax

The syntax is:

```
CREATE TRIGGER trigger_name
ON table
[WITH ENCRYPTION]
{
    {FOR {[,] [INSERT] [,] [UPDATE] [,] [DELETE]}
        [WITH APPEND]
        [NOT FOR REPLICATION]
        AS
            sql_statement [, ...n]
    }
    |
    {FOR {[,] [INSERT] [,] [UPDATE]}
        [WITH APPEND]
        [NOT FOR REPLICATION]
        AS
        IF UPDATE (column)
        [{AND | OR} UPDATE (column) [, ...n]]
```

```
            sql_statement [, ...n]
            | IF (COLUMNS_UPDATED() {bitwise_operator} updated_bitmask)
               { comparison_operator} column_bitmask [...n]
    }
}
```

The arguments are:

trigger_name	Trigger_name is the name of the trigger using the rules for identifiers and are unique in the database.
table	Table is the table the trigger executes against.
WITH ENCRYPTION	WITH ENCRYPTION encrypts the *syscomments* system table rows for the trigger.
{[,] [INSERT] [,] [UPDATE] [,] [DELETE]} | {[,] [INSERT] [,] [UPDATE]}	INSERT, UPDATE, AND DELETE are the data modification statements that cause the trigger to fire or execute. Use any of these together in any order, comma-delimited.
WITH APPEND	WITH APPEND means that another trigger of an existing type is to be added (this is only for backward compatibility when the compatibility level is less than 70).
NOT FOR REPLICATION	If replication modifies the table, the trigger is not executed if NOT FOR REPLICATION is used.
AS	AS precedes the statements the trigger performs.
sql_statement	Transact-SQL statements are creating the trigger and should not be used to return data to the user. Special tables only used for a trigger called deleted and inserted are conceptual tables. They resemble the table on which the trigger is placed and hold the old values or new values of the rows that are changing. You can refer to them within the trigger.

Example

Here's an example of the CREATE TRIGGER statement:

```
CREATE TRIGGER MyTrigger
ON MyTable
```

```
FOR INSERT, UPDATE, DELETE
AS
EXEC master..xp_sendmail 'gaylecof', 'MyTable has changed.'
GO
```

In this example, a trigger is created that sends mail when a table changes.

CREATE VIEW

The CREATE VIEW statement creates a virtual table that represents a logical view of the data rather than accessing the physical tables directly. You cannot use ORDER BY, COMPUTE, or COMPUTE BY clauses, or the INTO keyword; nor can you reference a temporary table.

Syntax

The syntax is:

```
CREATE VIEW view_name [(column [, ...n])]
WITH ENCRYPTION]
AS
    select_statement
[WITH CHECK OPTION]
```

The arguments are:

view_name	View_name is the name of the view using the rules for identifiers.
column	Column is the name of a column in a view.
n	N means column is repeatable.
WITH ENCRYPTION	Encrypts the *syscomments* system table rows for the view.
AS	The actions for the view.
select_statement	Transact-SQL SELECT statements that define the view.
WITH CHECK OPTION	WITH CHECK OPTION ensures that the data is visible with the view after data modifications have been made to the view.

Example

Here's an example of a CREATE VIEW statement:

```
CREATE VIEW MyView (Column1, Column2, Column3)
WITH ENCRYPTION
AS
SELECT    a.Column1,
        a.Column2,
          b.Column3
FROM    MyTable a,
        YourTable b
WHERE a.Column1 = b.Column1
GO
```

In this example, a view is created.

CURRENT_TIMESTAMP

CURRENT_TIMESTAMP can be used as a function or with DEFAULT constraints in the CREATE TABLE or ALTER TABLE statements to create a default value for a column holding the current date and time.

Syntax

The syntax is:

```
CURRENT_TIMESTAMP
```

Example

Here's an example of the CURRENT_TIMESTAMP function:

```
DECLARE @myvariable datetime
SET @myvariable = CURRENT_TIMESTAMP
```

In this example, the local variable myvariable is populated with the current date and time.

CURRENT_USER

CURRENT_USER can be used as a function or with DEFAULT constraints in the CREATE TABLE or ALTER TABLE statements to create a default value for a column holding the current user.

Syntax

The syntax is:

```
CURRENT_USER
```

Example

Here's an example of the CURRENT_USER function:

```
DECLARE @myvariable sysname
SET @myvariable = CURRENT_USER
```

In this example, the local variable myvariable is populated with the current user.

cursor data type

The cursor data type is used to create a cursor variable; you need to use it as a cursor OUTPUT argument, and it cannot be used in the CREATE TABLE statement. The only operations you can use with the cursor data type are the SET *@local_variable* statement and the CURSOR_STATUS function.

CURSOR_STATUS

CURSOR_STATUS is a scalar function that allows the caller of a stored procedure to know whether or not the procedure has returned a cursor and result set for a given parameter.

If 1 is returned, the result set of the cursor has at least one row for sensitive, insensitive, and for dynamic cursors; the result set has zero, one, or more rows. The cursor is open. If 0 is returned, the result set of the cursor is empty. If -1 is returned, the cursor is closed. If -2 is returned, there is no cursor assigned to a declared cursor variable. If -3 is returned, a cursor with the specified name does not exist or it has not yet had a cursor allocated to it.

Syntax

The syntax is:

```
CURSOR_STATUS
     (
          {
               {'local', cursor_name}
               | {'global', cursor_name}
               | {'variable', cursor_variable}
```

```
            }
        )
```

The arguments are:

'local'	Local is a constant that means the cursor is a local cursor.
cursor_name	Cursor_name is the name of the cursor using rules for identifiers.
'global'	Global is a constant that means the cursor is a global cursor.
'variable'	Variable is a constant that means the source of the cursor is a local variable.
cursor_variable	Cursor is the name of the cursor variable defined using the CURSOR data type.

cursors

Cursors are used when it is best to process a result set one row at a time. You can now assign a cursor to a variable or parameter with the cursor data type. The following statements are used with cursors: DECLARE CURSOR, CLOSE, DECLARE @local_variable, DEALLOCATE, OPEN, UPDATE, SET, DELETE, FETCH, CREATE PROCEDURE. The following global variables are used with cursors: @@cursor_rows, @@fetch_status, CURSOR_STATUS. And the following system stored procedures are used with cursors: *sp_describe_cursor, sp_describe_cursor_columns, sp_describe_cursor_tables, sp_cursor_list.*

DATABASEPROPERTY

DATABASEPROPERTY returns the named database property value when supplied a database and property name. The values are 1=True, 0=False and NULL=Input if flawed.

Syntax

The syntax is:

```
DATABASEPROPERTY('database', 'property')
```

The arguments are:

'database'	Database is the name of the database for which you want information.
'property'	Property is the name of the database property to return information. The properties are: IsAnsiNullDefault=SQL-92 nullability. IsAnsiNullsEnabled=Comparisons to null evaluate to unknown. IsAnsiWarningsEnabled=Warning messages are given when errors happen. IsAutoClose=Database shuts down after the last user logs off. IsAutoShrink=Automatically shrinking database files. IsBulkCopy=Logging may not occur for some operations. IsCloseCursorsOnCommitEnabled=Cursorclosed when a transaction is committed. IsDboOnly=Only Database Owners have access to the database. IsDetached=Database was detached using sp_detach_db. IsEmergencyMode=Emergency mode allows use of suspect database. IsFulltextEnabled=Database is enabled for full text. IsInLoad=Database is being restored. IsInRecovery=Recovering database. IsInStandBy=Database is readonly, with restore log. IsLocalCursorsDefault=Default is declaring a cursor makes it LOCAL. IsNotRecovered=Database did not recover. IsNullConcat=Null concatenation operand gives a NULL result set. IsOffline=Offline database. IsQuotedIdentifiersEnabled=Double quotation marks are allowed for valid identifiers. IsReadOnly=Readonly database. IsRecursiveTriggersEnabled=Recursive triggers. IsShutDown=Startup problem encountered for database. IsSingleUser=Only one user can use the database. IsSuspect=Suspect database. IsTruncLog=Checkpoints truncates the transaction log of the database. Version=Version number of the or NULL for closed database.

Example

Here's an example of the DATABASEPROPERTY function:

```
USE master
SELECT DATABASEPROPERTY('master', 'IsTruncLog')
```

In this example, the setting for the *IsTruncLog* property for the *master* system database is returned. Return values are 1 meaning true, 0 meaning false, and NULL meaning value not found.

Data Types

Data types determine the data characteristics of columns, stored procedure parameters, and local variables. There are system-supplied data types and user-defined data types. The system-supplied data types are listed in the following sections.

Binary Data

The data types for binary data are:

binary	Binary is a fixed-length data type with a maximum of 8,000 bytes of binary data.
varbinary	Varbinary is a variable-length data type with a maximum of 8,000 bytes of binary data.

Character Data

The data types for character data are:

char	Char is a fixed-length data type with a maximum of 8,000 ANSI characters.
varchar	Varchar is a variable-length data type with a maximum of 8,000 ANSI characters.
nchar	Nchar is a fixed-length data type with a maximum of 4,000 Unicode characters. Storage for Unicode characters is 2 bytes per character. UNICODE includes all international characters.
nvarchar	Nvarchar is a variable-length data type with a maximum of 4,000 Unicode characters. Storage for Unicode characters is 2 bytes per character. UNICODE includes all international characters.

Date and Time Data

The data types for date and time data are:

datetime	Datetime is a data type with possible values starting at January 1, 1753, and ranging to December 31, 9999.
smalldatetime	Smalldatetime is not as accurate as datetime (datetime is accurate to one three-hundredth of a second, while smalldatetime is accurate to one minute), with possible values starting at January 1, 1900, and ranging through June 6, 2079. Datetime consumes 8 bytes, while smalldatetime consumes 4 bytes.

Exact Numeric Data

The data types for exact numeric data are:

decimal	Decimal is an exact numeric data type with possible values starting at -10^{38} -1 and ranging through 10^{38} -1.
numeric	This is the same as the decimal data type.
int	Int is a data type holding only whole numbers starting at -2^{31} (-2,147,483,648) and ranging through 2^{31} - 1 (2,147,483,647).
smallint	Smallint is a data type holding only whole numbers starting at -2^{15} (-32,768) and ranging through 2^{15} - 1 (32,767).
tinyint	Tinyint is a data type holding only whole numbers starting at 0 and ranging through 255.

Approximate Numeric Data

The data types for approximate numeric data are:

float	Float is a data type for floating point numbers. The default is 15-digit precision with a positive range starting at 2.23E - 308 and ranging through 1.79E + 308 and a negative range starting at -2.23E - 308 and ranging through -1.79E + 308.

real	A data type that can hold positive or negative floating point numbers similar to float. The real data type has 7-digit precision and has a range of positive values of approximately 1.18E - 38 through 3.40E + 38, zero can be stored, and the range of negative values is approximately -1.18E - 38 through -3.40E + 38.

Monetary Data

The data types for monetary data are:

money	Money is a data type for monetary values starting at -922,337,203,685,477.5707 and ranging through +922,337,203,685,477.5807, with accuracy to a ten-thousandth of a monetary unit.
smallmoney	A data type that stores monetary values in the range of -214,748.3648 through +214,748.3647, with accuracy to a ten-thousandth of a monetary unit. When smallmoney values are displayed, they are rounded up to two decimal places.

Special data

A special data type is a bit which is a 1 or 0 value. Integers greater than 0 are all considered 1 by SQL Server.

Cursor

A cursor data type is used with a cursor variable and is only used in the context of a cursor.

Sysname

Sysname is a SQL Server data type defined by SQL Server as nvarchar(128), 128 Unicode characters , 256 bytes. SQL Server needs a common data type between system tables and stored procedures and SQL Server uses sysname as the common data type.

timestamp

Timestamp is a data type that is updated by SQL Server any time the row is inserted or updated; they are limited to one per table and are binary(8) or varbinary(8).

uniqueidentifier

Uniqueidentifier is a 16-byte globally unique identifier, also called a GUID.

user-defined

A user-defined data type is based on a SQL Server data type, defined using the sp_addtype system stored procedure.

Text and Image Data

The data types for text and image data are:

text	Text is a data type that can hold up to $2^{31} - 1$ or 2,147,483,647 characters and has a variable default length of 16.
ntext	Ntext is a data type that can hold up to $2^{30} - 1$ or 1,073,741,823 characters and is of variable length.
Image	Image is a data type that can hold up to $2^{31} - 1$ or 2,147,483,647 bytes of binary data and is of variable length.

Unicode Data

Nchar (n prefix is a SQL-92 Unicode standard)	Nchar is Unicode data up to 4,000 fixed characters.
nvarchar	Nvarchar is Unicode data up to 4,000 variable characters.
Ntext	Ntext is Unicode data up to 1,073,741,823 variable characters.

DATALENGTH

DATALENGTH is a system function that returns the length of any data type expression.

Syntax

The syntax is:

```
DATALENGTH(expression)
```

The argument, expression, is a constant, column name, function, and subquery and arithmetic, bitwise, and string operators.

Example

Here's an example of the DATALENGTH system function:

```
SELECT DATALENGTH(Column1)
FROM MyTable
GO
```

In this example, an integer is returned representing the length in bytes of Column1. Use DATALENGTH with varchar, varbinary, text, image, nvarchar, and ntext datatypes to see how long they are. If the column is null, a null will be returned. The storage for numeric data types is different in this version, and DATALENGTH for numeric expressions returns 5, 9, 13 or 17.

DATEADD

DATEADD returns a datetime-based adding of any of the units enumerated in the datepart list to a date.

Syntax

The syntax is:

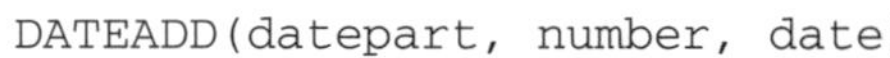

```
DATEADD(datepart, number, date)
```

Date Functions

The following table applies to all date functions that take a *datepart* parameter:

Date part	Abbreviation	Values
Year	yy	1753-9999
Quarter	qq	1-4
Month	mm	1-12
Day-of-year	dy	1-366
Day	dd	1-31
Week	wk	1-53
Weekday	dw	1-7 (Sun.-Sat.)
Hour	hh	0-23
Minute	mi	0-59
Second	ss	0-59
Millisecond	ms	0-999

The arguments are:

Argument	Description
datepart	Datepart is part of a date used in a calculation. See the table under Date Functions.
number	Number is how many dateparts to increase the date argument.
date	Date is GETDATE function; a character string formatted as a date; or the name of a column, variable, or parameter of a datetime data type.

Example

Here's an example of the DATEADD function:

```
SELECT DATEADD(day, 7, DateColumn1)
FROM MyTable
GO
```

In this example, 7 days are added to the value in DateColumn1.

DATEDIFF

DATEDIFF returns the difference in dateparts between two specified dates.

Syntax

The syntax is:

```
DATEDIFF(datepart, date, date)
```

The arguments are:

Argument	Description
Datepart	Datepart is part of a date used in a calculation. See the table under Date Functions.
Date	Date is GETDATE function; a character string formatted as a date; or the name of a column, variable, or parameter of a datetime data type.

Example

Here's an example of the DATEDIFF function:

```
SELECT DATEDIFF(day, DateColumn1, getdate())
FROM Mytable
```

In this example, the number of days difference between the value in DateColumn1 and the current date is returned.

DATENAME

DATENAME returns the name of the datepart of a date.

Syntax

The syntax is:

```
DATENAME(datepart, date)
```

The arguments are:

Datepart	Datepart is part of a date used in a calculation. See the table under Date Functions.
Date	Date is GETDATE function, a character string formatted as a date, or the name of a column of a datetime data type.

Example

Here's an example of the DATENAME function:

```
SELECT DATENAME(dw, getdate())
```

In this example, if today is Monday, you will receive in character data the word 'Monday'.

DATEPART

DATEPART returns an integer representing the date part of the date.

Syntax

The syntax is:

```
DATEPART(datepart, date)
```

The arguments are:

Datepart	Datepart is part of a date used in a calculation. See the table under Date Functions.

Date	Date is GETDATE function, a character string formatted as a date, or the name of a column of a datetime data type.

Example

Here's an example of the DATEPART function:

```
SELECT DATEPART(month, getdate())
GO
```

In this example, the number of the month within a 12-month year is returned.

DAY

DAY displays an integer and the day part of the supplied date.

Syntax

The syntax is:

```
DAY(date)
```

The argument, date, is a smalldatetime or datetime data type.

DB_ID

DB_ID is a system function that returns the database identification number.

Syntax

The syntax is:

```
DB_ID(['database_name'])
```

The argument, database_name, is the database name for which you want the database identification number, and the default is the database in use.

Example

Here's an example of the DB_ID function run in the *master* database:

```
SELECT DB_ID('master')
```

In this example, 1 is returned as the database identification number for the *master* system database.

DB_NAME

DB_NAME returns the database name when you pass in a database identification number.

Syntax

The syntax is:

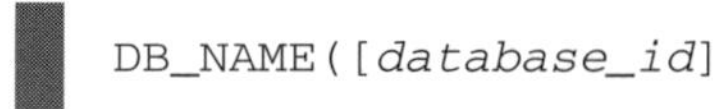

```
DB_NAME([database_id])
```

The argument database_id is the database identification number of the database whose name you wish to see, and the default is the database in use.

Examples

Here's an example of the DB_NAME system function:

```
SELECT DB_NAME(1)
```

In this example, the name of the database with a database identification number of 1 is returned. The database name is *master* in this case.

DBCC CHECKALLOC

The Database Consistency Checker statement, DBCC CHECKALLOC, checks allocation usage of all the pages in the database.

Syntax

The syntax is:

```
DBCC CHECKALLOC
(     'database_name'
[,      NOINDEX |
       {     REPAIR_ALLOW_DATA_LOSS
           | REPAIR_FAST
           | REPAIR_REBUILD
        }
]

)
[WITH {ALL_ERRORMSGS | NO_INFOMSGS}]
```

The arguments are:

'database_name'	Database_name is the name of the database affected by the statement. You can run this command in the current database without a database_name.
NOINDEX	NOINDEX means that nonclustered indexes for user-defined tables are not included in the check of the database.
REPAIR_ALLOW_DATA_LOSS	REPAIR_ALLOW_DATA_LOSS does repairs that REPAIR_REBUILD does; it also fixes allocation errors and structural row or page errors and removes corrupted text objects which can cause data loss.
REPAIR_FAST	REPAIR_FAST does small, fast repair actions such as small index repairs. No data loss occurs.
REPAIR_REBUILD	REPAIR_REBUILD does repairs that REPAIR_FAST does and also more time-consuming repairs to indexes. No data loss occurs.
WITH NO_INFOMSGS | ALL_ ERRORMSGS	WITH NO_INFOMSGS means the report will not include informational messages and space used. Only error messages are reported. WITH ALL_ERRORMSGS means display all error messages.

DBCC CHECKCATALOG

DBCC CHECKCATALOG checks the integrity of the system tables.

Syntax

The syntax is:

```
DBCC CHECKCATALOG [('database_name')]

[WITH NO_INFOMSGS]
```

The arguments are:

'database_name'	Database_name is the name of the database affected by the statement. You can run this command in the current database without a database_name.

WITH NO_INFOMSGS	WITH NO_INFOMSGS means the report will not include informational messages and space used. Only error messages are reported.

DBCC CHECKDB

DBCC CHECKDB checks the integrity of everything in the database. You do not need to run DBCC CHECKALLOC or CHECKTABLE when you run DBCC CHECKDB.

Syntax

The syntax is:

```
DBCC CHECKDB
('database_name'
[, NOINDEX |
      {REPAIR_ALLOW_DATA_LOSS
         | REPAIR_FAST
         | REPAIR_REBUILD
       }
]
)
[WITH {ALL_ERRORMSGS | NO_INFOMSGS}]
```

The arguments are:

'database_name'	Database_name is the name of the database affected by the statement. You can run this command in the current database without a database_name.
NOINDEX	NOINDEX means that nonclustered indexes for user-defined tables are not included in the check of the database.
REPAIR_ALLOW_DATA_LOSS	REPAIR_ALLOW_DATA_LOSS does repairs that REPAIR_REBUILD does; it also fixes allocation errors and structural row or page errors and removes corrupted text objects which can cause data loss.
REPAIR_FAST	REPAIR_FAST does small, fast repair actions such as small index repairs. No data loss occurs.
REPAIR_REBUILD	REPAIR_REBUILD does repairs that REPAIR_FAST does and also does more time-consuming repairs to indexes. No data loss occurs.

WITH NO_INFOMSGS | ALL_ ERRORMSGS	WITH NO_INFOMSGS means the report will not include informational messages and space used. Only error messages are reported. WITH ALL_ ERRORMSGS means display all error messages.

DBCC CHECKFILEGROUP

DBCC CHECKFILEGROUP checks the allocation of all tables in the filegroup.

Syntax

The syntax is:

```
DBCC CHECKFILEGROUP
[( [ {'filegroup_name' | filegroup_id} ] [, NOINDEX] ) ]
[WITH NO_INFOMSGS | ALL_ ERRORMSGS]
```

The arguments are:

'filegroup_name'	Filegroup_name is the name of the filegroup affected by the DBCC statement.
filegroup_id	Filegroup_id is the ID of the filegroup in the sysfilegroups system table.
NOINDEX	NOINDEX means that nonclustered indexes for user-defined tables are not included in the check of the database.
WITH NO_INFOMSGS | ALL_ ERRORMSGS	WITH NO_INFOMSGS means the report will not include informational messages and space used. Only error messages are reported. WITH ALL_ERRORMSGS means display all error messages.

DBCC CHECKIDENT

DBCC CHECKIDENT checks the current identity value for the table and can correct identity values.

Syntax

The syntax is:

```
DBCC CHECKIDENT ('table_name'
[, { NORESEED | {RESEED [, new_reseed_value] } } ] )
```

The arguments are:

'table_name'	Table_name is the name of the table affected by the DBCC statement.
NORESEED	NORESEED tells SQL Server not to correct identity values.
RESEED	RESEED tells SQL Server to correct identity values to that of the maximum value of the identity column in the table if no new_reseed_value is supplied.
new_reseed_value	New_reseed_value is the new value to start at in the identity column.

DBCC CHECKTABLE

DBCC CHECKTABLE checks and optionally repairs the integrity of all the pages for the table.

Syntax

The syntax is:

```
DBCC CHECKTABLE
('table_name'
[, NOINDEX | index_id |
      {REPAIR_ALLOW_DATA_LOSS
            | REPAIR_FAST
            | REPAIR_REBUILD
      }
]
)
[WITH NO_INFOMSGS]
```

The arguments are:

'table_name'	Table_name is the name of the table affected by the DBCC statement.
NOINDEX	NOINDEX means that nonclustered indexes for user-defined tables are not included in the check of the table.
index_id	Index_id is the ID of the index the DBCC statement affects.

REPAIR_ALLOW_ DATA_LOSS	REPAIR_ALLOW_DATA_LOSS does repairs that REPAIR_REBUILD does; it also fixes allocation errors and structural row or page errors and removes corrupted text objects which can cause data loss.
REPAIR_FAST	REPAIR_FAST does small, fast repair actions such as small index repairs. No data loss occurs.
REPAIR_REBUILD	REPAIR_REBUILD does repairs that REPAIR_FAST does and also does more time-consuming repairs to indexes. No data loss occurs.
WITH NO_INFOMSGS | ALL_ ERRORMSGS	WITH NO_INFOMSGS means the report will not include informational messages and space used. Only error messages are reported. WITH ALL_ERRORMSGS means display all error messages.
WITH NO_INFOMSGS	WITH NO_INFOMSGS means the report will not include informational messages and space used. Only error messages are reported.

DBCC DBREPAIR

DBCC DBREPAIR is for backward compatibility only. Use DROP DATABASE now.

Syntax

The syntax is:

```
DBCC DBREPAIR ( database_name, DROPDB [, NOINIT] )
```

The arguments are:

database_name	Database_name is the name of the database you wish to get rid of.
DROPDB	DROPDB means to drop the database.
NOINIT	NOINIT means the allocation pages for the database are not changed.

DBCC DBREINDEX

DBCC DBREINDEX rebuilds the index(es) for a table and can be used instead of dropping and recreating the index to preserve the associated constraints reducing the overhead of dropping and recreating the constraints.

Syntax

The syntax is:

```
DBCC DBREINDEX (['database.owner.table_name' [, index_name
[, fillfactor ]]])
[WITH NO_INFOMSGS]
```

The arguments are:

'database.owner.table_name'	Database.owner.table_name is the fully qualified name of the table on which you are rebuilding the index(es).
index_name	Index_name is the name of the index to rebuild. Use two single quotes to indicate to SQL Server to rebuild all the indexes on the table. You only need to do this if you need to specify a fillfactor; otherwise, the last two arguments can be omitted.
fillfactor	Fillfactor is a percentage of space on each index leaf page to store data and is used only when the index is created. If 0, the original fillfactor is used.
WITH NO_INFOMSGS	WITH NO_INFOMSGS means the report will not include informational messages and space used. Only error messages are reported.

DBCC dllname(FREE)

DBCC dllname(FREE) takes a dynamic-link library (DLL) from an extended stored procedure out of memory.

Syntax

The syntax is:

```
DBCC dllname (FREE)
```

The argument, dllname, is the name of the dll to remove from memory.

DBCC HELP

DBCC HELP diplays syntax information for the DBCC statement you supply.

Syntax

The syntax is:

```
DBCC HELP ('dbcc_statement' | @dbcc_statement_var | '?')
```

The arguments are:

dbcc_statement | @dbcc_statement_var	DBCC_statement is the name of the DBCC statement or a part after 'DBCC' (e.g., CHECKTABLE).
?	? displays the DBCC statements with help information.

DBCC INPUTBUFFER

DBCC INPUTBUFFER shows you the last Transact-SQL statement sent from a client to SQL Server.

Syntax

The syntax is:

```
DBCC INPUTBUFFER (spid)
```

The argument, spid, is the system process ID for the user connection. (A spid can be selected by executing the system stored procedure, *sp_who*.)

DBCC MEMUSAGE

DBCC MEMUSAGE shows buffer and procedure cache information about memory usage in 8K pages.

Syntax

The syntax is:

```
DBCC MEMUSAGE( ['BUFFER'] [,] [ 'PROCEDURE'])
```

The arguments are:

'BUFFER'	BUFFER means that buffer cache information is shown.
'PROCEDURE'	PROCEDURE means procedure cache information is shown.

DBCC NEWALLOC

DBCC NEWALLOC checks the allocation of data and index pages for each table in the database; however, DBCC CHECKALLOC does the same thing. This is for backward compatibility only. Use DBCC CHECKALLOC instead.

Syntax

The syntax is:

```
DBCC NEWALLOC [('database_name'[, NOINDEX])]
[WITH NO_INFOMSGS]
```

The arguments are:

Argument	Description
'database_name'	Database_name is the name of the database affected by the statement. You can run this command in the current database without a database_name.
NOINDEX	NOINDEX means that nonclustered indexes for user-defined tables are not included in the check of the database.
WITH NO_INFOMSGS	WITH NO_INFOMSGS means the report will not include informational messages and space used. Only error messages are reported.

DBCC OPENTRAN

DBCC OPENTRAN shows information about the oldest active and distributed and nondistributed replicated transactions in the database. An open transaction can be identified by the spid and terminated.

Syntax

The syntax is:

```
DBCC OPENTRAN [('database_name'| database_id)]
[WITH TABLERESULTS[,NO_INFOMSGS]]
```

The arguments are:

Argument	Description
'database_name'	Database_name is the database affected by the DBCC statement.
database_id	Database_id is the database identification number.

WITH TABLERESULTS	WITH TABLERESULTS places the results into a format that can be put in a table.
WITH NO_INFOMSGS	WITH NO_INFOMSGS means the report will not include informational messages and space used. Only error messages are reported.

DBCC OUTPUTBUFFER

DBCC OUTPUTBUFFER shows the contents of the output buffer for a spid.

Syntax

The syntax is:

```
DBCC OUTPUTBUFFER (spid)
```

The argument, spid, is the system process ID for the user connection.

DBCC PERFMON

DBCC PERFMON displays the three types of SQL Server performance information, IOSTATS, LRUSTATS, and NETSTATS.

Syntax

The syntax is:

```
DBCC PERFMON
```

DBCC PINTABLE

DBCC PINTABLE pins a table, meaning that the table pages are kept in and updated in memory and not flushed out when SQL Server needs room to read in a new page. It is a good idea to limit the use of DBCC PINTABLE to small tables that are used often.

Syntax

The syntax is:

```
DBCC PINTABLE (database_id, table_id)
```

The arguments are:

database_id	Database_id is the database identification number of the pinned table.
table_id	Table_id is the id of the table to be pinned.

DBCC PROCCACHE

DBCC PROCCACHE is used by Microsoft SQL Server Performance Monitor to monitor the procedure cache.

Syntax

The syntax is:

```
DBCC PROCCACHE
```

DBCC ROWLOCK

DBCC ROWLOCK activated Insert Row Locking (IRL) on tables in Microsoft SQL Server 6.5 and is supported for backwards compatibility only. Using DBCC ROWLOCK in version 7.0 does nothing. Microsoft SQL Server 7.0 has dynamic row level locking.

DBCC SHOWCONTIG

DBCC SHOWCONTIG shows the fragmentation for data and indexes on a table. Drop and re-create the clustered index without the SORTED_DATA option to reduce fragmentation.

Syntax

The syntax is:

```
DBCC SHOWCONTIG (table_id [, index_id])
```

The arguments are:

table_id	Table_id is the OBJECT_ID of the table affected by the DBCC statement. All the tables are affected if no table_id is provided.
index_id	Index_id is the indid of the index affected by the DBCC statement. All the indexes on a table are affected if index_id is not provided.

DBCC SHOW_STATISTICS

DBCC SHOW_STATISTICS shows the distribution page statistics for the index or column on a table. The higher the density, the lower the selectivity (and thus the lower the usefulness of an index). If you are interested in knowing when the statistics were last updated, use the system function STATS_DATE.

Syntax

The syntax is:

```
DBCC SHOW_STATISTICS (table, target)
```

The arguments are:

Table	Table is the name of the table for which you would like to see statistics.
Target	Target is the index name or column name.

DBCC SHRINKDATABASE

DBCC SHRINKDATABASE shrinks the data files in a database.

Syntax

The syntax is:

```
DBCC SHRINKDATABASE
    (    database_name [, target_percent]
        [, {NOTRUNCATE | TRUNCATEONLY}]
    )
```

The arguments are:

database_name	Database_name is the name of the database you are shrinking.
Target_percent	Target_percent is the percentage of free space you wish to remain in the database file after shrinking.
NOTRUNCATE	NOTRUNCATE means the freed file space should stay in the database files with a default to release the space to the operating system.
TRUNCATEONLY	TRUNCATEONLY means any unused space in the data files is released to the operating system. Rows are not moved to unallocated pages and target_percent is ignored.

DBCC SHRINKFILE

DBCC SHRINKFILE shrinks the data file for the database.

Syntax

The syntax is:

```
DBCC SHRINKFILE
    (    {file_name | file_id } [, target_size]
             [, {EMPTYFILE | NOTRUNCATE | TRUNCATEONLY}]
    )
```

The arguments are:

file_name	File_name is the logical name of the database file you are shrinking.
file_id	File_id is the FILE_ID of the database file you are shrinking in the *sysfiles* system table.
target_size	Target_size is the size you wish to shrink the data file to in megabytes; if the target_size is not given, the file is shrunk as much as it can be.
EMPTYFILE	EMPTYFILE moves data from the file to other files in the same filegroup, then the file can be dropped using the ALTER DATABASE statement.
NOTRUNCATE	NOTRUNCATE means the freed file space should stay in the database files. The default is to release the space to the operating system.
TRUNCATEONLY	TRUNCATEONLY means any unused space in the data files is released to the operating system. Rows are not moved to unallocated pages and target_size is ignored.

DBCC TEXTALL

DBCC TEXTALL executes TEXTALLOC on the tables with text, ntext, or image columns. This is included in Microsoft SQL Server 7.0 for backward compatibility only. Use DBCC CHECKDB instead.

Syntax

The syntax is:

```
DBCC TEXTALL (['database_name'|database_id] [,'FULL' | 'FAST'])
```

DBCC SQLPERF

DBCC SQLPERF displays statistics on the use of transaction log space in all databases.

Syntax

The syntax is:

```
DBCC SQLPERF (LOGSPACE)
```

DBCC TEXTALL

DBCC TEXTALL runs DBCC TEXTALLOC on tables in the database with text, ntext, or image columns. This is included in Microsoft SQL Server 7.0 for backward compatibility only. Use DBCC CHECKTABLE instead.

Syntax

The syntax is:

```
DBCC TEXTALL
```

DBCC TEXTALLOC

DBCC TEXTALLOC checks a table with text, ntext, or image columns. This is included in Microsoft SQL Server 7.0 for backward compatibility only. Use DBCC CHECKTABLE instead.

Syntax

The syntax is:

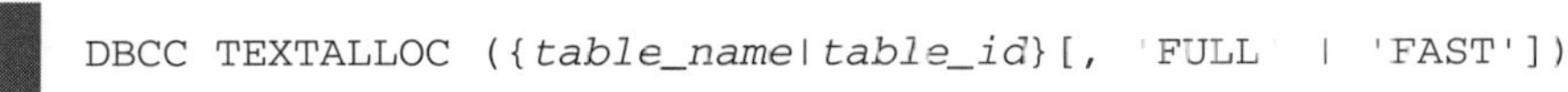

```
DBCC TEXTALLOC ({table_name|table_id}[, 'FULL' | 'FAST'])
```

DBCC TRACEOFF

DBCC TRACEOFF removes a trace flag from affecting the SQL Server.

Syntax

The syntax is:

```
DBCC TRACEOFF (trace# [,…trace#])
```

The arguments are:

trace#	Trace# is the trace flag number.

DBCC TRACEON

DBCC TRACEON turns on a trace flag to affect a server.

Syntax

The syntax is:

```
DBCC TRACEON (trace# [,…trace#])
```

The arguments are:

trace#	Trace# is the trace flag number.

DBCC TRACESTATUS

DBCC TRACESTATUS shows the status of trace flags. SQL Server will return 1 if the trace flag is on or 0 if the trace flag is off. Use a trace# of –1 (negative 1) to see all the trace flags that are affecting a server.

Syntax

The syntax is:

```
DBCC TRACESTATUS (trace# [, ...trace#])
```

The arguments are:

Trace#	Trace# is the trace flag number.

DBCC UNPINTABLE

DBCC UNPINTABLE unpins table pages in the buffer cache.

Syntax

The syntax is:

```
DBCC UNPINTABLE (database_id, table_id)
```

The arguments are:

database_id	Database_id is the database identification number of the database containing the table to be unpinned.
table_id	Table_id is the OBJECT_ID of the table to be unpinned.

DBCC UPDATEUSAGE

DBCC UPDATEUSAGE updates the *sysindexes* system table and removes any old statistics that could result in inaccurate reports from the *sp_spaceused* system stored procedure.

Syntax

The syntax is:

```
DBCC UPDATEUSAGE ({'database_name'| 0} [, 'table_name' [, index_id]])
    [WITH [NO_INFOMSGS]    [[,] COUNT_ROWS]
```

The arguments are:

'database_name' | 0	Database name is the database affected by the DBCC statement. If 0 is given as this argument, the current database is affected.
'table_name'	Table_name is the table affected by the DBCC statement.
index_id	Index_id is the indid of the index affected. The default is all indexes on the table.
WITH NO_INFOMSGS	WITH NO_INFOMSGS means the report will not include informational messages and space used. Only error messages are reported.
WITH COUNT_ROWS	WITH COUNT_ROWS updates the rows column of the *sysindexes* system table with the number of rows currently in the table. This takes longer on large tables.

Example

Here's an example of the DBCC UPDATEUSAGE statement:

```
DBCC UPDATEUSAGE (0)
GO
```

In this example, the sysindexes table is updated for all tables and all indexes in the current database.

DBCC USEROPTIONS

DBCC USEROPTIONS displays the SET options that are active for the current connection.

Syntax

The syntax is:

```
DBCC USEROPTIONS
```

DEALLOCATE

DEALLOCATE is a statement used to remove a reference to a cursor either by name or variable name. Data structures and locks are freed when the last reference to the cursor is deallocated.

Syntax

The syntax is:

```
DEALLOCATE { { [GLOBAL] cursor_name } | cursor_variable_name}
```

The arguments are:

cursor_name	The cursor_name has been declared and is local unless specified as GLOBAL or if no local cursor exists with that name.
cursor_variable_name	Cursor_variable_name is the name of a cursor variable.

decimal data type

The *decimal* datatype is exactly numeric and accurate down to the smallest part of the number. The other exact numeric data type is *numeric*. Both can contain values ranging from 10^{38} - 1 through - 10^{38} - 1.

```
decimal[(p[, s])] and numeric[(p[, s])]
```

The arguments are:

precision	Precision (p) means the maximum number of decimal digits to store on both sides of the decimal.
scale	Scale is the maximum number of decimal digits to the right of the decimal, a value from 0 through whatever your precision argument is.

DECLARE @local_variable

Variables are declared in a batch or stored procedure or trigger with the DECLARE statement. Values are assigned to a variable with either a SET or SELECT statement. All declared local variables are initialized as NULL.

Syntax

The syntax is:

```
DECLARE
    {
        {@local_variable data_type}
        | {cursor_variable_name CURSOR}
    } [, …n]
```

The arguments are:

@local_variable	The @ sign at the beginning of the local variable name is how SQL server identifies a local variable. Variables in Transact SQL statements cannot be used for database objects only as constants. A local variable is local within a procedure, trigger, or batch or if no local cursor exists with that name.
data_type	Data_type is a system or user-defined data type but not image, text, or ntext data type.
cursor_variable_name	Cursor_variable_name is the name of a cursor variable and uses the same specifications of a local variable but does not start with @.
CURSOR	CURSOR means the variable is a local cursor variable.
N	N means the preceding syntax is repeatable.
SET | SELECT	SET | SELECT sets the variable to the value in the expression.

Expression	An expression can be a column name(s), a constant, a function, a variable, a subquery, and constants and functions, arithmetic, bitwise, and string operators.

DECLARE CURSOR

DECLARE CURSOR declares the attributes of a Transact-SQL cursor.

Syntax

The syntax is:

```
DECLARE cursor_name [INSENSITIVE] [SCROLL] CURSOR
FOR select_statement
[FOR {READ ONLY | UPDATE [OF column_list]}]
```

or

```
DECLARE cursor_name CURSOR
[LOCAL | GLOBAL]
[FORWARD_ONLY | SCROLL]
[STATIC | KEYSET | DYNAMIC]
[READ_ONLY | SCROLL_LOCKS | OPTIMISTIC]
FOR select_statement
[FOR {READ ONLY | UPDATE [OF column_list]}]
```

The arguments are:

cursor_name	The name of the cursor you are declaring using the rules for identifiers.
INSENSITIVE	INSENSITIVE declares a cursor that copies the data for the cursor, and changes to the base rows are not shown when the fetch statement gets rows from the cursor. The cursor cannot update.
SCROLL	Scroll means that you can scroll through the cursor using first, last, prior, next, relative, and absolute fetches.
select_statement	Select_statement is a SELECT statement that determines the result set of the cursor. COMPUTE, COMPUTE BY, FOR BROWSE, and INTO are not allowed.

READ_ONLY	READ_ONLY means a read only cursor allowing no updates.
UPDATE [OFcolumn_list]	UPDATE [OFcolumn_list] determines updatable columns within the cursor. If no list, all columns are updateable.
LOCAL	LOCAL means the scope of the cursor is local to the batch, stored procedure, or trigger in which it is declared.
GLOBAL	GLOBAL means that the scope of the cursor is global to the connection.
FORWARD ONLY	FORWARD ONLY means the cursor can scroll forward, first row to last row.
STATIC	STATIC declares a cursor that copies the data for the cursor; changes to the base rows are not shown when the fetch statement gets rows from the cursor. The cursor cannot update.
KEYSET	KEYSET means that members and order of rows is set when the cursor is opened, and changes to the tables are visible as the owner scrolls around the cursor. Inserts made by other users are not visible; however, if a row is deleted, the global variable @@fetch_status is -2. Updates behave as a delete and insert.
DYNAMIC	A DYNAMIC cursor is aware of all data changes made to the rows in its result set as you scroll around the cursor. The rows can change on each fetch with no absolute and relative fetch options.
SCROLL_LOCKS	SCROLL_LOCKS mean that updates or deletes made through the cursor are sure to succeed. SQL Server locks the rows.
OPTIMISTIC	OPTIMISTIC means that updates or deletes made through the cursor won't succeed if the row has been updated since it was read into the cursor.

DEGREES

DEGREES provides a numeric expression in degrees for the supplied number of radians of an angle.

Syntax

The syntax is:

```
DEGREES(numeric_expression)
```

The argument, numeric_expression, is an expression using the decimal, float, int, tinyint, money, numeric, real, smallint, or smallmoney data types.

DELETE

The DELETE statement deletes rows from a table.

Syntax

The syntax is:

```
DELETE [FROM {table_name | view_name}
[  <from_clause> : : =
    FROM
    {    <table_or_view>
        | (select_statement) [AS] alias
        | <table_or_view> CROSS JOIN <table_or_view>
        | <table_or_view>
            [{    INNER | {LEFT | RIGHT | FULL} [OUTER] }]
            [<join_hint>] JOIN
            <table_or_view> ON search_conditions
    }[,…n]
]
[WHERE { search_conditions } |
    {CURRENT OF { { [ GLOBAL ] cursor_name } | cursor_variable_name } } ]
[OPTION (<query_hint> [, ...n] ) ]


<table_or_view> ::=
    { table [[AS] alias] [<table_hint>]
    | view [[AS] alias] }
    | OpenRowset('provider_name', {'datasource';'user_id';'password' |
            'provider_string'}, {[catalog.][schema.]object_name | 'query'})
    | OpenQuery(linked_server, 'query')}


<table_hint> ::=
    ([INDEX = {index_name | index_id}[, …n]] [FASTFIRSTROW]
        [HOLDLOCK] [NOLOCK] [PAGLOCK] [READCOMMITTED]
        [READPAST] [READUNCOMMITTED] [REPEATABLEREAD]
        [ROWLOCK] [SERIALIZABLE] [TABLOCK] [TABLOCKX]
```

```
        [UPDLOCK])

<join_hint> ::=
    {LOOP | HASH | MERGE}

<query_hint> ::=
    {     {HASH | ORDER} GROUP
        | {MERGE | HASH | CONCAT} UNION
        | FAST n
        | FORCE ORDER
        | ROBUST PLAN
    }
```

The arguments are:

FROM	FROM indicates the table or view from which the rows are deleted.
table_name | view_name	table_name | view_name is the table or view from which the rows are deleted.
Alias	Alias is the name of an alias for *table* or *view.*
CROSS JOIN	CROSS JOIN is the cross-product of two tables.
<join_hint>	<join_hint> tells the query optimizer to use one *join_hint* for each join in the query's FROM clause.
LOOP | HASH | MERGE	LOOP | HASH | MERGE determines that the joins in the query are using looping, hashing, or merging.
JOIN	JOIN is an indication that an SQL-92 join is used in the DELETE operation.
ON search_conditions	ON search_conditions are the conditions of the join.
N	N means the preceding items are repeatable.
WHERE	WHERE determines the conditions to filter the rows that are to be deleted.
Search_conditions	Search_conditions are the restricting conditions for the rows to be deleted.

CURRENT OF	CURRENT OF means DELETE from the current position of the cursor.
GLOBAL	GLOBAL means the cursor is a global cursor.
cursor_name	Cursor_name is the name of the open cursor from which the fetch is made.
cursor_variable_name	Cursor_variable_name is the name of a cursor variable.
OpenRowset	OpenRowset has all connection information to access remote data from a data source.
OpenQuery	OpenQuery runs the pass-through query.
<table_hint>	<table_hint> is a table scan, indexe(s) to be used by the optimizer or a locking method.
INDEX = index_name | index_id	The INDEX name to use.
OPTION (<query_hint>, [,...n])	OPTION means that optimizer hints follow.
{HASH | ORDER} GROUP	{HASH | ORDER} GROUP means that the aggregations specified in the GROUP BY or COMPUTE clause of the query should use hashing or ordering.
{MERGE | HASH | CONCAT} UNION	{MERGE | HASH | CONCAT} UNION means that UNION operations are done by merging, hashing, or concatenating UNION sets.
FAST	FAST means that the query has fast retrieval of the first *n* rows returning the entire result set.
N	N indicates the number of rows to be retrieved.
FORCE ORDER	FORCE ORDER means the join order in the query syntax is the same during query optimization.
ROBUST PLAN	ROBUST PLAN means the query plan works for the maximum potential row size.

DENY

DENY is a statement that is used not only to deny permission from a security account but also to prevent permission inheritance from other group or role memberships. In conflict situations the most restrictive permission applies. You can also use DENY with the *public* role and the *guest* user. You will have to use the REVOKE statement to remove a denied permission from a security account.

Syntax

The syntax is:

```
DENY{ALL | statement[,…n]}
TO security_account[,…n]
```

The arguments are:

ALL	ALL means that all permissions are denied.
statement	Statement is the statement whose permission is being denied. DENY can deny a user the following statements; CREATE DATABASE, CREATE DEFAULT, CREATE PROCEDURE, CREATE RULE, CREATE TABLE, CREATE VIEW, BACKUP DATABASE, BACKUP TRANSACTION, and BACKUP TABLE.
TO	TO indicates the next word is a security account.
Security_account	The security account can be a SQL Server user, SQL Server role, Windows NT user, or Windows NT group.
PRIVILEGES	Optional keyword for SQL-92 compliance.
permission	Permission is the statement permission, a table or a view, denied. The permission list is: SELECT, INSERT, DELETE, and UPDATE, and also REFERENCES for a table. The permission list for columns is: SELECT and UPDATE. For stored procedures it is EXECUTE.
n	N means the preceding item is repeatable.
column	Column is the name of the column to which permissions are denied.
Table	Table is the name of the table to which permissions are denied.
view	View is the name of the view to which permissions are denied.
procedure	Procedure is the name of the stored procedure to which permissions are denied.

extended_procedure	Extended_procedure is the name of an extended stored procedure to which permissions are denied.
CASCADE	CASCADE means that permissions will be denied from a security_account as well as any other security accounts granted permissions by that security_account. You can get an error if you do not use CASCADE and the user was granted WITH GRANT OPTION permission.

Examples

Here's an example of the DENY statement:

```
DENY INSERT, UPDATE, DELETE
ON MyTable
TO SecAcct1, SecAcct2, SecAcct3
```

In the preceding example, the security accounts have been denied permissions on MyTable.

DIFFERENCE

DIFFERENCE shows what is different between two character expressions by the SOUNDEX function.

Syntax

The syntax is:

```
DIFFERENCE(character_expression, character_expression)
```

The arguments are:

Character_expression	Character_expression is char or varchar data type, a constant, variable, or column.

Example

Here's an example of the DIFFERENCE function:

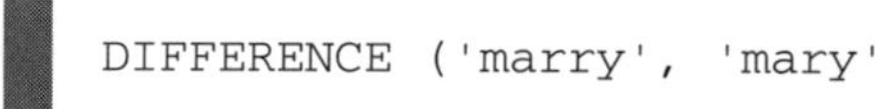

```
DIFFERENCE ('marry', 'mary')
```

In this example, 4 is the least possible difference, 0 is the most possible difference.

DROP DATABASE

DROP DATABASE physically removes a database(s).

Syntax

The syntax is:

```
DROP DATABASE database_name [,...n]
```

The arguments are:

database_name	Database_name is the database to be dropped.
n	N means the preceding entry is repeatable.

Example

Here's an example of the DROP DATABASE statement:

```
DROP DATABASE pubs,mydb
```

In this example, the pubs and mydb databases are removed.

DROP DEFAULT

DROP DEFAULT is a statement that removes a DEFAULT object that a user has created, but it will not remove a DEFAULT CONSTRAINT. To remove a DEFAULT CONSTRAINT, you must use ALTER TABLE.

Syntax

The syntax is:

```
DROP DEFAULT default [,...n]
```

The arguments are:

Default	Default is the default to be dropped.
n	N means the preceding entry is repeatable.

Example

Here's an example of the DROP DEFAULT statement:

```
DROP DEFAULT usrdefdflt
```

In this example, the user-defined default is removed.

DROP INDEX

DROP INDEX is a statement that removes an INDEX except indexes created by PRIMARY KEY or UNIQUE constraints.

Syntax

The syntax is:

```
DROP INDEX {'table.index'} [, ...n]
```

The arguments are:

Table	Table is the location of the indexed column.
Index	Index is the index you are dropping.
n	N means the preceding entry is repeatable.

Example

Here's an example of the DROP INDEX statement:

```
DROP INDEX 'MyTable.idx1'
```

In this example, the index, idx1, on MyTable is removed.

DROP PROCEDURE

DROP PROCEDURE is a statement that removes a stored procedure or stored procedure groups from the database.

Syntax

The syntax is:

```
DROP PROCEDURE procedure [, ...n]
```

The arguments are:

Procedure	Procedure is the name of the stored procedure you are dropping.
n	N means the preceding entry is repeatable.

Example

Here's an example of the DROP PROCEDURE statement:

```
DROP PROCEDURE MyProcedure
```

In this example, a stored procedure is removed.

DROP RULE

DROP RULE is a statement that removes a user-defined rule as a database object.

Syntax

The syntax is:

```
DROP RULE rule [, ...n]
```

The arguments are:

Rule	Rule is the name of the user-defined rule to drop.
n	N means the preceding entry is repeatable.

Example

Here's an example of the DROP RULE statement:

```
DROP RULE MyRule
```

In this example, a rule is removed.

DROP STATISTICS

Drops Statistics removes statistics for a column(s).

Syntax

The syntax is:

```
DROP STATISTICS table.column [, ...n]
```

The arguments are:

Table	Table is the name of the table.
Column	Column is the name of the column.
n	N means the preceding entry is repeatable.

DROP TABLE

DROP TABLE removes a table and its indexes, triggers, constraints, and permissions; however, views using the table must be dropped using DROP VIEW.

Syntax

The syntax is:

```
DROP TABLE table_name
```

The argument, table_name, is the table you wish to drop.

DROP TRIGGER

DROP TRIGGER removes a trigger as a database object.

Syntax

The syntax is:

```
DROP TRIGGER trigger_name [, ...n]
```

The argument, trigger_name, is the name of the trigger to drop from the database.

DROP VIEW

DROP VIEW removes a view and is used because views are not automatically dropped when a table is dropped.

Syntax

The syntax is:

```
DROP VIEW view_name [, ...n]
```

The argument, view_name, is the view you wish to drop as a database object.

DUMP

DUMP is for backwards compatibility only, use BACKUP instead.

ELSE (IF ... ELSE)

ELSE (IF ... ELSE) is a conditional set of statements. If the condition returns true, the statements are executed; when the IF condition is false, the ELSE statements are executed.

Syntax

The syntax is:

```
IF Boolean_expression
    {sql_statement | statement_block}
[ELSE
    {sql_statement | statement_block}]
```

The arguments are:

Boolean_expression	Boolean_expression returns true or false.
{sql_statement | statement_block}	Transact-SQL statement, or statements.

Example

Here's an example of the IF (IF … ELSE) set of conditional statements.

```
IF (SELECT count(Column1)
    FROM MyTable
    WHERE Column1 = 1 ) > 0
     BEGIN
          SELECT Column2
         FROM MyTable
     END
ELSE
     BEGIN
         SELECT Column3
         FROM MyTable
     END
```

In this example, if the number of rows selected by the query from MyTable is greater than zero, Column2 is selected; otherwise, Column3 is selected.

END (BEGIN ... END)

BEGIN …. END surrounds a set of Transact-SQL statements, making it possible to execute a set of statements as a block as in the case of IF … ELSE logic.

Syntax

The syntax is:

```
BEGIN
    {sql_statement | statement_block}
END
```

The argument, sql_statement or statement block, is a Transact-SQL statement, or statements.

Example

Here's an example of the BEGIN … END statements.

```
IF (SELECT count(Column1)
    FROM MyTable
    WHERE Column1 = 1 ) > 0
     BEGIN
          SELECT Column2
         FROM MyTable
     END
ELSE
     BEGIN
         SELECT Column3
         FROM MyTable
     END
```

In this example, if the number of rows selected by the query from MyTable is greater than zero, Column2 is selected; otherwise, Column3 is selected.

EXECUTE

EXECUTE executes a stored procedure or an extended stored procedure. You can also execute a character string in a Transact-SQL batch.

Syntax

The syntax to execute a stored procedure is:

```
[[EXEC[UTE]]
    {
        [@return_status =]
            {procedure_name [;number] | @procedure_name_var
    }
    [[@parameter =] {value | @variable [OUTPUT] | [DEFAULT]] [, …n]
[WITH RECOMPILE]
```

The syntax to execute a character string is:

```
EXEC[UTE] ({@string_variable | 'tsql_string' | expression} [+...n])
```

The arguments are:

@return_status	@return_status stores the return status of a stored procedure and must be declared.
procedure_name	Procedure name is the stored procedure to execute.
number	Number groups stored procedures together so that they can be dropped at once.
@procedure_name_var	@procedure_name_var is a local variable that holds the stored procedure name.
@parameter	@parameter is the parameter for the stored procedure.
Value	Value is the value to put into the parameter varaiable.
@variable	@variable is a local variable that holds a parameter.
OUTPUT	OUTPUT means that the stored procedure will return a parameter.
DEFAULT	DEFAULT is the default value of the parameter .
n	N means the preceding entry is repeatable.
WITH RECOMPILE	WITH RECOMPILE forces a new query plan to be developed for the stored procedure by query processor.
@string_variable	@string_variable is the name of a local string variable that holds a Transact-SQL statement that has been concatenated together.
'tsql_string'	'tsql_string' is a string in quotes that is a Transact-SQL statement or statements.
Expression	Expression is a constant, column name, function, subquery, and arithmetic, bitwise, and string operators.

[NOT] EXISTS

EXISTS or NOT EXISTS tests for the existence of rows returned by the subquery by returning a true or a false.

Syntax

The syntax is:

```
[NOT] EXISTS (subquery)
```

The arguments are:

NOT	NOT is the negative indicator of a boolean expression.
Subquery	Subquery is a SELECT statement where ORDER BY, COMPUTE, and INTO cannot be used.

Example

Here's an example of a NOT EXISTS test:

```
SELECT DISTINCT name
FROM MyTable
WHERE NOT EXISTS
    (SELECT *
    FROM MyTable2
    WHERE MyTable_ID = MyTable.MyTable_ID)
```

In this example, a distinct name is returned if the ID exists in the second table.

EXP

EXP returns the exponential value of a float expression.

Syntax

The syntax is:

```
EXP(float_expression)
```

The argument, float_expression, is a float data type.

FETCH

FETCH returns a row from a Transact-SQL cursor.

Syntax

The syntax is:

```
FETCH
[ [NEXT | PRIOR | FIRST | LAST
| ABSOLUTE {n | @nvar} | RELATIVE {n | @nvar}]
```

```
FROM ] { { [GLOBAL] cursor_name } | cursor_variable_name}
[INTO @variable_name[,...n] ]
```

The arguments are:

NEXT	NEXT retrieves the next row following the current row and is the default FETCH option.
PRIOR	PRIOR retrieves the row preceding the current row.
FIRST	FIRST retrieves the first row in the cursor.
LAST	LAST retrieves the last row in the cursor.
ABSOLUTE {n | @nvar}	If n or @nvar is positive, ABSOLUTE makes the row n rows from the front of the cursor the current row and retrieves it. If n or @nvar is negative, the row n rows before the end of the cursor is retrieved.
RELATIVE {n | @nvar}	If n or @nvar are positive, RELATIVE retrieves the row n rows after the current row. If n or @nvar are negative, RELATIVE returns the row that is n rows before of the current row.
GLOBAL	GLOBAL means a global cursor.
cursor_name	Cursor_name is the name of the cursor you are fetching from.
cursor_variable_name	Cursor_variable_name is the name of a cursor variable.
INTO @variable_name[,...n]	INTO places the data into local variables.

FILE_ID

FILE_ID returns the file identification number for a logical file name in the current database.

Syntax

The syntax is:

```
FILE_ID('file_name')
```

The argument, file_name, is the logical name of the file in the *sysfiles* system table.

FILE_NAME

FILE_NAME returns the file name for a file identification number in the current database.

Syntax

The syntax is:

```
FILE_NAME(file_id)
```

The argument, file_id, is the fileid column in *sysfiles* system table.

FILEGROUP_ID

FILEGROUP_ID returns the filegroup identification number for a filegroup name in the current database.

Syntax

The syntax is:

```
FILEGROUP_ID('filegroup_name')
```

The argument, filegroup_name, is the filegroup name and matches the groupname column in the *sysfilegroups* system table.

FILEGROUP_NAME

FILEGROUP_NAME returns the filegroup name for a filegroup identification number in the current database.

Syntax

The syntax is:

```
FILEGROUP_NAME(filegroup_id)
```

The argument, filegroup_id, is the groupid column in *sysfilegroups* system table.

FILEGROUPPROPERTY

FILEGROUPPROPERTY returns the filegroup property value of '1 = true', '0 = false', and 'NULL = value not found' for the property names, IsReadOnly, IsDefault, and IsUserDefinedFG when a filegroup and property name are supplied as arguments.

Syntax

The syntax is:

```
FILEGROUPPROPERTY('filegroup_name', 'property')
```

The arguments are:

'filegroup_name'	Filegroup_name is the name of the filegroup.
'property'	Property is the name of the filegroup property, IsReadOnly, IsDefault, and IsUserDefinedFG.

FILEPROPERTY

FILEPROPERTY returns the file property value of '1 = true', '0 = false', and 'NULL = value not found' for the property names, IsLogFile, SpaceUsed, IsReadOnly, and IsPrimaryFile.

Syntax

The syntax is:

```
FILEPROPERTY('file_name', 'property')
```

The arguments are:

'file_name'	File_name is the name of the file.
'property'	Property is the name of the file property, IsLogFile, SpaceUsed, IsReadOnly, and IsPrimaryFile.

float and real

See DataTypes.

FLOOR

FLOOR returns the integer that is less than or equal to the numeric expression argument.

Syntax

The syntax is:

```
FLOOR(numeric_expression)
```

The argument, numeric_expression, is a decimal, float, int, money, numeric, real, smallint, smallmoney, or tinyint expression.

Example

Here's an example of the FLOOR function:

```
SELECT FLOOR(2.3), FLOOR(-2.3)
GO
```

In this example, 2 is returned for FLOOR(2.3), and -3 is returned for FLOOR(-2.3).

FORMATMESSAGE

FORMATMESSAGE formats a message from system messages in the *sysmessages* system table and returns the formatted message.

Syntax

The syntax is:

```
FORMATMESSAGE(msg_number, param_value[,…n])
```

The arguments are:

msg_number — Msg_number is the identifier for the message that exists as a row in the *sysmessages* system table in the *master* system database.

param_value — Param_value represents the positional values that replace the variables in the message (maximum of 20).

FREETEXT

FREETEXT is for searching character full-text enabled columns for matches on meaning. The 'freetext_string' is divided into weighted search terms before retrieving the matches.

Syntax

The syntax is:

```
FREETEXT(    {column | * }, 'freetext_string'    )
```

The arguments are:

Column	Column is the name of a character column enabled for full-text searching.
*	* means search all full-text enabled columns for a match on meaning to the freetext_string argument.
Freetext_string	Freetext_string represents the characters to search for matches on meaning in the column.

Example

Here's an example of using FREETEXT:

```
SELECT MyColumn
FROM MyTable
WHERE FREETEXT (MyFullTextEnabledColumn, 'planets in the universe' )
GO
```

In this example, MyFullTextEnabledColumn is searched for items similar in meaning to the argument 'planets in the universe', a search less exact than using the CONTAINS syntax, another full-text search facility.

FREETEXTTABLE

FREETEXTTABLE provides a result set as a table of rows with RANK for each row for character column values that match in meaning the characters in the 'freetext_string' argument. The syntax allows you to use FREETEXTTABLE in the FROM clause of SELECT statement queries that use FREETEXT searching.

Syntax

The syntax is:

```
FREETEXTTABLE (table, {column | *}, 'freetext_string')
```

The arguments are:

table	Table is the name of the full-text enabled table.

column	Column is the name of the full-text enabled column you are searching.
*	* means search all full-text enabled columns for a match on meaning to the freetext_string argument.
freetext_string	Freetext_string represents the characters to search for matches on meaning in the column.

FROM

The FROM clause precedes the tables, views, derived tables, and joined tables used in DELETE, INSERT, SELECT, and UPDATE statements.

Syntax

The syntax is:

```
FROM
{<table_or_view> | (select_statement) [AS] alias | <table_or_view>
[{CROSS | INNER|{FULL | LEFT | RIGHT } [OUTER] [<join_hint>] JOIN
<table_or_view> ON search_conditions]
| CONTAINSTABLE ( table, { column | *},
'<contains_search_condition>' )
| FREETEXTTABLE
( table, {column | * }, 'freetext_string'))}[, …n]

<table_or_view> ::=
{ table [[AS] alias] [WITH(<table_hint> [ ...m])]
| view [[AS] alias]
| OPENROWSET( 'provider_name',
{'datasource';'user_id';'password' | 'provider_string'},
{[catalog.][schema.]object_name | 'query'})
| OPENQUERY(linked_server, 'query')}

<table_hint> ::=
([INDEX =
{
index_name
| index_id]
} [, …n]
[FASTFIRSTROW] [HOLDLOCK] [NOLOCK] [PAGLOCK]
[READCOMMITTED] [READPAST] [READUNCOMMITTED]
[REPEATABLEREAD] [ROWLOCK] [SERIALIZABLE] [TABLOCK]
[TABLOCKX] [UPDLOCK]
```

```
)
          <join_hint> ::=
{
HASH
| LOOP
| MERGE
}
```

The arguments are:

<table_or_view>	Table_or_view is the table or view referenced in the FROM clause.
alias	Each table or view can be given an alias, a shortened version of the table/view name. An alias makes it easier to refer to a column in the table later in a fully qualified manner in the likely event there are two columns of the same name in the two tables.
<table_hint>	Table hint determines indexes used, a table scan, or a locking strategy. See Chapter 6 for the new optimizer hints.
n	N means the preceding entry is repeatable.
OPENROWSET	OPENROWSET defines the connection information to access remote data from a data source. See "OPENROWSET" later in this chapter.
OPENQUERY	OPENQUERY executes a pass-through query. See "OPENQUERY" later in this chapter.
select_statement	The statement responsible for the return of rows from the database.
CROSS	Cross is the cross product of two tables.
FULL [OUTER]	When FULL [OUTER] is provided in the SELECT statement and there is no match between the tables, you will still receive the row from the both tables with the columns of the unmatched row being shown as NULL.
INNER	An INNER join is the default and means that only the matching pairs of rows are returned.
LEFT [OUTER]	A LEFT [OUTER] join means matching rows are returned and, for unmatched rows, that rows from the left table are included in the result set with the other table's columns set to NULL.

RIGHT [OUTER]	A RIGHT [OUTER] join means matching rows are returned and, for unmatched rows, that rows from the right table are included in the result set with the other table's columns set to NULL.
JOIN	JOIN indicates the join operation is to occur.
<join_hint>	Join_hint is given to the query optimizer to instruct how to perform the join with one join hint per join in the FROM clause.
Search_conditions	Search_conditions sets forth the limits for the rows returned by using WHERE clause Transact-SQL syntax.
n	N means the preceding entry is repeatable.
CONTAINSTABLE	CONTAINSTABLE returns a table when searching character full-text enabled columns for precise or close matches to a word or a phrase, words near one another, and weighted matches.
FREETEXTTABLE	FREETEXTTABLE returns a table for character free-text enabled columns with matches in meaning.

Example

Here's an example of an ANSI FULL OUTER JOIN.

```
SELECT Column1, Column2
FROM MyTable a FULL OUTER JOIN MyTable2 b
    ON a.My_Id = b.My_Id
WHERE MyTable.My_OtherId IN (987, 346, 985)
```

In this example, a full outer join is performed.

FULLTEXTCATALOGPROPERTY

FULLTEXTCATALOGPROPERTY displays information relating to full-text catalog properties.

Syntax

The syntax is:

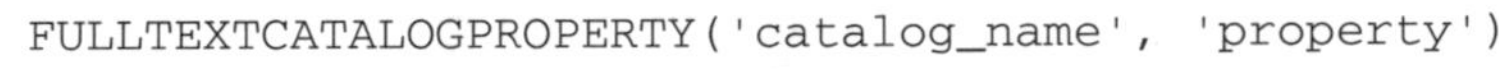

```
FULLTEXTCATALOGPROPERTY('catalog_name', 'property')
```

The arguments are:

'catalog_name'	Catalog_name is the name of the full-text catalog.
'property'	The full-text catalog properties are: PopulateStatus 0=Idle, 1=Population in progress, 2=Paused, 3=Throttled, 4=Recovering, 5=Shutdown, 6=Incremental population in progress, 7=Updating index. ItemCount: a count of entries in the full-text catalog. IndexSize: size in MB of the full-text index. UniqueKeyCount, the count of unique keys in the full-text index. LogSize: size in MB of the last full-text index population. PopulateCompletionAge: the age of the completion of the last population is calculated in seconds by subtracting the date of the completion and 01/01/1990 00:00:00.

FULLTEXTSERVICEPROPERTY

FULLTEXTSERVICEPROPERTY displays information related to full-text service properties.

Syntax

The syntax is:

```
FULLTEXTSERVICEPROPERTY('property')
```

The arguments are:

'property'	The full-text service properties are: ResourceUsage, 1=background through 5=dedicated. ConnectTimeout, multiply by 4 and you get the seconds for Microsoft Search Service, initiate the full-text index population. IsFulltextInstalled, 1=Microsoft Search Service is installed and 0= Microsoft Search Service is not installed.

GETANSINULL

GETANSINULL is a function that returns 1 if the database follows the ANSI default of the nullability allowing nulls and returns 0 if the nullability is not the ANSI default. You can override this by specifying NULL in the CREATE TABLE or ALTER TABLE statements. You can also set the default behavior by using either sp_dboption 'ANSI

NULL DEFAULT', {true | false} or SET ANSI_NULL_DFLT_ON {ON | OFF} or SET ANSI_NULL_DEFLT_OFF {ON | OFF}.

```
GETANSINULL(['database'])
```

The argument, database, is the name of the database.

GETDATE

GETDATE is a function that returns the system date and time.

Syntax

The syntax is:

```
GETDATE()
```

GO

GO is the command to execute the batch of Transact-SQL statements.

Syntax

The syntax is:

```
GO
```

GOTO

GOTO is the statement that transfers the programmatic flow of control to a label.

Syntax

The syntax is:

```
GOTO label
```

The argument, label, is the point in Transact-SQL where programmatic control is passed by the GOTO statement.

GRANT

See Chapter 5.

GROUP BY

See "SELECT" later in this chapter.

GROUPING

GROUPING creates an additional column for output containing the value 1 when the row is inserted by the CUBE or ROLLUP clause. The additional column contains zero (0) when the inserted row is not because of CUBE or ROLLUP and is used with a GROUP BY clause with CUBE or ROLLUP.

Syntax

The syntax is:

```
GROUPING(column_name)
```

The argument, column_name, represents the additional column in the GROUP BY clause you are checking for CUBE or ROLLUP indicators.

HAVING

HAVING is a search condition for a grouping (usually using an aggregate function) used with the SELECT … GROUP BY. It is much like the WHERE clause.

Syntax

The syntax is:

```
HAVING <search_condition>
```

The argument, search_condition, is the criteria for the group that must be satisfied.

HOST_ID

HOST_ID is a function that returns the identification number of the workstation.

Syntax

The syntax is:

```
HOST_ID( )
```

HOST_NAME

HOST_NAME is a function that returns the name of the workstation.

Syntax

The syntax is:

```
HOST_NAME( )
```

IDENT_INCR

IDENT_INCR is a function the returns the identity increment value of a table or a view that was specified when the table or view was created with an identity column.

Syntax

The syntax is:

```
IDENT_INCR('table_or_view')
```

The argument, table_or_view, is the table or view for which you wish to see the identity increment value.

IDENT_SEED

IDENT_SEED is a function the returns the initial (seed) value of a table or a view that was specified when the table or view was created with an identity column.

Syntax

The syntax is:

```
IDENT_SEED('table_or_view')
```

The argument, table_or_view, is the table or view for which you wish to see the identity seed value.

IDENTITY

An identity column provides a unique, automatically generated value in a column.

Syntax

The syntax is:

```
IDENTITY(data_type[, seed, increment])
```

Example

Here's an example of an identity column:

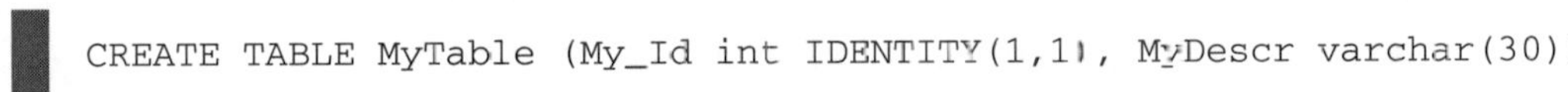

```
CREATE TABLE MyTable (My_Id int IDENTITY(1,1), MyDescr varchar(30))
```

In this example, the column, My_Id , is created as an identity column.

IF ... ELSE

See "ELSE" later in this chapter.

IN

The IN clause checks to see if a value is in a list of other values.

Syntax

The syntax is:

```
expression IN
( subquery | expression [,...n] )
```

The arguments are:

Expression	Expression is any valid SQL expression.
Subquery	The result set of the subquery must have one column and the expressions must match in data type.

Example

Here's an example of the IN clause:

```
SELECT MyColumn, MyId
FROM MyTable
WHERE MyId IN
(SELECT MyId
FROM MyOtherTable
WHERE MyOtherColumn LIKE (%this%))
```

In this example, MyColumn and MyId are returned when MyId is found in MyOtherTable.

INDEXPROPERTY

INDEXPROPERTY returns an index property value for an index on a table. The index properties are: IndexDepth, IsClustered, IsUnique, IndexFillFactor, IsPadIndex, IsFullTextKey with 1 = true, 0 = false, and NULL = value not found.

Syntax

The syntax is:

```
INDEXPROPERTY(table_ID, 'index', 'property')
```

The arguments are:

table_ID	Table_ID is the OBJECT_ID the table.
'index'	Index is the name of the index.
'property'	Property is the name of the index property.

INDEX_COL

INDEX_COL is a function that returns the indexed column name.

Syntax

The syntax is:

```
INDEX_COL('table', index_id, key_id)
```

The arguments are:

'table'	Table is the name of the table.
Index_id	Index_id is the indid of the index.
key_id	Key_id is the the cardinal number (1 through 16) of the column in the index of the key.

INSERT

The INSERT statement inserts a row(s) into a table or view.

Syntax

The syntax is:

```
INSERT [INTO] {<table_or_view>}
{
{
[(column_list)] VALUES
(
{
DEFAULT
| constant_expression
}[,...n]
)
| select_statement
| execute_statement
}
| DEFAULT VALUES
}
<table_or_view> ::=
{
table [[AS] alias] [WITH(<table_hint> [ ...m])]
| view [[AS] alias]
| OPENROWSET( 'provider_name',
{
'datasource';'user_id';'password'
| 'provider_string'
},
{
[catalog.][schema.]object_name
| 'query'
})
| OPENQUERY(linked_server, 'query')
}
<table_hint> ::=
([INDEX =
{
index_name
| index_id]
} [, …n]
[HOLDLOCK] [PAGLOCK] [READCOMMITTED]
[READUNCOMMITTED] [REPEATABLEREAD]
[ROWLOCK] [SERIALIZABLE] [TABLOCK] [TABLOCKX]
)
```

The arguments are:

INTO	INTO is the keyword before the name of the table or view.
Column_list	Column list is a list of column(s).
VALUES	VALUES are the data values you are placing in the list of columns with a one-to-one correspondence.
DEFAULT	DEFAULT indicates the default value for the column will be placed in the column. This will not work with an identity column.
Constant_expression	Constant_expression is an expression, a constant, or a variable.
n	N means the preceding value is repeatable.
Select_statement	SELECT statement is the query used to get the data to place in the table.
Execute_statement	Execute_statement is any valid EXECUTE statement that returns a result set whose columns match those to be inserted.
DEFAULT VALUES	DEFAULT VALUES means the new row will contain the default values for each column.
<table_or_view>	Table_or_view is the header for the name of the table or view.
table	Table is the name of a table where the data is being placed.
alias	Alias is the short name given to a table or view.
view	View is the name of a view.
OPENROWSET	OPENROWSET contains connection definitions to use remote data from a data source.
OPENQUERY	OPENQUERY runs the pass-through query. See "OPENQUERY" later in this chapter.
<table_hint>	Table-hint tells the SQL Server query optimizer how to perform the query. See "New Optimizer Hints" in Chapter 6.
INDEX = index_name | index_id	The index to use to process the query if giving an index optimizer hint.

Example

Here's an example of an INSERT statement:

```
INSERT MyTable
(Column1, Column2, Column3)
VALUES
(1, DEFAULT, 'Value for column 3')
```

In this example the values 1, the default value for column2, and the value for column3 is inserted as a row into MyTable.

int, smallint, and tinyint

See datatype.

IS_MEMBER

IS_MEMBER is a function that returns 0 if the current user is not a member of the group or role or 1 if the current user is a member of the group or role or NULL if the group or role does not exist.

Syntax

The syntax is:

```
IS_MEMBER ({'group' | 'role'})
```

The arguments are:

'group'	Group is the name of the Windows NT group and is referenced by domain\group.
'role'	Role is the name of the SQL Server role but cannot be a server role. Use IS_SRVROLEMEMBER for server role.

IS_SRVROLEMEMBER

IS_SRVROLEMEMBER is a function that returns 0 if the current user is not a member of the server role or 1 if the current user is a member of the server role or NULL if the server role does not exist.

Syntax

The syntax is:

```
IS_SRVROLEMEMBER ( 'role' [,'login'])
```

The arguments are:

'role'	Role is the name of the server role, sysadmin, dbcreator, diskadmin, processadmin, serveradmin, setupadmin, securityadmin.
'login'	Login is the name of the login to check. If this argument is not provided, the login account for the current user is used.

ISDATE

ISDATE is a function that examines a variable or varchar column and returns a 1 when the expression contains a valid date or 0 if the content does not contain a date.

Syntax

The syntax is:

```
ISDATE(expression)
```

The argument, expression, is a variable or varchar column.

IS [NOT] NULL

IS [NOT] NULL checks to see if an expression is NULL.

Syntax

The syntax is:

```
expression IS [NOT] NULL
```

The arguments are:

Expression	Expression is any expression.
NOT	NOT is the negative aspect of a boolean expression.

ISNULL

ISNULL is a function that substitutes a NULL value for something not null.

Syntax

The syntax is:

```
ISNULL(expression, substitution_value)
```

The arguments are:

expression	Expression is what is checked for null.
substitution_value	Substitution_value is what is returned if the expression is NULL.

ISNUMERIC

ISNUMERIC is a function that returns 1 if the expression is an integer, float, money, or decimal type and returns 0 if the expression is not numeric.

Syntax

The syntax is:

```
ISNUMERIC(expression)
```

The argument, expression, must be expressed as a string.

KILL

The KILL command ends a process.

Syntax

The syntax is:

```
KILL {spid} [WITH {ABORT | COMMIT}]
```

The argument, spid, is the process ID to stop.

LEFT

LEFT is a function that returns a certain number of bytes from the left of the character expression. NULL is returned if the integer is negative.

Syntax

The syntax is:

```
LEFT(character_expression, integer_expression)
```

The arguments are:

Character_expression	Character_expression is a variable, a constant, or a column in a table.
Integer_expression	Integer_expression is a variable, a constant, or a column in a table that indicates the number of characters to return.

LEN

LEN is a function that provides the length in characters of the string expression.

Syntax

The syntax is:

```
LEN(string_expression)
```

The argument, string_expression, is a variable, constant, or a column. It can also be any expression that returns a character datatype (like the concatenation of strings, a function that returns a string, etc.).

LIKE

Use the LIKE clause with a character string to pattern match with wildcard characters.

Syntax

The syntax is:

```
match_expression [NOT] LIKE pattern
```

The arguments are:

match_expression	Match_expression is any valid character SQL expression.

pattern	Pattern is what you are looking for in the argument, match_expression. You can use wildcards in your pattern: % - Looks for anything, any length _ - Looks for any one character [] - contains a range or a list of characters [^] – characters to exclude

Example

Here's an example of the LIKE clause:

```
SELECT *
FROM Mytable
WHERE Column1 LIKE "%MS%"
```

In this example, all rows with the two consecutive letters MS anywhere in the table column, Column1, are returned.

LOAD

Load is present for backward compatibility only. Use the RESTORE command instead. See "RESTORE" later in this chapter.

LOG

When passed a float expression, LOG is a function that returns the natural logarithm for that float expression.

Syntax

The syntax is:

```
LOG(float_expression)
```

The argument is a float expression.

LOG10

When passed a float expression, LOG10 is a function that returns the base-10 logarithm for that float expression.

Syntax

The syntax is:

```
LOG10(float_expression)
```

The argument is a float expression.

LOWER

LOWER is a function that converts uppercase characters to lowercase.

Syntax

The syntax is:

```
LOWER(character_expression)
```

The argument is a character expression.

LTRIM

LTRIM removes leading blanks from a character expression.

Syntax

The syntax is:

```
LTRIM(character_expression)
```

The argument is a character expression.

MAX

MAX returns the maximum value in the expression and cannot be used with bit columns.

Syntax

The syntax is:

```
MAX([ALL | DISTINCT] expression)
```

The arguments are:

ALL	ALL is the default.

DISTINCT	DISTINCT means unique values. The usage here is ANSI compatible but meaningless.
expression	Expression is a constant, column, or function and can contain arithmetic, bitwise, and string operators.

Example

Here's an example of the MAX function.

```
SELECT MAX(Column1)
FROM MyTable
```

In this example, the maximum value in the table for Column1 is returned.

MIN

MIN returns the minimum value in the expression and cannot be used with bit columns.

Syntax

The syntax is:

```
MIN([ALL | DISTINCT] expression)
```

The arguments are:

ALL	ALL is the default.
DISTINCT	DISTINCT means unique values. The usage here is ANSI compatible but meaningless.
expression	Expression is a constant, column, or function and can contain arithmetic, bitwise, and string operators.

Example

Here's an example of the MIN function:

```
SELECT MIN(Column1)
FROM MyTable
```

In this example, the minimum value in the table for Column1 is returned.

money and smallmoney

See "Data Types" earlier in this chapter.

MONTH

See "Date Functions" earlier in this chapter. MONTH(date) is the same as DATEPART(mm, date).

NCHAR

NCHAR returns the standard Unicode character for integer 0-65535.

Syntax

The syntax is:

```
NCHAR(integer_expression)
```

The argument is an integer 0-65535.

nchar and nvarchar

See "Data Types" later in this chapter.

NEWID

NEWID is a function that returns a *uniqueidentifier* value.

Syntax

The syntax is:

```
NEWID()
```

NOT

NOT is the negative of a boolean expression.

Syntax

The syntax is:

```
[NOT] boolean_expression
```

The argument is a valid SQL boolean expression.

ntext, text, and image

See "Data Types" earlier in this chapter.

NULLIF

If a pair of expressions are equal, NULLIF is a function that returns NULL. If they are not equal, it returns the value of the first expression.

Syntax

The syntax is:

```
NULLIF(expression, expression)
```

The argument, expression, is a constant, column, or function and can contain arithmetic, bitwise, and string operators.

numeric

See "Data Types" earlier in this chapter.

OBJECT_ID

OBJECT_ID returns the object identification number when passed the name of the object in the database in use.

Syntax

The syntax is:

```
OBJECT_ID('object')
```

The argument, object_id, is the name of the object.

OBJECT_NAME

OBJECT_NAME is a function that returns the name of an object when passed the identification number of the object in the database in use.

Syntax

The syntax is:

```
OBJECT_NAME(object_id)
```

The argument, object_id, is the identification number of the object.

OBJECTPROPERTY

OBJECTPROPERTY is a function that produces a wealth of information about database objects by returning the values of the following properties: CnstIsClustKey, CnstIsColumn, CnstIsDisabled, CnstIsNonclustKey, CnstIsNotRepl, ExecIsAnsiNullsOn, ExecIsDeleteTrigger, ExecIsInsertTrigger, ExecIsQuotedIdentOn, ExecIsStartup, ExecIsTriggerDisabled, ExecIsUpdateTrigger, IsCheckCnst, IsConstraint, IsDefault, IsDefaultCnst, IsExecuted, IsExtendedProc, IsForeignKey, IsMSShipped, IsPrimaryKey, IsProcedure, IsReplProc, IsRule, IsSystemTable, IsTable, IsTrigger, IsUniqueCnst, IsUserTable, IsView, OwnerId, TableDeleteTrigger, TableDeleteTriggerCount, TableFulltextKeyColumn, TableFulltextCatalogId, TableHasActiveFulltextIndex, TableHasCheckCnst, TableHasClustIndex, TableHasDefaultCnst, TableHasDeleteTrigger, TableHasForeignKey, TableHasForeignRef, TableHasIdentity, TableHasIndex, TableHasInsertTrigger, TableHasNonclustIndex, TableHasPrimaryKey, TableHasRowGuidCol, TableHasTextImage, TableHasTimestamp, TableHasUniqueCnst, TableHasUpdateTrigger, TableInsertTrigger, TableInsertTriggerCount, TableIsPinned, TableUpdateTrigger, TableUpdateTriggerCount, TriggerDeleteOrder, TriggerInsertOrder, TriggerUpdateOrder.

Syntax

The syntax is:

```
OBJECTPROPERTY(id, 'property')
```

The arguments are:

id	Is the ID of the object.
'property'	Is the information to be returned for the object with *id*. *Property* can be one of the values listed above.

OPEN

The OPEN statement is used with a Transact-SQL server cursor to open it.

Syntax

The syntax is:

```
OPEN { { [GLOBAL] cursor_name } | cursor_variable_name}
```

The arguments are:

GLOBAL	GLOBAL means that if there is both a local and a global cursor with the same name, use the Global cursor.
Cursor_name	Cursor_name is the name of a cursor. A global cursor with the same name as a local cursor will be cursor used. If the optional keyword GLOBAL is specified, the local cursor will be used.
Cursor_variable_name	Cursor_variable is the name of a cursor variable.

OPENQUERY

OPENQUERY is a function used in the FROM clause of a query in place of a table name or can be the target table of INSERT, UPDATE, or DELETE statements (if the OLE DB provider has the capability). OPENQUERY runs a pass-through query on an OLE DB data source defined as a linked server. The linked server has already been created with the sp_addlinkedserver stored procedure.

Syntax

The syntax is:

```
OPENQUERY(linked_server, 'query')
```

The arguments are:

linked_server	Linked_server is the name of the linked server.
'query'	Query is the query executed on the linked server.

Example

Here's an example of the OPENQUERY function:

```
SELECT *
FROM OPENQUERY(Orcl_Linked_Srv1, 'SELECT Column1 FROM dbo.DBA_Table')
```

In this example, data from an Oracle server is selected.

OPENROWSET

OPENROWSET is a function used in the FROM clause of a query in place of a table name or can be the target table of INSERT, UPDATE, or DELETE statements (if the OLE DB provider has the capability). OPENROWSET delivers connection information to access remote data from an OLE DB data source. Use this as an alternative to OPENQUERY. Use this instead of accessing tables in a linked server as an ad hoc way to interrogate remote data with OLE DB.

Syntax

The syntax is:

```
OPENROWSET('provider_name'
{
'datasource';'user_id';'password'
| 'provider_string'
},
{
[catalog.][schema.]object
| 'query'
})
```

The arguments are:

'provider_name'	Provider is the friendly name of the OLE DB provider in the registry.
'datasource'	Datasource is an alphnumeric string of the OLE DB data source. This string is used by the provider to locate the database or file.
'user_id'	User_id is the user name sent to the OLE DB provider.
'password'	Password is for the user and is passed to the OLE DB provider.
'provider_string'	Provider_string is specific to the provider and is passed in as the DBPROP_INIT_PROVIDERSTRING property to initialize the OLE DB provider.
catalog	Catalog is the name of the catalog or database where the object is located.
schema	Schema is the name of the schema or object owner of the object.
object	Object is the object name.
'query'	Query is a pass-through executed by the provider. Pass-through queries are useful when used on providers that do not expose their tabular data through table names, but only through a command language.

Example

Here's an example of the OPENROWSET function:

```
SELECT t1.*
FROM OPENROWSET('MSDASQL',
'DRIVER={SQL Server};SERVER=server1;UID=sa;PWD=server1pwd',
db1.dbo.MyTable) AS t1
ORDER BY t1.Column1, t1.Column2
GO
```

In this example, the OLE DB Provider for ODBC and the SQL Server ODBC driver sends a query to run a remote server.

OR

OR examines two conditions and if either condition is TRUE, TRUE is returned. AND is evaluated first, but the placement of parentheses controls the order of evaluation.

Syntax

The syntax is:

```
boolean_expression OR boolean_expression
```

The argument, boolean expression, is any valid SQL expression that is TRUE, FALSE, or UNKNOWN.

ORDER BY

ORDER BY determines the sort order in a SELECT statement.

PARSENAME

PARSENAME returns object name, owner name, database name, and server name for an object but will not tell you if the object exists.

Syntax

The syntax is:

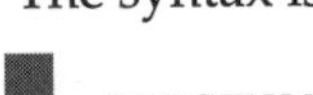

```
PARSENAME('object_name ', object_piece)
```

The arguments are:

'object_name'	Object_name is the name of the object and can be optionally qualified.

object_piece	Object_piece is the part of the object to return. The following values are valid for object_piece: 1 = Object name 2 = Owner name 3 = Database name 4 = Server name

Example

Here's an example of the PARSENAME function:

```
SELECT PARSENAME('mydb..MyTable', 2) AS 'Owner Name'
```

In this example, the owner name of the table, MyTable, in the database, mydb, is parsed and returns NULL.

PATINDEX

PATINDEX is a function that returns the beginning position of the first incidence of a pattern in an expression which returns zero if the pattern does not exist in the expression.

Syntax

The syntax is:

```
PATINDEX('%pattern%', expression)
```

The arguments are:

Pattern	Pattern is a string that may contain wildcard characters.
Expression	Expression is a string that is mostly a column name that is being searched.

Example

Here's an example of PATINDEX:

```
SELECT PATINDEX('%MS%', Column1)
FROM MyTable
WHERE My_id = 062554
```

PERMISSIONS

PERMISSIONS is a function that returns a 32-bit bitmap that shows the statement, object, or column permissions for the user in the current session. The stored procedure, *sp_helpprotect*, can also be used as an alternative to the PERMISSIONS function.

The lower 16 bits are permissions of the security account for the user in the current session. For example, a returned value of 12 (no objectid as an argument means the current user has permissions to execute the CREATE PROCEDURE (decimal value 4) and CREATE VIEW (value 8) statement permissions.

The upper 16 bits are permissions that the user in the current session can GRANT to other users. The upper 16 bits are interpreted exactly as those for the lower 16 bits, but they are multiplied by 65536.

Statement permission bitmap values returned are decimal, bit and permission; 1 =0x1=CREATE DATABASE, 2=0x2=CREATE TABLE, 4=0x4=CREATE PROCEDURE, 8=0x8=CREATE VIEW, 16=0x10=CREATE RULE, 32=0x20=CREATE DEFAULT, 64=0x40=BACKUP DATABASE, 128=0x80=BACKUP LOG, 256=0x100=BACKUP TABLE.

Object permission bitmap values returned when supplied an objectid are decimal, bit, and permission; 1=0x1=SELECT ALL, 2=0x2=UPDATE ALL, 4=0x4=REFERENCES ALL, 8=0x8=INSERT, 16=0x10=DELETE, 32=0x20=EXECUTE (stored procedures), 4096=0x1000=SELECT ANY, 8192=0x2000=UPDATE ANY, 16384=0x4000=REFERENCES ANY.

Column object permission bitmap values returned when supplied an objectid and a column are decimal, bit and permission; 1=0x1=SELECT, 2=0x2 =UPDATE, 4=0x4=REFERENCES.

If an objectid or column does not exist, NULL is returned.

Syntax

The syntax is:

```
PERMISSIONS([objectid [, 'column']])
```

The arguments are:

Objectid	Object is the OBJECT_ID of an object in the current database. If you do not supply objectid statement, permissions are returned for the current user.
'column'	Column is optional and is the column name for which to return permissions.

Example

Here's an example of the PERMISSIONS function:

```
IF PERMISSIONS()&1=1
CREATE TABLE DBA_Table (Column1 INT, Column2 VARCHAR)
ELSE
GOTO ErrorRtn
```

PI

The PI function returns the value of pi, 3.14159265358979.

Syntax

The syntax is:

```
PI()
```

Example

Here's an example of the PI function:

```
SELECT PI()
```

In this example, the value 3.14159265358979 is returned as the value for PI.

POWER

The POWER function returns a numeric expression to a supplied power.

Syntax

The syntax is:

```
POWER(numeric_expression, y)
```

The arguments are:

numeric_expression	Numeric_expression is of data type decimal, float, int, money, numeric, real, smallint, smallmoney, or tinyint.
y	Raise the expression to the power of y.

PRINT

The PRINT statement returns a user-defined message to the client up to 1024 characters.

Syntax

The syntax is:

```
PRINT {'any ASCII text' | @local_variable | @@global_variable | string_expr}
```

The arguments are:

'any ASCII text'	Any ASCII text is a string.
@local_variable	@local_variable is a local variable.
@@global_variable	@@global_variable is a global variable that returns a string.
string_expr	String_expr is an expression that returns a string.

QUOTENAME

The QUOTENAME function returns a Unicode string transforming the character string argument into a valid quoted identifier.

Syntax

The syntax is:

```
QUOTENAME('character_string'[, 'quote_character'])
```

The arguments are:

'character_string'	Character_string is a string of Unicode characters.
'quote_character'	Quote_character is a single character functioning as the delimiter. The possible values are single quote, a left or right bracket , or a double quote.

RADIANS

RADIANS is a function that returns radians when provided a numeric expression in degrees.

Syntax

The syntax is:

```
RADIANS(numeric_expression)
```

The argument, numeric_expression is decimal, float, int, money, numeric, real, smallint, smallmoney, or tinyint data type.

RAISERROR

RAISERROR is a function that returns a user-defined error message and sets a system flag to indicate that an error happened. The message can be a message from the *sysmessages* system table or can be built inside the function with a user-defined severity and state. If the error occurs at run-time, the message is sent to the client.

If the *sysmessages* system table is used, and the message was defined using the formatting options for the argument, msg_str, then arguments are passed to the msg_id. The system stored procedures, *sp_addmessage* and *sp_dropmessage*, are used to create and drop user-defined error messages.

@@ERROR stores the most recently generated error number and by default is set to 0 for severity of 1 through 10.

Syntax

The syntax is:

```
RAISERROR ({msg_id | msg_str}{, severity, state}
[, argument
[,...n]] )
[WITH option]
```

The arguments are:

msg_id	Msg_id is a user-defined error message stored in the *sysmessages* table. Make error numbers for user-defined error messages greater than 50,000. Ad hoc messages will raise an error of 50,000. The maximum value for msg_id is 2,147,483,647.

msg_str	Msg_str is an ad hoc message up to 8000 characters with a standard message ID of 14,000. The % character means that this is an ad hoc message formatted as: % [[*flag*] [*width*] [*precision*] [{h | l}]] *type* flag= a code that defines spacing and justification of the message used without single quotes. '-'=Left justification within the field +=Signs the value with plus or minus 0= Zero pads character data types #=Radix prefix for nondecimal numbers ' '=Space pads positive signed values and is ignored when the + flag is used. Width=integer and the minimum width with * meaning precision defines the width. Precision=maximum number of characters or the minimum number of digits with * meaning the argument defines the precision. {h|l}type=modifier (h for short int, or l for long int) used with numeric types to define the size of the numeric argument. The types are: Di= signed integer :u=unsigned integer :o=unsigned octal :x or X=unsigned hexadecimal :p=pointer
severity	Severity is the user-defined severity level for this message. 1–18: Any user 19–25: Sysadmin and must use WITH LOG 20–25: Fatal error with termination of client connection and logging in the SQL Server errorlog and the NT event log.
state	State is any integer from 1 through 127 about the state of the error.
argument	Argument represents the substitution parameters for variables in the msg-str with with a maximum of 20. The parameter can be a local variable or a constant of data type int1, int2, int4, char, varchar, binary, or varbinary.

option	Option represents the custom options for the error. LOG: Logs the error in the server error log and the event log and can only be used by sysadmin. NOWAIT: Messages are sent immediately to the client. SETERROR: @@error is msg_id or 50000 for ad hoc messages no matter the severity.

Example

Here's are two examples of the RAISERROR function:

```
RAISERROR ('Customerid 4 expects the district of 44.',16,-1)

RAISERROR ('The district for customer_id:%d should be between %d and %d.',
16, -1, @@customer_id, @@min_dist, @@max_dist)
```

In the first example, a simple message is created. The second raiserror dynamically builds the message.

RAND

RAND returns a random float value between 0 and 1.

Syntax

The syntax is:

```
RAND([seed])
```

The argument, seed, determines the starting value and is int, smallint, or tinyint data type.

READTEXT

READTEXT returns text, ntext, or image values from a text or image column, starting from a specified offset and returning a given number of bytes. You can use the TEXTPTR function to get a valid *text_ptr* value for the table. See "TEXTPTR" and "SET TEXTSIZE" later in this chapter.

Syntax

The syntax is:

```
READTEXT {table.column text_ptr offset size} [HOLDLOCK]
```

The arguments are:

table.column	The name of a table and column.
text_ptr	Text_ptr is a valid text pointer of binary (16).
offset	Offset is the number of characters (bytes) to overlook before positioning in the text or image data. Ntext data type must be given in characters (2 bytes each), and text or image data types given in bytes.
size	Size is the number of bytes of data to read with 0 meaning 4K bytes of data.
HOLDLOCK	HOLDLOCK locks the text value until the end of the transaction, and it can be read but not changed.

Example

Here's an example of the READTEXT function:

```
DECLARE @ varbinary(16)
SELECT @pntr = TEXTPTR(MyTable)
READTEXT MyTable.Column1 @pntr 2 55
```

This example reads the third through fifty-seventh characters of Column1 in MyTable.

real

See "Data Type" earlier in this chapter.

RECONFIGURE

RECONFIGURE updates the currently configured and, for some configuration options, the currently running value changed by the *sp_configure* system stored procedure. For some of the configuration options, Microsoft SQL Server must be stopped and started for the currently running value to be updated.

Syntax

The syntax is:

```
RECONFIGURE [WITH OVERRIDE]
```

The arguments are:

RECONFIGURE	RECONFIGURE updates the currently configured and, for some configuration options, the currently running value changed by the *sp_configure* system stored procedure; it also checks for invalid values or bad values.
WITH OVERRIDE	WITH OVERRIDE disables the check for the allow updates, recovery interval, or time slice configuration options and forces the reconfiguration with the value provided in *sp_configure*.

Example

Here's an example of the RECONFIGURE WITH OVERRIDE statement:

```
EXEC sp_configure 'allow updates', 1
RECONFIGURE WITH OVERRIDE
GO
```

In this example, the server is reconfigured to allow updates to the system tables. SQL Server will not inform you that the value is not recommended even though that is true.

REPLACE

REPLACE substitutes string_expression2 in string_expression1 with string_expression3.

Syntax

The syntax is:

```
REPLACE('string_expression1', 'string_expression2',
'string_expression3')
```

The arguments are:

'string_expression1'	String_expression1 is the string expression to search in string_expression2. Character or binary data can be used.
'string_expression2'	String_expression2 is the string expression to look for in string_expression1 and to substitute with string_expression3.

'string_expression3'	String_expression3 is the new string expression replacement for string_expression2.

Example

Here's an example of REPLACE:

```
SELECT REPLACE('MyDog','Dog','Cat')
```

In this example, Dog in MyDog is replaced with Cat. The result is MyCat.

REPLICATE

REPLICATE repeats a character expression a user-defined number of times.

Syntax

The syntax is:

```
REPLICATE(character_expression, integer_expression)
```

The arguments are:

character_expression	Character_expression is a character or binary constant, variable, or column.
integer_expression	Integer_expression is a positive whole number representing the number of times to replicate the character_expression.

RESTORE

The RESTORE statement restores a database, log, or database files. The following types of restores can occur: a standby server restore, a full database restore, a full database restore, a differential database restore (a differential backup is restored by using the RESTORE DATABASE statement), a transaction log restore, and individual file and filegroup restores. Files and filegroups can be restored from a file and/or filegroup backup or from a full database backup. When restoring files or filegroups, you must apply a transaction log.

Only RESTORE DATABASE affects the autoclose, autoshrink, autotruncate, dbo use only, readonly, single user, select into/bulkcopy, or torn page detection settings back to the database backup settings.

Syntax

The syntax to restore a complete database is:

```
RESTORE DATABASE {database_name | @database_name_var}
[FROM <backup_device> [, ... n]]
[WITH
[DBO_ONLY]
[[,] FILE = file_number]
[[,] MEDIANAME = {media_name | @media_name_variable}]
[[,] MOVE 'logical_file_name' TO 'operating_system_file_name']
[,…p]
[[,] {NORECOVERY | RECOVERY | STANDBY = undo_file_name}]
[[,] {NOUNLOAD | UNLOAD}]
[[,] REPLACE]
[[,] RESTART]
[[,] STATS [= percentage]]
]
```

The syntax to restore specific files or filegoup is:

```
RESTORE DATABASE {database_name | @database_name_var}
<file_or_filegroup> [, ...m]
[FROM <backup_device> [, …n]]
[WITH
[DBO_ONLY]
[[,] FILE = file_number]
[[,] MEDIANAME = {media_name | @media_name_variable}]
[[,] {NORECOVERY | RECOVERY | STANDBY = undo_file_name}]
[[,] {NOUNLOAD | UNLOAD}]
[[,] REPLACE]
[[,] RESTART]
[[,] STATS [= percentage]]
]
```

The syntax to restore a transaction log is:

```
RESTORE LOG {database_name | @database_name_var}
[FROM <backup_device> [, …n]]
[WITH
[DBO_ONLY]
[[,] FILE = file_number]
[[,] MEDIANAME = {media_name | @media_name_variable}]
[[,] MOVE 'logical_file_name' TO 'operating_system_file_name']
[,…p]
```

```
[[,] {NORECOVERY | RECOVERY | STANDBY = undo_file_name}]
[[,] {NOUNLOAD | UNLOAD}]
[[,] RESTART]
[[,] STATS [= percentage]]
[[,] STOPAT = {date_time | @date_time_var}]
]

<backup_device> :: =
{
{'backup_device_name' | @backup_device_name_var}
| {DISK | TAPE | PIPE} =
{'temp_backup_device' | @temp_backup_device_var}
}

<file_or_filegroup> :: =
{
FILE = {logical_file_name | @logical_file_name_var}
|
FILEGROUP = {logical_filegroup_name | @logical_filegroup_name_var}
}
```

The arguments are:

DATABASE	If DATABASE is used, it instructs Microsoft SQL Server to do a complete restore of the database. You can also use this with a list of files or filegroups limiting the database restore to the files and/or filegroups named. Microsoft SQL Server now backs up only enough of the log to create the database with transaction integrity when the backup file is restored.
{database_name | @database_name_var}	Database_name is the name of the database involved in the restore procedure. You can pass in the database name in the form of a variable or a constant string.
FROM	FROM defines the backup devices from which to restore. Omitting the FROM clause can be used to recover a non-suspect database that has been restored with the NORECOVERY option, or to switch over to a standby server. If the FROM clause is left out, NORECOVERY, RECOVERY, or STANDBY must be given.

<backup_device>	Backup_device is the logical name for the backup device created by sp_addumpdevice.
{DISK | TAPE | PIPE} = 'temp_backup_device' | @temp_backup_device_var	Allows backups to be restored from the named disk, tape, or pipe device. DISK = 'c:\mssql7\backup\myback.dat' or TAPE = '\\.\TAPE0'. A device type of pipe names the pipe used by the client application for use by third-party vendors.
n	N means the preceding entry is repeatable.
DBO_ONLY	DBO_ONLY means that only the Database Owner can access the restored database.
FILE = file_number	File_number is the number of the backup set to be restored as the set appears on the media.
MEDIANAME = {media_name | @media_name_variable}	MEDIANAME is the media name for the entire backup set. This must match the media name on the backup volume(s). Using media names in BACKUP and RESTORE operations is a safety check.
MOVE 'logical_file_name' TO 'operating_system_file_name'	MOVE determines that the logical_file_name be moved to operating_system_file_name with a default of restoring the logical_file_name to its starting location. You can use this to relocate a database to another server.
p	P means you can list multiple MOVE statements.
NORECOVERY	No uncommitted transactions will be rolled back. You must specify either the NORECOVERY or RECOVERY is the default. Use NORECOVERY on all but the final RESTORE when you are restoring a database and transaction logs. NORECOVERY makes the database unusable when all the transaction logs have not been applied. If you use STANDBY, the database will be usable in read-only mode. RECOVERY is the default.
RECOVERY	Uncommitted transactions will be rolled back, making the database available. RECOVERY should not be specified when another transaction log is to be applied to the database.

STANDBY = undo_file_name	This is the filename where the data is stored to undo the recovery efforts. You can look at the database between transaction log restores, unlike NORECOVERY. If the file is not on the operating system it will be created. If the file exists, it will be overwritten.
NOUNLOAD	NOUNLOAD means that the tape will not automatically unload from the tape drive after a restore. This setting is set this way until the UNLOAD is given in a restore command to change the setting.
UNLOAD	This argument determines that the tape automatically rewinds and unloads when the restore is complete. This is the default setting for this tape drive behavior. This setting is set this way until the NOUNLOAD is given in a restore command to change the setting.
REPLACE	REPLACE means that SQL Server will destroy the database and recreate it according to the specification in the backup set. If you do not use the REPLACE option, the database will not be restored under the following conditions: The database already exists on the server—without REPLACE, restore will not occur. The database name is different from the database name in the backup set—without REPLACE, restore will not occur. The set of files in the database is different from the set of database files contained in the backup set—without REPLACE, restore will not occur. File size differences are not recognized by Microsoft SQL Server in the restore process and they are not checked when a restore occurs.
RESTART	RESTART is the option that allows the restore to be restarted if it was interrupted. To restart the restore, repeat the RESTORE command and specify RESTART option. There is a caveat to this option, however: it can only be used for restores from tape media and restores that are written across multiple tape volumes.

STATS [= percentage]	The percent complete statistics will be shown if this is specified. If not provided, the default is 10 percent.
<file_or_filegroup>	Use this argument when the size of the database is so large that a full database backup is not advisable in terms of performance. This can be one file or multiple files or one filegroup or multiple filegroups.
FILE = {logical_file_name | @logical_file_name_var}	FILE defines the files to include in the database restore.
FILEGROUP = {logical_filegroup_name | @logical_filegroup_name_var}	FILEGROUP defines the filegroups to include in the database restore. You must apply the log to the database files immediately after the last file or filegroup restore operation to roll the files forward to the condition of the rest of the database. If the files were not modified since they were backed up, no log must be applied. If indexes were created on these filegroups since the last time these files were backed up, more than one filegroup may be required.
m	M means that multiple files and filegroups can be used in the one RESTORE statement.
LOG	Only a transaction log backup is restored. To apply more than one transaction log, the NORECOVERY argument must be used in all but the restore of the last log.
STOPAT = date_time | @date_time_var	STOPAT controls the date and time of exactly when to stop restoring. Only transactions committed before the STOPAT date and time will be restored to the database.

Example

Here's an example of restoring a database with files, a filegroup, and a transaction log:

```
RESTORE DATABASE MyDB
FILE = 'MyDB_data_1',
FILE = 'MyDB_data_2',
```

```
FILEGROUP = 'My_filegroup'
FROM MyDB_1
WITH NORECOVERY
GO
RESTORE LOG MyDB
FROM MyDBLog1
GO
```

In this example, a database is restored by restoring the files, filegroup, and log of the MyDB database.

Example

Here's an example of a full database and a differential backup:

```
RESTORE DATABASE MyDB
FROM MyDB_1
WITH NORECOVERY
GO
RESTORE DATABASE MyDB
FROM MyDB_1
WITH FILE = 2
GO
```

In this example, a full database restore and a differential database restore is done. The differential was placed as file 2 on the backup file.

Example

Here's an example of restoring a full database and transaction log:

```
RESTORE DATABASE MyNwind
FROM MyNwind_1
WITH NORECOVERY,
MOVE 'MyDB' TO 'c:\mssql7\data\MyNewDB.mdf',
MOVE 'MyDBLog1' TO 'c:\mssql7\data\MyNewDB.ldf'
RESTORE LOG MyDB
FROM MyDBLog1
WITH RECOVERY
```

In this example, a database and a transaction log are restored and the MOVE statement causes the data and log file to be restored to the locations provided.

Example

Here's an example of restoring to a point-in-time using STOPAT:

```
RESTORE DATABASE MyDB
FROM MyDB_1, MyDB_2
WITH NORECOVERY
GO
RESTORE LOG MyDB
FROM MyDBLog1
WITH NORECOVERY
GO
RESTORE LOG MyDB
FROM MyDBLog2
WITH RECOVERY, STOPAT = 'Sept 15, 1998 12:00 AM'
GO
```

In this example, a database is restored as of 12:00 A.M. on September 15, 1998.

Example

Here's an example of a full database backup:

```
RESTORE DATABASE MyDB
FROM MyDB_1
```

In this example, an entire database is restored.

RESTORE FILELISTONLY

RESTORE FILELISTONLY returns a listing of the database and log files in the backup set.

Syntax

The syntax is:

```
RESTORE FILELISTONLY
FROM <backup_device>
[WITH
[FILE = file_number]
[[, ] {NOUNLOAD | UNLOAD}]
]
```

```
<backup_device> :: =
{
{'backup_device_name' | @backup_device_namevar}
| {DISK | TAPE | PIPE} =
{'temp_backup_device' | @temp_backup_device_var}
}
```

See the RESTORE statement for the various arguments.

RESTORE HEADERONLY

RESTORE HEADERONLY returns the backup header information for all backup sets on a backup device.

Syntax

The syntax is:

```
RESTORE HEADERONLY
FROM <backup_device>
[WITH {NOUNLOAD | UNLOAD}]

<backup_device> :: =
{
{'backup_device_name' | @backup_device_name_var}
| {DISK | TAPE | PIPE} =
{'temp_backup_device' | @temp_backup_device_var}
}
```

See the RESTORE statement for the various arguments.

RESTORE LABELONLY

RESTORE LABELONLY returns information about the backup media of the backup device.

Syntax

The syntax is:

```
RESTORE LABELONLY
FROM <backup_device>
```

```
<backup_device> :: =
{
{'backup_device_name' | @backup_device_name_var}
| {DISK | TAPE | PIPE} =
{'temp_backup_device' | @temp_backup_device_var}
}
```

See the RESTORE statement for the various arguments.

RESTORE VERIFYONLY

RESTORE VERIFYONLY verifies that the backup set is all there and that all volumes can be read; it does NOT restore the backup or verify the data.

Syntax

The syntax is:

```
RESTORE VERIFYONLY
FROM <backup_device> [,…n]
[WITH
[FILE = file_number]
[[,] {NOUNLOAD | UNLOAD}]
[[,] LOADHISTORY]
]

<backup_device> :: =
{
{'backup_device_name' | @backup_device_name_var}
| {DISK | TAPE | PIPE} =
{'temp_backup_device' | @temp_backup_device_var}
}
```

See the RESTORE statement for the various arguments.

RETURN

The RETURN statement exits from a query or procedure without executing statements following the RETURN statement. User-defined return status values should not conflict with those reserved by SQL Server, 0 through negative 99.

If no return value is provided, the SQL Server value is used. The values 0 through -14 are currently used by SQL Server. Value and description are as follows: 0=Procedure was executed successfully, -1=Object is missing, -2=Data type error occurred, -3=Process was chosen as deadlock victim, -4=Permission error occurred, -5=Syntax error occurred, -6=Miscellaneous user error occurred, -7=Resource error occurred, -8=Nonfatal internal problem was encountered, -9=System limit was reached, -10=Fatal internal inconsistency occurred, -11=Fatal internal inconsistency occurred, -12=Table or index is corrupt, -13=Database is corrupt, -14=Hardware error occurred.

Syntax

The syntax is:

```
RETURN [(integer_expression)]
```

The argument, integer_expression, is the integer value returned to the calling stored procedure or application.

Example

Here's an example of using RETURN:

```
CREATE PROC MyProc
AS
DECLARE @rtn int
SELECT *
FROM SYSOBJECTS
If @@error = 0
BEGIN
SELECT @rtn = 0
END
ELSE
BEGIN
SELECT @rtn = 1
RETURN @rtn
@END
GO
```

In this example, you can take it further by executing the stored procedure, MyProc, and checking the return code for success or failure.

```
DECLARE @rtn int
EXEC @rtn = MyProc
IF @rtn = 0
PRINT 'Successful execution of MyProc stored procedure'
```

```
ELSE
PRINT 'Failed execution of MyProc stored procedure'
GO
```

REVERSE

REVERSE returns the reverse of a character expression. If you pass in 'pam', you will receive 'map' back.

Syntax

The syntax is:

```
REVERSE(character_expression)
```

The argument, character_expression, is an alphanumeric character or binary expression, a constant, variable, or column.

REVOKE

See Chapter 5.

RIGHT

RIGHT returns a character string beginning a given number of characters from the right.

Syntax

The syntax is:

```
RIGHT(character_expression, integer_expression)
```

The arguments are:

character_expression	Character_expression is a character or binary alphanumeric expression, a constant, variable, or column.
integer_expression	Integer_expression is a positive whole number.

ROLLBACK TRANSACTION

ROLLBACK TRANSACTION removes any data changes made since the beginning of the transaction; this is called rolling back a transaction to a savepoint or all the way to the beginning of the transaction.

Syntax

The syntax is:

```
ROLLBACK [TRAN[SACTION] [transaction_name |
@tran_name_variable |
savepoint_name |
@savepoint_variable] ]
```

The arguments are:

transaction_name	Transaction_name is the name given the transaction by BEGIN TRANSACTION.
@tran_name_variable	@tran_name_variable is the name of a user-defined variable holding a transaction name of data type CHAR, VARCHAR, NCHAR, or NVARCHAR.
savepoint_name	Savepoint_name is the *savepoint_name* given by a SAVE TRANSACTION statement.
@savepoint_variable	@savepoint_variable is the name of a user-defined variable holding a savepoint name of data type CHAR, VARCHAR, NCHAR, or NVARCHAR.

ROLLBACK WORK

ROLLBACK WORK is the same as ROLLBACK TRANSACTION, except that ROLLBACK TRANSACTION accepts a transaction name.

Syntax

The syntax is:

```
ROLLBACK [WORK]
```

ROUND

ROUND returns the numeric expression it is given, rounded to the length or precision provided.

Syntax

The syntax is:

```
ROUND(numeric_expression, length[, function])
```

The arguments are:

numeric_expression	Numeric_expression is an expression of decimal, float, int, money, numeric, real, smallint, smallmoney, or tinyint.
Length	Length is the precision to round to and is tinyint, smallint, or int. When length is negative, numeric_expression is rounded on the left side of the decimal point.
Function	Function is is tinyint, smallint, or int and is the operation to perform. If the value is 0, numeric_expression is rounded. If the value is not 0, numeric_expression is truncated.

RTRIM

RTRIM removes trailing blanks.

Syntax

The syntax is:

```
RTRIM(character_expression)
```

The argument character_expression, is a character or binary alphanumeric expression, a constant, variable, or column.

SAVE TRANSACTION

SAVE TRANSACTION creates a savepoint in a transaction.

Syntax

The syntax is:

```
SAVE TRAN[SACTION] {savepoint_name | @savepoint_variable}
```

The arguments are:

savepoint_name	The name of the savepoint.
@savepoint_variable	The name of a user-defined variable holding a savepoint name of data type CHAR, VARCHAR, NCHAR, or NVARCHAR.

SELECT

The SELECT statement returns rows from a database table.

Syntax

The syntax is:

```
SELECT
[ALL | DISTINCT]
[
TOP n [PERCENT] [WITH TIES]
]
{ <result_data> :: =
{ *
| [column_heading = ] column_name
| column_name [[AS] column_heading]
| column_name AS expression
| expression [AS] column_heading]
| GROUPING (column_name)
| IDENTITYCOL
| ROWGUIDCOL
| local_or_global_variable
| new_column_name = IDENTITY(data_type, seed, increment)
| fulltext_table.RANK
} [, …n]
| <variable_assignment> :: = {@local_variable = expression } [, …n]
}
[INTO new_table_name]
[FROM
{
<table_or_view>
| (select_statement) [AS] alias
| <table_or_view>
[ {CROSS | INNER }
|
{
FULL
| LEFT
| RIGHT
} [OUTER] [<join_hint>] JOIN <table_or_view>
ON search_conditions
]
```

```
| CONTAINSTABLE
( table, { column | *}, '<contains_search_condition>'
)
| FREETEXTTABLE
( table, {column | * }, 'freetext_string'
)
}[, …n]
]
[ WHERE
{ [ <search_conditions> ::=
[NOT] <predicate> [{AND | OR} [NOT] <predicate>]
] [, ...n]
[ | CONTAINS
( {column | *}, '<contains_search_condition>'
)
| FREETEXT
(
{column | * }, 'freetext_string'
)
] [, ...n]
| fulltext_table.fulltext_key_column = alias.[KEY]
}
]
[{
GROUP BY [ALL] {column_name} [, …n]]
[WITH {CUBE | ROLLUP}]
}]
[HAVING search_conditions]
[ORDER BY
{
{
{table. | view.}column_name
| select_list_number
| expression
} [ASC | DESC]
} [, …n]
]
[COMPUTE row_aggregate({expression | column_name}[, …n])
[BY {expression | column_name}[, …n]]
]
[FOR BROWSE]
[OPTION (<query_hint> [, ... n])]
```

```
<table_or_view> ::=
{
table [[AS] alias] [WITH(<table_hint> [ ...m])]
| view [[AS] alias]
| OPENROWSET( 'provider_name',
{
'datasource';'user_id';'password'
| 'provider_string'
},
{
[catalog.][schema.]object_name
| 'query'
})
| OPENQUERY(linked_server, 'query')
}

<table_hint> ::=
([INDEX =
{
index_name
| index_id]
} [, …n]
[FASTFIRSTROW]
[HOLDLOCK] [NOLOCK] [PAGLOCK] [READCOMMITTED]
[READPAST] [READUNCOMMITTED] [REPEATABLEREAD]
[ROWLOCK] [SERIALIZABLE] [TABLOCK] [TABLOCKX]
[UPDLOCK])

<join_hint> ::=
{
HASH
| LOOP
| MERGE
}

<query_hint> :: =
{ {HASH | ORDER} GROUP
| {MERGE | HASH | CONCAT} UNION
| FAST n
| FORCE ORDER
| ROBUST PLAN
}
```

The arguments are:

SELECT ALL	ALL allows duplicate rows in the result set.
DISTINCT	DISTINCT retrieves only unique rows for the result set.
TOP n	TOP means only the first n rows are returned.
PERCENT	PERCENT returns the first n % of the rows.
WITH TIES	WITH TIES is only used with an ORDER BY clause and is used with TOP and PERCENT. WITH TIES sometimes returns more rows than the number n (user specified number) if the rows are tied to each other by having the same value in the ORDER BY columns.
<result_data>	Result data is what you want SQL Server to return back to you. It can be a column(s), expression, or an assignment of a variable or an asterisk (*) meaning all the columns in a table.
Column_heading	Column_heading is used if you would like to create a column heading as you wish to see it, instead of the column heading SQL Server supplies. You can choose from the following syntax: column_name AS column_heading column_heading = column_name. column_name column_heading.
GROUPING	GROUPING is used with GROUP BY and CUBE or ROLLUP and is applied to a column name in the result set, which is also a GROUP BY column. It outputs an extra column where a value of 1 signifies that CUBE or ROLLUP added the summary row and the value is NULL, or a value of 0, which means the null value is in the result set for the column.
IDENTITYCOL	IDENTITYCOL means the column name of the identity column in the table.
ROWGUIDCOL	ROWGUIDCOL means the uniqueidentifier column is a row global unique identifier column.

local_or_global_variable	Local_or_global_variable specifies a local or global variable name.
new_column_name	New_column_name defines a new column of NOT NULL tinyint, smallint, int, decimal, or numeric data type.
IDENTITY	IDENTITY is used with SELECT INTO and means the column will use the IDENTITY property.
data_type	Data_type refers to the data type of the identity column and can be int, smallint, tinyint, decimal, or numeric.
seed	Seed is used with IDENTITY and is the value of the first row in the table. The default is 1.
increment	Increment is the value to increment the seed value by when adding the next row to a table. It will then increment from the last row added to insert the next rows in the table.
n	N means the preceding entry is repeatable.
fulltext_table	Fulltext_table is the table marked for full-text querying.
RANK	RANK is used with a full-text query and displays the ranking value for each row.
<variable_assignment>	Variable_assignment is the assignment of a value to a local variable.
@local_variable = expression	@ local_variable = expression is the assignment of a value to a local variable. If possible, it is better to use the SET statement to do this because if your SELECT statement returns more than one value, the variable is set to the last row returned. If no rows are returned, the variable keeps the value it had before the execution of the SELECT statement. If a subquery is making the assignment and there are no rows returned, the value is set to NULL.
INTO new_table_name	INTO new_table_name creates a table with the columns in the return set.
<table_or_view>	Table_or_view is the name of the table or view.

alias	Alias is the name of a column or view alias and is required for derived tables. It is usually shorter than the actual name, which makes it easier to use to qualify ambiguous duplicate column names when two tables with columns of the same name are used in the SELECT statement.
<table_hint>	Table_hint instructs SQL Server on optimization methods. Table hints should be placed within parentheses. This is provided, but SQL Server can usually find the most optimal method by itself. Available table hints consist of PAGLOCK, NOLOCK, ROWLOCK, TABLOCK, TABLOCKX, HOLDLOCK, NOLOCK, READCOMMITTED, REPEATABLEREAD, SERIALIZABLE, NOLOCK and READPAST.
INDEX = {index_name | index_id}	INDEX = the index names or index object IDs to use for a table. Clustered index presence means that INDEX = 0 uses the clustered index; INDEX = 1 also causes a clustered index scan. No clustered index and use of INDEX = 0 causes a table scan, and use of INDEX = 1 causes an error.
n	n means the preceding is repeatable.
FASTFIRSTROW	FASTFIRSTROW is the same as using FAST 1, which means the optimizer will return the first row as fast as it can and then continue to produce the remainder of the rows in the query.
HOLDLOCK	HOLDLOCK is the same as SERIALIZABLE and is mutually exclusive of the FOR BROWSE clause. It holds shared locks for the duration of the transaction instead of releasing access of the page that is complete.
NOLOCK	NOLOCK does dirty reads and does not perform shared or exclusive locks. It is possible uncommitted transactions can be read, which means NOLOCK can result in the reading of inconsistent data and could result in errors 605, 606, 624, or 625; this means you should try the statement again.

PAGLOCK	PAGLOCK issues shared page locks instead of a shared table lock.
READCOMMITTED	READCOMMITTED provides for a higher consistency when reading data by holding shared locks and not allowing dirty reads but allowing the data to be updated. This can cause non-repeatable reads.
READPAST	READPAST skips rows with row level locks.
READUNCOMMITTED	READUNCOMMITTED is the same as NOLOCK.
REPEATABLEREAD	REPEATABLEREAD usage places locks on all the data in the query but still allows rows to be inserted by someone else and can still result in phantom rows and allows less concurrency that the default.
ROWLOCK	ROWLOCK issues a shared row lock instead for a shared page or table lock.
SERIALIZABLE	SERIALIZABLE is the same as HOLDLOCK.
TABLOCK	TABLOCK issues a shared table lock on the table until the end of the statement.
TABLOCKX	TABLOCKX issues an exclusive table lock until the end of the statement or the transaction.
UPDLOCK	UPDLOCK issues update locks until the end of the statement or the transaction.
<join_hint>	<join_hint> instructs SQL Server in the execution strategy of the join.
{LOOP | HASH | MERGE}	{LOOP | HASH | MERGE} allows you to control the join strategy used by the query optimizer and performs a nested loop join, a hash join, or a merge join depending on what is specified.
OpenRowset	OpenRowset defines connection information to query remote data from a data source.
OpenQuery	OpenQuery usage results in the execution of a pass-through query.
select_statement	Select_statement is a query that returns rows from a database.

CROSS JOIN	CROSS JOIN is the cross product of two tables returning rows as if there is no WHERE clause.
INNER	INNER join is the default and returns matching rows.
LEFT [OUTER]	LEFT [OUTER] join returns all rows from the left table even if they do not have corresponding rows in the RIGHT table; however, the columns for the RIGHT table are NULL.
RIGHT [OUTER]	RIGHT [OUTER] join returns all rows from the right table even if they do not have corresponding rows in the LEFT table; however, the columns for the LEFT table are returned as NULL
FULL [OUTER]	FULL [OUTER] join usage results in rows returned from either the left or right table that do not meet the join criteria with the rows in the other table returned as NULL in addition to the other matching rows that do meet the join criteria.
CONTAINSTABLE	CONTAINSTABLE returns a result table for character columns for precise or less precise matches.
FREETEXTTABLE	FREETEXTTABLE returns a result table for character columns matching the meaning rather that the wording.
<search_conditions>	<search_conditions> are the limiting conditions in the query.
CONTAINS	CONTAINS is a character column search for precise and less precise matches.
FREETEXT	FREETEXT is a character column search for matches of the meaning.
fulltext_table	Fulltext_table is the name of the table or alias marked for full-text querying.
fulltext_key_column	Fulltext_key_column is the full-text key column in the fulltext_table marked for full-text querying.
[KEY]	[KEY] indicates that rows meeting the <contains_search_condition> are chosen for selection.

GROUP BY	GROUP BY groups the rows into groups that have the same values in the GROUP BY column(s); the SELECT statement may also contain aggregate functions for summarization of the columns per group.
ALL	ALL specifies that all groups and result sets are returned even if they do not meet the search conditions of the WHERE clause and returns NULL in the summary columns for the groups not meeting the search conditions. This ALL must follow the GROUP BY clause.
CUBE	CUBE not only returns the GROUP BY aggregate rows but also summary rows created by grouping on a subset of the expressions or columns in the GROUP BY clause called super-aggregate rows.
ROLLUP	ROLLUP indicates a subset of super-aggregates and is created along with the usual aggregate rows in the GROUP BY clause.
HAVING	HAVING defines the conditions for the GROUP BY clause the same way the WHERE clause defines conditions for the SELECT statement individual rows.
ORDER BY	ORDER BY determines the sort order of the columns returned by SQL Server.
select_list_number	Select_list_number is the position of the expression in the <result_data> and this number may be used instead of the expression in the ORDER BY clause.
ASC	ASC (ascending) indicates the sorted data resulting from an ORDER BY clause is returned smallest to largest.
DESC	DESC (descending) indicates the sorted data resulting from an ORDER BY clause is returned largest first.

COMPUTE	COMPUTE creates summary rows in the result set for row aggregate functions. The COMPUTE clause is used to calculate summary values for subgroupings or for calculating multiple aggregate functions for the same group breaking at summary changes in the groups for the aggregate functions SUM, AVG, MIN, MAX, and COUNT. You can then see the detail and the summary rows. Using COMPUTE BY means you must also use the ORDER BY clause; however, ORDER BY is optional if you use COMPUTE without BY.
row_aggregate	Row_aggregate functions are AVG, COUNT, MAX, MIN, and SUM.
BY	BY indicates you would like row-aggregate functions to calculate for subgroups. When the value of the subgroup changes, a break occurs and the aggregate function values are created as a new row in the result set. Use of BY means that ORDER BY must be used with COMPUTE BY. If there is more than one expression after the BY, it causes the aggregate function to summarize at each level.
FOR BROWSE	FOR BROWSE allows updates if data is being viewed in applications using DB-Library.
<query_hint>	<query_hint> instructs the query optimizer how to optimize the query; however, SQL Server usually knows how to optimize without the user specifying a query hint.
{HASH | ORDER} GROUP	{HASH | ORDER} GROUP instructs SQL Server to use hashing or ordering for the aggregations in the ORDER BY or COMPUTE clause.
{MERGE | HASH | CONCAT} UNION	{MERGE | HASH | CONCAT} UNION instructs SQL Server to use merging, hashing, or concatenating for UNION operations.
FAST n	FAST n means the optimizer will return the first n rows as fast as it can and will then continue to produce the remainder of the rows in the query.

FORCE ORDER	FORCE ORDER instructs SQL Server to keep the join order specified in the query syntax during query optimization.
ROBUST PLAN	ROBUST PLAN instructs the SQL Server query optimizer to create a query plan for the maximum potential row size.

Example

Here's an example of the SELECT statement:

```
SELECT a.Column1, b.Column2
FROM    MyTable a,
         YourTable b
WHERE a.Column3 = b.Column3
ORDER BY a.Column1
```

In this example, an INNER JOIN is performed and the result set is sorted.

SESSION_USER

SESSION_USER is a niladic function supplying the value of the user name running the current session.

Syntax

The syntax is:

```
SESSION_USER
```

SET @local_variable

SET @local_variable sets a local variable to some value.

Syntax

The syntax is:

```
SET
{
{@local_variable = expression}
| { @cursor_variable =
{ @cursor_variable
| cursor_name
```

```
| { CURSOR
[FORWARD_ONLY | SCROLL]
[STATIC | KEYSET | DYNAMIC]
[READ_ONLY | SCROLL_LOCKS | OPTIMISTIC]
FOR select_statement
[FOR {READ ONLY | UPDATE [OF column_list] } ]}}}}
```

The arguments are:

@local_variable	@local_variable is a variable but not a cursor variable.
expression	Expression is any Microsoft SQL Server expression.
cursor_variable	Cursor_variable refers to the name of a cursor variable.
cursor_name	Cursor_name refers to the name of a cursor.
CURSOR	CURSOR means that this SET statement has a declaration of a cursor.
SCROLL	SCROLL describes the cursor, indicating that the FIRST, LAST, NEXT, PRIOR, RELATIVE, and ABSOLUTE scrolling of the cursor can occur.
FORWARD_ONLY	FORWARD_ONLY usage restricts the scrolling of the cursor to the FETCH NEXT.
STATIC	A STATIC cursor uses a temporary table in tempdb to hold cursor data, and updates to the data in the database are not noticed by the cursor fetches.
KEYSET	KEYSET usage means the order and the rows in the cursor are fixed when the cursor is opened. The set of unique keys is inserted into a tempdb table called the keyset. Changes to nonkey values by the current user or other users can be seen as the cursor is scrolled, but inserts made by concurrent users cannot be seen. Attempts to fetch a deleted row returns an @@FETCH_STATUS value of –2. Key column updates from other users are an insert and delete, and the insert cannot be seen. Attempts to fetch the deleted row results in an @@FETCH_STATUS value of –2. However, usage of the WHERE CURRENT OF syntax will result in the new rows being visible.

DYNAMIC	DYNAMIC usage for a cursor makes all data changes visible as the cursor scrolls, and every fetch changes the cursor. This means that absolute and relative fetch aren't used with DYNAMIC.
READ_ONLY	READ_ONLY defines a read-only cursor that cannot perform updates.
SCROLL LOCKS	SCROLL LOCKS means the cursor rows are locked as they are read and updates made later will proceed unhampered.
OPTIMISTIC	OPTIMISTIC usage means that updates or deletes by cursor will not be made if the row has changed since it was fetched. This is accomplished by comparisons of timestamp values or checksum if there is not timestamp column.
FOR select_statement	FOR select_statement is the query returning the data for the cursor.
READ ONLY	READ ONLY is the same as READ_ONLY.
UPDATE [OF column_list]	UPDATE [OF column_list] lists the updateable columns for the cursor.

Example

Here's an example of the SET statement:

```
DECLARE Cursor1 CURSOR GLOBAL FOR SELECT * FROM MyTable
DECLARE @Cursor1_variable CURSOR
SET @Cursor1_variable = Cursor1
DEALLOCATE Cursor1 /* There is now only a LOCAL variable
reference (@my_variable) to the my_cursor
cursor. */
```

In this example, a local variable is set with a reference to the cursor called Cursor1.

SET

The SET statement alters the current session's behavior based on the value of certain settings.

SET ANSI_DEFAULTS

SET ANSI_DEFAULTS turns on or off the Microsoft SQL Server settings determining SQL-92 standard behavior.

Syntax

The syntax is:

```
SET ANSI_DEFAULTS {ON | OFF}
```

SET ANSI_NULL_DFLT_OFF

SET ANSI_NULL_DFLT_OFF to ON to change the default of allowing null in the new column when a column is added with the CREATE or ALTER statement. If this setting is ON, the new column will require a value other than NULL.

Syntax

The syntax is:

```
SET ANSI_NULL_DFLT_OFF {ON | OFF}
```

SET ANSI_NULL_DFLT_ON

SET ANSI_NULL_DFLT_ON to OFF to change the default of allowing null in the new column when a column is added with the CREATE or ALTER statement. If this setting is OFF, the column will require a value other than NULL.

Syntax

The syntax is:

```
SET ANSI_NULL_DFLT_ON {ON | OFF}
```

SET ANSI_NULLS

SET ANSI_NULLS to ON to have the equal sign and the not equal sign evaluate a value compared to a NULL value to unknown. Set it to OFF to have a value compared to a NULL evaluate to true if the value was NULL and false if it wasn't.

Syntax

The syntax is:

```
SET ANSI_NULLS {ON | OFF}
```

SET ANSI_PADDING

SET ANSI_PADDING to ON is recommended for this setting and determines how trailing blanks are stored for char, binary, varchar, and varbinary data types. When set to ON for new char columns, trailing blanks are inserted to fill the length of the column; for new binary columns, trailing zeroes are inserted to fill the length of the column. For new varchar and varbinary columns, inserted values with trailing values are not trimmed, and trailing values are not added to fill the length of the column. When this setting is OFF, char and binary columns that are NOT NULL are padded with trailing values to fill the length of the column, but char and binary columns that are NULL behave the same as varchar and varbinary. In these cases, trailing values are trimmed and trailing values are not padded to the length of the new column.

Syntax

The syntax is:

```
SET ANSI_PADDING {ON | OFF}
```

SET ANSI_WARNINGS

SET ANSI_WARNINGS to ON warns with a message if NULL appears in aggregate functions. Divide by zero and overflow errors roll back the statement and warn with a message. INSERT and UPDATE statements are aborted if the length of the new value is longer than the char, Unicode, or binary column.

SET ANSI_WARNINGS to OFF does not warn with a message if NULL appears in aggregate functions. Divide by zero or overflow errors returns NULL. INSERT and UPDATE returns NULL values if the length of the new value is longer than the char, Unicode, or binary column.

Syntax

The syntax is:

```
SET ANSI_WARNINGS {ON | OFF}
```

SET ARITHABORT

If you SET ARITHABORT to ON, divide by zero and overflow error will cause Transact-SQL to terminate and/or rollback the transaction.

If you SET ARITHABORT to OFF, divide by zero and overflow error will cause a warning with a message but Transact-SQL continues to execute.

Syntax

The syntax is:

```
SET ARITHABORT {ON | OFF}
```

SET ARITHIGNORE

If SET ARITHIGNORE is set to OFF and SET ANSI_WARNINGS is set to OFF, a warning on a divide by zero or arithmetic overflow will not be issued.

Syntax

The syntax is:

```
SET ARITHIGNORE {ON | OFF}
```

SET CONCAT_NULL_YIELDS_NULL

SET CONCAT_NULL_YIELDS_NULL to ON and the result of concatenating a NULL value with a string returns NULL.

SET CONCAT_NULL_YIELDS_NULL to OFF and the result of concatenating a NULL value with a string returns the string.

Syntax

The syntax is:

```
SET CONCAT_NULL_YIELDS_NULL {ON | OFF}
```

SET CURSOR_CLOSE_ON_COMMIT

SET CURSOR_CLOSE_ON_COMMIT to ON closes open cursors on commit. SET CURSOR_CLOSE_ON_COMMIT to OFF does not close open cursors on commit.

Syntax

The syntax is:

```
SET CURSOR_CLOSE_ON_COMMIT {ON | OFF}
```

SET DATEFIRST

SET DATEFIRST determines the first day of the week where 1 is Monday, 2 is Tuesday, etc., to a number from 1 through 7. The U.S. English default is 7 (Sunday).

Syntax

The syntax is:

```
SET DATEFIRST {number | @number_var}
```

The argument number | @number_var is an integer with Sunday the default for U.S. English.

SET DATEFORMAT

SET DATEFORMAT determines the order of the date parts, month, day, and year, for the date data types.

Syntax

The syntax is:

```
SET DATEFORMAT {format | @format_var}
```

The argument, format | @format_var, has valid values of mdy, dmy, ymd, ydm, myd, and dym with a U.S. English default of mdy.

SET DEADLOCK_PRIORITY

SET DEADLOCK PRIORITY determines what happens in the current session when a deadlock occurs.

Syntax

The syntax is:

```
SET DEADLOCK_PRIORITY {LOW | NORMAL | @deadlock_var}
```

The arguments are:

LOW	LOW chooses the current session as the deadlock victim and rolls back the transaction.
NORMAL	NORMAL allows SQL Server to determine the deadlock victim according to default behavior.
@deadlock_var	*@deadlock_var* is a string variable.

SET DISABLE_DEF_CNST_CHK

This setting is for backward compatibility only and cannot be turned ON in this version.

SET FIPS_FLAGGER

SET FIPS_FLAGGER controls the level of compliance threshold for warning messages with the FIPS 127-2 standard based on the SQL-92 standard.

Syntax

The syntax is:

```
SET FIPS_FLAGGER 'level'
```

The argument, level, must be ENTRY, FULL, INTERMEDIATE, or OFF.

SET FMTONLY

SET FMTONLY to ON returns no rows, only metadata.

Syntax

The syntax is:

```
SET FMTONLY {ON | OFF}
```

SET FORCEPLAN

SET FORCEPLAN instructs SQL Server to process joins in the order that the join tables are in the FROM clause.

Syntax

The syntax is:

```
SET FORCEPLAN {ON | OFF}
```

SET IDENTITY_INSERT

SET IDENTITY_INSERT to ON permits the insertion of user-defined values into an identity column.

Syntax

The syntax is:

```
SET IDENTITY_INSERT [database.[owner.]]{table} {ON | OFF}
```

The arguments are:

database — Database is the database name.

owner — Owner is the owner of the affected table.

table — Table is the name of a table containing the identity column.

SET IMPLICIT_TRANSACTIONS

SET IMPLICIT_TRANSACTIONS to ON sets the connection to implicit transaction mode, which means if a connection is not in a transaction, FETCH, DROP, OPEN, DELETE, SELECT, REVOKE, CREATE, ALTER TABLE, TRUNCATE TABLE, GRANT, INSERT, UPDATE starts a transaction. If the setting is OFF, the connection is in autocommit transaction mode.

Syntax

The syntax is:

```
SET IMPLICIT_TRANSACTIONS {ON | OFF}
```

SET LANGUAGE

SET LANGUAGE determines the language for the session in terms of date formats and system messages.

Syntax

The syntax is:

```
SET LANGUAGE {language | @language_var}
```

The argument, language | @language_var, is the name of the language in the syslanguages system table. The variable must be of data type sysname.

SET LOCK_TIMEOUT

SET LOCK_TIMEOUT is the number of milliseconds a process waits when it needs a locked resource.

Syntax

The syntax is:

```
SET LOCK_TIMEOUT [timeout_period]
```

The argument *timeout_period* is the number of milliseconds before the lock is released or an error is returned with a default of –1 no waiting.

SET NOCOUNT

SET NOCOUNT to ON keeps the informational message about the count of rows from being displayed in the return set.

Syntax

The syntax is:

```
SET NOCOUNT {ON | OFF}
```

SET NOEXEC

SET NOEXEC to ON does not execute the Transact-SQL statements that follow until you SET NOEXEC to OFF; however, the statements still go through the compilation stage.

Syntax

The syntax is:

```
SET NOEXEC {ON | OFF}
```

SET NUMERIC_ROUNDABORT

SET NUMERIC_ROUNDABORT to ON causes an error to occur when a loss of precision occurs in an expression by rounding into a column with less precision than the result.

Syntax

The syntax is:

```
SET NUMERIC_ROUNDABORT {ON | OFF}
```

SET OFFSETS

SET OFFSETS is used for DB-Library applications and returns the position relative to the start of a statement of a user-defined, comma-separated list of Transact-SQL keywords from the following selection: SELECT, FROM, ORDER, COMPUTE, TABLE, PROCEDURE, STATEMENT, PARAM, and EXECUTE.

Syntax

The syntax is:

```
SET OFFSETS keyword_list
```

The argument, keyword_list, is a comma-separated list of Transact-SQL keywords.

SET PARSEONLY

SET PARSEONLY checks syntax but does not compile or execute the Transact-SQL statement.

Syntax

The syntax is:

```
SET PARSEONLY {ON | OFF}
```

SET PROCID

If you use SET PROCID ON, the identification number of the stored procedure is sent to DB-Library applications before sending the result sets generated by that stored procedure.

Syntax

The syntax is:

```
SET PROCID {ON | OFF}
```

SET QUERY_GOVERNOR_COST_LIMIT

SET QUERY_GOVERNOR_COST_LIMIT allows all queries to run if the argument is 0 and will not run the queries that have a cost greater than the integer supplied in the argument.

Syntax

The syntax is:

```
SET QUERY_GOVERNCR_COST_LIMIT value
```

The argument, value, is an integer.

SET QUOTED_IDENTIFIER

If you use SET QUOTED_IDENTIFIER ON, names for identifiers are allowed to be key words and can also contain special characters when placed in double quotation marks. Literals must be placed in single quotation marks. The case may arise when a single quote is contained in the literal; in that case, substitute it with two single quotes to keep the syntax from failing.

If you use SET QUOTED_IDENTIFIER OFF, identifier name cannot be double-quoted and must play by the rules, while literals can be placed in pair single or double quotation marks and can contain single quotes if quoted in double quotes. If you use SET QUOTED_IDENTIFIER inside a stored procedure, it will be ignored. SET QUOTED_IDENTIFIER for a stored procedure is determined by what the setting was at compile time. The sp_dboption stored procedure using the quoted identifier argument can also affect this setting.

SET QUOTED_IDENTIFIER can cause confusion because it changes the functionality of the double-quote symbol. For this reason, it is wise practice to always use single quotes to delimit string literals and to use square brackets ([,]) to get the same functionality as Quoted Identifiers without changing the usage rules for double quotes. See Chapter 23 for this and other system stored procedures.

Syntax

The syntax is:

```
SET QUOTED_IDENTIFIER {ON | OFF}
```

SET REMOTE_PROC_TRANSACTIONS

If you use SET REMOTE_PROC_TRANSACTIONS ON, notice that a distributed transaction is started and managed by the Microsoft Distributed Transaction Coordinator, MS DTC, when a remote stored procedure is executed.

If you use SET REMOTE_PROC_TRANSACTIONS OFF, notice that a distributed transaction is not started.

Syntax

The syntax is:

```
SET REMOTE_PROC_TRANSACTIONS {ON | OFF}
```

SET ROWCOUNT

If you use SET ROWCOUNT and set it to a specific number, the query will quit processing after the rows are returned.

Syntax

The syntax is:

```
SET ROWCOUNT {number | @number_var}
```

The argument, number | @number_var, is an integer.

SET SHOWPLAN_ALL

If you use SET SHOWPLAN_ALL ON, the Transact-SQL statement will not be executed. Information is returned instead about how the query optimizer plans to execute the Transact-SQL statement and about the cost of the query from the cost-based optimizer. SET SHOWPLAN_ALL was written to format the output in a consistent way for programs scanning through and processing the output.

Syntax

The syntax is:

```
SET SHOWPLAN_ALL {ON | OFF}
```

SET SHOWPLAN_TEXT

If you use SET SHOWPLAN_TEXT ON, the Transact-SQL statement will not be executed. Information is returned instead about how the query optimizer plans to execute the Transact-SQL statement. This version of showplan is for a human being to process and examine the output.

Syntax

The syntax is:

```
SET SHOWPLAN_TEXT {ON | OFF}
```

SET STATISTICS IO

If you use SET STATISTICS IO ON, information about the name of the table, the scan count, the logical reads (the number of pages read from the data cache), physical reads (the number of pages read from disk), and read-ahead reads (the number of pages placed into the cache for the query) is displayed.

Syntax

The syntax is:

```
SET STATISTICS IO {ON | OFF}
```

SET STATISTICS PROFILE

SET STATISTICS PROFILE shows the profile information for ad hoc queries, views, triggers, and stored procedures.

Syntax

The syntax is:

```
SET STATISTICS PROFILE {ON | OFF}
```

SET STATISTICS TIME

If you use SET STATISTICS TIME ON, the number of milliseconds it takes to parse, compile, and execute the Transact-SQL statement is displayed.

Syntax

The syntax is:

```
SET STATISTICS TIME {ON | OFF}
```

SET TEXTSIZE

SET TEXTSIZE to a user-defined number and the length of the text and ntext data type is set to that number for display when a SELECT statement is issued.

Syntax

The syntax is:

```
SET TEXTSIZE {number | @number_var}
```

The argument, number | @number_var, is an integer with a maximum of 2GB.

SET TRANSACTION ISOLATION LEVEL

If you use SET TRANSACTION ISOLATION LEVEL and set it to one of the available choices of READ COMMITTED, READ UNCOMMITTED, REPEATABLE READ, or SERIALIZABLE, the default transaction locking will change to the selected choice for the current session's SELECT statements.

Syntax

The syntax is:

```
SET TRANSACTION ISOLATION LEVEL
{READ COMMITTED |READ UNCOMMITTED | REPEATABLE READ | SERIALIZABLE}
```

The arguments are:

READ COMMITTED	READ COMMITTED is the isolation level that holds shared locks for SELECT statements and is the Microsoft SQL Server default. This isolation level prevents dirty reads, meaning data is not read that has not been committed. This isolation level can produce the situation of a non-repeatable read, meaning the data can be changed by some other session and, when the data is read again, it may have changed prior to the end of the transaction. This transaction can also produce the case of phantom data, meaning that someone can add new data before the transaction has finished.

READ UNCOMMITTED	READ UNCOMMITTED (also called isolation level 0) allows a dirty read. This isolation level issues no locks and ignores any exclusive locks made by other users, the consequences of which are dirty reads, non-repeatable reads, and phantom data. This isolation level provides the most concurrency and least consistency and is the same as using NOLOCK.
REPEATABLE READ	REPEATABLE READ isolation level keeps other users from updating the data by placing locks on all the data used by the current transaction; however, phantom rows can still occur. This option can affect concurrency in a negative way and should be used with care and out of necessity.
SERIALIZABLE	SERIALIZABLE isolation level keeps other users from updating the data the transaction is using or from inserting new rows by placing a range lock on the data. This provides the least concurrency and the most consistency but should be used with care because other users are affected, and concurrency is affected in a negative way and is the same as using HOLDLOCK.

SET XACT_ABORT

If you use SET XACT_ABORT ON, the current transaction will roll back on a run-time error.

Syntax

The syntax is:

```
SET XACT_ABORT{ON | OFF}
```

SETUSER

SETUSER is not recommended for use in Microsoft SQL Server and is present only for backward compatibility. The SETUSER function is used by the system administrator and the database owner in order to assume the permissions of another user.

Syntax

The syntax is:

```
SETUSER ['username' [WITH NORESET]]
```

The arguments are:

'username'	The name of the security account that the SA or DBO is assuming permissions. If this is not given as a parameter, the original identity is assumed.
WITH NORESET	WITH NORESET determines that SETUSER statements issued later without using a supplied user name, do not reset to SA or DBO.

SHUTDOWN

The SHUTDOWN command stops Microsoft SQL Server.

Syntax

The syntax is:

```
SHUTDOWN [WITH NOWAIT]
```

The argument, WITH NOWAIT, does not perform checkpoints before stopping SQL Server. A rollback will occur for all transactions that are running.

SIGN

The SIGN function returns 1 if the expression is positive, -1 if it is negative, and 0 if it is 0.

Syntax

The syntax is:

```
SIGN(numeric_expression)
```

The argument, numeric_expression, is a decimal, float, int, money, numeric, real, smallint, smallmoney, or tinyint data type.

SIN

The SIN system stored procedure displays the trigonometric sine of the angle in a float expression in radians.

Syntax

The syntax is:

```
SIN(float_expression)
```

The argument, float_expression, is a float data type expression.

smalldatetime

See "Data Types" in this chapter.

smallint

See "Data Types" in this chapter.

smallmoney

See "Data Types" in this chapter.

SOME | ANY

SOME is also known as ANY, and both return true if the comparison of the initial expression and at least one of the values in the subquery returns true; otherwise it returns false.

Syntax

The syntax is:

```
scalar_expression { = | <> | != | > | >= | !> | < | <= | !< }
{SOME | ANY} (subquery)
```

The arguments are:

scalar_expression	Scalar_expression is any valid SQL expression.
{ = | <> | != | > | >= | !> | < | <= | !< }	These are the Microsoft SQL Server operators that can be used for comparison operations.
SOME | ANY	SOME or ANY are keywords indicating a comparison will take place.
Subquery	SUBQUERY used in this context must return only one column of the same data type as the scalar expression in the argument list.

SOUNDEX

SOUNDEX is used to determine if two strings are similar in sound and returns a four-character code. The first byte of the code is a character and is the first letter of the argument. The rest of the code contains numbers. Vowels are ignored unless they are the first position in the string. The letter *y*, doubled letters, and the letter *h* are ignored as well. A related function is the DIFFERENCE function. See "DIFFERENCE" in this chapter.

Syntax

The syntax is:

```
SOUNDEX(character_expression)
```

The argument, character_expression, is a string and can be a variable, a constant, or a column in a table.

Example

Here's an example of the SOUNDEX function:

```
SELECT SOUNDEX ('FOREX'), SOUNDEX ('FORX')
```

In this example, F620 is returned for 'FOREX' and for 'FORX' because they sound very similar.

SPACE

SPACE returns a string of repeated spaces; however, if you want to include spaces in Unicode data, use the REPLICATE function instead.

Syntax

The syntax is:

```
SPACE(integer_expression)
```

The argument, integer_expression, is an integer. This function returns a NULL value if integer_expression is a negative number.

SQUARE

SQUARE is a function that multiples a number of float data type by itself.

Syntax

The syntax is:

```
SQUARE(float_expression)
```

The argument, float_expression, is a float data type.

SQRT

SQRT is a function that returns the square root of a float data type.

Syntax

The syntax is:

```
SQRT(float_expression)
```

The argument, float_expression, is a float data type.

STATS_DATE

STATS_DATE is a function that returns the date and time the statistics for an index were updated last.

Syntax

The syntax is:

```
STATS_DATE(table_id, index_id)
```

The arguments are:

table_id	Table_id is the OBJECT_ID of the table.
index_id	Index_id is the indid of the index.

STDEV

STDEV is an aggregate function that returns the standard deviation. This functions much in the same way that other aggregate functions, such as SUM function, do and must be used with numeric data types only. NULL values in the supplied column are excluded from the input data set.

Syntax

The syntax is:

```
STDEV(expression)
```

The argument, expression, can be a constant, column name, or function and can also be expressed with the inclusion of operators.

Example

Here's an example of the STDEV function:

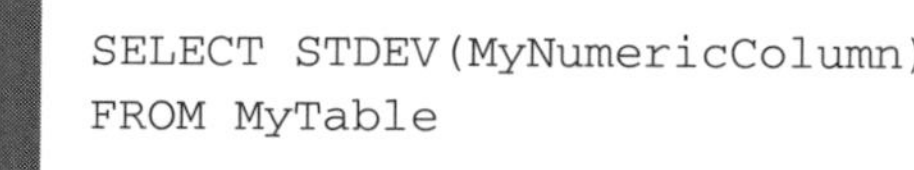

```
SELECT STDEV(MyNumericColumn)
FROM MyTable
```

In this example, the standard deviation is returned for all the numeric values in the column MyNumericColumn in the table, MyTable.

STDEVP

STDEVP is an aggregate function that returns the standard deviation for the population. This functions much in the same way that other aggregate functions, such as SUM function, do and must be used with numeric data types only. NULL values are ignored.

Syntax

The syntax is:

```
STDEVP(expression)
```

The argument, expression, can be a constant, column name, or function and can also be expressed with the inclusion of operators.

Example

Here's an example of the STDEVP function:

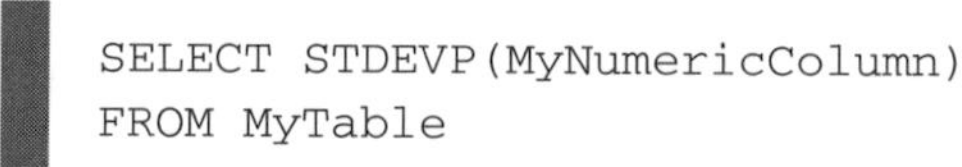

```
SELECT STDEVP(MyNumericColumn)
FROM MyTable
```

In this example, the standard deviation of the population is returned for all the numeric values in the column MyNumericColumn in the table, MyTable.

STR

The STR function returns character data by changing it to character data from numeric data and offers more than the CAST function in terms of functionality because it allows control over formatting of decimals. If the length is not large enough, asterisks are returned.

Syntax

The syntax is:

```
STR(float_expression[, length[, decimal]])
```

The arguments are:

float_expression	Float_expression is an expression with data type of float and can contain a decimal point.
length	Length is the entire length of the desired string with a default of 10 if this optional parameter is not supplied.
decimal	Decimal is the count of the places to the right of the decimal point.

STUFF

The STUFF function replaces one part of a character expression with another supplied part. The part is defined by a starting position and a length.

Syntax

The syntax is:

```
STUFF(character_expression, start, length, character_expression)
```

The arguments are:

character_expression	Character expression can be a character or binary constant, variable, or column.
Start	Start is an integer defining the starting position of the part of the character expression to begin replacing. If a negative value is supplied for this parameter or if the value is larger than the entire length of the character expression, NULL is returned.
length	LENGTH is an integer which determines the number of characters to replace.

Example

Here's an example of the STUFF function.

```
SELECT STUFF('My dog Fido', 8, 4, 'Sally')
GO
```

In this example, Fido is replaced with Sally starting at position 8 and deleting 4 characters and inserting 5 characters where the 4 characters were. That's why it is called STUFF. You can stuff in more that what was previously there if you wish; however, you can also replace with the same or fewer bytes.

SUBSTRING

The SUBSTRING function returns part of a character, binary, text, or image expression.

Syntax

The syntax is:

```
SUBSTRING(expression, start, length)
```

The arguments are:

expression	Expression in this case is a character string, binary string, text, image, or a column name, but not an aggregate function.
start	Start is an integer that tells where the part of the expression begins.
Length	Length is an integer determining the length of the part of the expression.

Example

Here's an example of the SUBSTRING function:

```
SELECT SUBSTRING('Microsoft',6,4)
```

In this example, the 4 characters, soft, part of the expression, Microsoft, are returned.

SUM

SUM is an aggregate function that returns the sum of all the numeric selected columns in selected rows in a table, or only the DISTINCT values of the numeric selected columns in selected rows in a table. A NULL value in one of the selected columns in a selected row means the row will be excluded.

Syntax

The syntax is:

```
SUM([ALL | DISTINCT] expression)
```

ALL	The ALL keyword is separate from DISTINCT and is the default that means all selected values are summed.
DISTINCT	The DISTINCT keyword usage determines that only the unique values are summed.
expression	Expession is any valid SQL Server expression returning a numeric value with the exception of aggregate functions and subqueries.

SUSER_ID

The SUSER_ID function returns the identification number of a SQL Server user and is used for backward compatibility only. A person coding in 7.0 will use SUSER_SID instead.

Syntax

The syntax is:

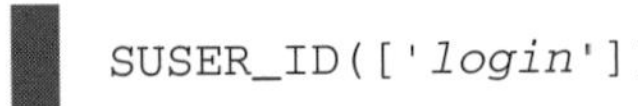

```
SUSER_ID(['login'])
```

The argument, login, is optional and is the name of a login ID. If not supplied, the default is the current user.

SUSER_NAME

The SUSER_NAME function returns the name of the login ID of a SQL Server user and is used for backward compatibility only. A person coding in 7.0 will use SUSER_SNAME instead.

Syntax

The syntax is:

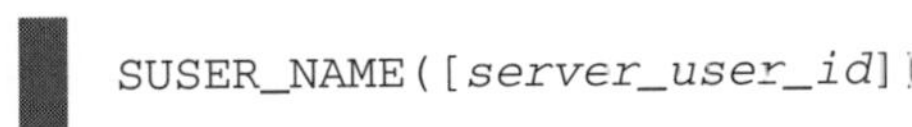

```
SUSER_NAME([server_user_id])
```

The argument, server_user_id, is optional and is the login ID number. If not supplied, the default is the current user.

SUSER_SID

SUSER_SID returns the security identification number also called the SID for the user-supplied Microsoft SQL Server security account name.

Syntax

The syntax is:

```
SUSER_SID(['login'])
```

The argument, login, is optional and is the name of a security account. If not supplied, the default is the current user.

SUSER_SNAME

SUSER_SNAME returns the Microsoft SQL Server security account name from a user's security identification number also called the SID.

Syntax

The syntax is:

```
SUSER_SNAME([server_user_sid])
```

The argument, server_user_sid, is optional and is the security identification number. If not supplied, the default is the current user.

SYSTEM_USER

SYSTEM_USER is a function that provides a system-supplied value of the NT account name if NT Authentication is used to authenticate the user, or it provides a system-supplied value of the SQL Server authenticated security account name if SQL Server Authentication is used. This function can be used either as a regular function, the default value for insertion into a table if no other default exists, or in a DEFAULT CONSTRAINT.

Syntax

The syntax is:

```
SYSTEM_USER
```

TAN

TAN returns the tangent of the float argument.

Syntax

The syntax is:

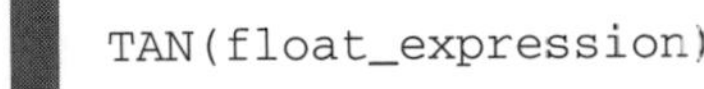

```
TAN(float_expression)
```

The argument, float_expression, is radians and is of float or real data type.

text

See Data Type in this chapter.

TEXTPTR

The TEXTPTR function is used to point to the first text page, and the result is in the form of varbinary.

Syntax

The syntax is:

```
TEXTPTR(column)
```

The argument, column, is the name of the column.

TEXTVALID

TEXTVALID is a function used for text, ntext, or image columns to check to see if a text pointer is valid returning 1 for valid and 0 for invalid. UPDATETEXT, WRITETEXT, and READTEXT depend upon the use of this function.

Syntax

The syntax is:

```
TEXTVALID('table.column', text_ ptr)
```

The arguments are:

table	Table is the name of the table.
Column	Column is the name of the column.
Text_ptr	Text_ptr is the text pointer to be validated.

timestamp

Timestamp is a data type for a column with only one per table and holds a binary(8) (or varbinary(8) if nullable) value that is unique in the database with the column being updated every time the row is inserted or updated.

tinyint

See "Data Type" in this chapter.

TRIGGER_NESTLEVEL

TRIGGER_NESTLEVEL returns how many triggers execute on a table for an UPDATE, INSERT, or DELETE operation.

Syntax

The syntax is:

```
TRIGGER_NESTLEVEL( [ object_id ] )
```

The argument, object_id, is the ID of the trigger. If not supplied, the integer returned represents how many times all triggers fired for the UPDATE, INSERT, or DELETE operation.

TRUNCATE TABLE

The TRUNCATE_TABLE statement deletes all rows from a table without logging but does not fire triggers.

Syntax

The syntax is:

```
TRUNCATE TABLE name
```

The argument, name, is the name of the table to truncate.

TYPEPROPERTY

TYPEPROPERTY is a function that returns types of information in the form of properties for a character or binary data type.

Syntax

The syntax is:

```
TYPEPROPERTY ( type, property )
```

The arguments are:

type	Type is the data type.

property	Property can be one of the following: Precision (the number of digits or characters) Scale (the number of decimals) AllowsNull (0=FALSE, 1=TRUE) UsesAnsiTrim (0=FALSE, 1=True)

UNICODE

UNICODE is a function that returns the Unicode standard integer value for the first byte of the argument.

Syntax

The syntax is:

```
UNICODE('ncharacter_expression')
```

The argument, ncharacter_expression, is nchar or nvarchar.

UNION

The UNION statement takes the results of more than one SELECT statement and merges the results.

Syntax

The syntax is:

```
select_statement
UNION [ALL]
select_statement
[UNION [ALL] select_statement][,...n]
```

The arguments are:

select_statement	Select_statement is a query that returns data.
UNION	UNION merges result sets from more than one query.
ALL	ALL returns all rows including duplicates; however, if this keyword is not supplied, duplicates will not be returned.
n	N means that the preceding entry is repeatable.

Example

Here's an example of the UNION statement:

```
SELECT FirstName, LastName
FROM MyFirstTable
UNION
SELECT FirstName, LastName
FROM MySecondTable
```

In this example, the results from MyFirstTable will be combined in the result set of MySecondTable and will return as one result set.

uniqueidentifier

See "Data Type" in this chapter.

UPDATE

The UPDATE statement modifies data in a table by changing a row(s) already in the table.

Syntax

The syntax is:

```
UPDATE {<table_or_view>}
SET
{column_name = {expression | DEFAULT}
| @variable = expression} [,…n]
[FROM
{
<table_or_view>
| (select_statement) [AS] table_alias [ (column_alias [,…m]) ]
| <table_or_view> CROSS JOIN <table_or_view>
| INNER [<join_hints>] JOIN
<table_or_view> ON <join_condition>
| <rowset_function>
}[, …n]
]
[WHERE
<search_conditions>
| CURRENT OF
{ { [GLOBAL] cursor_name } | cursor_variable_name} }
```

```
]
[OPTION (<query_hints>, [,...n] )]

<table_or_view> :: =
{ table_name [ [AS] table_alias ] [ <table_hints> [...m] ]
| view_name [ [AS] table_alias ]
}

<table_hints> ::=
{ INDEX = {index_name | index_id} [, …n]
| FASTFIRSTROW
| READPAST
| { HOLDLOCK | PAGLOCK | READCOMMITTED
| READUNCOMMITTED | REPEATABLEREAD
| ROWLOCK | SERIALIZABLE | TABLOCK | TABLOCKX
}

<table_hints> ::=
{ INDEX(index_name | index_id)
| FASTFIRSTROW
| HOLDLOCK
| PAGLOCK
| READCOMMITTED
| READPAST
| READUNCOMMITTED
| REPEATABLEREAD
| ROWLOCK
| SERIALIZABLE
| TABLOCK
| TABLOCKX}

<join_hints> ::=
{ HASH | LOOP | MERGE }

<query_hints> :: =
{ { HASH | ORDER } GROUP
| { CONCAT | HASH | MERGE } UNION
| FAST number_rows
| FORCE ORDER
| ROBUST PLAN}

<join_condition> :: =
```

```
{ table_name | table_alias | view_name }.column_name
<logical_operator>
{ table_name | table_alias | view_name }.column_name

<logical_operator>:: =
{ = | > | < | >= | <= | <> | != | !< | !> }

<rowset_function> :: =
{ OPENQUERY (linked_server, 'query')
| OPENROWSET
( 'provider_name',
{'datasource';'user_id';'password' | 'provider_string'},
{[catalog.][schema.]object_name | 'query'}))}

<search_conditions> ::=
{ [ NOT ] <predicate> [ { AND | OR } [ NOT ] <predicate> ]
} [, ...n]

<predicate> ::=
{
expression { = | <> | != | > | >= | !> | < | <= | !< } expression
| string_expression [NOT] LIKE string_expression
[ESCAPE 'escape_character']
| expression [NOT] BETWEEN expression AND expression
| expression IS [NOT] NULL
| expression [NOT] IN (subquery | expression [,...n])
| expression { = | <> | != | > | >= | !> | < | <= | !< }
{ALL | SOME | ANY} (subquery)
| EXISTS (subquery)}
```

The arguments are:

<table_or_view>	Table_or_view is the header for the name of the table or view.
table_name | view_name	table_name | view_name is the name of a table or view where the data is being updated. Only one table can be updated in a view.
table_alias	Alias is the short name given to a table or view.
column_alias	Column_alias is an alternate column heading.

<table_hints>	Table_hint tells the SQL Server query optimizer how to perform the query. See new optimizer hints in Chapter 6.
INDEX(index_name | index_id)	The index to use to process the query if giving an index optimizer hint.
m	M means the column alias is repeatable.
OPENQUERY	OPENQUERY runs the pass-through query. See "OPENQUERY" in this chapter.
OPENROWSET	OPENROWSET contains connection definitions to use remote data from a data source.
SET	The columns after the SET keyword are the columns being updated.
column_name	Column_name is the comma-separated list of terms of the form, column_name = expression.
expression	Expression is any valid SQL expression.
DEFAULT	DEFAULT sets the value in the column to the default value defined by the DEFAULT constraint for the column.
@variable	Is a declared variable that is set to the value returned by expression.
n	N means the preceding is repeatable.
FROM	FROM determines the table used to provide the values for the UPDATE.
CROSS JOIN	CROSS JOIN is the cross product of two tables returning rows as if there is no WHERE clause.
INNER	INNER join is the default and returns matching rows.
<join_hints>	<join_hint> instructs SQL Server in the execution strategy of the join.
ON <join_condition>	ON <join_condition> are the conditions of the join.
WHERE <search_conditions>	WHERE <search_conditions> are the limiting conditions in the query.
CURRENT OF	CURRENT OF is the current position of the cursor and points to the row affected by the update.

GLOBAL	GLOBAL indicates that the cursor is a GLOBAL cursor.
cursor_name	Cursor_name is the name of the cursor determining the updateable data set.
cursor_variable_name	Cursor_variable_name is the name of a cursor variable.
OPTION (<query_hints>, [,...n])	OPTION (<query_hints>, [,...n] instructs the query optimizer how to optimize the query; however, SQL Server usually knows how to optimize without the user specifying a query hint.
{HASH | ORDER} GROUP	{HASH | ORDER} GROUP instructs SQL Server to use hashing or ordering for the aggregations in the ORDER BY or COMPUTE clause.
{MERGE | HASH | CONCAT} UNION	{MERGE | HASH | CONCAT} UNION instructs SQL Server to use merging, hashing, or concatenating for UNION operations.
FAST n	FAST n (number_of_rows) means the optimizer will return the first n rows as fast as it can and will then continue to produce the remainder of the rows in the query.
FORCE ORDER	FORCE ORDER instructs SQL Server to keep the join order specified in the query syntax during query optimization.
ROBUST PLAN	ROBUST PLAN instructs the SQL Server query optimizer to create a query plan for the maximum potential row size.

Example

Here's an example of the UPDATE statement:

```
UPDATE MyTable
SET Column1 = b.Column1
FROM MyTable a,
     MyTable2 b
WHERE a.MyId = b.MyId
```

In this example, Column1 in MyTable is updated to Column1 in MyTable2 for the rows in MyTable that have matching values in the MyId column in MyTable and MyTable2.

UPDATE STATISTICS

The UPDATE STATISTICS statement refreshes information in the system tables related to the indexes in a table. This information is distribution data of the column values that SQL Server uses to construct its plan. This data should be updated after a significant portion of the data has changed, and the user can take advantage of the automatic statistics feature (via sp_autostats) to accomplish this rather than performing update statistics.

Syntax

The syntax is:

```
UPDATE STATISTICS {table} [index | (index_or_column[, ...n])]
[WITH [[FULLSCAN]| SAMPLE number {PERCENT | ROWS}]
[[,] [ALL | COLUMNS | INDEX][[,] NORECOMPUTE]]
```

The arguments are:

table	Table is the table name.
index	Index is the index name.
index_or_column	Index or column is the name of the column(s) or index(es) for which statistics are being updated. Index and column names must conform to the rules for identifiers. index_or_column is required only when the INDEX or COLUMN options are specified.
n	N means the preceding is repeatable.
FULLSCAN	FULLSCAN does a full scan of the table as opposed to sampling the table.
SAMPLE *number* {PERCENT | ROWS}	SAMPLE *number* {PERCENT | ROWS} represents the percentage of the rows in a table or the number of rows sampled. If the percent or number are too few to give a good representation, Microsoft SQL Server corrects the number.
ALL | COLUMNS | INDEX	ALL | COLUMNS | INDEX determines whether column statistics, index statistics, or all statistics are affected with a default of affecting indexes only.

NORECOMPUTE	NORECOMPUTE disables Microsoft SQL Server from automatically rebuilding statistics and disables automatic statistics rebuilding. Execute the *sp_autostats* system stored procedure to restore the automatic computation of statistics or run UPDATE STATISTICS without NORECOMPUTE.

UPDATETEXT

UPDATETEXT is used to update only a portion of a text, ntext, or image column. WRITETEXT is used to replace the whole text, ntext, or image column.

Syntax

The syntax is:

```
UPDATETEXT {table_name.dest_column_name dest_text_ptr}
{NULL | insert_offset} {NULL | delete_length}
[WITH LOG]
[inserted_data | [{table_name.src_column_name src_text_ptr}]
```

The arguments are:

table_name.dest_column_name	Table_name.dest_column_name is the name of the table and text, ntext, or image column.
dest_text_ptr	Dest_text_ptr is returned by the TEXTPTR function and points for the data you are updating.
insert_offset	Insert_offset is the beginning point for the insertion of new data and if the first character has an offset of 0, the second has an offset of 1, etc. If the column is a text or image column, insert_offset represents how many bytes are passed over from the beginning of the column before finding the point to insert the data. If the column is ntext data type, insert_offset represents the number of characters rather than bytes since ntext data type takes two bytes. If zero is supplied, the data is inserted at the beginning and NULL appends to the end of the data.

delete_length	Delete_length is the number of characters to be deleted. If the column is a text or image column, delete_length represents how many bytes are passed over from the beginning of the insert_offset position before finding the point to delete the data. If the column is ntext data type, delete_length represents the number of characters rather than bytes since ntext data type takes two bytes. If zero is supplied, no data is deleted and NULL deletes all data from the insert_offset to the end of the data.
WITH LOG	WITH LOG specifies that the UPDATETEXT operation is logged but quickly increases the size of the log file. If WITH LOG is not supplied, the select into/bulkcopy database option must be on and can be turned on using the system stored procedure, *sp_dboption*. See Chapter 23 for system stored procedures.
inserted_data	Inserted_data represents the data to be inserted into the column of data type text, ntext, or image at the insert_offset position.
table_name.src_column_name	The table qualified column name of data type text, ntext, or image holding the inserted data.
src_text_ptr	Use the TEXTPTR function to get the pointer into a text, ntext, or image column holding the inserted data.

Example

Here's an example of the UPDATETEXT statement:

```
EXEC sp_dboption 'MyDB', 'select into/bulkcopy', 'true'
GO
DECLARE @pointervar binary(16)
SELECT @pointervar = TEXTPTR(MyTable)
FROM MyTable a, MyTable2 b
WHERE a.MyId = b.MyId
UPDATETEXT MyTable.MyColumn @pointervar 56 3 'COM'
GO
EXEC sp_dboption 'MyDB', 'select into/bulkcopy', 'false'
GO
```

In this example, the TEXTPTR is placed into a local variable and MyColumn is updated.

UPPER

The UPPER function substitutes uppercase characters for lowercase characters.

Syntax

The syntax is:

```
UPPER(character_expression)
```

The argument, character_expression, is a character or binary constant, variable, or column.

USE

The USE statement determines which database you are using.

Syntax

The syntax is:

```
USE {database}
```

The argument, database, is the database name.

USER

This statement is the same as USER_NAME.

USER_ID

USER_ID is a system function that returns the database user identification number of the user.

Syntax

```
USER_ID(['user'])
```

The argument, user, is the user name.

USER_NAME

USER_NAME is a function returning the database username when supplied the identification number of a user.

Syntax

The syntax is:

```
USER_NAME([id])
```

The argument, id, is the identification number of the user.

VAR

VAR is an aggregate function returning the variance of all values in the numeric column or expression. If the value in the column is NULL, the column is excluded.

Syntax

The syntax is:

```
VAR(expression)
```

The argument, expression, is a constant, column name, or function and can include operators but not aggregate functions and subqueries.

varbinary

See "Data Type" in this chapter.

varchar

See "Data Type" in this chapter.

VARP

VARP is an aggregate function returning the variance for the population of all values in the numeric column or expression. If the value in the column is NULL, the column is excluded.

Syntax

The syntax is:

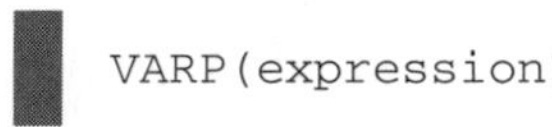

```
VARP(expression)
```

The argument, expression, is a constant, column name, or function and can include operators but not aggregate functions and subqueries.

WAITFOR

WAITFOR is a statement that allows a time factor to pass before processing continues.

Syntax

The syntax is:

```
WAITFOR {DELAY 'time' | TIME 'time'}
```

The arguments are:

DELAY	DELAY is the keyword followed by the amount of time to wait to a maximum of 24 hours.
'time'	Time is expressed as hh:mm:ss. You can use a local variable.
TIME	TIME is the keyword followed by the time to wait until.

WHERE

The WHERE clause determines rows to retrieve when used in a SELECT, UPDATE, INSERT, or DELETE statement.

Syntax

The syntax is:

```
WHERE <search_conditions>
```

The argument, <search_conditions>, defines the limiting conditions for the rows affected by the statement.

WHILE

WHILE sets a condition for the repeated execution of an *sql_statement* or statement block. The statements are executed repeatedly as long as the specified condition is true. The execution of statements in the WHILE loop can be controlled from inside the loop with the BREAK and CONTINUE keywords.

Syntax

The syntax is:

```
WHILE Boolean_expression
{sql_statement | statement_block}
[BREAK]
{sql_statement | statement_block}
[CONTINUE]
```

The arguments are:

Boolean_expression	A Boolean_expression returns TRUE or FALSE.
{sql_statement | statement_block}	{sql_statement | statement_block} is Transact-SQL statements with blocks using BEGIN and END syntax.
BREAK	BREAK exits from the inside WHILE loop.
CONTINUE	CONTINUE goes to the start of the WHILE loop, skipping statements after the CONTINUE but before the end of the WHILE loop.

WRITETEXT

WRITETEXT permits nonlogged, interactive updating of an existing text, ntext, or image column. This statement completely overwrites any existing data in the column it affects. WRITETEXT cannot be used on text, ntext, and image columns in views. By default, WRITETEXT statements are not logged; therefore, the transaction log does not fill up with the large amounts of data that often make up these data types.

Syntax

The syntax is:

```
WRITETEXT {table.column text_ptr}
[WITH LOG] {data}
```

The arguments are:

table.column	Table.column is the table qualified name of the text, ntext, or image column.
text_ptr	Use the TEXTPTR function to get the pointer into a text, ntext, or image column holding the data you are writing.

WITH LOG	WITH LOG specifies that the WRITETEXT operation is logged but quickly increase the size of the log file. If WITH LOG is not supplied, select into/bulkcopy database option must be on and can be turned on using the system stored procedure, *sp_dboption*. See Chapter 23 for system stored procedures.
data	Data is the text, ntext, or image data type getting written to the database with a maximum length of 120 kilobytes.

Example

Here's an example of the WRITETEXT statement:

```
EXEC sp_dboption 'MyDB', 'select into/bulkcopy', 'true'
GO
DECLARE @pointervar binary(16)
SELECT @pointervar = TEXTPTR(MyTable)
FROM MyTable a, MyTable2 b
WHERE a.MyId = b.MyId
WRITETEXT MyTable.MyColumn @pointervar 'These types of columns are
used to hold long text ntext or image data and can hold up to 120
kilobytes at a time.'
GO
EXEC sp_dboption 'MyDB', 'select into/bulkcopy', 'false'
GO
```

In this example, the TEXTPTR is placed into a local variable and receives a value.

YEAR

The YEAR function returns an integer indicating the year date part of the supplied date.

Syntax

The syntax is:

```
YEAR( date)
```

The argument, date, is a date expression.

Chapter 22

System Tables

The System Tables

The information used by Microsoft SQL Server is stored in special tables known as system tables. All databases contain system tables; these tables include information about Microsoft SQL Server and about each user database. Each user database has its own set of system tables, and many are found in the *master* database, which holds system tables that are server-wide.

The following system tables are located in the master system database; all others are located in the *msdb* system database in the distribution system database (or other Replication-involved databases) or in user databases:

- sysobjects
- sysindexes
- syscolumns
- systypes
- syscomments
- sysfiles1
- syspermissions
- sysusers
- sysdepends
- sysreferences
- sysfulltextcatalogs
- sysindexkeys
- sysforeignkeys
- sysmembers
- sysprotects
- sysdatabases
- sysperfinfo
- sysprocesses
- sysxlogins
- syslocks
- sysdevices
- sysmessages
- sysconfigures
- syscurconfigs
- sysservers
- syslockinfo
- syslanguages
- syscharsets
- syscursorrefs
- syscursors
- syscursorcolumns
- syscursortables
- syscacheobjects
- sysaltfiles
- sysfiles
- sysfilegroups
- sysallocations
- SYSREMOTE_PROVIDER_TYPES
- SYSREMOTE_TABLE_PRIVILEGES
- SYSREMOTE_COLUMN_PRIVILEGES
- SYSREMOTE_PRIMARY_KEYS
- SYSREMOTE_FOREIGN_KEYS
- SYSREMOTE_CATALOGS
- SYSREMOTE_SCHEMATA
- SYSREMOTE_TABLES
- SYSREMOTE_VIEWS
- SYSREMOTE_COLUMNS
- SYSREMOTE_INDEXES
- SYSREMOTE_STATISTICS

Use the Allow Updates option to allow direct updates to system tables. By default, this option is turned off so users cannot update system tables through ad hoc updates. If the allow updates option is not on (1), users can only update system tables using system stored procedures. When allow updates is off (0), updates are not allowed. When allow updates is on, any user who has permission can update system tables directly with ad hoc updates and can create stored procedures that update system tables.

Updating system tables can prevent SQL Server from starting and can cause inconsistencies; it is generally not recommended by Microsoft. Additionally, if you create stored procedures while the allow updates option is on, those stored procedures can update system tables even after the allow updates option is turned off. You can stop others from using SQL Server while you are directly updating system tables by starting SQL Server from a command prompt with the following syntax:

```
sqlservr -m
```

This will start SQL Server in a single-user mode and turn on the Allow Updates option.

The Allow Updates option is a dynamic option and is turned on or off without restarting SQL Server, requiring the use of the RECONFIGURE WITH OVERRIDE statement.

To allow direct updates to the system tables the syntax is:

```
sp_configure 'Allow Updates', 1
GO
RECONFIGURE WITH OVERRIDE
GO
```

To disallow direct updates to the system tables the syntax is:

```
sp_configure 'Allow Updates', 0
GO
RECONFIGURE WITH OVERRIDE
GO
```

The system tables have changed dramatically in SQL Server 7.0 and many new system tables have been added; others have been modified. Views also have been added.

The following sections name each system table and, following that, Information Schema Views are introduced.

backupfile

The *backupfile* system table resides in the *msdb* system database and has backup information for data and log files. The columns are:

- backup_set_id
- first_family_number
- first_media_number
- filegroup_name
- page_size
- file_number
- backed_up_page_count
- file_type
- source_file_block_size
- file_size
- logical_name
- physical_drive
- physical_name.

backupmediafamily

The backupmediafamily system table resides in the *msdb* system database and has backup information for a media family. The columns are:

- media_set_id
- family_sequence_number
- media_family_id
- media_count
- logical_device_name
- physical_device_name
- device_type
- physical_block_size

backupmediaset

The backupmediaset system table resides in the *msdb* system database and has backup information for a backupmedia set. The columns are:

- media_set_id
- media_uuid
- media_family_count
- name
- description
- software_name
- software_vendor_id
- MTF_major_version

backupset

The backupset system stored procedure resides in the *msdb* system database and has backup information for a backup set. The columns are:

- backup_set_id
- backup_set_uuid
- media_set_id
- first_family_number
- first_media_number
- last_family_number
- last_media_number
- catalog_family_number
- catalog_media_number
- position
- expiration_date
- software_vendor_id
- name
- description
- user_name
- software_major_version
- software_minor_version
- software_build_version
- time_zone
- mtf_minor_version
- first_lsn
- last_lsn
- checkpoint_lsn
- database_backup_lsn
- database_creation_date
- backup_start_date
- backup_finish_date
- type
- sort_order
- code_page

- compatibility_level
- database_version
- backup_size
- database_name
- server_name
- machine_name

MSagent_parameters

The MSagent_parameters system table resides in the *msdb* system database and has parameter information for an agent profile. The columns are:

- profile_id
- parameter_name
- value

MSagent_profiles

The MSagent_profiles system table resides in the *msdb* system database and has information about an agent profile. The columns are:

- profile_id
- profile_name
- agent_type
- type
- description
- def_profile

MSarticles

The MSarticles system table resides in the *distribution* system database and has information about replicated articles. The columns are:

- publisher_id
- publisher_db
- publication_id
- article
- article_id
- destination_object
- source_owner
- source_object
- description

MSdistpublishers

The MSdistpublishers system table resides in the *msdb* system database and has information about each remote publisher supported by the local Distributor. The columns are:

- name
- distribution_db
- working_directory
- security_mode
- login
- password
- active
- trusted
- thirdparty_flag

MSdistributiondbs

The MSdistributiondbs system table resides in the *msdb* system database and has information for the distribution database(s) relating to the local Distributor. The columns are:

- name
- min_distretention
- max_distretention
- history_retention

MSdistribution_agents

The MSdistribution_agents system table resides in the distribution system database and has information for the Distribution Agent(s) running on the Distributor. The columns are:

- id
- name
- publisher_database_id
- publisher_id
- publisher_db
- publication
- subscriber_id
- subscriber_db
- subscription_type
- local_job

- job_id
- subscription_guid
- profile_id
- anonymous_subid
- subscriber_name
- virtual_agent_id
- anonymous_agent_id

MSdistribution_history

The MSdistribution_history system table resides in the distribution system database and has historical information pertaining to the Distribution Agents on the Distributor. The columns are:

- agent_id
- runstatus
- start_time
- time
- duration
- comments
- xact_seqno
- current_delivery_rate
- current_delivery_latency
- delivered_transactions
- delivered_commands
- average_commands
- delivery_rate
- delivery_latency
- total_delivered_commands
- error_id
- updateable_row
- timestamp

MSdistributor

The MSdistributor system table resides in the *msdb* system database and has the properties of the Distributor. The columns are property and value.

MSlogreader_agents

The MSlogreader_agents system table resides in the distribution system database and has information pertaining to the Log Reader Agent(s) running on the Distributor. The columns are:

- id
- name
- publisher_id
- publisher_db
- publication

- local_job
- job_id
- profile_id

MSlogreader_history

The MSlogreader_history system table resides in the *distribution* system database and has historical information pertaining to the Log Reader Agents relating to the Distributor. The columns are:

- agent_id
- runstatus
- start_time,time
- duration,comments
- xact_seqno
- delivery_time
- delivered_transactions
- delivered_commands
- average_commands
- delivery_rate
- delivery_latency
- error_id
- timestamp

MSmerge_contents

The MSmerge_contents system table resides in the published database and has information about which rows have been modified in the database during the time it was published for the default priority-based conflict resolver used in merge replication. The columns are:

- tablenick
- rowguid
- generation
- partchangegen
- joinchangegen
- lineage
- colv1

MSmerge_delete_conflicts

The MSmerge_delete_conflicts system table resides in the published database (but can be in the subscribing database if you have decided to have decentralized conflict logging) and has information for deleted rows that were rolled back because of a conflict. The columns are:

- tablenick
- rowguid
- origin_datasource
- conflict_type
- reason_code
- reason_text
- pubid

MSmerge_genhistory

The MSmerge_genhistory system table resides in the distribution system database and has historical information pertaining to a generation(s) known by a Subscriber to prevent the exchange of common generations and to resynchronize Subscribers after they have been restored. The columns are:

- guidsrc
- guidlocal
- pubid
- generation
- art_nick
- nicknames
- coldate

MSmerge_history

The MSmerge_history system table resides in the distribution system database and has historical information pertaining to updates to the Subscriber. The columns are:

- agent_id
- runstatus
- start_time
- time
- duration
- comments
- delivery_time
- delivery_rate
- publisher_insertcount
- publisher_updatecount
- publisher_deletecount
- publisher_conflictcount
- subscriber_insertcount
- subscriber_updatecount

- subscriber_deletecount
- subscriber_conflictcount
- error_id
- timestamp

MSmerge_replinfo

The MSmerge_replinfo system table resides in the published database and has generation information pertaining to replication(s) created from the server by merge jobs. The columns are:

- repid
- replnickname
- recgen
- recguid
- sentgen
- sentguid
- schemaversion
- schemaguid
- merge_jobid
- snapshot_jobid

MSmerge_subscriptions

The MSmerge_subscriptions system table resides in the distribution database and has generation information that contains one row for each subscription serviced by the Merge Agent at the Subscriber. The columns are:

- publisher_id
- publisher_db
- publication_id
- subscriber_id
- subscriber_db
- subscription_type
- sync_type
- status
- subscription_time

MSmerge_tombstone

The MSmerge_tombstone system table resides in the published database and has information for deleted rows while facilitating the replication of deletes to other Subscribers. The columns are:

- rowguid
- tablenick
- type
- lineage
- generation
- reason

MSpublication_access

The MSpublication_access system table resides in the distribution database and has information about a SQL Server login with permission to publications and the Publisher. The columns are:

- publisher_id
- publication_id
- login

Mspublications

The MSpublications system table resides in the distribution database and has information for each publication replicated by a Publisher. The columns are:

- publisher_id
- publisher_db
- publication
- publication_id
- publication_type
- thirdparty_flag
- independent_agent
- immediate_sync
- allow_push
- allow_pull
- allow_anonymous
- description
- vendor_name
- default_access

MSpublisher_databases

The MSpublisher_databases system table resides in the distribution database and identifies the Publisher's database on the Distributor. The columns are:

- publisher_id
- publisher_db
- id (the id of the row)

MSreplication_objects

The MSreplication_objects system table resides in the subscriber database and identifies the objects involved in replication in the Subscriber database. The columns are:

- publisher
- publisher_db
- publication
- object_name
- object_type (u=table, t=trigger)

MSreplication_subscriptions

The MSreplication_subscriptions system table resides in the subscriber database and has replication information for Distribution Agents replicating to the subscriber database. The columns are:

- publisher
- publisher_db
- publication
- independent_agent
- subscription_type (0=push, 1=pull, 2=anonymous)
- distribution_agent
- time
- description
- transaction_timestamp
- update_mode
- agent_id
- subscription_guid
- subid
- reinit

MSrepl_commands

The MSrepl_commands system table resides in the distribution database and has replication information about replicated commands. The columns are:

- publisher_database_id
- xact_seqno
- type
- article_id
- originator_id
- command_id
- partial_command
- command

MSrepl_errors

The MSrepl_commands system table resides in the distribution database and has replication information about extended replication agent failures. The columns are:

- id
- time
- error_type_id
- source_type_id
- source_name
- error_code
- error_text

MSrepl_originators

The MSrepl_originators system table resides in the distribution database and has replication information about updatable Subscribers that began the transaction. The columns are:

- id
- publisher_database_id
- srvname
- dbname

MSrepl_transactions

The MSrepl_transactions system table resides in the distribution database and has replication information about replicated transactions. The columns are:

- publisher_database_id
- xact_id
- xact_seqno
- entry_time

MSrepl_version

The MSrepl_version system table resides in the distribution database and has replication information about the version of replication. The columns are:

- major_version
- minor_version
- revision
- db_existed

MSsnapshot_agents

The MSsnapshot_agents system table resides in the distribution database and has replication information about Snapshot Agents related to the Distributor. The columns are:

- id
- name
- publisher_id
- publisher_db
- publication
- publication_type
- local_job
- job_id
- profile_id

MSsnapshot_history

The MSsnapshot_history system table resides in the distribution database and has historical replication information about the Snapshot Agents related to the Distributor. The columns are:

- agent_id
- runstatus
- start_time
- time
- duration
- comments
- delivered_transactions
- delivered_commands
- delivery_rate
- error_id
- timestamp

MSsubscriber_info

The MSsubscriber_info system table resides in the distribution database and has replication information about Publisher and Subscriber and their pushed subscriptions from the Distributor. The columns are:

- publisher
- subscriber
- type
- login
- password
- description
- security_mode

MSsubscriber_schedule

The MSsubscriber_schedule system table resides in the distribution database and has replication information about default merge and transactional synchronization schedules for Publisher and Subscriber. The columns are:

- publisher
- subscriber
- agent_type
- frequency_type
- frequency_interval
- frequency_relative_interval
- frequency_recurrence_factor
- frequency_subday
- frequency_subday_interval
- active_start_time_of_day
- active_end_time_of_day
- active_start_date
- active_end_date

MSsubscriptions

The MSsubscriptions system table resides in the distribution database and has replication information about the subscriptions related to the Distributor. The columns are:

- publisher_database_id
- publisher_id
- publisher_db
- publication_id
- article_id
- subscriber_id
- subscriber_db
- subscription_type
- sync_type
- status
- subscription_seqno
- snapshot_seqno_flag
- independent_agent
- subscription_time
- loopback_detection
- agent_id
- update_mode
- publisher_seqno

MSsubscription_properties

The MSsubscription_properties system table resides in the distribution database and has replication information about the parameters for pull Distribution Agents. The columns are:

- publisher
- publisher_db
- publication
- publication_type (0=snapshot, 1=transactional)
- publisher_login
- publisher_password
- publisher_security_mode (0=SQL Server Authentication, 1=Windows NT Authentication)
- encrypted_publisher_password
- distributor_login
- distributor_password
- distributor_security_mode
- encrypted_distributor_password

restorefile

The restorefile system table resides in the msdb database and has information about restored files. The columns are:

- restore_history_id
- file_number
- destination_phys_driv
- destination_phys_name

restorefilegroup

The restorefilegroup system table resides in the msdb database and has information about restored filegroups. The columns are restore_history_id and filegroup_name.

restorehistory

The restorehistory system table resides in the msdb database and has information about restored objects. The columns are:

- restore_history_id
- restore_date
- destination_database_name
- user_name
- backup_set_id
- restore_type
- replace
- recovery
- restart
- stop_at
- device_count

sysalerts

The sysalerts system table resides in the msdb database and has information about alerts (e-mail, pager, etc.) raised by events on the server. The columns are:

- id
- name
- event_source
- event_category_id
- event_id
- message_id
- severity
- enabled
- delay_between_responses
- last_occurrence_date
- last_occurrence_time
- last_response_date
- last_response_time
- notification_message

- include_event_description
- database_name
- event_description_keyword
- occurrence_count
- count_reset_date
- count_reset_time
- job_id
- has_notification
- flags
- performance_condition
- category_id

sysallocations

The sysallocations system table resides in every database and has information about allocation units. The columns are:

- objid
- indid
- fileid
- gaminterval
- iampage

sysaltfiles

The sysaltfiles system table resides in the master database and has information about the files in a database. The columns are:

- fileid
- groupid
- size
- maxsize
- growth
- status
- perf
- dbid
- name
- filename

sysarticles

The sysarticles system table resides in the publisher database and has replication information about articles in the database. The columns are:

- artid
- columns
- creation_script
- del_cmd
- description
- dest_table
- filter
- filter_clause

- ins_cmd
- name
- objid
- pubid
- pre_creation_cmd
- status
- sync_objid
- type
- upd_cmd
- schema_option
- dest_owner

sysarticleupdates

The sysarticleupdates system table resides in the publisher database and has replication information about the articles of updatable subscriptions. The columns are:

- artid
- pubid
- sync_ins_proc
- sync_upd_proc
- sync_del_proc
- autogen

syscategories

The syscategories system table resides in the msdb database and has information about the categories used to categorize jobs, alerts, and operators. The columns are:

- category_id
- category_class
- category_type
- name

syscharsets

The syscharsets system table resides in the master database and has information about the character sets and sort orders available when using Microsoft SQL Server (only one is actually in use). The columns are:

- type
- id
- csid
- status,name

- description
- binarydefinition
- definition

syscolumns

The syscolumns system table resides in every database and has information about columns in all tables and views, and each argument in a stored procedure. The columns are:

- name
- id
- xtype
- typestat
- xusertype
- length
- xprec
- xscale
- colid
- xoffset
- bitpos
- reserved
- colstat
- cdefault
- domain
- number
- colorder
- autoval
- offset
- status
- type
- usertype
- printfmt
- prec
- scale
- iscomputed
- isoutparam
- isnullable

syscomments

The syscomments system table resides in every database and has information about CHECK constraints, DEFAULT constraints, defaults, rules, stored procedures, triggers, and views. The columns are:

- id
- number
- colid
- status
- ctext
- texttype
- language
- encrypted
- compressed
- text

In this version, do not delete from syscomments, use CREATE PROCEDURE with the ENCRYPTION instead.

sysconfigures

The sysconfigures system table resides in the master database and has information about configuration options. The columns are:

- value
- config
- comment
- status

sysconstraints

The sysconstraints system table resides in every database and has information about constraints and constraint owners. The columns are:

- constid
- id
- colid
- spare1
- status
- actions
- error

syscurconfigs

The syscurconfigs system table resides in the master database and has information about current configuration options. The columns are:

- value
- config
- comment
- status

sysdatabases

The sysdatabases system table resides in the master database and has information about databases. The columns are:

- name
- dbid
- sid
- mode

- status
- status2
- crdate
- reserved
- category
- cmptlevel
- filename
- suid
- version

sysdepends

The sysdepends system table resides in the master database and has information about dependency information between objects. The columns are:

- id
- depid
- number
- depnumber
- status
- depdbid
- depsiteid
- selall
- resultobj
- readobj

sysdevices

The sysdevices system table resides in the master system database and has information about database file, disk backup file, and tape backup file. This table is for backward compatibility only. Look in sysfiles instead. The columns are:

- name
- size
- low
- high
- status
- cntrltype
- phyname

sysdownloadlist

The sysdownloadlist system table resides in the msdb system database and has information about the download instructions for target servers. The columns are:

- instance_id
- source_server
- operation_code
- object_type
- object_id
- target_server

- error_message
- date_posted
- date_downloaded
- status
- deleted_object_name

sysfiles

The sysfiles virtual system table resides in the master system database and has information about database files. The columns are:

- fileid
- groupid
- size
- maxsize
- growth
- status
- perf
- name
- filename

sysfilegroups

The sysfilegroups system table resides in the master system database and has information about database filegroups. The columns are:

- groupid
- allocpolicy
- status
- groupname

sysforeignkeys

The sysforeignkeys system table resides in every database and has information about the FOREIGN KEY constraints. The columns are:

- constid
- fkeyid
- rkeyid
- fkey
- rkey
- keyno

sysfulltextcatalogs

The sysfulltextcatalogs system table resides in every database and has information about full-text catalogs. The columns are:

- ftcatid
- name
- status
- path

sysindexes

The sysindexes system table resides in every database and has information about indexes and tables. The columns are:

- id
- status
- first
- indid
- root
- minlen
- keycnt
- groupid
- dpages
- reserved
- used
- rowcnt
- rowmodctr
- soid
- csid
- xmaxlen
- maxirow
- OrigFillFactor
- reserved1
- reserved2
- FirstIAM
- impid
- lockflags
- pgmodctr
- keys
- name
- statblob
- maxlen
- rows

sysindexkeys

The sysindexkeys system table resides in every database and has information about the columns in an index. The columns are:

- id
- indid
- colid
- keyno

sysjobhistory

The sysjobhistory system table resides in the msdb system database and has information about scheduled jobs. The columns are:

- instance_id
- job_id
- step_id
- step_name
- sql_message_id
- sql_severity
- message
- run_status
- run_date
- run_time
- run_duration
- operator_id_emailed
- operator_id_netsent
- operator_id_paged
- retries_attempted
- server

sysjobschedules

The sysjobschedules system table resides in the msdb system database and has information about job schedules. The columns are:

- schedule_id
- job_id
- name
- enabled
- freq_type
- freq_interval
- freq_subday_type
- freq_subday_interval
- freq_relative_interval
- freq_recurrence_factor
- active_start_date
- active_end_date
- active_start_time
- active_end_time
- next_run_date
- next_run_time
- date_created

sysjobs

The sysjobs system table resides in the msdb system database and has information about scheduled jobs. The columns are:

- job_id
- originating_server
- name
- enabled
- description
- start_step_id
- category_id
- owner_sid

- notify_level_eventlog
- notify_level_email
- notify_level_netsend
- notify_level_page
- notify_email_operator_id
- notify_netsend_operator_id
- notify_page_operator_id
- delete_level
- date_created
- date_modified
- version_number

sysjobservers

The sysjobservers system table resides in the msdb system database and has information about a job and its target servers. The columns are:

- job_id
- server_id
- last_run_outcome
- last_outcome_message
- last_run_date
- last_run_time
- last_run_duration

sysjobsteps

The sysjobsteps system table resides in the msdb system database and has information about job steps. The columns are:

- job_id
- step_id
- step_name
- subsystem
- command
- flags
- additional_parameters
- cmdexec_success_code
- on_success_action
- on_success_step_id
- on_fail_action
- on_fail_step_id
- server
- database_name
- database_user_name
- retry_attempts
- retry_interval
- os_run_priority
- output_file_name
- last_run_outcome
- last_run_duration
- last_run_retries
- last_run_date
- last_run_time

syslanguages

The syslanguages system table resides in the master system database and has information about each language available to Microsoft SQL Server. The columns are:

- langid
- dateformat
- datefirst
- upgrade
- name
- alias
- months
- shortmonths
- days
- lcid
- msglangid

syslockinfo

The syslockinfo system table resides in the master database and has information about lock requests. The columns are:

- rsc_text
- rsc_bin
- rsc_valblk
- rsc_dbid
- rsc_indid
- rsc_objid
- rsc_type
- rsc_flag
- req_mode
- req_status
- req_refcnt
- req_cryrefcnt
- req_lifetime
- req_spid
- req_ecid
- req_ownertype

syslogins

The syslogins system table resides in the master database and has information about login accounts. The columns are:

- suid
- sid
- status
- createdate
- updatedate
- accdate
- totcpu
- totio
- spacelimit
- timelimit
- resultlimit
- name
- dbname
- password

- language
- denylogin
- hasaccess
- isntname
- isntgroup
- isntuser
- sysadmin
- securityadmin
- serveradmin
- setupadmin
- processadmin
- diskadmin
- dbcreator
- loginname

sysmembers

The sysmembers system table resides in every database and has information about members of a database role. The columns are memberuid and groupuid.

sysmergearticles

The sysmergearticles system table resides in the publisher database and has information about merge articles. The columns are:

- name
- type
- objid
- sync_objid
- view_type
- artid
- description
- pre_creation_command
- pubid
- nickname
- column_tracking
- status
- conflict_table
- creation_script
- conflict_script
- article_resolver
- ins_conflict_proc
- insert_proc
- update_proc
- select_proc
- schema_option
- destination_object
- resolver_clsid
- subset_filterclause
- missing_col_count
- missing_cols
- columns
- resolver_info
- view_sel_proc

sysmergepublications

The sysmergepublications system table resides in the publisher database and has information about merge publications. The columns are:

- publisher
- publisher_db
- name
- description
- retention
- publication_type
- pubid
- designmasterid
- parentid
- sync_mode
- allow_push
- allow_pull
- allow_anonymous
- centralized_conflicts
- status
- snapshot_ready
- enabled_for_internet
- default_access
- dynamic_filters

sysmergeschemachange

The sysmergeschemachange system table resides in the publisher database and has information about schema modifications. The columns are:

- pubid
- artid
- schemaversion
- schemaguid
- schematype
- schematext

sysmergesubscriptions

The sysmergesubscriptions system table resides in the publisher database and has information about Subscribers. The columns are:

- subid
- partnerid
- datasource_type
- datasource_path
- srvid
- db_name

- pubid
- status
- subscriber_type
- subscription_type
- priority
- sync_type
- description
- login_name
- last_validated

sysmergesubsetfilters

The sysmergesubsetfilters system table resides in the publisher database and has information about Contains join filter information for partitioned articles. The columns are:

- filtername
- join_filterid
- pubid
- artid
- art_nickname
- join_articlename
- join_nickname
- join_unique_key
- expand_proc
- join_filterclause

sysmessages

The sysmessages system table resides in the master database and has information about system errors or warnings The columns are:

- error
- severity
- dlevel
- description
- msglangid

sysnotifications

The sysnotifications system table resides in the msdb database and has information about notifications. The columns are:

- alert_id
- operator_id
- notification_method

sysobjects

The sysobjects system table resides in every database and has information about objects in a database. The columns are:

- name
- id
- xtype
- uid
- info
- status
- base_schema_ver
- replinfo
- parent_obj
- crdate
- ftcatid
- schema_ver
- stats_schema_ver
- type
- userstat
- sysstat
- indexdel
- refdate
- version
- deltrig
- instrig
- updtrig
- seltrig
- category
- cache

sysoledbusers

The sysoledbusers system table resides in the master database and has information about users and password mapping for a linked server. The columns are:

- rmtsrvid
- rmtloginame
- rmtpassword
- loginsid
- status
- changedate

sysoperators

The sysoperators system table resides in the msdb database and has information about operators. The columns are:

- id
- name
- enabled
- email_address

- last_email_date
- last_email_time
- pager_address
- last_pager_date
- last_pager_time
- weekday_pager_start_time
- weekday_pager_end_time
- saturday_pager_start_time
- saturday_pager_end_time
- sunday_pager_start_time
- sunday_pager_end_time
- pager_days
- netsend_address
- last_netsend_date
- last_netsend_time
- category_id

sysperfinfo

The sysperfinfo system table resides in the master database and has information about SQL Server performance counters in the Windows NT Performance Monitor. The columns are:

- object_name
- counter_name
- instance_name
- cntr_value
- cntr_type

syspermissions

The syspermissions system table resides in every database and has information about permissions in the database. The columns are:

- id
- grantee
- grantor
- actadd
- actmod
- seladd
- selmod
- updadd
- updmod
- refadd
- refmod

sysprocesses

The sysprocesses system table resides in the master database and has information about processes running on Microsoft SQL Server. The columns are:

- spid
- kpid
- blocked
- waittype
- dbid
- uid
- cpu
- physical_io
- memusage
- login_time
- last_batch
- ecid
- open_tran
- status
- sid
- hostname
- program_name
- hostprocess
- cmd
- nt_domain
- nt_username
- net_address
- net_library
- loginame
- suid

sysprotects

The sysprotects system table resides in every database and has information about permissions of security accounts. The columns are:

- id
- uid
- action
- protecttype
- columns
- grantor

syspublications

The syspublications system table resides in the publisher database and has information about publications in the database. The columns are:

- description
- name
- pubid
- repl_freq
- status
- sync_method
- snapshot_jobid
- independent_agent

- immediate_sync
- enabled_for_internet
- allow_push
- allow_pull
- allow_anonymous
- immediate_sync_ready
- allow_sync_tran
- autogen_sync_procs
- retention
- default_access

sysreferences

The sysreferences system table resides in every database and has information about FOREIGN KEY constraints to referenced columns. The columns are:

- constid
- fkeyid
- rkeyid
- rkeyindid
- keycnt
- forkeys
- refkeys
- fkeydbid
- rkeydbid
- fkey1
- fkey2
- fkey3
- fkey4
- fkey5
- fkey6
- fkey7
- fkey8
- fkey9
- fkey10
- fkey11
- fkey12
- fkey13
- fkey14
- fkey15
- fkey16
- rkey1
- rkey2
- rkey3
- rkey4
- rkey5
- rkey6
- rkey7
- rkey8
- rkey9
- rkey10
- rkey11
- rkey12
- rkey13
- rkey14
- rkey15
- rkey16

sysremotelogins

The sysremotelogins system table resides in the master database and has information about remote users. The columns are:

- remoteserverid
- remoteusername
- suid
- status
- sid
- changedate

sysreplicationalerts

The sysreplicationalerts system table resides in the msdb system database and has information about causes of a replication alert. The columns are:

- alert_id
- status
- agent_type
- agent_id
- error_id
- alert_error_code
- time
- publisher
- publisher_db
- publication
- publication_type
- subscriber
- subscriber_db
- article
- destination_object
- source_object
- alert_error_text

sysservers

The sysservers system table resides in the master database and has information about remote servers and the local server. The columns are:

- srvid
- srvstatus
- srvname
- srvproduct
- providername
- datasource
- location
- providerstring

- schemadate
- topologyx
- topologyy
- catalog
- srvnetname

syssubscriptions

The syssubscriptions system table resides in the publisher database and the publisher database and has information about subscription. The columns are:

- artid
- srvid
- dest_db
- status
- sync_type
- login_name
- subscription_type
- distribution_jobid
- timestamp
- update_mode
- loopback_detection

systargetservergroupmembers

The systargetservergroupmembers system table resides in the msdb database and has information about target servers are currently enlisted in a Multi Server group. The columns are servergroup_id and server_id.

systargetservergroups

The systargetservergroups system table resides in the msdb database and has information about which target server groups are enlisted in a Multi Server scenario. The columns are servergroup_id and name.

systargetservers

The systargetservers system table resides in the msdb database and has information about target servers that are currently enlisted in a Multi Server scenario. The columns are:

- server_id
- server_name
- location
- time_zone_adjustment
- enlist_date
- last_poll_date
- status
- local_time_at_last_poll
- enlisted_by_nt_user
- poll_interval

systaskids

The systaskids system table resides in the msdb database and has information about tasks created in earlier versions and jobs in version 7.0. The columns are task_id and job_id.

systypes

The systypes system table resides in every database and has information about data types. The columns are:

- name
- xtype
- status
- xusertype
- length
- xprec
- xscale
- tdefault
- domain,uid
- reserved
- usertype
- variable
- allownulls
- type
- printfmt
- prec
- scale

sysusers

The sysusers system table resides in every database and has information about database users. The columns are:

- uid
- status
- name
- sid
- roles
- createdate
- updatedate
- altuid
- password
- suid
- gid
- environ
- hasdbaccess
- islogin
- isntname
- isntgroup
- isntuser
- issqluser
- isaliased
- issqlrole
- isapprole

In the next section, Information Schema Views used to view SQL Server metadata in the system tables are described.

Information Schema Views

Microsoft SQL Server returns information on system tables by stored procedures or information schema views.

To retrieve information from these views, supply the fully qualified name, INFORMATION_SCHEMA.*view_name*.

An example is:

```
select * from  INFORMATION_SCHEMA.CHECK_CONSTRAINTS
```

In this example, information from the *sysobjects* and *sycomments* system tables is returned.

CHECK_CONSTRAINTS

The Information Schema View CHECK_CONSTRAINTS has information about check constraints from the *sysobjects* and *sycomments* system tables. The columns are:

- CONSTRAINT_CATALOG
- CONSTRAINT_SCHEMA
- CONSTRAINT_NAME
- CHECK_CLAUSE

COLUMN_DOMAIN_USAGE

The Information Schema View COLUMN_DOMAIN_USAGE has information about user-defined data type columns owned by the user in the database in use from the *sysobjects*, *syscolumns*, and *systypes* system tables. The columns are:

- DOMAIN_CATALOG
- DOMAIN_SCHEMA
- DOMAIN_NAME
- TABLE_CATALOG
- TABLE_SCHEMA
- TABLE_NAME
- COLUMN_NAME

COLUMN_PRIVILEGES

The Information Schema View COLUMN_PRIVILEGES has information about privileges on columns granted to or by the user in the database in use from the *sysprotects*, *sysobjects*, and *syscolumns* system tables. The columns are:

- GRANTOR
- GRANTEE
- TABLE_CATALOG
- TABLE_SCHEMA
- TABLE_NAME
- COLUMN_NAME
- PRIVILEGE_TYPE
- IS_GRANTABLE

COLUMNS

The Information Schema View COLUMNS has information for columns of the user in the database in use from the *sysobjects*, *spt_data type_info*, *systypes*, *syscolumns*, *syscomments*, *sysconfigures*, and *syscharsets* system tables. The columns are:

- TABLE_CATALOG
- TABLE_SCHEMA
- TABLE_NAME
- COLUMN_NAME
- ORDINAL_POSITION
- COLUMN_DEFAULT
- IS_NULLABLE
- DATA_TYPE
- CHARACTER_MAXIMUM_LENGTH
- CHARACTER_OCTET_LENGTH
- NUMERIC_PRECISION
- NUMERIC_PRECISION_RADIX
- NUMERIC_SCALE
- DATETIME_PRECISION

- CHARACTER_SET_CATALOG
- CHARACTER_SET_SCHEMA
- CHARACTER_SET_NAME
- COLLATION_CATALOG
- COLLATION_SCHEMA
- COLLATION_NAME
- DOMAIN_CATALOG
- DOMAIN_SCHEMA
- DOMAIN_NAME

CONSTRAINT_COLUMN_USAGE

The Information Schema View CONSTRAINT_COLUMN_USAGE has information for constrained columns of the user in the database in use from the *sysobjects*, *syscolumns*, and *systypes* system tables. The columns are:

- TABLE_CATALOG
- TABLE_SCHEMA
- TABLE_NAME
- COLUMN_NAME
- CONSTRAINT_CATALOG
- CONSTRAINT_SCHEMA
- CONSTRAINT_NAME

CONSTRAINT_TABLE_USAGE

The Information Schema View CONSTRAINT_TABLE_USAGE has information for each constrained table accessible to the user in the database in use from the *sysobjects* system table. The columns are:

- TABLE_CATALOG
- TABLE_SCHEMA
- TABLE_NAME
- CONSTRAINT_CATALOG
- CONSTRAINT_SCHEMA
- CONSTRAINT_NAME

DOMAIN_CONSTRAINTS

The Information Schema View DOMAIN_CONSTRAINTS has information for data types with rules of the user in the database in use from the *sysobjects* and *systypes* system tables. The columns are:

- CONSTRAINT_CATALOG
- CONSTRAINT_SCHEMA
- CONSTRAINT_NAME
- DOMAIN_CATALOG
- DOMAIN_SCHEMA
- DOMAIN_NAME
- IS_DEFERRABLE
- INITIALLY_DEFERRED

DOMAINS

The Information Schema View DOMAINS has information for data types of the user in the database in use from the *spt_data type_info, systypes, syscomments, sysconfigures,* and *syscharsets* system tables. The columns are:

- DOMAIN_CATALOG
- DOMAIN_SCHEMA
- DOMAIN_NAME
- DATA_TYPE
- CHARACTER_MAXIMUM_LENGTH
- CHARACTER_OCTET_LENGTH
- COLLATION_CATALOG
- COLLATION_SCHEMA
- COLLATION_NAME
- CHARACTER_SET_CATALOG
- CHARACTER_SET_SCHEMA
- CHARACTER_SET_NAME
- NUMERIC_PRECISION
- NUMERIC_PRECISION_RADIX

- NUMERIC_SCALE
- DATETIME_PRECISION
- DOMAIN_DEFAULT

KEY_COLUMN_USAGE

The Information Schema View KEY_COLUMN_USAGE has information for columns owned by the user in the database in use from the *sysobjects, syscolumns, sysreferences, spt_values,* and *sysindexes* system tables. The columns are:

- CONSTRAINT_CATALOG
- CONSTRAINT_SCHEMA
- CONSTRAINT_NAME
- TABLE_CATALOG
- TABLE_SCHEMA
- TABLE_NAME
- COLUMN_NAME
- ORDINAL_POSITION

(2)REFERENTIAL_CONSTRAINTS

The Information Schema View REFERENTIAL_CONSTRAINTS has information for foreign constraints owned by the user in the database in use from the *sysreferences, sysindexes,* and *sysobjects* system tables. The columns are:

- CONSTRAINT_CATALOG
- CONSTRAINT_SCHEMA
- CONSTRAINT_NAME
- UNIQUE_CONSTRAINT_CATALOG
- UNIQUE_CONSTRAINT_SCHEMA
- UNIQUE_CONSTRAINT_NAME
- MATCH_OPTION
- UPDATE_RULE
- DELETE_RULE

SCHEMATA

The Information Schema View SCHEMATA has information for each database with permissions for the user from the *sysdatabases, sysconfigures,* and *syscharsets* system tables. The columns are:

- CATALOG_NAME
- SCHEMA_NAME
- SCHEMA_OWNER
- DEFAULT_CHARACTER_SET_CATALOG
- DEFAULT_CHARACTER_SET_SCHEMA
- DEFAULT_CHARACTER_SET_NAME

TABLE_CONSTRAINTS

The Information Schema View TABLE_CONSTRAINTS has information for table constraints owned by the user in the database in use from the *sysobjects* system table. The columns are:

- CONSTRAINT_CATALOG
- CONSTRAINT_SCHEMA
- CONSTRAINT_NAME
- TABLE_CATALOG
- TABLE_SCHEMA
- TABLE_NAME
- CONSTRAINT_TYPE
- IS_DEFERRABLE
- INITIALLY_DEFERRED

TABLE_PRIVILEGES

The Information Schema View TABLE_PRIVILEGES has information for each table privilege granted to or by the user in the database in use from the *sysprotects* and *sysobjects* system tables. The columns are:

- GRANTOR
- GRANTEE
- TABLE_CATALOG
- TABLE_SCHEMA
- TABLE_NAME

- PRIVILEGE_TYPE
- IS_GRANTABLE

TABLES

The Information Schema View TABLES has information for each table with permissions for the user in the database in use from the *sysobjects* system table. The columns are:

- TABLE_CATALOG
- TABLE_SCHEMA
- TABLE_NAME
- TABLE_TYPE

VIEW_COLUMN_USAGE

The Information Schema View VIEW_COLUMN_USAGE has information for each column owned by the user in the database in use from the *sysobjects* and *sysdepends* system tables. The columns are:

- VIEW_CATALOG
- VIEW_SCHEMA
- VIEW_NAME
- TABLE_CATALOG
- TABLE_SCHEMA
- TABLE_NAME
- COLUMN_NAME

VIEW_TABLE_USAGE

The Information Schema View VIEW_TABLE_USAGE has information for each table used by a view and owned by the user in the database in use from the *sysobjects* and *sysdepends* system tables. The columns are:

- VIEW_CATALOG
- VIEW_SCHEMA
- VIEW_NAME
- TABLE_CATALOG
- TABLE_SCHEMA
- TABLE_NAME

VIEWS

The Information Schema View VIEWS has information for views accessible by the user in the database in use from the *sysobjects* and *syscomments* system tables. The columns are:

- TABLE_CATALOG
- TABLE_SCHEMA
- TABLE_NAME
- VIEW_DEFINITION
- CHECK_OPTION
- IS_UPDATABLE

The new Information Schema Views provide an easy way to look at metadata that previously required the join of system tables. In the next chapter, we will examine system stored procedures that are another way to manipulate and view the system tables without accessing them directly.

Chapter 23

System Stored Procedures

SQL Server system stored procedures have been written to prevent users from accessing the system tables directly while providing the functionality to perform all of the database administration tasks. A listing of the system stored procedures is available by using the Enterprise Manager, expanding the server and the master database, and double-clicking on stored procedures. By default, the master database does not appear in Enterprise Manager. To turn on the ability to see system databases, the user must select Show System Database and System Objects in the Registered SQL Server Properties window. Select a system stored procedure and double-click to see the Transact-SQL code for the selected system stored procedure. Other system stored procedures are located in the msdb system database and can be seen and accessed by using the same method, the difference being to expand the msdb database instead of master.

System stored procedures can be grouped by functional area in the following categories:

- **Catalog** Data dictionary functionality
- **Cursors** Cursor functionality
- **Distributed Queries** Distributed query functionality
- **SQL Server Agent** Task management functionality
- **Replication** Replication functionality
- **Security** Security management functionality
- **System** SQL Server maintenance functionality
- **Web Assistant** Web functionality
- **Extended Procedures** SQL Server interface to external programs
- **OLE Automation** OLE automation within Transact-SQL
- **Data Transformation Services** Datawarehousing procedures

Extended stored procedures can be futher broken down into General, SQL Mail, and SQL Server Profiler.

The Microsoft SQL Server system stored procedures are presented here in alphabetical order.

sp_add_agent_parameter

The sp_add_agent_parameter system stored procedure is used in snapshot, merge, and transaction replication to add a parameter and its value to the replication agent profile.

Syntax

The syntax is:

```
sp_add_agent_parameter [@profile_id =] 'profile_id',
[@parameter_name =] 'parameter_name',
[@parameter_value =] 'parameter_value'
```

The arguments are:

[@profile_id =] 'profile_id'	Profile_id is an integer identifying the configuration in the MSagent_configurations system table.
[@parameter_name =] 'parameter_name'	Parameter_name is the sysname of the parameter.
[@parameter_value =] 'parameter_value'	Parameter_value is the nvarchar(255) value for the parameter.

sp_add_agent_profile

The sp_add_agent_profile system stored procedure adds a replication agent profile to the Msagent_profiles table for use in snapshot, merge, and transaction replication.

Syntax

The syntax is:

```
sp_add_agent_profile [[@profile_id =] 'profile_id' OUTPUT]
{,[@profile_name =] 'profile_name' [,[@agent_type =] 'agent_type'}
[,[@profile_type =] 'profile_type'] {,[@description =] 'description',}
[,[@default =] 'default']
```

The arguments are:

[@profile_id =] 'profile_id'	Profile_id is an integer identifying the configuration in the MSagent_configurations system table and can be used as an OUTPUT parameter. A result of profile_id is returned if the profile_id is not supplied.

[@profile_name =] 'profile_name'	The sysname of the profile.
[@agent_type =] 'agent_type'	Agent_type is an integer and the replication agent where 1=Snapshot Agent, 2=Log Reader Agent, 3=Distribution Agent, 4=Merge Agent.
[@profile_type =] 'profile_type'	Profile_type is an integer where 0=system profile (the default), 1=custom profile.
[@description =] 'description'	Description is nvarchar(3000) and describes the profile.
[@default =] 'default'	Default is a bit that determines if the profile is the default for the type of replication agent and 0=not a default profile, 1=a default profile.

sp_add_alert

The sp_add_alert system stored procedure adds a new alert.

Syntax

The syntax is:

```
sp_add_alert {'name'} [, message_id] [, severity] [, enabled]
[, delay_between_responses] [, 'notification_message']
[, include_event_description_in] [, 'database']
[, 'event_description_keyword_pattern'] [, {job_id | 'job_name'}]
[, raise_snmp_trap] [, 'performance_condition'] [, 'category']
```

The arguments are:

'name'	Name is the varchar(100) name of the alert.
message_id	Message_id is the integer message error number in the sysmessages system table. If severity is used instead, message_id must be zero or NULL.
severity	Severity can also be used to identify the alert with integer values of 9 through 25, 110, 120, 130, or 140 and a default of 0. If message_id is used instead, severity must have a value of 0.
enabled	Enabled is tinyint where 1=enabled (the default), 0=not enabled.

delay_between_responses	Delay_between_responses is integer and expresses in seconds (with default of zero) the delay before sending the next alert. This is used when you wish to avoid having multiple alerts occurring in the space of a short time.
'notification_message'	Notification_message is varchar(255) with a default of NULL and can be used to send additional information to the recipient of the alert.
include_event_description_in	Include_event_description_in is tinyint (with a default of zero) and determines whether the description of the SQL Server error in the NT Event Log is part of the notification message that is sent to the recipient. 0= None, 1=Email, 2=Pager, 4=NetSend, 7=All.
'database'	Database is varchar(64) and the name of the database in with a default of NULL which means the alert will occur on error in any database on the server.
'event_description_keyword'	Event_description_keyword is varchar(100) with a default of NULL and describes the SQL Server error in the Windows NT event log. LIKE expression wildcard characters can be used to for object names.
job_id	Job is the uniqueidentifier of the job with default of NULL. Supply job_id or job_name as an argument.
'job_name'	Job_name is the CmdExec or Transact-SQL varchar(100) job name to run when an alert is given with a default of NULL.

sp_addalias

The sp_addalias is provided for backward compatibility. A version 7.0 programmer will use Roles instead.

sp_addapprole

The sp_addapprole system stored procedure creates a database role used for security in an application.

Syntax

The syntax is:

```
sp_addapprole [@rolename =] 'role', [@password =] 'password'
```

The arguments are:

[@rolename =] 'role'	Role is the sysname of a new database role.
[@password =] 'password'	Password is the sysname and the password to access the permissions granted to the database role.

sp_addarticle

The ap_addarticle system stored procedure adds a new article to a publication for use in snapshot, merge, and transaction replication.

Syntax

The syntax is:

```
sp_addarticle [@publication =] 'publication',
[@article =]'article', [@source_table =] 'source_table'
[,[@destination_table =] 'destination_table']
[,[@vertical_partition =] 'vertical_partition']
[,[@type =] 'type'] [,[@filter =] 'filter'] [,[@sync_object =] 'sync_object']
[,[@ins_cmd =] 'ins_cmd'] [,[@del_cmd =] 'del_cmd']
[,[@upd_cmd =] 'upd_cmd'] [,[@creation_script =] 'creation_script']
[,[@description =] 'description']
[,[@pre_creation_cmd =] 'pre_creation_cmd']
[,[@filter_clause =] 'filter_clause'] [,[@schema_option =] schema_option]
[,[@destination_owner =] 'destination_owner'] [,[@status =] status]
[,[@source_owner =] 'source_owner'][,[@sync_object_owner =] 'source_owner']
[,[@filter_owner =] 'filter_owner'] [,[@source_object =] 'source_object']
```

The arguments are:

[@publication =] 'publication'	Publication is the sysname of the publication that contains the article.
[@article =]'article'	Article is the sysname of the new article.
[@source_table =] 'source_table'	Source_table is the nvarchar(92) name of the table where the data originates.
[@destination_table =] 'destination_table'	Destination table is the sysname of the destination table. The default means use the source_table name for the destination table.
[@vertical_partition =] 'vertical_partition'	Vertical_partition is nchar(5) and holds the values of true or false, the default. If false, all columns are published; if true, it only uses the primary key, and if an article is vertically partitioned, you can add columns using the system stored procedure, sp_articlecolumn.
[@type =] 'type'	Type is the sysname article type where logbased=Log-based article logbased manualfilter=Log-based article with manual filter logbased manualview=Log-based article with manual view logbased manualboth=Log-based article with manual filter and manual view proc exec=Replicates the execution of the stored procedure to the article's Subscribers and serializable proc exec= Replicates the execution of the stored procedure (if it is within a serializable transaction). Type defaults to NULL.
[@filter =] 'filter'	Filter is the nvarchar(92) name of a FOR REPLICATION stored procedure that horizontally filters the table with a default of NULL (the filter procedure is created). You must have previously executed the system stored procedures sp_articleview and sp_articlefilter to create a view and stored procedure if you give a value.

[@sync_object =] 'sync_object'	Sync_object is the nvarchar(92) name (default is NULL) of the table or view used for producing a synchronization output file. If NULL, the view that synchronizes the output file is created automatically when adding columns with the system stored procedure, sp_articlecolumn.
[@ins_cmd =] 'ins_cmd'	Ins_cmd is nvarchar(255) and is the method used for replicating inserts where NONE=No action, CALL customproc=Creates a stored procedure call for the insert to be applied at the Subscriber (you have the task of creating the stored procedure in the destination database to be passed each column in the insert), SQL (default) or NULL=replicates an insert statement by using the syntax insert into <table name> values (column1value, column2value, etc.).
[@del_cmd =] 'del_cmd'	Del_cmd is nvarchar(255) and is the method used for replicating deletes; it is the same as ins_cmd except that deletes are done by primary key values.
[@upd_cmd =] 'upd_cmd'	Upd_cmd is nvarchar(255) and is the method used for replicating deletes; it is the same as ins_cmd except that updartes are done by passing primary key values and the other columns of the article.
[@creation_script =] 'creation_script'	Creation_script is the nvarchar(127) path and name of an article schema script used to create target tables with a NULL default value.
[@description =] 'description'	Description is nvarchar(255) and describes the article and defaults to NULL.
[@pre_creation_cmd =] 'pre_creation_cmd'	Pre_creation_cmd is nvarchar(10) a pre-creation command for drop table, delete table, or truncate where None=No command, Delete=Deletes destination table, drop (default)=Drops destination table, Truncate=Truncates destination table.
[@filter_clause =] 'filter_clause'	Filter_clause is ntext WHERE clause for horizontal partitioning with a default of empty string.

[@schema_option =] schema_option	Schema_option is binary(8) where 0x00=Disables scripting by Snapshot and uses the supplied CreationScript; 0x01=Generates the object creation CREATE TABLE, CREATE PROCEDURE; 0x10=Creates a clustered index; 0x20=Converts user-defined data types to base data types; 0x40=Creates nonclustered indexes; 0x80=Includes declared referential integrity on the primary keys; 0x71=Creates the create table, clustered index, and nonclustered index(es)and converts user-defined data types to base data types (the default); 0x01=Default for stored procedure articles.
[@destination_owner =] 'destination_owner'	Owner is the sysname and represents the owner of the destination object with a NULL default value. If the publication has ODBC Subscribers, use NULL.
[@status =] status	Status is the tinyint bitmask of the article options where 0, 8=include the column name in insert statements, 16=use parameterized statements, 24=use column name and use parameterized statements.
[@source_owner =] 'source_owner'	Source_owner is the sysname and the owner of the source object set to NULL for Microsoft SQL Server 6.5 Publishers.
[@sync_object_owner =] 'sync_object_owner'	Sync_object_owner is the sysname and the owner of the synchronization object set to NULL for Microsoft SQL Server 6.5 Publishers.
[@filter_owner =] 'filter_owner'	Filter is the sysname and the owner of the filter set to NULL for Microsoft SQL Server 6.5 Publishers.
[@source_object =] 'source_object'	Source_object is the sysname and the owner of the source object. If source_table is NULL, this argument must be used instead.

sp_adddistpublisher

The sp_adddistpublisher system stored procedure adds a remote Publisher using the local Distributor for use in snapshot, merge, and transaction replication.

Syntax

The syntax is:

```
sp_adddistpublisher {[@publisher =] 'publisher',
[@distribution_db =] 'distribution_db'} [,[@security_mode =] security_mode]
[,[@login =] 'login'] [,[@password =] 'password']
{,[@working_directory =] 'working_directory'},
[,[@trusted =] 'trusted'] [,[@encrypted_password =] encrypted_password]
[,[@thirdparty_flag =] thirdparty_flag]
```

The arguments are:

[@publisher =] 'publisher'	Publisher is the syname of the Publisher.
[@distribution_db =] 'distribution_db'	The sysname of the distribution database.
[@security_mode =] security_mode	Security_mode is the integer security mode where 0=SQL Server Authentication, 1=Distributor is running on Windows NT, 2=Distributor is running on Windows 95, NULL=default.
[@login =] 'login'	Login is the sysname, defaults to sa and is needed if security_mode is 0=SQL Server Authentication.
[@password =] 'password']	Password is the sysname password for the login used by replication agents to connect to the Publisher.
[@working_directory =] 'working_directory'	Working_directiory is the nvarchar(255) name of the directory where the data and schema files for the publication reside in UNC fomat.
[@trusted =] 'trusted'	Trusted with a nchar(5) value of true means whether the remote Publisher uses the same password as the local Distributor. Two trusted login mappings are added: sa to sa and distributor_admin to distributor_admin. A password is not needed at the remote Publisher to connect to the Distributor. Trusted with a nchar(5) value of false means one non-trusted mapping is added, distributor_admin to distributor_admin. A password is needed at the remote Publisher to connect to the Distributor.
[@encrypted_password =] encrypted_password	Encrypted password is bit data type with default of 0 used by scripting.

[@thirdparty_flag =] thirdparty_flag]	Thirdparty_flag is a bit and determines if the publication is a data source other than Microsoft SQL Server, where 0=Microsoft SQL Server database and 1=data source other than Microsoft SQL Server.

sp_adddistributiondb

The sp_adddistributiondb adds a new Distributor database with the Distributor schema to hold the procedures for distribution and its history for use in snapshot, merge, and transaction replication.

Syntax

The syntax is:

```
sp_adddistributiondb {[@database =] 'database'}
[,[@data_folder =] 'data_folder'] [,[@data_file =] 'data_file']
[,[@data_file_size =] 'data_file_size'] [,[@log_folder =] 'log_folder']
[,[@log_file =] 'log_file'] [,[@log_file_size =] log_file_size]
[,[@min_distretention =] min_distretention]
[,[@max_distretention =] max_distretention]
[,[@history_retention =] history_retention]
[,[@security_mode =] security_mode] [,[@login =] 'login']
[,[@password =] 'password']
[,[@encrypted_password =] encrypted_password]
[,[@createmode =] createmode]
```

The arguments are:

[@database =] 'database'	Database is the sysname of the database.
[@data_folder =] 'data_folder'	Data_folder is the nvarchar(255) name of the directory holding the database files defaulting to the path where SQL Server was installed (if you installed and let the default hold, this would default to \mssql7\data).
[@data_file =] 'data_file'	Data_file represents the nvarchar(255) name of the database file. The database name is used to create the name if none is supplied.
[@data_file_size =] 'data_file_size'	Data_file_size is an integer in megabytes and represents the beginning data file size and defaulting to 2MB.
[@log_folder =] 'log_folder'	Log_folder is the nvarchar(255) name of the directory for the database log file.

[@log_file =] 'log_file'	Log_file is the nvarchar(255) name of the log file. If not supplied, the log_file name is created using the database name.
[@log_file_size =] log_file_size	Log_ file_size is an integer in megabytes and represents the beginning log file size and defaulting to 0MB meaning 512KB.
[@min_distretention =] min_distretention	Min_distretention is an integer and represents the minimum hours prior to the removal of transactions with default of zero.
[@max_distretention =] max_distretention	Max_distretention is an integer and represents the maximum hours prior to the removal of transactions with default of 24 hours. Inactive Subscriptions after this time are deactivated with a Raiserror 21011 for each deactivated subscription.
[@history_retention =] history_retention	History_retention is an integer and represents the number of hours to keep history defaulting to 48 hours.
[@security_mode =] security_mode	Security_mode is an integer and represents what is on the Distributor, where 0=SQL Server Authentication or 1=Windows NT Authentication defaulting to 0.
[@login =] 'login'	Login is the sysname, defaults to sa and is needed if security_mode is 0=SQL Server Authentication.
[@password =] 'password'	Password is the sysname password for the login which is used by replication agents to connect to the Distributor.
[@encrypted_password =] encrypted_password	Encrypted password is bit data type with default of 0 used by scripting.
[@createmode =] createmode	Createmode is an integer where 0=Use create db for attach, 1=Create db or use existing but no attach (the default), and 2=Create for instdist and detach only.

sp_adddistributor

The sp_adddistributor system stored procedure adds an entry in the sysservers table for the Distributor with property data for use in snapshot, merge, and transaction replication.

Syntax

The syntax is:

```
sp_adddistributor {[@distributor =] 'distributor'},
[,[@heartbeat_interval =] 'heartbeat_interval'] [,[@login =] 'login']
[,[@password =] 'password']
```

The arguments are:

[@distributor =] 'distributor'	Distributor is the sysname server name.
[@heartbeat_interval =] 'heartbeat_interval'	Heartbeat_interval is an integer that creates a job to check the replication agents and represents the maximum minutes that an agent can go without logging a message defaulting to 10 minutes.
[@login =] 'login'	Login is the distributor_admin login sysname defaulting to sa.
[@password =] 'password']	Password is the sysname password of distributor_admin login defaulting to NULL for linked server entry for distributor RPC connection. If the distributor is local the password for distributor_admin is set to new value.

sp_addextendedproc

The sp_addextendedproc system stored procedure registers the name of an extended stored procedure and must be run within the context of the master system database and creates rows in the *syscomments* and *sysobjects* system tables.

Syntax

The syntax is:

```
sp_addextendedproc [@functname =] 'procedure', [@dllname =] 'dll'
```

The arguments are:

[@functname =] '*procedure*'	Procedure is nvarchar(257) and is the name of the function to call within the dynamic-link library (DLL).
[@dllname =] '*dll*'	DLL is the varchar(255) name of the DLL.

sp_addgroup

The sp_addgroup system stored procedure adds a role in the current database and is used for backward compatibility. A version 7.0 programmer uses roles instead.

Syntax

The syntax is:

```
sp_addgroup [@rolename =] 'role'
```

The argument, role, is the name of the role to add.

sp_add_category

The sp_add_category system stored procedure adds a category to a server.

Syntax

The syntax is:

```
sp_add_category [[@class =] 'class',] [[@type =] 'type',] {[@name =] 'name'}
```

The arguments are:

[@class =] 'class'	Class is the varchar(8) class of the category where JOB= Add a job (type must be MULTISERVER), ALERT=Add an alert, OPERATOR=Add an operator.
[@type =] 'type'	Type is the varchar(12) type of category to be added where LOCAL =Local computer (the default), MULTI SERVER=Member of the MSX domain, and `NONE=None.
[@name =] 'name'	Name is the varchar(100) name of the server.

sp_add_job

The sp_add_job system stored procedure creates a new job.

Syntax

The syntax is:

```
sp_add_job [@job_name =] 'job_name'}
[, [@enabled =] enabled] [, [@description =] 'description']
[, [@start_step_id =] step_id] [, [@category_name =] 'category']
[, [@category_id =] category_id] [, [@owner_login_name =] 'login']
[, [@notify_level_eventlog =] eventlog_level]
[, [@notify_level_email =] email_level]
[, [@notify_level_netsend =] netsend_level]
[, [@notify_level_page =] page_level]
[, [@notify_email_operator_name =] 'email_name']
[, [@notify_netsend_operator_name =] 'netsend_name']
[, [@notify_page_operator_name =] 'page_name']
[, [@delete_level =] delete_level] [, [@job_id =] job_id OUTPUT]
```

The arguments are:

'job_name'	Job_name is the sysname of the job.
Enabled	Enabled determines if the job is enabled or not enabled where 1=Enabled and 0=disabled and defaults to 1.
'description'	Description is the nvarchar(512) description of the job and defaults to 'No description available.'
step_id	Step_id is the integer that is the number of the first step of the job with a default of 1.
'category'	Category is the sysname category for the job and defaults to NULL.
category_id	Category is the integer identifying a job category and defaults to NULL.
'login'	Login is the sysname of the login whose permissions are used to run the job and defaults to NULL.
eventlog_level	Eventlog_level is an integer that determines when the NT event log entries occur for the job being created where 0=Never, 1=On Success, 2=On Failure, 3=Always, and the default is 2.
email_level	Email_level is an integer that determines when an e-mail is sent where 0=Never, 1=On Success, 2=On Failure, 3=Always, and the default is 0.

netsend_level	Netsend_level is an integer that determines when a network message is sent where 0=Never, 1=On Success, 2=On Failure, 3=Always, and the default is 0.
page_level	Page_level is an integer that determines when a page is sent to a pager where 0=Never, 1=On Success, 2=On Failure, 3=Always, and the default is 0.
'email_name'	E-mail_name is the nvarchar(100) name of the person to e-mail on email_level and defaults to NULL.
'netsend_name'	Netsend_name is the nvarchar(100) name of the operator to send a network message on netsend_level and defaults to NULL.
'page_name'	Page_name is the nvarchar(100) name of the person to page on page_level and defaults to NULL.
delete_level	Delete_level is an integer that determines when the job is deleted where 0=Never, 1=On Success, 2=On Failure, 3=Always, and the default is 0.
job_id	Job_id is the uniqueidentifer of the job and defaults to NULL.

sp_add_jobschedule

The sp_add_jobschedule system stored procedure puts the job on a schedule.

Syntax

The syntax is:

```
sp_add_jobschedule {[@job_id =] job_id | [@job_name =] 'job_name'}
{[@name =] 'name'} [,[@enabled =] enabled] [,[@freq_type =]
freq_type]
[,[@freq_interval =] freq_interval]
[,[@freq_subday_type =] freq_subday_type]
[,[@freq_subday_interval =] freq_subday_interval]
[,[@freq_relative_interval =] freq_relative_interval]
[,[@freq_recurrence_factor =] freq_recurrence_factor]
[,[@active_start_date =] active_start_date]
[,[@active_end_date =] active_end_date]
[,[@active_start_time =] active_start_time]
[,[@active_end_time =] active_end_time]
```

The arguments are:

job_id	Job_id is the uniqueidentifier of the job and defaults to NULL. Supply either job_id or name.
'job_name'	Job_name is the varchar(100) name of the job to put on a schedule and defaults to NULL. Supply either job_id or name.
'name'	Name is the varchar(100) name of the schedule entry the job.
Enabled	Enabled is tinyint and determines if the job is enabled or not enabled to run on schedule where 1=Enabled and 0=disabled and defaults to 1.
freq_type	Freq_type is an integer determining when the job is run with a default of 0 where 1=Once, 4=Daily, 8=Weekly, 16=Monthly, 32=Monthly (according to the freq interval), 64=Run when SQL Server Agent starts.
freq_interval	Freq_interval is an integer determining the days the job runs with a default of 0 where 1=Sunday, 2=Monday, 3=Tuesday, 4=Wednesday, 5=Thursday, 6=Friday, 7=Saturday, 8=day, 9=weekdays, 10=weekend days.
freq_subday_type	Freq_subday_type is an integer representing the units for freq_subday_interval and has a default of 0 where 1=At the specified time, 2=Seconds, 3=Minutes, 4=Hours.
freq_subday_interval	Freq_subday_interval is an integer defaulting to 0 and determining the number of freq_subday_type units between each job run.
freq_relative_interval	Freq_relative_interval is an integer and determines the freq_interval in each month with a default of 0, where 1=First, 2=Second, 4=Third, 8=Fourth, 16=Last.
freq_recurrence_factor	Freq_recurrence_factor is an integer that represents the number of months between the job run and defaults to 0.
active_start_date	Active_start_date is an integer that represents the date to start running the job with a default of NULL and a format of YYYYMMDD.
active_end_date	Active_end_date is an integer that represents the date to stop running the job with a default of 99991231 (December 31, 9999).

active_start_time	Active_start_time is an integer representing the time to start running the job with a default of 000000 (12:00:00 A.M.) and a format of HHMMSS.
active_end_time	Active_end_time is an integer representing the time to start running the job with a default of 235959 (11:59:59 P.M.).

sp_add_jobserver

The sp_add_jobserver system stored procedure adds the server to servers that are capable of running jobs.

Syntax

The syntax is:

```
sp_add_jobserver [{job_id | 'job_name'}, ] {'server'} [automatic_post]
```

The arguments are:

job_id	Job_id is the uniqueidentifer of the job to add to the server and defaults to NULL. Supply either job_id or name.
'job_name'	Job_name is the varchar(100) name of the job to put on a schedule and defaults to NULL. Supply either job_id or name.
'server'	Server is the varchar(30) name of the server to add to run jobs and is (Local) or target server name.

sp_add_jobstep

The sp_add_jobstep system stored procedure creates a step for a job. You can add the step to the schedule by using the sp_add_jobschedule system stored procedure.

Syntax

The syntax is:

```
sp_add_jobstep {[@job_id =] job_id | [@job_name =] 'job_name']}
[, [@step_id =] step_id] , {[@step_name =] 'step_name'}
[, [@subsystem =] 'subsystem'] [, [@command =] 'command']
[, [@additional_parameters =] 'parameters']
[, [@cmdexec_success_code =] code]
[, [@on_success_action =] success_action]
[, [@on_success_step_id =] success_step_id]
[, [@on_fail_action =] fail_action]
```

```
[, [@on_fail_step_id =] fail_step_id] [, [@server =] 'server']
[, [@database_name =] 'database'] [, [@database_user_name =] 'user']
[, [@retry_attempts =] retry_attempts] [, [@retry_interval =] retry_interval]
[, [@os_run_priority =] run_priority] [, [@output_file_name =] 'file_name']
[, [@flags =] flags]
```

The arguments are:

job_id	Job_id is the uniqueidentifer of the job and defaults to NULL. Supply either job_id or name.
'job_name'	Job_name is the varchar(100) name of the job and defaults to NULL. Supply either job_id or name.
step_id	Step_id is the integer for the job step with a default of NULL.
'step_name'	Step_name is the sysname of the step.
'subsystem'	Subsystem is varchar(60) and the subsystem used by SQL Server Enterprise Manager to execute command. The default is TSQL.
'command'	Command is the nvarchar(3200) command(s) sent to SQL Server Agent for execution with a default of NULL. Command can have tokens where [A-DBN]=Database name, [A-SVR]=Server name, [A-ERR]=Error number, [A-SEV]=Error severity, [A-MSG]=Message text, [DATE]=Current date formatted as YYYYMMDD, [JOBID]=Job ID, [MACH]=Computer name, [MSSA]=Master SQLServerAgent name, [SQLDIR]=Installation directory of SQL Server (C:\MSSQL7), [STEPCT]=Number of times this step has run., [STEPID]=Step ID, [TIME]=Current time formatted as HHMMSS, [STRTTM]=The time the job started formatted as HHMMSS, [STRDT]=The date the job started formatted as YYYYMMDD.
code	Code is the integer return value for successful completion and defaults to 0.
success_action	Success_action is tinyint and determines what to do when a success code is returned, where1 =Quit With Success and is the default, 2=Quit With Failure, 3=Goto Next Step, 4=Goto Step success_step_id.

success_step_id	Success_step_id is the step in this job to run, where success code and success_action is 4 with a default of 0.
fail_action	Fail_action is tinyint and is a return value that is not code, where 1=Quit With Success, 2 (default)=Quit With Failure, 3=Goto Next Step, 4=Goto Step fail_step_id.
fail_step_id	Fail_step_id is the step in this job to run when not code and success_action is 4 with default of 0.
'server'	Server is the nvarchar(30) name of the server to run the step and defaults to NULL.
'database'	Database is the sysname of the database to run the step and defaults to NULL.
'user'	User is the sysname of the user account used to run this step and defaults to NULL.
retry_attempts	Retry_attempts is the integer determining how many times to retry when the step fails and defaults to 0.
retry_interval	Retry_interval is the integer representing the number of seconds between retries with a default of 0.
run_priority	Run_priority is an integer representing the OS priority to use to run the step, where –15=Idle, -1=Below Normal, 0 =Normal (the default), 1=Above Normal, 15=Time Critical.
'file_name'	File_name is the nvarchar(200) name of the output file in which the output of this step is saved and can include the command tokens.

sp_addlinkedserver

The sp_addlinkedserver system stored procedure defines a linked server that allows access to distributed queries through OLE DB data sources; it also allows remote stored procedure calls between two SQL Servers. The DataSource, Location, and ProviderString arguments identify the database for the linked server. If any of these arguments are NULL, then the corresponding OLE DB initialization property is not set. If you want the data source to be Microsoft SQL Server, use NULL values for the ProviderName, the DataSource, the Location, and the ProviderString. The SQL Server OLE DB will be used. Provide the ProductName and Server arguments only.

SQL Server OLE DB Provider	Product_name= 'SQL Server' (default)	Provider_name= N'SQLOLEDB' data_source is server

Microsoft OLE DB Provider for Jet	Product_name=' '	Provider_name= 'Microsoft.Jet.OLEDB.4.0' data_source= path\ filename of Microsoft Access .mdf database file.
Microsoft OLE DB Provider for Oracle	Product_name=' Oracle'	Provider_name= 'MSDAORA' data_source= the SQL*Net Alias for an Oracle database instance created on the server SQL Server
OLE DB Provider for ODBC (Using data_source parameter)	Product_name=' '	Provider_name= 'MSDASQL' data_source= 'LocalServer'
OLE DB Provider for ODBC	Product_name=' '	Provider_name = 'MSDASQL' provider_string= 'DRIVER={SQL Server};SERVER=servername; UID=login;PWD=password;'

Syntax

The syntax is:

```
sp_addlinkedserver
{
[@server = ] 'server',
[@srvproduct = ] 'product_name',
[@provider = ] 'provider_name',
[@datasrc = ] 'data_source',
[@location = ] 'location',
[@provstr = ] 'provider_string',
[@catalog = ] 'catalog'
}
```

The arguments are:

ServerName	ServerName is the name of the linked server.
ProductName	ProductName is the name of the product you will be using as an OLE DB provider. It has a default of NULL. This is nvarchar datatype to 128 characters. The datatype nvarchar is to store Unicode character data.

ProviderName	Provider name must be a unique name and represents the OLE DB provider specified in *ProductName.* The provider name is nvarchar datatype to 128 characters. The datatype nvarchar is to store Unicode character data and has a default of NULL. The ProviderName must be registered in the NT registry. Data providers present different data sources to OLE DB interface calls. The OLE DB providers available from Microsoft are the ones that work with SQL Server data sources, the SQLOLEDB native provider, and the OLE DB provider for ODBC.
DataSource	Data source is the name of the data source given to the OLE DB provider. The provider name is nvarchar datatype to 4000 characters.
Location	Location is the location of the database as interpreted by the OLE DB provider. The provider name is nvarchar datatype to 4000 characters. The datatype nvarchar is to store Unicode character data and has a default of NULL.
ProviderString	ProviderString indicates a unique data source. The provider name is nvarchar datatype to 4000 characters. The datatype nvarchar is to store Unicode character data and has a default of NULL.
[@catalog =] '*catalog*'	Catalog is the sysname of the catalog to be used when making a connection to the OLE DB provider and defaults to NULL.

Example

Here's an example of the sp_addlinkedserver stored procedure:

```
sp_addlinkedserver    'RemoteServerName',    '',     'MSDASQL',
'LocalServerName',    NULL,     NULL
```

In this example, a remote linked server is defined that uses an OLE DB ODBC provider and the Data Source DSN arguments.

Example

Here's another example of the sp_addlinkedserver stored procedure:

```
EXEC sp_addlinkedserver 'RemoteServerName', 'SQL Server',
NULL,NULL,    NULL,    NULL
```

In this example, a linked server is defined that uses the OLE DB provider.

Example

Here's another example of the sp_addlinkedserver stored procedure:

```
sp_addlinkedserver 'RemoteServerName', 'MSDASQL', NULL,NULL,
'DRIVER={SQL Server};SERVER=LocalServer;UID=sa:PWD=;'
```

In this example, a linked server is defined that uses the OLE DB ODBC provider and the provider string argument.

Example

Here's another example of the sp_addlinkedserver stored procedure:

```
sp_addlinkedserver     'AccessRemoteServer', '', 'Microsoft.Jet.OLEDB.4.0',
    'C:\MSOffice\Access\Samples\Northwind.mdb',     NULL,     NULL
```

In this example, a linked server is defined using Microsoft Access OLE DB provider. You must have Microsoft Access installed on your machine.

sp_addlinkedsrvlogin

The sp_addlinkedsrvlogin stored procedure maps a login ID from one local server to a login ID on another remote server. The way this works is that a user logs into the local database and runs a query that uses a table on another server. This determines whose permissions the user will use to connect to the remote server from this local server.

This stored procedure is a little different in that if the UseSelf argument is set to true, it will not use the other arguments of RemoteUser and RemotePassword even if they are supplied. If the LocalLogin argument is set to NULL or not indicated at all, the mapping of RemoteUser and RemotePassword applies to all logins connecting to the remote server.

It is important to note that a default mapping always exists and is created by executing the new stored procedure sp_addlinkedserver. The default mapping is that the permissions of the local login ID are used when connecting to the linked server on behalf of the login ID. The new stored procedure sp_addlinkedsrvlogin can be used to change the default mapping and to create mappings tailored to each login ID. Permissions for the user are determined by what permissions are given to the login ID on the remote server. These may differ from the permissions given on the local server.

Syntax

The syntax is:

```
sp_addlinkedsrvlogin [@rmtsrvname =] 'rmtsrvname'
[,[@useself =] 'useself' [,[@locallogin =] 'locallogin'
[,[@rmtuser =] 'rmtuser' [,[@rmtpassword =] 'rmtpassword']]]]
```

The arguments are:

[@rmtsrvname =] 'rmtsrvname'	Rmtsrvname is the sysname of the remote server.
[,[@useself =] 'useself'	Useself is varchar(8) with a value of true or false. A value of true means that logins will use their SQL Server authentication permissions to connect to the remote server. (True is not valid for NT authenticated users). If true is used, the RemoteUser and the RemotePassword arguments will not be used. A value of false means that the RemoteUser and the RemotePassword arguments will be used to connect to the remote server. If NULL is used, rmtuser and rmtpassword are used to connect.
[,[@locallogin =] 'locallogin'	LocalLogin is the sysname and defaults to NULL, which means this argument refers to all local logins trying to connect to the remote server. This login ID must have a row in the syslogins table on the local server if it is not NULL.
[,[@rmtuser =] 'rmtuser'	Rmtuser is the sysname and used when the argument UseSelf is set to NULL. This is the user that will be used to connect to the remote server. This argument has a default of NULL.
[,[@rmtpassword =] 'rmtpassword']	This is a remote password associated with the remote user. This argument has a default of NULL.

sp_addlogin

The sp_addlogin stored procedure adds a SQL Server authenticated login to connect to Microsoft SQL Server.

Syntax

The syntax is:

```
sp_addlogin [@loginame =] 'login' [,[@passwd =] 'password'
[,[@defdb =] 'database' [,[@deflanguage =] 'language'
[,[@sid =] 'sid' [,[@encryptopt =] 'encryption_option']]]]]
```

The arguments are:

[@loginame =] 'login'	Login is the sysname of the login.
[@passwd =] 'password'	Password is the sysname of the password and defaults to NULL.
[@defdb =] 'database'	Database is the default database sysname of the database the login uses after logging in and the default is the master system database. It is best not to let users login with a default of the master database. Make this a user database.
[@deflanguage =] 'language'	Language is the default language a user uses after logging in to SQL Server. The default is what is defined by sp_configure.
[@sid =] 'sid'	SID is the varbinary(16) security identification number. This parameter is only used when a database user has no login and is an orphan. The security identification number you supply must not exist. Supply this and SQL Server will not generate its own.
[@encryptopt =] 'encryption_option'	Encryption_option determines if the password is encrypted where NULL=The password is encrypted, skip_encryption=The password is not encrypted, skip_encryption_old=The password is not encrypted but was encrypted by an earlier version of SQL Server (for upgrade only).

sp_addmergearticle

The sp_addmergearticle system stored procedure adds an article to a merge publication.

Syntax

The syntax is:

```
sp_addmergearticle {@publication =] 'publication', [@article =] 'article',
[@source_object =] 'source_object'}
 [,[@type =] 'type']
```

```
[,[@description =] 'description']
[,[@column_tracking =] 'column_tracking'] [,[@status =] 'status']
[,[@pre_creation_cmd =] 'pre_creation_cmd']
[,[@creation_script =] 'creation_script']
[,[@schema_option =] schema_option]
[,[@subset_filterclause =] 'subset_filterclause']
[,[@article_resolver =] 'article_resolver']
[,[@resolver_info =] 'resolver_info']
[,[@source_owner =] 'source_owner']
```

The arguments are:

[@publication =] 'publication'	Publication is the sysname of the publication with the article.
[@article =] 'article'	Article is the sysname of the article which must be a tablename (e.g., MyTable).
[@source_object =] 'source_object'	Source_object is the nvarchar(386) name of the source object from which to add the article (e.g., dbo.MyTable).
[@type =] 'type'	Type is the sysname of the type of article with only a type of table allowed for now.
[@description =] 'description'	Description is the nvarchar(255) descriptions of the article and defaults to NULL.
[@column_tracking =] 'column_tracking'	Column_tracking is the nvarchar(10) true false indicator for column level tracking which defaults to false for column tracking turned off. If the table is already published using merge replication, use the same column tracking value and set this to true.
[@status =] 'status'	Status is the nvarchar(10) status of the article and defaults to unsynced, meaning the initial data is assumed there. If the status is active, the initial processing script runs.
[@pre_creation_cmd =] 'pre_creation_cmd'	Pre_creation_cmd is the nvarchar(10) pre-creation method where None=If the table already exists at the Subscriber it does nothing, Delete=Deletes and filters on the WHERE clause in the subset filter, Drop=Drops the table before recreating it and is the default, Truncate=Same as delete, but deletes pages (no WHERE clause).

[@creation_script =] 'creation_script'	Creation_script is the nvarchar(255) pre-creation script for the article (optional and defaults to NULL).
[@schema_option =] schema_option	Schema_option is a binary(8) bitmap of the schema generation for the article where 0x00=Disables scripting by Snapshot and uses the provided CreationScript; 0x01=Generates the object creation (CREATE TABLE, CREATE PROCEDURE); 0x10=Generates a clustered index; 0x20=Converts user-defined data types to base data types; 0x40=Generates nonclustered indexes; 0x80=Provides declared referential integrity on the primary keys; 0xf1 (default)=Makes the create table, creates clustered indexes, creates nonclustered index(es), converts user-defined data types to base data types; 0x01=The default for stored procedure articles.
[@subset_filterclause =] 'subset_filterclause'	Subset_filterclause is a nvarchar(2000) WHERE clause determining the horizontal filtering.
[@article_resolver =] 'article_resolver'	Article_resolver is the varchar(255) custom resolver for the article. The stored procedure, sp_enumcustomsolvers, lists the custom resolvers. If left NULL, a system-supplied resolver is used.
[@resolver_info =] 'resolver_info']	Resolver_info is the sysname of the stored procedure used as a custom resolver and defaults to NULL.
[,[@source_owner =] 'source_owner']	Source_owner is the sysname and the owner of the source object. If this is left NULL, the current user is the default.

Example

Here's an example of the sp_addmergearticle stored procedure:

```
EXEC sp_addmergearticle @publication = 'mergeMyDB ,
@article = 'MyTable', @source_object = 'dbo.MyTable',
@type = 'table', @description = null, @column_tracking = 'true',
@status = 'unsynced', @pre_creation_cmd = 'drop',
@creation_script = null, @schema_option = 0x0000000000000071,
@article_resolver = null, @subset_filterclause = null
```

In this example, a merge article is added to a publication.

sp_addmergefilter

The sp_addmergefilter adds a merge filter to make a partition by joining another table and is used in articles with foreign keys to a published primary key table with a filter.

Syntax

The syntax is:

```
sp_ addmergefilter {[@publication =], 'publication',
[@article =] 'article', [@filtername =] 'filtername',
[@join_articlename =] 'join_articlename'}
[,[@join_filterclause =] join_filterclause]
[,[@join_unique_key =] join_unique_key]
```

The arguments are:

[@publication =], 'publication'	Publication is the sysname of the publication.
[@article =] 'article'	Article is the sysname of the article.
[@filtername =] 'filtername'	Filtername is the sysname of the filter.
[@join_articlename =] 'join_articlename'	Join article name is the nvarchar(258) name of the table joined with the base table and contained in the publication.
[@join_filterclause =] join_filterclause	Join_filterclause is the nvarchar(2000) filter clause qualifying the join and defines only boolean filters in this stored procedure.
[@join_unique_key =] join_unique_key	Join_unique_key is an integer and defaults to 0.

sp_addmergepublication

The sp_addmergepublication system stored procedure adds a merge publication.

Syntax

The syntax is:

```
sp_addmergepublication {[@publication =] 'publication'}
[,[@description =] 'description' [,[@retention =] retention]
[,[@sync_mode =] 'sync_mode', [@allow_push =] 'allow_push']
```

```
[,[@allow_pull =] 'allow_pull'] [@allow_anonymous =] 'allow_anonymous']
[,[@enabled_for_internet =] 'enabled_for_internet']
[,[@centralized_conflicts =] 'centralized_conflicts']
[,[@default_access =] 'default_access']
 [,[@dynamic_filters =] 'dynamic_filters']
```

The arguments are:

[@publication =] 'publication'	Publication is the sysname of the new merge publication.
[@description =] 'description'	Description is the nvarchar(255) publication description.
[@retention =] retention	Retention is an integer representing how many days to save the given publication with a default of 60 days. The subscription has to merge in the retention period or it will not sync.
[@sync_mode =] 'sync_mode'	Sync_mode is the nvarchar(10) mode of the synchronization and defaults to native. Native=bulk copy Character=character bulk copy
[@allow_push =] 'allow_push'	Allow_push is true or false (nvarchar(5)) determining if push subscriptions are permitted for the publication.
[@allow_pull =] 'allow_pull'	Allow_pull is true or false (nvarchar(5)) determining if pull subscriptions are permitted for the publication.
[@allow_anonymous =] 'allow_anonymous'	Allow_anonymous is true or false (nvarchar(5)) determining if anonymous subscriptions are permitted for the publication.
[@enabled_for_internet =] 'enabled_for_internet'	Enabled_for_internet is nvarchar(5), with a default of false, and determines whether the publication is enabled for the Internet. FTP is used to send the snapshot to the Subscriber.
[@centralized_conflicts =] 'centralized_conflicts'	Centralized_confilicts is nvarchar(5) and determines if conflict records are stored on the Publisher and defaults to true. False means the storage occurs at the Subscriber.
[@default_access =] 'default_access'	Default_access is nvarchar(5) and defaults to true.

[,[@dynamic_filters =] 'dynamic_filters']	Dynamic_filters is nvarchar(5) and determines if the publication filters on a dynamic clause and defaults to false.

sp_addmergepullsubscription

The sp_addmergepullsubscription system stored procedure creates a pull merge subscription.

Syntax

The syntax is:

```
sp_addmergepullsubscription {[@publication =] 'publication'}
[,[@publisher =] 'publisher'] [,[@publisher_db =] 'publisher_db']
[,[@subscriber_type =] 'subscriber_type']
[,[@subscription_priority =] subscription_priority]
[,[@sync_type =] 'sync_type'] [,[@description =] 'description']
```

The arguments are:

[@publication =] 'publication'	Publication is the sysname of the publication.
[@publisher =] 'publisher'	Publisher is the sysname (server name) of the Publisher.
[@publisher_db =] 'publisher_db	Publisher_db is the sysname of the Publisher database and defaults to NULL.
[@subscriber_type =] 'subscriber_type'	Subscriber_type is nvarchar(15) and defaults to local with values of global, local, or anonymous.
[@subscription_prirority =] subscription_prirority	Subscription priority is real data type and defaults to NULL and is used to resolve conflicts. Local = 0.0 Anonymous=0.0
[@sync_type =] 'sync_type'	Sync_type is the nvarchar(15) subscription synchronization type and defaults to automatic. Automatic=schema and data transfer Nosync=no schema and data transfer.

[@description =] 'description'	Description is a varchar(255) pull subscription description and defaults to NULL.

sp_addmergepullsubscription_agent

The sp_addmergepullsubscription_agent system stored procedure is used to add a merge pull subscription agent at the Subscriber.

Syntax

The syntax is:

```
sp_addmergepullsubscription_agent [[@name =] 'name']
{,[@publisher =]'publisher , [@publisher_db =] 'publisher_db',
[@publication =] 'publication'}
[,[@publisher_security_mode =] publisher_security_mode]
[,[@publisher_login =] 'publisher_login']
[,[@publisher_password =] 'publisher_password']
[,[@publisher_encrypted_password =] publisher_encrypted_password]
[,[@subscriber =] 'subscriber']
[,[@subscriber_db =] 'subscriber_db']
[,[@subscriber_security_mode =] subscriber_security_mode]
[,[@subscriber_login =] 'subscriber_login']
[,[@subscriber_password =] 'subscriber_password']
[,[@distributor =] 'distributor']
[,[@distributor_security_mode =] distributor_security_mode]
[,[@distributor_login =] 'distributor_login ]
[,[@distributor_password =] 'distributor_password']
[,[@encrypted_password =] encrypted_password]
[,[@frequency_type =] frequency_type]
[,[@frequency_interval =] frequency_interval]
[,[@frequency_relative_interval =] frequency_relative_interval]
[,[@frequency_recurrence_factor =] frequency_recurrence_factor]
[,[@frequency_subday =] frequency_subday]
[,[@frequency_subday_interval =] frequency_subday_interva]
[,[@active_start_time_of_day =] active_start_time_of_day]
[,[@active_end_time_of_day =] active_end_time_of_day]
[,[@active_start_date =] active_start_date]
[,[@active_end_date =] active_end_date]
[,[@optional_command_line =] 'optional_command_line']
[,[@merge_jobid =] merge_jobid]
[,[@agent_mode =] agent_mode]
```

The arguments are:

[@name =] 'name'	Name is the sysname of the agent and defaults to NULL.
[@publisher =] 'publisher'	Publisher is the sysname (server name) of the Publisher.
[@publisher_db =] 'publisher_db'	Publisher_db is the sysname of the Publisher database.
[@publication =] 'publication'	Publication is the sysname of the publication.
[@publisher_security_mode =] publisher_security_mode	Publisher_security_mode is an integer and the security mode at the Publisher with a default of 1.
[@publisher_login =] 'publisher_login'	Publisher_login is the sysname and defaults to NULL.
[@publisher_password =] 'publisher_password'	Publisher_password is the sysname and defaults to NULL.
[@publisher_encrypted_password =] publisher_encrypted_password	Publisher_encrypted_password is a bit datatype and defaults to 0.
[@subscriber =] 'subscriber'	Subscriber is the sysname of the subscriber.
[@subscriber_db =] 'subscriber_db'	Subscriber_db is the sysname of the subscriber database.
[@subscriber_security_mode =] subscriber_security_mode	Subscriber_security_mode is an integer that represents the security mode of the Subscriber with default of 1. 0=SQL Server Authentication 1=Windows NT Authentication
[@subscriber_login =] 'subscriber_login'	Subscriber login is used for SQL Server Authentication (subscriber security mode) with a default of NULL.
[@subscriber_password =] 'subscriber_password'	Subscriber password is the sysname used for SQL Server Authentication (subscriber security mode of 0) with a default of NULL.
[@distributor =] 'distributor'	Distributor is the sysname of the Distributor with a default of the Publisher server.
[@distributor_security_mode =] distributor_security_mode	Distributor_security_mode is an integer that represents the security mode of the Distributor with a default of 1. 0=SQL Server Authentication 1=Windows NT Authentication

[@distributor_login =] 'distributor_login'	Distributor login is used for SQL Server Authentication (subscriber security mode) with a default of sa.
[@distributor_password =] 'distributor_password'	Distributor password is the sysname used for SQL Server Authentication (subscriber security mode) with a default of NULL.
[@encrypted_password =] encrypted_password	Encrypted_password is a bit data type used by scripting to determine if the password is encrypted and defaults to 0.
[@frequency_type =] frequency_type	Frequency_type is an integer that determines how to schedule the Distribution Agent. 1=One Time, 2=On Demand, 4=Daily, 8=Weekly, 16=Monthly, 32=Monthly Relative, 64=Autostart, 124=Recurring, NULL=the default value.
[@frequency_interval =] frequency_interval	Frequency interval is an integer that represents the run days of the Distribution Agent. 1=Sunday, 2=Monday, 3=Tuesday, 4=Wednesday, 5=Thursday, 6=Friday, 7=Saturday, 8=day, 9=weekdays, 10=weekend days, NULL=the default value.
[@frequency_relative_interval =] frequency_relative_interval	Frequency_relative_interval is an integer used for a frequency_type of monthly relative. 1=First, 2=Second, 4=Third, 8=Fourth, 16=Last, NULL=the default.
[@frequency_recurrence_factor =] frequency_recurrence_factor	Frequency_recurrence_factor is an integer used in conjunction with frequency_type and defaults to NULL.
[@frequency_subday =] frequency_subday	Frequency_subday is an integer representing when to schedule again during the selected time period. 1=Once, 2=Second, 4=Minute, 8=Hour, NULL=the default.
[@frequency_subday_interval =] frequency_subday_interval	Frequency_subday_interval is an integer representing the interval for frequency_subday and defaults to NULL.
[@active_start_time_of_day =] active_start_time_of_day	Active_start_time_of_day is an integer representing the first time the Distribution Agent is scheduled and defaults to NULL (HHMMSS).

[@active_end_time_of_day =] active_end_time_of_day	Active_end_time_of_day is an integer representing the time the Distribution Agent stops being scheduled with a default of NULL (HHMMSS).
[@active_start_date =] active_start_date	Active_start_date is an integer representing the first date the Distribution Agent is scheduled and defaults to NULL (YYYYMMDD).
[@active_end_date =] active_end_date	Active_end_date is an integer representing the date when the Distribution Agent stops being scheduled and defaults to NULL (YYYMMDD).
[@optional_command_line =] 'optional_command_line'	Optional_command_line is nvarchar(255) commands given to the Distribution Agent. and defaults to NULL.
[@merge_jobid =] merge_jobid	Merge_jobid is binary(16) and is an output parameter which defaults to NULL.
[@agent_mode =] agent_mode	Agent_mode is nvarchar(200) and the mode in which the agent is created and can be one of the following values: none=No agent sqlagent=SQL Server Agent mobilesync=Mobile synchronization agent both=SQL Server Agent and mobile synchronization agent.

sp_addmergesubscription

The sp_addmergesubscription system stored procedure adds a push or pull merge subscription.

Syntax

The syntax is:

```
sp_addmergesubscription {[@publication =] 'publication'}
[,[@subscriber =] 'subscriber'] [,[@subscriber_db =]
'subscriber_db']
[,[@subscription_type =] 'subscription_type']
[,[@subscriber_type =] 'subscriber_type']
[,[@subscription_priority =] subscription_priority]
[,[@sync_type =] 'sync_type']
[,[@frequency_type =] frequency_type]
[,[@frequency_interval =] frequency_interval]
```

```
[,[@frequency_relative_interval =] frequency_relative_interval]
[,[@frequency_recurrence_factor =] frequency_recurrence_factor]
[,[@frequency_subday =] frequency_subday]
[,[@frequency_subday_interval =] frequency_subday_interval]
[,[@active_start_time_of_day =] active_start_time_of_day]
[,[@active_end_time_of_day =] active_end_time_of_day]
[,[@active_start_date =] active_start_date]
[,[@active_end_date =] active_end_date]
[,[@optional_command_line =] 'optional_command_line']
[,[@description =] 'description']
```

The arguments are:

[@publication =] 'publication'	Publication is the sysname of the publication.
[@subscriber =]'subscriber'	Subscriber is the sysname (server name) of the Subscriber.
[@subscriber _db =] ' subscriber_db'	Subscriber_db is the sysname of the Subscriber database.
[@subscriber_type =] 'subscriber_type'	Subscriber_type is nvarchar(15) and defaults to local with values of global, local, or anonymous.
[@subscription_type =] 'subscription_type'	Subscription_type is the nvarchar(15) type of subscription with a default of push. Push=push subscription and the Merge Agent at the Distributor Pull=pull subscription without a Merge Agent at the Distributor
[@subscription_prirority =] subscription_prirority	Subscription priority is real data type and defaults to NULL and is used to resolve conflicts. Local=0.0 Anonymous=0.0
[@sync_type =] 'sync_type'	Sync_type is the nvarchar(15) subscription synchronization type and defaults to automatic. Automatic=schema and data transfer Nosync=no schema and data transfer.
[@frequency_type =] frequency_type	Frequency_type is an integer that determines when the Merge Agent runs. 1=One Time, 2=On Demand, 4=Daily, 8=Weekly, 16=Monthly, 32=Monthly Relative, 64=Autostart, 124=Recurring, NULL=the default value.

[@frequency_interval =] frequency_interval	Frequency interval is an integer that represents the run days of the Merge Agent. 1=Sunday, 2=Monday, 3=Tuesday, 4=Wednesday, 5=Thursday, 6=Friday, 7=Saturday, 8=day, 9=weekdays, 10=weekend days, NULL=the default value.
[@C =] frequency_relative_interval	Frequency_relative_interval is an integer used for a frequency_type of monthly relative. 1=First, 2=Second, 4=Third, 8=Fourth, 16=Last, NULL=the default.
[@frequency_recurrence_factor =] frequency_recurrence_factor	Frequency_recurrence_factor is an integer used in conjunction with frequency_type and defaults to NULL.
[@frequency_subday =] frequency_subday	Frequency_subday is an integer representing when to schedule again during the selected time period. 1=Once, 2=Second, 4=Minute, 8=Hour, NULL=the default.
[@frequency_subday_interval =] frequency_subday_interval	Frequency_subday_interval is an integer representing the interval for frequency_subday to occur between each merge and defaults to NULL.
[@active_start_time_of_day =] active_start_time_of_day	Active_start_time_of_day is an integer representing the first time the Merge Agent is scheduled and defaults to NULL (HHMMSS).
[@active_end_time_of_day =] active_end_time_of_day	Active_end_time_of_day is an integer representing the time the Merge Agent stops being scheduled with a default of NULL (HHMMSS).
[@active_start_date =] active_start_date	Active_start_date is an integer representing the first date the Merge Agent is scheduled and defaults to NULL (YYYYMMDD).
[@active_end_date =] active_end_date	Active_end_date is an integer representing the date when the Merge Agent stops being scheduled and defaults to NULL (YYYMMDD).
[@optional_command_line =] 'optional_command_line'	Optional_command_line is nvarchar(255) commands (output capture to a file, configuration file, or attribute) with a default of NULL.
[@description =] 'description'	Description is the nvarchar(255) merge subscription description and defaults to NULL.

sp_addmessage

The sp_addmessage system stored procedure creates a new error message row in the sysmessages system table. To add a message in another language, the English version of the message must already exist in the sysmessages system table. In the case of adding the same message in another language, if the message contains arguments, the arguments must have the same numbers as the English message with an exclamation mark (!) after each argument. Use the SET LANGUAGE statement before attempting to add a message in a different language or the system defaults to the language of the current connection. Use @@langid to check the current connection language.

Syntax

The syntax is:

```
sp_addmessage {number, severity, 'msg' } [, 'language'] [, 'with_log ]
[, 'replace']
```

The arguments are:

number	Number is the integer identifying the message and the default is NULL and must start at 50001 as these are user messages and not system messages.
severity	Severity is the smallint 1-25 severity level of the error with a default of NULL. SA must add 19-25.
'msg'	Msg is the nvarchar(255) error message that defaults to NULL.
'language'	Language is the sysname language for the message being added and defaults to NULL.
'with_log'	With_log is varchar(5) (true or false) and determines if the message is written to the errorlogs (NT and SQL Server). A value of true writes the message to the logs; false can be written to the logs also, depending on how the message was raised.
'replace'	Replace is used as a varchar(7) flag to indicate that the error message already exists and replaces the error message and severity level. NULL=the default Replace=replace the error message and severity.

sp_add_notification

The sp_add_notification system stored procedure adds an alert notification.

Syntax

The syntax is:

```
sp_add_notification {'alert'} [, 'operator'] [, notification_method]
```

The arguments are:

'alert'	The varchar(100) notification alert description of your choice.
'operator'	Operator (varchar(100)) is the operator notified on the alert.
notification_method	Notification_method is a tinyint that represents how the operator is notified when the alert occurs. 1=E-mail (the default and SQL Mail must be configured), 2=Pager, 4=NetSend, 7=All

sp_add_operator

The sp_add_operator system stored procedure must be run in the msdb system database and adds an operator to be notified when an alert occurs. Your e-mail system must have e-mail-to-pager functionality if you want to send notification to a pager.

Syntax

```
sp_add_operator {'name'} [, enabled] [, 'email_address'] [, 'pager_address']
[, weekday_pager_start_time] [, weekday_pager_end_time]
[, saturday_pager_start_time] [, saturday_pager_end_time]
[, sunday_pager_start_time] [, sunday_pager_end_time] [, pager_days]
[, 'netsend_address'] [, 'category']
```

The arguments are:

'name'	Name is the varchar(100) operator notified in the event of an alert.
enabled	Enabled is a tinyint representing the status of the operator where 1=enabled (the default), 0=not enabled.
'email_address'	Email_address is the varchar(100) e-mail address of the operator.
'pager_address'	Pager_address is the varchar(100) pager address of the operator and defaults to NULL.

weekday_pager_start_time	Weekday_pager_start_time is an integer format of HHMMSS with a default of 090000, 9:00 A.M. on a 24-hour clock, representing the time to start sending pager notification to the operator Monday through Friday.
weekday_pager_end_time	Weekday_pager_end_time is an integer format of HHMMSS with a default of 180000, 6:00 P.M. on a 24-hour clock, representing the time to stop sending pager notification to the operator Monday through Friday.
saturday_pager_start_time	Saturday_pager_start_time is an integer format of HHMMSS with a default of 090000, 9:00 A.M. on a 24-hour clock, representing the time to start sending pager notification to the operator on Saturday.
saturday_pager_end_time	Saturday_pager_end_time is an integer format of HHMMSS with a default of 180000, 6:00 P.M. on a 24-hour clock, representing the time to stop sending pager notification to the operator on Saturday.
sunday_pager_start_time	Sunday_pager_start_time is an integer format of HHMMSS with a default of 090000, 9:00 A.M. on a 24-hour clock, representing the time to start sending pager notification to the operator on Sunday.
sunday_pager_end_time	Sunday_pager_end_time is an integer format of HHMMSS with a default of 180000, 6:00 P.M. on a 24-hour clock, representing the time to stop sending pager notification to the operator on Sunday.
pager_days	Pager_days is tinyint 1-127 representing the days the operator can be paged with a default of 0=Never. Add the values for each day where 1=Sunday, 2=Monday, 4=Tuesday, 8=Wednesday, 16=Thursday, 32=Friday, 64=Saturday. Monday through Friday is 2+4+8+16+32=62 or Saturday=64.
'netsend_address'	Netsend_address is the varchar(100) e-mail address of the operator to be notified by the network message popup on their computer screen. The default is NULL.
'category'	Category is the varchar(100) category name. The default is NULL.

sp_addpublication

The sp_addpublication system stored procedure adds a publication and is for snapshot, transactional, and merge replication. This is for backward compatibility only. Use sp_addpublication70 instead of sp_addpublication.

Syntax

The syntax is:

```
sp_addpublication {[@publication =] 'publication'} [,[@taskid =] taskid]
[,[@restricted =] 'restricted'] [,[@sync_method =] 'sync_method']
[,[@repl_freq =] 'repl_freq'] [,[@description =] 'description']
[,[@status =] 'status'] [,[@independent_agent =] 'independent_agent']
[,[@immediate_sync =] 'immediate_sync']
[,[@enabled_for_internet =] 'enabled_for_internet']
[,[@allow_push =] 'allow_push', [,[@allow_pull =] 'allow_pull']
[,[@allow_anonymous =] 'allow_anonymous']
[,[@allow_sync_tran =] 'allow_sync_tran']
[,[@autogen_sync_procs =] 'autogen_sync_procs']
[,[@retention =] retention]
[,[@default_access =] 'default_access'
```

The arguments are:

[@publication =] 'publication'	Publication is the sysname of the publication.
[@taskid =] taskid	Taskid is an integer representing a previously created scheduler task. This argument is for backward compatibility only. Use sp_addpublication_snapshot.
[@restricted =] 'restricted'	Restricted is nvarchar(10) true or false of who can look at the publication. False=can be seen by all True=seen only by authorized Subscribers
[@sync_method =] 'sync_method'	Sync_mode is the nvarchar(13) method of synchronization and defaults to native. Native=bulk copy Character=character bulk copy
[@repl_freq =] 'repl_freq'	Repl_freq is the nvarchar(10) replication frequency type. Continuous=Publisher sends every log-based transaction Snapshot=Publisher sends scheduled synchronization events

[@description =] 'description'	Description is nvarchar(255) publication description and defaults to NULL.
[@status =] 'status'	Status is nvarchar(8) and determines if the publication data is available to the Subscribers when the publication is initially created and defaults to inactive. Inactive=publication data is not immediately available Active=Publication data is immediately available
[@independent_agent =] 'independent_agent'	Independent_agent is nvarchar(5) true or false. True indicates a separate Distribution Agent.
[@immediate_sync =] 'immediate_sync'	Immediate_sync agent is nvarchar(5) true or false. True=Synchronization files are created with the Snapshot Agent running and Subscribers have synchronization files immediately after the subscription is created and a separate Distribution Agent is present. False=synchronization files are created only if there are new subscriptions. Subscribers do not get synchronization files after the subscription is created until the Snapshot Agents have successfully finished running (the default).
[@enabled_for_internet =] 'enabled_for_internet'	Enabled_for_internet is nvarchar(5) true or false. False=the default True=synchronization files for the publication are placed in \repldata\ftp folder previously manually created.
[@allow_push =] 'allow_push'	Allow_push is nvarchar(5) true or false. True=push subscriptions are allowed by the publication (the default) False=not allowed
[@allow_pull =] 'allow_pull'	Allow_pull is nvarchar(5) true or false. True=pull subscriptions are allowed by the publication (the default) False=not allowed
[@allow_anonymous =] 'allow_anonymous'	Allow_anonymous is nvarchar(5) true or false. True=anonymous are allowed if immediate_sync is true False=the default
[@allow_sync_tran =] 'allow_sync_tran'	Allow_sync_tran is nvarchar(5) true false and defaults to false.

[@autogen_sync_procs =] 'autogen_sync_procs'	Autogen_sync_procs is nvarchar(5) true or false and defaults to true.
[@retention =] retention]	Retention is an integer representing the retention term and defaults to 1.
[,[@default_access =] 'default_access'	Default_access is nvarchar(5) (true or false) and determines if you are to use the Publisher's default publication access list and defaults to NULL.

sp_addpublication_snapshot

The sp_addpublication_snapshot system stored procedure adds a Snapshot Agent.

Syntax

The syntax is:

```
sp_addpublication_snapshot {[@publication =] 'publication'}
[,[@frequency_type =] frequency_type]
[,[@frequency_interval =] frequency_interval]
[,[@frequency_subday =] frequency_subday]
[,[@frequency_subday_interval =] frequency_subday_interval]
[,[@frequency_relative_interval =] frequency_relative_interval]
[,[@frequency_recurrence_factor =] frequency_recurrence_factor]
[,[@active_start_date =] active_start_date]
[,[@active_end_date =] active_end_date]
[,[@active_start_time_of_day =] active_start_time_of_day]
[,[@active_end_time_of_day =] active_end_time_of_day]
```

The arguments are:

[@publication =] 'publication'	Publication is the sysname of the publication.
[@frequency_type =] frequency_type	Frequency_type is an integer that determines when the Snapshot Agent runs. 1=Once, 4=Daily (the default), 8=Weekly, 10=Monthly, 20=Monthly, relative to the frequency interval, 40=Run when SQL Server Agent starts.
[@frequency_interval =] frequency_interval	Frequency interval is an integer representing the frequency set by frequency_type and defaults to 1=daily.

[@frequency_subday =] frequency_subday	Frequency_subday is an integer representing the units for freq_subday_interval. 1=Once, 2=Second, 4=Minute (the default), 8=Hour
[@frequency_subday_interval =] frequency_subday_interval	Frequency_subday_interval is the integer representing the interval for frequency_subday and default to 5=every 5 minutes.
[@frequency_relative_interval =] frequency_relative_interval	Frequency_relative_interval is an integer and represents the date the Snapshot Agent runs and defaults to 1.
[@frequency_recurrence_factor =] frequency_recurrence_factor	Frequency_recurrence_factor is an integer representing the recurrence factor used by frequency_type and defaults to 0.
[@active_start_date =] active_start_date	Active_start_date is an integer representing the first date the Snapshot Agent is scheduled and defaults to 0 (YYYYMMDD).
[@active_end_date =] active_end_date	Active_end_date is an integer representing the date when the Snapshot Agent stops being scheduled and defaults to 99991231 (YYYMMDD).
[@active_start_time_of_day =] active_start_time_of_day	Active_start_time_of_day is an integer representing the first time the Snapshot Agent is scheduled and defaults to 0 (HHMMSS).
[@active_end_time_of_day =] active_end_time_of_day	Active_end_time_of_day is an integer representing the time the Snaphot Agent stops being scheduled with a default of 235959 (HHMMSS).

sp_addpublisher70

The sp_addpublisher70 system stored procedure adds a version 7.0 Publisher at a version 6.5 Subscriber. You must run a script on the 6.5 SQL Server that adds the sp_addpublisher70 stored procedure to the 6.5 SQL Server. The script is in the file Replp70.sql located in the \Mssql7\Install directory.

Syntax

The syntax is:

```
sp_addpublisher70 {[@publisher =] 'publisher',
[@dist_account =] 'dist_account'}
```

The arguments are:

[@publisher =] 'publisher'	Publisher is the varchar(3) name of the Publisher.
[@dist_account =] 'dist_account'	Dist_account is the varchar(255) NT account that the Distribution Agent uses on the Distributor. Usually it is the SQL Server Agent account on the Distributor.

sp_addpullsubscription

The sp_addpullsubscription system stored procedure adds a pull or an anonymous subscription to the Subscriber database.

Syntax

The syntax is:

```
sp_addpullsubscription {[@publisher =] 'publisher',
[@publisher_db =] 'publisher_db'] [@publication =] 'publication']
[,[@independent_agent =] 'independent_agent']
[,[@subscription_type =] 'subscription_type']
[,[@description =] 'description'] [,[@update_mode =] 'update_mode']
[,[@immediate_sync =] immediate_sync]
```

The arguments are:

[@publisher =] 'publisher'	Publisher is the sysname of the Publisher.
[@publisher_db =] 'publisher_db'	Publisher_db is the sysname of the Publisher database.
[@publication =] 'publication'	Publication is the sysname of the publication.

[@independent_agent =] 'independent_agent'	Independent_agent is nvarchar(5) and defaults to true, meaning the Distributor is separate and defaults to true.
[@subscription_type =] 'subscription_type'	Subscription_type is nvarchar(9) and the publication subscription type of pull or anonymous (the default).
[@description =] 'description'	Description is the nvarchar(100) description of the publication and defaults to NULL.
[@update_mode =] 'update_mode'	Update_mode is nvarchar(15) and read-only (the default) or synctran.
[,[@immediate_sync =] immediate_sync]	Immediate_sync is a bit (default of 1) that determines if the synchronization files are created when the Snapshot Agent runs and must be the same value as immediate_sync in sp_addpublication.

sp_addpullsubscription_agent

The sp_addpullsubscription_agent system stored procedure adds a new agent to the database of the Subscriber and is for snapshot, transactional, and merge replication.

Syntax

The syntax is:

```
sp_addpullsubscription_agent {[@publisher =]'publisher',
[@publisher_db =] 'publisher_db', [@publication =] 'publication'},
[,[@subscriber =] 'subscriber']
[,[@subscriber_db =] 'subscriber_db']
[,[@subscriber_security_mode =] subscriber_security_mode]
[,[@subscriber_login =] 'subscriber_login']
[,[@subscriber_password =] 'subscriber_password']
[,[@distributor =] 'distributor', [,[@distribution_db =] 'distribution_db']
[,[@distributor_security_mode =] distributor_security_mode]
[,[@distributor_login =] 'distributor_login']
[,[@distributor_password =] 'distributor_password']
[,[@optional_command_line =] 'optional_command_line']
[,[@frequency_type =] frequency_type]
[,[@frequency_interval =] frequency_interval]
[,[@frequency_relative_interval =] frequency_relative_interval]
[,[@frequency_recurrence_factor =] frequency_recurrence_factor]
[,[@frequency_subday =] frequency_subday]
```

```
[,[@frequency_subday_interval =] frequency_subday_interval]
[,[@active_start_time_of_day =] active_start_time_of_day]
[,[@active_end_time_of_day =] active_end_time_of_day]
[,[@active_start_date =] active_start_date]
[,[@active_end_date =] active_end_date]
[,[@distribution_jobid =] distribution_jobid]
[,[@encrypted_distributor_password =] encrypted_distributor_password]
[,[@agent_mode =] agent_mode]
```

The arguments are:

[@publisher =]'publisher'	Publisher is the sysname (server name) of the Publisher.
[@publisher_db =] 'publisher_db'	Publisher_db is the sysname of the Publisher database.
[@publication =] 'publication'	Publication is the sysname of the publication.
[,[@subscriber =] 'subscriber']	Subscriber is the sysname of the Subscriber.
[,[@subscriber_db =] 'subscriber_db']	Subscriber_db is the sysname of the subscription database.
[@subscriber_security_mode =] subscriber_security_mode	Subscriber_security_mode is an integer that represents the security mode of the Subscriber with a default of 1. 0=SQL Server Authentication 1=Windows NT Authentication
[@subscriber_login =] 'subscriber_login'	Subscriber login is used for SQL Server Authentication (subscriber security mode) with default of NULL.
[@subscriber_password =] 'subscriber_password'	Subscriber password is the sysname used for SQL Server Authentication (subscriber security mode) with default of NULL.
[@distributor =] 'distributor'	The sysname of the Distributor that defaults to the Publisher (server name).
[@distributor_security_mode =] distributor_security_mode	Distributor_security_mode is an integer that represents the security mode of the Distributor with a default of 1. 0=SQL Server Authentication 1=Windows NT Authentication

[@distributor_login =] 'distributor_login'	Distributor login is used for SQL Server Authentication (subscriber security mode) with default of sa.
[@distributor_password =] 'distributor_password'	Distributor password is the sysname used for SQL Server Authentication (subscriber security mode) with default of NULL.
[@optional_command_line =] 'optional_command_line'	Optional_command_line is nvarchar(255) commands given to the Distribution Agent and defaults to NULL.
[@frequency_type =] frequency_type	Frequency_type is an integer that determines how to schedule the Distribution Agent. 1=One Time, 2=On Demand, 4=Daily, 8=Weekly, 16=Monthly, 32=Monthly Relative, 64=Autostart, 124=Recurring, NULL=the default value.
[@frequency_interval =] frequency_interval	Frequency interval is an integer that represents the run days of the Distribution Agent. 1=Sunday, 2=Monday, 3=Tuesday, 4=Wednesday, 5=Thursday, 6=Friday, 7=Saturday, 8=day, 9=weekdays, 10=weekend days, NULL=the default value.
[@C =] frequency_relative_interval	Frequency_relative_interval is an integer used for a frequency_type of monthly relative. 1=First, 2=Second, 4=Third, 8=Fourth, 16=Last, NULL=the default.
[@frequency_recurrence_factor =] frequency_recurrence_factor	Frequency_recurrence_factor is an integer used in conjunction with frequency_type and defaults to NULL.
[@frequency_subday =] frequency_subday	Frequency_subday is an integer representing when to schedule again during the selected time period. 1=Once, 2=Second, 4=Minute, 8=Hour, NULL=the default.
[@frequency_subday_interval =] frequency_subday_interval	Frequency_subday_interval is an integer representing the interval for frequency_subday and defaults to NULL.

[@active_start_time_of_day =] active_start_time_of_day	Active_start_time_of_day is an integer representing the first time the Distribution Agent is scheduled and defaults to NULL (HHMMSS).
[@active_end_time_of_day =] active_end_time_of_day	Active_end_time_of_day is an integer representing the time the Distribution Agent stops being scheduled with a default of NULL (HHMMSS).
[@active_start_date =] active_start_date	Active_start_date is an integer representing the first date the Distribution Agent is scheduled and defaults to NULL (YYYYMMDD).
[@active_end_date =] active_end_date	Active_end_date is an integer representing the date when the Distribution Agent stops being scheduled and defaults to NULL (YYYMMDD).
[@distribution_jobid =] distribution_jobid	Distribution_jobid is binary(16) and is an output parameter which defaults to NULL.
[@encrypted_distributor_password =] encrypted_distributor_password	Encrypted_distributor_password is a bit data type used by scripting determining if the distributor password is encrypted and defaults to 0.
[,[@agent_mode =] agent_mode]	Agent_mode is nvarchar(20), represents the mode when the agent is created, and can be one of the following values: none=No agent sqlagent=SQL Server Agent mobilesync=Mobile synchronization agent both=SQL Server Agent and mobile synchronization agent.

sp_addremotelogin

The sp_addremotelogin system stored procedure creates a new remote login on the local server.

Syntax

The syntax is:

```
sp_addremotelogin [@remoteserver =] 'remoteserver' [,[@loginame =]
'login' [,[@remotename =] 'remote_name']]
```

The arguments are:

[@remoteserver =] 'remoteserver'	Remoteserver is the sysname of the remote server. The users on the remote server are given the same logins as those on the local server unless the other arguments are supplied.
[@loginame =] 'login'	Login is the sysname of the login of the user on the local SQL Server.
[@remotename =] 'remote_name'	Remote is the sysname of the login of the user on the remote server.

sp_addrole

The sp_addrole system stored procedure adds a database role in the database in use.

Syntax

The syntax is:

```
sp_addrole [@rolename =] 'role' [,[@ownername =] 'owner']
```

The arguments are:

[@rolename =] 'role'	Role is the sysname of the new role.
[@ownername =] 'owner'	Owner is the sysname of the owner of the role and defaults to dbo (database owner).

sp_addrolemember

The sp_addrolemember system stored procedure adds a security account to a database role in the database in use.

Syntax

The syntax is:

```
sp_addrolemember [@rolename =] 'role', [@membername =] 'security_account'
```

The arguments are:

[@rolename =] 'role'	Rolename is the sysname of the database role.
[@membername =] 'security_account'	Security_account is the sysname of security account added to the database role. If the account does not exist in the database in use, it is added.

sp_addserver

The sp_addserver system stored procedure places a row in the sysservers system table for a remote server and is used for backward compatibility. The system stored procedure sp_addlinkedserver is used in version 7.0 instead of sp_addserver.

Syntax

The syntax is:

```
sp_addserver [@server =] 'server' [,[@local =] 'local']
[,[@duplicate_ok =] 'duplicate_OK']
```

The arguments are:

[@server =] 'server'	Server is the sysname of the server.
[@local =] 'LOCAL'	LOCAL is varchar(10) and indicates the sysname of the server is a local server and defaults to NULL.
[@duplicate_ok =] 'duplicate_OK'	Duplicate_OK is varchar(13) and values are duplicate_OK or NULL. Duplicate_OK means a duplicate server name can exist without the report of an error.

sp_addsrvrolemember

The sp_addsrvrolemember system stored procedure adds a login to a fixed server role.

Syntax

The syntax is:

```
sp_addsrvrolemember [@loginame =] 'login' [,[@rolename =] 'role']
```

The arguments are:

[@loginame =] 'login'	Login is the sysname of the login being added to the fixed server role. If the login does not exist on the SQL Server it will be added.
[@rolename =] 'role'	Role is the sysname of the fixed server role, sysadmin, securityadmin, serveradmin, setupadmin, processadmin, diskadmin, or dbcreator.

sp_addsubscriber

The sp_addsubscriber system stored procedure creates a new Subscriber for snapshot, transactional, and merge replication.

Syntax

The syntax is:

```
sp_addsubscriber {[@subscriber =] 'subscriber'} [,[@type =] type]
[,[@login =] 'login'] [,[@password =] 'password']
[,[@commit_batch_size =] commit_batch_size]
[,[@status_batch_size =] status_batch_size]
[,[@flush_frequency =] flush_frequency]
[,[@frequency_type =] frequency_type]
[,[@frequency_interval =] frequency_interval]
[,[@frequency_relative_interval =] frequency_relative_interval]
[,[@frequency_recurrence_factor =] frequency_recurrence_factor]
[,[@frequency_subday =] frequency_subday]
[,[@frequency_subday_interval =] frequency_subday_interval]
[,[@active_start_time_of_day =] active_start_time_of_day]
[,[@active_end_time_of_day =] active_end_time_of_day]
[,[@active_start_date =] active_start_date]
[,[@active_end_date =] active_end_date]
[,[@description =] 'description'] [,[@security_mode =] security_mode]
[,[@encrypted_password =] encrypted_password]
```

The arguments are:

[@subscriber =] 'subscriber'	Subscriber is the sysname of the server added as a Subscriber.
[@type =] type	Type is the tinyint type of Subscriber. 0=Microsoft SQL Server Subscriber 1=ODBC data source server
[@login =] 'login'	Login is the sysname of the SQL Server Authenticated login and defaults to SA.
[@password =] 'password	Password is the sysname password for the SQL Server Authenticated login and defaults to NULL.
[@commit_batch_size =] commit_batch_size	Commit_batch_size is an integer determining how many transactions are sent to the Subscriber and committed together and defaults to 100.

[@flush_frequency =] flush_frequency	Flush_frequency is an integer determining how often transactions are deleted from the distribution database tables after distributiom to the Subscriber and defaults to 0.
[@frequency_type =] frequency_type	Frequency_type is an integer that determines how to schedule the Distribution Agent. 1=One Time, 2=On Demand, 4=Daily, 8=Weekly, 16=Monthly, 32=Monthly Relative, 64=Autostart, 124=Recurring, NULL=the default value.
[@frequency_interval =] frequency_interval	Frequency interval is an integer that represents the run days of the Distribution Agent. 1=Sunday, 2=Monday, 3=Tuesday, 4=Wednesday, 5=Thursday, 6=Friday, 7=Saturday, 8=day, 9=weekdays, 10=weekend days, NULL=the default value.
[@frequency_relative_interval =] frequency_relative_interval	Frequency_relative_interval is an integer used for a frequency_type of monthly relative. 1=First, 2=Second, 4=Third, 8=Fourth, 16=Last, NULL=the default.
[@frequency_recurrence_factor =] frequency_recurrence_factor	Frequency_recurrence_factor is an integer used in conjunction with frequency_type and defaults to NULL.
[@frequency_subday =] frequency_subday	Frequency_subday is an integer representing when to schedule again during the selected time period. 1=Once, 2=Second, 4=Minute, 8=Hour, NULL=the default.
[@frequency_subday_interval =] frequency_subday_interval	Frequency_subday_interval is an integer representing the interval for frequency_subday and defaults to NULL.
[@active_start_time_of_day =] active_start_time_of_day	Active_start_time_of_day is an integer representing the first time the Distribution Agent is scheduled and defaults to NULL (HHMMSS).
[@active_end_time_of_day =] active_end_time_of_day	Active_end_time_of_day is an integer representing the time the Distribution Agent stops being scheduled with a default of NULL (HHMMSS).

[@active_start_date =] active_start_date	Active_start_date is an integer representing the first date the Distribution Agent is scheduled and defaults to NULL (YYYYMMDD).
[@active_end_date =] active_end_date	Active_end_date is an integer representing the date when the Distribution Agent stops being scheduled and defaults to NULL (YYYMMDD).
[@description =] 'description'	Description is the nvarchar(255) description of the Subscriber and defaults to NULL.
[@security_mode =] security_mode	Security_mode is an integer and represents the security mode where 0=SQL Server authentication and 1=Windows NT authentication (the default).
[@encrypted_password =] encrypted_password	Encrypted_password is a bit data type used by scripting determining if the password is encrypted and defaults to 0.

sp_addsubscriber_schedule

The sp_addsubscriber_schedule system stored procedure adds a Distribution Agent or Merge Agent schedule for snapshot, transactional, and merge replication.

Syntax

The syntax is:

```
sp_addsubscriber_schedule {[@subscriber =] 'subscriber'}
[,[@agent_type =] agent_type] [,[@frequency_type =] frequency_type]
[,[@frequency_interval =] frequency_interval]
[,[@frequency_relative_interval =] frequency_relative_interval]
[,[@frequency_recurrence_factor =] frequency_recurrence_factor]
[,[@frequency_subday =] frequency_subday]
[,[@frequency_subday_interval =] frequency_subday_interval]
[,[@active_start_time_of_day =] active_start_time_of_day]
[,[@active_end_time_of_day =] active_end_time_of_day]
[,[@active_start_date =] active_start_date]
[,[@active_end_date =] active_end_date]
```

The arguments are:

[@subscriber =] 'subscriber'	Subscriber is the sysname of the Subscriber.

[@agent_type =] agent_type	Agent_type is the smallint type of agent where 0=Distribution Agent and 1=Merge Agent with a default of 0.
[@frequency_type =] frequency_type	Frequency_type is an integer that determines how to schedule the Distribution Agent. 1=One Time, 2=On Demand, 4=Daily, 8=Weekly, 16=Monthly, 32=Monthly Relative, 64=Autostart, 124=Recurring, NULL=the default value.
[@frequency_interval =] frequency_interval	Frequency interval is an integer that represents the run days of the Distribution Agent. 1=Sunday, 2=Monday, 3=Tuesday, 4=Wednesday, 5=Thursday, 6=Friday, 7=Saturday, 8=day, 9=weekdays, 10=weekend days, NULL=the default value.
[@frequency_relative_interval =] frequency_relative_interval	Frequency_relative_interval is an integer used for a frequency_type of monthly relative. 1=First, 2=Second, 4=Third, 8=Fourth, 16=Last, NULL=the default.
[@frequency_recurrence_factor =] frequency_recurrence_factor	Frequency_recurrence_factor is an integer used in conjunction with frequency_type and defaults to NULL.
[@frequency_subday =] frequency_subday	Frequency_subday is an integer representing when to schedule again during the selected time period. 1=Once, 2=Second, 4=Minute, 8=Hour, NULL=the default.
[@frequency_subday_interval =] frequency_subday_interval	Frequency_subday_interval is an integer representing the interval for frequency_subday and defaults to NULL.
[@active_start_time_of_day =] active_start_time_of_day	Active_start_time_of_day is an integer representing the first time the Distribution Agent is scheduled and defaults to NULL (HHMMSS).
[@active_end_time_of_day =] active_end_time_of_day	Active_end_time_of_day is an integer representing the time the Distribution Agent stops being scheduled with a default of NULL (HHMMSS).

[@active_start_date =] active_start_date	Active_start_date is an integer representing the first date the Distribution Agent is scheduled and defaults to NULL (YYYYMMDD).
[@active_end_date =] active_end_date	Active_end_date is an integer representing the date when the Distribution Agent stops being scheduled and defaults to NULL (YYYYMMDD).

sp_addsubscription

The sp_addsubscription system stored procedure adds a subscription to an article. If a Subscriber is to view articles in a restricted publication article, a dummy subscription must be added with a status of inactive.

Syntax

The syntax is:

```
sp_addsubscription {[@publication =] 'publication'}
[,[@article =] 'article'] [,[@subscriber =] 'subscriber']
[,[@destination_db =] 'destination_db', [@sync_type =] 'sync_type']
[,[@status =] 'status' [@subscription_type =] 'subscription_type']
[,[@update_mode =] 'update_mode']
[,[@loopback_detection =] 'loopback_detection']
[,[@frequency_type =] frequency_type]
[,[@frequency_interval =] frequency_interval]
[,[@frequency_relative_interval =] frequency_relative_interval]
[,[@frequency_recurrence_factor =] frequency_recurrence_factor]
[,[@frequency_subday =] frequency_subday]
[,[@frequency_subday_interval =] frequency_subday_interval]
[,[@active_start_time_of_day =] active_start_time_of_day]
[,[@active_end_time_of_day =] active_end_time_of_day]
[,[@active_start_date =] active_start_date]
[,[@active_end_date =] active_end_date]
[,[@optional_command_line =] 'optional_command_line']
[,[@reserved =] 'reserved'] [,[@agent_mode =] agent_mode]
```

The arguments are:

[@publication =] 'publication'	Publication is the sysname of the publication.

[@article =] 'article'	Article is the sysname of the article. If not given, the subscription is for every article in the publication.
[@subscriber =] 'subscriber'	Subscriber is the sysname of the Subscriber and defaults to NULL.
[@destination_db =] 'destination_db'	Destination_db is the sysname of the destination database which holds the replicated data (should be the same name as the Publication database).
[@sync_type =] 'sync_type'	Sync_type is nchar(15) and the subscription synchronization type. Automatic=synchronization is done at the Subscriber through the distribution process (the default). Manual=synchronization file is automatically produced and manually applied at the Subscriber None=no initial synchronization
[@status =] 'status'	Status is the sysname of the subscription status. Sync_type=none and status is active else Subscribed Sync_type=automatic and status is inactive
[@subscription_type =] 'subscription_type'	Subscription_type is the nvarchar type of subscription of push (the default) or pull.
[@update_mode =] 'update_mode'	Update_mode is the nvarchar(15) type of update where read-only is the default and synctran is the other type.
[,[@loopback_dectection =] 'loopback_detection']	Loopback_detection is nvarchar(5) and determines if the Distribution Agent will send transactions originating at the Subscriber to the Subscriber. True=Distribution Agent does not send transactions back. False=Distribution Agent sends transactions back. NULL=The value will be set to true when update_mode is synctran and the article has a published timestamp column (the default).

[@frequency_type =] frequency_type	Frequency_type is an integer that determines how to schedule the Distribution Agent. 1=One Time, 2=On Demand, 4=Daily, 8=Weekly, 16=Monthly, 32=Monthly Relative, 64=Autostart, 124=Recurring, NULL=the default value.
[@frequency_interval =] frequency_interval	Frequency interval is an integer that represents the run days of the Distribution Agent. 1=Sunday, 2=Monday, 3=Tuesday, 4=Wednesday, 5=Thursday, 6=Friday, 7=Saturday, 8=day, 9=weekdays, 10=weekend days, NULL=the default value.
[@frequency_relative_interval =] frequency_relative_interval	Frequency_relative_interval is an integer used for a frequency_type of monthly relative. 1=First, 2=Second, 4=Third, 8=Fourth, 16=Last, NULL=the default.
[@frequency_recurrence_factor =] frequency_recurrence_factor	Frequency_recurrence_factor is an integer used in conjunction with frequency_type and defaults to NULL.
[@frequency_subday =] frequency_subday	Frequency_subday is an integer representing when to schedule again during the selected time period. 1=Once, 2=Second, 4=Minute, 8=Hour, NULL=the default.
[@frequency_subday_interval =] frequency_subday_interval	Frequency_subday_interval is an integer representing the interval for frequency_subday and defaults to NULL.
[@active_start_time_of_day =] active_start_time_of_day	Active_start_time_of_day is an integer representing the first time the Distribution Agent is scheduled and defaults to NULL (HHMMSS).
[@active_end_time_of_day =] active_end_time_of_day	Active_end_time_of_day is an integer representing the time the Distribution Agent stops being scheduled with a default of NULL (HHMMSS).
[@active_start_date =] active_start_date	Active_start_date is an integer representing the first date the Distribution Agent is scheduled and defaults to NULL (YYYYMMDD).

[@active_end_date =] active_end_date	Active_end_date is an integer representing the date when the Distribution Agent stops being scheduled and defaults to NULL (YYYYMMDD).
[@optional_command_line =] 'optional_command_line'	Optional_command_line is the nvarchar(4000) command line you wish to run and defaults to NULL.
[@reserved =] 'reserved'	Reserved and defaults to NULL.
[,[@agent_mode =] agent_mode]	Agent_mode is nvarchar(200) and the mode in which the agent is created and can be one of the following values: none=No agent sqlagent=SQL Server Agent mobilesync=Mobile synchronization agent both=SQL Server Agent and mobile synchronization agent

sp_addsynctriggers

The sp_addsynctriggers system stored procedure will add synchronous transaction triggers at the Subscriber.

Syntax

The syntax is:

```
sp_addsynctriggers {[@source_table =] 'source_table',
[@publisher =] 'publisher', [@publisher_db =] 'publisher_db',
[@ins_proc =] 'ins_proc', [@upd_proc =] 'upd_proc'
[,[@del_proc =] 'del_proc'} [,[@identity_col =] 'identity_col']
[,[@ts_col =] 'ts_col'] [,[@filter_clause =] 'filter_clause']
```

The arguments are:

[@source_table =] 'source_table'	Source_table is nvarchar(92) and the name of the source table.
[@publisher =] 'publisher'	Publisher is the sysname of the Publisher (server name).

[@publisher_db =] 'publisher_db'	Publisher_db is the sysname of the publishing database and defaults to the database in use.
[@ins_proc =] 'ins_proc'	Ins_proc is the sysname of the article's stored procedure for synchronous transaction inserts.
[@upd_proc =] 'upd_proc'	Upd_ proc is the sysname of the article's stored procedure for synchronous transaction updates.
[@del_proc =] 'del_proc'	Del_ proc is the sysname of the article's stored procedure for synchronous transaction deletes.
[@identity_col =] 'identity_col'	Identity_col is the sysname of the identity column.
[@ts_col =] 'ts_col'	Ts_col is the sysname of the time stamp column.
[@filter_clause =] 'filter_clause'	Filter_clause is nvarchar(4000) and contains a WHERE clause to filter the source table.

sp_addtask

The sp_addtask system stored procedure is for backward compatibility only. A Microsoft SQL Server 7.0 programmer uses sp_add_job.

sp_addtype

The sp_addtype system stored procedure adds a data type created by the user for the application.

Syntax

The syntax is:

```
sp_addtype [@typename =] type,
[@phystype =] system_data_type
[, [@nulltype =] 'null_type']
```

The arguments are:

type	Type is the sysname of the user created data types.
[@phystype =] system_data_type	The SQL Server system data type that serves as the basis for the user created type. The following are the values for this argument: 'binary(n)', image, smalldatetime, bit, int smallint, 'char(n)', 'nchar(n)', text, datetime, ntext, tinyint, decimal, numeric, uniqueidentifier, 'decimal[(p[, s])]', 'numeric[(p[, s])]', 'varbinary(n)', Float, 'nvarchar(n)', 'varchar(n)', 'float(n)', and real. N, P, and S are described in the following rows in this table.
n	N represents a positive non-zero integer for the length for the user created data type.
p	P represents a positive non-zero integer for the total of decimal digits that can be stored on either side of the decimal point.
s	S represents a positive non-zero integer for the total of decimal digits that can be stored on the right side of the decimal point; it has to be less than or equal to P, the preceding argument.
[@nulltype =] 'null_type']	Null_type is varchar(8) with values of 'NULL' or 'NOT NULL' (enclose in single quotation marks).

sp_add_targetservergroup

The sp_add_targetservergroup system stored procedure adds the target server group name.

Syntax

The syntax is:

```
sp_add_targetservergroup {'name'}
```

The argument, name, is the varchar(100) name of the target server group.

sp_addumpdevice

The sp_addumpdevice system stored procedure adds a dump device used for backing up the different parts of a database.

Syntax

The syntax is:

```
sp_addumpdevice {'device_type', 'logical_name', 'physical_name'}
[, {{controller_type]}|'device_status'}}]
```

The arguments are:

'device_type' Device_type is the varchar(10) type of dump device where Disk=disk file, pipe=named pipe, tape=tape device.

'logical_name' Logical_name is the sysname backup device for BACKUP and RESTORE.

'physical_name' Physical is the physical nvarchar(260) name of the dump device and is an operating system path\file. An example for a tape device is \\.\\TAPE0.

controller_type Controller_type is ignored in version 7.0 but values are 5=tape, 6=pipe.

'device_status' Device_status is varchar(40) and characterizes tape labels as noskip=read (the default) or skip=ignored.

sp_add_targetsvrgrp_member

The sp_add_targetsvrgrp_member system stored procedure adds a server to the target server group.

Syntax

The syntax is:

```
sp_add_targetsvrgrp_member {'group_name'} [, 'server_name']
```

The arguments are:

'group_name' Group_name is varchar(100) and the name of the target server group.

'server_name' Server_name is varchar(30) and the name of the server to add to the target server group.

sp_adduser

The sp_adduser system stored procedure is for backward compatibility. A version 7.0 programmer uses sp_grantdbaccess.

Syntax

The syntax is:

```
sp_adduser [@loginame =] 'login' [,[@name_in_db =] 'user'
[,[@rolename =] 'role']]
```

The arguments are:

'[@loginame =] login'	Login is the sysname of the login.
[@name_in_db =] 'user'	User is the sysname for the new user and defaults to the login.
[@rolename =] 'role'	Role is the role in which the user will be placed.

sp_altermessage

The sp_altermessage system stored procedure alters the state of whether a message is written to the error logs.

Syntax

The syntax is:

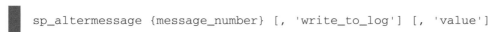

```
sp_altermessage {message_number} [, 'write_to_log'] [, 'value']
```

The arguments are:

message_number	Message_number is the integer ID of the sysmessages error.
[, 'write_to_log'] [, 'value']	If 'write to log' has a value of WITH_LOG, the message is written to the NT errorlog. A value of true writes the message to the NT error log. A value of false means the error is not automatically written to the NT error log. (The error can still be written to the NT error log with a value of false depending on how the error was raised.)

Example

Here's an example of the sp_altermessage system stored procedure.

```
sp_altermessage 255101, 'WITH_LOG', 'true'
```

In this example, the message, 255101, is written to the error logs.

sp_apply_job_to_targets

The sp_apply_job_to_targets system stored procedure adds a job to target servers or target server groups.

Syntax

The syntax is:

```
sp_apply_job_to_targets {job_id | 'job_name'}
[,'target_server_groups']
[,'target_servers'] [, 'operation']
```

The arguments are:

job_id	Job_id is the uniqueidentifier of the job and defaults to NULL.
'job_name'	Job_name is the varchar(100) name of the job and defaults to NULL.
'target_server_groups'	Target_server_groups is varchar(1024) and one or more target server groups which you can delineate with commas if there are more than one; it defaults to NULL.
'target_servers'	Target_servers is varchar(1024) and one or more target servers which you can delineate with commas if there is more than one; it defaults to NULL.
'operation'	Operation is varchar(7) and determines how the job is removed from the servers. APPLY=remove from servers where applied (the default) REMOVE= remove from servers where not applied

sp_approlepassword

The sp_approlepassword system stored procedure modifies the password of an application role in the database in use.

Syntax

The syntax is:

```
sp_approlepassword [@rolename =] 'role' [,[@newpwd =] 'password']
```

The arguments are:

[@rolename =] 'role'	Role is the sysname of the application role.
[@newpwd =] 'password'	Password is the sysname of the new password and defaults to NULL.

sp_article_validation

The sp_article_validation system stored procedure validates the article's data.

Syntax

The syntax is:

```
sp_article_validation [@publication =] 'publication' [,[@article =]'article']
[,[@rowcount_only =] rowcount_only]
[,[@full_or_fast =] full_or_fast]
[,[@shutdown_agent =] shutdown_agent]
```

The arguments are:

[@publication =] 'publication'	Publication is the sysname of the publication for the article.
[@article =]'article'	Article is the sysname of the article.
[,[@rowcount_only =] rowcount_only]	Rowcount_only is bit data type and determines if only the rowcount is returned for the table. Values are: NULL=Rowcount only returned 1=Rowcount and checksum returned

[,[@full_or_fast =] full_or_fast]	Full_or_fast is tinyint and determines how to calculate the rowcount. 0=Full count using COUNT(*). 1= Does fast count from sysindexes (may not be accurate if statistics are not current) 2= Fast counting by doing fast count and going to full if the system detects a need.
[@shutdown_agent =] shutdown_agent	Shutdown_agent is a bit and determines if the replication agent shutsdown when the validation finishes. 0=replication agent does not shut down 1= replication agent shuts down after validation.

sp_articlecolumn

The sp_articlecolumn system stored procedure defines the columns in an article.

Syntax

The syntax is:

```
sp_articlecolumn {[@publication =] 'publication', [@article =] 'article'}
[,[@column =] 'column'] [,[@operation =] 'operation']
[,[@refresh_synctran_procs =] refresh_synctran_procs]
```

The arguments are:

[@publication =] 'publication'	Publication is the sysname of the publication with the article.
[@article =] 'article'	Article is the sysname of the article.
[@column =] 'column'	Column is the sysname of the column and defaults to NULL, all columns.
[@operation =] 'operation'	Operation is nvarchar(4) and represents the status of the column. Add=replicate the column Drop=do not replicate the column

[@refresh_synctran_procs =] refresh_synctran_procs	Refresh_synctran_procs is a bit. 1=make the stored procedures supporting synchronous transactions match the replicated columns 0=do not make the stored procedures supporting synchronous transactions match the replicated columns

sp_articlefilter

The sp_articlefilter system stored procedure adds a filter stored procedure which horizontally partitions data from a published table.

Syntax

The syntax is:

```
sp_articlefilter {[@publication =] 'publication', [@article =] 'article'}
[,[@filter_name =] 'filter_name'] [,[@filter_clause =] 'filter_clause']
```

The arguments are:

[@publication =] 'publication'	Publication is the sysname of the publication.
[@article =] 'article	Article is the sysname of the article.
[@filter_name =] 'filter_name'	Filter_name is the nvarchar(46) name of the stored procedure that will be created with the same name as the filter with a default of NULL.
[@filter_clause =] 'filter_clause'	Filter_clause is text and the WHERE clause that horizontally partitions the data without the keyword WHERE.

sp_articlesynctranprocs

The sp_articlesynctranprocs system stored procedure adds synchronous transaction stored procedures at the Publisher for use by the synchronout transaction triggers at the Subscriber and triggers created by the sp_addsynctriggers system stored procedure.

Syntax

The syntax is:

```
sp_articlesynctranprocs {[@publication =] 'publication',
[@article =] 'article', [@ins_proc =] 'ins_proc',
[@upd_proc =] 'upd_proc', [@del_proc =] 'del_proc'}
[,[@autogen =] 'autogen']
```

The arguments are:

[@publication =] 'publication'	Publication is the sysname of the publication.
[@article =] 'article'	Article is the sysname of the article.
[@ins_proc =] 'ins_proc'	Ins_ proc is the sysname of the article's stored procedure for synchronous transaction inserts.
[@upd_proc =] 'upd_proc'	Upd_proc is the sysname of the article's stored procedure for synchronous transaction updates.
[@del_proc =] 'del_proc'	Del_proc is the sysname of the article's stored procedure for synchronous transaction deletes.
[@autogen =] 'autogen'	Autogen in nvarchar(5) with values of true or false and a default of true determining whether synchronous transaction stored procedures are automatically created.

sp_articleview

The sp_articleview system system stored procedure adds the article view that vertically or horizontally partitions a table for data delivery to the destination.

Syntax

The syntax is:

```
sp_articleview {[@publication =] 'publication', [@article =] 'article'}
[,[@view_name =] 'view_name'] [,[@filter_clause =] 'filter_clause']
```

The arguments are:

[@publication =] 'publication'	Publication is the sysname of the publication.
[@article =] 'article'	Article is the sysname of the article.
[@view_name =] 'view_name'	View_name is the name of the view created to partition the article (table) and the default is NULL.

[@filter_clause =] 'filter_clause'	Filter_clause is text and the WHERE clause that horizontally partitions the data without the keyword WHERE.

sp_attach_db

The sp_attach_db system stored procedure can attach a database to SQL Server. This can be used in the upgrade process, if necessary, after sp_detach_db has detached the database files from SQL Server.

Syntax

The syntax is:

```
sp_attach_db [@dbname =] 'dbname',
[@filenamen =] 'filename_n' [,…n]
```

The arguments are:

[@dbname =] 'dbname'	Dbname is the sysname of the database to be attached to SQL Server.
[@filenamen =] 'filename_n'	Filename_n is the nvarchar(260) path and physical name of a database file with up to 16 filenames.

sp_attach_single_file_db

The sp_attach_single_file_db system stored procedure attaches a database with one database file to SQL Server. This can be used in the upgrade process, if necessary, after sp_detach_db has detached the database file from SQL Server.

Syntax

The syntax is:

```
sp_attach_single_file_db [@dbname =] 'dbname',
[@physname =] 'physical_name'
```

The arguments are:

[@dbname =] 'dbname'	Dbname is the sysname of the database to be attached to SQL Server.

[@physname =] 'phsyical_name'	Filename_n is the nvarchar(260) path and physical name of the database file.

sp_autostats

The sp_autostats system stored procedure can display or modify the setting that determines whether UPDATE STATISTICS is automatically enabled for the index(es) on a table.

Syntax

The syntax is:

```
sp_autostats 'table_name' [, 'stats_flag'] [, 'index_name']
```

The arguments are:

'table_name'	Table_name is the sysname of the table.
'stats_flag'	Stats_flag is varchar(10) and defaults to NULL. ON=automatic UPDATE STATISTICS setting enabled OFF=disabled
'index_name'	Index_name is the sysname of the index and defaults to NULL.

sp_bindefault

The sp_bindefault system stored procedure binds a DEFAULT to a column or to a data type created by a user.

Syntax

The syntax is:

```
sp_bindefault [@defname =] 'default',
[@objname =] 'object_name'
[, [@futureonly =] 'futureonly_flag']
```

The arguments are:

'default'	Default is the nvarchar(386) name of the previously created DEFAULT.

'object_name'	Object_name is nvarchar(257) in the format of table.column and is also the name of a data type.
'futureonly_flag'	Futureonly_flag is varchar(15) and is used when binding a DEFAULT to a data type created by a user. Futureonly=stops existing columns bound to the data type from inheriting the default; however, all future columns will assume the characteristics of the DEFAULT. NULL=the default

sp_bindrule

The sp_bindrule system stored procedure binds a rule to a column or to a data type created by a user.

Syntax

The syntax is:

```
sp_bindrule {'rule'} [, 'object_name' [, 'futureonly_flag']
```

The arguments are:

'rule'	Rule is the nvarchar(386) name of the previously created RULE.
'object_name'	Object_name is nvarchar(257) in the format of table.column or is also the name of a data type.
'future_only_flag'	Futureonly_flag is varchar(15) and is used when binding a DEFAULT to a data type created by a user. Futureonly=stops existing columns bound to the data type from inheriting the default; however, all future columns will assume the characteristics of the DEFAULT. NULL=the default

sp_bindsession

The sp_bindsession system stored procedure binds or unbinds a connection to other connections.

Syntax

The syntax is:

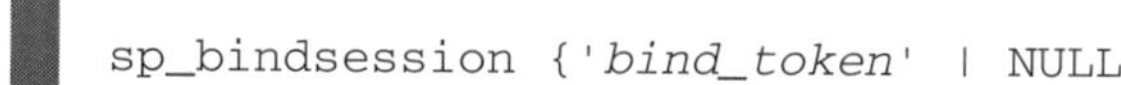

```
sp_bindsession {'bind_token' | NULL}
```

The argument, bind_token, is varchar(255) and is acquired by using sp_getbindtoken or srv_getbindtoken. This system stored procedure finds the transaction space to allow connections to use the same transaction.

sp_browsereplcmds

The sp_browsereplcmds system stored procedure displays the replicated commands in the distribution database.

Syntax

The syntax is:

```
sp_browsereplcmds [[@xact_seqno_start =] 'xact_seqno_start']
    [,[@xact_seqno_end =] 'xact_seqno_end']
    [,[@originator_id =] 'originator_id']
    [,[@publisher_database_id =] 'publisher_database_id']
    [,[@article_id =] 'article_id']
    [,[@command_id =] command_id]
```

The arguments are:

[@xact_seqno_start =] 'xact_seqno_start'	Xact_seqno_start is nchar(22) and the lowest exact sequence number you wish to see displayed. Default is 0x00000000000000000000.
[@xact_seqno_end =] 'xact_seqno_end'	Xact_seqno_end is nchar(22) and the highest exact sequence number you wish to see displayed. Default is 0xFFFFFFFFFFFFFFFFFFFF.
[@originator_id =] 'originator_id'	Originator_id is an integer and displays commands with a specific originator_id.
[@publisher_database_id =] 'publisher_database_id'	Publisher_database_id is integer and displays commands with a specific publisher_database_id.
[@article_id =] 'article_id'	Article_id is an integer and displays commands related to a specific article_id.
[@command_id =] command_id	Command_id is an integer and is the location of the command in MSrepl_commands. All of the other arguments must be used and xact_seqno_start must equal xact_seqno_end.

sp_catalogs

The sp_catalogs system stored procedure displays a catalog listing of a linked server. If SQL Server is being accessed it is equivalent to a database listing.

Syntax

The syntax is:

```
sp_catalogs {'linked_svr'}
```

The argument, linked_svr, is the sysname of a linked server.

sp_certify_removable

The sp_certify_removable system stored procedure certifies that a database can be placed on removable media.

Syntax

The syntax is:

```
sp_certify_removable [@dbname = ] 'dbname' [, [@autofix = ] 'auto']
```

The arguments are:

[@dbname =] 'dbname'	Dbname is the sysname of the database.
[@autofix =] 'auto']	Auto changes the database and transfers ownership of the database and objects to sysadmin, drops database users created by users including permissions that are not native to Microsoft SQL Server 7.

sp_change_agent_parameter

The sp_change_agent_parameter system stored procedure updates an argument in MSAgent_parameters system table of a replication agent profile and can be used for all types of replication.

Syntax

The syntax is:

```
sp_change_agent_parameter [@profile_id =] profile_id,
[@parameter_name =] 'parameter_name',
[@parameter_value =] 'parameter_value'
```

The arguments are:

[@profile_id =] profile_id,	Profile_id is an integer and the profile identifier.
[@parameter_name =] 'parameter_name'	Parameter_name is sysname and the parameter name found in the MSAgent_parameters system table.
[@parameter_value =] 'parameter_value'	Parameter_value is nvarchar(255) and the new parameter value.

sp_change_agent_profile

The sp_change_agent_profile system stored procedure updates an argument in MSAgent_profiles system table of a replication agent profile and can be used for all types of replication.

Syntax

The syntax is:

```
sp_change_agent_profile [@profile_id =] profile_id,
[@property_name =] 'property_name',
[@property_value =] 'property_value'
```

The arguments are:

[@profile_id =] profile_id,	Profile_id is an integer and the profile identifier.
[@property_name =] 'property_name'	Property_name is sysname and the property name found in the MSAgent_profiles system table.
[@property_value =] 'property_value'	Property_value is nvarchar(255) and the new property value.

sp_changearticle

The sp_changearticle system stored procedure modifies an unsubscribed article for snapshot and transactional replication.

Syntax

The syntax is:

```
sp_changearticle [[@publication =] 'publication'] [,[@article =]'article']
[,[@property =] 'property'] [,[@value =] 'value']
```

The arguments are:

[@publication =] 'publication'	Publication is the sysname of the publication.
[@article =]'article'	Article is the sysname of the article.
[@property =] 'property'	Property, of sysname data type, represents the article characteristics to change.
[@value =] 'value'	Value is nvarchar(255) and holds the value for the properties of the article.

The article properties to change and the values for the properties are:

Name	Name is the modified name of the article.
Description	Description is the modified description for the publication job.
sync_object	Sync_object is the name of the table or view that creates the synchronization output file.
Type	The article types are: Logbased=Log-based article Logbased manualfilter=Log-based article with manual filter Logbased manualview=Log-based article with manual view Logbased manualboth=Log-based article with manual filter and manual view.
ins_cmd ins_cmd	Ins_cmd ins_cmd is the INSERT statement to execute or SQL Server generates it.
del_cmd del_cmd	Del_cmd del_cmd is the DELETE statement to execute or SQL Server generates it.
upd_cmd upd_cmd	Upd_cmd upd_cmd is the UPDATE statement to execute or SQL Server generates it.
Filter	Filter is a stored procedure used for horizontal partitioning of the table with default of NULL.
dest_table (dest_object)	Dest_table is the destination table name if it is not the same name as the source table.
creation_script creation_script	Creation_script creation_script is the Path\name of an article schema script file that creates the target tables.

pre_creation_cmd	Pre_creation_cmd is the pre-creation command to drop, delete, or truncate the destination table prior to synchronization. Values are: None=No command Drop=Drop the destination table Delete=Delete the destination table Truncate=Truncate the destination table.
Status	Status is the modified status of the property.
include column names	Include column names is what is allowed for column names in the INSERT statement. The values are: No column names=column names not allowed Owner qualified=owner qualified table names allowed Not owner qualified=not owner qualified table names allowed String literals | parameters=determines if the string_literal command format or the parameterized command is used for the commands generated by the logreader.
schema option	Schema option is the binary(8) bitmap of the article's schema generation option for the article. The values are: 0x00=Uses the CreationScript provided by the user 0x01=CreationScript is generated 0x11=Bitmap for generating the CREATE TABLE, clustered index, nonclustered index, and changing user created data types to base types 0x10=Creates a clustered index 0x20=Changes user created data types to base data types 0x40=Creates a nonclustered index(es) 0x80=Declared referential integrity on primary keys.
destination_owner	Destination_owner is the name of the owner of the destination object.
NULL	NULL means all property values are displayed.

sp_changedbowner

The sp_changedbowner system stored procedure is run in the database in use to change the database owner. The new database owner must not exist as a user in the database in use. If you do not supply the drop_alias_flag, the default will drop the aliases for the old database owner.

Syntax

The syntax is:

```
sp_changedbowner [@loginame =] 'login' [,[@map =] drop_alias_flag]
```

The arguments are:

[@loginame =] 'login'	Login is the login ID of the new database owner.
[@map =] drop_alias_flag	Drop_alias_flag is varchar(5) holding the values of TRUE or FALSE. If the value is TRUE, users aliased to the old database owner will be dropped. If you do not supply the drop_alias_flag, the default will drop the aliases for the old database owner.

sp_changedistpublisher

The sp_changedistpublisher system stored procedure modifies some characteristics of the distribution Publisher.

Syntax

The syntax is:

```
sp_changedistpublisher [@publisher =] 'publisher'
[,[@property =] 'property'] [,[@value =] 'value']
```

The arguments are:

[@publisher =] 'publisher'	Publisher is the sysname of the Publisher.
[@property =] 'property'	Property defines the modifiable characteristics of the Publisher where Active=the value of the active registry key, Distribution_db=the value in the distribution database registry key, Login=the value in the login registry key, Password=the value in the password registry key, Security_mode=the value in the security mode registry key, Working_directory=the value in the working directory registry key, and NULL=the existing properties and values.

[@value =] 'value'	Value is nvarchar(255) and holds the value for the properties of the Publisher.

sp_changedistributiondb

The sp_changedistributiondb system stored procedure modifies some characteristics of the distribution database.

Syntax

The syntax is:

```
sp_changedistributiondb [@database =] 'database'
[,[@property =] 'property'] [,[@value =] 'value']
```

The arguments are:

[@database =] 'database'	Database is the sysname of the database.
[@property =] 'property'	Property is of sysname datatype and represents the property to change for the Publisher and can be one of the following: History_retention=the retention period for the history table Max_distretention=the maximum retention period for distribution Min_distretention= the minimum retention period for distribution Security_mode=the value of the security mode registry key NULL=displays existing properties and values.
[@value =] 'value'	Value is nvarchar(255) and holds the value for the properties of the distribution database.

sp_changedistributor_property

The sp_changedistributor_property system stored procedure modifies some characteristics of the Distributor for all types of replication.

Syntax

The syntax is:

```
sp_changedistributor_property [[@property =] 'property']
[,[@value =] 'value']
```

The arguments are:

[@property =] 'property'	Property is the sysname property for a given Distributor where working_directory=the value of the working directory registry key, NULL=existing properties and values are listed.
[@value =] 'value'	Value is nvarchar(255) and holds the value for the properties of the Distributor.

sp_changedistributor_password

The sp_changedistributor_password system stored procedure is used on all types of replication to create a new password for a Distributor and, in the case of a local Distributor, is used to modify the distributor_admin password.

Syntax

The syntax is:

```
sp_changedistributor_password [@password =] 'password'
```

The argument, [@password =] 'password', is the new password replacing the old one.

sp_changegroup

The sp_changegroup system stored procedure is provided for backward compatibility. A Microsoft SQL Server 7 programmer uses sp_addrolemember instead of sp_changegroup to change the role membership for a database user. Using sp_changegroup will allow the database user to be placed in only one role by dropping other role memberships while the newer role paradigm in version 7 allows a user to be placed in more than one role.

Syntax

The syntax is:

```
sp_changegroup [@grpname =] 'role', [@username =] 'user'
```

The arguments are:

[@grpname =] 'role'	Role is the role the database user is assuming and must be an existing database role.
[@username =] 'user'	User is the sysname for the database user to change into a new role.

sp_changemergearticle

The sp_changemergearticle system stored procedure modifies some characteristics of the merge article.

Syntax

The syntax is:

```
sp_changemergearticle [@publication =] 'publication' [,[@article =]'article']
[,[@property =] 'property'] [,[@value =] 'value']
```

The arguments are:

[@publication =] 'publication'	Publication is the sysname of the publication with the article.
[@article =] 'article'	Article is the sysname of the article which must be a tablename (e.g., MyTable).
[@property =] 'property'	Property, of sysname data type, represents the article characteristics to change.
[@value =] 'value'	Value is nvarchar(255) and holds the value for the properties of the article.

The merge article properties to change and the values for the properties are:

name	Name is the new name of the merger article.
[@description =] 'description'	Description is the nvarchar(255) descriptions of the article and defaults to NULL.
[@column_tracking =] 'column_tracking'	Column_tracking is the nvarchar(10) true false indicator for column level tracking which defaults to false for column tracking turned off. If the table is already published using merge replication, use the same column tracking value and set this to true.
[@status =] 'status'	Status is the nvarchar(10) status of the article and defaults to unsynced, meaning the initial data is assumed already at the destination. If the status is active, the initial processing script runs or you can set the status to inactive.

[@pre_creation_cmd =] 'pre_creation_cmd'	Pre_creation_cmd is the nvarchar(10) pre-creation method where None=if the table already exists at the Subscriber, does nothing, Delete=deletes and filters on the WHERE clause in the subset filter, Drop=drops the table before recreating it and is the default, Truncate=same as delete, but deletes pages (no WHERE clause needed).
[@creation_script =] 'creation_script'	Creation_script is the nvarchar(255) pre-creation script for the article (optional and defaults to NULL).
[@schema_option =] schema_option	Schema_option is a binary(8) bitmap of the schema generation for the article where 0x00=Disables scripting by Snapshot and uses the provided CreationScript, 0x01=Generates the object creation (CREATE TABLE, CREATE PROCEDURE), 0x10=Generates a clustered index, 0x20=Converts user-defined data types to base data types, 0x40=Generates nonclustered indexes, 0x80=Provides declared referential integrity on the primary keys, 0xf1 (default)=Makes the create table, creates clustered indexes, creates nonclustered index(es), converts user-defined data types to base data types, 0x01=The default for stored procedure articles.
[@subset_filterclause =] 'subset_filterclause'	Subset_filterclause is a nvarchar(2000) WHERE clause determining the horizontal filtering.
[@article_resolver =] 'article_resolver'	Article_resolver is the varchar(255) custom resolver for the article. The stored procedure, sp_enumcustomsolvers, lists the custom resolvers. If left NULL, a system-supplied resolver is used.
[@resolver_info =] 'resolver_info']	Resolver_info is the sysname of the stored procedure used as a custom resolver and defaults to NULL.

sp_changemergefilter

The sp_changemergefilter system stored procedure modifies some of the characteristics of a filter.

Syntax

The syntax is:

```
sp_changemergefilter [@publication =] 'publication' [,[@article =]'article']
[,[@filtername =] 'filtername' [,[@property =] 'property'] [,[@value =]  value']
```

The arguments are:

[@publication =] 'publication'	Publication is the sysname of the publication.
[@article =]'article'	Article is the sysname of the article.
[@filtername =] 'filtername'	The filter is the sysname of a filter.
[@property =] 'property'	Property is the characteristic of the merge filter. The following can be changed: Filtername=sysname of the filter Join_filterclause=a WHERE clause minus the WHERE Join_table_name=sysname of the join table
[@value =] 'value'	Value is the nvarchar(2000) value for the modifiable property.

sp_changemergepublication

The sp_changemergepublication system stored procedure modifies some of the characteristics of a merge publication.

Syntax

The syntax is:

```
sp_changemergepublication [@publication =] 'publication'
[,[@property =] 'property'] [,[@value =] 'value']
```

The arguments are:

[@publication =] 'publication'	Publication is the sysname of the publication.
[@property =] 'property'	Property, of sysname data type, represents the Publication characteristics to change.
[@value =] 'value'	Value is nvarchar(255) and holds the value for the properties of the Publication.

The merge publication properties to change and the values for the properties are:

[@description =] 'description'	Description is the nvarchar(255) publication description.
status	Status is the status of the Publication with modifiable values of unsynced, active, or inactive.
[@retention =] retention	Retention is an integer representing how many days to save the given publication with a default of 60 days. The subscription has to merge in the retention period or it will not sync.
[@sync_mode =] 'sync_mode'	Sync_mode is the nvarchar(10) mode of the synchronization and defaults to native. Native=bulk copy Character=character bulk copy
[@allow_push =] 'allow_push'	Allow_push is true or false (nvarchar(5)) determining if push subscriptions are permitted for the publication.
[@allow_pull =] 'allow_pull'	Allow_pull is true or false (nvarchar(5)) determining if pull subscriptions are permitted for the publication.
[@allow_anonymous =] 'allow_anonymous'	Allow_anonymous is true or false (nvarchar(5)) determining if anonymous subscriptions are permitted for the publication.
[@enabled_for_internet =] 'enabled_for_internet'	Enabled_for_internet is nvarchar(5), with a default of false, and determines whether the publication is enabled for the Internet. FTP is used to send the snapshot to the Subscriber.
[@centralized_conflicts =] 'centralized_conflicts'	Centralized_confilicts is nvarchar(5) and determines if conflict records are stored on the Publisher and defaults to true. False means the storage occurs at the Subscriber.
[@default_access =] 'default_access'	Default_access is nvarchar(5) and defaults to true.

sp_changemergepullsubscription

The sp_changemergepullsubscription system stored procedure modifies some of the characteristics of a merge pull subscription. The subscriber is the server in use and the subscriber_db is the database in use.

Syntax

The syntax is:

```
sp_changemergepullsubscription [[@publication =] 'publication']
[,[@publisher =] 'publisher'] [,[@publisher_db =] 'publisher_db']
[,[@property =] 'property'] [,[@value =] 'value']
```

The arguments are:

[@publication =] 'publication'	Publication is the sysname of the publication.
[@publisher =] 'publisher'	Publisher is the sysname (server name) of the Publisher.
[@publisher_db =] 'publisher_db	Publisher_db is the sysname of the Publisher database and defaults to NULL.
[@property =] 'property'	Property, of sysname data type, represents the merge pull subscription characteristics to change.
[@value =] 'value'	Value is nvarchar(255) and holds the value for the properties of the merge pull subscription.

The merge pull subscription properties and values to change are:

[@priority =] priority	Subscription priority is real data type and defaults to NULL and is used to resolve conflicts. Local = 0.0 Anonymous=0.0
[@sync_type =] 'sync_type'	Sync_type is the nvarchar(15) subscription synchronization type and defaults to automatic. Automatic=schema and data transfer Nosync=no schema and data transfer.
[@description =] 'description'	Description is a varchar(255) pull subscription description and defaults to NULL.

sp_changemergesubscription

The sp_changemergesubscription system stored procedure modifies some of the characteristics of a merge push or pull subscription.

Syntax

The syntax is:

```
sp_changemergesubscription [[@publication =] 'publication']
[,[@subscriber =] 'subscriber' [,[@subscriber_db =]
'subscriber_db'] [,[@property =] 'property'] [,[@value =] 'value']
```

The arguments are:

[@publication =] 'publication'	Publication is the sysname of the publication.
[@subscriber =]'subscriber'	Subscriber is the sysname (server name) of the Subscriber.
[@subscriber _db =] ' subscriber_db'	Subscriber_db is the sysname of the Subscriber database.
[@property =] 'property'	Property, of sysname data type, represents the merge subscription characteristics to change.
[@value =] 'value'	Value is nvarchar(255) and holds the value for the properties of the merge subscription.

The merge subscription properties and values to change are:

[@priority =] priority	Subscription priority is real data type and defaults to NULL and is used to resolve conflicts. Local = 0.0 Anonymous=0.0
[@sync_type =] 'sync_type'	Sync_type is the nvarchar(255) subscription synchronization type and defaults to automatic. Automatic=schema and data transfer None=no schema but data transfer.
[@description =] 'description'	Description is the nvarchar(255) merge subscription description and defaults to NULL.

sp_changeobjectowner

The sp_changeobjectowner system stored procedure is run in the database in use to change the object owner.

Syntax

The syntax is:

```
sp_changeobjectowner [@objname =] 'object' [,[@newowner =] 'owner']
```

The arguments are:

[@objname =] 'object'	Object is the optionally owner qualified nvarchar(517) name of a table, view, or stored procedure in the database in use.
[@newowner =] 'owner'	Owner is the sysname of a database user (security account).

sp_changepublication

The sp_changepublication system stored procedure modifies some of the characteristics of a publication.

Syntax

The syntax is:

```
sp_changepublication [[@publication =] 'publication']
[,[@property =] 'property'] [,[@value =] 'value']
```

The arguments are:

[@publication =] 'publication'	Publication is the sysname of the publication.
[@property =] 'property'	Property, of sysname data type, represents the Publication characteristics to change.
[@value =] 'value'	Value is nvarchar(255) and holds the value for the properties of the Publication.

The publication properties and values to change are:

[@description =] 'description'	Description is nvarchar(255) publication description and defaults to NULL.

[@taskid =] taskid	Taskid is integer representing a previously created scheduler task. This argument is for backward compatibility only. Use sp_addpublication_snapshot.
[@restricted =] 'restricted'	Restricted is nvarchar(10) true or false of who can look at the publication. False=can be seen by all True=can be seen only by authorized Subscribers
[@sync_method =] 'sync_method'	Sync_method is the nvarchar(13) method of synchronization and defaults to native. Native=bulk copy Character=character bulk copy
[@repl_freq =] 'repl_freq'	Repl_freq is the nvarchar(10) replication frequency type. Continuous=Publisher sends every log-based transactions Snapshot=Publisher sends scheduled synchronization events
[@status =] 'status'	Status is nvarchar(8) determines if the publication data is available to the Subscribers when the publication is initially created and defaults to inactive. Inactive=publication data is not immediately available Active=Publication data is immediately available
immediate_sync	Immediate_sync, if set to true, determines that the synchronization files for the publication are created each time the Snapshot Agent runs. If set false, the synchronization files are created if new subscriptions are detected.
independent_agent	Independent_agent, if set to true, determines that there is a stand-alone Distribution Agent for the publication. If set to false, there is one Distribution Agent for each Publisher and Subscriber combination.
enabled_for_internet	Enabled_for_internet, if set to true, determines the publication is enabled for the Internet and the sync files for the publication reside in \Repldata\Ftp.
allow_push	Allow_push, if set to true, determines that push subscriptions are allowed for the publication.
allow_pull	Allow_pull, if set to true, determines that pull subscriptions are allowed for the publication.

allow_anonymous	Allow_ anonymous, if set to true, determines that anonymous subscriptions are allowed for the publication.
retention	The retention period for subscription activity expressed in days.
default_access	Default_access, if set to true, determines that the Publisher's default publication access list is used.

sp_changesubscriber

The sp_changesubscriber system stored procedure modifies some of the characteristics of a Subscriber.

Syntax

The syntax is:

```
sp_changesubscriber {[@subscriber =] 'subscriber'} [,[@type =] type]
[,[@login =] 'login'] [,[@password =] 'password']
[,[@commit_batch_size =] commit_batch_size]
[,[@status_batch_size =] status_batch_size]
[,[@flush_frequency =] flush_frequency]
[,[@frequency_type =] frequency_type]
[,[@frequency_interval =] frequency_interval]
[,[@frequency_relative_interval =] frequency_relative_interval]
[,[@frequency_recurrence_factor =] frequency_recurrence_factor]
[,[@frequency_subday =] frequency_subday]
[,[@frequency_subday_interval =] frequency_subday_interval]
[,[@active_start_time_of_day =] active_start_time_of_day]
[,[@active_end_time_of_day =] active_end_time_of_day]
[,[@active_start_date =] active_start_date]
[,[@active_end_date =] active_end_date]
[,[@description =] 'description'] [,[@security_mode =] security_mode]
```

The arguments are:

[@subscriber =] 'subscriber'	Subscriber is the sysname of the server added as a Subscriber.
[@type =] type	Type is the tinyint type of Subscriber. 0=Microsoft SQL Server Subscriber 1=ODBC data source server

[@login =] 'login'	Login is the sysname of the SQL Server Authenticated login and defaults to SA.
[@password =] 'password	Password is the sysname password for the SQL Server Authenticated login and defaults to %, no change to the password property.
[@commit_batch_size =] commit_batch_size	Commit_batch_size is an integer determining how many transactions are sent to the Subscriber and committed together and defaults to NULL.
[@status_batch_size =] status_batch_size	Status_batch_size is reserved for future use with default of NULL.
[@flush_frequency =] flush_frequency	Flush_frequency is an integer determining how often transactions are deleted from the distribution database tables after distributiom to the Subscriber and defaults to NULL.
[@frequency_type =] frequency_type	Frequency_type is an integer that determines how to schedule the Distribution Agent. 1=One Time, 2=On Demand, 4=Daily, 8=Weekly, 16=Monthly, 32=Monthly Relative, 64=Autostart, 128=Recurring, NULL=the default value.
[@frequency_interval =] frequency_interval	Frequency interval is an integer that represents the run days of the Distribution Agent. 1=Sunday, 2=Monday, 3=Tuesday, 4=Wednesday, 5=Thursday, 6=Friday, 7=Saturday, 8=day, 9=weekdays, 10=weekend days, NULL=the default value.
[@frequency_relative_interval =] frequency_relative_interval	Frequency_relative_interval is an integer used for a frequency_type of monthly relative. 1=First, 2=Second, 4=Third, 8=Fourth, 16=Last, NULL=the default.
[@frequency_recurrence_factor =] frequency_recurrence_factor	Frequency_recurrence_factor is an integer used in conjunction with frequency_type and defaults to NULL.
[@frequency_subday =] frequency_subday	Frequency_subday is an integer representing when to schedule again during the selected time period. 1=Once, 2=Second, 4=Minute, 8=Hour, NULL=the default.

[@frequency_subday_interval =] frequency_subday_interval	Frequency_subday_interval is an integer representing the interval for frequency_subday and defaults to NULL.
[@active_start_time_of_day =] active_start_time_of_day	Active_start_time_of_day is an integer representing the first time the Distribution Agent is scheduled and defaults to NULL (HHMMSS).
[@active_end_time_of_day =] active_end_time_of_day	Active_end_time_of_day is an integer representing the time the Distribution Agent stops being scheduled with a default of NULL (HHMMSS).
[@active_start_date =] active_start_date	Active_start_date is an integer and represents the first date the Distribution Agent is scheduled and defaults to NULL (YYYYMMDD).
[@active_end_date =] active_end_date	Active_end_date is an integer representing the date when the Distribution Agent stops being scheduled and defaults to NULL (YYYYMMDD).
[@description =] 'description'	Description is the nvarchar(255) description of the Subscriber and defaults to NULL.
[@security_mode =] security_mode	Security_mode is an integer and represents the security mode where 0=SQL Server authentication and 1=Windows NT authentication (the default).

sp_changesubscriber_schedule

The sp_changesubscriber_schedule system stored procedure modifies some of the characteristics of a Distribution Agent and Merge Agent. Use sp_changesubscriber to modify the schedule for a Distribution Agent or create a default schedule for the Merge Agent.

Syntax

The syntax is:

```
sp_changesubscriber_schedule [@subscriber =] 'subscriber',
[@agent_type =] type [,[@frequency_type =] frequency_type]
[,[@frequency_interval =] frequency_interval]
[,[@frequency_relative_interval =] frequency_relative_interval]
```

```
[,[@frequency_recurrence_factor =] frequency_recurrence_factor]
[,[@frequency_subday =] frequency_subday]
[,[@frequency_subday_interval =] frequency_subday_interval]
[,[@active_start_time_of_day =] active_start_time_of_day]
[,[@active_end_time_of_day =] active_end_time_of_day]
[,[@active_start_date =] active_start_date]
[,[@active_end_date =] active_end_date]
```

The arguments are:

[@subscriber =] 'subscriber'	Subscriber is the sysname of the Subscriber.
[@agent_type =] agent_type	Agent_type is the smallint type of agent where 0=Distribution Agent and 1=Merge Agent with a default of 0.
[@frequency_type =] frequency_type	Frequency_type is an integer that determines how to schedule the Distribution Agent. 1=One Time, 2=On Demand, 4=Daily, 8=Weekly, 16=Monthly, 32=Monthly Relative, 64=Autostart, 124=Recurring, NULL=the default value.
[@frequency_interval =] frequency_interval	Frequency interval is an integer that represents the run days of the Distribution Agent. 1=Sunday, 2=Monday, 3=Tuesday, 4=Wednesday, 5=Thursday, 6=Friday, 7=Saturday, 8=day, 9=weekdays, 10=weekend days, NULL=the default value.
[@frequency_relative_interval =] frequency_relative_interval	Frequency_relative_interval is an integer used for a frequency_type of monthly relative. 1=First, 2=Second, 4=Third, 8=Fourth, 16=Last, NULL=the default.
[@frequency_recurrence_factor =] frequency_recurrence_factor	Frequency_recurrence_factor is an integer used in conjunction with frequency_type and defaults to NULL.
[@frequency_subday =] frequency_subday	Frequency_subday is an integer representing when to schedule again during the selected time period. 1=Once, 2=Second, 4=Minute, 8=Hour, NULL=the default.

[@frequency_subday_interval =] frequency_subday_interval	Frequency_subday_interval is an integer representing the interval for frequency_subday and defaults to NULL.
[@active_start_time_of_day =] active_start_time_of_day	Active_start_time_of_day is an integer representing the first time the Distribution Agent is scheduled and defaults to NULL (HHMMSS).
[@active_end_time_of_day =] active_end_time_of_day	Active_end_time_of_day is an integer representing the time the Distribution Agent stops being scheduled with a default of NULL (HHMMSS).
[@active_start_date =] active_start_date	Active_start_date is an integer and represents the first date the Distribution Agent is scheduled and defaults to NULL (YYYYMMDD).
[@active_end_date =] active_end_date	Active_end_date is an integer representing the date when the Distribution Agent stops being scheduled and defaults to NULL (YYYYMMDD).

sp_changesubstatus

The sp_changesubstatus system stored procedure procedure modifies a status of an existing Subscriber.

Syntax

The syntax is:

```
sp_changesubstatus [[@publication =] 'publication'] [,[@article =] article']
[,[@subscriber =] 'subscriber'] {,[@status =] 'status'}
[,[@previous_status =] 'previous_status']
[,[@destination_db =] 'destination_db']
[,[@frequency_type =] frequency_type]
[,[@frequency_interval =] frequency_interval]
[,[@frequency_relative_interval =] frequency_relative_interval]
[,[@frequency_recurrence_factor =] frequency_recurrence_factor]
[,[@frequency_subday =] frequency_subday]
[,[@frequency_subday_interval =] frequency_subday_interval]
[,[@active_start_time_of_day =] active_start_time_of_day]
[,[@active_end_time_of_day =] active_end_time_of_day]
[,[@active_start_date =] active_start_date]
[,[@active_end_date =] active_end_date]
[,[@optional_command_line =] 'optional_command_line']
[,[@distribution_jobid =] distribution_jobid]
[,[@from_auto_sync =] from_auto_sync]
[,[@ignore_distributor =] ignore_distributor]
```

The arguments are:

[@publication =] 'publication'	Publication is the sysname of the publication. The default of % means all.
[@article =] 'article'	Article is the sysname of the article. If not given, the subscription is for every article in the publication. The default of % means all.
[@subscriber =] 'subscriber'	Subscriber is the sysname of the Subscriber and defaults to NULL. The default of % means all.
[@status =] 'status'	Status is the sysname of the subscription status. Active=subscriber synced and data is being transferred Inactive=subscriber entry without a subscription for restricted publications Subscribed=Subscribed but not synced
[@previous_status =] 'previous_status'	Previous status is the sysname and represents the previous status for the subscription. This allows you to to change a set of subscriptions with a previous status to another status.
[@destination_db =] 'destination_db'	Destination_db is the sysname of the destination database which holds the replicated data (should be the same name as the Publication database). The default of % means all.
[@frequency_type =] frequency_type	Frequency_type is an integer that determines how to schedule the Distribution Agent. 1=One Time, 2=On Demand, 4=Daily, 8=Weekly, 16=Monthly, 32=Monthly Relative, 64=Autostart, 124=Recurring, NULL=the default value.
[@frequency_interval =] frequency_interval	Frequency interval is an integer that represents the run days of the Distribution Agent. 1=Sunday, 2=Monday, 3=Tuesday, 4=Wednesday, 5=Thursday, 6=Friday, 7=Saturday, 8=day, 9=weekdays, 10=weekend days, NULL=the default value.
[@frequency_relative_interval =] frequency_relative_interval	Frequency_relative_interval is an integer used for a frequency_type of monthly relative. 1=First, 2=Second, 4=Third, 8=Fourth, 16=Last, NULL=the default.

[@frequency_recurrence_factor =] frequency_recurrence_factor	Frequency_recurrence_factor is an integer used in conjunction with frequency_type and defaults to NULL.
[@frequency_subday =] frequency_subday	Frequency_subday is an integer representing when to schedule again during the selected time period. 1=Once, 2=Second, 4=Minute, 8=Hour, NULL=the default.
[@frequency_subday_interval =] frequency_subday_interval	Frequency_subday_interval is an integer representing the interval for frequency_subday and defaults to NULL.
[@active_start_time_of_day =] active_start_time_of_day	Active_start_time_of_day is an integer representing the first time the Distribution Agent is scheduled and defaults to NULL (HHMMSS).
[@active_end_time_of_day =] active_end_time_of_day	Active_end_time_of_day is an integer representing the time the Distribution Agent stops being scheduled with a default of NULL (HHMMSS).
[@active_start_date =] active_start_date	Active_start_date is an integer and represents the first date the Distribution Agent is scheduled and defaults to NULL (YYYYMMDD).
[@active_end_date =] active_end_date	Active_end_date is an integer representing the date when the Distribution Agent stops being scheduled and defaults to NULL (YYYYMMDD).
[@optional_command_line =] 'optional_command_line'	Optional_command_line is the nvarchar(4000) command line you wish to run and defaults to NULL.
[@distribution_jobid =] distribution_jobid	Distribution_jobid is binary(16), with a default of NULL and the job identifier of the distribution agent at the distributor for the subscription. This argument is only used when changing the status from active to inactive.
[@from_auto_sync =] from_auto_sync	From_auto_sync is bit datatype with default of 0.
[@ignore_distributor =] ignore_distributor	Ignore_distributor is bit, with default of 0.

sp_change_subscription_properties

The sp_change_subscription_properties system stored procedure modifies the security accounts and passwords for the Publisher and Distributor of a subscription.

Syntax

The syntax is:

```
sp_change_subscription_properties [,[@publisher =] 'publisher']
[,[@publisher_db =] 'publisher_db'] [,[@publication =]
'publication'] [,[@property =] 'property'] [,[@value =] 'value']
```

The arguments are:

[@publisher =] 'publisher'	Publisher is the sysname of the Publisher.
[@publisher_db =] 'publisher_db'	Publisher_db is the sysname of the Publisher database.
[@publication =] 'publication'	Publication is the sysname of the publication.
[@property =] 'property'	Property is the characteristics to modify of publisher_login, publisher_password, publisher_security_mode (values of 0=SQL Server Authentication and 1=Windows NT Authentication), encrypted_publisher_password, distributor_login, distributor_password, distributor_security_mode (values of 0=SQL Server Authentication and 1=Windows NT Authentication), encrypted_distributor_password.
[@value =] 'value'	Value is nvarchar(255) and holds the value for the property.

sp_change_users_login

The sp_change_users_login system stored procedure is used to modify user login information.

Syntax

The syntax is:

```
sp_change_users_login [@Action =] 'action' [,[@UserNamePattern =] 'user'
[,[@LoginName =] 'login']]
```

The arguments are:

[@Action =] 'action'	Action is varchar(10) and the action to be taken. Auto_Fix=Updates the database users (sysusers system table) to correspond to the login of the same name in the login table (syslogins system table). Provide the UserNamePattern but not the LoginName. Report=Reports the database users that are orphaned and have no corresponding login. Do not provide the LoginName or the UserNamePattern for this report. Update_One=Provide a LoginName and the UserNamePattern and the database UserName will be updated in the sysusers table in the database in use to the LoginName you provide.
[@UserNamePattern =] 'user'	User is the sysname of a database user.
[@LoginName =] 'login'	Login is the sysname of a SQL Server login name existing in the syslogins table on the Microsoft SQL Server.

sp_column_privileges

The sp_column_privileges system stored procedure displays the column privileges of a table in the database in use.

Syntax

The syntax is:

```
sp_column_privileges {'table_name'} [, 'table_owner'] [, 'table_qualifier']
[, 'column']
```

The arguments are:

'table_name'	Table_name is the sysname of the table.
'table_owner'	Table_owner is the sysname of the owner of the table.

'table_qualifier'	Table_qualifier is the database sysame in SQL Server. It may represent other things in other products with different source data set names.
'column'	Column is the nvarchar(384) name of a column. If this argument is omitted, all columns are returned. This is the only argument for this system stored procedure that allows wildcard characters.

sp_column_privileges_ex

The sp_column_privileges_ex system stored procedure displays the column privileges for a table on a linked server.

Syntax

The syntax is:

```
sp_column_privileges_ex {'table_server'} [, 'table_name'] [, 'table_schema']
[, 'table_catalog'] , 'column_name'
```

The arguments are:

'table_server'	Table_server is the sysname of the linked server.
'table_name'	Table_name is the sysname of the table.
'table_schema'	Table_schema is the sysname of the table schema default of NULL.
'table_catalog'	Table_catalog is the sysname of the database with default of NULL.
column_name	Column is the nvarchar(384) name of a column.

sp_columns

The sp_columns system stored procedure displays catalog information for tables or views in the database in use.

Syntax

The syntax is:

```
sp_columns {object} [, owner] [, qualifier] [, column] [, ODBCVer]
```

The arguments are:

object	Object is the nvarchar(384) name of the table or view.
owner	Owner is the nvarchar(384) name of the owner of the table or view.
qualifier	Qualifier is the database sysame in SQL Server. It may represent other things in other products with different source data set names.
column	Column is the nvarchar(384) name of a column.
ODBCVer	ODBCVer is an integer representing the ODBC version in use with default of 2 and possible values of 2 or 3.

sp_columns_ex

The sp_columns_ex system stored procedure displays the catalog information for the column(s).

Syntax

The syntax is:

```
sp_columns_ex {'table_server'} [, 'table_name'] [, 'table_schema']
[, 'table_catalog'] [, 'column']
```

The arguments are:

'table_server'	Table_server is the sysname of the linked server.
'table_name'	Table_name is the sysname of the table.
'table_schema'	Table_schema is the sysname of the table schema default of NULL.
'table_catalog'	Table_catalog is the sysname of the database with default of NULL.
'column'	Column is the nvarchar(384) name of a column.

sp_configure

The sp_configure system stored procedure displays or changes global configuration settings for the current server. See Chapter 10, "Simplifying the Role of the Database Administrator."

Syntax

The syntax is:

```
sp_configure ['name'] [, 'value']
```

The arguments are:

'name'	Name is varchar(35) and the configuration option and can be any string that is a subset of the name if it is not duplicated in another option. Not supplying the name returns all available options.
'value'	Value is an integer and is the value assigned to the configuration option. For many of the configuration options, 0=Off or FALSE, 1=On or TRUE.

sp_createstats

The sp_createstats system stored procedure runs UPDATE STATISTICS WITH COLUMNS while excluding columns of bit, text, image, or timestamp datatypes and columns with statistics.

Syntax

The syntax is:

```
sp_createstats [@indexonly =] 'indexonly', [@fullscan =] 'fullscan'
```

The arguments are:

[@indexonly =] 'indexonly'	Indexonly is char(9) and defaults to NO. Supplying this argument further limits the columns marked for UPDATE STATISTICS WITH COLUMNS to only indexed columns.
[@fullscan =] 'fullscan'	FULLSCAN is char(9) and must be supplied if you want the entire table scanned, otherwise a sample scan will be done.

sp_create_removable

The sp_create_removable system stored procedure is used to make a removable media database which can be placed on a CD-ROM or other removable media. This stored procedure puts the database on a file that holds the system tables, a file that holds the transaction log, and on 1 to 16 data files depending on the amount of data. It can be useful to send a database to another location.

Syntax

The syntax is:

```
sp_create_removable [@dbname = ] 'dbname',
[@syslogical = ] 'syslogical',
[@sysphysical = ] 'sysphysical',
[@syssize = ] syssize,
[@loglogical = ] 'loglogical',
[@logphysical = ] 'logphysical',
[@logsize = ] logsize,
[@datalogical1 = ] 'datalogical1',
[@dataphysical1 = ] 'dataphysical1',
[@datasize1 = ] datasize1
[... , [@datalogical16 = ] 'datalogical16',
[@dataphysical16 = ] 'dataphysical16',
[@datasize16 = ] datasize16]
```

The arguments are:

'dbname'	Dbname is the sysname of the database.
'syslogical'	Syslogical is the logical name (sysname datatype) of the file that will be created to hold the system tables.
'sysphysical'	Sysphysical is the physical name (path\file format of nvarchar(260)) of the file that will be created to hold the system tables.
syssize	Syssize is an integer representing in megabytes, with a minimum of 1MB, the size of the file this stored procedure creates to hold the system tables.
'loglogical'	Loglogical is the logical name (sysname datatype) of the file that will be created to hold the transaction log.
'logphysical'	Logphysical is the physical name (path\file format of nvarchar(260)) of the file that will be created to hold the the transaction log.
logsize	Logsize is an integer representing in megabytes, with a minimum of 1MB, the size of the file this stored procedure creates to hold the transaction log.
'datalogical'	Datalogical is the logical name (sysname datatype) of the file that will be created to hold the data tables. For large databases there can be up to 16 data files.

'dataphysical' Dataphysical is the physical name (path\file format of nvarchar(260)) of the file that will be created to hold the the data tables.

'datasize' Datasize is an integer representing in megabytes, with a minimum of 1MB, the size of the file this stored procedure creates to hold the data tables.

sp_cursor_list

The sp_cursor_list system stored procedure returns scroll and update information on the open server cursors for the connection.

Syntax

The syntax is:

```
sp_cursor_list {[@cursor_return = ] cursor_variable_name OUTPUT }
{, [@cursor_scope = ] cursor_scope}
```

The arguments are:

cursor_variable_name Cursor_variable_name is the declared name of an existing cursor variable.

cursor_scope Cursor_scope is an integer where 1=local cursors, 2=global cursors.3=local and global cursors.

sp_cycle_errorlog

The sp_cycle_errorlog system stored procedure closes the in-use error log file opens a new one behaving just as if you had stopped and restarted SQL Server.

Syntax

The syntax is:

```
sp_cycle_errorlog
```

sp_databases

The sp_databases system stored procedure returns the Microsoft SQL Server databases on the server and the databases available through a database gateway.

Syntax

The syntax is:

```
sp_databases
```

sp_datatype_info

The sp_datatype_info system stored procedure lists the data types created on the Microsoft SQL Server in use if you pass it no arguments. You can also pass the data type as an argument.

Syntax

The syntax is:

```
sp_datatype_info [data_type] [, odbc_version]
```

The arguments are:

data_type	Data_type integer values can be obtained by running this same system stored procedure (sp_datatype_info) without parameters and reviewing the values in the output column called data_type.
odbc_version	ODBC version is the version of ODBC being used. odbc_version is tinyint, with a default of 2.

sp_dbcmptlevel

The sp_dbcmptlevel system stored procedure determines how the server will behave to be compatible with specified previous versions of Microsoft SQL Server.

Syntax

The syntax is:

```
sp_dbcmptlevel [[@dbname =] name] [, [@new_cmptlevel =] version]
```

The arguments are:

[@dbname =] name	Dbname is the sysname of the database.
[@new_cmptlevel =] version	Version is the integer compatiblility level for the database with values of 60, 65, or 70.

sp_dbfixedrolepermission

The sp_dbfixedrolepermission system stored procedure returns permissions for all fixed database roles or a selected role.

Syntax

The syntax is:

```
sp_dbfixedrolepermission [[@rolename =] 'role']
```

The argument, role, is the name of a fixed database role. If this argument is not supplied the permissions for all roles will be returned.

sp_dboption

The sp_dboption system stored procedure lists all database options or changes an option.

Syntax

The syntax is:

```
sp_dboption ['database'] [, 'option_name'] [, 'value']
```

The arguments are:

'database'	Database is the sysname of the database. If no arguments are supplied, all database options that can be changed are listed.
'option_name'	Option is the varchar(35) name of the database option to change. If this argument is not supplied but the database argument is supplied, its current database options are returned.
'value'	Value is the varchar(10) new value for the database option.

sp_dbremove

The sp_dbremove system stored procedure is provided for backward compatibility. A Microsoft SQL Server 7 programmer uses sp_detach_db to remove a removable media database from a Microsoft SQL Server. The sp_dbremove stored procedure removes a database and its files.

Syntax

The syntax is:

```
sp_dbremove [@dbname =] 'database'[, [@dropdev = ] 'dropdev']
```

The arguments are:

[@dbname =] 'database'	Database is the sysname of the database.
[@dropdev =] 'dropdev'	Dropdev is a flag that is ignored on version 7.0 with the value 'dropdev'.

sp_defaultdb

The sp_defaultdb system stored procedure creates a new default database for a login. Executing sp_defaultdb does not give the login access to the default database unless there is a guest user; otherwise the dbo must execute the sp_grantdbaccess sytem stored procedure to explicitly give database access to the login.

Syntax

The syntax is:

```
sp_defaultdb [@loginame =] 'login' [,[@defdb =] 'database']
```

The arguments are:

[@loginame =] 'login'	Login is the sysname of the login. If login is a Windows NT user or group that does not exist, it will be added.
[@defdb =] 'database'	Database is the sysname of an existing database that becomes the default database for the user.

sp_defaultlanguage

The sp_defaultlanguage system stored procedure changes the default language of a login to another.

Syntax

The syntax is:

```
sp_defaultlanguage [@loginame =] 'login' [,[@language =] 'language']
```

The arguments are:

[@loginame =] 'login'	Login is the sysname of the login. If login is a Windows NT user or group that does not exist, it will be added.
[@language =] 'language'	Language is the sysname of an existing language that becomes the default language for the user. Use the system stored procedure sp_helplanguage to get the available languages.

sp_delete_alert

The sp_delete_alert system stored procedure deletes a SQL Server alert when executed in the msdb system database.

Syntax

The syntax is:

```
sp_delete_alert {'name'}
```

The argument, name, is the varchar(100) name of the alert to delete.

sp_delete_category

The sp_delete_category system stored procedure deletes a category from a server.

Syntax

The syntax is:

```
sp_delete_category {'class'} [, 'name']
```

The arguments are:

'class'	Class is the varchar(8) category class to delete with possible values of JOB, ALERT, and OPERATOR. Be aware that removing an alert removes any jobs, categories, or operators with membership in the category.
'name'	Name is the sysname name of the server.

sp_delete_job

The sp_delete_job system stored procedure removes a job from the SQL Server. Supply the job_id argument or the job_name argument.

Syntax

The syntax is:

```
sp_delete_job {[@job_id =] job_id | [@job_name =] 'job_name'}
[, [@originating_server =] 'server'] [, [@delete_history =] delete_history]
```

The arguments are:

job_id	Job_id is the uniqueidentifier of the job.
'job_name'	Job_name is the varchar(100) name of the job to be deleted.
'server'	Server is the varchar(30) name of the server where the job originated.
delete_history	Delete_history is a bit flag where 0=false and 1=true. Default is 1.

sp_delete_jobschedule

The sp_delete_jobschedule system stored procedure deletes a job from the scheduled jobs available for execution on a server. Supply the job_id argument or the job_name argument.

Syntax

The syntax is:

```
sp_delete_jobschedule {[@job_id =] job_id | [@job_name =] 'job_name'}
{, [@name =] 'sched_job_name'}
```

The arguments are:

job_id	Job_id is the uniqueidentifier of the job to remove from the job schedule.
'job_name'	Job_name is the varchar(100) name of the job to be removed from the schedule.

'sched_job_name'	Sched_job_name is the varchar(100) name of the job in the schedule.

sp_delete_jobserver

The sp_delete_jobserver system stored removes a server from functioning as a job server for a job.

Syntax

The syntax is:

```
sp_delete_jobserver {job_id | 'job_name'}{, 'server'}
```

The arguments are:

job_id	Job_id is the uniqueidentifier of the job to remove from the job server.
'job_name'	Job_name is the varchar(100) name of the job to be removed from the job server.
'server'	Server is the varchar(30) name of the server to remove as a job server.

sp_delete_jobstep

The sp_delete_jobstep system stored procedure deletes a job step from a job. Supply the job_id argument or the job_name argument.

Syntax

The syntax is:

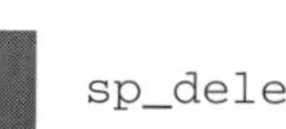

```
sp_delete_jobstep {[@job_id =] job_id | [@job_name =] 'job_name'}
{, [@step_id =] step_id}
```

The arguments are:

job_id	Job_id is the uniqueidentifier of the job containing the job step to remove from the job server.
'job_name'	Job_name is the varchar(100) name of the job containing the job step to be removed from the job server.
step_id	Step_id is the integer representing the step you are deleting.

sp_delete_notification

The sp_delete_notification system stored procedure deletes a notification sent to an operator by an alert.

Syntax

The syntax is:

```
sp_delete_notification {'alert', 'operator'}
```

The arguments are:

'alert'	Alert is the varchar(100) name of the alert.
'operator'	Operator is the varchar(100) name of the operator.

sp_delete_operator

The sp_delete_operator system stored procedure deletes an operator.

Syntax

The syntax is:

```
sp_delete_operator {'name'} [, 'reassign_operator']
```

The arguments are:

'name'	Name is the varchar(100) name of the operator to delete.
'reassign_operator'	Reassign_operator allows you to reassign alerts for the deleted operator to this operator and is varchar(100).

sp_delete_targetserver

The sp_delete_targetserver system stored procedure removes the server from the list of job servers (target servers).

Syntax

The syntax is:

```
sp_delete_targetserver {'server'} [, clear_downloadlist] [, post_defection]
```

The arguments are:

'server'	Server is varchar(100) and the name of the server to remove as a target server.
clear_downloadlist	Reserved for use by SQL Server.
post_defection	Reserved for use by SQL Server.

sp_delete_targetservergroup

The sp_delete_targetservergroup system stored procedure removes a target server group.

Syntax

The syntax is:

```
sp_delete_targetservergroup {'name'}
```

The argument, name, is varchar(100) and the name of the target server group to remove.

sp_delete_targetsvrgrp_member

The sp_delete_targetsvrgrp_member system stored procedure deletes the server from the target server group.

Syntax

The syntax is:

```
sp_delete_targetsvrgrp_member {'group_name'} [, 'server_name']
```

The arguments are:

'group_name'	Group_name is the varchar(100) target server group from which to remove the server.
'server_name'	Server is the varchar(30) name of the server you are removing from the target server group.

sp_deletemergeconflictrow

The sp_deletemergeconflictrow system stored procedure removes rows that are in conflict from merge replication from the msmerge_delete_conflicts system table.

Syntax

The syntax is:

```
sp_deletemergeconflictrow [[@conflict_table =]  conflict_table']
[,[@source_object =] 'source_object'] {,[@rowguid =] 'rowguid',
[@origin_datasource =] 'origin_datasource']}
[,[@drop_table_if_empty =] 'drop_table_if_empty']
```

The arguments are:

[@conflict_table =] 'conflict_table'	Conflict_table is the sysname of the conflict table. You can leave this argument NULL and a delete conflict is assumed with rows where the rowguid and origin_datasource and source_object are equal to the arguments for this stored procedure deleted from the msmerge_delete_conflicts system table. The default is % for all conflict tables.
[@source_object =] 'source_object'	Source_object is the nvarchar(386) name of the source table.
[@rowguid =] 'rowguid'	Rowguid is the delete conflict's row identifier, a uniqueidentifier.
[@origin_datasource =] 'origin_datasource'	Origin_datasource is varchar(255) conflict origination.
[@drop_table_if_empty =] 'drop_table_if_empty'	Drop_table_if_ empty is varchar(10) and if set to true will drop the conflict table if it has no rows. The default is false.

sp_denylogin

The sp_denylogin system stored procedure denies a login access to the SQL Server in use.

Syntax

The syntax is:

```
sp_denylogin [@loginame =] 'login'
```

The argument, login, in the format of domain\user is the sysname of the Windows NT user or group and if it does not exist it will be added.

sp_depends

The sp_depends system stored procedure returns the object dependencies.

Syntax

The syntax is:

```
sp_depends {'object'}
```

The argument, object, is the object for which to return the dependency information.

sp_describe_cursor

The sp_describe_cursor system stored procedure returns information about a server cursor.

Syntax

The syntax is:

```
sp_describe_cursor {[@cursor_return = ] 'cursor_variable_name' | OUTPUT}
{
[, [@cursor_source = ] 'local', [@cursor_identity = ]
'local_cursor_name'] |
[, [@cursor_source = ] 'global', [@cursor_identity = ]
'global_cursor_name'] |
[, [@cursor_source = ] 'variable', [@cursor_identity = ]
'cursor_variable_name']
}
```

The arguments are:

'cursor_variable_name'	Cursor_variable_name is the name of an existing cursor variable.
'local_cursor_name'	Local_cursor_name is the name of the local cursor.
'global_cursor_name'	Global_cursor_name is the name of the global cursor.

sp_describe_cursor_columns

The sp_describe_cursor_columns system stored procedure exports the attributes of the columns in the result set of a server cursor.

Syntax

The syntax is:

```
sp_describe_cursor_columns {[@cursor_return = ] 'cursor_variable_name'
OUTPUT}
{
[, [@cursor_source = ] 'local', [@cursor_identity = ] 'local_cursor_name'] |
[, [@cursor_source = ] 'global', [@cursor_identity = ] 'global_cursor_name'] |
[, [@cursor_source = ] 'variable', [@cursor_identity = ]
'cursor_variable_name']
}
```

The arguments are:

'cursor_variable_name'	Cursor_variable_name is the name of an existing cursor variable.
'local_cursor_name'	Local_cursor_name is the name of the local cursor.
'global_cursor_name'	Global_cursor_name is the name of the global cursor.

sp_describe_cursor_tables

The sp_describe_cursor_tables system stored procedure returns information on the base tables of a server cursor.

Syntax

The syntax is:

```
sp_describe_cursor_tables {[@cursor_return = ] 'cursor_variable_name'
OUTPUT}
{
[, [@cursor_source = ] 'local', [@cursor_identity = ] 'local_cursor_name'] |
[, [@cursor_source = ] 'global', [@cursor_identity = ] 'global_cursor_name'] |
[, [@cursor_source = ] 'variable', [@cursor_identity = ]
'cursor_variable_name']
}
```

The arguments are:

'cursor_variable_name'	Cursor_variable_name is the name of an existing cursor variable.
'local_cursor_name'	Local_cursor_name is the name of the local cursor.

'global_cursor_name'	Global_cursor_name is the name of the global cursor.

sp_detach_db

The sp_detach_db system stored procedure detaches a database from a SQL Server and can run UPDATE STATISTICS before the database is detached.

Syntax

The syntax is:

```
sp_detach_db [@dbname =] 'dbname'
[, [@skipchecks =] 'skipchecks']
```

The arguments are:

[@dbname =] 'dbname'	Dbname is sysname and the name of the database.
[@skipchecks =] 'skipchecks'	Skipchecks is nvarchar(10). TRUE=do not run UPDATE STATISTICS FALSE=run UPDATE STATISTICS

sp_distcounters

The sp_distcounters system stored procedure returns the Subscribers distribution information. You can also get this information through the Performance Monitor.

Syntax

The syntax is:

```
sp_distcounters
```

sp_drop_agent_parameter

The sp_drop_agent_parameter system stored procedure removes parameters from profiles used in a replication agent.

Syntax

The syntax is:

```
sp_drop_agent_parameter [@profile_id =] 'profile_id',
[@parameter_name =] 'parameter_name'
```

The arguments are:

[@profile_id =] 'profile_id'	Profile_id is an integer and the profile with the parameter to be dropped.
[@parameter_name =] 'parameter_name'	Parameter_name is the sysname of the parameter to be dropped. % is the default meaning all.

sp_drop_agent_profile

The sp_drop_agent_profile system stored procedure drops profiles for a replication agent.

Syntax

The syntax is:

```
sp_MSdrop_agent_profile [@profile_id =] 'profile_id'
```

The argument, profile, is the integer ID of the profile.

sp_dropalias

The sp_dropalias system stored procedure is for backward compatibility. A Microsoft SQL Server 7.0 programmer uses roles.

Syntax

The syntax is:

```
sp_dropalias [@loginame =] 'login'
```

The argument login is the login or Window NT user or group for which to drop the alias.

sp_dropapprole

The sp_dropapprole system stored procedure drops an application role in the database in use.

Syntax

The syntax is:

```
sp_dropapprole [@rolename =] 'role'
```

The argument, role, is the sysname and the application role you are dropping.

sp_droparticle

The sp_droparticle system stored procedure removes an unsubscribed article. This is used in the context of replication to change a publication.

Syntax

The syntax is:

```
sp_droparticle [@publication =] 'publication', [@article =]'article'
[,[@ignore_distributor =] ignore_distributor]
```

The arguments are:

[@publication =] 'publication'	Publication is the sysname of the publication.
[@article =]'article'	Article is the sysname of the article. You may use 'all'.
[@ignore_distributor =] ignore_distributor	Ignore_distributor indicator is a bit and defaults to 0 or false. You can use this if you want to ignore the clean-up tasks at the distributor.

sp_dropdevice

The sp_dropdevice system stored procedure drops a database device.

Syntax

The syntax is:

```
sp_dropdevice [@logicalname =] 'device'
[, [@delfile =] 'delfile']
```

The arguments are:

[@logicalname =] 'device'	Device is the logical name of the database device.
[@delfile =] 'delfile'	A value of 'delfile' deletes the physical backup file (varchar(7)). If this parameter is omitted, the physical file is closed but not deleted.

sp_dropdistpublisher

The sp_dropdistpublisher system stored procedure removes a Publisher that is its own Distributor.

Syntax

The syntax is:

```
sp_dropdistpublisher [@publisher =] 'publisher' [,[@no_checks =] no_checks]
```

The arguments are:

[@publisher =] 'publisher'	Publisher is the sysname of the Publisher. You may use 'all'.
[@no_checks =] no_checks	The no_checks indicator is a bit and defaults to 0.

sp_dropdistributiondb

The sp_dropdistributiondb system stored procedure removes a Distributor database and the associated database files.

Syntax

The syntax is:

```
sp_dropdistributiondb [@database =] 'database'
```

The argument, database, is the sysname of the database.

sp_dropdistributor

The sp_dropdistributor system stored procedure deletes the Distributor from the NT registry of a server registered as a Distributor.

Syntax

The syntax is:

```
sp_dropdistributor [@no_checks =] no_checks]
[,[@ignore_distributor =] ignore_distributor
```

The arguments are:

[@no_checks =] no_checks	The no_checks indicator is a bit and defaults to 0.
[@ignore_distributor =] ignore_distributor	Ignore_distributor indicator is a bit and defaults to 0 or false. You can use this if you want to ignore the clean-up tasks at the distributor.

sp_dropextendedproc

The sp_dropextendedproc system stored procedure removes an extended stored procedure.

Syntax

The syntax is:

```
sp_dropextendedproc {'procedure'}
```

The argument, procedure, is the nvarchar(257) name of the extended stored procedure.

sp_dropgroup

The sp_dropgroup system stored procedure drops a role from the database in use. This stored procedure is for backward compatibility only. A Microsoft SQL Server 7 programmer uses roles instead of groups.

Syntax

The syntax is:

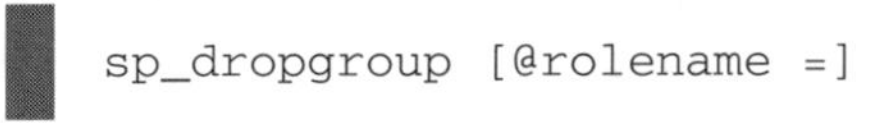

```
sp_dropgroup [@rolename =] 'role'
```

The argument, role, is the sysname and the role to drop.

sp_droplinkedsrvlogin

The sp_droplinkedsrvlogin system stored procedure drops the connection between a login on the local SQL Server and a linked server login that has been mapped to it.

Syntax

The syntax is:

```
sp_droplinkedsrvlogin [@rmtsrvname =] 'rmtsrvname',
[@locallogin =] 'locallogin'
```

The arguments are:

[@rmtsrvname =] 'rmtsrvname'	Rmtsrvname is the sysname name of a linked server.
[@locallogin =] 'locallogin'	LocalLogin is the sysname SQL Server login on the local server.

sp_droplogin

The sp_droplogin system stored procedure drops a Microsoft SQL Server login.

Syntax

The syntax is:

```
sp_droplogin [@loginame =] 'login
```

The argument, login, is the sysname SQL Server login you are dropping.

sp_dropmergearticle

The sp_dropmergearticle system stored procedure drops a merge publication article.

Syntax

The syntax is:

```
sp_dropmergearticle [@publication =] 'publication', [@article =]'article'
[,[@ignore_distributor =] ignore_distributor
```

The arguments are:

[@publication =] 'publication'	Publication is the sysname of the publication. You may use 'all'.
[@article =]'article'	Article is the sysname of the article. You may use 'all'.
[@ignore_distributor =] ignore_distributor	Ignore_distributor indicator is a bit and defaults to 0 or false. You can use this if you want to ignore the clean-up tasks at the distributor.

sp_dropmergefilter

The sp_dropmergefilter system stored procedure removes a merge filter.

Syntax

The syntax is:

```
sp_dropmergefilter [@publication =] 'publication' [,[@article =]'article']
[,[@filtername =] 'filtername']
```

The arguments are:

[@publication =] 'publication'	Publication is the sysname of the publication.
[@article =]'article'	Article is the sysname of the article.
[@filtername =] 'filtername'	Filter is the sysname of the filter.

sp_dropmergepublication

The sp_dropmergepublication system stored procedure drops a merge publication and its associated Snapshot Agent.

Syntax

The syntax is:

```
sp_dropmergepublication [@publication =] 'publication'
[,[@ignore_distributor =] ignore_distributor]
```

The arguments are:

[@publication =] 'publication'	Publication is the sysname of the publication. You may use 'all'.
[@ignore_distributor =] ignore_distributor	Ignore_distributor indicator is a bit and defaults to 0 or false. You can use this if you want to ignore the clean up tasks at the distributor.

sp_dropmergepullsubscription

The sp_dropmergepullsubscription system stored procedure deletes a merge pull subscription. Execute on the Subscriber with the current database being the Subscriber database

Syntax

The syntax is:

```
sp_dropmergepullsubscription [[@publication =] 'publication']
[,[@publisher =] 'publisher'] [,[@publisher_db =] 'publisher_db']
```

The arguments are:

[@publication =] 'publication'	Publication is the sysname of the publication. You may use 'all'.
[@publisher =] 'publisher'	Publisher is the sysname of the Publisher.
[@publisher_db =] 'publisher_db'	Publisher_db is the sysname of the Publisher database.

sp_dropmergesubscription

The sp_dropmergesubscription system stored procedure deletes a merge publication subscription from its Merge Agent.

Syntax

The syntax is:

```
sp_dropmergesubscription [[@publication =] 'publication']
[,[@subscriber =] 'subscriber' [,[@subscriber_db =]
'subscriber_db']
[,[@subscription_type =] 'subscription_type']
[,[@ignore_distributor =] ignore_distributor]
```

The arguments are:

[@publication =] 'publication'	Publication is the sysname of the publication. You may use 'all'.
[@subscriber =] 'subscriber'	Subscriber is the sysname of the Subscriber.
[@subscriber_db =] 'subscriber_db'	Subscriber_db is the sysname name of the database of the Subscriber.

[@subscription_type =] 'subscription_type'	Subscription_type is nvarchar(15) where Push=push subscription (the default), Pull=pull subscription, or Both=a push and pull subscription
[@ignore_distributor =] ignore_distributor	Ignore_distributor indicator is a bit and defaults to 0 or false. You can use this if you want to ignore the clean-up tasks at the distributor.

sp_dropmessage

The sp_dropmessage system stored procedure deletes an error message from the sysmessages system table in the master database.

Syntax

The syntax is:

```
sp_dropmessage [message_number] [, 'language']
```

The arguments are:

message_number	The user created integer of the message to delete.
'language'	Language is the sysname of the language associated with the message.

sp_droppublication

The sp_droppublication system stored procedure removes a publication and all of its articles. The sync task is also removed.

Syntax

The syntax is:

```
sp_droppublication [@publication =] 'publication'
[,[@ignore_distributor =] ignore_distributor]
```

The arguments are:

[@publication =] 'publication'	The sysname of the publication to remove. You may use 'all'.
[@ignore_distributor =] ignore_distributor	Ignore_distributor indicator is a bit and defaults to 0 or false. You can use this if you want to ignore the clean-up tasks at the distributor.

sp_droppullsubscription

The sp_droppullsubscription system stored procedure drops a subscription at the current database of the Subscriber. This also removes the Distributor Agent at the Subscriber.

Syntax

The syntax is:

```
sp_droppullsubscription [@publisher =] 'publisher',
[@publisher_db =] 'publisher_db', [@publication =] 'publication'
[,[@reserved =] 'reserved']
```

The arguments are:

[@publisher =] 'publisher'	Publisher is the sysname of the Publisher. You may use 'all'.
[@publisher_db =] 'publisher_db'	Publisher is the sysname of the Publisher database. You may use 'all'.
[@publication =] 'publication'	Publication is the sysname of the publication name. You may use 'all'.
[@reserved =] 'reserved'	Reserved is nvarchar(8) and is reserved for SQL Server.

sp_dropremotelogin

The sp_dropremotelogin system stored procedure removes a remote user login from a local SQL Server. A Microsoft SQL Server 7.0 programmer uses linked servers instead of remote servers.

Syntax

The syntax is:

```
sp_dropremotelogin [@remoteserver =] 'remoteserver' [,[@loginname =] 'login'
[,[@remotename =] 'remote_name']]
```

The arguments are:

Argument	Description
[@remoteserver =] 'remoteserver'	Remoteserver is the sysname of the remote server. Supplying only this one parameter removes all the remote logins to the remote server from the local server.
[@loginname =] 'login'	Login is the sysname of the local server login name that is associated with the remote server login name. (optional)
[@remotename =] 'remote_name'	Remote_name is the sysname of the remote login mapped to the local login. (optional)

sp_droprole

The sp_droprole system stored procedure drops a Microsoft SQL Server role from the database in use.

Syntax

The syntax is:

```
sp_droprole [@rolename =] 'role'
```

The argument, role, is the sysname of the role to drop.

sp_droprolemember

The sp_droprolemember system stored procedure drops a SQL Server login, role, NT user, or group (these are also known as security accounts) from a SQL Server role in the database in use.

Syntax

The syntax is:

```
sp_droprolemember [@rolename =] 'role',
[@membername =] 'security_account'
```

The arguments are:

'role'	Role is the sysname of the role.
'security_account'	Security_account is the sysname of the security account being dropped as a member of a role.

sp_dropserver

The sp_dropserver system stored procedure drops a server from being a remote or linked server on the local server.

Syntax

The syntax is:

```
sp_dropserver [@server =] 'server' [, {[@droplogins =] 'droplogins' | NULL}]
```

The arguments are:

[@server =] 'server'	Server is the sysname of the server.
[@droplogins =] 'droplogins' | NULL	Droplogins is char(10) with a value of 'droplogins' telling SQL Server to also remove the remote logins associated with the server being dropped. A value of NULL does not drop the remote logins.

sp_dropsrvrolemember

The sp_dropsrvrolemember system stored procedure drops a SQL Server login, Windows NT user, or Windows NT group from a fixed server role.

Syntax

The syntax is:

```
sp_dropsrvrolemember [@loginame =] 'login' [,[@rolename =] 'role']
```

The arguments are:

[@loginame =] 'login'	Login is the sysname of the SQL Server login, Windows NT user, or Windows NT group to drop from membership in the role.
[@rolename =] 'role'	Role is the sysname of the server role and can be NULL. Role must be a valid fixed server role and can be sysadmin, securityadmin, serveradmin, setupadmin, processadmin, diskadmin, or dbcreator.

sp_dropsubscriber

The sp_dropsubscriber system stored procedure deletes the Subscriber from the NT registry of a server registered as a Subscriber. This also revokes the sa (system administrator) login mapping for the repl_subscriber login.

Syntax

The syntax is:

```
sp_dropsubscriber [@subscriber =] 'subscriber' [,[@reserved =] 'reserved']
[,[@ignore_distributor =] ignore_distributor]
```

The arguments are:

[@subscriber =] 'subscriber'	Subscriber is the sysname of the Subscriber.
[@reserved =] 'reserved'	Reserved for SQL Server.
[@ignore_distributor =] ignore_distributor	Ignore_distributor indicator is a bit and defaults to 0 or false. You can use this if you want to ignore the clean-up tasks at the distributor.

sp_dropsubscription

The sp_dropsubscription system stored procedure is used on a Publisher to remove subscriptions to a publication, article, or subscriptions set. You will not be able to read the subscription on an article in an immediate_sync publication if you drop it without dropping the subscriptions on all the articles in the publication and read them all.

Syntax

The syntax is:

```
sp_dropsubscription [[@publication =] 'publication'] [,[@article =] article']
{,[@subscriber =] 'subscriber'} [,[@destination_db =]  destination_db']
[,[@ignore_distributor =] ignore_distributor] [,[@reserved =] 'reserved']
```

The arguments are:

[@publication =] 'publication'	Publication is the sysname of the publication. Using 'all' removes all subscriptions for all publications for a Subscriber.
[@article =]'article'	Article is the sysname of the article. Using 'all' drops all subscriptions to all articles for a Publication and Subscriber for immediate-sync publications. If this argument is not given, all subscriptions for all articles of the publication are dropped.
[@subscriber =] 'subscriber'	Subscriber is the sysname of the Subscriber. Using 'all' drops all Subscriptions for all the Subscribers.
[@destination_db =] 'destination_db'	Destination_db is the sysname of the destination database. If NULL is supplied for this argument all the subscriptions from the named Subscriber are dropped.
[@ignore_distributor =] ignore_distributor]	Ignore_distributor indicator is a bit and defaults to 0 or false. You can use this if you want to ignore the clean-up tasks at the distributor.
[@reserved =] 'reserved'	Reserved is nvarchar(10) and reserved for SQL Server.

sp_droptask

The sp_droptask system stored procedure removes scheduled tasks and is for backward compatibility only. A SQL Server 7 programmer uses jobs instead of tasks.

sp_droptype

The sp_droptype system stored procedure drops a user created data type.

Syntax

The syntax is:

```
sp_droptype {'type'}
```

The argument, type, is the name of a user created data type to drop,

sp_dropuser

The sp_dropuser system stored procedure is for backward compatibility and drops a SQL Server user, or Windows NT user, or Windows NT group from the database in use. A Microsoft SQL Server programmer uses sp_revokedbaccess instead.

Syntax

The syntax is:

```
sp_dropuser [@name_in_db =] 'user'
```

The argument, user, is the sysname of the user to drop.

sp_dropwebtask

The sp_dropwebtask system stored procedure drops an existing Web task. Supply one or both arguments.

Syntax

The syntax is:

```
sp_dropwebtask [[@procname=]'procname'|NULL][, 'outputfile']
```

The arguments are:

'procname'	Procname is the name of the stored procedure housing the query for the Web task.
'outputfile'	Outputfile is the name of the HTML output file you are removing.

sp_dsninfo

The sp_dsninfo system stored procedure displays information about ODBC data source names from the user-created replication Distributor of the local server. This shows what databases are available on the network for querying and what databases are available for replication. The information includes databases and datasources from other database vendors and of different file types.

Syntax

The syntax is:

```
sp_dsninfo {'dsn'} [, 'info_type' ] [, 'login' ] [, 'password' ]
```

The arguments are:

'dsn'	DSN is the required varchar(128) ODBC data source name.
'info_type'	Info_type is varchar(128) and what type of information you wish to see where DBMS_NAME=database vendor name, DBMS_VERSION=version, DATABASE_NAME=database name, SQL_SUBSCRIBER=Subscriber. If not given or NULL all types are shown.
'login'	Login is the varchar(128) ODBC data source name login. The DSN may contain the login and password, in which case you should omit the login and password arguments here.
'password'	Password is the varchar(128) password for the login of the ODBC data source name.

sp_enumcodepages

The sp_enumcodepages system stored procedure is used when you are making a Web task and are interested in knowing which character sets and code pages are available when running sp_makewebtask (.nls files must have been previously installed by the operating system.).

Syntax

The syntax is:

```
sp_enumcodepages
```

sp_enumcustomresolvers

The sp_enumcustomresolvers system stored procedure shows all custom resolvers located on a distributor and used by merge replication to resolve conflicts.

Syntax

The syntax is:

```
sp_enumcustomresolvers ['distributor']
```

The argument, distributor, is the sysname of the distributor.

sp_enumdsn

The sp_enumdsn system stored procedure shows all ODBC data source names available for the user account running this SQL Server.

Syntax

The syntax is:

```
sp_enumdsn
```

sp_enumfullsubscribers

The sp_enumfullsubscribers system stored procedure shows Subscribers subscribed to all of the articles in a publication.

Syntax

The syntax is:

```
sp_enumfullsubscribers ['publication']
```

sp_executesql

The sp_executesql system stored procedure is used to execute a Transact-SQL statement(s) and can contain arguments.

Syntax

The syntax is:

```
sp_executesql [@stmt =] stmt
[
{, [@params =] N'@parameter_name  data_type [,…n]' }
{, [@param1 =] 'value1'[,…n] }
]
```

The arguments are:

[@stmt =] stmt	Stmt is a Unicode string or a variable (concatenation in not allowed). If a constant is given it must be prefixed with an N. Each parameter used must have a corresponding entry in both the @params parameter and @parm1 (the other arguments to sp_executesql) .
[@params =] N'@parameter_name data_type [,...n]'	@params is one string of all the parameters in stmt. A data_type or the parameter must also be given. This is only used for embedded parameters in @stmt. The n means this is repeatable and separated by commas.
[@param1 =] 'value1'	Value1 is a constant or variable value for the first parameter defined in the @params string. Each parameter_name must have a corresponding value.

sp_fkeys

The sp_fkeys system stored procedure is a catalog system stored procedure that returns foreign key relationship information.

Syntax

The syntax is:

```
sp_fkeys      {'pktablename'} [, 'pktableowner'] [,  pktablequalifier']
    {, 'fktablename'} [, 'fktableowner'] [, 'fktablequalifier']
```

The arguments are:

Pktablename	Pktablename is a sysname and the primary key table. You must supply this argument and/or the Fktablename argument.
Pktableowner	Pktableowner is a sysname and the object owner of the primary key table for which you would like to see foreign key information. This is an optional argument; if you do not specify an owner, the system will default to what is available as the default visibility of the current user or the DBO in that order.

Pktablequalifier	Pktablequalifier is the sysname and the database name for the primary key table for which you would like to see foreign key information.
Fktablename	Fktablename is the sysname and the name of the foreign key table. You must supply this argument and/or the Pktablename argument.
Fktableowner	Fktableowner is the sysname and the object owner of the foreign key. This is an optional argument and if you do not specify an owner, the system will default to what is available as the default visibility of the current user or the DBO in that order.
Fktablequalifier	Fktablequalifier is the sysname and the database name for the foreign key table.

sp_foreignkeys

The sp_foreignkeys system stored procedure displays the foreign keys of the table in a server referencing primary keys of a remote table in a linked server.

Syntax

The syntax is:

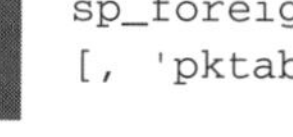

```
sp_foreignkeys {'table_server'} [, 'pktab_name'] [, 'pktab_schema']
[, 'pktab_catalog'] [, 'fktab_name'] [, 'fktab_schema'] [, 'fktab_catalog']
```

The arguments are:

'table_server'	Table_server is the sysname of the remote server.
'pktab_name'	Pktab_name is the sysname of the table with the primary key (default is NULL).
'pktab_schema'	Pktab_schema is the sysname of the schema with the primary key (default is NULL).
'pktab_catalog'	Pktab_catalog is the sysname of the catalog with the primary key (default is NULL).
'fktab_name'	Fktab_name is the sysname of the table with the foreign key (default is NULL).
'fktab_schema'	Fktab_schema is the sysname of the schema with the foreign key (default is NULL).

'fktab_catalog'	Fktab_catalog is the sysname of the catalog with the foreign key (default is NULL).

sp_fulltext_catalog

The sp_fulltext_catalog system stored procedure creates a full-text catalog, drops a full-text catalog, starts indexing action for a catalog, or stops the indexing action for a catalog.

Syntax

The syntax is:

```
sp_fulltext_catalog [@ftcat =] 'fulltext_catalog_name',
[@action =] 'action'
[, [@path =] 'root_directory']
```

The arguments are:

[@ftcat =] 'fulltext_catalog_name'	Fulltext_catalog_name is the sysname of the full-text catalog.
[@action =] 'action'	Action is varchar(20). Create=makes a full-text catalog as an operating system file and inserts a row in the sysfulltextcatalogs system table, Drop=drops fulltext_catalog_name Start_incremental=starts a differential index population for fulltext_catalog_name with only changed rows as denoted by the existing timestamp column being affected Start_full=starts a full population for fulltext_catalog_name Stop=Stops a population for fulltext_catalog_name Rebuild=rebuilds fulltext_catalog_name from scratch without repopulating.
[@path =] 'root_directory'	Root_directory is the varchar(100) root directory with a default of NULL which is C:\msssql7\Ftdata. This must be NULL for every action but create.

sp_fulltext_column

The sp_fulltext_column system stored procedure determines whether a table column will have full-text indexing. The unactivated table should have been previously flagged for full-text indexing.

Syntax

The syntax is:

```
sp_fulltext_column [@tabname =] 'qualified_table_name',
[@colname =] 'column_name',
[@action =] 'action'
```

The arguments are:

[@tabname =] 'qualified_table_name'	Qualified_table_name is the nvarchar(517) table in the format of database.owner.table or owner.table.
[@colname =] 'column_name'	Column_name is the sysname of a table column.
[@action =] 'action'	Action is the varchar(20) action to be performed. Possible values: Add=adds a column to inactive full-text index for a table. Drop=drops a column from inactive full-text index for a table.

sp_fulltext_database

The sp_fulltext_database system stored procedure enables full-text indexing in a database, drops all full-text catalogs from the current database, or disables full-text indexing in a database (without deleting rows from sysfulltextcatalog system table), depending on the action argument you supply in the database in use. To populate the full-text index you must run sp_fulltext_catalog with start_full or start_incremental arguments on each catalog.

Syntax

The syntax is:

```
sp_fulltext_database [@action =] 'action'
```

The argument, action, is varchar(20) where Enable=enables full-text indexing by dropping any existing full-text catalogs and re-creating any full-text indexing as defined in the system tables, Disable=drops all full-text catalogs operating system files and marks the database as being disabled for full-text indexing.

sp_fulltext_service

The sp_fulltext_service system stored procedure is used to modify the full-text properties of the Microsoft Search Service.

Syntax

The syntax is:

```
sp_fulltext_service [@action =] 'action'
[, [@value =] 'value']
```

The arguments are:

[@action =] 'action'	Action is the varchar(20) name of the property where Resource_usage=the amount of resources to be used by the Microsoft Search Service, Clean_up=deletes full-text orphaned operating system files that do not have entries in sysfulltextcatalogs system table, Connect_timeout=the seconds to give the Microsoft Search Service to init the full-text population before failing the population.
[@value =] 'value'	Value is the integer representing the value of the property where Connect_timeout=is a value between 1 and 32767, Resource_usage=the resources used by the Microsoft Search Service 1 (background) through 5 (dedicated) with a default of 3, Clean_up=NULL to clean up.

sp_fulltext_table

The sp_fulltext_table system stored procedure flags a table for full-text indexing. You must also use sp_fulltext_catalog system stored procedure with the start_incremental or start_full arguments to have full-text search capability.

Syntax

The syntax is:

```
sp_fulltext_table [@tabname =] 'qualified_table_name',
[@action =] 'action'
```

```
[, [@ftcat =] 'fulltext_catalog_name',
[@keyname =] 'unique_index_name']
```

The arguments are:

[@tabname =] 'qualified_table_name'	Qualified_table_name is the nvarchar(517) table in the format of database, owner table, or owner table.
[@action =] 'action'	Action is varchar(20) where Create=creates the rows in the system tables for a full-text index, Drop=deletes the rows in the system tables and deactivates a full-text index. Activate=Activates but does not populate the full-text index, Deactivate=deactivates the full-text index but keeps the metadata in place but not used in full-text searching.
[@ftcat =] 'fulltext_catalog_name'	Full-text catalog name is the sysname of a previously created full-text catalog. This must be NULL for every action but create.
[@keyname =] 'unique_index_name'	Unique_index_name is a previously uniquely indexed column used for the full-text index column search. This must be NULL for every action but create.

sp_generatefilters

The sp_generatefilters system stored procedure generates filters on foreign key tables when replication is in place for a table.

Syntax

The syntax is:

```
sp_generatefilters [@publication =] 'publication'
```

The argument, publication, is the sysname of the publication for which you are generating filters.

sp_getbindtoken

The sp_getbindtoken system stored procedure returns a string to use as a token when you have clients that are planning to use the same transaction and share the same lock space; it is used with the sp_bindsession system stored procedure to bind new sessions to the same transaction.

Syntax

The syntax is:

```
sp_getbindtoken {'return_value'} OUTPUT [, @for_xp_flag]
```

The arguments are:

'return_value'	Return_value is nvarchar(255) and returned as the token to use to pass in as an argument to sp_bindsession system stored procedure which enables connections to share a transaction context.
OUTPUT	OUTPUT indicates the return_value will be placed in the output argument.
@for_xp_flag	For_xp_flag is a flag that when 1 is the value, indicates the creation of a bind token you can pass to an extended stored procedure for it to send back to SQL Server.

sp_getmergedeletetype

The sp_getmergedeletetype system stored procedure displays the merge delete type of user delete, partial delete, or system delete.

Syntax

The syntax is:

```
sp_getmergedeletetype [@source_object =] 'source_object',
[@rowguid =] 'rowguid'
```

The arguments are:

[@source_object =] 'source_object'	Source_object is the nvarchar(386) name of the source object for replication.
[@rowguid =] 'rowguid'	Rowguid is the uniqueidentifier for the row for which you wish to see the delete type.

sp_get_distributor

The sp_get_distributor system stored procedure displays the merge delete type of user delete, partial delete, or system delete for the destributor.

Syntax

The syntax is:

```
sp_get_distributor
```

sp_grant_publication_access

The sp_grant_publication_access system stored procedure gives a login access to a Publication.

Syntax

The syntax is:

```
sp_grant_publication_access [@publication = ] 'publication',
[@login =] 'login'
```

The arguments are:

[@publication =] 'publication'	Publication is the sysname of the publication. If this agrument is NULL, the login will be placed on the server global access list. A SQL Server authenticated login must have been created on the publisher and distributor SQL Servers. A Windows NT authenticated security account must have been created on the publisher SQL Server.
[@login =] 'login'	Login is the sysname of the login ID.

sp_grantdbaccess

The sp_grantdbaccess system stored procedure creates a security account in the database in use for a SQL Server authenticated login or Windows NT user or group. (sp_revokedbaccess is the opposite of this.)

Syntax

The syntax is:

```
sp_grantdbaccess [@loginame =] 'login' [,[@name_in_db =] 'name_in_db']
```

The arguments are:

[@loginame =] 'login'	Login is the sysname of the login for which you are creating a security account in the database in use. Windows NT groups and users must be formatted as Domain\User.
[@name_in_db =] 'name_in_db'	Name_in_db is the sysname for the account in the database. If left NULL the login will be used.

sp_grantlogin

The sp_grantlogin system stored procedure permits a Windows NT user or group account to connect to Microsoft SQL Server as a Windows NT authenticated user and can also be used to grant access that has been denied through the execution of the sp_denylogin system stored procedure (use sp_addlogin for a SQL Server authenticated login).

Syntax

The syntax is:

```
sp_grantlogin [@loginame =] 'login'
```

The argument, login, is the sysname of the Windows NT user or group in the format Domain\User.

sp_help

The sp_help system stored procedure gives information on database objects except triggers (use sp_helptrigger) and including data types in the database in use.

Syntax

The syntax is:

```
sp_help [name]
```

The argument, name, is the sysname of any object in the sysobjects system table. If an argument is not supplied, all database objects except triggers will be listed.

sp_help_agent_default

The sp_help_agent_default system stored procedure returns the integer ID of the default configuration for the Replication agent type.

Syntax

The syntax is:

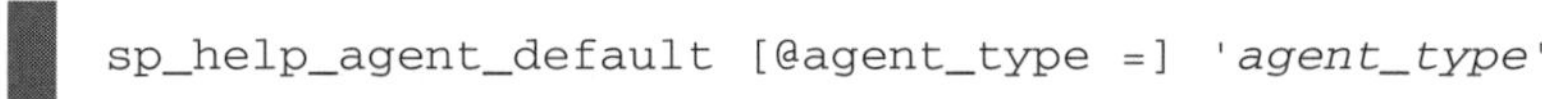

```
sp_help_agent_default [@agent_type =] 'agent_type'
```

The argument, agent_type, is an integer where 1=Snapshot Agent, 2=Log Reader Agent, 3=Distribution Agent, 4=Merge Agent.

sp_help_agent_parameter

The sp_help_agent_parameter system stored procedure displays the parameters of a profile of a Replication agent.

Syntax

The syntax is:

```
sp_help_agent_parameter [@profile_id =] 'profile_id'
```

The argument, profile_id, is the integer ID of the profile from the MSagent_configurations system table with a default of -1 (all parameters).

sp_help_agent_profile

The sp_help_agent_profile system stored procedure returns the profile of an agent.

Syntax

The syntax is:

```
sp_help_agent_profile [[@agent_type =] 'agent_type']
[,[@profile_id =] 'profile_id']
```

The arguments are:

[@agent_type =] 'agent_type'	Agent_type is an integer where 0=all, 1=Snapshot Agent, 2=Log Reader Agent, 3=Distribution Agent, 4=Merge Agent

[@profile_id =] 'profile_id'	Profile_id is the integer of the profile and defaults to –1 (all profiles).

sp_help_alert

The sp_help_alert system stored procedure must be run in the msdb system database to display information about previously created alerts on the current SQL Server.

Syntax

The syntax is:

```
sp_help_alert ['alert_name'] [, 'order_by'] [, alert_id] [, 'category']
```

The arguments are:

'alert_name'	Alert_Name is the sysname of the alert. If this argument is not supplied, information on all alerts on the server is returned.
'order_by'	Order_by is the sysname sort order for the result set and defaults to name.
alert_id	Alert_id is the integer ID of the alert with a default of NULL.
'category'	Category is the sysname for the category of the alert and defaults to NULL.

sp_helparticle

The sp_helparticle system stored procedure returns information about replication article(s).

Syntax

The syntax is:

```
sp_helparticle [@publication =] 'publication' [,[@article =] 'article']
[,[@returnfilter =] returnfilter]
```

The arguments are:

[@publication =] 'publication'	Publication is the sysname of the Publication.

[@article =] 'article'	Article is the sysname of the article. If this argument is not supplied, information on all articles for the Publication is returned.
[@returnfilter =] returnfilter	Returnfilter is a bit where 1=return the filter clause and 0=do not return the filter clause.

sp_helparticlecolumns

The sp_helparticlecolumns system stored procedure lists all columns in the table of the article for checking a vertical partition involved in replication.

Syntax

The syntax is:

```
sp_helparticlecolumns [@publication =] 'publication', [@article =] 'article'
```

The arguments are:

[@publication =] 'publication'	Publication is the sysname of the Publication.
[@article =] 'article'	Article is the sysname of the article.

sp_help_category

The sp_help_category system stored procedure returns information about the classes of jobs, alerts, or operators. Execute this system stored procedure without parameter to see the values for the available arguments.

Syntax

The syntax is:

```
sp_help_category ['class'] [, 'type'] [, 'name'] [, suffix]
```

The arguments are:

'class'	Class is the varchar(8) class with possible values of JOB (the default), ALERT or OPERATOR.
'type'	Type is varchar(12) and the type to report information about. Values are LOCAL, MULTI-SERVER, NONE, and NULL (the default).

'name'	Name is the sysname NULL=the default.
suffix	Suffix is a bit flag where 1=instructs SQLServer to add a suffix to define the searching for local and multiserver category name.

sp_helpconstraint

The sp_helpconstraint system stored procedure provides information about the constraints on a table.

Syntax

The syntax is:

```
sp_helpconstraint {'table'} [, 'no_message']
```

The arguments are:

'table'	Table is the nvarchar(776) name of the table.
'no_message'	No_message is varchar(5) where nomsg=suppress table name, msg=do not suppress (the default).

sp_helpdb

The sp_helpdb system stored procedure returns information about a database, or, if no argument is supplied, all databases.

Syntax

The syntax is:

```
sp_helpdb ['name']
```

The argument, name, is the sysname of the database.

sp_helpdbfixedrole

The sp_helpdbfixedrole system stored procedure displays information about a fixed database role(s).

Syntax

The syntax is:

```
sp_helpdbfixedrole [[@rolename =] 'role']
```

The argument, role, is the sysname of a fixed database role. Execute this system stored procedure without paramters to see a list of all fixed database roles.

sp_helpdevice

The sp_helpdevice system stored procedure is for backward compatibility. A Microsoft SQL Server 7 programmer uses files and filegroups.

Syntax

The syntax is:

```
sp_helpdevice ['name']
```

The argument, name, is the sysname of the device.

sp_helpdistpublisher

The sp_helpdistpublisher system stored procedure displays information on about a publisher that is also its own distributor.

Syntax

The syntax is:

```
sp_helpdistpublisher [[@publisher = ] 'publisher']
```

The argument, publisher, is the sysname of the publisher.

sp_helpdistributiondb

The sp_helpdistributiondb system stored procedure displays information about the distribution database.

Syntax

The syntax is:

```
sp_helpdistributiondb [[@database =] 'database']
```

The argument, database, is the sysname of the database.

sp_helpdistributor

The sp_helpdistributor system stored procedure displays information about the distributor.

Syntax

The syntax is:

```
sp_helpdistributor [[@publisher =] 'publisher'] [,[@local =] 'local']
```

The arguments are:

[@publisher =] 'publisher'	Publisher is the sysname of the publisher.
[@local =] 'local'	Local is nvarchar(5) true or false indicator, with a default of NULL that indicates a local distributor.

sp_help_downloadlist

The sp_help_downloadlist system stored procedure displays the contents of the sysdownloadlist system table by job or for all jobs. Supply no argument, or else job_id or jobname, but not both arguments.

Syntax

The syntax is:

```
sp_help_downloadlist [{job_id | 'job_name'}] [, 'operation'] [, 'object_type']
[, 'object_name'] [, 'target_server'] [, has_error] [, status] [, date_posted]
```

The arguments are:

job_id	Job_id is the uniqueidentifier for a job.
'job_name'	Job is the varchar(100) name of the job.

'operation'	Operation is varchar(64) the operation for the job where DEFECT =release the target server, DELETE=delete the job, INSERT=insert a new job or refreshes a job, RE-ENLIST=resend enlistment information to the multi-server domain and download the information from the MSXOperator to the target server again, SET-POLL=set the seconds ranging from 1 to 28,800 for target servers to poll the multiserver domain, START=start job execution, STOP=stop job execution, SYNC-TIME=the target server synchs its clock with that of the multi-server domain, UPDATE=update the sysjobs information for a job.
'object_type'	Object_type is the varchar(64) with values of JOB or SERVER.
'object_name'	Object_name is varchar(100) and the name of the JOB or SERVER depending on object_type.
'target_server'	Target_server is varchar(30) and the name of the target server.
has_error	Has_error is a tinyint flag where 1=acknowledge all errors and NULL=acknowledge no errors.
status	Status is the tinyint job status.
date_posted	Date-posted is datetime for the cutoff point for the result set of on the time or after the time.

sp_helpextendedproc

The sp_helpextendedproc system stored procedure returns information about extended stored procedures.

Syntax

The syntax is:

```
sp_helpextendedproc ['procedure']
```

The argument, procedure, is the sysname of the extended stored procedure.

sp_helpfile

The sp_helpfile system stored procedure displays information about the database files for the database in use.

Syntax

The syntax is:

```
sp_helpfile [@filename= ] 'name''
```

The argument, name, is the logical sysname of a database file associated with the database in use. If the argument is not supplied, all the database s files are displayed.

sp_helpfilegroup

The sp_helpfilegroup system stored procedure displays information about the filegroups belonging to the database in use.

Syntax

The syntax is:

```
sp_helpfilegroup [@filegroupname = ] 'name'
```

The argument, name, is the logical sysname of a filegroup belonging to the database in use. If no argument is supplied, all the database's filegroups are displayed.

sp_help_fulltext_catalogs

The sp_help_fulltext_catalogs system stored procedure displays information about a full-text catalog or all catalogs if no argument is supplied.

Syntax

The syntax is:

```
sp_help_fulltext_catalogs [@fulltext_catalog_name =] 'fulltext_catalog_name'
```

The argument, fulltext_catalog_name, is the sysname of a full-text catalog.

sp_help_fulltext_catalogs_cursor

The sp_help_fulltext_catalogs_cursor system stored procedure deploys a cursor to display detailed information about a full-text catalog or all full-text catalogs in the database in use if no argument is supplied.

Syntax

The syntax is:

```
sp_help_fulltext_catalogs [@cursor_return =] @cursor_variable OUTPUT,
[@fulltext_catalog_name =] 'fulltext_catalog_name'
```

The arguments are:

[@cursor_return =] @cursor_variable OUTPUT	Cursor_variable is the output variable of a cursor.
[@fulltext_catalog_name =] 'fulltext_catalog_name'	Fulltext_catalog_name is the sysname of the full-text catalog.

sp_help_fulltext_columns

The sp_help_fulltext_columns system stored procedure displays information about the columns marked for full-text indexing.

Syntax

The syntax is:

```
sp_help_fulltext_columns [@table_name =] 'table_name',
[@column_name =] 'column_name'
```

The arguments are:

[@table_name =] 'table_name'	Table_name is nvarchar(517) and the optionally owner-qualified table name. If this argument is not supplied all tables marked for full-text indexing are involved.
[@column_name =] 'column_name'	Column_name is the sysname of the column. If this argument is not supplied all columns for the tables involved are displayed.

sp_help_fulltext_tables

The sp_help_fulltext_tables system stored procedure displays information about tables marked for full-text indexing.

Syntax

The syntax is:

```
sp_help_fulltext_tables [@fulltext_catalog_name =] 'fulltext_catalog_name',
[@table_name =] 'table_name'
```

The arguments are:

[@fulltext_catalog_name =] 'fulltext_catalog_name'	Fulltext_catalog_name is the sysname of the full-text catalog. If this argument is not supplied or is NULL, all in the database are returned.
[@table_name =] 'table_name'	Table_name is nvarchar(517) and the optionally owner-qualified table name.

sp_help_fulltext_tables_cursor

The sp_help_fulltext_tables_cursor system stored procedure deploys a cursor to display the tables that are registered for full-text indexing.

Syntax

The syntax is:

```
sp_help_fulltext_tables_cursor [@cursor_return =] @cursor_variable OUTPUT,
[@fulltext_catalog_name =] 'fulltext_catalog_name',
[@table_name =] 'table_name'
```

The arguments are:

[@cursor_return =] @cursor_variable OUTPUT	Cursor_variable is the output variable of a cursor.
[@fulltext_catalog_name =] 'fulltext_catalog_name'	Fulltext_catalog_name is the sysname of the full-text catalog.
[@table_name =] 'table_name'	Table_name is nvarchar(517) and the optionally owner-qualified table name.

sp_help_fulltext_columns_cursor

The sp_help_fulltext_columns_cursor system stored procedure deploys a cursor to return information about columns marked for full-text indexing.

Syntax

The syntax is:

```
sp_help_fulltext_columns_cursor [@cursor_return =] @cursor_variable OUTPUT,
[@table_name =] 'table_name',
[@column_name =] 'column_name'
```

The arguments are:

[@cursor_return =] @cursor_variable OUTPUT	Cursor_variable is the output variable of a cursor.
[@table_name =] 'table_name'	Table_name is nvarchar(517) and the optionally owner-qualified table name. If this argument is not supplied, all tables marked for full-text indexing are involved.
[@column_name =] 'column_name'	Column_name is the sysname of the column. If this argument is not supplied, all columns for the tables involved are displayed.

sp_helpgroup

The sp_helpgroup system stored procedure is for backward compatibility and displays information about roles in the database in use. A Microsoft SQL Server 7 programmer uses database roles instead of database groups.

Syntax

The syntax is:

```
sp_helpgroup [[@grpname =] 'role']
```

The argument, role, is the sysname of a database role. If this argument is not supplied, information about all roles in the database in use is returned.

sp_helphistory

The sp_helphistory system stored procedure is for backward compatibility only. A Microsoft SQL Server programmer uses jobs instead (sp_help_jobhistory).

sp_help_job

The sp_help_job system stored procedure displays information about jobs. Supply the job_id or the job_name argument, but not both.

Syntax

The syntax is:

```
sp_help_job {[@job_id =] job_id | [@job_name =] 'job_name'}
```

```
[, [@job_aspect =] 'job_aspect'] [, [@job_type =] 'job_type']
[, [@owner_login_name =] 'login_name'] [, [@subsystem =] 'subsystem']
[, [@category_name =] 'category'] [, [@enabled =] enabled]
[, [@execution_status =] status] [, [@date_comparator =] 'date_comparison']
[, [@date_created =] date_created] [, [@date_last_modified =] date_modified]
[, [@description =] 'description_pattern']
```

The arguments are:

job_id	Job_id is the uniqueidentifier for a job.
'job_name'	Job is the varchar(100) name of the job.
'job_aspect'	Job_aspect is the varchar(9) job characteristic to display where possible values are ALL, JOB, SCHEDULES, STEPS, or TARGETS.
'job_type'	Job_type is varchar(12) with values of LOCAL, MULTI-SERVER, or NULL.
'login_name'	Login_name is the varchar(64) job owner's login name and defaults to NULL.
'subsystem'	Subsystem is the varchar(60) name of the subsystem and defaults to NULL.
'category'	Category is the varchar(100) name of the category and defaults to NULL.
enabled	Enabled is a tinyint where 1=enabled jobs, 0=disabled jobs, NULL=the default.
status	Status is an integer representing the job status where 0=not idle or suspended jobs, 1=executing jobs, 2=jobs waiting for thread, 3=jobs between retries, 4=idle jobs, 5=suspended jobs, 7=completing jobs.
'date_comparison'	Date_comparison is char(1) with possible values of =, <, or > and is used to compare the date_created and date_modified.
date_created	Date_created is the datetime job creation date and defaults to NULL.
date_modified	Date_modified is the datetime job modification date and defaults to NULL.
'description_pattern'	Description_pattern is varchar(512) and is the description of the job.Wildcard characters can be used.

sp_help_jobhistory

The sp_help_jobhistory system stored procedure displays information about the jobs for servers in a multiserver environment.

Syntax

The syntax is:

```
sp_help_jobhistory [job_id] [, 'job_name'] [, step_id] [, sql_message_id]
[, sql_severity] [, start_run_date] [, end_run_date] [, start_run_time]
[, end_run_time] [, minimum_run_duration] [, run_status]
[, minimum_retries] [, oldest_first] [, 'server'] [, 'mode']
```

The arguments are:

job_id	Job_id is the uniqueidentifier for a job.
'job_name'	Job is the sysname of the job.
step_id	Step_id is an integer and defaults to NULL.
sql_message_id	SQL_message_id is the integer error message ID that is returned when the job runs. The default is NULL.
sql_severity	SQL_severity is the integer severity level of the error message. Default is NULL.
start_run_date	Start_run_date is an integer in the year, month, day format YYYYMMDD representing the date the job began.
end_run_date	End_run_date is an integer in the year, month, day format YYYYMMDD representing the date the job ended.
start_run_time	Start_run_time is an integer in the hour, minute, second format HHMMSS representing the time the job began.
end_run_time	End_run_time is an integer in the hour, minute, second format HHMMSS representing the time the job ended.
minimum_run_duration	Minimum_run_duration is an integer in the hour, minute, second format HHMMSS representing the smallest amount of time for the job to complete.

run_status	Run_status is an integer representing the state of execution for the job where 0=Failed, 1=Succeeded, 2=Retry, 3=Cancelled, 4=In-progress message, 5=Unknown
minimum_retries	Minimum_retries is an integer representing the smallest number of times to retry executing the job.
oldest_first	Oldest_first is an integer where a value of 1 shows the output oldest jobs first and 0 (the default) shows the output newest jobs first.
'server'	Server is the varchar(30) name of the server where the job ran.
'mode'	Mode is varchar(7) where FULL=prints all columns, and SUMMARY=prints a summary.

sp_help_jobschedule

The sp_help_jobschedule system stored procedure displays information about job scheduling. Arguments are used in combination with each other. The syntax @argument_name = supplied_value is used in this stored procedure. Supply either job_id or job_name, but not both.

Syntax

The syntax is:

```
sp_help_jobschedule
{
{[@job_id =] job_id | [@job_name =] 'job_name'}
[, [@schedule_name =] 'schedule_name']
|
[, [@schedule_name =] 'schedule_name', ]
{[@schedule_id =] schedule_id}
```

The arguments are:

job_id	Job_id is the uniqueidentifier job number. This argument cannot be used with schedule_id or job_name but can be used with schedule_name.
'job_name'	Job_name is the sysname of the job. This argument cannot be used with schedule_id or job_id but can be used with schedule_name.

'schedule_name'	Schedule_name is the varchar(100) name of the job's schedule.
schedule_id	Schedule_id is the integer identifying the job's schedule.

sp_help_ jobserver

The sp_help_jobserver system stored procedure displays information about a job. Supply either job_id or job_name but not both.

Syntax

The syntax is:

```
sp_help_jobserver {job_id | 'job_name'} [, show_last_run_details]
```

The arguments are:

job_id	Job_id is the uniqueidentifier of the job.
'job_name'	Job_name is the sysname of the job.
show_last_run_details	Show_last_run_details is of tinyint data type where 1=show the details of the last time this job ran and 0=do not show the details of the last time this job ran.

sp_help_ jobstep

The sp_help_jobstep system stored procedure displays information about the job steps for a job. Supply either job_id or job_name, but not both.

Syntax

The syntax is:

```
sp_help_jobstep {[@job_id =] job_id | [@job_name =] 'job_name'}
[, [@step_id =] step_id] [,[@step_name =] step_name] [, [@suffix =] suffix]
```

The arguments are:

job_id	Job_id is the uniqueidentifier of the job.
'job_name'	Job_name is the sysname of the job.
step_id	Step_id is the integer job step number. If this argument is not supplied, all steps for the job are displayed.

step_name	Step_name is the sysname of the job step.
suffix	Suffix is a bit flag where 1=text description is included and 0=text description is not included (the default).

sp_helpindex

The sp_helpindex system stored procedure displays information about a table's indexes.

Syntax

The syntax is:

```
sp_helpindex {'name'}
```

The argument, name, is nvarchar(776) and is the name of a table in the database in use.

sp_helplanguage

The sp_helplanguage system stored procedure displays information about languages for Microsoft SQL Server residing in the syslanguages system table.

Syntax

The syntax is:

```
sp_helplanguage ['language']
```

The argument, language, is the sysname of the language. If this argument is not supplied, all languages are displayed.

sp_helplinkedsrvlogin

The sp_helplinkedsrvlogin system stored procedure displays the login mapped for a linked server.

Syntax

The syntax is:

```
sp_helplinkedsrvlogin [[@rmtsrvname =] 'rmtsrvname',]
    [[@locallogin =] 'locallogin']
```

The arguments are:

[@rmtsrvname =] 'rmtsrvname'	Rmtsrvname is sysname and the name of the linked server.
[@locallogin =] 'locallogin'	Locallogin is sysname and the local SQL Server login mapped to the linked server rmtsrvname.

sp_helplogins

The sp_helplogins system stored procedure returns information pertaining to SQL Server logins and the database accounts for the login. The sp_helplogins stored procedure shows LoginName, SID (login security identifier), DefaultDBName, DefaultLanguageName, IsDatabaseUserYesOrNo, and DefaultDatabaseName. The report also shows the databases, roles, and database user accounts for each database where the login has accounts.

Syntax

The syntax is:

```
sp_helplogins [[@LoginNamePattern =] 'login']
```

The argument, login, is the sysname of a login.

sp_helpmergearticle

The sp_helpmergearticle system stored procedure displays information about an article used in merge replication.

Syntax

The syntax is:

```
sp_helpmergearticle [[@publication =] 'publication'] [,[@article =]'article']
```

The arguments are:

[@publication =] 'publication'	Publication is the sysname of the publication. If this argument is not supplied, the default is % for all.
[@article =]'article'	Article is the sysname of the article. If this argument is not supplied, the default is % for all.

sp_helpmergearticleconflicts

The sp_helpmergearticleconflicts system stored procedure lists the articles in the publication with conflicts.

Syntax

The syntax is:

```
sp_helpmergearticleconflicts [[@publication =] 'publication']
```

The argument, publication, is the sysname of the publication. If this argument is not supplied, the default is % for all.

sp_helpmergeconflictrows

The sp_helpmergeconflictrows system stored procedure returns information about merge replication publications and their conflicts in the conflict table.

Syntax

The syntax is:

```
sp_helpmergeconflictrows [[@publication =] 'publication']
{,[@conflict_table =] 'conflict_table'}
```

The arguments are:

[@publication =] 'publication'	Publication is the sysname of the publication. If this argument is not supplied, the default is % for all.
[@conflict_table =] 'conflict_table'	Conflict_table is the sysname of the conflict table.

sp_helpmergedeleteconflictrows

The sp_helpmergedeleteconflictrows system stored procedure returns information about merge replication publications and their conflicts as represented in the msmerge_delete_conflicts replication table.

Syntax

The syntax is:

```
sp_helpmergedeleteconflictrows [[@publication =] 'publication']
[,[@source_object =] 'source_object']
```

The arguments are:

[@publication =] 'publication'	Publication is the sysname of the publication. If this argument is not supplied, the default is % for all.
[@source_object =] 'source_object'	Source_object is sysname of the source object.

sp_helpmergefilter

The sp_helpmergefilter system stored procedure shows information about filters used in merge replication.

Syntax

The syntax is:

```
sp_helpmergefilter [@publication =] 'publication', [@article =]'article'
[,[@filtername =] 'filtername']
```

The arguments are:

[@publication =] 'publication'	Publication is the sysname of the publication.
[@article =]'article'	Article is the sysname of the article. If this argument is not supplied, the default is % for all.
[@filtername =] 'filtername'	Filtername is the sysname of the filter. If this argument is not supplied, the default is % for all.

sp_helpmergepublication

The sp_helpmergepublication system stored procedure shows information about the publications used in merge replication.

Syntax

The syntax is:

```
sp_helpmergepublication [[@publication =] 'publication']
[,[@found =] 'found'] [,[@publication_id =] 'publication_id']
[,[@reserved =] 'reserved']
```

The arguments are:

[@publication =] 'publication'	Publication is the sysname of the publication. If this argument is not supplied, the default is % for all.
[@found =] 'found'	Found is an integer where 1=publication is found and 2=publication is not found.
[@publication_id =] 'publication_id'	Publication_id is the uniqueidentifier of the publication.
[@reserved =] 'reserved'	Reserved for Microsoft SQL Server.

sp_helpmergepullsubscription

The sp_helpmergepullsubscription system stored procedure displays information about a pull subscription used in merge replication.

Syntax

The syntax is:

```
sp_helpmergepullsubscription [[@publication =] 'publication ]
[,[@publisher =] 'publisher'] [,[@publisher_db =] 'publisher_db']
[,[@subscription_type =] 'subscription_type']
```

The arguments are:

[@publication =] 'publication'	Publication is the sysname of the publication. If this argument is not supplied, the default is % for all.
[@publisher =] 'publisher'	Publisher is the sysname of the publisher. If this argument is not supplied, the default is % for all.
[@publisher_db =] 'publisher_db'	Publisher_db is the sysname of the publisher database. If this argument is not supplied, the default is % for all.
[@subscription_type =] 'subscription_type'	Subscription_type is nvarchar(10) with values push, pull (the default), or both.

sp_helpmergesubscription

The sp_helpmergesubscription system stored procedure displays information about a push subscription used in merge replication.

Syntax

The syntax is:

```
sp_helpmergesubscription [[@publication =] 'publication']
[,[@subscriber =] 'subscriber'] [,[@subscriber_db =] 'subscriber_db']
[,[@publisher =] 'publisher'] [,[@publisher_db =] 'publisher_db']
[,[@subscription_type =] 'subscription_type']
```

The arguments are:

[@publication =] 'publication'	Publication is the sysname of the publication. If this argument is not supplied, the default is % for all.
[@subscriber =] 'subscriber'	Subscriber is the sysname of the subscriber. If this argument is not supplied, the default is % for all.
[@subscriber_db =] 'subscriber_db'	Subscriber_db is the sysname of the subscription database. If this argument is not supplied, the default is % for all.
[@publisher =] 'publisher'	Publisher is the sysname of the publisher. If this argument is not supplied, the default is % for all.
[@publisher_db =] 'publisher_db']	Publisher_db is the sysname of the publisher database. If this argument is not supplied, the default is % for all.
[@subscription_type =] 'subscription_type'	Subscription_type is nvarchar(10) with values push, pull (the default), or both.

sp_help_notification

The sp_help_notification system stored procedure displays information about notifications for automated alerts.

Syntax

The syntax is:

```
sp_help_notification {'object_type'} [, 'name'] [, 'enum_type']
[ , notification_method] [, 'target_name']
```

The arguments are:

'object_type'	Object_type is char(9) where ALERTS=the alerts for an operator and OPERATORS=the operators for an alert.

'name'	Name is char(100) and is the name of the alert if the object_type argument is ALERTS or the name of an operator if the object_type argument is OPERATORS.
'enum_type'	Enum_type is char(10) and represents the information returned where ACTUAL=the 'name' object_types, ALL=all the object_types (even those not belonging to the 'name') and TARGET= the 'target_name' object_types.
notification_method	Notification_method is tinyint data type where 1=returns e-mail information, 2=returns pager information, 4=returns NetSend information, 7=returns all information.
'target_name'	Target_name is char(100) and is used if enum_type is TARGET. If object_type is ALERTS is target_name is the alert name and if object_type is OPERATORS it is the operator name.

sp_helpntgroup

The sp_helpntgroup system stored procedure displays information about Microsoft Windows NT groups with database accounts in the database in use.

Syntax

The syntax is:

```
sp_helpntgroup [[@ntname =] 'name']
```

The argument, name, is the sysname of the Microsoft Windows NT group. If the name is not supplied, all NT groups with database accounts in the database in use are displayed.

sp_help_operator

The sp_help_operator system stored procedure displays information about the operators for the Microsoft SQL Server in use.This stored procedure must be run from the msdb system database.

Syntax

The syntax is:

```
sp_help_operator ['operator_name'] [, operator_id]
```

The arguments are:

'operator_name'	Operator_Name is the sysname of the operator. If this argument is not supplied, information about all operators is returned.
operator_id	Operator_id is an integer and is the ID of the operator.

sp_helppublication

The sp_helppublication system stored procedure returns information about a publication used in replication.

Syntax

The syntax is:

```
sp_helppublication [[@publication =] 'publication']
```

The argument, publication, is the sysname of the publication. If this argument is not supplied, information for all publications for the local SQL Server is returned.

sp_help_publication_access

The sp_help_publication_access system stored procedure displays all granted logins for a publication.

Syntax

The syntax is:

```
sp_help_publication_access [@publication = ] 'publication'
[@return_granted =] 'return_granted'] [,[@login =] 'login']
```

The arguments are:

[@publication =] 'publication'	Publication is the sysname of the publication. If this argument is not supplied, global access logins are returned.
[@return_granted =] 'return_granted'	Return_granted is bit where 0=all the logins at the publisher that are not granted and 1=all the logins at publisher that are granted.
[@login =] 'login'	Login is the sysname of the SQL Server authenticated login ID. If this argument is not supplied, the default is % for all.

sp_helppublication_snapshot

The sp_helppublication_snapshot system stored procedure displays information about the publication snapshot and is used in the context of replication.

Syntax

The syntax is:

```
sp_helppublication_snapshot [@publication =] 'publication'
```

The argument, publication, is the sysname of the publication.

sp_helppullsubscription

The sp_helppullsubscription system stored procedure displays information about one or more subscriptions at the subscriber.

Syntax

The syntax is:

```
sp_helppullsubscription [[@publisher =] 'publisher']
[,[@publisher_db =] 'publisher_db'] [,[@publication =] 'publication']
[,[@show_push =] 'show_push']
```

The arguments are:

[@publisher =] 'publisher'	Publisher is the sysname of the publisher. If this argument is not supplied, the default is % for all.
[@publisher_db =] 'publisher_db'	Publisher_db is the sysname of the publisher database. If this argument is not supplied, the default is % for all.
[@publication =] 'publication'	Publication is the sysname of the publication. If this argument is not supplied, the default is % for all.
[@show_push =] 'show_push'	Show_push is nvarchar(5) where FALSE=do not display push subscriptions and TRUE=do display push subscriptions.

sp_helpremotelogin

The sp_helpremotelogin system stored procedure displays information about remote logins defined on the local server.

Syntax

The syntax is:

```
sp_helpremotelogin [[@remoteserver =] 'remoteserver'
[,[@remotename =] 'remote_name']]
```

The arguments are:

[@remoteserver =] 'remoteserver'	Remoteserver is the sysname of the remote server. If this argument is not supplied, the default is % for all.
[@remotename =] 'remote_name'	Remote_name is the sysname of a remote login. If this argument is not supplied, the default is % for all.

sp_helpreplicationdb

The sp_helpreplicationdb system stored procedure displays information about publication databases on the local server.

Syntax

The syntax is:

```
sp_helpreplicationdb [[@dbname =] 'dbname'] [,[@type =] 'type']
```

The arguments are:

[@dbname =] 'dbname'	Dbname is the sysname of the database. If this argument is not supplied, the default is % for all.
[@type =] 'type'	Type is the sysname of the type of information where Pub=publication database and Sub=subscription database.

sp_helpreplicationdboption

The sp_helpreplicationdboption system stored procedure is used on a local SQL Server to list the databases with replication.

Syntax

The syntax is:

```
sp_helpreplicationdboption [[@dbname =] 'dbname'] [,[@type =] 'type']
```

The arguments are:

[@dbname =] 'dbname'	Dbname is the sysname of the database. If this argument is not supplied, the default is % for all.
[@type =] 'type'	Type is the sysname determining if replication is allowed and defaults to replication allowed.

sp_helpreplicationoption

The sp_helpreplicationoption system stored procedure displays information about replication options.

Syntax

The syntax is:

```
sp_helpreplicationoption [[@optname =] 'optname']
```

The argument, optname, is the sysname of the replication option, where Transactional=transactional replication, Merge=merge replication, and NULL=the default (which shows all).

sp_helprole

The sp_helprole system stored procedure displays information about the roles in the database in use.

Syntax

The syntax is:

```
sp_helprole [[@rolename =] 'role']
```

The argument, role, is the sysname of a role in the current database. If this argument is not supplied, the default is % for all.

sp_helprolemember

The sp_helprolemember system stored procedure displays information pertaining to the members of a database role in the database in use.

Syntax

The syntax is:

```
sp_helprolemember [[@rolename =] 'role']
```

The argument, role, is the sysname of a database role in the current database. If this argument is not supplied, all roles with at least one member in the database in use are returned.

sp_helprotect

The sp_helprotect system stored procedure displays information about user permissions and runs in the database in use.

Syntax

The syntax is:

```
sp_helprotect [[@name =] 'object_statement']
[,[@username =] 'security_account']
[,[@grantorname =] 'grantor'] [,[@permissionarea =] 'type']
```

The arguments are:

[@name =] 'object_statement'	Object_statement is nvarchar(776) and is an object in the database. It can also be all the CREATE statements and the BACKUP DATABASE and BACKUP LOG statements.
[@username =] 'security_account'	Security_account is the sysname of the security account. If this argument is not supplied, permission for all security accounts in the database in use are returned.
[@grantorname =] 'grantor'	Grantor is the sysname of the security account that originally granted the permissions. If this argument is not supplied, all the grantors are displayed.
[@permissionarea =] 'type'	Type is varchar(10) where o=object permissions and s=statement permissions. Any combination of o and s may be used with or without commas.

sp_helpserver

The sp_helpserver system stored procedure displays information about remote or replication servers.

Syntax

The syntax is:

```
sp_helpserver ['server'] [, 'option'] [, 'show_topology']
```

The arguments are:

'server'	Server is the sysname of the server. If this argument is not supplied, all the servers in the sysservers system table are reported upon.
'option'	Option is varchar(35) describing the type of server, where Dist=Distributor, dpub=Remote Publisher for the local Distributor, dsn=DSN server, dsub=Remote Subscriber to the local Distributor, fallback=Fallback server, pullpub=Pull Publisher, pub=Publisher, rpc=Remote server, and sub=Subscriber.
'show_topology'	Show_topology is varchar(1) where t=yes show server relationships along with the other information returned and NULL=no do not show server relationships along with the other information returned.

sp_helpsort

The sp_helpsort system stored procedure returns the sort order and character set for the local server.

Syntax

The syntax is:

```
sp_helpsort
```

sp_helpsrvrole

The sp_helpsrvrole system stored procedure displays the fixed server roles.

Syntax

The syntax is:

```
sp_helpsrvrole [[@srvrolename =] 'role']
```

The argument, role, is the name of the fixed server role, where sysadmin=system administrators, securityadmin=security administrators, serveradmin=server administrators, setupadmin=setup administrators, processadmin=process administrators, diskadmin=disk administrators, and dbcreator=database creators. If this argument is not supplied, information on all server roles is returned.

sp_helpsrvrolemember

The sp_helpsrvrolemember system stored procedure displays information about fixed server role members.

Syntax

The syntax is:

```
sp_helpsrvrolemember [[@srvrolename =] 'role']
```

The argument, role, is the sysname of the fixed server role, where sysadmin=system administrators, securityadmin=security administrators, serveradmin=server administrators, setupadmin=setup administrators, processadmin=process administrators, diskadmin=disk administrators, and dbcreator=database creators. If this argument is not supplied, information on all server roles is returned.

sp_helpsubscriber

The sp_helpsubscriber system stored procedure displays subscription information on the subscriber.

Syntax

The syntax is:

```
sp_helpsubscriber [[@subscriber =] 'subscriber']
```

The argument, subscriber, is the sysname of the subscriber and defaults to all subscribers (%).

sp_helpsubscriberinfo

The sp_helpsubscriberinfo system stored procedure returns information on a replication subscriber on the local Microsoft SQL Server.

Syntax

The syntax is:

```
sp_helpsubscriberinfo [[@subscriber =] 'subscriber']
```

The argument, subscriber, is the sysname of the subscriber. If this argument is not supplied, the default is % for all subscribers.

sp_helpsubscription

The sp_helpsubscription system stored procedure returns information about subscriptions.

Syntax

The syntax is:

```
sp_helpsubscription [[@publication =] 'publication'] [,[@article =] 'article']
[,[@subscriber =] 'subscriber'] [,[@destination_db =] 'destination_db']
```

The arguments are:

Argument	Description
[@publication =] 'publication'	Publication is the sysname of the publication. If this argument is not supplied, the default is % for all.
[@article =] 'article'	Article is the sysname of the articles. If this argument is not supplied, the default is % for all subscription information for publications and subscribers. All=return a full subscription on a publication in one row.
[@subscriber =] 'subscriber'	Subscriber is the sysname of the subscriber viewing subscriptions. If this argument is not supplied, the default is % for all subscription information for the publications and articles.
[@destination_db =] 'destination_db'	Destination_db is the sysname of the destination database. If this argument is not supplied, the default is % for all.

sp_helpsubscription_properties

The sp_helpsubscription_properties system stored procedure displays information from the MSsubscription_properties replication table pertaining to security.

Syntax

The syntax is:

```
sp_helpsubscription_properties [[@publisher =] 'publisher'] [,[@publisher_db =]
'publisher_db'] [,[@publication =] 'publication']
[,[@publication_type =] 'publication_type']
```

The arguments are:

[@publisher =] 'publisher']	Publisher is the sysname of the publisher. If this argument is not supplied, the default is % for all.
[@publisher_db =] 'publisher_db'	Publisher_db is the sysname of the publisher database. If this argument is not supplied, the default is % for all.
[@publication =] 'publication'	Publication is the sysname of the publication. If this argument is not supplied, the default is % for all.
[@publication_type =] 'publication_type'	Publication_type is the type of publication. It is an integer, with a default of 0=Snapshot, while 1=Transactional.

sp_help_targetserver

The sp_help_targetserver system stored procedure returns information pertaining to target servers.

Syntax

The syntax is:

```
sp_help_targetserver ['server_name']
```

The argument, server_name, is the nvarchar(30) name of the target server. If this argument is not supplied, information for all target servers is returned.

sp_help_targetservergroup

The sp_help_targetservergroup system stored procedure displays the target servers in the target server group.

Syntax

The syntax is:

```
sp_help_targetservergroup ['name']
```

The argument, name, is the sysname of the target server group. If this argument is not supplied, information for all target server groups is returned.

sp_helptask

The sp_helptask system stored procedure is for backward compatibility only. A Microsoft SQL Server 7 programmer uses jobs instead of tasks.

sp_helptext

The sp_helptext system stored procedure returns the Transact-SQL code of a rule, a default, or a stored procedure, trigger, or view stored in the syscomments system table in the database in use. However, if the object was created encrypted, the text for the object is not readable.

Syntax

The syntax is:

```
sp_helptext {'name'}
```

The argument, name, is the nvarchar(776) name of the database object in the database in use.

sp_helptrigger

The sp_helptrigger system stored procedure displays the trigger types on a table located in the database in use.

Syntax

The syntax is:

```
sp_helptrigger {'table'} [, 'type']
```

The arguments are:

'table'	Table is the nvarchar(776) name of the table.
'type'	Type is the char(6) trigger type where DELETE=delete trigger, INSERT=insert trigger, UPDATE= update trigger. The default is NULL.

sp_helpuser

The sp_helpuser system stored procedure displays information about database users in the database in use.

Syntax

The syntax is:

```
sp_helpuser [[@name_in_db =] 'security_account']
```

The argument, security_account, is the sysname of a SQL Server user, Windows NT user, or database role. If this argument is not supplied, information for all security accounts in the database in use is displayed.

sp_indexes

The sp_indexes system stored procedure displays index information for a remote table. If either the table_name or table_schema parameters are NULL, then sp_indexes returns only the rows with NULL values for those corresponding columns.

Syntax

The syntax is:

```
sp_indexes {'table_server'} [, 'table_name'] [, 'table_schema'] [, 'table_db']
[, 'index'] [, 'is_unique']
```

The arguments are:

'table_server'	Table_server is the sysname of the server of the remote table.
'table_name'	Table_name is the sysname of the remote table. Use % for all database tables.
'table_schema'	Table schema is the sysname of the table schema. Use % for all schemas or databases.

'table_db'	Table_db is the name of the database.
'index'	Index is the sysname of the index.
'is_unique'	Is_unique is a bit flag where 1 returns information for unique indexes only and 0 returns information for all indexes.

sp_indexoption

The sp_indexoption system stored procedure allows you to choose a type of lock for user-created indexes. This is for advanced users, as Microsoft SQL Server does this automatically.

Syntax

The syntax is:

```
sp_indexoption {[@IndexNamePattern = ] 'index_name'}[,
[@OptionName = ] 'option_name'] [,
[@OptionValue = ]'value']
```

The arguments are:

'index_name'	Index_name is the nvarchar(1035) name of a user-created table or index. If you choose to qualify the name with a database name, the database in use must be the database name. Giving a table name with no index name sets the option for all indexes on the table.
'option_name'	Option_name is varchar(35) where AllowRowLocks=row locks are used when 'value' is TRUE (set 'value' to FALSE and only page and table locks are used). AllowPageLocks= page locks are not be used when 'value' is FALSE (only row and table locks are used for the named index).
'value'	Value is the varchar(12) setting that determines the 'option_name' value of TRUE or FALSE. If you let this default to NULL, the current settings for the 'index_name' are displayed.

sp_link_publication

The sp_link_publication system stored procedure defines the security used by synchronization triggers when connecting to the publisher for push and pull subscriptions creating entries in the MSsubscription_properties system table. Use sp_helpsubscription_properties and sp_subscription_cleanup to view and clear entries in the MSsubscription_properties system table.

Syntax

The syntax is:

```
sp_link_publication [@publisher = ] 'publisher',
[@publisher_db = ] 'publisher_db', [@publication = ] 'publication',
[@security_mode =] security_mode [,[@login = ] 'login']
[,[@password = ] 'password']
```

The arguments are:

Argument	Description
[@publisher =] 'publisher'	Publisher is the sysname of the publisher.
[@publisher_db =] 'publisher_db'	Publisher_db is the sysname of the publisher database.
[@publication =] 'publication'	Publication is the sysname of the publication.
[@security_mode =] security_mode	Security_mode is the integer security mode when linking to the publisher. 0 means the synchronization triggers use a dynamic remote procedure call connection to the publisher, and 2 means the synchronization triggers needs a sysservers system table entry to do remote procedure calls. (Use sp_addlinkedserver to add the entry to sysservers.)
[@login =] 'login'	Login is the sysname of the login.
[@password =] 'password'	Password is the sysname of the password.

sp_linkedservers

The sp_linkedservers system stored procedure displays the linked servers for the local server.

Syntax

The syntax is:

```
sp_linkedservers
```

sp_lock

The sp_lock system stored procedure displays information pertaining to locks. Use sp_who to get spid numbers.

Syntax

The syntax is:

```
sp_lock [spid1] [, spid2]
```

The arguments are:

spid1	Spid1 is the integer process ID number from the sysprocesses system table. If this argument is not given, information on all processes is displayed.
spid2	Spid2 is another process ID number to return locking information.

sp_makewebtask

The sp_makewebtask system stored procedure produces an HTML document through the creation of a task. The HTML document holds data created by executing a query.

A template file is used to format the HTML document with the following methods of controlling the placement of query results in the template:

- You can use the "insert data here" tag. <%insert_data_here%> indicates the position to add the query results in an HTML table and uses @fixedfont, @bold, @italic, @colheaders, and @tabborders to format the query results.
- You can define the more exact complete row format which will cause the system to ignore the @colheaders, @reftext, @URL, @fixedfont, @resultstitle, @url_query, @HTMLHeader, @singlerow, @webpagetitle, @italic, and @tabborder arguments in sp_makewebtask.
    - <%begindetail%> and <%enddetail%> keywords contain the row format.
    - <TR>, </TR>, <TD>, and </TD> HTML tags occur between the row format keywords.
    - <%insert_data_here%> is used within the row format keywords to place each column in the result set.

Syntax

The syntax is:

```
sp_makewebtask {[@outputfile =] 'outputfile'} [, [@query =] 'query']
[, [@fixedfont =] fixedfont] [, [@bold =] bold] [, [@italic =] italic]
[, [@colheaders =] colheaders] [, [@lastupdated =] lastupdated]
[, [@HTMLHeader =] HTMLHeader] [, [@username =] username]
[, [@dbname =] dbname] [, [@templatefile =] 'templatefile']
[, [@webpagetitle =] 'webpagetitle'] [, [@resultstitle =] 'resultstitle']
[
[, [@URL =] 'URL', [@reftext =] 'reftext']
| [, [@table_urls =] table_urls, [@url_query =] 'url_query']
]
[, [@whentype =] whentype] [, [@targetdate =] targetdate]
[, [@targettime =] targettime] [, [@dayflags =] dayflags]
[, [@numunits =] numunits] [, [@unittype =] unittype]
[, [@procname =] procname ] [, [@maketask =] maketask]
[, [@rowcnt =] rowcnt] [, [@tabborder =] tabborder]
[, [@singlerow =] singlerow] [, [@blobfmt =] blobfmt]
[, [@nrowsperpage =] n] [, [@datachg =] table_column_list]
[, [@charset =] characterset]]
[, [@codepage =] codpage]]
```

The arguments are:

@outputfile	Outputfile is the varchar(255) path and filename of the HTML file. Use a UNC name if the file is stored on a remote machine. Otherwise, it will be placed on the local SQL Server.
@query	@query is the text datatype of the query to be run. More than one SELECT query can be defined.
@fixedfont	@fixedfont is tinyint where 1=fixed font and 0=proportional font. The default is 1.
@bold	@bold is tinyint where 1=bold font and 0=not bold font. The default is 0.
@italic	@italic is tinyint where 1=italic font and 0=not italic font.The default is 0.
@colheaders	@colheaders is tinyint where 1=column headers and 0=no column headers. The default is 1.

@lastupdated	@lastupdated is tinyint where 1=display last updated date and time on the HTML page right before the query results and 0=do not display the last updated date and time. The default is 1.
@HTMLHeader	@HTMLHeader is the tinyint that indicates the HTML formatting code for the content in the @resultstitle variable where 1=H1, 2=H2, 3=H3, 4=H4, 5=H5, and 6=H6.
@username	Username is nvarchar(128) under whose permissions the query will be executed. The default is the current database user.
@dbname	Dbname is the nvarchar(128) database name where the query will be executed. The default is the database in use.
@templatefile	Templatefile is the path of the HTML template file. The formatting details and the <%insert_data_here%> tag are contained in the template file.
@webpagetitle	@webpagetitle is the varchar(255) title of the HTML document.
@resultstitle	@resultstitle is the varchar(255) title above the query results and defaults to "Query Results".
@URL	@URL is a varchar(255) link to another HTML document placed at the end of the document. The argument @reftext must be used in conjunction with this argument, but @table_urls and @url_query must not be used. Use either the @URL and @reftext arguments or the @url_query and @table_urls arguments.
@reftext	@reftext is the varchar(255) hyperlink text which is the destination. The address is the URL defined in the @URL argument.
@table_urls	@table_urls is tinyint where 1=hyperlinks are on the HTML document and the hyperlinks come from a SELECT statement (@url_query creates a list of hyperlinks and @URL and @reftext arguments must not be given. Use @url_query with @table_urls) and 0= there is no query creating hyperlinks for the HTML (the default).
@url_query	@url_query is a varchar(255) SELECT statement to generate multiple URLs and hyperlink text from a SQL Server table. Use @url_query with @table_urls. The url_query variable returns two columns: the address of a hyperlink, and the description of the hyperlink.

@whentype	@whentype is tinyint and represents when to run the task to create the HTML document where 1=now (the default), 2=later with @targetdate and @targettime used in conjunction with this argument to define when, 3=create the page every n day(s) of the week with @dayflags and @targettime starting on @targetdate (use sp_dropwebtask to remove the task), 4=make the Web page every n minutes, hours, days, or weeks starting on @targetdate and @targettime (use @numunits and @unittype agruments with 4), 5=on demand (use sp_runtask with no automatic sheduling to occur), 6=make Web page now and again later with @targetdate and @targettime used in conjunction with this argument to define when, 7=make page now and create the page every n day(s) of the week with @dayflags and @targettime, 8=create page now and periodically after make the Web page every n minutes, hours, days, or weeks starting now and @targettime (use @numunits and @unittype arguments), 9=make Web page now and on demand, 10=make Web page now and when the data on the database changes (use @datachg argument).
@targetdate	@targetdate is the date the page is made (in the YYYYMMDD format). Today's date is used if the argument is not supplied but needed. @whentypes of 2, 3, 4, and 6 require this argument.
@targettime	@targettime is the time the HTML document is created in the format HHMMSS with a default of 12:00 A.M.
@dayflags	@dayflags are days to update the HTML document. Add the values together to schedule on multiple days where 1=Sunday (the default), 2=Monday, 4=Tuesday, 8=Wednesday, 16=Thursday, 32=Friday, and 64=Saturday. (Required for @whentypes 3 and 7.)
@numunits	@numunits is a tinyint representing how often to update the HTML document. Possible values are from 1 to 255 with default of 1. This argument is used in conjunction with a @whentype 4 and 8 and @unittype.
@unittype	@unittype is a tinyint representing how often the HTML document should be updated where 1=hours (the default), 2=days, 3=weeks, and 4=minutes. This argument is used in conjunction with @whentype 4 and 8 and @numunits.
@procname	@procname is the varchar(128) procedure or task name for the HTML document with default Web_YYMMDDHHMMSS<spid>. varchar(28).

@maketask	@maketask is an integer that determines if a task is created to generate an HTML document where 0=creates an unencrypted stored procedure but not the task, 1=creates an encrypted stored procedure and the task, and 2=creates an unencrypted stored procedure and the task (the default).
@rowcnt	@rowcnt is an integer representing the maximum number of rows to display in the HTML document. The default is 0 for all rows.
@tabborder	@tabborder is a tinyint representing if a border is placed around the results table where 1=yes (the default) and 0=no.
@singlerow	@singlerow is tinyint representing if the results occur as one row per page where 1= yes and 0=no (the default).
@blobfmt	@blobfmt is ntext data type and determines if all columns of text or image data types should be placed in the same results page where NULL=yes (the default) or the columns are saved in another page and linked to the HTML document by another URL using the format: "%n% FILE=output_filename use TPLT=template_filename URL=url_link_name..." where n= the column number in the result list corresponding to a text field, and n+1 is the URL hyperlink text to another text or image HTML file. Without a template_file name use <%insert_data_here%> to determine where the data will be placed. The url_link_name is the http:// link to the file. The same syntax in @blobfmt (%n% FILE=...) can be repeated for multiple text or image columns. Do not put filenames in quotation marks.
@nrowsperpage	@nrowsperpage is an integer representing rows on each page with pages linked with NEXT and PREVIOUS URLs. The default is 0 for all. This argument is mutually exclusive of @singlerow.
@datachg	@datachg is text datatype and required when @whentype parameter is 10. It is the table and column name(s) causing the HTML document to be recreated. The syntax is: {TABLE=name[COLUMN=name]}[,...] UPDATE, INSERT, and DELETE triggers are created on the table that execute the Web task. sp_runwebtask is added to the end of any triggers already in existence (if the triggers have not been compiled with encryption leaving them not modifiable).

@charset	@charset is nvarchar(25) and represents the character set alias code used by browsers. It defaults to 'utf-8'.
@codepage	@codepage is a numeric value relating to the character set with a default of 65001 relating to the default character set UTF-8. Use sp_enumcodepages to obtain a list of codepages.

sp_manage_jobs_by_login

The sp_manage_jobs_by_login system stored procedure updates jobs owned by a login.

Syntax

The syntax is:

```
sp_manage_jobs_by_login {'action'} [, 'current_owner_login_name']
[, 'new_owner_login_name']
```

The arguments are:

'action'	Action is the varchar(10) action to take where DELETE deletes all jobs for the current_owner_login_name and REASSIGN reassigns all jobs to the new_owner_login_name.
'current_owner_login_name'	Current_owner_login_name is sysname and is the login name of the current job owner.
'new_owner_login_name'	New_owner_login_name is sysname and is the login name of the new job owner.

sp_mergedummyupdate

The sp_mergedummyupdate system stored procedure is used in merge replication so that updates to text columns made using UPDATETEXT or WRITETEXT are sent in the next merge.

Syntax

The syntax is:

```
sp_mergedummyupdate [@source_object =] 'source_object',
[@rowguid =] 'rowguid'
```

The arguments are:

[@source_object =] 'source_object'	Source_object is the nvarchar(386) name of the source object.
[@rowguid =] 'rowguid'	Rowguid is the row identifier (uniqueidentifier).

sp_mergesubscription_cleanup

The sp_mergesubscription_cleanup system stored procedure cleans up triggers and rows in the sysmergesubscription and sysmergearticles system tables after a subscriber's merge subscription is dropped.

Syntax

The syntax is:

```
sp_mergesubscription_cleanup [@publisher =] 'publisher',
    [@publisher_db =] 'publisher_db' [,[@publication =] 'publication']
```

The arguments are:

[@publisher =] 'publisher'	Publisher is the sysname of the publisher.
[@publisher_db =] 'publisher_db'	Publisher_db is the sysname of the publisher database.
[@publication =] 'publication'	Publication is the sysname of the publication.

sp_monitor

The sp_monitor system stored procedure returns statistical information about how SQL Server is using resources.

Syntax

The syntax is:

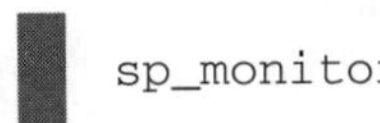

```
sp_monitor
```

sp_msx_defect

The sp_msx_defect system stored procedure edits the registry and takes the local server out of multiserver operations.

Syntax

The syntax is:

```
sp_msx_defect [forced_defection]
```

The argument, forced_defection, is a bit datatype where 1=yes and 0=no. This is used in case the Master SQL Server Agent has been lost or corrupted.

If 1 is used sa (system administrator) must run the following command:

```
EXECUTE msdb.dbo.sp_delete_targetserver @server_name = 'xxxxxxx',
@post_defection = 0
```

sp_msx_enlist

The sp_msx_defect system stored procedure edits the registry and adds the local server to multiserver operations.

Syntax

The syntax is:

```
sp_msx_enlist {'msx_server'} [, 'location']
```

The arguments are:

'msx_server'	Msx_server is varchar(30) and is the name of the multiserver administration server to add.
'location'	Location is varchar(100) and is the user-supplied location of the multiserver administration server (e.g. South Computer Room E45).

sp_OACreate

The sp_OACreate system stored procedure creates an OLE object on a Microsoft SQL Server, used in SQL-DMO. An OLE object can be created by using the progid argument (SQL-DMO.SQLServer) or the clsid argument, '{00026BA1-0000-0000-C000-000000000046}' and by making object token an integer local variable (DECLARE @object1 INT).

Syntax

The syntax is:

```
sp_OACreate {progid | clsid} {, objecttoken OUTPUT} [, context]
```

The arguments are:

progid	Progid is a character string of a valid class of the OLE object you are creating in the format 'OLEComponent.Object' where OLEComponent is the name of the OLE Automation server, and Object is the name of the OLE object supporting the IDispatch interface (e.g. SQLDMO.SQLServer).
clsid	Clsid is the character string of the class identifier of the OLE object you are creating in the format '{nnnnnnnn-nnnn-nnnn-nnnn-nnnnnnnnnnnn}' (e.g. '{00026BA1-0000-0000-C000-000000000046}' for the SQL-DMO SQLServer object).
objecttoken OUTPUT	Objecttoken OUTPUT is an integer, local variable and is the returned object token. This object token identifies the newly created OLE object when calling other OLE Automation stored procedures.
context	Context is an interger representing the execution context of the created OLE object where 1=in process, a .dll and OLE server allowed, 4=Local, .exe and OLE server allowed, and 5=both in process and local OLE server allowed (the default). If an in-process OLE server is allowed, it has access to resources owned by SQL Server while a local OLE server does not have access to any SQL Server resources.

sp_OADestroy

The sp_OADestroy system stored procedure destroys a user-created OLE object.

Syntax

The syntax is:

```
sp_OADestroy {objecttoken}
```

The argument, objecttoken, is the object token of a user-created OLE object.

sp_OAGetErrorInfo

The sp_OAGetErrorInfo system stored procedure returns OLE Automation error information. Each time an OLE Automation stored procedure is called, the error information is reset.

Errors are:

- **bad variable type** (0x80020008)=SQL Server data type passed as a method parameter did not match the Microsoft Visual Basic data type or NULL was passed
- **unknown name** (0x8002006)=specified property or method name was not found for the specified object
- **invalid class string** (0x800401f3)=ProgID or CLSID has not been registered as an OLE object on SQL Server
- **server execution failed** (0x80080005)=OLE object is registered as a local OLE server and .exe file, and it could not be found or started
- **the module could not be found** (0x8007007e)=OLE object is registered as an in-process OLE server and .DLL file, but it could not be found
- **type mismatch** (0x80020005)=data type of a local variable for a property value or a method did not match the Visual Basic data type
- **parameter not found** (0x80020004)=argument was defined before a positional argument
- **the parameter is incorrect** (0x80070057)=the number specified as the context parameter of sp_OACreate is not valid

Syntax

The syntax is:

```
sp_OAGetErrorInfo [objecttoken [, source OUTPUT [, description OUTPUT
[, helpfile OUTPUT [, helpid OUTPUT ]]]]]
```

The arguments are:

objecttoken	Objecttoken is the object token of a user created OLE object.
source OUTPUT	Source OUTPUT is a local char or varchar variable and the source of the error information.
description OUTPUT	Description OUTPUT is a local char or varchar variable and the description of the error.
helpfile OUTPUT	Helpfile OUTPUT is a local char or varchar variable and the Help file for the OLE object.
helpid OUTPUT	Helpid OUTPUT is a local integer variable and the Help file context ID.

sp_OAGetProperty

The sp_OAGetProperty system stored procedure returns a property value of an OLE object.

Syntax

The syntax is:

```
sp_OAGetProperty {objecttoken, propertyname} [, propertyvalue OUTPUT]
[, index...]
```

The arguments are:

objecttoken	Objecttoken is the object token of a user-created OLE object.
propertyname	Propertyname is the name of the property.
propertyvalue OUTPUT	Propertyvalue OUTPUT is a local variable of the correct data type to hold the returned property value.
index	Index is a value of the correct data type and index parameter as some properties have one or more parameters.

sp_OAMethod

The sp_OAMethod system stored procedure calls a method of an OLE object and can also be used to get a property value. For the OUTPUT local variable, be sure to use the right data type for the value returned.

Syntax

The syntax is:

```
sp_OAMethod {objecttoken, methodname} [, returnvalue OUTPUT
[, [@parametername =] parameter [OUTPUT] [...n]]]
```

The arguments are:

Objecttoken	Objecttoken is the object token of a user-created OLE object.
Methodname	Methodname is the method name of the OLE object to call.

Returnvalue OUTPUT	Returnvalue OUTPUT is a local variable, and it returns the value of the method of the OLE object.
[@parametername =] parameter [OUTPUT]	Parameter is the parameter of a method. The parameter must be the name of the Microsoft Visual Basic named parameter.
n	N means the preceeding entry is repeatable.

sp_OASetProperty

The sp_OASetProperty system stored procedure changes the setting of a property of an OLE object to another value.

Syntax

The syntax is:

```
sp_OASetProperty {objecttoken, propertyname, newvalue} [, index...]
```

The arguments are:

objecttoken	Objecttoken is the object token of a user-created OLE object.
propertyname	Propertyname is the name of the property.
newvalue	Newvalue is the changed value of the property.
index	Index is a value of the correct data type and index parameter as some properties have one or more parameters.

sp_OAStop

The sp_OAStop system stored procedure terminates the OLE Automation stored procedure execution environment for a server. This stored procedure does not have to be explicitly called, as the environment will terminate when SQL Server is cycled. It starts when sp_OACreate is called by a client session. If one client session issues sp_OAStop, then all other SQL-DMO procedures will fail until sp_OACreate is called again.

Syntax

The syntax is:

```
sp_OAStop
```

sp_password

The sp_password system stored procedure updates the password for a Microsoft SQL Server login.

Syntax

The syntax is:

```
sp_password [[@old =] 'old_password',] {[@new =] 'new_password'}
[,[@loginame =] 'login']
```

The arguments are:

[@old =] 'old_password'	Old_password is the sysname of the old password.
[@new =] 'new_password'	New_password is the sysname of the new value for the password.
[@loginame =] 'login'	Login is the sysname of the SQL Server login.

sp_pkeys

The sp_pkeys system stored procedure displays the primary key information for a table in the database in use.

Syntax

The syntax is:

```
sp_pkeys {'name'} [, 'owner'] [, 'qualifier']
```

The arguments are:

'name'	Name is the sysname of the table.
'owner'	Owner is the sysname of the table owner.
'qualifier'	Qualifier is the sysname of the table qualifier (or database qualifier for Microsoft SQL Server).

sp_primarykeys

The sp_primarykeys system stored procedure displays the primary key columns for a table.

Syntax

The syntax is:

```
sp_primarykeys {'table_server'} [, 'table_name'] [, 'table_schema']
[, 'table_catalog']
```

The arguments are:

'table_server'	Table_server is the sysname of the server.
'table_name'	Table_name is the sysname of the table where % is used for all tables.
'table_schema'	Table_schema is the sysname of the table schema. Use % for all databases or all schemas.
'table_catalog'	Table_catalog is the sysname of the database.

sp_post_msx_operation

The sp_post_msx_operation system stored procedure is used to populate the sysdownloadlist system table. This process is used to post job operations for target servers to download.

Syntax

The syntax is:

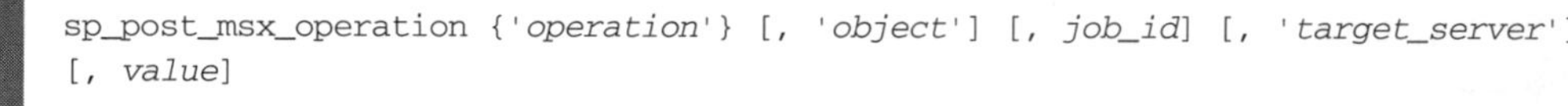

```
sp_post_msx_operation {'operation'} [, 'object'] [, job_id] [, 'target_server']
[, value]
```

The arguments are:

'operation'	Operation is varchar(64) and is the type of posted operation. Execute the system stored procedure sp_help_downloadlist to see the available values for operation.
'object'	Object is the varchar(64) object for the operation. JOB is the default. When SERVER is used, the job_id argument is not necessary.
job_id	Job_id is the uniqueidentifier for the job where 0x00 = all jobs.

'target_server'	Target_server is the varchar(30) name of the target server for the operation.
value	Value is an integer and is the polling interval in seconds.

sp_processmail

The sp_processmail system stored procedure processes incoming mail messages from the inbox and return the result set of the query to the message sender. Incoming mail is expected to contain a query and a known Subject argument. You can set this up as a SQL Server Agent task, and you can associate the filetype with an application on the server and the receiving client to get the proper icon on the result set.

Syntax

The syntax is:

```
sp_processmail [[@subject=]'subject'][, @filetype=]'filetype'][,
[@separator=]'separator'][, [@user=]['user'][, [@dbuse=]'dbname']
```

The arguments are:

'subject'	Subject is the varchar(255) subject line queries for SQL Server.
'filetype'	Filetype is the varchar(3) file extension to use for sending back the result set. The default is txt.
'separator'	Separator is the varchar(3) column separator for the result set. The default is TAB.
'user'	User is the sysname of the security account with permission to run the query. The default is guest.
'dbname'	Dbname is the sysname of the database to run the query and defaults to master.

sp_procoption

The sp_procoption system stored procedure defines procedure options. Use the stored procedure with no arguments to see the available options.

Syntax

The syntax is:

```
sp_procoption ['procedure'] [, 'option'] [, 'value']
```

The arguments are:

'procedure'	Procedure is the nvarchar(776) name of the stored procedure affected.
'option'	Option is the varchar(35) option to set, where Startup=define a stored procedure as a startup stored procedure that will automatically execute when SQL Server is started, and Allow updates=allow the stored procedure to be altered.
'value'	Value is varchar(12) where TRUE=on and FALSE=off.

sp_publication_validation

The sp_publication_validation system stored procedure is used in snapshot and merge replication, and it validates the article's data. Use row count validation or a full checksum validation of the article data. You can schedule this through the SQL Server Agent to run periodically.

Syntax

The syntax is:

```
sp_publication_validation [@publication =] 'publication'
[,[@rowcount_only =] rowcount_only]
[,[@full_or_fast =] full_or_fast]
[,[@shutdown_agent =] shutdown_agent]
```

The arguments are:

[@publication =] 'publication'	Publication is the sysname of the publication.
[@rowcount_only =] *rowcount_only*	Rowcount_only is a bit where 1=return only the rowcount for the table and 0=do a checksum validation.
[@full_or_fast =] full_or_fast	Full_or_fast is the tinyint rowcount calculation type where 0=full count(*), 1= fast count from sysindexes.rows (may produce inaccurate rowcount), 2=revert to full if fast count is inconsistent.
[@shutdown_agent =] shutdown_agent	Shutdown_agent is a bit where 0=Distribution agent shuts down after validation and 1=It does not shut down.

sp_purgehistory

The sp_purgehistory system stored procedure is for backward compatibility only and removes information from the history table for a task.

Syntax

The syntax is:

```
sp_purgehistory ['task_name'] [, task_id]
```

The arguments are:

'task_name'	Task_name is the varchar(100) name of the task.
task_id	Task_id is an integer and is the task identifier.

sp_purge_jobhistory

The sp_purge_jobhistory system stored procedure deletes the job history rows. If you do not provide the job arguments all history records are deleted. Only one argument can be supplied, not both.

Syntax

The syntax is:

```
sp_purge_jobhistory {[@job_name =] 'job_name' | [@job_id =] job_id}
```

The arguments are:

'job_name'	Job_Name is the varchar(100) name of the job for the records to be deleted.
job_id	Job-id is the uniqueidentifier for the job.

sp_reassigntask

The sp_reassigntask system stored procedure is for backward compatibility only. See version 6.5 documentation for more information.

sp_recompile

The sp_recompile system stored procedure marks the stored procedures and trigger for a table for recompilation (reading from the syscomments system table and placing the procedure in cache) next time they execute.

Syntax

The syntax is:

```
sp_recompile {'table'}
```

The argument, table, is nvarchar(776) and is the name of a table.

sp_refreshsubscriptions

The sp_refreshsubscriptions system stored procedure is used in pull replication (snapshot, transactional, and merge) to add subscriptions to new articles for all the subscribers.

Syntax

The syntax is:

```
sp_refreshsubscriptions [@publication =] 'publication'
```

The argument, publication, is the sysname of the publication.

sp_refreshview

The sp_refreshview system stored procedure refreshes the view due to changes in the underlying dependent objects.

Syntax

The syntax is:

```
sp_refreshview [@viewname = ] 'viewname'
```

The argument, viewname, is the nvarchar name of the view.

sp_reinitmergepullsubscription

The sp_reinitmergepullsubscription system stored procedure flags a merge pull subscription for reinitialization when the Merge Agent runs.

Syntax

The syntax is:

```
sp_reinitmergepullsubscription [@publisher =] 'publisher',
[@publisher_db =] 'publisher_db', [@publication =] 'publication'
```

The arguments are:

[@publisher =] 'publisher'	Publisher is the sysname of the publisher.
[@publisher_db =] 'publisher_db'	Publisher_db is the sysname of the publisher database.
[@publication =] 'publication'	Publication is the sysname of the publication.

sp_reinitmergesubscription

The sp_reinitmergesubscription system stored procedure flags a merge subscription for reinitialization when the Merge Agent runs and can be called from the Publisher. Rerun the Snapshot agent also.

Syntax

The syntax is:

```
sp_reinitmergesubscription [@publisher =] 'publisher',
[@publisher_db =] 'publisher_db', [@publication =] 'publication'
```

The arguments are:

[@publisher =] 'publisher'	Publisher is the sysname of the publisher.
[@publisher_db =] 'publisher_db'	Publisher_db is the sysname of the publisher database.
[@publication =] 'publication'	Publication is the sysname of the publication.

sp_reinitpullsubscription

The sp_reinitpullsubscription system stored procedure flags a merge subscription for reinitialization when the Merge Agent or Distribution Agent runs and can be called from the subscriber side (except for non_immediate_sync publications).

Syntax

The syntax is:

```
sp_reinitpullsubscription [@publisher =] 'publisher',
[@publisher_db =] 'publisher_db', [@publication =] 'publication'
```

The arguments are:

[@publisher =] 'publisher'	Publisher is the sysname of the publisher.
[@publisher_db =] 'publisher_db'	Publisher_db is the sysname of the publisher database.
[@publication =] 'publication'	Publication is the sysname of the publication.

sp_reinitsubscription

The sp_reinitsubscription system stored procedure synchronizes the subscription for snapshot, transactional, and merge replication. Run the Snapshot Agent also if auto_sync subscriptions on a nonimmediate_sync publication are involved. If no_sync subscriptions are involved, it is up to you to ensure that the destination tables at the subscriber are in sync and there are no undelivered replication commands. Anonymous subscribers are synchronized by using all or NULL for the subscriber argument.

Syntax

The syntax is:

```
sp_reinitsubscription [@publication =] 'publication', [@article =] 'article',
[@subscriber =] 'subscriber', [@destination_db =] 'destination_db'
```

The arguments are:

[@publication =] 'publication'	Publication is the sysname of the publication.
[@article =] 'article'	Article is the sysname of the article. Use the default, ALL, for an immediate_sync publication.

[@subscriber =] 'subscriber'	Subscriber is the sysname of the subscriber. The default is ALL, and NULL is for an anonymous subscription.
[@destination_db =] 'destination_db'	Destination_db is the sysname of the destination database and defaults to all.

sp_remoteoption

The sp_remoteoption system stored procedure displays or changes options for a remote login defined on the local server running Microsoft SQL Server.

Syntax

The syntax is:

```
sp_remoteoption [[@remoteserver =] 'remoteserver ]
[,[@loginame =] 'loginame'] [,[@remotename =]  remotename']
[,[@optname =] 'optname'] [,[@optvalue =] 'optvalue']
```

The arguments are:

[@remoteserver =] 'remoteserver'	Remoteserver is the sysname of the remote server.
[@loginame =] 'loginame'	Loginame is the sysname of the login of the user on the local SQL Server.
[@remotename =] 'remotename'	Remotename is the sysname of the login of the user on the remoteserver.
[@optname =] 'optname'	Optname is the varchar(35) name of the option you are to set.
[@optvalue =] 'optvalue'	Optvalue is the varchar(10) value for optname, with a default of NULL, where TRUE=trusted (integrated login) or FALSE=untrusted (standard login).

sp_removedbreplication

The sp_removedbreplication system stored procedure is used when restoring a replicated database and no replication objects need to be restored with the database. It deletes all replication objects from a database. No data is updated on the distributor database.

Syntax

The syntax is:

```
sp_removedbreplication [@dbname =] 'dbname'
```

The argument, dbname, is the sysname of the database.

sp_remove_job_from_targets

The sp_remove_job_from_targets system stored procedure removes a job from the target servers or groups. Supply the job_id argument or the job_name argument, but not both.

Syntax

The syntax is:

```
sp_remove_job_from_targets {job_id | 'job_name'} [, 'target_server_groups']
[, 'target_servers']
```

The arguments are:

job_id	Job_id is the uniqueidentifier of the job.
'job_name'	Job_name is the sysname of the job.
'target_server_groups'	Target_server_groups is nvarchar(1024) and holds a list of target server groups. Separate multiple groups with commas.
'target_servers'	Target_servers is nvarchar(1024) and holds a list of target servers. Separate more than one with commas.

sp_rename

The sp_rename system stored procedure gives a new name to an existing user-created object. Use this procedure in the database in use.

Syntax

The syntax is:

```
sp_rename {'object_name'} [, 'new_name'] [, 'object_type']
```

The arguments are:

'object_name'	Object_name is the nvarchar(776) old name of the object. Use table.column and table.index for columns and indexes.
'new_name'	New_name is the new sysname given to the object. Do not use the qualifying table name here if it is a column or index.
'object_type'	Object_type is varchar(13) and determines what type the object is where COLUMN=column, DATABASE=user created database, INDEX=user created index, OBJECT=item of an object type in sysobjects system table, and USERDATATYPE=user-defined data type.

sp_renamedb

The sp_renamedb system stored procedure gives a new name to an existing user-created database. (The database must be in single-user mode to rename it.)

Syntax

The syntax is:

```
sp_renamedb {'old_name', 'new_name'}
```

The arguments are:

'old_name'	Object_name is the old sysname of the database.
'new_name'	New_name is the new sysname given to the database.

sp_replcmds

The sp_replcmds system stored procedure used in transactional replication that designates the first client that executes the sp_replcmds stored procedure in a database to be the log reader. This stored procedure is used by the Logreader Agent. It returns the transaction's commands, as well as information about replication transactions in the transaction log not yet designated as sent to the distributor. It also returns information about the publication database from where it runs. Only one client can run this stored procedure in a database at a time (error 18752). Only run this to trouble-shoot replication when necessary.

Error 18759 will occur if a text command cannot be replicated because the text pointer was not retrieved in the same transaction.

Syntax

The syntax is:

```
sp_replcmds [@maxtrans =] maxtrans
```

The argument, maxtrans, is an integer and is the number of transactions to examine. The default is one transaction.

sp_replcounters

The sp_replcounters system stored procedure is used in transactional replication to display information about latency, throughput, and transaction-count of undelivered transactions, as well as transactions per second for the generated listing of published databases on the SQL Server.

Syntax

The syntax is:

```
sp_replcounters
```

sp_repldone

The sp_repldone system stored procedure is used in transactional replication by the Logreader Agent to mark the record that identifies the SQL Server's last distributed transaction. You should not execute this manually unless you know what to do. You can disrupt the replication process, however, by using sp_repldone system stored procedure. Also, you can mark that a transaction has been sent to the distributor, or designate the transaction as the next one to replicate, by using the arguments xactid and xact_seqno. You can get the arguments by running sp_repltrans or sp_replcmds system stored procedures. All transactions less than or equal to that transaction are designated distributed. To designate that all are replicated transactions in the transaction log as distributed, specify sp_repldone NULL, NULL, 0, 0, 1. To view the replicated transactions in the transaction log, specify sp_repldone NULL, NULL, 0, 0, 0.

Syntax

The syntax is:

```
sp_repldone [@xactid =] xactid, [@xact_seqno =] xact_seqno
[,[@numtrans =] numtrans] [,[@time =] time [,[@reset =] reset]
```

The arguments are:

[@xactid =] xactid	Xactid is the log sequence number of the *first* record for the last distributed transaction.
[@xact_seqno =] xact_seqno	Xact_seqno is the log sequence number of the *last* record for the last distributed transaction.
[@numtrans =] numtrans]	Numtrans is the number of distributed transactions.
[@time =] time	Time is the number of milliseconds needed to distribute the last batch of transactions.
[@reset =] reset	Reset is a bit reset status where 1=mark all replicated transactions in the log distributed and 0=reset the transaction log to the first replicated transaction and do not designate replicated transactions as distributed. This argument requires xactid and xact_seqno to be NULL.

sp_replflush

The sp_replflush system stored procedure is used in snapshot, transactional, and merge replication to flush the article cache. It is used by other replication stored procedures when an article definition is changed, and it is not usually manually executed.

The syntax is:

Syntax

```
sp_replflush
```

sp_replicationdboption

The sp_replicationdboption system stored procedure is used for snapshot, transactional, and merge replication in the database in use to set a replication database option. It sets the category bit in the sysdatabases system table and creates the replication system tables.

Syntax

The syntax is:

```
sp_replicationdboption [@dbname =] 'db_name', [@optname =] 'optname',
[@value =] 'value' [,[@ignore_distributor =] ignore_distributor]
```

The arguments are:

[@dbname =] 'dbname'	DB_name is the syname of the database to drop.
[@optname =] 'optname'	Optname is the sysname of the option to create or drop where merge publish=database is for merge publications, and publish=database is for other types of publications.
[@value =] 'value'	Value is the sysname holding the values true or false (false also drops merge subscriptions).
[@ignore_distributor =] ignore_distributor]	Ignore_distributor is bit, where 1=true and 0=false (the default).

sp_replicationoption

The sp_replicationoption system stored procedure adds or drops replication stored procedures and is used in snapshot, transactional, and merge replication to enable replication.

Syntax

The syntax is:

```
sp_replicationoption [@optname =] 'optname',
[@value =] 'value' [,[@security_mode =] security_mode] [,[@login =] 'login']
[,[@password =] 'password'] [,[@reserved =] 'reserved']
```

The arguments are:

[@optname =] 'optname'	Option is the sysname of the replication option where transactional=transactional replication, and merge=merge replication.
[@value =] 'value'	Value is nvarchar(5) where true=create the option, and false=delete the option.
[@security_mode =] security_mode	Security_mode is integer and the security mode of the distributor where 0=SQL Server authentication (the default) and 1= Windows NT authentication.
[@login =] 'login'	Login is the sysname of the distributor login and defaults to system administrator (sa).

[@password =] 'password'	Password is the sysname password of the distributor login.
[@reserved =] 'reserved'	Reserved is for use by Microsoft SQL Server and defaults to NULL.

sp_replication_agent_checkup

The sp_replication_agent_checkup system stored procedure is used in snapshot, transactional, and merge replication to check distribution databases for replication agents that are running but have not written to the history table within the heartbeat interval. It raises error 14151 when appropriate.

Syntax

The syntax is:

```
sp_replication_agent_checkup [[@heartbeat_interval =] 'heartbeat_interval']
```

The argument, heartbeat_interval, is the number of minutes that an agent can go without writing to the history table and without raising an error. It defaults to 10 minutes.

sp_replshowcmds

The sp_replshowcmds system stored procedure displays the commands for transactions marked for replication and can only be used when all client connections do not access replicated log transactions.

Syntax

The syntax is:

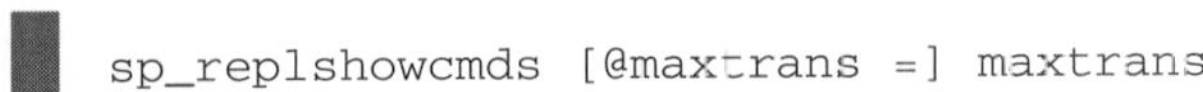

```
sp_replshowcmds [@maxtrans =] maxtrans
```

The argument [@maxtrans =] maxtrans is an integer and represents the number of transactions for which you would like to see information. The default is 1.

sp_repltrans

The sprepltrans system stored procedure is used in transactional replication to display a list of replication transactions in the publication database transaction log that have not been designated distributed. Execute this from the publication database. It is like sp_replcmds but does not return the transaction commands.

Syntax

The syntax is:

```
sp_repltrans
```

sp_resync_targetserver

The sp_resync_targetserver system stored procedure synchronizes the server in the multiserver domain.

Syntax

The syntax is:

```
sp_resync_targetserver {'server'}
```

The argument, server, is the nvarchar(30) name of the server where ALL causes all servers to be resynchronized in the multiserver domain.

sp_revoke_publication_access

The sp_revoke_publication_access system stored procedure is used in snapshot, transactional, and merge replication to delete the login from a publications access list.

Syntax

The syntax is:

```
sp_revoke_publication_access [@publication = ] 'publication',
[@login =] 'login'
```

The arguments are:

[@publication =] 'publication'	Publication is the sysname of the publication. If this argument is not supplied, the login is removed from the server global access list.
[@login =] 'login'	Login is the sysname of the login.

sp_revokedbaccess

The sp_revokedbaccess system stored procedure deletes any security account , permissions, and aliases from the database in use.

Syntax

The syntax is:

```
sp_revokedbaccess {[@name_in_db =] 'name'}
```

The argument, name, is the sysname of the deleted database user.

sp_revokelogin

The sp_revokelogin system stored procedure deletes the login entries for a Microsoft Windows NT user or group that were added when sp_grantlogin or sp_denylogin was executed for the login.

Syntax

The syntax is:

```
sp_revokelogin {[@loginame =] 'login'}
```

The argument, login, is the sysname of the Windows NT user or group. The format is Domain\User.

sp_runwebtask

The sp_runwebtask system stored procedure runs an existing Web task and generates the HTML document.

Syntax

The syntax is:

```
sp_runwebtask [[@procname =] 'procname'] [,[@outputfile = ] 'outputfile']
```

The arguments are:

'procname'	Procname is the nvarchar(128) name of the stored procedure belonging to the Web task.
'outputfile'	Outputfile is the nvarchar(255) name of the output file for the Web task.

sp_script_synctran_commands

The sp_script_synctran_commands system stored procedure is used in snapshot and transactional replication to create a script with sp_addsyntrigger calls for each article for application at the subscribers.

Syntax

The syntax is:

```
sp_script_synctran_commands [@publication =] 'publication'
[,[@article =] 'article']
```

The arguments are:

[@publication =] 'publication'	Publication is the sysname of the publication.
[@article =] 'article'	Article is the sysname of the article. The default is ALL.

sp_scriptdelproc

The sp_scriptdelproc system stored procedure is used in snapshot and transactional replication to automatically create the CREATE PROCEDURE statement for a custom stored procedure that contains a delete statement.

Syntax

The syntax is:

```
sp_scriptdelproc [@artid =] 'artid'
```

The argument, artid, is an integer identifying the article.

sp_scriptinsproc

The sp_scriptinsproc system stored procedure is used in snapshot and transactional replication to automatically create the CREATE PROCEDURE statement for a custom stored procedure that contains an insert statement.

Syntax

The syntax is:

```
sp_scriptinsproc [@artid =] 'artid'
```

The argument, artid, is an integer and is the identifier of the article.

sp_scriptupdproc

The sp_scriptupdproc system stored procedure is used in snapshot and transactional replication to automatically create the CREATE PROCEDURE statement for a custom stored procedure that contains an update statement.

Syntax

The syntax is:

```
sp_scriptupdproc [@artid =] 'artid'
```

The argument, artid, is an integer identifying the article.

sp_server_info

The sp_server_info system stored procedure displays information about Microsoft SQL Server, the database gateway, or other data sources.

Syntax

The syntax is:

```
sp_server_info [[@attribute_id =] attribute_id]
```

The argument, attribute_id, is the integer identifier of the attribute.

sp_serveroption

The sp_serveroption system stored procedure defines server options for remote and linked servers, and it defines options for distributed queries.

Syntax

The syntax is:

```
sp_serveroption [[@server = ]'server',
[@optname = ]'option_name',
[@optvalue = ]'option_value']
```

The arguments are:

'server'	Server is the sysname of the server. If this argument is not supplied, a list of server options is displayed.

'option_name'	Option_name is the varchar(35) name of the option. If this argument is not supplied a list of server options is displayed where collation compatible=true designates the distributed query execution as compatible when executed against linked servers, false and SQL Server compares locally, data access=enables or disables a linked server for distributed query access, dist=distributor, dpub=remote publisher to this distributor, pub=publisher, rpc=true is Remote Prodedure Calls from the server, rpc out=true is Remote Procedure Calls to the server, sub=subscriber, system=used by Microsoft SQL Server.
'option_value'	Option_value is varchar(10) and determines if the option is True=on or False=off. If this argument is not supplied, option values are displayed.

sp_setapprole

The sp_setapprole system stored procedure causes other permissions associated with the user to be ignored while the application role in the database is in effect. Only the application role permissions are permitted for the user while the application role is set.

Syntax

The syntax is:

```
sp_setapprole {[@rolename =] 'name' ,[@password =] 'password'}
[,[@encrypt =] 'encrypt_style']
```

The arguments are:

[@rolename =] 'name'	Name is the sysname of the application role in the database.
[@password =] 'password'	Password is sysname and is the password for the application role.
[@encrypt =] 'encrypt_style'	Encrypt is varchar(10) and determines the type of encryption where none=the password is not encrypted (the default), ODBC=the password is encrypted using the ODBC canonical encrypt function.

sp_setnetname

The sp_setnetname system stored procedure is used to place the name of remote servers that have invalid characters for execution of remote stored procedures. The name is placed into the sysservers column, srvnetname, in the event of an incompatibility between the name of the remote server and what SQL Server allows in the table.

Syntax

The syntax is:

```
sp_setnetname {'server'} [, 'network_name']
```

The arguments are:

'server'	Server is the sysname of the remote server used in the remote stored procedure call. The server must have been previously added to the sysservers table.
'network_name'	Network_name is the network name of the remote computer.

sp_spaceused

The sp_spaceused system stored procedure returns information about the disk space used by a table or a database. The updateusage argument will make updates to the sysindexes table so that the space information will be up-to-date in the event the information in the sysindexes system table is out of date. Be wary of using this argument on a large table. It may take a while.

The syntax is:

Syntax

```
sp_spaceused ['objname'] [, 'updateusage']
```

The arguments are:

'objname'	Objname is the nvarchar(776) name of the table or database. A default of NULL runs this on the database.
'updateusage'	Updateusage is varchar(5), can be true or false (the default) and determines if DBCC UPDATEUSAGE is run on the table or database.

sp_special_columns

The sp_special_columns system stored procedure displays uniquely identifying columns and automatically updated columns in a table.

Syntax

The syntax is:

```
sp_special_columns {'name'} [, 'owner'] [, 'qualifier'] [, 'col_type']
[, 'scope']
[, 'nullable'] [, 'ODBCVer']
```

The arguments are:

'name'	Name is the sysname of the table.
'owner'	Owner is the sysname of the owner of the table.
'qualifier'	Qualifier is the sysname of the table qualifier (the database name for SQL Server).
'col_type'	Col_type is char(1) and the type of the column, where R=returns uniquely identifying columns, and V= returns columns in the table that are automatically updated.
'scope'	Scope is char(1) and represents the scope of the ROWID where C=the ROWID is valid when positioned on the row and T=the ROWID is valid for duration of the transaction (the default).
'nullable'	Nullable is char(1) where U=the special column allows null values (the default), and O=the special column does not allow null values.
'ODBCVer'	ODBCVer is an integer representing the ODBC version being used. The default is 2 (ODBC version 2.0).

sp_sproc_columns

The sp_sproc_columns system stored procedure displays information about the arguments and the result set for a stored procedure in the database in use.

Syntax

The syntax is:

```
sp_sproc_columns ['name'] [, 'owner'] [, 'qualifier'] [, 'column_name']
[, 'ODBCVer']
```

The arguments are:

'name'	Name is the nvarchar(390) name of the stored procedure and defaults to % for all stored procedures in the database in use.
'owner'	Owner is the nvarchar(384) name of the owner of the stored procedure.
'qualifier'	Qualifier is the sysname of the procedure qualifier (database name in SQL Server).
'column_name'	Column_name is the nvarchar(384) name of a column. All columns are returned when this column is not supplied. The % and _ wildcard characters are supported.
'ODBCVer'	ODBCVer is an integer representing the ODBC version being used. The default is 2 (ODBC version 2.0).

sp_srvrolepermission

The sp_srvrolepermission system stored procedure displays the permissions of a fixed server role.

Syntax

The syntax is:

```
sp_srvrolepermission [[@srvrolename =] 'role']
```

The argument, role, is the name of the fixed server role with the following possible values: sysadmin, securityadmin, serveradmin, setupadmin, processadmin, diskadmin, and dbcreator.

sp_start_job

The sp_start_job system stored procedure is used to start the job running. Use either the job_name argument or the job_id argument, not both.

Syntax

The syntax is:

```
sp_start_job {[@job_name =] 'job_name' | [@job_id =] job_id}
[, [@error_flag =] error_flag]
[, [@server_name =] 'server_name']
[, [@step_name =] 'step_name']
[, [@output_flag = ] output_flag]
```

The arguments are:

'job_name'	Job_name is the sysname of the job.
job_id	Job_id is the uniqueidentifier of the job. The default is NULL.
error_flag	Errorlog is reserved for SQL Server.
'server_name'	Server_name is the nvarchar(30) name of the server running the job. The default is NULL.
'step_name'	Step_name is the sysname of the step where execution starts. The default is NULL.
output_flag	Output_flag is reserved for SQL Server.

sp_statistics

The sp_statistics system stored procedure displays all indexes on a table.

Syntax

The syntax is:

```
sp_statistics {'name'} [, 'owner'] [, 'qualifier'] [, 'index_pattern']
[, 'is_unique']
[, 'accuracy']
```

The arguments are:

'name'	Name is the sysname of the table.
'owner'	Owner is the sysname of the table owner.
'qualifier'	Qualifier is the sysname of the table qualifier (the database name for SQL Server).
'index_pattern'	Index_pattern is the sysname of the index with default of % for all indexes.
'is_unique '	Is_unique is char(1) where Y=unique are returned and N=nonunique are returned.
'accuracy'	Accuracy is char(1) data type and the page accuracy for statistics where E=ensure that statistics are updated and Q=do not ensure that statistics are updated (the default).

sp_stop_job

The sp_stop_job system stored procedure is used to cancel the execution of a job. If the type of job is CmdExec, use this stored procedure carefully because unpredictable behavior—including files left in use—could result. Use either the job_name argument or the job_id argument, not both.

Syntax

The syntax is:

```
sp_stop_job [@job_name =] 'job_name' | [@job_id =] job_id |
[@originating_server =] 'server' | [@server_name =] 'target_server'
```

The arguments are:

'job_name'	Job_name is the sysname of the job.
job_id	Job_id is the uniqueidentifier of the job with a default of NULL.
'server'	Originating_server is the nvarchar(30) name of the server that initiated the job.
'server_name'	Server_name is the nvarchar(30) name of the server running the job with a default of NULL.

sp_stored_procedures

The sp_stored_procedures system stored procedure displays the stored procedures in the database in use.

Syntax

The syntax is:

```
sp_stored_procedures ['name'] [, 'owner'] [, 'qualifier']
```

The arguments are:

'name'	Name is the nvarchar(390) name of a stored procedure. The % and _ wildcard characters are supported.
'owner'	Owner is the nvarchar(384) name of the owner of the stored procedure. The % and _ wildcard characters are supported.
'qualifier'	Qualifier is the sysname of the table qualifier (the database name for SQL Server).

sp_subscription_cleanup

The sp_subscription_cleanup system stored procedure is used in all types of replications to clean up the entry in MSreplication_subscriptions replication table and for a synchronizing transaction subscription. It also cleans up synctran triggers.

Syntax

The syntax is:

```
sp_subscription_cleanup [@publisher =] 'publisher',
[@publisher_db =] 'publisher_db' [,[@publication =] 'publication']
```

The arguments are:

[@publisher =] 'publisher'	Publisher is the sysname of the publisher.
[@publisher_db =] 'publisher_db'	Publisher_db is the sysname of the publisher database.
[@publication =] 'publication'	Publication is the sysname of the publication and defaults to NULL.

sp_table_privileges

The sp_table_privileges system stored procedure displays tables and their permissions for the database in use.

Syntax

The syntax is:

```
sp_table_privileges {'table_name_pattern'} [, 'table_owner_pattern']
[, 'table_qualifier']
```

The arguments are:

'table_name_pattern'	Table_name_pattern is the nvarchar(384) name of the table. There is no default. The % and _ wildcard characters are supported.
'table_owner_pattern'	Table_owner_pattern is the nvarchar(384) table owner of the table. The % and _ wildcard characters are supported.

'table_qualifier'	Qualifier is the sysname of the table qualifier (the database name for SQL Server).

sp_table_privileges_ex

The sp_table_privileges system stored procedure displays tables and their permissions in the database on a linked server.

Syntax

The syntax is:

```
sp_table_privileges_ex {'table_server'} [, 'table_name'] [, 'table_schema']
[, 'table_catalog']
```

The arguments are:

'table_server'	Table_server is the sysname of the linked server.
'table_name'	Table_name is the sysname of the table.
'table_schema'	Table_schema is the sysname of the table schema.
'table_catalog'	Table_catalog is the sysname of the table's database.

sp_table_validation

The sp_table_validation system stored procedure is used in replication to return rowcount or checksum information for a table. It also can be used to ascertain the differences in the provided rowcount or checksum information of a table by displaying the difference between the expected number of rows and the actual number of rows.

Syntax

The syntax is:

```
sp_table_validation [@table =] 'table'
[,[@expected_rowcount =] expected_rowcount]
[,[@expected_checksum =] expected_checksum]
[,[@rowcount_only =] rowcount_only] [,[@owner =] 'owner']
[,[@full_or_fast =] full_or_fast]
[,[@shutdown_agent =] shutdown_agent]
```

The arguments are:

[@table =] 'table'	Table is the sysname of the table.
[@expected_rowcount =] expected_rowcount	Expected_rowcount is an integer where NULL=return the actual rowcount and value=value to check against the actual rowcount.
[@expected_checksum =] expected_checksum	Expected_checksum is numeric where NULL=returns the actual checksum and value=value to check against the actual checksum.
[@rowcount_only =] rowcount_only	Rowcount_only is bit where 1=return only the rowcount for the table and 0=return both rowcount and checksum (the default).
[@owner =] 'owner'	Owner is the sysname of the owner of the table.
[@full_or_fast =] full_or_fast	Full_or_fast is a tinyint representing how the rowcount is determined, where 0=full count using COUNT(*), 1=fast count from sysindexes.rows but is only as accurate as the last time sysindexes was updated and 2=conditional fast counting—if discrepancies are detected, full count is used.
[@shutdown_agent =] shutdown_agent	Shutdown_agent is a bit where 0=replication agent does not shut down and 1= replication agent does shut down.

sp_tableoption

The sp_tableoption system stored procedure is used to set options for user-created tables.

Syntax

The syntax is:

```
sp_tableoption {'table'} [, 'option_name'] [, 'value']
```

The arguments are:

'table'	Table is the nvarchar(776) name of user created database table.
'option_name'	Option_name is varchar(35) and is the name of the option where NULL=lists all options and their default values.
'value'	Value is varchar(12), determining whether the option is on or off, where true=on and false=off.

sp_tables

The sp_tables system stored procedure displays a list of table objects in the database in use.

Syntax

The syntax is:

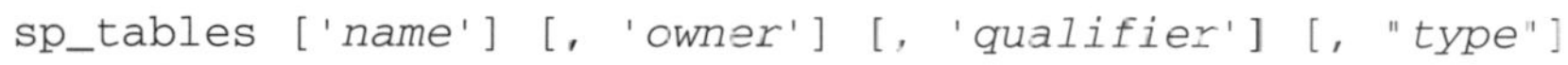

```
sp_tables ['name'] [, 'owner'] [, 'qualifier'] [, "type"]
```

The arguments are:

'name'	Name is the nvarchar(384) name of the table with a default of NULL. The % and _ wildcard characters are supported.
'owner'	Owner is the nvarchar(384) table owner. The % and _ wildcard characters are supported.
'qualifier'	Qualifier is the sysname of the table qualifier with default of NULL.
"type"	Type is varchar(100) and is a comma-separated list of table types (TABLE, SYSTEM TABLE, or VIEW).

sp_tables_ex

The sp_tables_ex stored procedure displays a list of queriable objects from the specified linked server.

Syntax

The syntax is:

```
sp_tables_ex {'table_server'} [, 'table_name'] [, 'table_schema']
[, 'table_catalog'] [, 'table_type']
```

The arguments are:

'table_server'	Table_server is the sysname of the linked server.
'table_name'	Table_name is the sysname of the table.
'table_schema'	Table_schema is the sysname of the table schema.
'table_catalog'	Table_catalog is the sysname of the database of the table.
'table_type'	Table_types is sysname and is a comma-separated list of table types: ALIAS, GLOBAL TEMPORARY, LOCAL TEMPORARY, SYNONYM, SYSTEM TABLE, VIEW, and TABLE.

sp_unbindefault

The sp_unbindefault system stored procedure unbinds a default on a column or on a user-defined data type.

Syntax

The syntax is:

```
sp_unbindefault {'object_name'} [, 'futureonly_flag']
```

The arguments are:

object_name	Object_name is nvarchar(776) and is the table and column, or a user-defined data type.
'futureonly_flag'	Futureonly_flag is varchar(15) and is used only for unbinding a default from a user-defined data type by keeping existing columns of that data type from having the default removed.

sp_unbindrule

The sp_unbindrule system stored procedure unbinds a rule on a column or on a user-defined data type.

Syntax

The syntax is:

```
sp_unbindrule { object_name'} [, 'futureonly_flag']
```

The arguments are:

'object_name'	Object_name is nvarchar(776) and is the table and column or a user-defined data type.
'futureonly_flag'	Futureonly_flag is varchar(15) and is used only for unbinding a rule from a user-defined data type by keeping existing columns of that data type from having the rule removed.

sp_update_alert

The sp_update_alert system stored procedure must be run in the msdb database if you want to update an alert.

Syntax

The syntax is:

```
sp_update_alert {'name'} [, 'new_name'] [, enabled] [, message_id]
[, severity]
[, delay_between_responses] [, 'notification_message']
[, include_event_description_in] [, 'database_name']
[, 'event_description_keyword'] [, job_id][, 'job_name']
[, occurrence_count] [, count_reset_date] [, count_reset_time]
[, last_occurrence_date] [, last_occurrence_time] [, last_response_date]
[, last_response _time][, raise_snmp_trap][, 'performance_condition']
[, 'category']
```

The arguments are:

[@name =] 'name'	Name is sysname and is the name of an existing alert.
[, [@new_name =] 'new_name']	New_name is sysname and is the new name of the alert.
[, [@enabled =] enabled]	Enabled in tinyint where 1=enabled (the default) and 0=not enabled.

[, [@message_id =] message_id]	Message_id is the integer error number in the sysmessages table that is associated with the alert. (You can add your own with sp_addmessage where the argument WITH_LOG will write the error message to the NT Event log.) If you supply the severity argument, this argument must be null or zero. You must also write to the Microsoft Windows NT application event log to set off an alert.
[, [@severity =] severity]	Severity is an integer representing the severity level of the error associated with an alert. Any message written to the NT Event log of this severity will set off the alert. If you are using the message_id argument, this argument must be null or zero.
[, [@delay_between_responses =] delay_between_responses]	Delay_between_responses is an integer and is the number of seconds to wait before issuing the next alert. This can prevent repeated e-mail or pages for the same alert. The default is zero.
[, [@notification_message =] 'notification_message']	Notification_message is nvarchar(512) with a default of NULL and can be used to send additional information to the recipient of the alert. You can include troubleshooting messages here.
[, [@include_event_description_in =] include_event_description_in]	Include_event_description_in (with a default of zero) is tinyint and determines whether the description of the SQL Server error in the NT Event Log is part of the notification message that is sent to the recipient, where 0=None, 1=Email, 2=Pager, 4=NetSend, 7=All.
[, [@database_name =] 'database_name']	Database is the sysname and is the name of the database in use. The default is NULL, which means the alert will occur on errors in any database on the server.
[, [@event_description_keyword =] 'event_description_keyword']	Event_description_keyword is nvarchar(100) with a default of NULL and describes the SQL Server error in the Windows NT event log. LIKE expression wildcard characters can be used for object names.

[, [@job_id =] job_id | [@job_name =] 'job_name']	Job_id is the unicueidentifier of the job with a default of NULL. Supply job_id or job_name as an argument. Job_name is the CmdExec or Transact-SQL sysname job name to run when an alert is given. The default is NULL.
[, [@occurrence_count =] occurrence_count]	Occurrence_count is the integer number of times the alert has fired and can be reset to zero.
[, [@count_reset_date =] count_reset_date]	Count_reset_date is an integer and is the date the occurrence count was reset.
[, [@count_reset_time =] count_reset_time]	Count_reset_time is an integer and is the time the occurrence count was reset. It can be reset to zero.
[, [@last_occurrence_date =] last_occurrence_date]	Last_occurrence_date is an integer; it's the last date the alert occurred and can only be reset to zero.
[, [@last_occurrence_time =] last_occurrence_time]	Last_occurrence_time is an integer; it's the last time the alert occurred and can only be reset to zero.
[, [@last_response_date =] last_response_date]	Last_response_date is an integer; it's the last date SQL Server Agent responded to the alert and can only be reset to zero.
[, [@last_response_time =] last_response _time]	Last_response_time is an integer; it's the last time SQL Server Agent responded to the alert and can only be reset to zero.
[, [@raise_snmp_trap =] raise_snmp_trap]	Raise_snmp_trap is reserved for Microsoft SQL Server.
[, [@performance_condition =] 'performance_condition']	Performance_condition is reserved for Microsoft SQL Server.
[, [@category_name =] 'category']	Category is reserved for Microsoft SQL Server.

sp_updatecategory

The sp_updatecategory system stored procedure modfies the name of a category.

Syntax

The syntax is:

```
sp_update_category {[@class =] 'class' [, [@name =] 'old_name']
[,[@new_name =] 'new_name']
```

The arguments are:

[@class =] 'class'	Class is the varchar(8) class of the category where JOB=update a job (type must be MULTISERVER), ALERT=update an alert, and OPERATOR=update an operator.
[, [@name =] 'old_name']	Old_name is sysname and is the old name of the category.
[,[@new_name =] 'new_name']	New_name is sysname and is the new name of the category.

sp_update_job

The sp_update_job system stored procedure modifies a job. Supply the job_id or the job_name argument, but not both.

Syntax

The syntax is:

```
sp_update_job {[@job_id =] job_id | [@job_name =] 'job_name'}
[, [@new_name =] 'new_name'] [, [@enabled =] enabled]
[, [@description =] 'description'] [, [@start_step_id =] step_id]
[, [@category_name =] 'category'] [, [@owner_login_name =] 'login']
[, [@notify_level_eventlog =] eventlog_level]
[, [@notify_level_email =] email_level]
[, [@notify_level_netsend =] netsend_level]
[, [@notify_level_page =] page_level]
[, [@notify_email_operator_name =] 'email_name']
[, [@notify_netsend_operator_name =] 'netsend_operator']
[, [@notify_page_operator_name =] 'page_operator']
[, [@delete_level =] delete_level] [, @automatic_post =]
automatic_post]
```

The arguments are:

[@job_id =] job_id | [@job_name =] 'job_name'	Job_id is the uniqueidentifier of the job. Job_name is the sysname of the job.
[, [@new_name =] 'new_name']	New_name is the new sysname of the job.
[, [@enabled =] enabled]	Enabled determines if the job is enabled or not enabled where 1=enabled and 0=disabled. The default is 1.
[, [@description =] 'description']	Description is the nvarchar(512) description of the job and defaults to 'No description available.'
[, [@start_step_id =] step_id]	Step_id is an integer and is the number of the first step of the job. The default is 1.
[, [@category_name =] 'category']	Category is the sysname category for the job and defaults to NULL.
[, [@owner_login_name =] 'login']	Login is the sysname of the login whose permissions are used to run the job, and it defaults to NULL.
[, [@notify_level_eventlog =] eventlog_level]	Eventlog_level is an integer that determines when the NT event log entries occur for a job, where 0=Never, 1=On Success, 2=On Failure, 3=Always and the default is 2.
[, [@notify_level_email =] *email_level*]	Email_level is an integer that determines when an e-mail is sent where 0=Never, 1=On Success, 2=On Failure, 3=Always and the default is 0.
[, [@notify_level_netsend =] *netsend_level*]	Netsend_level is an integer that determines when a network message is sent where 0=Never, 1=On Success, 2=On Failure, 3=Always and the default is 0.
[, [@notify_level_netsend =] netsend_level]	Page_level is an integer that determines when a page is sent to a pager where 0=Never, 1=On Success, 2=On Failure, 3=Always and the default is 0.

[, [@notify_level_eventlog =] eventlog_level]	E-mail_name is the nvarchar(100) name of the person to e-mail on email_level. The default is NULL.
[, [@notify_netsend_operator_name =] 'netsend_operator']	Netsend_operator is the nvarchar(100) name of the operator to send a network message on netsend_level. The default is NULL.
[, [@notify_page_operator_name =] '*page_operator*']	Page_operator is the nvarchar(100) name of the person to page on page_level. The default is NULL.
[, [@delete_level =] *delete_level*]	Delete_level is an integer that determines when the job is deleted where 0=Never, 1=On Success, 2=On Failure, 3=Always and the default is 0.
[, [@automatic_post =] automatic_post]	Automatic_post is reserved for Microsoft SQL Server.

sp_update_jobschedule

The sp_update_jobschedule system stored procedure modifies the job's schedule and updates its version number.

Syntax

The syntax is:

```
sp_update_jobschedule {[@job_id =] job_id | [@job_name =]
'job_name'}
{, [@name =] 'name'] [, [@newname =] 'new_name']
[, [@enabled =] enabled] [, [@freq_type =] freq_type]
[, [@freq_interval =] freq_interval]
[, [@freq_subday_type =] freq_subday_type]
[, [@freq_subday_interval =] freq_subday_interval]
[, [@freq_relative_interval =] freq_relative_interval]
[, [@freq_recurrence_factor =] freq_recurrence_factor]
[, [@active_start_date=] active_start_date]
[, [@active_end_date =] active_end_date]
[, [@active_start_time =] active_start_time]
[, [@active_end_time=] active_end_time]
```

The arguments are:

[@job_id =] job_id | [@job_name =] 'job_name'	Job_id is the uniqueidentifier of the job and defaults to NULL. Supply either job_id or name. Job_name is the sysname name of the job to put on a schedule and defaults to NULL.
[@name =] 'name']	Name is the sysname name of the schedule entry for the job.
[, [@newname =] 'new_name']	New_name is the sysname new name of the schedule entry for the job.
[, [@enabled =] enabled]	Enabled determines if the job is enabled or not enabled to run on schedule where 1=enabled and 0=disabled. The default is 1.
[, [@freq_type =] freq_type]	Freq_type is an integer determining when the job is run with a default of 0 where 1=once, 4=daily, 8=weekly, 16=monthly, 32=monthly (according to the freq interval), 64=run when SQL Server Agent starts.
[, [@freq_interval =] freq_interval]	Freq_interval is an integer determining the days the job runs (with a default of 0) where 1=Sunday, 2=Monday, 3=Tuesday, 4=Wednesday, 5=Thursday, 6=Friday, 7=Saturday, 8=Sunday, 9=weekdays, 10=weekend days.
[, [@freq_subday_type =] freq_subday_type]	Freq_subday_type is an integer representing the units for freq_subday_interval and has a default of 0 where 1=at the specified time, 2=seconds, 3=minutes, 4=hours.
[, [@freq_subday_interval =] freq_subday_interval]	Freq_subday_interval is an integer defaulting to 0 and determining the number of freq_subday_type units between each job run.
[, [@freq_relative_interval =] freq_relative_interval]	Freq_relative_interval is an integer and determines the freq_interval in each month (with a default of 0) where 1=first, 2=second, 4=third, 8=fourth, 16=last.
[, [@freq_recurrence_factor =] freq_recurrence_factor]	Freq_recurrence_factor is an integer that represents the number of months between the job run and defaults to 0.

[, [@active_start_date=] active_start_date]	Active_start_date is an integer that represents the date to start running the job (with a default of NULL) and has a format of YYYYMMDD.
[, [@active_end_date =] active_end_date]	Active_end_date is an integer that represents the date to stop running the job with a default of 99991231 (December 31, 9999).
[, [@active_start_time =] active_start_time]	Active_start_time is an integer representing the time to start running the job with a default of 000000 (12:00:00 A.M.) and has a format of HHMMSS.
[, [@active_end_time=] active_end_time]	Active_end_time is an integer representing the time to start running the job with a default of 235959 (11:59:59 P.M.).

sp_update_jobstep

The sp_update_jobstep system stored procedure modifies a job step and updates its version number.

Syntax

The syntax is:

```
sp_update_jobstep {[@job_id =] job_id | [@job_name =] 'job_name'}
{, [@step_id =] step_id} [, [@step_name =] 'step_name']
[, [@subsystem =] 'subsystem'] [, [@command =] 'command']
[, [@additional_parameters =] 'parameters']
[, [@cmdexec_success_code =] success_code]
[, [@on_success_action =] success_action]
[, [@on_success_step_id =] success_step_id]
[, [@on_fail_action =] fail_action] [, [@on_fail_step_id =] fail_step_id]
[, [@server =] 'server'] [, [@database_name =] 'database']
[, [@database_user_name =] 'user'] [, [@retry_attempts =] retry_attempts]
[, [@retry_interval =] retry_interval] [, [@os_run_priority =] run_priority]
[, [@output_file_name =] 'file_name'] [, [@flags =] flags]
```

The arguments are:

[@job_id =] job_id | [@job_name =] 'job_name'	Job_id is the uniqueidentifer of the job and defaults to NULL. Job_name is the sysname name of the job and defaults to NULL. Supply either job_id or name.
{, [@step_id =] step_id} [, [@step_name =] 'step_name']	Step_id is the integer for the job step with a default of NULL. Step_name is the sysname of the step.
[, [@subsystem =] 'subsystem'] [,	Subsystem is the nvarchar(40)subsystem used by SQL Server Enterprise Manager to execute command with a default of TSQL.
[@command =] 'command']	Command is the nvarchar(3200) command sent to SQL Server Agent for execution with a default of NULL. Command can have tokens where [A-DBN]=database name, [A-SVR]=server name, [A-ERR]=error number, [A-SEV]=error severity, [A-MSG]=message text, [DATE]=current date formatted as YYYYMMDD, [JOBID]=job ID, [MACH]=computer name, [MSSA]=Master SQLServerAgent name, [SQLDIR]=installation directory of SQL Server (C:\MSSQL7), [STEPCT]=number of times this step has run, [STEPID]=step ID, [TIME]=current time formatted as HHMMSS, [STRTTM]=the time the job started formatted as HHMMSS, [STRDT]=the date the job started formatted as YYYYMMDD.
[, [@additional_parameters =] 'parameters']	Parameter is reserved for Microsoft SQL Server.
[, [@cmdexec_success_code =] success_code]	Success_code is the integer return value for successful completion and defaults to 0.

[, [@on_success_action =] success_action]	Success_action is tinyint and determines what to do when a success code is returned where1 =Quit With Success and is the default, 2=Quit With Failure, 3=Go to Next Step, 4=Go to Step success_step_id.
[, [@on_success_step_id =] success_step_id]	Success_step_id is an integer and is the step in this job to run when success_code and success_action are 4. The default is 0.
[, [@on_fail_action =] fail_action]	Fail_action is tinyint and is a return value that is not code where 1=Quit With Success, 2 (default)=Quit With Failure, 3=Go to Next Step, 4=Go to Step fail_step_id.
[, [@on_fail_step_id =] fail_step_id]	Fail_step_id is the integer step in this job to run when not_code and success_action are 4. The default is 0.
[, [@server =] 'server']	Server is the nvarchar(30) name of the server to run the step and defaults to NULL.
] [, [@database_name =] 'database']	Database is the sysname of the database to run the step and defaults to NULL.
[, [@database_user_name =] 'user']	User is the sysname of the user account used to run this step and defaults to NULL.
[, [@retry_attempts =] retry_attempts]	Retry_attempts is the integer determining how many times to retry when the step fails. The default is 0.
[, [@retry_interval =] retry_interval]	Retry_interval is the integer representing the number of seconds between retries with a default of 0.
[, [@os_run_priority =] run_priority]	Run_priority is an integer representing the OS priority to use to run the step where –15=Idle, –1=Below Normal, 0 =Normal (the default), 1=Above Normal, and 15=Time Critical.
[, [@output_file_name =] 'file_name']	File_name is the nvarchar(200) name of the output file in which the output of this step is saved and can include the command tokens.
[, [@flags =] flags]	Flags is reserved for Microsoft SQL Server.

sp_update_notification

The sp_update_notification system stored procedure modifies the notification method of an alert notification and must be run in the msdb system database.

Syntax

The syntax is:

```
sp_update_notification [@alert_name =] 'alert',
[@operator_name =] 'operator',
[@notification_method =] notification
```

The arguments are:

[@alert_name =] 'alert'	The sysname alert name of your choice.
[@operator_name =] 'operator'	Operator sysname is the operator notified on the alert.
[@notification_method =] notification	Notification_method is a tinyint that represents how the operator is notified when the alert occurs where 1=E-mail (the default and SQL Mail must be configured), 2=Pager, 4=NetSend, 7=All.

sp_update_operator

The sp_update_operator system stored procedure is run from the msdb system database to modify information about an operator.

Syntax

The syntax is:

```
sp_update_operator [@name =] 'name
[, [@new_name =] 'new_name']
[, [@enable =] enabled]
[, [@email_address =] 'email_address']
[, [@pager_address =] 'pager_number']
[, [@weekday_pager_start_time =] weekday_pager_start_time]
[, [@weekday_pager_end_time =] weekday_pager_end_time]
[, [@saturday_pager_start_time =] saturday_pager_start_time]
[, [@saturday_pager_end_time =] saturday_pager_end_time]
```

```
[, [@sunday_pager_start_time =] sunday_pager_start_time]
[, [@sunday_pager_end_time =] sunday_pager_end_time]
[, [@pager_days =] pager_days]
[, [@netsend_address =] 'netsend_address']
[, [@category_name =] 'category']
```

The arguments are:

[@name =] 'name'	Name is the sysname name of an existing operator.
[, [@new_name =] 'new_name']	New_name is the sysname new name of an existing operator.
[, [@enable =] enabled]	Enabled is a tinyint representing the status of the operator where 1=enabled (the default), and 0=not enabled.
[, [@email_address =] 'email_address']	Email_address is the varchar(100) e-mail address of the operator.
[, [@pager_address =] 'pager_number']	Pager_address is the varchar(100) pager address of the operator and defaults to NULL.
[, [@weekday_pager_start_time =] weekday_pager_start_time]	Weekday_pager_start_time is an integer of format HHMMSS with a default of 090000, 9:00 A.M. on a 24-hour clock, representing the time to start sending pager notification to the operator (Monday through Friday).
[, [@weekday_pager_end_time =] weekday_pager_end_time]	Weekday_pager_end_time is an integer format HHMMSS with a default of 180000, 6:00 P.M. on a 24-hour clock, representing the time to stop sending pager notification to the operator (Monday through Friday).
[, [@saturday_pager_start_time =] saturday_pager_start_time]	Saturday_pager_start_time is an integer format HHMMSS with a default of 090000, 9:00 A.M. on a 24-hour clock, representing the time to start sending pager notification to the operator on Saturday.

[, [@saturday_pager_end_time =] saturday_pager_end_time]	Saturday_pager_end_time is an integer of format HHMMSS with a default of 180000, 6:00 P.M. on a 24-hour clock, representing the time to stop sending pager notification to the operator on Saturday.
[, [@sunday_pager_start_time =] sunday_pager_start_time]	Sunday_pager_start_time is an integer of format HHMMSS with a default of 090000, 9:00 A.M. on a 24-hour clock, representing the time to start sending pager notification to the operator on Sunday.
[, [@sunday_pager_end_time =] sunday_pager_end_time]	Sunday_pager_end_time is an integer of format HHMMSS with a default of 180000, 6:00 P.M. on a 24-hour clock, representing the time to stop sending pager notification to the operator on Sunday.
[, [@pager_days =] pager_days]	Pager_days is tinyint 1-127 representing the days the operator can be paged with a default of 0=Never. Add the values for each day where 1=Sunday, 2=Monday, 4=Tuesday, 8=Wednesday, 16=Thursday, 32=Friday, 64=Saturday. Monday through Friday=62.
[, [, [@netsend_address =] 'netsend_address']	Netsend_address is the varchar(100) e-mail address of the operator to be notified by the network message pop-up. The default is NULL.
[@category_name =] 'category']	Category is the sysname category name. The default is NULL.

sp_updatestats

The sp_updatestats system stored procedure executes UPDATE STATISTICS for all user-created tables in the database in use.

Syntax

The syntax is:

```
sp_updatestats
```

sp_update_targetservergroup

The sp_update_targetservergroup system stored procedure modifies the name of the target server group.

Syntax

The syntax is:

```
sp_update_targetservergroup [@name =] 'current_name'
[, [@new_name =] 'new_name']
```

The arguments are:

[@name =] 'current_name'	Current_name is the sysname name of the existing target server group
[, [@new_name =] 'new_name']	New_name is the sysname new name of the existing target server group.

sp_updatetask

The sp_updatetask system stored procedure is provided for backward compatibility only and is used to modify a task. Microsoft SQL Server 7 programmers use jobs instead of tasks and the SQL Server Agent instead of the SQL Executive.

sp_validname

The sp_validname system stored procedure is used to see if an identifier name is a valid SQL Server identifier.

Syntax

The syntax is:

```
sp_validname [@name =] 'name'
[, [@raise_error =] raise_error]
```

The arguments are:

[@name =] 'name'	Name is the sysname of the string to validate.
[, [@raise_error =] raise_error]	Raise_error is a bit where 1=show error messages and 0=do not show error messages.

sp_validatelogins

The sp_validatelogins system stored procedure displays Windows NT users and groups that no longer exist but have rows in the SQL Server system tables.

Syntax

The syntax is:

```
sp_validatelogins
```

sp_who

The sp_who system stored procedure displays users and processes currently running on SQL Server.

Syntax

The syntax is:

```
sp_who ['login ]
```

The argument, login, is the user's sysname login name on SQL Server. If the login is not supplied all users and processes are displayed.

xp_cmdshell

The xp_cmdshell extended stored procedure executes a command as if you were at the operating system command prompt. Note that when using with Window 95/98, the return code will always be zero (0).

Syntax

The syntax is:

```
xp_cmdshell {'command_string'} [, no_output]
```

The arguments are:

'command_string'	Command string is the varchar(255) or nvarchar(4000) command you wish to execute as if you were at the operating system command prompt.
no_output	No_output is an optional parameter that will not return the output to the client.

xp_deletemail

The xp_deletemail system stored procedure removes a message from the SQL Server inbox.

Syntax

The syntax is:

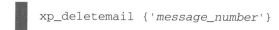

```
xp_deletemail {'message_number'}
```

The argument, message_number, is varchar(255) and is the number of the mail message to remove.

xp_enumgroups

The xp_enumgroups system stored procedure displays the Windows NT groups in a Windows NT domain.

Syntax

The syntax is:

```
xp_enumgroups ['domain_name']
```

The argument, domain_name, is the sysname of the Windows NT domain. If no domain is supplied or the SQL Server computer has the same name as the domain, local groups are returned. Otherwise, global groups are returned.

xp_findnextmsg

The xp_findnextmsg system stored procedure is used with sp_processmail to find the next message by accepting a message_id and returning the next message_id.

Syntax

The syntax is:

```
xp_findnextmsg [[@msg_id = ] msg_id [OUTPUT]]
[,[@type = ] type]
[,[@unread_only = ] 'unread_value'])
```

The arguments are:

[@msg_id =] msg_id	Msg_id serves as both an input and output argument that accepts the string of the message on input and displays the next message on output.
OUTPUT	OUTPUT places the the msg_id as output.
[@type =] type	Type is the input message types beginning with IPM that will appear. If you are after types beginning with IPC, you must set this argument, which defaults to NULL.
[@unread_only =] 'unread_value'	Unread_value can be true or false where true=only unread messages and false=all messages.

xp_grantlogin

The xp_grantlogin system stored procedure gives a Windows NT group or user a SQL Server login and is used for backward compatibility. A Microsoft SQL Server programmer uses sp_grantlogin.

Syntax

The syntax is:

```
xp_grantlogin {[@loginame =] 'login'} [,[@logintype =] 'logintype']
```

The arguments are:

[@loginame =] 'login'	Login is the sysname of the Windows NT user or group in the format Domain\User.
[@logintype =] 'logintype'	Logintype is varchar(5) and the security level where admin=add login to the sysadmin fixed server role.

xp_logevent

The xp_logevent system stored procedure writes a user-created message in the SQL Server errorlog and/or in the Windows NT Event Viewer, which is used to raise an alert without notifying the client.

Syntax

The syntax is:

```
xp_logevent {error_number, 'message'} [, 'severity']
```

The arguments are:

error_number	Error_number is a user-created error number larger than 50,000.
'message'	Message is a character string up to 8,000 characters that is logged to the SQL Server errorlog file or the NT Event Viewer.
'severity'	Severity is a string INFORMATIONAL, WARNING, or ERROR. The default is INFORMATIONAL.

xp_loginconfig

The xp_loginconfig system stored procedure displays the security configurations related to Microsoft SQL Server.

Syntax

The syntax is:

```
xp_loginconfig ['config_name']
```

The argument, config_name, is the configuration value to be displayed. Supply no argument to see them all.

xp_logininfo

The xp_logininfo system stored procedure displays information related to the Microsoft SQL Server security account.

Syntax

The syntax is:

```
xp_logininfo ['account_name' [, 'all' | 'members']
[,[@privilege =] variable_name OUTPUT]]
```

The arguments are:

'account_name'	Account_name is the name of a Windows NT user or group with SQL Server security. If no account_name is supplied, all accounts are displayed.
'all' | 'members'	All or members is a string where all=all permission for the account and members= members of the Windows NT group. The default is members.
[@privilege =] variable_name	Privilege is an output argument of nchar(21) that returns the privilege level of the Windows NT account user: admin or repl.
OUTPUT	OUTPUT uses the value of the variable_name as an output argument.

xp_msver

The xp_msver system stored procedure provides SQL Server version information.

Syntax

The syntax is:

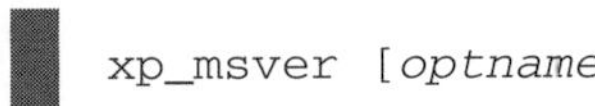

```
xp_msver [optname]
```

The argument, optname, is the name of an option. All can be viewed by supplying no argument.

xp_readmail

The xp_readmail system stored procedure reads a mail message from an e-mail inbox.

Syntax

The syntax is:

```
xp_readmail [[@msg_id = ] 'message_number'] [, [@type = ] 'type' [OUTPUT]]
[, [@peek = ] 'peek']
[, [@suppress_attach = ] 'suppress_attach']
[, [@orginator = ] 'sender' OUTPUT]
[, [@subject = ] 'subject_line' OUTPUT]
[, [@message = ] 'body_of_message' OUTPUT]
[, [@recipients = ] 'recipient_list' OUTPUT]
[, [@cc_list = ] 'cc_list' OUTPUT]
```

```
[, [@bcc_list = ] 'bcc_list' OUTPUT]
[, [@date_received = ] 'date' OUTPUT]
[, [@unread = ] 'value' OUTPUT]
[, [@attachments = ] 'temp_file_paths' OUTPUT])
[, [@skip_bytes = ] bytes_to_skip OUTPUT]
[, [@msg_length = ] length_in_bytes OUTPUT]
[, [@originator_address = ] 'originator_address' OUTPUT]]
```

The arguments are:

[@msg_id =] 'message_number'	The number of the message to be read.
'type'	The varchar(255) message type as defined by MAPI mail. If the type begins with IPM, the message will appear in the inbox of the mail client. Message types beginning with IPC do not appear in the client inbox. If the message type starts with IPC, the mail will only appear in the inbox if the type argument is set.
OUTPUT	OUTPUT uses the value of the type argument as an output variable.
[@peek =] 'peek'	Peek is varchar(5) where true=you can read the mail without marking it as read and false=mail is marked as read (the default).
[@suppress_attach =] 'suppress_attach'	Supress_attach is true=do not create temporary files and false=go ahead and create temporary files for attachments.
[@orginator =] 'sender'	Sender is varchar(255) and the e-mail name of the sender.
[@subject =] 'subject_line'	Subject_line is varchar(255) and a summary of the intent of the e-mail message.
[@message =] 'body_of_message'	Message is varchar(255) and is the text of the message.
[@recipients =] 'recipient_list'	Recipients are the individuals receiving the mail message. Separate names with semicolons.

[@cc_list =] 'cc_list'	Individuals you are sending a copy of the mail. Separate names with semicolons.
[@bcc_list =] 'bcc_list'	The other recipients will not know you are copying the blind copy recipients with the mail message.
[@date_received =] 'date'	Date is the varchar(255) date the mail message was received.
[@unread =] 'value'	Unread is varchar(5) where true=the message has not been read and false=the message has been read.
[@attachments =] 'temp_file_paths'	Temp_file_paths is varchar(255) and the temporary paths of the mail attachments. Separate paths with semicolons.
[@skip_bytes =] bytes_to_skip OUTPUT	Bytes_to_skip is the number of bytes to skip before reading the next number of bytes (defined by length_in_bytes argument) into the output argument. The default is 0.
[@msg_length =] length_in_bytes OUTPUT	Length_in_bytes is the number of bytes in a message. Use with bytes_to_skip to read messages 255 bytes at a time. The default is 255 bytes.
[@originator_address =] 'originator_address'	Originator_address is varchar(255) and is the sender of the e-mail message.

xp_revokelogin

The xp_revokelogin system stored procedure removes a SQL Server login from a Windows NT group or user. It is used for backward compatibility. A Microsoft SQL Server 7 programmer uses sp_revokelogin (a stored procedure instead of an extended stored procedure).

Syntax

The syntax is:

```
xp_revokelogin {[@loginame =] 'login'}
```

The argument, login, is the sysname of the Windows NT user or group in the format domain\user (e.g. CONTINUUM\wccomp).

xp_sendmail

The xp_sendmail system stored procedure sends an electronic mail message, a query result set, or an attachment. SQL Mail must be running.

Syntax

The syntax is:

```
xp_sendmail {[@recipients =] 'recipients [,…n]'}
[,[@message =] 'message']
[,[@query =] 'query']
[,[@attachments =] attachments]
[,[@copy_recipients =] 'copy_recipients [,…n]'
[,[@blind_copy_recipients =] 'blind_copy_recipients [,…n]'
[,[@subject =] 'subject']
[,[@type =] type]
[,[@attach_results =] 'attach_value']
[,[@no_output =] 'output_value']
[,[@no_header =] 'header_value']
[,[@width =] width]
[,[@separator =] separator]
[,[@echo_error =] 'echo_value']
[,[@set_user =] user]
[,[@dbuse =] database]
```

The arguments are:

[@recipient =] 'recipients'	Recipients are the individuals receiving the mail message. Names are separated by semicolons.
n	N means the preceding entry is repeatable.
[@message =] 'message'	The text of the message to the recipient.
[@query =] 'query'	An SQL query with the results being sent in mail.
[@attachments =] attachments	A file attached to the mail message.
[@copy_recipients =] 'copy_recipients'	Individuals you are sending a copy of the mail. Names are separated by semicolons.
[@blind_copy_recipients =] 'blind_copy_recipient'	The other recipients will not know you are copying the blind copy recipients with the mail message.

[@subject =] 'subject'	If you do not specify the subject of the mail message, 'SQL Server Message' appears as the subject.
[@type =] type	The message type as defined by MAPI mail. If the type begins with IPM, the message will appear in the inbox of the mail client if the type is NULL. Message types beginning with IPC do not appear in the client inbox. If the message type starts with IPC, the mail will only appear in the inbox if the type argument is set.
[@attach_results =] 'attach_value'	TRUE = send results in an attached file. The file name will be the first file name in attachments. If attachments is NULL, the file name will have a .txt extension. FALSE = append the result set to the message.
[@no_output =] 'output_value'	TRUE = no output is sent to the client session that sent the mail. FALSE = the default, the client session sending mail receives output.
[@no_header =] 'header_value'	TRUE = no column headers are sent with query results. FALSE = the default, column headers are sent with the query results.
[@width =] width	The line width of the results for a query. The default is 80 characters.
[@separator =] separator	The column separator for query result set.
[@echo_error =] 'echo_value'	TRUE = append errors, messages, and row counts that are generated by the query to the mail message. FALSE = do not append errors, messages, and row counts generated by the query to the mail message.
[@set_user =] user	User is the user with permissions to run the query. The default is guest user.

[@dbuse =] database	The database where the query will run. The default is NULL and the database becomes the default database of the user.

xp_snmp_getstate

The xp_snmp_getstate system stored procedure tells you if the SQL Server Simple Network Management Protocol (SNMP) agent is available to query SQL Server by an SNMP client—possibly from another operating system (e.g. mainframe or UNIX). You can use this to query the state of the agent if you have stored procedures that depend upon the SNMP agent.

Syntax

The syntax is:

```
xp_snmp_getstate [return_status OUTPUT]
```

The arguments are:

return_status	Return_status is an integer status of the SNMP agent. Use not argument to see the result status.
OUTPUT	OUTPUT makes return_status an output argument.

xp_snmp_raisetrap

The xp_snmp_raisetrap system stored procedure is used to communicate with an SNMP client and allows the client to check on SQL Server. In the Windows Network control panel, you can control which SNMP clients will receive the alert.

Syntax

The syntax is:

```
xp_snmp_raisetrap {'server', 'database', 'error_message', message_number,
severity, 'user', 'comment', date_and_time, return_status OUTPUT}
```

The arguments are:

'server'	Server is varchar(30) and the name of the server raising the alert.

'database'	Database is varchar(30) and is the name of the database raising the alert.
'error_message'	Error_message is varchar(255) and is the error message for the alert.
Message_number	Message_number is the sysmessages system table message error number for the alert.
Severity	Severity is integer and the severity of message_number (1-25).
'user'	User is the varchar(30) name of the user raising the alert.
'comment'	Comment is varchar(255) and is a comment about what to do once the alert is received.
date_and_time	Date_and_time is datetime and the date and the time the alert happened.
return_status	Return_status is an integer representing the status of the statement where 0=the alert was sent, 2=memory error, 3=network error, 4=SQL SNMP agent time out waiting for the SNMP client, 5=SQL SNMP agent is stopped.
OUTPUT	OUTPUT puts the return_status in an output variable.

xp_sprintf

The xp_sprintf system stored procedure is used to format and hold characters in the output parameter after formatting it.

Syntax

The syntax is:

```
xp_sprintf {string OUTPUT, format}
[, argument [, ...n]]
```

The arguments are:

string	String is varchar and is a variable storing the output.
OUTPUT	OUTPUT puts the string in an output variable.
format	Format is a format character string with % representing the argument values.

argument	Argument is a string of the value of the corresponding format argument.
n	N means the preceding entry is repeatable to 50 times.

Example

Here's an example of xp_sprintf:

```
DECLARE @mystring varchar (255)

EXEC xp_sprintf @mystring OUTPUT, 'SELECT * FROM %s WHERE %s = %s',
'MyTable', 'MyId', '1'
```

In this example, 'SELECT * FROM MyTable WHERE MyId = 1' is returned.

xp_sqlinventory

The xp_sqlinventory system stored procedure stores SQL Server configuration information in a database and table of your choice.

Syntax

The syntax is:

```
xp_sqlinventory {'database', 'table', {interval | STOP}}
```

The arguments are:

'database'	Database is varchar(30) and is the name of the database to store configuration information.
'table'	Table is varchar(30) and is the name of the table to store configuration information. This table will be created automatically.
Interval	Interval is an integer and is the number of seconds (valid values are 1 through 3600 (one hour)) to wait before checking again for SQL Server inventory messages.
STOP	STOP terminates inventory actions currently running.

xp_sqlmaint

The xp_sqlmaint system stored procedure calls the sqlmaint utility with a string containing sqlmaint switches in order to execute a set of maintenance operations on databases.

Syntax

The syntax is:

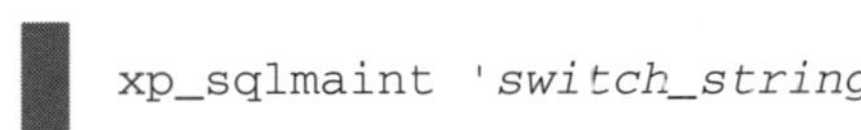

```
xp_sqlmaint 'switch_string'
```

The argument, switch_string, is a string containing the sqlmaint utility switches. See Chapter 8, "Utility Changes," for more information on the SQLMAINT utility.

xp_sscanf

The xp_sscanf system stored procedure extracts data from a string into the argument placeholders given by the format arguments.

Syntax

The syntax is:

```
xp_sscanf {string OUTPUT, format}
[, argument [,…n]]
```

The arguments are:

String	String is varchar and is a variable storing the output.
OUTPUT	OUTPUT puts the string in an output variable.
format	Format is a format character string with % representing the argument values.
argument	Argument is a string of the value of the corresponding format argument.
n	N means the preceding entry is repeatable up to 50 times.

Example

Here's an example of xp_sscanf:

```
DECLARE @table_name varchar (30), @column_name varchar (30)

EXEC xp_sscanf 'SELECT * FROM MyTable WHERE MyId = 1', 'SELECT *
FROM %s WHERE %s = 1', @table_name OUTPUT, @column_name OUTPUT
```

In this example, MyTable and MyId are returned.

xp_startmail

The xp_startmail system stored procedure starts a Microsoft SQL Server mail client session.

Syntax

The syntax is:

```
xp_startmail [[@user = ] 'user'] [, [@password = ] 'password']
```

The arguments are:

[@user =] 'user'	The user sysname can be supplied if you want to start mail under a different mailbox than what was defined as the startup mailbox of SQL Mail.
[@password =] 'password'	Password is a sysname mailbox password for the user. If the mail client is running locally, password can be NULL.

xp_stopmail

The xp_stopmail system stored procedure terminates SQL Mail.

Syntax

The syntax is:

```
xp_stopmail
```

Appendix A

Pre-installation Preparation Checklist

Checklist Item	Your Choices and Information
Verify that you have the required hardware	❑
Verify that you have the required software	❑
Installation Type:	
Typical	❑
Compact	❑
Custom	❑
Domain Name	______________
SQL Server Name (taken from the Windows NT computer name)	______________
Windows NT user account that starts the SQL Server service (SQL Server and SQL Server Agent can use the same or different accounts)	______________
Windows NT user account that starts the SQL Server Agent service	______________
Windows NT user account with Administrator privileges to run SQL Server setup	______________
Character Set	______________
Sort Order	______________
Unicode Collation	______________
Authentication Mode (NT Authentication or Mixed)	______________
User Name of primary responsible user of SQL Server	______________
User Organization Name *(Optional)*	______________
Product ID *(Optional but needed for technical support)*	______________
Network Protocols	______________
Install Online Books	❑
Location of Utilities Files	______________

Checklist Item	Your Choices and Information
Location of Data Files	____________________
Location of Program Files	____________________
Autostart SQL Server	❑
Autostart SQL Server Agent	❑
Program Group for SQL Server	____________________

Index

D

J

K

L

M

S

T

X

Notes